Windows NT Heterogeneous Networking

Steven B. Thomas

201 West 103rd Street, Indianapolis, Indiana 46290

Windows NT Heterogeneous Networking

International Standard Book Number: 1-57870-064-7

Library of Congress Catalog Card Number: 98-84229

2001 00 99 3 2 1

Interpretation of the printing code: The rightmost double-digit number is the year of the book's printing; the rightmost single-digit, the number of the book's printing. For example, the printing code 99-1 shows that the first printing of the book occurred in 1999.

Composed in Sabon and MCPdigital by Macmillan Computer Publishing.

Printed in the United States of America.

Warning and Disclaimer

This book is designed to provide information about Windows NT heterogeneous networking. Every effort has been made to make this book as complete and as accurate as possible, but no warranty or fitness is implied.

The information is provided on an as-is basis. The authors and Macmillan Technical Publishing shall have neither liability nor responsibility to any person or entity with respect to any loss or damages arising from the information contained in this book or from the use of the discs or programs that may accompany it.

Associate Publisher *Jim LeValley*

Executive Editor *Linda Ratts Engelman*

Managing Editor *Caroline Roop*

Acquisitions Editor
Karen Wachs

Development Editor
Lisa M. Gebken

Copy Editors
Keith Cline
Howard Jones

Indexer
Craig Small

Manufacturing Coordinator
Brook Farling

Book Designer
Gary Adair

Cover Designer
Aren Howell

Proofreaders
Tricia Sterling
Megan Wade

Production Team Supervisor
Daniela Raderstorf

Production
Wil Cruz
Liz Johnston
Cheryl Lynch

About the Author

Steven B. Thomas has been involved in teaching various areas of Windows NT for the past several years. As president of Gate City Consulting, Steven created a firm dedicated to providing consulting, training, and course-development services to clients for the purpose of establishing real-world implementations of business solutions. For more than two years, Steve has been a contract trainer and course director at the American Research Group Global Knowledge Network (ARG), where he developed public-training curriculum for three NT courses, including one entitled "Internetworking with NT."

Steve is also a Microsoft Certified Systems Engineer (MCSE) and Microsoft Certified Trainer (MCT). Due to his UNIX and Novell background, Steve is also a Certified NetWare Administrator (CNA).

Trademark Acknowledgments

About the Technical Reviewers

These reviewers contributed their considerable practical, hands-on expertise to the entire development process for *Windows NT Heterogeneous Networking*. As the book was being written, these folks reviewed all the material for technical content, organization, and flow. Their feedback was critical to ensuring that *Windows NT Heterogeneous Networking* fits our reader's need for the highest quality technical information.

Marcus D. Nelson is a consultant and Microsoft Certified Systems Engineer and trainer with 15 years of experience in information systems. Marcus spent 15 years in the Infantry and Military Intelligence branches of the U.S. Army, including tours with the 82nd Airborne Division and the Multinational Peacekeeping Forces. During his military career, Marcus began working with computer systems and received awards for his efforts in Computer Security and Administration. While in the Army, Marcus provided security and support to military information systems worldwide. Upon leaving the military, Marcus became a consultant with Digital Equipment Corporation where he provided Windows NT support to a myriad of customers. Marcus is currently employed as principal consultant with RABA Technologies of Columbia, Maryland, where he provides a variety of support to commercial, local/county/state governments, and federal agencies. Marcus lives in Maryland with his wife Kelly and their three children: Gunner, Zachary, and Megan.

Marc Charney has 12 years of experience in the computer industry. Upon receiving his degree from the University of California, Berkeley in 1987, Marc went to work for the Federal Reserve Bank of San Francisco. At the Federal Reserve, he was involved in the design of computer models of the United States economy. After the Federal Reserve, Marc moved on to Sybase where he helped develop its sales-office integration, automation and networking strategy. While at Sybase, Marc concentrated his efforts on networking and systems integration including PCs, Macintoshes, UNIX, and VAX. Following Sybase, Marc went to work for Delta Life & Annuity where he managed a complete overhaul of its network and systems infrastructure. This process involved a large network redesign effort as well as a method for seamlessly integrating Windows NT, Novell Netware, AS400s, and UNIX systems. Marc is currently working at First Tennessee Bank as an Internet security and intranet development manager. His current efforts are focused on Web integration of current bank systems.

Overview

Table of Contents

Acknowledgments

San Francisco, Chicago, Pittsburgh, West Palm Beach, Raleigh, Charlotte, Aberdeen, Columbus, Orlando, New York, Dublin! Every week, MTP kept hearing "My number this week is..." Yet they dealt with me. I was a pain in the neck to work with due to my hectic activities. One of the first things I failed to realize when I accepted this book deal was the fact that things were going to change drastically for me following the birth of my child. This caused for me a major shift in priorities. It was also a period of everything going wrong all at the same time. My music composition teacher in college taught me this expression, "You need to find a good place to put a double-bar on this one." I am ecstatic that I am available to follow through on this and reach the double-bar.

It was during the course of writing this book that I decided to get a pager. I never thought it would come to that, but now I have lost total independence. However the staff at MTP was very excited about it, except when I was out of the country and the pager was not receiving messages. I only wish that they realized how appreciative I am of their effort in helping me maintain the course.

To Linda Engelman: It is amazing how much Norman Vincent Peale has been incarnated into Linda Engelman.

To Jane Brownlow: She did not work with me very long, but she was very nice. She moved on to other projects during my book and was replaced by Karen Wachs.

To Karen Wachs: She came on in the middle of this project and quickly learned the importance of email in communicating with me. If I am not mistaken, I believe she has placed my face on a dartboard (just kidding!).

To Lisa Gebken: I am responsible for the increase in her blood pressure. She did an excellent job at making me write my own material and keeping the text objective. Some of those jokes would have gone over real well if I could have kept them, but we must not forget the purpose of the book.

To Marcus Nelson: He was the technical editor and author of two chapters, Chapter 11, "Enterprise Management," and Chapter 13, "Emerging Enterprise Concerns." I appreciated his expertise and effort in making this book a success. He, in many ways, rescued me!

On a personal note, I would like to thank my mother and father for all of their support in helping me to get my career and family started. My father and mother are a unique and interesting pair with my mother as the wacky one and my father as the quick-witted straight man. I feel that I am definitely the product of these two minds, so they deserve some credit for the book.

To my wife: She is incredible! She puts up with a very trying husband who spends a large amount of time on the road. I pledge to keep myself more at home in the future. She also told me to stop forgetting to mention her by name when I acknowledge her. So thank you, Kristie!!

Finally to my son: Six months old as I am writing this and he is growing as fast as NT's market share. He keeps me occupied at home and gave me a wonderful excuse to procrastinate while at the same time I was driving the publication team at MTP to a mental asylum.

Introduction

When I started working for a university in its instructional and research computing department, one of the first things that I noticed was that the network was a hybrid one. The term *hybrid* meant many vendors and many products. I found it fascinating to read the documentation and to hear terms such as *open architecture*, *open drivers*, and *seamless integration*. Then I realized the pain involved in trying to get all of these products connected. We had vaxes, DEC stations, Macintoshes, NetWare servers, Sun servers, XTs, ATs and VT100s running DOS, Windows, System 6, System 7, VMS, Solaris, Xenix, Ultrix, and UNIX. Establishing seamless integration led me to realize that the term *open systems* in the practical sense is more of a goal for the future rather than the status quo.

Why did the university have so many different platforms? Most organizations must recycle whatever they can because technology budgets are often tight. In the case of the university, it had to plan its budgets with the anticipation of a 10 percent budget cut. There are other reasons as well. The programmers may like one while the accountants like another. One group may be more security-conscious and want a secure-tested operating system. The administrative data is often kept on mainframes because of the still apparent mistrust of PCs.

There also are the less-technical reasons. While the analysts like command-line interfaces, the users prefer the user-friendly operating system. In some cases, the advertisements for one operating system look better than the others, so some choose on that basis.

In the end it doesn't really matter what systems are chosen—heterogeneous connectivity is needed.

In recent years, the bulk of my time has dealt with UNIX, NetWare, and Windows NT. Lately it seems Windows NT is the common denominator. This serves as the major inspiration for this book. Trying to implement, manage, and maintain Windows NT in a multi-vendor environment is becoming a major necessity because many organizations do not move directly to NT or build Windows NT networks from the ground up. As a result, they must gradually integrate NT into their networks.

The Contents

Chapter 1, "Developing an Enterprise Model," deals with developing a Windows NT-centered enterprise model using current and forthcoming technologies. Chapter 2, "LAN/WAN Protocol Management," and Chapter 3, "Managing Enterprise Services," discuss the management of essential components involved with Windows NT connectivity. Chapter 4, "Remote Administrative Services," is concerned with possible options for controlling Windows NT remotely by using both interactive and non-interactive means. Chapter 5, "Network Management and Monitoring," and Chapter 6, "Optimization and Capacity Planning," deal with monitoring, managing, and optimizing a heterogeneous networking environment by using Windows NT.

The second half of the book covers information about specific vendors for connectivity. Those that are prevalent, especially in larger environments, were chosen. Chapter 7, "UNIX Integration," deals with UNIX connectivity. Chapter 8, "Integration with NetWare Bindery-based Servers," and Chapter 9, "Integration with NetWare Directory Services," discuss NetWare connectivity. Chapter 10, "Apple Integration," discusses integration with Apple Macintosh networks.

Chapter 11, "Enterprise Management," deals with troubleshooting, and Chapter 12, "Inventory Management," discusses inventory management. The last part of the book deals with current migration steps and emerging enterprise concerns, discussed in Chapter 13, "Emerging Enterprise Concerns."

Goals to Accomplish

I strongly recommend using heterogeneous components and protocols whenever possible, for reasons mostly related to TCP/IP. I do want to state that this book is not (and administrators are not) limited to using only TCP/IP. This book enables you as an administrator to learn the following:

- Information regarding Windows NT interconnectivity with major operating systems.
- Information regarding built-in and external methods for managing, monitoring, and optimizing Windows NT.
- Information that will help people do their jobs better.

On the Web

Updates and additional information are available on the Macmillan Technical Publishing Web site (`http://www.macmillantech.com/thomas`). Among any updates to this material are additional articles relating to the following topics:

- Heterogeneous printing
- Client management with Windows clients
- Client management with DOS clients
- Connectivity with Banyan VINES networks

There also are links to additional helpful articles as well as shareware and utilities relating to the topics covered in this book.

Conventions Used in This Book

The following conventions are used in this book:

Tip

Tips provide you with helpful ways of completing a task.

Troubleshooting Tip

Troubleshooting tips provide resolutions of problems you may encounter during deployment.

Warning

Warnings provide you with information you need to know to avoid damage to data, hardware, or software, and to avoid error messages.

Author's Note

In these areas, I relate personal experiences that give you a real-life understanding of a topic.

Part I

Planning and Managing the Network Architecture

Chapter 1

Developing an Enterprise Model

- **The Concept of Directory Services**
  Directory Services help organize network resources into a directory of objects.
- **Different Types of Directory Services**
  Directory Services fall into two main categories. Structure may also differ across vendors.
- **The Various Enterprise Naming Services Built into Windows NT**
  In complex TCP/IP internetworks, naming services help facilitate the accessibility of user-friendly names.
- **Geographical Distribution of Domain Controllers and Servers**
  It is important to strategically place domain controllers (directory servers) where wide-area bandwidth is not consumed by authentication traffic.

The Directory Service Model

Lately, there has been a recurring theme in the networking organization of data. With the success of personal computers, we are finding that storing information in some type of hierarchical fashion (such as directories and folders) is the most consistent and practical method. After all, this "filing cabinet" approach is something with which we are all familiar. We can therefore easily transcend knowledge levels from the advanced administrator to the basic user.

The *Directory Service Model* is a directory of services, resources, user and group entities, and properties. The latter two usually deal with a certain context of security. This directory is made available to users who require a map to guide them towards the resources and/or services they need to access.

The directory itself is nothing but a collection of objects. Each object maps to a specific entitity. All of this information is then placed in a database that is stored on a designated server. In some cases, especially for larger models, the database can be divided up for distribution and replication.

Types of Directory Services

There are two common schools of thought in the design and implementation of Directory Services: the tree-based method and the flat method.

Tree Method

The *tree standard* is a full-fledged, object-oriented, context-dependent method of directory services (see Figure 1.1). You could say that this is the true approach to directory services since it is a hierarchical structure with a clearly defined root. NetWare's NDS (NetWare Directory Services), Banyan's StreetTalk, and other CCITT X.500-based implementations use this standard.

The tree-based standard organizes network resources hierarchically uses container objects. *Container objects* are objects within the enterprise directory that can hold other containers and leaf objects. *Leaf objects* are objects that map to a specific resource and/or service. You could say that a container object is analogous to a folder (file system directory) while a leaf object is analogous to a file.

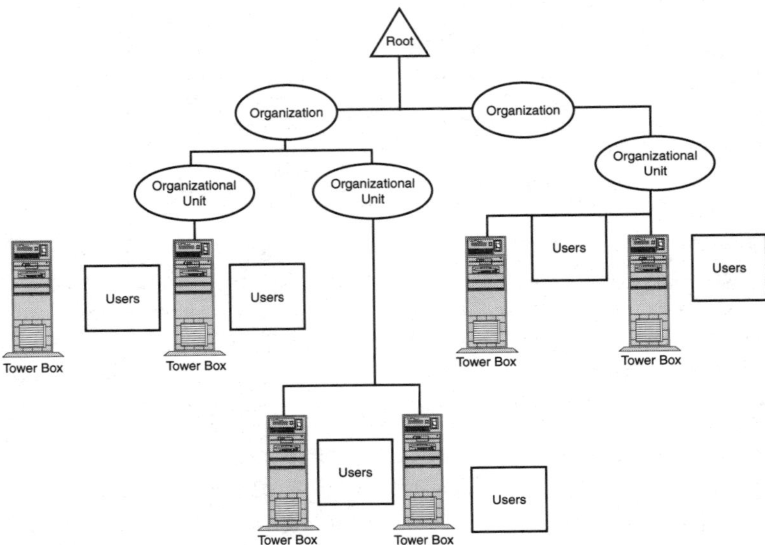

Figure 1.1. *An example of the tree method of directory services.*

Flat Method

A *flat model* is based less on context and more on the centralization of management, preferably security (see Figure 1.2). While the flat model is considered less complicated, there is still a learning curve. There is also little room for post-implementation changes. The flat model is very dependent on preplanning. The flat model is currently the Microsoft Directory Services standard for Windows NT.

In fact, Microsoft used the term *domain models* to describe its enterprise model for NT Server 3.50 and 3.51, but used the term *directory services* for NT 4.0. Administrators who worked with Windows NT 3.50 thought these two models would be different, but soon learned that Microsoft simply just made a semantic change.

Whatever it is called, there are many distinctions that make it stand alone as a method:

- First of all, there is no defined root. All entities exist at the same level and may choose to have relationships with one another depending on how the administrators set it up.
- When domains link up with each other via trust relationships, the databases are not merged, they are still kept separate.
- The domain controllers (directory servers) always maintain a complete copy of the database.
- It is heavily dependent upon planning because it characteristically is not known for its flexibility and mobility.

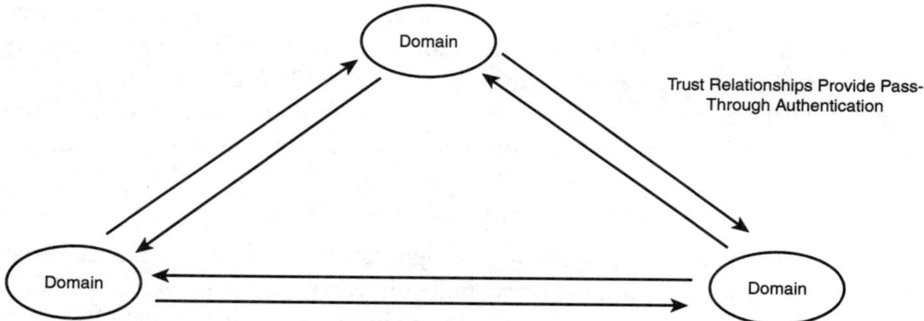

Figure 1.2. *An example of a flat directory service method.*

Directory Service Implementations

The Microsoft Domain Model concept is unique when comparing it to the other directory service models. But it is not the only model that uses the flat structure in the same sense that NetWare Directory Services (NDS) is not the only tree-based model. Below are a few examples of Directory Service implementations:

Implementation	Vendor	Type	Use
NDS (NetWare Directory Services)	Novell	Tree	Used as an enterprise management model.
NTDM (NT Domain Models)	Microsoft	Flat	Used as an enterprise security model.
NIS (Network Information System)	Sun	Flat	No longer vendor-specific, used as a UNIX enterprise security model.
SNMP (Simple Network Management Protocol)	None	Tree	Used as an internetwork management interface and designed to be cross-platform.
StreetTalk	Banyan	Tree	Used as a total enterprise management model.
DNS (Domain Name System)	None	Tree	Used as a naming model for the global Internet.

Distributed Directory Databases

Another major aspect in deciding on a directory service standard is the method of storing the directory database. One approach is to divide up the database into portions and to distribute the portions among multiple servers all across the internetwork. Novell NetWare does this in NetWare Directory Services by using partitions. These partitions are referred to as *replicas*. Certain servers contain master replicas, while others contain either Read-Only or Read-Write replicas. Each branch of the directory can be stored on a separate replica.

Decentralized Directory Databases

Microsoft uses a decentralized model to maintain its directory database. A centralized database is maintained on a single directory server. In Windows NT these are domain controllers. What happens in this environment is a Read-Write database server replicates the database to servers with Read-Only copies of the database. This makes fault tolerance easier and more simplistic.

Extensible Versus Fixed Schemas

Schemas define the guidelines and blueprints of a Directory Service Model. Some vendors offer schemas, which can be extended to include additional manageable objects. Banyan's StreetTalk and Novell's NetWare Directory Services offer extensible schemas while models like NIS and Microsoft's domain models do not.

Microsoft Domain Models

Windows NT Server Directory Services are based on the configuration and use of Windows NT Server Domains (see Figure 1.3).

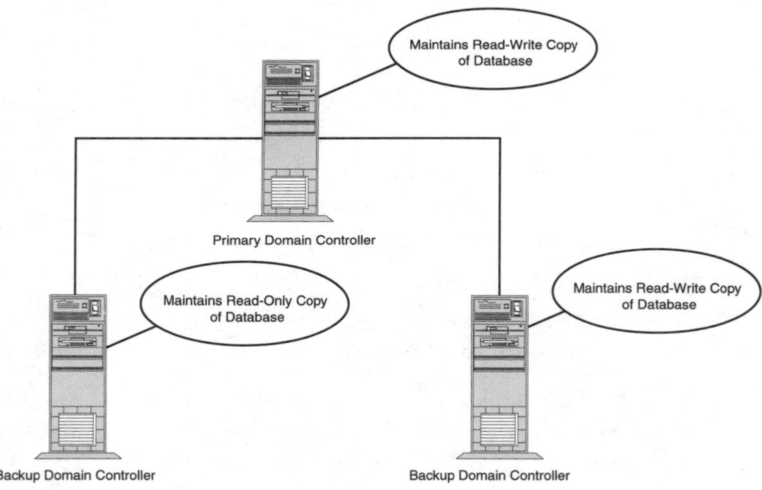

Figure 1.3. *The concept of a Microsoft domain.*

These are the same organizational units that have been in place for Microsoft PC-based networks since LAN Manager. Domains are NetBIOS-based logical groups that are joined together for the sole purpose of security. While workgroups offer logical groups of computers as well, they maintain a decentralized approach to management. In the case of Windows NT, each computer in a workgroup maintains a local security accounts database. Each administrator of each computer (or delegated administrators) is responsible for the management of that computer. Domains allow a single point of administration and access control as well as a single point of login for the users. They are the single, fundamental component of the Microsoft Enterprise Model.

A *domain model*, therefore, is a grouping of one or more domains, with administration and communications links between the domains (called *trust relationships*), arranged for the purpose of user and resource management. Once logged on, users can access all the resources they have rights to access including files, directories, servers, applications, and printers.

Windows NT Server Directory Services (multiple domain models) allow the administrator to maintain one user account for each user regardless of the number of servers in the distributed system. Users log on only once to gain access to all the different files, printers, and other network resources they need to use.

Domain Organization

The domain consists primarily of a single administrative unit with the capabilities of maintaining the following:

- *Centralized accounts*. The user must receive validation from the domain's Account database before s/he can access any resource on any node controlled by that domain.
- *Centralized account policies*. The Account, Audit, and User Rights policies are established domain-wide (network wide) instead of on a per-computer basis.
- *Centralized permissions*. File, directory, and printing permissions can be locally established to all users within the domain.
- *Centralized profiles*. This provides centralized control of the user's environment either via logon scripts or through per-user or mandatory profiles.

Trust Relationships

Trust relationships are the building blocks of the Microsoft Domain Model. These are the elements that link multiple SAM databases together for the pass-through authentication. When one domain trusts another, this allows the potential of the users and groups in the trusted domain to access resources in the trusting domain. This access is not automatic except for those resources granted to the Everyone group, as well as any users that have matching user names and passwords.

When one domain trusts another, it is acting as the *trusting domain* while the other domain is considered the *trusted domain*. Figure 1.4 shows the trust relationship between DOMAIN A and DOMAIN B where DOMAIN A trusts DOMAIN B.

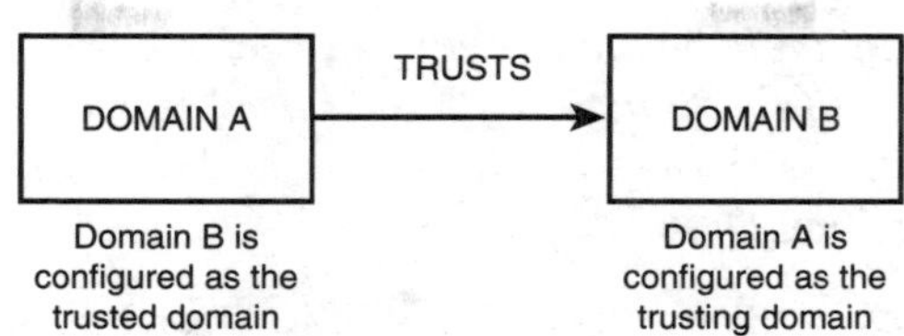

Figure 1.4. *DOMAIN A trusts DOMAIN B.*

Here, DOMAIN B users and groups now have the potential to access resources in DOMAIN A. Ultimately the decision will be determined by the trusting domain administrators.

Trusts are set up, by navigating to the User Manager for Domains and selecting Trust Relationships from the Policies menu. Figure 1.5 displays the Trust Relationships dialog box.

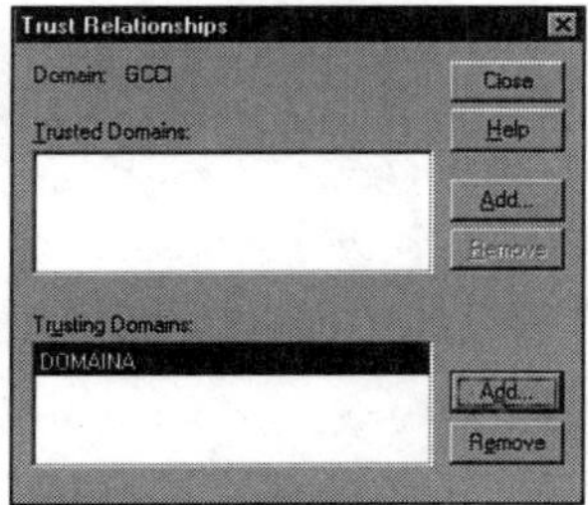

Figure 1.5. *Setting up trust relationships using the User Manager for Domain's utility.*

In this dialog box, the domain that is going to be trusted must first "permit" that domain to trust it. In doing so, you have the opportunity to set a password to ensure the security of the trust. This helps when you set this part up in advance. The domains that are listed in this dialog box do not have to exist, so you can begin to set up your multi-domain models before they even exist.

Troubleshooting Tip

Proper planning is essential when setting up domain models and trust relationships. You will need to know all of the domains that exist on your network/internetwork. Only one domain controller in each domain will need to actually set up the trust relationships. Writing information down will be very beneficial as well as mapping out the logical drawing of the domain model.

You can use the table below to help you keep track of the trust relationships. For each of the domains, you will need to know which domains you will put in the Trusted Domain field, and which domains you will put in the Trusting Domains field.

Domain	Trusted Domain	Trusting Domain

Based upon the information in this table, set up your trust relationships. The Trusting Domains field should be set up first, otherwise the domain controllers will not be able to verify the trusted domains through the secure channel. Remember the following information:

- *If you attempt to add a trusted domain and that domain controller cannot be located, you will receive the message* `The domain controller cannot be found.`
- *If attempt to add a trusted domain and that domain has not added you as a trusting domain, you will get a message* `The trust relationship cannot be verified at this time.`
- *If you attempt to add a trusted domain and the password is incorrect, you will get a message stating that the password is incorrect.*

Single Domain Model

The *Single Domain Model* consists of only one domain. Users at client workstations log on to the domain for the Primary Domain Controller (PDC) or one of the servers (see Figure 1.6). With a Single Domain Model, there are no trust relationships involved. This is the easiest and most common of the domain models.

This configuration consists of one domain. There is one PDC with potentially multiple Backup Domain Controllers (BDCs). In a single domain network, network administrators can always administer all network servers because the ability to administer servers is performed at the domain level.

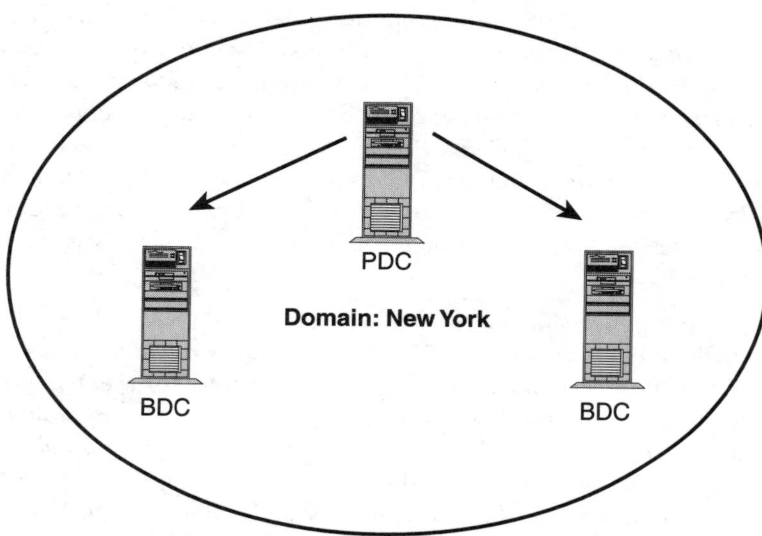

Figure 1.6. *Primary and Backup Domain Controllers within a domain.*

Author's Note

The Single Domain Model uses a single domain containing all of the users and resources within your organization. The Single Domain Model is the best choice for small-to-medium–sized networks. Those that do not have a large user base and will not need to divide up resource administration will benefit from this model. It is also important to note that a PDC contains a Read-Write copy of the database while the BDCs maintain only a Read-Only copy. The main purpose of having the BDCs are to help load-balance authentication. If the PDC is brought down, the BDCs can still authenticate logon requests.

The major downside to all of this is without a PDC, no changes to the domain database can be made. This wipes out administrative capabilities. Since the BDC has a complete copy of the database, it can easily be promoted to a PDC using the Server Manager.

Troubleshooting Tip

If you are working with a Single Domain Model that is going to be logically superimposed on top of a physical internetwork, you need to ensure that all of your connectivity is in place from the Physical Layer all of the way up to the Transport Layer. This is because this Domain Model is exclusively an Application Layer Model. If this is not possible, you will need to set up your PDC and BDCs on the same network or subnetwork. The reason for this is that a BDC cannot complete its installation until it links up with the PDC. If the BDC cannot link up with the PDC, then it will not be able to complete its installation unless it installs instead as a PDC.

The mistake people make is that they install a PDC with the same domain name as the existing PDC. As a result, you will not have two PDCs in the same domain. Even though the names for the domains match, they see each other internally as being from different domains. Windows NT does not like this and even worse, will not resolve from this particular situation because of the conflict in SIDs. When a computer is installed, it is given a SID. For a Windows NT workstation, Windows NT member server, or a Windows NT PDC, that SID is computed to contain a statistically unique 96-bit number. For a Windows NT BDC, that SID is identical to the SID of the PDC for the domain. If the SIDs between domain controllers do not match, they will not initially authenticate with each other, no secure channel can be established between the different domain controllers, and as a result, are never seen as belonging to the same domain.

The primary SID for a domain is generated during the installation of the first Windows NT domain controller installed (the PDC) and is the prefix of the SIDs for all the user accounts and group accounts created on the computer. The SID is concatenated with the RID (Resource Identifier) of the account to create each account's unique identifier. For example, the accounts for the built-in accounts, Administrator and Guest, are Resource IDs 500 and 501 respectively.

Master Domain Model

In the *Master Domain Model*, a single domain is used to validate the accounts for the members of all domains (see Figure 1.7). Other domains contain the resources to be shared among users. You will want to use this model when the total number of users and groups is less than 10,000. The master domain is a trusted domain in the sense that the domain, which is connected to the master by a one-way relationship, trusts the other domains.

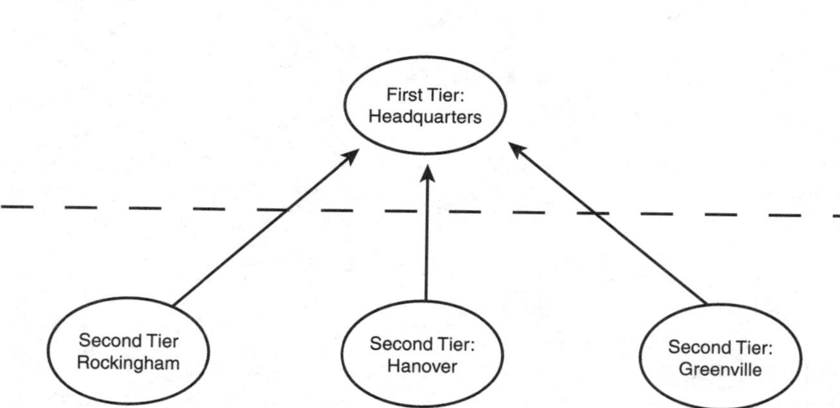

Figure 1.7. *The two-tier Master Domain Model.*

The NT servers in the master domain only have copies of the account database for all domains. Users with accounts in the Master Domain can use resources in the other domains. Users with accounts in any of the trusting domains can use resources in their own domains but not in the master or any of the other domains unless accounts are set for them individually.

A special type of group called a global group can be used to reference across domains in the Master Domain Model. Global groups from the master domain are added to the local groups of the trusted domains. Once global groups have been added to local groups, users can be added to global groups to permit access to local resources. This strategy allows all of the enterprise's user's and group's access to resources to be managed from the domain controller in the master domain.

The model uses a "pseudo-hierarchical" structure in that there is a single domain containing all of the user and group accounts. This domain is referred to as the *domain master* while the subordinate domains are referred to as *resource domains* since they are existing primarily for the purpose of resource administration. The terms *first-tier* and *second-tier* domains are also used to label domain masters and subordinates respectively (refer to Figure 1.7).

The major benefit of a Single Master Domain Model is that it gives the administrator a centralized control of all of the users and their accounts database.

Users will always know where their accounts reside. It also satisfies administrators in the medium-sized environments as well as the large environments with a single user domain. The resource domains or second-tier domains can be used to group resources into different domains and place the administrators you want to manage those domains in those different domains.

These administrators will also govern which users have access and the level access they will have through the one-way trust relationship with the master domain.

The fact that there are one-way trusts between the tiers allows for a centralized pool of users with a decentralized approach to resource administration. This also satisfies the various resource administrators in your organization for the second-tier domains are given complete autonomy. They have control over their specific resources yet they do not have control over any first-tier domains nor any other second-tier domains.

Multiple Master Domain Model

Microsoft prescribes the primary criteria for implementation of the multiple Master Domain Model is more than 10,000 accounts. There may be no MIS department to be given centralized control, so the administration needs to be at the department level. Each large department can be a *master*, a trusted domain. The multiple master domains function together as account domains. All users' accounts must be defined in one of these domains (see Figure 1.8).

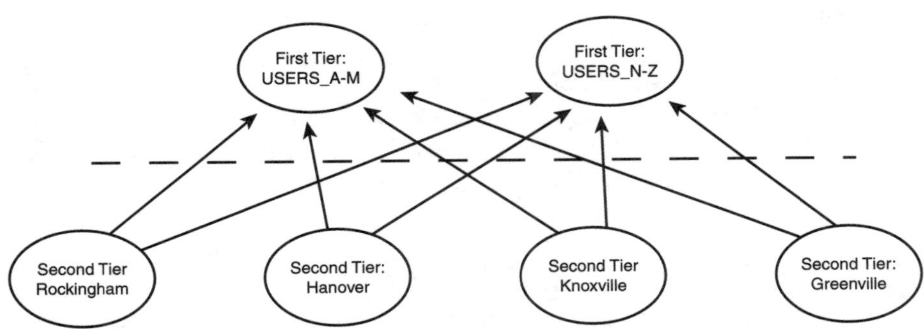

Figure 1.8. *The Multiple Master Domain model.*

Two-way trusts are necessary between each master domain because pass-through account validation isn't transitive. Domains that are not account domains are effectively resource domains. Resource domains do not need to trust each other. Each resource domain trusts all of the master domains.

Like the Master Domain Model (refer to Figure 1.7), each account is only defined once within a single master domain. All domains trust every master domain, and every user account in the set of domains is usable in all domains. Users receive authentication from the master domain that contains their account. Each master domain should contain two or more servers to validate user logons.

Complete Trust Model

All domains trust each other. Each department manages its own domain and defines its own users and global groups. The complete trust model distributes the administration of users and groups among different organizations (see Figure 1.9). Its other features include:

- No centralized MIS departments
- Local user or administrator trusts the administrator of the trusted domain to manage and assign users to global groups in the other domains
- The number of trust relationships for a company with *n* domains is:

    n * (n-1)

A network of 10 domains requires 90 trust relationships, or

    10 * (10-1)

Once you grant permissions to a global group from another domain by placing the global group in a local group in your domain, you trust that inappropriate users aren't added to the global group later.

Troubleshooting Tip

If you do not want to use one of the four sanctioned domain models that Microsoft recommends, you can create your own custom Multiple Domain Model (Directory Service Model). Even something simple such as two domains with a single one-way trust relationship technically counts as a domain model.

One of the most common of these models includes the Headquarters domain model. Often, when people troubleshoot the Master Domain Model, they determine that in order to secure and allow the necessary different types of access to the master domain, they must create two-way trust relationships between the master and the resource domains. If you enable this, you will no longer be adhering to a Master Domain Model, but that is fine if it suits your organizational needs. Figure 1.10 shows this example.

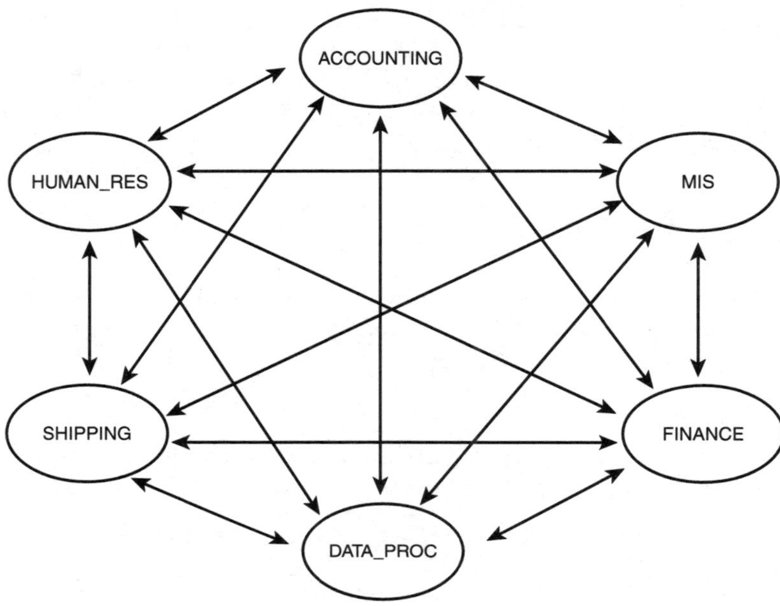

Figure 1.9. *The complete trust domain model.*

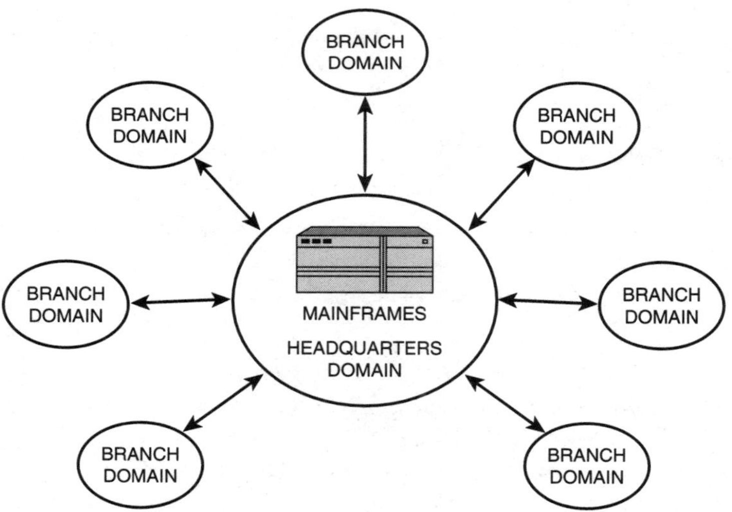

Figure 1.10. *Using the Headquarters Domain Model to keep resource domains separate (as branches) and access to centralized resources two-way.*

X.500 Directory Service Model

With the forthcoming release of Windows NT 5.0, X.500 is the OSI (Open Systems Interconnect) directory service standard. X.500 defines the following components:

- *An information model.* Determines the form and character of information in the directory.
- *A namespace.* Allows the information to be referenced and organized.
- *A functional model.* Determines what operations can be performed on the information.
- *An authentication framework.* Allows information in the directory to be secured.
- *A distributed operation model.* Determines how data is distributed and how operations are carried out.

The information model is centered on entries, which are composed of attributes. Each attribute has a type and one or more values. The type determines the attribute's syntax, which defines what kind of information is allowed in the values.

To determine the attribute types that are allowed and/or required, a special type of attribute called `objectClass` is included in every entry in the directory. The attributes tell the application, management utility, or other component what type of entry (such as person or organization) is being used. It then tells you individual attribute requirements followed by the optional requirements. For example, the object class `person` will require the `surname` (user's last name) and `commonName` (the actual username on the network) attributes, but `description`, `seeAlso` and others are optional.

Entries are arranged in a tree structure and divided among servers in a geographical and organizational distribution (see Figure 1.11). Entries are named according to their position in this hierarchy by a *distinguished name (DN)*. Each component of the DN is called a *relative distinguished name (RDN)*. *Alias entries*, which point to other entries, are allowed, circumventing the hierarchy.

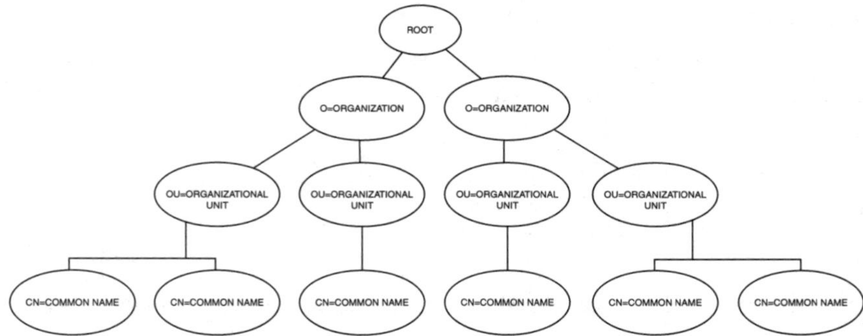

Figure 1.11. *The X.500 hierarchy.*

Enterprise Services

When planning an enterprise model, you need to consider certain services and their relevancy. I will refer to these services as *Enterprise Services*. They are large-scale server portions of client-server solutions. In addition to determining the placement of domain controllers, the placement of these critical application servers is very important as well. The majority of these services relate to groupware, messaging, network management, and relational databases.

In its BackOffice suite, Microsoft offers many integrated enterprise-oriented services with Windows NT. Windows NT also comes with integrated services for wide-area network (WAN) browsing, hosting, and naming.

Microsoft BackOffice

The BackOffice suite includes the following packages:

- *Exchange Server*. An integrated groupware package allowing for SMTP, POP3, MS Mail, X.500, and scheduling support.
- *SQL Server*. The Relational Database Management System (RDMS), designed to serve as the back end to a variety of client/server application solutions.
- *Systems Management Server*. The inventory management/network management platform, designed to work with Microsoft's SQL Server package.
- *Systems Network Architecture (SNA) Server*. The IBM/SNA gateway solution for host and mainframe connectivity.

- *Proxy Server*. The Internet solution for intranet/Internet boundary management, security, and address sharing.
- *Transaction Server*. The solution for providing secure transactions and other electronic-commerce–building strategies over the Internet.

Inherent Utilities:

The enterprise services that are shipped along with Windows NT include:

- *Internet Information Server*. Offers HTTP (Web), file transfer protocol (FTP), and Gopher services for Windows NT. The latest version includes support for SQL integration via Active Server Pages, PERL scripting, and MS FrontPage extensions.
- *Dynamic Host Configuration Protocol*. Allows for centralized management of addresses for TCP/IP networks.
- *Windows Internet Naming Service*. Offers NetBIOS naming services for NT networks using TCP/IP.
- *Domain Name System Server*. Offers Internet and intranet name services for all TCP/IP-compliant hosts.

The Dynamic Addressing Solution

With its release of Windows NT 4.0, Microsoft introduced a complete dynamic solution to centralized TCP/IP configuration. There is a three-service process centering on the Windows Internet Naming Service (WINS). It provides the complete capability of centralizing the administration and distribution of TCP/IP configuration and naming.

In the Microsoft DNS Server Service, host records are usually stored in a flat text file referred to as a *zone file*. This, by nature, is not dynamic content. In Microsoft's DNS Server, DNS zones can be linked to WINS servers for host-name querying. Although this will eventually be replaced by Dynamic DNS, using zone links to WINS avoids the normal static configuration of DNS zones.

In figure 1.12 you see a DNS request for `hoss.gcci.com`. The DNS server that maintains the database for `gcci.com` can forward that request to a WINS server. If the WINS server contains a name entry for `hoss`, it can return the IP address to the DNS server. The DNS server can then forward that request back to the client making the original DNS query.

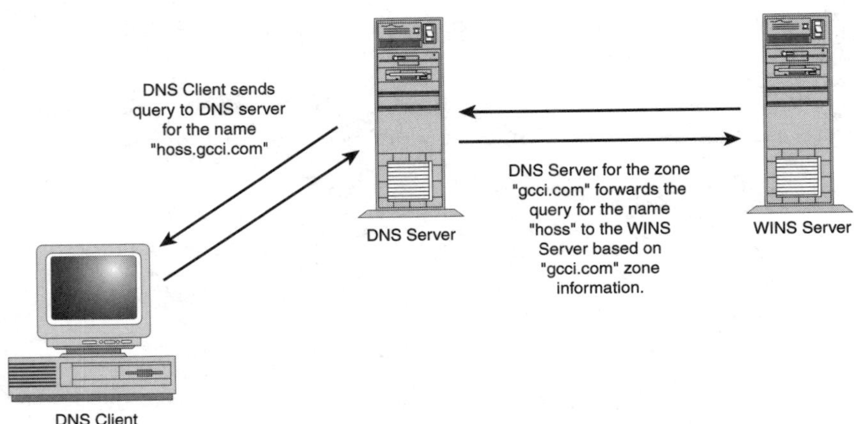
DNS Client sends
query to DNS server
for the name
"hoss.gcci.com"
DNS Server
WINS Server
DNS Server for the zone
"gcci.com" forwards the
query for the name
"hoss" to the WINS
Server based on
"gcci.com" zone
information.
DNS Client

Figure 1.12. *Part 1 of the dynamic addressing solution focusing on DNS and WINS.*

The *Dynamic Host Configuration Protocol (DHCP)* allows for a centralized configuration of TCP/IP configuration. Pools of addresses, called *scopes*, can be activated to service DNCP clients. These clients are not manually assigned any TCP/IP configuration. They initially use broadcasts to obtain auto-configuration from DHCP servers.

These DHCP scopes can be linked to WINS servers for computer names to be dynamically updated when IP addresses change. What basically happens is the DHCP client obtains its TCP/IP configuration. If this configuration contains the IP address of a WINS server, the client will then register its name and IP address with a WINS server. This is normally used for NetBIOS name resolution over TCP/IP. In NT 4.0, you can use this as a means of resolving DNS queries as I mentioned in the previous paragraph.

In Figure 1.13, the host `hoss` has obtained its IP address from a DHCP server. It then registered its NetBIOS hostname and IP address with the WINS server. We will discuss these services more in Chapter 3.

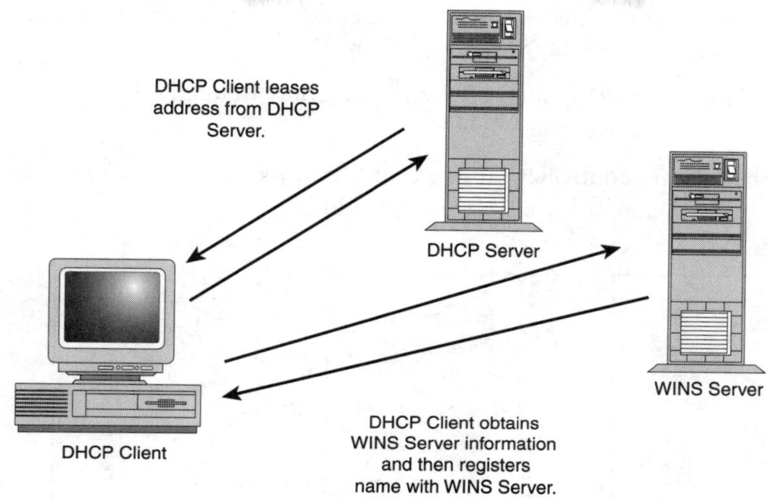
DHCP Client leases
address from DHCP
Server.
DHCP Server
WINS Server
DHCP Client
DHCP Client obtains
WINS Server information
and then registers
name with WINS Server.

Figure 1.13. *Part 2 of the dynamic addressing solution focusing on DHCP and WINS.*

Geographical Distribution of Domain Controllers

Certain issues arise when deciding where to place domain controllers in WAN and metropolitan area networks. This is the point of actually combining a logical model with a physical model. One of the major issues is to isolate and segment network traffic to where only necessary traffic is going out across an external link.

In Figure 1.14, a Master Domain Model is being implemented where DOMAIN A is the domain master and DOMAINS B, C, D, and E are the resource domains. Since the user pool is being stored in one domain and users from every other resource domain need to have access to that domain, a BDC for the domain master is placed at each resource domain location.

In a Single Domain Model that spans multiple sites, network engineers need to either:

- Distribute domain controllers to each site so only domain SAM database replication occurs over the WAN.
- Place the domain controllers at one centralized location where all authentication on other sites have to cross WAN links.

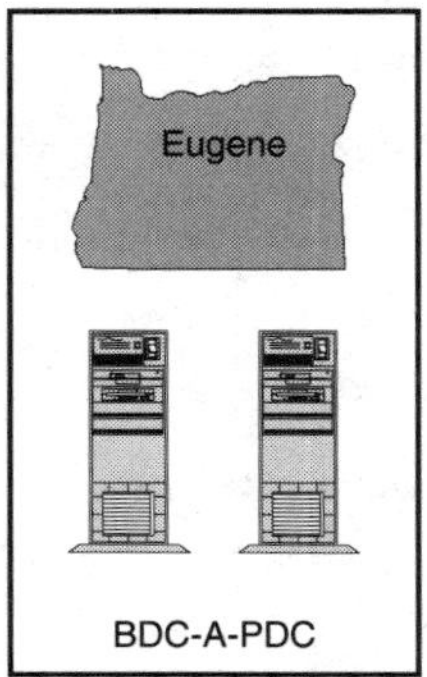

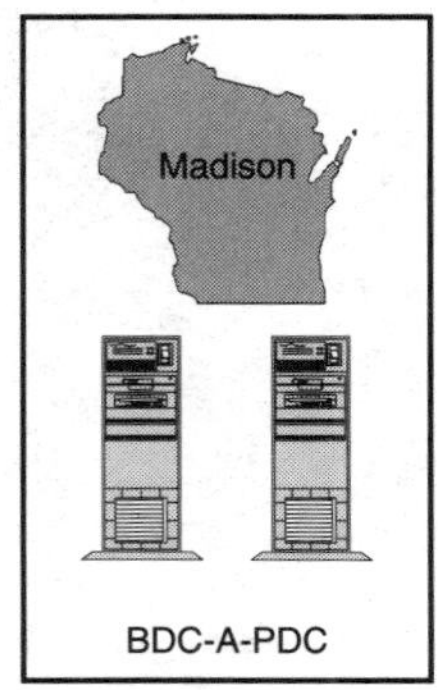

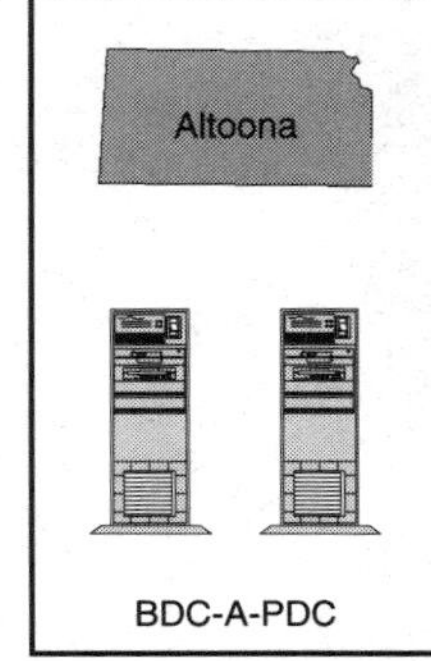

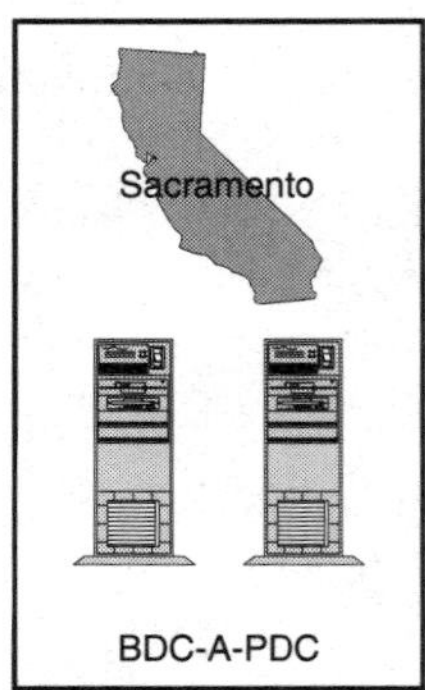

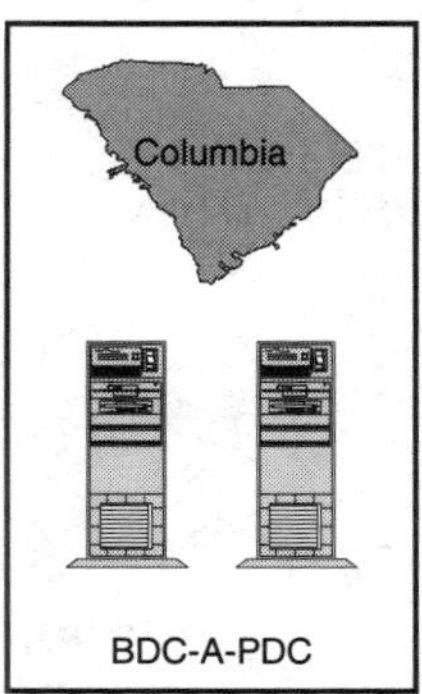

Figure 1.14. *Domain controller placement in a Master Domain Model.*

In a Master or a Multiple Master Domain Model, it is recommended to either:

- Place BDCs for all master domains at each site represented by a resource domain.
- Place all domain controllers for domain masters at one particular site in order to simplify administrative tasks, while having all clients from resource domains authenticate across the WAN link.

Network Bandwidth

Tables 1.1 through 1.3 list the most common network links and group them in three categories:

- Low-to-medium bandwidth
- Medium-to-high bandwidth
- Very high bandwidth

Generally, sites should be designed so that their servers can connect through links in the medium-to-high and very high bandwidth range.

Table 1.1. Low-to-medium bandwidth connections.

Network link	Bandwidth
Dial-Up phone line	2.4Kbp/s to 33.6Kbp/s
X.25 (leased lines)	19.2, 56, and 64KB/s
Frame relay (leased lines)	64 to 512KB/s
Fractional T-1	64KB/s

Table 1.2. Medium-to-high bandwidth connections.

Network link	Bandwidth
Integrated Services Digital Network (ISDN)	64K to 1.544Mbp/s
T-1	1.544MB/s
ArcNet	2.5MB/s
Token Ring	4 or 16MB/s
Thin Ethernet	10MB/s
Thick Ethernet	10MB/s
Fiber optic	10 to 100MB/s
10-BaseX Ethernet	10 to 100MB/s

Common Use	Description
Single user, remote connections to LANs and WANs	Copper, voice-grade wire. Bandwidths of up to 33.6KB/s are possible with high-speed modems configured with the same encoding and compression technology on both ends.
WANs	Provides permanent connections between LAN segments. Access to an X.25 network is through leased or dial-up lines.
WANs	Provides permanent connections between LAN segments. Frame Relay provides better performance than X.25 because it reduces some of the overhead used in X.25.
WANs and redundant	A fraction of a T-1 line. Channels can be added to expand bandwidth up to a full T-1 line.

Common Use	Description
LANs and WANs	High-speed, digital dial-up lines based on the Integrated Services Digital Network standard. Personal computers users benefit the most from these lines.
High-use WAN links	A high-quality digital line that runs over two twisted copper wires. T-1's bandwidth of 1.544MB/s can be divided into 24 64KB/s channels each carrying one voice or data transmission.
LANs	Arranged in a star or bus topology and use a token-passing access method with coaxial cable.
LANs	Arranged in star and ring topologies and use a token-passing access method with shielded or unshielded twisted pair cable.
Single LANs	Arranged in a linear bus topology and use a Carrier Sense Multiple Access with Collision Detection (CSMA/CD) access method with thin or twisted-pair cable.
Multiple LANs	Same as thin Ethernet but with thick cable.
High-use MAN links	Fiber-optic cable that usually follows the Fiber Distributed Data Interface (FDDI) standard. It is used as backbone connections in MANs. Large networks with many LAN segments and heavy traffic benefit from FDDI fiber optic cable.
Campus and Large Office LANs	Twisted-Pair Cable Category 5 specifications designed for mid-size and large LANs.

Table 1.3. Very high bandwidth connections.

Network link	Bandwidth
Satellite connections	128KB/s to 1.544MB/s
Microwave connections	1.544MB/s
T-3	44.184MB/s
Synchronous Optical Network (SONET)	51.8MB/s to 2.5GB/s
Asynchronous Transfer Mode (ATM)	100, 200, and 400MB/s up to 9.6GB/s

Common Use	Description
Wireless WANs (many use them as backup connections)	Wireless connections that provide global data links. AT&T, Tridom, Comsat General Corporation, and GTE Spacenet Corporation offer satellite links.
Wireless LANs	Wireless connections that use waves at the microwave frequency.
High-use WAN links	Similar to T-1 but has higher bandwidth and can be divided microwave into 28 T-1 channels.
WANs	High-speed, fiber-optic connections defined by the SONET set of standards. SONET is an underlying transport network (similar to Ethernet) with a maximum bandwidth that is equivalent to 48 T-3 lines.
WANs, LAN-to-WAN connections	Data transfer technology that provides a way to simultaneously send packets of information from many sources across a high-speed line, where it is reassembled and transferred to each destination point. ATM supports voice and video. ATM can be used on existing fractional T-1, T-1, T-3, and SONET connections as its physical medium.

Chapter 2

LAN/WAN Protocol Management

- **Network Services**
  This chapter examines many service-layer components, including network file systems, network application programming interfaces, and various interprocess communication mechanisms.
- **Network Transport Protocols**
  This section looks at Transport Layer protocols that are often the major component of network stacks.
- **Routing Strategies**
  Learn about options for routing, including software and hardware solutions.
- **Network Access Support**
  Data link and logical link-based standards are discussed, especially those that are implemented at the Enterprise Level.

Understanding NT's Network Architecture

In Windows NT, various software components work together to define a network environment, as shown in Figure 2.1. Each networking component typically provides some complete network function, and also defines an interface through which data can move into or out of or that function to or from other system components.

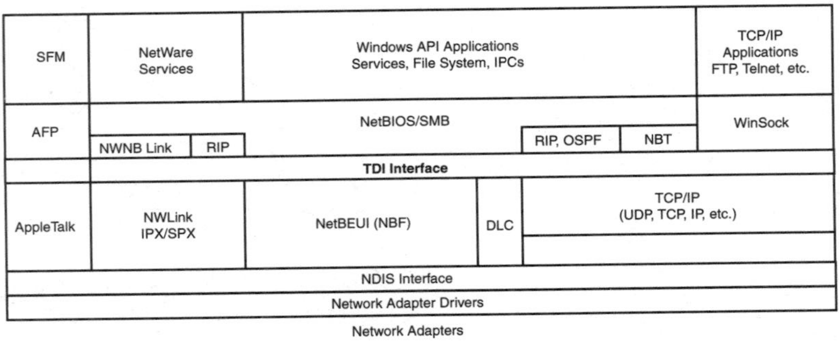

SFM
NetWare Services
Windows API Applications Services, File System, IPCs
TCP/IP Applications FTP, Telnet, etc.
AFP
NetBIOS/SMB
WinSock
NWNB Link
RIP
RIP, OSPF
NBT
TDI Interface
AppleTalk
NWLink IPX/SPX
NetBEUI (NBF)
DLC
TCP/IP (UDP, TCP, IP, etc.)
NDIS Interface
Network Adapter Drivers
Network Adapters

Figure 2.1. *The Windows NT network architecture.*

Components can be added to or deleted from a system without affecting the functionality of other components, unless such components are bound to those other components (binding is discussed later in this chapter). New components can be added to existing networks to add new services, communications, or other capabilities.

Components intercommunicate through interfaces called *boundary layers*, which translate data from a format that's intelligible to the sending component to one that's meaningful to the receiving component. Regardless of the components installed and their design in nature, they all meet at two distinct boundary layers:

- TDI (Transport Driver Interface)
- NDIS (Network Driver Interface Specification)

These are where the upper- and lower-layer bindings are maintained respectively.

TDI is a boundary layer that maintains the upper-layer bindings for services to link up with network protocol drivers. TDI does not exist as a driver, but as an interface standard for passing information between these two areas.

NDIS originated as a joint project between 3Com and Microsoft as an interface for communicating between the protocol driver and the MAC sublayer of the Data-Link OSI layer. Earlier versions of NDIS required a Protocol Manager such as PROTMAN. NT uses an NDIS wrapper (NDIS.SYS) along with an NDIS network driver to communicate with the network interface card.

Using an Internet Service Provider

One major decision that occurs early in the process is whether or not Internet connectivity will be a design goal. You connect to the Internet telecommunications infrastructure by using the services of an *Internet Service Provider (ISP)*.

ISPs can provide both dial-up connectivity for occasional connection to the Internet or dedicated digital lines for high-speed continuous 24-hour connectivity.

Troubleshooting Tip

Be careful not to get caught paying unnecessary Internet access charges. Often smaller companies lease massive amounts of bandwidth from larger telecommunication companies. They then divide it up and sublease the bandwidth to other organizations. For smaller speeds of digital lines, this is often the most convenient route. But often, higher speeds are not recommended through this route due to support issues and higher costs.

If you are leasing digital lines at speeds of 1 Mbps or greater, I recommend going through the larger telecommunications companies like MCI, BellSouth, or Pacific Bell.

There are a number of different corporate, non-profit, and government entities that help make up the Internet infrastructure. Larger telecommunications corporations make up the primary backbone of the U.S. portion of the Internet (see Figure 2.2). There are smaller companies that are designed to provide lower cost access as well as dial-up access for people to the Internet. Often these smaller ISPs lease bandwidth from these larger Network Service Providers (NSPs).

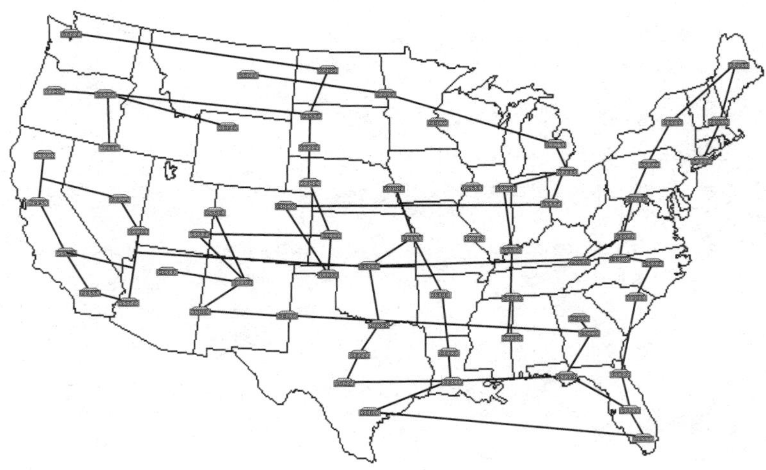

Figure 2.2. *The Internet infrastructure.*

The point where the ISP layer ends and the NSPs begin is often confusing. This is especially true recently since more and more organizations are deciding to go directly with NSPs instead of local ISPs because of fluctuating costs of dedicated lines. While these ISPs are great for dynamic dial-up users, companies that need guaranteed 24-hour connectivity find the extra middle point more of a hassle and not all that cost-effective. One of the terms that has grown in popularity recently is "Don't get caught on the low end of the ISP food chain."

Connecting Directly to the Internet

A dedicated connection to the Internet was required in most cases prior to the National Information Infrastructure Act in 1995. Those who wanted dial-up connection could do so for their users by providing them SLIP or PPP access through the company's dedicated connection. Now the term *dedication* has evolved into obtaining access through either a direct point-of-presence on the Internet backbone, usually through an NSP.

Worldwide Internet Connectivity

As far as other countries are concerned, the same issues exist there as well, especially in recent years. Take Europe for example: European networks use the European Internet backbone also referred to as the *EBONE*. There are some places where this has become obsolete due to the transmission mediums being used and the prevalence of limited bandwidth.

Due to these inefficiencies, many of these countries route traffic through the U.S. backbone via the prime transatlantic gateway.

In this chapter, we talk only about those services primarily offered in the United States and North America.

Author's Note

To find out more about worldwide Internet connectivity, available telecommunication services, and ISPs, search the International Telecommunications Union Web server at: `http://www.itu.ch`. *You can also contact public telecommunication carriers in your area for additional information.*

Network APIs

This section investigates the various individual components of the Windows NT network architecture. As mentioned earlier, three major layers can summarize the Windows NT architecture separated via two boundary layers. The next few pages analyze the various component options available at each layer, starting with the network application programming interfaces that facilitate applications and services exchanging network information to and from the lower layers.

Author's Note

This section will discuss the network components of Windows NT starting from the top of the Network Layer Model. However, when planning the infrastructure of any network or internetwork, you would normally work from the bottom layers on up. When we speak of layers, *we speak of the OSI Model.*

- *Layer 1 is the Physical Layer. At this layer, you would be concerned with the layout of your network physically including the placement of hubs, repeaters, transceivers, and network interface cards. You would also be concerned with the wiring layouts including cabling type, patch panels, and wiring closet locations.*
- *Layer 2 is the Data Link Layer. The IEEE later divided this into two sub-layers: the logical link (LLC) and the Media Access Control (MAC). Layer 2 is where you would be concerned with logical topology, data-link switching, and bridging.*
- *Layer 3 is the Network Layer. This is where you would deal with network protocols and routing strategies, as well as network addressing. Example protocols include IP (Internet Protocol), IPX (Internet Packet Exchange), and the DDP (Datagram Delivery Protocol).*

The first few layers will not be discussed to the degree that they deserve due to the focus of this book. When possible, this section goes into concepts and issues relating specifically to Windows NT at these levels. This section will speak more at the software levels, which are as follows:

- *Layer 4 is the Transport Layer. This includes host-to-host and reliable protocols such as TCP (Transmission Control Protocol), SPX (Sequenced Packet Exchange), and NetBEUI.*
- *Layer 5 is the Session Layer. This includes accessing services via NetBIOS names and Service IDs as well as Windows sockets.*
- *Layer 6 is the Presentation Layer. This area deals with data format translation including character-code translation, such as from ASCII to EBCDIC, as well as local file system to network file system translation, which may or may not incorporate issues such as data compression and encryption.*
- *Layer 7 is the Application Layer. These elements include all components that deal directly with user interaction ranging from a Telnet application all the way to the Directory Service Model.*

NetBIOS

NetBIOS is *still* the native Net API for Windows NT. Many services and security parameters are dependent upon the NetBIOS API. As of Windows NT 4.0, NetBIOS is an imperative component of Windows NT's architecture. *LANA numbers* identify NetBIOS routes. The NetBIOS route consists of the Protocol Helper driver and the network driver that will be used to facilitate NetBIOS commands.

There are certain NetBIOS-dependent services in Windows NT that are common necessities for basic to complex Microsoft Windows-based networks. Their subsequent image files are found in the \%SystemRoot%\system32\drivers directory:

- *The Workstation Service (RDR.SYS).* The service that provides for network connections and communication. This element makes it possible to access resources through shares.
- *Multiple Universal Naming Convention Provider (MUP.SYS).* The element that uses the Universal Naming Convention \\computer\share\directory\etc to redirect I/O requests to the proper destination.
- *The Multi-Provider Router (MPR.SYS).* The element that provides a communication layer between applications that make Win32 Network API calls and the redirectors installed on the Windows NT computer.
- *The Server Service (SVR.SYS).* The service that allows resources on a computer to be made available for access via the network. It also provides for print, named pipe, and file sharing as well as RPCs.

Server Message Blocks

Server Message Blocks (SMBs) are the messages that Microsoft clients and servers use to communicate with each other. SMBs are a higher level protocol and can be transported over NetBEUI, NetBIOS over IPX, and NetBIOS over TCP/IP.

One of the major strengths of SMB is its initial support for Windows NT security. It also defines a security mechanism that enables the network software to offer the protection where it is missing from the operating system (Windows 95/98, and Windows for Workgroups), and supports user-based protection where it is provided by the operating system. The mechanism also allows machines with no concept of user ID to demonstrate access authorization to machines that do have a permission mechanism (DOS, Windows connectivity to Windows NT). Finally, the permission protocol is designed so that it can be omitted if both machines share a common permission mechanism.

SMB uses four message types:

- *Session Control messages.* Commands that start and end a connection with a server.
- *File messages.* Enable you to gain access to directories, files, and name pipes.
- *Printer messages.* Enable you to gain access to and send data to a printer. They also get information from the printer.
- *Messaging messages.* Enables message transfer between computers.

The SMB protocol is also called the *tree connection* protocol. It connects to all server object resources as if it were traversing a local filesystem directory. This occurs even during an interprocess communication. For example, when a user pulls up the Registry Editor REGEDT32.EXE, he or she can select Select Computer and then connect to a remote computer.

With SMB, what actually occurs in this situation is an initial connection to a virtual IPC root using the same UNC syntax as a filesystem directory share (`\\Computername\IPC$`). After the virtual root connection is established, a map is established to a handle that represents the server object resource. In the case of this example, it is `\winreg`. So the mapping from the client process to the server process is similar to that of a tree-based directory (`\\Computername\\IPC$\\winreg`).Service Pack 3, when applied, allows additional support for security signatures. This can provide yet additional security in which a client can be forced to use SMB security signatures in order to establish a connection. If you want to enable support for SMB signatures on an NT server, you will need to perform the following steps:

1. Open one of the Registry Editors (REGEDIT.EXE or REGEDT32.EXE).
2. Navigate to HKEY_LOCAL_MACHINE System\CurrentControlSet\Services\LanManServer\Parameters.
3. Add the following two Registry values:

```
EnableSecuritySignature
Data Type: REG_DWORD
Data: 0 (disable), 1 (enable)

RequireSecuritySignature
Type: REG_DWORD
Value: 0 (disable), 1 (enable)
```

4. Shut down and restart Windows NT.

If you want to enable this support on an NT Workstation acting as a client:

1. Open one of the Registry Editors.
2. Navigate to HKEY_LOCAL_MACHINE\System\CurrentControlSet\Services\Rdr\Parameters.
3. Add the following two values:

```
EnableSecuritySignature
Data Type: REG_DWORD
Data: 0 (disable), 1 (enable)

RequireSecuritySignature
Type: REG_DWORD
Value: 0 (disable), 1 (enable)
```

4. Shut down and restart Windows NT.

Author's Note

If you enable support for SMB signing, you may risk slowing down the overall system performance from 10 to 15 percent.

Common Internet File System

Microsoft was responsible for the development of SMB. They, along with AT&T, Hewlett-Packard, IBM, and Sun Microsystems, are developing the *Common Internet File System (CIFS)*. The CIFS is significantly faster than SMB or NFS (Network File System) because it allows write ahead and has native support for locks. It also has inherent support for TCP/IP and the Domain Name System, and steers away from NetBIOS, unlike the SMB protocol.

Distributed Component Object Model

DCOM is the new client-server standard that takes concepts originating in OLE (Object Linking and Embedding) and extends them into a form of network interprocess communication. DCOM, like OLE, builds its strength around object libraries and containers, which are implemented in DLLs. DCOM's system of these types of software objects is designed to be reusable and replaceable. DCOM is platform-dependent and supports any 32-bit application that is DCOM-aware.

Remote Procedure Calls

RPCs were originally a client-server mechanism developed by Sun Microsystems. RPCs later evolved into the DCE (Distributed Computing Environment) RPC standard developed by the OSF (Open Software Foundation). Windows NT's RPC mechanism is compatible with other DCE-based mechanisms including most flavors of UNIX.

Microsoft's RPC Facility

Microsoft has a proprietary implementation that enables it to also use the other IPC mechanisms (named pipes, mailslots, and so on) to establish communication between a client and a server.

If the client process and the server process exist on the same machine, then local procedure calls (LPCs) are used via the LPC facility.

Named Pipes

A *pipe* is an object handle resident in memory that can be used by a client process to pass information to another pipe used by a server process. This method also works in reverse, from server to client. *Named pipes* are connection-oriented and originate from OS/2 routines that were ported over to the Win32 API. An example of named pipe usage includes SQL connectivity, domain authentication, and remote registry management.

Mailslots

Mailslots provide connectionless oriented communication for broadcasts. There is no guarantee for delivery but the overhead on machines is minimal. The Browser services as well as other mechanisms used to identify servers make use of this mechanism.

Named pipes and mailslots are actually written as file system drivers so that these requests can be processed into SMB commands and so that some of the same characteristics of file systems, such as path structures and access control lists, can be shared. An example of mailslot usage includes the Browser Service.

Windows Sockets

Windows Sockets is the preferred API for integrated client/server computing over TCP/IP networks. Because of this inclusion, third-party Windows Sockets APIs like Trumpet Winsock are no longer needed. Standard Internet applications like Telnet, FTP, and Web browsers use this API.

Windows Sockets provides a standard, widely used Interface-to-Transport Layer that now maps to the TCP/IP and IPX. Windows Sockets was originally developed to make it easier to migrate UNIX applications written to the Berkeley Sockets specification. Not coincidentally, this approach has also made it easier to standardize how protocols are used across multiple platforms (at a certain level, one socket interface is quite like another).

Programs that originated as or descended from UNIX programs most commonly use Windows Sockets. They use service/port identifiers as governed by the IANA (Internet Assigned Numbers Association). The reserved numbers commonly used for Internet applications can be found in the SERVICES file located in the %SYSTEMROOT%\System32\drivers\etc directory under Windows NT. The service number is appended to an IP address or a host name to constitute a socket address.

NWNBLink

Also known as *NBIPX*, NWNBLink is the NetBIOS service driver for IPX/SPX. NWNBLink (see Figure 2.3) is a very fast, routable combination stack that is compatible with Novell's IPX/SPX protocols and provides a NetBIOS Layer. This protocol provides all of the extensions and functionality of NetBEUI and adds routing capability through IPX/SPX.

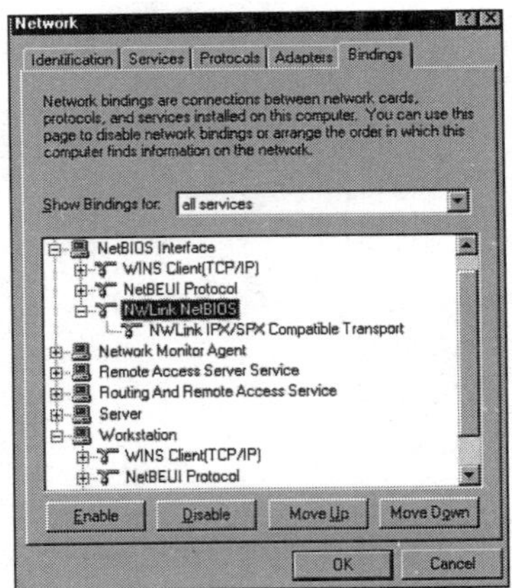

Figure 2.3. *NWNBLink as found in the Bindings tab.*

Transport Protocols

The next several pages discuss Transport Layer protocols supported in Windows NT. Both inherent and non-inherent protocols supported by Windows NT are examined.

NetBEUI

NetBEUI stands for *NetBIOS Enhanced User Interface* and is a protocol design for small LANs with primarily workgroup-based needs. This protocol works at the Logical Link subcomponent of the OSI Data Link Layer. IBM originally developed NetBEUI in 1985.

NetBEUI has several disadvantages: It is not routable, it causes increased network overhead, and it is very dependent upon upper layers for throughput. It is, however, the fastest of all protocols by nature and it is the easiest protocol to set up under Windows NT.

IPX/SPX (NWLink)

NWLink is Microsoft's IPX/SPX implementation that has been modified to support NDIS technology. It is a full 32-bit implementation that provides support for two network APIs.

Features of NWLink include:

- *SPX II.* SPX II is a new Novell implementation of the SPX protocol that has been enhanced to support windowing and has the ability to set a maximum frame size.
- *Multiple bindings.* NWLink, on NT Server, can be bound to multiple network adapters with multiple frame types. Normally, IPX/SPX can be bound using one frame type. The frame type refers to the data link method of packaging the IPX information. Multiple bindings are difficult on NT Workstation since the IPX/SPX dialog box only allows one frame type. This can, however, be overridden via the Registry.
- *Auto-detection of frame types.* NWLink automatically detects which frame type is being used on the network during initial startup and uses that frame type. If there are no frame types on the existing network, NT defaults to 802.2.
- *Direct hosting over IPX.* Increases performance 20 percent on client computers. This also means sessions can be established independently away from NetBIOS. This is helpful, especially for client/server applications.

Configuring IPX/SPX (NWLink)

There are three major options for configuring IPX/SPX (NWLink) with Windows NT:

- The frame type
- The frame type's associated network node number
- The internal network number that can be automatically obtained (as mentioned earlier)

Figure 2.4 shows the NWLink IPX/SPX Properties dialog box, where you can select the internal network number and frame type.

Tip

On NT Workstation, it is often not recommended to do manual configuration if NT servers or NetWare servers are present on the network. On NT Server, you may need to adjust these settings, especially if no NetWare servers are present or if you plan to use the File and Print Services for NetWare (discussed later in this book).

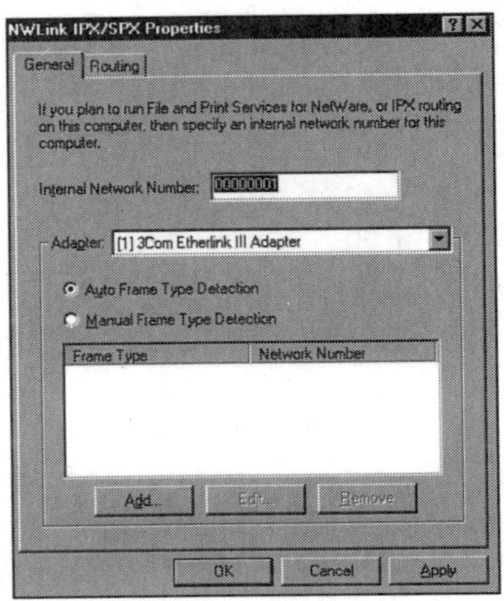

Figure 2.4. *The NWLink configuration dialog box.*

Frame Type

One feature of NWLink IPX/SPX is that it can automatically detect which frame type is being used on the network during boot-up, and resolve to that frame type. If one frame type is detected, it defaults to 802.2. You can manually assign multiple frame types, but of course this causes a little more network traffic.

Tip

Make sure that the IPX/SPX package on a Windows NT computer is configured with the same frame type as the one the NetWare server is using. The NWLink IPX/SPX compatible protocol runs on Ethernet, Token Ring, FDDI, and ARCnet. Each of these topologies requires a specific frame type. If the frame types mismatch, then you will have connectivity problems.

Network Number

Windows NT uses an IPX network number that can be assigned to frame types. This is used primarily for routing purposes. This number is sometimes referred to as the *external network number*, and it must be unique for each network segment.

Internal Network Number

When working with NetWare, every NetWare network has an *internal network number*. This number identifies a logical grouping of NetWare servers. When you install NWLink, this number defaults to zero. When the number is defaulted to zero, it enables auto-detection of the network number. Defaulting the, network number to zero is not recommended for those networks which contain multiple logical IPX networks.

Windows NT also uses an internal network number for internal routing purposes. The internal network number is also known as a *virtual network number*. The internal network number uniquely identifies the computer on the internetwork.

Enabling IPX Routing

IPX routing can be enabled to allow the use of IPX in a multiple segment environment. It can also allow certain NetBIOS-services, such as browsing, to perform across internetworks. We will discuss browsing later in Part III.

To enable IPX routing:

1. Choose the Network icon in the Control Panel.
2. In the Protocols tab, select NWLink IPX/SPX Compatible Transport, and then click Properties.
3. In the Routing tab, select the Enable RIP Routing checkbox, then click OK. You are then prompted to allow NetBIOS propagation over IPX (type 30 packets), as shown in Figure 2.5. Click Yes if you want to allow the encapsulation of NetBIOS information to cross routers.

Author's Note

The initial release of Windows NT 4.0 does not provide LAN to WAN to LAN routing. If you want to enable this feature, you will need to obtain Microsoft's Routing and Remote Access Services upgrade from `http://www.backoffice.microsoft.com`.

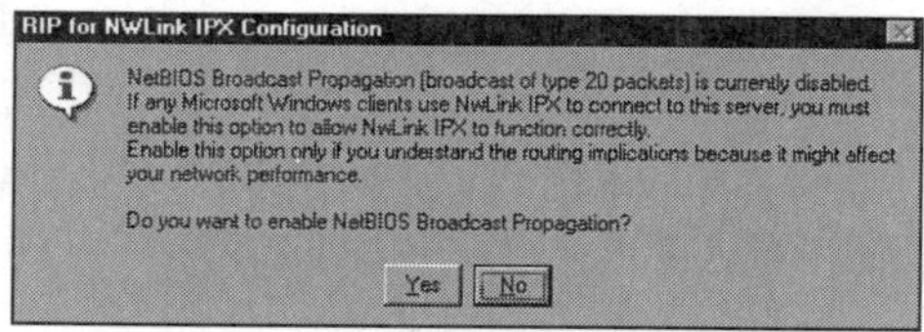

Figure 2.5. *The NetBIOS propagation over IPX dialog box.*

Using IPX and RIP

Windows NT includes RIP (Routing Information Protocol) for IPX. This allows for dynamic routing over Windows NT using an intelligent routing algorithm. The concept of routing and routing protocols is discussed later in this section.

If you are using RIP for IPX, the IPXROUTE utility is excellent for helping you manage and troubleshoot IPX RIP source routing. In addition to current source routing information, the IPXROUTE utility provides information on RIP, SAP, and statistics. Use the IPXROUTE utility to display and modify information about the source routing tables used by IPX. The IPXROUTE console utility can even be used remotely by means of the remote utility found in the Windows NT Resource Kit version 3.5 or later. The remote utility as well as other remote administration utilities are discussed in Chapter 4, "Remote Administrative Services."

The syntax for IPXROUTE is as follows:

```
ipxroute board=n [clear] [def] [gbr] [mbr] [remove=xxxxx]
ipxroute config
ipxroute table
ipxroute servers [/type=xxx]
ipxroute stats [/show] [/clear]
```

The IPXROUTE `board` option allows the management of static routes and source routes. This also has several additional sub-options:

`board=`*n*	Specifies the network adapter card for which to query or set parameters.
`clear`	Clears the source routing table.
`def`	Sends packets to the `ALL ROUTES` broadcast. If a packet is transmitted to a unique media access control (MAC) address that is not in the source routing table, the default is to send the packet to the `SINGLE ROUTES` broadcast.
`gbr`	Sends packets to the `ALL ROUTES` broadcast. If a packet is transmitted to the broadcast address (`FFFF FFFF FFFF`), the default is to send the packet to the `SINGLE ROUTES` broadcast.
`mbr`	Sends packets to the `ALL ROUTES` broadcast. If a packet is transmitted to a multicast address (`C000 xxxx xxxx`), the default is to send the packet to the `SINGLE ROUTES` broadcast.
`remove=xxxxx`	Removes the given node address from the source routing table.

When a computer using NWLink receives an IPX/SPX broadcast packet or an IPX/SPX packet with its node address not in its source routing table, the computer forwards the packet as a Single Route Broadcast frame by default. `ipxroute table` displays the current source routing table. The `ipxroute config` displays information on all the bindings for which IPX is configured. The `ipxroute table` displays the IPX routing table. The `ipxroute servers` displays the SAP table. It contains the following sub-options:

`/type=xxx`	*xxx* refers to server type. The default is all server types.
`stats`	Displays or clears IPX internal routing statistics.
`/show`	Displays the internal routing table. This is the default option.
`/clear`	Clears the internal routing table.

Author's Note

The IPXROUTE utility changes NWLINK parameters only for the current Windows NT session. In order to permanently change NWLink parameters, you must set them in the Registry under HKEY_LOCAL _MACHINE\System\CurrentControlSet\Services\NWLnkipx. This will prevent the administrator from having to keep doing it every time you boot up Windows NT.

AppleTalk

AppleTalk is Apple's network protocol for Macintosh networks. A Windows NT machine can use this protocol for connecting to Macintosh Hosts. A Windows NT server can use AppleTalk as a protocol with Services for Macintosh, providing a full Server service for Macintosh computers.

Windows NT also supports EtherTalk, Apple's AppleTalk over Ethernet support. EtherTalk is much faster than regular AppleTalk (LocalTalk).

Service for Macintosh networks allow File and Print Services for Macintosh clients. Macintosh workstations view the network as a true AppleTalk network. Users make connections with the AppleShare Chooser. As a result, Macintosh and PC users see one seamless network.

AppleTalk transport technology comes with its own set of terminology. Before we discuss the configuration of AppleTalk networks, we need to become familiar with these terms.

AppleTalk Nodes

AppleTalk networks communicate with each other using a unique logical addressing scheme. The address consists of a network ID that identifies a subnet and the node address. These are separated by periods. For example, Node 5, a computer running AppleTalk, running on the subnet 13, would have an AppleTalk node address of 5.13.

In order for an AppleTalk node to communicate with other nodes, it must first obtain this information through dynamic assignment. While other protocols offer dynamic node assignment as an option (TCP/IP uses DHCP and BOOTP), AppleTalk makes all node assignments automatically. When the computer boots up, it obtains its node address and its subnet's network range from its network's routers. The network routers will have this information already configured in order to route frames between subnets.

AppleTalk Phase 1

The first AppleTalk implementation was called *AppleTalk Phase 1*. Phase 1 networks offered an 8-bit field for the node address. This gives the network a maximum node range of 256. When this was being developed, the only transmission medium used was the LocalTalk cabling. In fact, due to physical limitations, the maximum recommended limit was 32 nodes for a LocalTalk network. Logical routing was not available, therefore, when Ethernet support became available, there was a need for revamping the standard.

AppleTalk Phase 2

In 1989, AppleTalk revised AppleTalk. The basic idea of this revision was to break the restriction of a single network number per cable segment. A 16-bit network field was made available, giving a maximum support of more than 65,000 networks available for assignment, with 253 nodes available per network. This gave a mathematical possibility of over 16 million AppleTalk nodes. In AppleTalk Phase 2, the last portion of the range (networks 65,280 through 65,534) are reserved as the startup range, leaving the previous numbers available for assignment.

AppleTalk Routing

Windows NT includes the complete AppleTalk stack, which facilitates routing. AppleTalk routers rely on routing tables just like other routable protocols. Routing is discussed in general later in this section. AppleTalk uses the *RTMP* or *Routing Table Maintenance Protocol* to maintain routing tables. RTMP updates these routing tables via a broadcast every 10 seconds. This is similar in concept and design to the Routing Information Protocol (RIP).

Seed Routing

Every router must be informed of the network range of each subnet that it is connected to. It must also have at least one path to each subnet on the network and it must know the network range assigned to each subnet. Each router keeps track of paths and network ranges in its routing table. Since manually entering the complete table into each router would be extraneous, the administrator instead pre-configures the routing table of at least one router on each subnet along with its network range.

This process is referred to as *seed routing* and these computers are referred to as *seed routers*. Each seed router broadcasts its *seed ranges* to each of its subnets. Non-seed routers on these subnets receive this information and add it to their routing tables, and every 10 seconds each router (seed router or otherwise) rebroadcasts its entire routing table to each of its subnets.

AppleTalk has limitations on routing. For example, the datagram component of AppleTalk, the Datagram Delivery Protocol, has a limitation on the amount of interfaces it can cross. Usually these interfaces are AppleTalk routers. When describing routing, the term *hop* is used to describe the units crossed during a route. AppleTalk has a maximum hop count of 15.

Zones

Seed routers are also responsible for the creation and management of AppleTalk zones. A *zone* is a logical grouping of computers. It is written in many sources that a zone can be analogous to an NT domain. I find it more analogous to a workgroup or a TCP/IP domain. When routers update their routing tables, they also periodically update their listing of zones.

Each AppleTalk subnet has a default zone. When a node boots and contacts a router for network range information, the reply also includes the name of the AppleTalk subnet's default zone. Unlike Windows NT domains, zones are voluntary associations: a user can make a node leave one zone to join another at any time.

The AppleTalk routers use the *Zone Information Protocol (ZIP)* to determine which networks are associated with each zone. These zone-to-network mappings are kept in a Zone Information Table. This table then can be sent to applications that may request it, such as the Macintosh Chooser. It also can be sent when a user clicks the Get Zones button under the Services for Macintosh properties option in the Network Control Panel.

Author's Note

Zone names can contain up to 32 characters that are not case-insensitive. Spaces are accepted as part of the zone name.

Configuring AppleTalk

You can configure AppleTalk once it is set up. For the changes to take effect, you must stop and restart the AppleTalk Protocol (through the Devices icon in Control Panel) or reboot the computer.

To configure AppleTalk:

1. In the Network Control Panel, select the Services tab. In the Services tab, select Services for Macintosh and then click Properties.
2. In the Network box, select the network adapter card you want.
3. For computers running Windows NT Server, in the Zone box, select the zone in which you want Services for Macintosh to appear to Macintosh users. For computers running Windows NT Workstation, in the Zone box, select the zone in which you will use AppleTalk.
4. Click OK.
5. To enable AppleTalk routing (Windows NT Server only), select the Enable Routing checkbox (see Figure 2.6). On computers running Windows NT Server, the AppleTalk protocol will become a router. This means that if the AppleTalk protocol is bound to more than one network card, the computer running Windows NT Server will be seen from Macintoshes connected to all the bound networks.

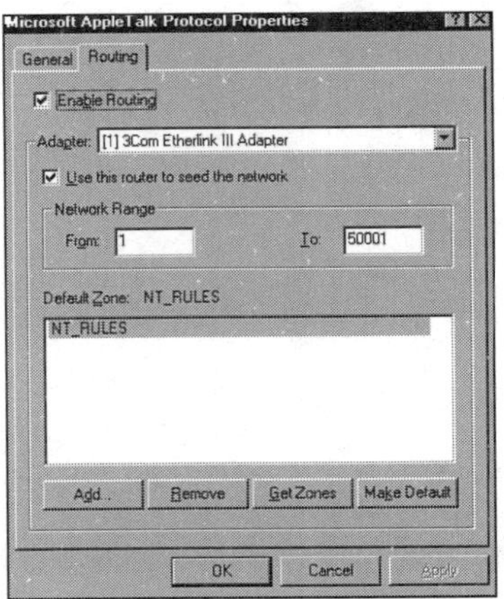

Figure 2.6. *The AppleTalk Network Configuration dialog box.*

To seed the network:

1. Select the Seed the Network box. The Network Range and Zone Information options become available.

2. Enter a start and end number in the appropriate Network Range boxes. The values you specify must be from 1 through 65,279. Setting zone information is part of seeding a network. You can see the current list of zones, add and remove zones, and set the default zone. The default zone is the zone in which all AppleTalk devices will appear if a desired zone has not been specified for them.

To set zone information, choose among the following options: New Zone and Add button. Add a zone by typing the name in the New Zone box and clicking Add. The new zone is added to the Zone list.

TCP/IP

TCP/IP (Transmission Control Protocol/Internet Protocol) is actually a suite of protocols developed for connectivity in the early 1970s by the Department of Defense. This *de juro* standard provides connectivity primarily to UNIX hosts, as well as other operating systems and hardware platforms. It has full routing support and is the global standard that has evolved into what is known as today's Internet.

As you can see in Figure 2.7, Windows NT provides support for all of the core network and host-to-host layer components. TCP/IP under Windows NT also allows for SNMP (Simple Network Management Protocol) support as well as DHCP (Dynamic Host Configuration Protocol) support.

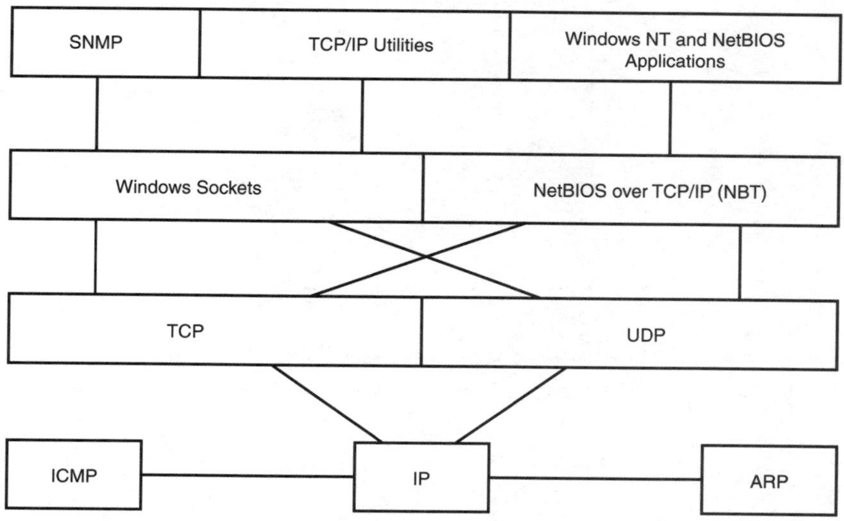

Figure 2.7. *The TCP/IP protocol stack as it is implemented in Windows NT.*

Microsoft's TCP/IP NDIS-Based Suite

When you install TCP/IP, it requires certain unique configuration information:

- *IP address*. A unique 32-bit address that identifies a TCP/IP host. This IP address is often referred to as a *dotted quad address*. The address has two or three parts: a network number, an optional subnet number, and a host number.
- *Subnet mask*. An address that specifies whether an IP address is on a local or a remote network. Also known as an *address mask*, the subnet mask is an address that is used to identify which bits in an IP address are network significant, subnet significant, and host significant.
- *Default gateway (router)*. The IP address of the interface to remote networks.

Configuring TCP/IP Manually

Manual TCP/IP configuration means that the administrator manually assigns the three required configuration components. However, if the TCP/IP network is local only, the default gateway address isn't needed. In Figure 2.8, you can see the TCP/IP dialog box where you can opt to manually configure TCP/IP or obtain the TCP/IP configuration from a DHCP server.

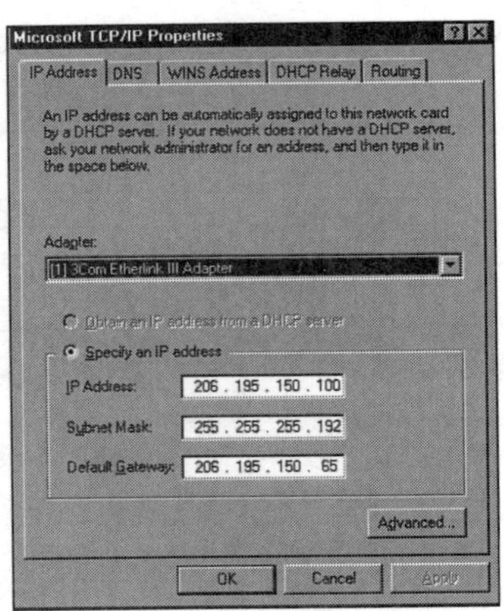

Figure 2.8. *The TCP/IP Configuration dialog box.*

For TCP/IP to work on your computer, it must be configured with the IP addresses, subnet mask, and default gateway for each network adapter on the computer.

Configuring TCP/IP Automatically

The best method for ensuring easy and accurate installation of TCP/IP is to use automatic DHCP configuration, which uses DHCP to configure your local computer with the correct IP address, subnet mask, and default gateway.

You can take advantage of this method for configuring TCP/IP if there is a DHCP server installed on your network. You cannot use DHCP configuration for a server that you are installing as a DHCP server.

To configure TCP/IP using DHCP, make sure the Enable Automatic DHCP Configuration option is checked in either the Windows NT TCP/IP Installation Options dialog box or the TCP/IP Configuration dialog box, which is shown in Figure 2.8.

When you restart the computer after completing TCP/IP installation, the DHCP server automatically provides the correct configuration information for your computer.

Warning

After installing TCP/IP and electing to use DHCP, if you then try to configure TCP/IP in the Network Control Panel, the system will warn you that any manual settings will override the automatic settings provided by DHCP. This is actually only true for the default gateway, plus any advanced options such as DNS or WINS. It is recommended that you not change the automatic settings unless you specifically want to override a setting provided by DHCP.

IP Addressing

All network interface devices, both physical and virtual, are identified by a unique 32-bit dotted decimal address. This address also specifies routing information in an internetwork. An IP address looks like this:

206.195.150.122

Network ID and Host ID

While the IP address is designed to be unique and singular, it actually contains two pieces of information. The leftmost portion is the *network ID* and the second-most portion is the *host ID*.

If you plan on connecting computers to the Internet, you must obtain an official network ID from the Network Information Center. This is how all of the addresses on the Internet are kept unique. The InterNIC can be contacted via email at `info@internic.net` (for the United States, 1-800-444-4345 or, for Canada and overseas, 619-455-4600). Internet registration requests can be sent to `hostmaster@internic.net`. You can also use FTP to connect to `is.internic.net`, then log in as **anonymous**, and change to the /INFOSOURCE/FAQ directory.

IP Address Classes

IP addresses are divided into different classes. These classes determine the maximum number of hosts per network ID. Only three classes are actually used for network connectivity. The following table lists all of the address classes.

Class A Addresses	Values 0-126	0XXXXXXX
Reserved Loopback	Address Value-127	01111111
Class B Addresses	Values 128-191	10XXXXXX
Class C Addresses		110XXXXX
Reserved Multicast Addresses	Values 224-239	1110XXXX
Reserved Experimental Addresses	Values 240-255	1111XXXX

Because the sender's IP address is included in every outgoing IP packet, it is useful for the receiving computer system to derive the originating network ID and host ID from the IP address field. Using subnet masks, as described in the following section, does this.

Proxy Server Issues

There are some problems that arise in those networks which use proxy servers for isolation. They often use a single address and share it via certain mechanisms. One of those methods is the *Internal Network-Internet approach*. To facilitate this, the IANA (The Internet Assigned Numbers Authority) reserved some Class A, B, and C networks for use by internal networks isolated via a proxy server. They are as follows:

Class A: 10.0.0.0

Class B: 172.162.0.0 to 172.31.0.0

Class C: 192.168.1.0 to 192.168.255

Subnet Masks

Subnet masks are determined by assigning 1s to bits that belong to the network ID and 0s to the bits that belong to the host ID. Once the bits are in place, the 32-bit value is converted to dotted decimal notation, as shown in the following table.

Default Subnet Masks for Standard IP Address Classes

The following table lists the default subnet masks for each available class of TCP/IP networks. Bear in mind that a default Class C subnet mask is identical to a Class B network that has been subnetted into 254 subnets.

Address Class	Bits for Subnet Mask	Subnet Mask
Class A	11111111 00000000 00000000 00000000	255.0.0.0
Class B	11111111 11111111 00000000 00000000	255.255.0.0
Class C	11111111 11111111 11111111 00000000	255.255.255.0

TCP/IP Utilities

The following sections discuss some utilities found in Windows NT that can be used to test TCP/IP connectivity. PING and TRACERT use ICMP (Internet Control Message Protocol) to diagnose connectivity. Each of the others use primarily TCP and UDP to provide the application services the connectivity.

PING

PING stands for *Packet InterNet Grouper*. PING uses the ICMP (Internet Control Message Protocol) component to verify configurations and tests connections. PING is the most popular error-testing protocol.

Syntax:

```
ping [-t] [-a] [-n count] [-l size] [-f] [-i TTL] [-v TOS] [-r count] [-s
count] [[-j host-list] ¦ [-k host-list]] [-w timeout] destination-list
```

`-t`	Pings the specified host until interrupted.
`-a`	Resolves addresses to hostnames.
`-n` *count*	Number of echo requests to send.
`l` *size*	Sends buffer size.
`-f`	Sets the "Don't Fragment" flag in packet.
`-i TTL`	Time To Live.
`-v TOS`	Type Of Service.
`-r` *count*	Record route for count hops.
`-s` *count*	Timestamp for count hops.
`-j` *host-list*	Loose source route along *host-list*.
`-k` *host-list*	Strict source route along *host-list*.
`-w` *timeout*	Timeout in milliseconds to wait for each reply.

TRACERT

TRACERT actually tests the route that travels from your computer to the remote hostname or IP address specified.

Syntax:

```
tracert [-d] [-h maximum_hops] [-j host-list] [-w timeout] target_name
```

`-d`	Do not resolve addresses to hostnames.
`-h` *`maximum_hops`*	Maximum number of hops to search for target.
`-j` *`host-list`*	Loose source route along host list.
`-w` *`timeout`*	Wait *`timeout`* milliseconds for each reply.

FTP

The File Transfer Protocol lets a user on one computer access and transfer files to and from another remote host using the TCP protocol.

Some of the available FTP commands include:

`?`	Displays help information.
`ascii`	Sets the file transfer mode to ASCII.
`binary`	Sets the file transfer mode to binary.
`bye`	Leaves FTP.
`cd`	Changes the working directory.
`close`	Closes the current connection.
`delete`	Deletes file.
`dir`	Prints current working directory.
`disconnect`	Closes current connection.
`get`	Gets file.
`help`	Displays information.
`lcd`	Changes the local directory.
`ls`	Lists remote directory.
`mdelete`	Multiple file delete.
`mdir`	Views multiple directories.
`mget`	Gets multiple directories.
`mkdir`	Creates a directory.
`mput`	Uploads multiple files.
`open`	Opens a remote connection.
`put`	Uploads file.

`pwd`	Prints current working directory.
`quit`	Leaves FTP.
`quote`	Sends a remote command.
`rename`	Renames file or directory.
`rmdir`	Removes directory.
`send`	Sends remote file.
`type`	Types a remote file.
`user`	Logs in remotely.

Ipconfig

Ipconfig displays all current TCP/IP network configuration values. This command is of particular use on systems running DHCP, allowing users to determine which TCP/IP configuration values have been configured by DHCP.

Syntax:

```
ipconfig [/? ¦ /all ¦ /release [adapter] ¦ /renew [adapter]]
```

`/?`	Displays the help message.
`/all`	Displays full configuration information.
`/release`	Releases the IP address for the specified adapter.
`/renew`	Renews the IP address for the specified adapter.

The default is to display only the IP address, subnet mask and default gateway for each adapter bound to TCP/IP. For `/release` and `/renew`, if no adapter name is specified, the IP address leases for all adapters bound to TCP/IP are released or renewed.

FINGER

FINGER displays information about a user on a specified system running the Finger service. The output varies based on the remote system. This command is available only if the TCP/IP protocol has been installed.

Syntax:

```
FINGER [-l] [user]@host [...]
```

`-l`	Displays information in long list format.
`user`	Specifies the user you want information about. Omit the *`user`* parameter to display information about all users on the specified host.
`@host`	Specifies the server on the remote system whose users you want information about.

ARP

ARP stands for the *Address Resolution Protocol* and displays a listing of the ARP cache. This cache contains the locally resolved IP addresses to MAC addresses.

Syntax:

```
ARP -s inet_addr eth_addr [if_addr]
ARP -d inet_addr [if_addr]
ARP -a [inet_addr] [-N if_addr]
```

`-a`	Displays current ARP entries by interrogating the current protocol data. If `inet_addr` is specified, the IP and physical addresses for only the specified computer are displayed. If more than one network interface uses ARP, entries for each ARP table are displayed.
`-g`	Same as `-a`.
`inet_addr`	Specifies an Internet address.
`-N if_addr`	Displays the ARP entries for the network interface specified by `if_addr`.
`-d`	Deletes the host specified by `inet_addr`.
`-s`	Adds the host and associates the Internet address `inet_addr` with the physical address `eth_addr`. The physical address is given as six hexadecimal bytes separated by hyphens. The entry is permanent.
`eth_addr`	Specifies a physical address.
`if_addr`	If present, specifies the Internet address of the interface with the address translation table that should be modified. If not present, the first applicable interface is used.
`HOSTNAME`	Returns the IP hostname of your computer.

DLC

The *Data Link Control (DLC) protocol* is a transport mechanism not really designed for connectivity between computers like the aforementioned transport protocols. Windows NT uses it for the purpose of connectivity to IBM mainframes (via 3270 terminal emulation) or accessing HP printers such as the 4si that is attached directly to the network.

Windows NT can also use DLC to facilitate the Remote Boot Service. This service allows RPL (Remote Program Load) clients to load MS-DOS, Windows for Workgroups, or Windows 95 operating system clients from images stored on the server.

DECnet/DEC Pathworks

Digital Equipment Corporation (DEC) provides support for the DECnet Protocol through DEC Pathworks integration (see Figure 2.9). The PATHWORKS version 5 package for OpenVMS server works well as a down-level server in a Windows NT domain. It can assume the role of a BDC, Member server, or Standalone server in a Windows NT domain as a down-level server. A *down-level server* is a Microsoft LAN Manager server running in a Windows NT domain that supports an SMB protocol level less than version 3.0.

Included with Windows NT is support for DECnet printing. The Digital Network Port print monitor, Decpsmon.dll, sends print jobs to DEC's PrintServer print devices and to other DEC print devices (such as the DEClaser 5100 and the DECcolorwriter 1000). Windows NT supplies the TCP/IP network protocol, but does not supply the DECnet protocol. If you want to use DECnet, you must contact DEC to obtain it.

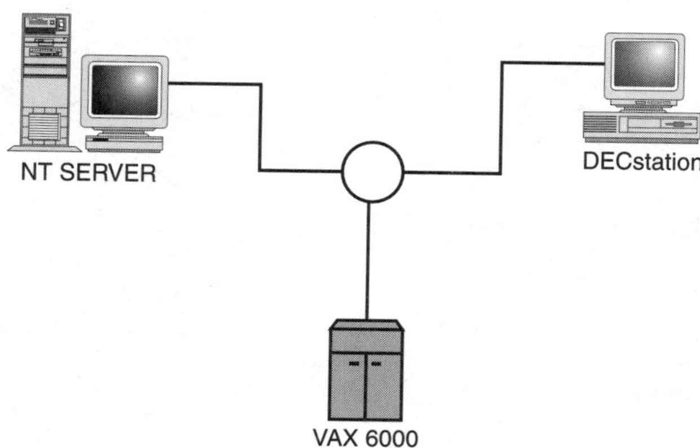

Figure 2.9. *DECnet integration.*

VINES/IP

VINES uses the VINES Internetwork Protocol (VIP) to perform Layer 3 activities (including internetwork routing). VINES also supports its own Address Resolution Protocol (ARP), its own version of the Routing Information Protocol (RIP) called the *Routing Table Protocol (RTP)*, and the *Internet Control Protocol (ICP)*, which provides exception handling and special routing cost information. ARP, ICP, and RTP packets are encapsulated in a VIP header.

VINES Internetwork Protocol (VIP)

VINES network-layer addresses are 48-bit entities subdivided into network (32 bits) and subnetwork (16 bits) portions. The network number is better described as a server number because it is derived directly from the *server's key* (a hardware module that identifies a unique number and the software options for that server). The subnetwork portion of a VINES address is better described as a host number because it is used to identify hosts on VINES networks.

Routing with RTP

The Vines/IP stack uses the RTP Protocol to provide routing capabilities. RTP (Routing Table Protocol) distributes network routing information. Routing update packets are broadcast periodically by both client and service nodes. These packets inform neighbors of a node's existence and also indicate whether the node is a client or a service node. Service nodes also include, in each routing update packet, a list of all known networks and the cost factors associated with reaching those networks. This is referred to as *Distance Vector Routing*. Different types of routing are discussed later in this chapter.

StreetTalk Directory Services

Windows NT connects to Banyan Enterprise environments using the StreetTalk Directory services client for Windows NT Workstation. The Enterprise Client allows for File and Print Access to allow NT servers and workstations the option of connecting to StreetTalk resources. As of this printing, the Enterprise Client is up to version 8.06.

Routing Strategies

It was mentioned in brief earlier that bridges, switches, and routers use tables of addresses to forward packets to the proper destination network and node. Routers differ from bridges and switches in that instead of just tracking Layer 2 addresses, routers maintain tables of logical addresses (Layer 3). Therefore, configuration of routers will be protocol-specific. With routers, segmenting along with subnetting is possible in that broadcast packets are typically not forwarded across the routers unless certain types have been configured to do so with protocol helpers. Since routers are highly configurable, packet forwarding can occur in a very controlled manner.

Developing solid routing strategies is important to designing solid Windows NT internetworks. To understand how routing fits in to Windows NT, you need to be sure to have a strong understanding of routing concepts. It is the responsibility of routers to direct traffic through an internetwork, based upon information learned from network protocols.

There are two approaches to routers:

- You could use Windows NT Server as a router using software services.

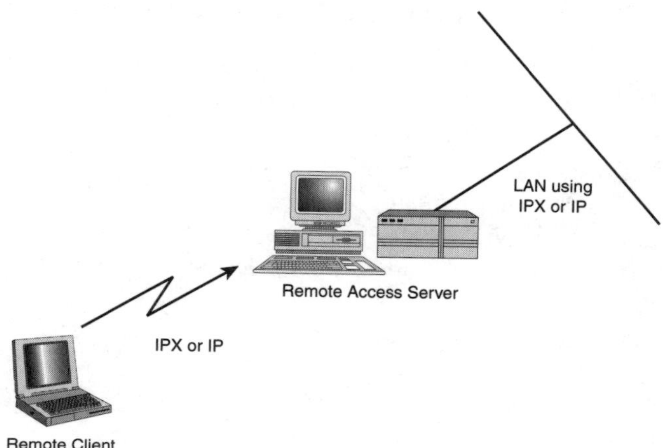

Figure 2.10. *Routing from a dial-up client to a LAN and from a LAN to another LAN.*

- You can use dedicated hardware routers such as Cisco, Bay, and/or IBM routers. (In Cisco routers, the operating system is called the *Internetwork Operating System*.)

Routing Design with Windows NT

Windows NT 4.0 includes a built-in Multi-Protocol Router. The Multi-Protocol Routing and the Routing Information Protocol (RIP) routing options allows your Windows NT Server computer to route network packets between two or more network adapters using RIP, as shown in Figure 2.10, on IP, IPX, or both. You can also configure your server to become a DHCP Relay Agent (depending on your configuration), which allows a computer to relay DHCP messages across an IP network (in a similar fashion to BOOTP).

It isn't possible to route between WANs over switched circuits or dial-up lines. The only exception to this rule is a WAN card (for example, T-1 or Frame Relay) that appears to the router as a LAN card.

Types of Routing Protocols

Routing can be managed using static routing or dynamic routing. *Static routing* requires an administrator to manually submit routes to a routing table while *dynamic routing* allows information relating to routing tables to be exchanged using intelligent algorithms.

When using routing protocols, deciding on a basic type to implement will depend on the interfaces involved. Within an autonomous system (your corporate internetwork, for example), it is recommended to use an interior routing protocol. When routing outside the autonomous system, an exterior routing protocol is recommended. Each type may employ one of two major types of routing algorithms, described in the following sections.

Distance Vector

The *distance vector algorithm* requires each router involved in the routing process to keep track of its distance from each other. A distance vector protocol will announce an update on a regular basis that contains all of its information contained on its local routing table. The other routers collect this information. Once these routers receive the update, they decide which entries should be put into the routing table. The distance is determined in *hops*, or metric costs. These units refer to the amount of interfaces the route crosses. Examples of Distance Vector Routing protocols include RIP (Routing Information Protocol), Apple's RTMP (Routing Table Maintenance Protocol), and Banyan's RTP (Routing Table Protocol).

Link State

A *link state algorithm* is much different from a distance vector. When a router first enters the network using a link state routing protocol, it will first find out which routers are directly connected to it. Each router then sends out and collects each other's *Link State Announcements (LSAs)*, which list the names and costs of its adjacent routers. Each router now knows the routes for the internetwork through cooperation and can use this database to help determine the most optimal route. Examples of Link State Routing Protocols include OSPF (Open Shortest Path First) and NLSP (Netware Link State Protocol).

Interior Versus Exterior Protocols

In addition to the type of routing algorithm being used, the next major area of categorizing protocols is whether a routing protocol is a host routing, interior, or exterior routing protocol. *Host routing* refers to those protocols that directly affect the router. *Interior routing protocols* are responsible for locating networks and routes within a common area of network management, or an autonomous system. *Exterior routing protocols* are used to connect different autonomous systems such as connecting to the Internet.

Examples of host routing protocols include:

- The Proxy Address Resolution Protocol (Proxy ARP)
- Static Configuration
- ICMP Router Discovery Protocol (IRDP)
- Gateway Discovery Protocol (GDP)

Examples of Interior Routing Protocols include:

- Routing Information Protocol (RIP)

- Interior Gateway Routing Protocol (IGRP)
- Enhanced IGRP (EIGRP)
- Integrated Intermediate System-to-Intermediate System (IS-IS)
- Open Shortest Path First (OSPF)

Examples of exterior routing protocols include:

- Border Gateway Protocol
- Exterior Gateway Protocol

Exterior Gateway Protocol

Exterior Gateway Protocol (EGP) is a link state Internet routing protocol by which gateways exchange information about what systems they can reach; this protocol is documented in RFC 904. Generally, an EGP is any internetworking prototcol used for passing routing information between autonomous systems.

EGP has three basic components:

- *Neighbor acquisition*: Allows routers to receive adjacent routing updates.
- *Neighbor reachability*: Allows cost information to be exchanged between routers.
- *Routing information*: Contains the routing table information.

Originally EGP reachability information was passed into ARPAnet/MILnet core gateways where the best routes were chosen and passed back out to all connected autonomous systems. As the Internet moved toward a less hierarchical architecture, EGP, an exterior routing protocol which assumes a hierarchical structure, became less effective.

Before EGP sends routing information to a remote router it must establish an adjacency with that router. This is accomplished by an exchange of Hello (not to be confused with the HELLO protocol, or OSPF HELLO messages) and I Heard You (I-H-U) messages with that router. Computers communicating via EGP are called *EGP neighbors*, and the exchange of Hello and I-H-U messages is referred to as *acquiring a neighbor*.

Border Gateway Protocol

Border Gateway Protocol (BGP) is a link state exterior gateway protocol used to exchange network reachability information with other BGP systems. BGP routers form relationships with other BGP routers. Using an entity called a *BGP speaker*, BGP routers transmit and receive current routing information over a reliable transport layer connection. Because a reliable transport mechanism is used, periodic updates are not necessary.

BGP was designed to be an improvement to EGP. BGP updates contain *path attributes* that describe the route to some set of destination networks. When multiple paths are available, BGP compares these path attributes to choose the preferred path.

Routing Information Protocol

Routing Information Protocol (RIP) is a distance vector protocol. A RIP router periodically broadcasts a routing update message that contains an entry for each network it can reach, as well as the cost to that network. RIP routers listen to all RIP broadcast messages. The message contains the destination address of host or network, the IP address of the gateway sending the address, and a metric cost to the destination.

RIPII is an enhancement to RIP; it includes the subnetwork mask in its routes. The lack of subnetwork mask information limits RIP to advertising only networks routes, or requires RIP routers to make assumptions about the subnetwork mask. When RIP is used in a network with subnetworks, all the subnetworks are usually required to use the same subnetwork mask.

RIPII can be used in network topologies requiring variable length subnetwork masks, and it can support subnet zero. RIPII can also authenticate routing message exchanges. RIPII uses multicast addresses instead of broadcast addresses. Not all RIP routers support RIPII.

RIP version I is supported inherently in Windows NT 4.0 for both IP and IPX. This is part of the Windows NT Multi-Protocol Router Service.

> **Tip**
>
> *RIP II is supported through the newly released Routing and Remote Access Services (RRAS) for NT, also known as Steelhead.*

> **Troubleshooting Tip**
>
> *In larger internetworks that connect serial-line WAN links to Ethernet LAN segments, RIP is not recommended because it only supports metric costs up to 15 and it does not carry subnet mask information. Also, RIP-enabled devices accept RIP information from anyone.*

Interior Gateway Routing Protocol

The *Interior Gateway Routing Protocol (IGRP)* is a proprietary, router-to-router, intra-area protocol developed by Cisco Systems for routing.

The big differences between IGRP and RIP are in the metric and default gateway options. One of the main functions of a router is to choose the "best" path between a source and a destination. Because each path might comprise many links, a method of comparing the links is required. Rather than characterizing each link along the path with only one metric (as does RIP—it counts only hops), IGRP uses five metrics.

The metrics evaluated are the link's speed (or available bandwidth), delay, packet size, loading, and reliability. In networks with diverse data link types, this can be an important improvement. Enhanced IGRP supports TCP/IP, IPX, and AppleTalk, and provides many of the benefits of link-state router-to-router protocols.

Open Shortest Path First

The *Open Shortest Path First (OSPF)* protocol is a shortest path first (SPF) or link-state protocol. OSPF is better suited than RIP for complex networks with many routers. OSPF is an interior gateway protocol that distributes routing information between routers in a single autonomous system (AS). OSPF chooses the least-cost path as the best path.

OSPF is regarded as suitable for complex networks with a large number of routers. OSPF provides equal-cost multipath routing where packets to a single destination can be sent via more than one interface simultaneously.

In OSPF, you will encounter four types of router roles:

- *Backbone routers*: These have their interface connected only to the router.
- *Area border routers*: These routers can attach to multiple areas.
- *Internal router*: These routers have all of their interfaces connected to the same area.
- *Autonomous system boundary router:* These routers exchange information with routers belonging to other autonomous systems.

OSPF allows networks to be grouped into areas. OSPF uses four different types of routes, listed here in order of preference:

- Intra-area
- Inter-area
- Type 1 external
- Type 2 external

Intra-area paths have destinations within the same area, inter-area paths have destinations in other OSPF areas, and Autonomous System External (ASE) routes are routes to destinations external to the AS.

Routes imported into OSPF as Type 1 routes are supposed to be from internal gateway protocols whose external metrics are directly comparable to OSPF metrics. When a routing decision is being made, OSPF will add the internal cost to the AS border router to the external metric. Type 2 ASEs are used for exterior gateway protocols with metrics that are not comparable to OSPF metrics. In this case, only the internal OSPF cost to the AS border router is used in the routing decision.

Windows NT supports OSPF directly, using the Routing and Remote Access Services update.

Data Link Switching

Data Link Switching, or *DLSw*, is a standard designed to allow the transportation of SNA and NetBIOS traffic over an IP wide area network. It is not a Layer 3 protocol, but is a Layer 2 protocol and should only be used if this information cannot otherwise be encapsulated.

WAN Connectivity

The following table can help guide you through the process of determining the type of WAN connectivity to use:

Line Type	Description	When to Use	Line Speed
Public dial-up network lines	Common telephone lines. They require users to manually make a connection for each communication session.	This connection type is slow and not totally reliable for transferring data. However, for some companies it may be practical to dial up a temporary link between sites daily to transfer files or update a database.	Carriers are continually improving their dial-up line service. Some digital lines claim data transmission speeds of up to 56 Kbit/sec by using error correction, data compression, and synchronous modems.
Leased or dedicated lines	Provide full-time dedicated connections that do not use a series of switches to complete the connection.	The quality of the line is often higher than that of a line designed only for voice transmissions.	Lines typically range in speed from 56 to 45 Mbps or more.

If your server is used infrequently by a small number of users, basic dial-up services may be the best option. However, if your NT server is accessed by a large number of simultaneous users or provides 24-hour continuous availability, you should choose a dedicated connection and line technology that provides adequate bandwidth and availability.

Dial-up telephone lines aren't the most cost effective option even when used with the fastest of modems and data compression. When using dial-up connections for demand-dial access purposes, a significant amount of delay time can occur as well, often being detrimental to those applications that are not prepared for it. *Leased lines*, which offer more continuous connections, wind up costing more for companies that want to provide continuous availability to remote users.

SLIP/PPP Access

Point-to-Point Protocol (PPP) has become the standard for remote access. PPP is supported through the Remote Access Services and the Routing and Remote Access Services provided as an update by Microsoft.

Remote Access protocol standards are defined in Requests for Comments (RFCs), which are published by the Internet Engineering Task Force and other working groups. The RFCs supported in this version of Windows NT RAS are as follows:

- *RFC 1548*. The Point-to-Point Protocol (PPP)
- *RFC 1549*. PPP in HDLC Framing
- *RFC 1552*. The PPP Internetwork Packet Exchange Control Protocol (IPXCP)
- *RFC 1334*. PPP Authentication Protocols
- *RFC 1332*. The PPP Internet Protocol Control Protocol (IPCP)

If your remote clients connect to third-party PPP servers, they will either have to interactively logon, connect using strict PPP, or use a non-interactive script to establish the PPP connection.

Author's Note

It is recommended that you use PPP instead of SLIP for several reasons. First of all, Windows NT only supports PPP on the server side. PPP is also more flexible in that it supports a variety of transport protocols as well as data encryption and authentication encryption options.

When using a non-MS PPP stack to dial into an NT server that is a part of a domain, but is not a BDC or PDC, the server only looks to its local Accounts database (rather than to the Domain Accounts database) for the account name and password you specified when dialing in. If it doesn't find it locally, it won't go look at the domain accounts—it will just deny you access.

On the other hand, a PDC or BDC doesn't have any local accounts that it can use to attempt to verify you, so it uses the only accounts it has access to—namely, the domain accounts.

RAS Connection Sequence under Windows NT 4.0

Upon connecting to a remote computer, PPP negotiation begins. The negotiation first begins by establishing framing rules. These are established using HDLC (High Data Link Control) framing. This enables the next step, which involves the Link Control Protocol if it is selected under the Dial-Up entry.

The RAS server then authenticates the remote connection using any one of the supported PPP authentication protocols (PAP, CHAP, Shiva-PAP, DES, Clear-Text, or MS-CHAP). The authentication protocol used depends on the security configurations of the remote client and server. The following table lists the supported encryption options:

Protocol	Description
PAP	The Password Authentication Protocol
CHAP	The Challenge Handshake Authentication Protocol
Shiva-PAP	The Shiva Password Authentication Protocol
DES	The Data Encryption Standard
MS-CHAP	The Microsoft Challenge Handshake Authentication Protocol

Once authenticated, there are options for additional callback security. This culminates in the Network Control Protocols negotiating the LAN protocol used on the remote client.

Point-to-Point Tunneling Protocol

With PPTP, you can establish an additional layer of security with the Point to Point Tunneling Protocol. PPTP is a networking technology that supports multi-protocol virtual private networks (VPNs), enabling remote users to access corporate networks securely across the Internet.

PPTP enables you to shift the burden of supporting hardware such as modems and ISDN cards from the NT RAS server to a Front-End Processor (FEP). PPTP also enables clients using PPTP to access their corporate LAN by dialing an ISP or by connecting directly through the Internet. The PPTP tunnel in all these scenarios is encrypted and secure, and works with any protocol (IP, IPX, and NetBEUI).

PSTN

PPP can be used over *Public Switched Telephone Networks (PSTNs)*, which are the standard analogous phone lines supplied by local telecommunication exchange providers, otherwise known as Baby Bells. This method is also referred to as *POTS (Plain Old Telephone Services)*. Figure 2.11 shows how to communicate externally using standard modems.

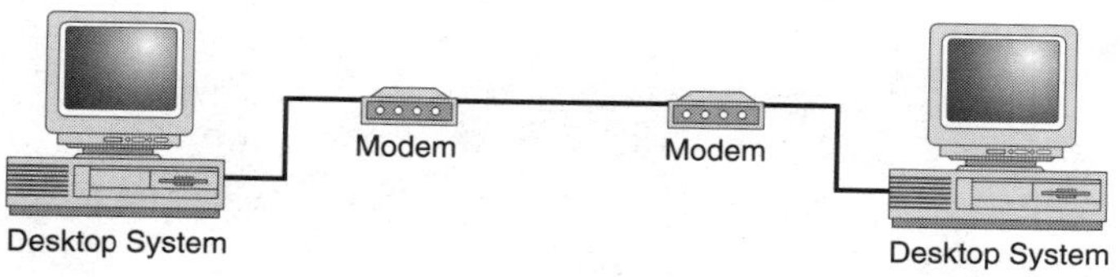

Figure 2.11. *Connecting over PSTNs using standard analogous modems.*

Integrated Services Digital Network

The Integrated Services Digital Network (ISDN) is also supported through PPP. ISDN is an international digital telephony standard defined by the International Telecommunications Union. ISDN protocols are mapped to OSI standards: to OSI Layer 2 for call setup, maintenance, and disconnect, and to OSI Layer 3 for basic call control.

ISDN provides end-to-end digital connectivity between a remote computer and another computer by using a local telephone line for network connection.

ISDN can provide data transfer rates of up to 128 Kbit/sec. These speeds are slower than those of LANs supported by high-speed data communications technology. However they are faster than those of analog telephone lines, which provide transfer rates of up to 28.8Kbps.

In addition to the difference in data transfer rates, ISDN calls can be set up much faster than analog phone calls. While an analog modem can take up to a minute to set up a connection, you usually can start transmitting data in about two seconds with ISDN. Because ISDN is fully digital, the lengthy handshaking process of analog modems (those piercing, screeching noises) is not required.

POTS (Plain Old Telephone Services) provides a single channel which can carry voice or digital communications but not both at the same time. ISDN service is available in several configurations of multiple channels that provide simultaneous voice and digital communications. In addition to increasing data throughput, multiple channels eliminate the need for separate voice and data phone lines:

ISDN—Basic Rate Interface (BRI)	Employs digital transmission that divides its available bandwidth into two 64Kbps B channels and one 16Kbps D channel, using existing regular telephone lines.
ISDN—Primary Rate Interface (PRI)	Has a larger bandwidth capacity than ISDN-BRI. PRI provides 23 64Kbps B channels and one 64Kbps D channel.

Using Multi-Link PPP

Windows NT supports the Multi-Link PPP implementation as legislated by the Internet Engineering Task Force in RFC 1717. The Multi-Link PPP protocol provides a cheap method of increasing bandwidth on your remote connection by aggregating multiple physical channels (connections) into a single virtual channel. While this can be used on both analog and digital connections, you will lose less overhead with digital lines.

Windows NT Server 4.0 includes RFC-compliant support for the Multilink protocol as part of the Windows NT Server RAS service. Any remote clients that connect to the RAS server must also support a PPP Multilink implementation compliant with RFC 1717.

X.25

X.25 is a set of protocols incorporated in a packet-switching network. An X.25 packet-switching network uses switches, circuits, and routes as available to provide the best routing and transmission of your data at any particular time. X.25 originally was set at 64K as its standard speed. There is a new 2.0MB standard developed in 1992 that is not supported currently by Windows NT RAS and RRAS.

Although it is not widely used in the United States, it is still very popular in Europe. X.25 networks are often referred to as *X-dot* networks because they use a series of protocols. At the physical layer, X.21 is used. The addressing scheme used by X.25 is the addressing standard, usually 12 characters representing the Logical Channel Number (8 bits) and the Logical Channel Group number (4 bits). Each node in an X.25 network uses an X.121 address. The X.121 addresses are also referred to as *network user addresses (NUAs)*. X.121 is actually just the specification for NUAs in public data networks. These digits can be at least 12 digits, with an option of 2 more.

The first four digits in the address are called the *DNIC (Data Network Identification Number)*. The first three identify the country. The fourth identifies the network within the country. The next eight are for the national number and the last two are optional for subnetting by the user.

Windows NT's RAS support for X.25 requires an Eicon Compatible PAD (Packet Assembler/Disassembler) adapter that converts the X.25 protocol to the RS-232 serial signal or sends information directly to the PAD without the Eicon protocol (X.3).

Windows NT RAS users, like traditional X.25 users, can use X.3 Eicon-compatible PADs to directly connect with an X.25 cloud. Most users actually use a modem to dial into the network provider, which routes from an incoming modem to a PAD adapter. This adheres to the RS-232 approach to accessing X.25. The user has to put in facilities information as well as additional user data, which is often required by many X.25 providers. The user data facility is also used for the purpose of initiating reverse charges. If you are in a situation where you have to connect using a post-dial terminal or a script, the user data facility is also available. It is important to note that if you elect to use a script, the default script to connect NT to X.25 is the PAD.INF file found in the %SystemRoot%\system32\ras subdirectory.

Routing and Remote Access Services (RRAS)

Routing and Remote Access Service, formerly codenamed Steelhead, is the new software-based dynamic routing solution for Windows NT Server. This service is designed to replace the default Multi-Protocol RRAS built into Windows NT.

RRAS is available for free from Microsoft and is included with Windows NT 5.0 Server.

RRAS supports the following:

- A full set of dynamic routing protocols for IP and IPX (including RIP, RIP II, and OSPF by Bay Networks)
- A graphical user interface and command line interface with scripting
- APIs for third-party routing protocols, user interface, and management
- Demand-dial routing
- PPTP server-to-server for secure VPNs
- RADIUS client support
- Regular Remote Access Services

Limits for RRAS are as follows:

- 16 LAN interfaces
- 48 demand-dial interfaces
- 256 RAS clients

Frame Relay

In many cases, Frame Relay can compete with technologies such as ATM. Like ATM, bandwidth is dynamically allocated, but frame uses a variable-length packet. This allows for less overhead in Frame Relay rather than the fixed-length ATM cell.

Most Frame Relay carriers offer similar bandwidth options to Fractional T-1 or Primary Rate ISDN. Some high speed providers are offering faster port access, ranging from 1.5 to 45Mbps comparable to T-1/T-3.

Switched Multimegabit Data Service

Switched Multimegabit Data Service (SMDS) is a connectionless public network that acts as a LAN at the WAN level. SMDS is much less complex than its WAN counterparts. Since it is a connectionless protocol at the network access level, it is also much less complex to design because each network is associated with one address, an E.164 address.

Speeds within an SMDS network range from 56Kbps to 34Mbps. SMDS does not give good support for intense applications such as voice and real-time video. This has placed significant limitations on SMDS.

Figure 2.12 shows how digital lines are implemented.

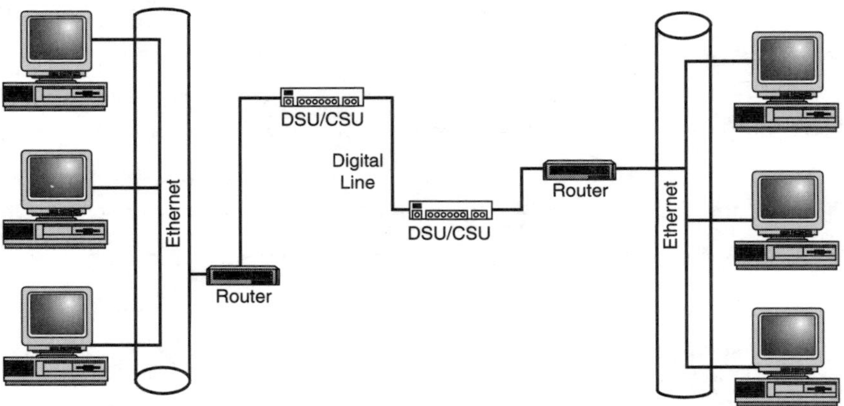

Figure 2.12. *T-1, Fractional T-1, SMDS, and Frame Relay are implemented through routers sending information from the LAN to digital services units to access the leased digital line.*

T-1/T-3

The T networks refer to a aggregated set of switched digital channels. Routers from LANs connect a serial link to a DSU/CSU (Digital Service Unit/Channel Services Unit) which connects to the T network. The two most frequent flavors are T-1 and T-3.

T-1 is an AT&T term for a digital carrier facility used to transmit a Digital Service 1 (DS-1) formatted digital signal at 1.544Mbps.

T-3 is a digital carrier facility used to transmit a Digital Service 3 (DS-3) formatted digital signal at 44.746Mbps.

The following table explains the relationship of channels to T lines as well as their alternate names.

Type	Speed	Number of Channels	Alternate Name	Number of T-1s
Fractional T-1 Channel	64KB	N/A	DS-0	N/A
T-1	1.544MB	24	DS-1	1
T-1C	3.152MB	48	DS-1C	2
T-3	44.736MB	672	DS-3	28
T-4	274.760MB	4032	DS-4	168

Copper-based cable can be used for lines up to a T-1C grade. Fiber-optics or the use of microwaves must be used for speeds faster then T-1Cs.

ATM

Asynchronous Transfer Mode (ATM) is a communication standard that facilitates the transmission of information across networks using a special format—a cell, as opposed to a frame. It is a 53-byte fixed length cell. Any type of information can be carried within the cell. All cells are the same size. The term *Transfer Mode* describes the fact that it is a cell-relay method while the term *Asynchronous* describes the order of the transfer process. It is not an ordered structure, but a more random and less periodic one. Since ATM is primarily a Layer 2 element, it does not route but rather acts as a media-independent, variable-speed packet-switching technology.

ATM offers a greater capacity for bandwidth. ATM can reach speeds in excess of 622Mbps and can handle a variety of different traffic types. Cell Relay offers voice, data, and video support.

The ATM forum is the organization responsible for setting the ATM standards. They defined four service categories for the ATM transmission formats. These formats include the following:

- *CBR (Constant Bit Rate).* A constant or guaranteed rate of supporting information. Used for multimedia applications such as video and voice.
- *VBR (Variable Bit Rate).* For packet-style video and sound. Designed for predictable data streams occurring within peak limits.
- *ABR (Available Bit Rate).* Supports applications such as Web browsers and other Internet applications. Internal and external feedback routines are used to manage traffic.
- *UBR (Unspecified Bit Rate).* Offers no traffic-related service guarantees.

ATM LANE

ATM LANE stands for *ATM LAN Emulation.* LAN emulation creates a single "logical" physical network and broadcast domain over multiple physical networks. LAN emulation allows existing LAN nodes transparently interface an ATM cell-relay network with workgroup switches. Most routers now support LANE for IP, IPX, and AppleTalk.

SONET

Synchronous Optical Network (SONET) is used as an underlying infrastructure for those ATM networks starting at speeds of 155 Mbps. SONET is also desired when networks depend upon ATM as their underlying infrastructure for many different services.

ADSL

Asymmetrical Digital Subscriber Line (ADSL) is a new protocol that delivers high-speed communication over the standard phone line. Rather than using modems to facilitate up to 33.6 or 56Kbps, ADSL technology can deliver upstream (from the user) speeds of 640Kbps and downstream (to the user) speeds of more than 6Mbps. ADSL uses the portion of a phone line's bandwidth not used by voice, allowing for simultaneous voice and data transmission. Many local exchange carriers are looking into ADSL and many ADSL deployments may begin this year.

Chapter 3

Managing Enterprise Services

- **Service Management**
  We will discuss the concept of a service process and how it differs from a regular application process that uses its own security context.
- **The Browser Service**
  This common service facilitates the advertisement of server resources on Microsoft networks.
- **Time Services**
  Learn the importance of Time Services in an enterprise environment and how NT lacks a strong implementation.
- **The Domain Name Service**
  DNS is the service that participates in the DNS Internet hierarchy by storing name records and serving name resolution requests.
- **The Dynamic Host Configuration Protocol**
  DHCP is the mechanism that enables clients to obtain their TCP/IP configuration from a server running this service.
- **The Windows Internet Naming Service**
  WINS provides NetBIOS name resolution over TCP/IP. Although this service was mentioned previously, it is discussed in much greater detail in this section.

Core Service Concepts

Windows NT uses *services* rather than *daemons* for background modules. Windows NT has several default services. As additional components and software are installed, these services will increase—especially network-related services. The Services icon in the Control Panel enables an administrator to start and stop services. Services can also be scheduled to start at boot time.

To open the Services Control Panel, navigate to the control panels from the Start menu or from My Computer. Click the Services icon. As Figure 3.1 shows, the available services installed on the server display with their current start and startup status.

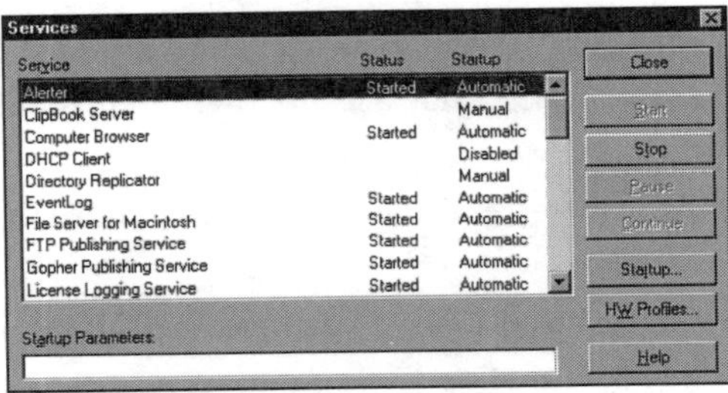

Figure 3.1. *The Services Control Panel.*

Service Configuration

The configuration information for services is found under the following path in the Registry:

HKEY_LOCAL_MACHINE\System\CurrentControlSet\Services

The Services subkey is one of four main subkeys found beneath the CurrentControlSet Registry subkey. Even more interesting, the Services Registry key contains configuration information for device drivers, file system drivers, filter drivers, and networking components as well. This makes it one of the most important single portions of the Registry. Table 3.1 displays and briefly describes the four subkeys of CurrentControlSet. All subkeys follow the format correlating to Table 3.1.

Table 3.1. `CurrentControlSet` *subkeys and their descriptions.*

Subkey	Description
Control	Static Windows NT tuning and configuration parameters.
Enum	Enumeration information collected when the drivers/services are started.

Subkey	Description
Hardware Profiles	Configuration information that relates to hardware profiles.
Services	Startup parameters and error controls for services and device drivers.

In both the Services and the Control subkeys, the subkey name correlates to the internal name rather than the display name. In the case of most drivers and services, it correlates to the actual binary file. For the serial mouse driver, for example, the driver name and driver subkey name are found under the Services key as Sermouse. The file location is actually %SystemRoot%\System32\Drivers\Sermouse.sys.

When a user clicks the Devices or the Services Control Panel, all the keys found under the Services subkey are examined to build the options available in either Control Panel applet. All keys that map to binary files ending with .SYS are viewed as devices, and those ending with .EXE are treated as services. The drivers are technically developed like dynamic link libraries (DLLs) in that they do not constitute processes in and of themselves. The operating system process NTOSKRNL.EXE loads them.

Author's Note

You can use the Resource Kit utility `DRIVERS.EXE` *to see a listing of all the drivers and Kernel Mode components that normally show up under the system process when viewing processes in the Task Manager.*

Each Services key can have additional subkeys. Many services have a Linkage subkey that provides data for binding networks. Many services also have a Parameters subkey that contains entries defined by the service, with values for configuring the specific service.

Each of the Services keys has subkeys relating to standard parameters. These subkeys include the following:

- ErrorControl
- Start
- Group
- Type

The Group and Type controls should *not* be adjusted because they are set to a specific value during the installation of that service. The Start option relates to how the service will be set to start up when the operating system boots. This is better adjusted using the Service Control Panel.

Some additional optional subkeys contain information specific to the service or driver. The most common of these is the Parameters subkey, a standard option for service-specific information.

The ErrorControl Value Entry

This basic value entry appears for each Services subkey in the CurrentControlSet path. It deals with service and device error/exception handling. For this reason, it is one of the most important subkeys.

The ErrorControl value has a data type of REG_DWORD. The type DWORD just states that it is a 32-bit integer. Its range is a particular error constant that specifies the level of error control for the service. Table 3.2 shows the ErrorControl value and its descriptions, listed in order from most severe to least severe.

Table 3.2. Error constants and their descriptions.

Error	Name	Description
0x3	Critical	Critical and security-related services use this key. This value fails the attempted system startup unless the startup is using the LastKnownGood configuration set. If the LastKnownGood configuration is being used and it is a noncritical service such as Workstation Service, a bug-check routine is run using DrWatson. If it is a critical service or a Kernel Mode device driver, a bug-check routine at the system level occurs. Users may know this by its infamous "Blue Screen of Death" (BSoD) name.
0x2	Severe	This error tells the system startup process to revert to the LastKnownGood configuration set. If the LastKnownGood configuration set is currently being used, then continue anyway.
0x1	Normal	If the driver fails to load or initialize, startup proceeds, but a warning message appears in two places. In the Event log, a message explaining which service/devices failed appears. A generic message also appears on the user's screen.
0x0	Ignore	If the driver fails to load or initialize, startup proceeds. No warning message appears.

Table 3.3 describes how Windows NT handles service and device failures. They are ranked in order of severity, with 0x3 being the highest and 0x0 being the lowest.

Table 3.3. Basic default services and NetBIOS-dependent services.

Service	Filename	Explanation
Alerter	Services.EXE	Along with the Messenger Service, generates warning messages to administrators about NetBIOS-based events, messages, and problems.
ClipBook Server	ClipSrv.EXE	Enables sharing ClipBook pages to network users.
Computer Browser	Services.EXE	Enables you to browse the network for resources shared by other workstations.
Directory Replicator	LMREPL.EXE	Performs Directory Replication Service enabling administrators to easily copy complete directories to multiple workstations.
Event Log	Services.EXE	Monitors the workstation's use of local and remote users by recording events of significance. Also reports internal error conditions such as malfunctioning hardware and other matters.
Messenger	Services.EXE	Sends and receives messages in conjunction with the Alerter Service. The main value of supporting the Messenger Service is that you can then receive service message blocks (SMBs) from other networked machines. The Messenger Service uses your username and your workstation name in the NetBIOS name table, with a `Hex 03` appended to each.
Net Logon	LSASS.EXE	Used to verify the authenticity of users logging on to a workstation, workgroup, or domain.
Network DDE	NETDDE.EXE	Required for dynamic data exchange (DDE) between workstations.
Network DDE DSDM	NETDDE.EXE	DDE Shared Database Manager. This service is used by Network DDE.
NT LM Security Support Provider	Services.EXE	Supplies Windows NT security to RPC applications that do not use LAN Manager-named pipe transports.
Plug-and-Play	Services.EXE	Microsoft's first attempt at automating SCSI device setups.
Remote Procedure Call Locator	Locater.EXE	Used by the RPC to locate available workstations to process Remote Procedure Calls (RPCs).

continues

Table 3.3. Continued

Service	Filename	Explanation
Remote Procedure Call	RPCSS.EXE	Supports client access to the Windows NT machines. Also a necessary interprocess communication mechanism for client/server computing.
Schedule	ATSVC.EXE	Required for prescheduled commands, such as automated backups, to run at a specified time.
Server	Services.EXE	Allows a device to accept requests from another computer's redirector. This is the MS-NET's server-side mounter.
Spooler	SpoolSS.EXE	Allows a workstation to spool printer files.
TCP/IP NetBIOS Helper	Services.EXE	Allows NetBIOS and SMB information to be encapsulated over UDP and TCP.
Telephony Services	TAPISrv.EXE	Enables application integration with the Telephony API.
UPS	UPS.EXE	Monitors the uninterruptible power supply (UPS) and instructs the system to issue warnings, save files, and shut down prior to power outages.
Workstation	Services.EXE	The redirector service that allows access to shared resources.

Service Management

Always remember that a service in Windows NT is another type of User Mode Win32 process. All the capabilities of Win32 are available to services. To convert a current Win32 application to a service, just use the SRVANY.EXE utility to configure it.

Author's Note

The SRVANY utility is found only in the Windows NT Server Resource Kit.

Command-Line Management

You can manage a Windows NT service from the command line instead of using the Services Control Panel. Using NET.EXE, you can start, pause, continue, and stop services

```
NET START service name
NET PAUSE service name
```

```
NET CONTINUE service name
NET STOP service name
```

`NET START` by itself displays the current running services.

Tip

These command-line options can also help automate the stopping or starting of services with batch files. These batch files can then be scheduled—using the AT.EXE utility—to run at a certain date or time.

The Browser Service

The Browser Service is an internal service that allows the computer to view all file and print resources on the network. It assigns browsing levels to specific computers on the network, which in turn provides a centralized list of available resources. These different browsing levels also reduce the amount of traffic on the network. Browsing in Windows NT is an internal process exclusive only to Microsoft networks (see Figure 3.2). It also has become quite an enigma because of its complex nature and varying behavior.

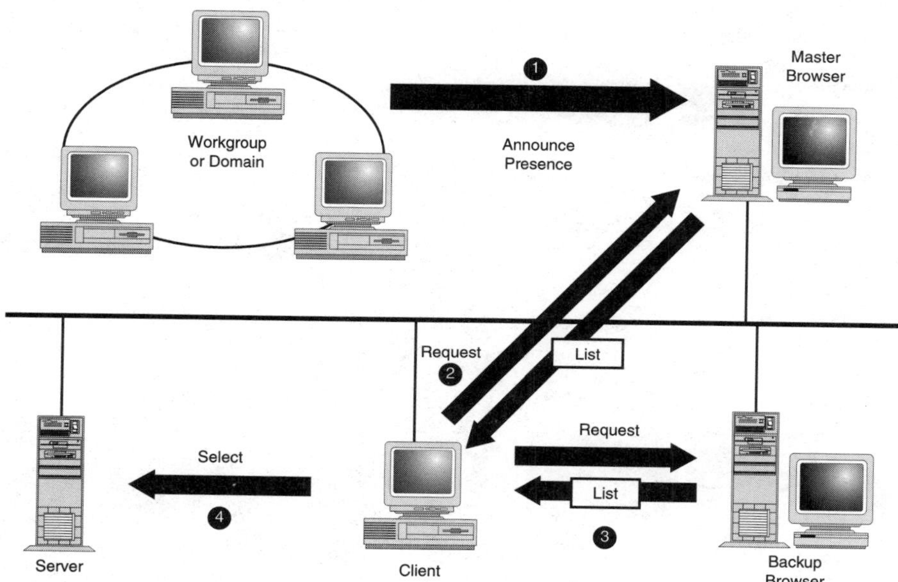

Figure 3.2. *Browsing: The advertising method on Microsoft Windows networks.*

There are five types of browsers, as follows:

- *Nonbrowser.* These computers have been adjusted in the Registry to not participate as a browser.
- *Potential browser.* A computer capable of maintaining a Browse List and participating in browser elections.
- *Backup browser.* These computers receive a copy of the Browse List from the Master Browser and distribute the list upon request to computers in the domain or workgroup. All domain controllers are automatically configured as Master or backup browsers.
- *Master browser.* The Master Browser is responsible for collecting the list of servers in a workgroup or a domain. It also includes a list of all other domains and workgroups on the network.
- *Domain Master Browser.* Only used for computers using TCP/IP (specifically, the NetBT LANA route). It is responsible for collecting announcements for the entire domain, including all network segments. It is also responsible for providing lists to all the Master Browsers on each segment. It is always the Primary Domain Controller of a domain. The NWLink and NetBEUI transports do not use the Domain Master Browser role because these transports use a single Master Browser for the entire network.

The following computers are potential browsers:

- Windows NT Server 3.5x/4.0
- Windows NT Advanced Server 3.1
- Windows NT Workstation 3.5x/4.0
- Windows NT 3.1
- Windows 95 workstations
- Windows for Workgroups 3.11
- MS-DOS Peer Servers

The Preferred Master Browser

The *Preferred Master Browser* is a server that has been configured to win browser elections and become the Master Browser. This will not, however, necessarily reduce broadcast traffic. Configuring the Master Browser is important in NetBEUI, NWLink, and TCP/IP networks (not using WINS) for NetBIOS computer name resolution.

To specify a computer as the preferred Master Browser, modify the following Registry entry:

```
\HKEY_LOCAL_MACHINE\SYSTEM\CurrentControlSet\Services\Browser\
```

Use the following parameters to modify the preceding Registry entry:

Entry:	`IsDomainMasterBrowser`
Data Type:	`REG_SZ`
Value:	`True`

Configuring the Computer Browser Service

You can adjust the Browser Service on Windows NT computers to control browser roles and behavior. The most crucial entry is found in HKEY_LOCAL_MACHINE\SYSTEM\CurrentControlSet\Browser\Parameters. The value is `MaintainServerList` and can have one of the following three values:

- `No`. Will not ever be a browser.
- `Yes`. The computer will be a browser. When it enters the network, it tries to get a Browse List from a Master Browser. If none is found, it forces an election. These computers either become Master or backup browsers. This is the default value for servers.
- `Auto`. This computer becomes a potential browser. It may or may not become a browser depending on the amount of browsers on the network. This is the default value for Windows NT Workstations.

The announcement period can be adjusted by going to the following Registry path:

HKEY_LOCAL_MACHINE\System\CurrentControlSet\Services\LanmanServer\Parameters

By adding the `Announce` value with a data type of `REG_DWORD`, you can add the amount of time for the browser to wait between announcements as the default value. The default is 720 for 12 minutes.

We can also adjust the domains made available to the Browser Service to cut down domain announcements. In the Network Control Panel applet, select the Computer Browser Service and click Configure. The Browser Configuration dialog box appears (see Figure 3.3).

Author's Note

It is important to note that this option works only in Windows NT Server, not Workstation.

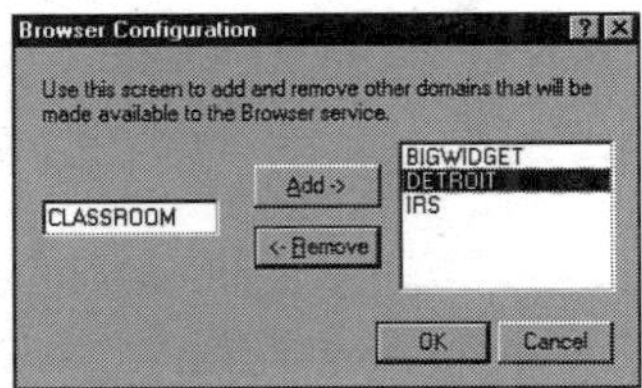

Figure 3.3. *Adding domains to the browser configuration.*

To make additional domains available to the browser, select the names in the left box, and then choose the Add button. To make domains unavailable to the browser, select the names in the right box, and then choose the Remove button.

Browsing Across a WAN with TCP/IP and IPX

Currently, browser/service communication relies almost entirely on broadcasts. In a WAN environment, such as TCP/IP, where domains are separated by routers, special broadcast problems can arise because broadcasts, by default, do not pass through routers. There are two issues to consider:

- How browsers separated by a router perform browser functions
- How local clients browse remote domains that are not on their local network segment

With IPX, it is just a matter of having the routers properly route packets using a static route or a routing protocol such as the Routing Information Protocol (RIP). Because the Browsing Service depends on NetBIOS, it requires NetBIOS propagating over IPX. This requires Type 20 packet support being enabled on the IPX router.

With TCP/IP, you likewise have to have proper routing enabled. NetBIOS information must also be passed over the TCP and UDP protocols. There are several methods of resolving NetBIOS for the purpose of facilitating services such as browsing.

If the workgroup or domain spans more than one subnet, the Master Browser maintains the list for all the computers on its own subnet as well as for the backup browsers. If a domain or workgroup is spanning multiple subnets and is using TCP/IP, each subnet functions as an independent browsing entity with its own Master Browser and backup browsers.

The Master Browser of each subnet announces itself as the domain master to the Domain Master Browser. The Domain Master merges all these lists into a global Browse List every 15 minutes.

The Windows Internet Naming Service

The *Windows Internet Naming Service (WINS)* resolves NetBIOS names to IP addresses so that datagrams can be sent to the targeted computer. Implementing WINS eliminates the need to use a static file called the *LMHOSTS file* or to enable UDP port 137. Using WINS requires the following configuration:

- WINS is configured on a computer running Windows NT Server 3.5 or later.
- Clients are WINS-enabled.

WINS clients can be configured with Windows NT 3.5 or later, Windows 95, Windows for Workgroups 3.11b running TCP/IP-32, LAN Manager 2.2c for MS-DOS, or Microsoft Network Client 3.0 for MS-DOS. The last two are provided on the compact discs for versions 3.5 or later of Windows NT Server.

Microsoft usually recommends implementing WINS for name resolution and browsing support. As an alternative, it is possible to have full domain browsing by using only LMHOSTS files on all computers, but this limits browsing to the local domain. Non-WINS clients still need the LMHOSTS file to browse a WAN, even if WINS has been implemented in the domain.

WINS is being phased out with Windows NT 5.0, although Windows NT 5.0 will still support WINS for backward compatibility.

Using the Browser Monitor (Resource Kit Utility)

The Browser Monitor utility monitors the status of browsers on selected domains. Browsers are shown on a per-domain and per-transport basis. In the main window, Browser Monitor displays various status icons and identifies the domain, transport, and Master Browser. Browser Monitor connects to servers to retrieve status information using the current user's username and password. Therefore if the current user account doesn't exist in a domain, the status query may fail. Any user who is logged on can query the status information.

Troubleshooting Browsing and Naming

If, for some reason, browsing across routers is becoming a problem in exclusive TCP/IP networks, you could have a problem with browsing roles or with naming.

If you pull up the Network Neighborhood and notice that there is not a complete list because you can only view computers on your current segment, you can follow these simple steps to determine whether the problem is with browsing or with naming:

1. Verify all physical connections are established with your computer's interface to the network, the router's interface to the network, and so on.

2. Verify that the routers are configured to forward the name resolution requests and the browser requests across its interfaces. Most routers have debugging features which allow an administrator to see the packet types traveling across its interfaces. Figure 3.4 displays this method on Cisco series routers. In this example, the command `debug ip udp` is being run on the router. The UDP Port 137 traffic refers to the WINS resolution traffic while the UDP Port 138 traffic refers to browsing traffic.

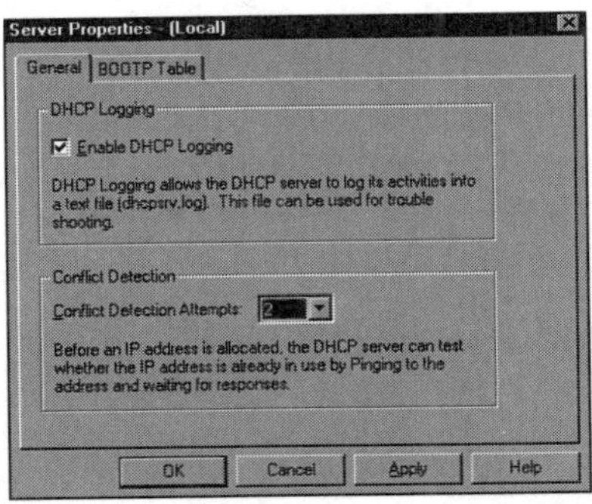

Figure 3.4. *Viewing WINS resolution and browser traffic on a router.*

3. If the routers are properly configured, then the problem is likely one of three things. The first is a possible error in NetBIOS naming. WINS client configuration may not be correct, LMHosts configuration may be wrong, or there could even be in error in the IP configuration on that machine. To verify that naming works correctly, you can type the command:

   ```
   net view \\servername
   ```

   and if you get a positive response (other than `Network name cannot be found`) then naming is working properly. If you get a negative response, you try the same command with the IP address instead of the name, as in:

   ```
   net view \\202.126.12.146
   ```

   If this works, then IP configuration is correct; if not, then the problem is likely an error in IP configuration.

4. Once you have determined that naming is not the problem, then you need to verify that the Computer Browser service has been started on that machine you are trying to connect to, or your machine. If both machines have the Browser service started, then you will need to make sure that each of the different segments are either configured to be different workgroups, or at least in one Microsoft domain. If you have a single workgroup spanning multiple IP segments, browsing will encounter problems.

Time Services

In larger enterprise environments, the issue of Time Services comes to the forefront because of the need to ensure time synchronization. Organizations such as banks rely heavily on date and timestamps for validating various transactions. In Windows NT, there is no built-in method for having an automatic reference server for clients to perform automatic synchronization. Time synchronization can be set either manually or automatically using the `NET TIME` command.

The following command sets the local machine's workstation with the remote machine *machine_name*:

```
NET TIME \\machine_name /set /yes
```

Time Source Creation

To have a Windows NT Workstation or Server point to a specific machine as a time source, use the Registry Editor to add a parameter:

Value Name:	`TimeSource`
Data Type:	`REG_DWORD`
Value:	`1`
Location:	HKEY_LOCAL_MACHINE\SYSTEM\CurrentControlSet\Services\LanManServer\Parameters

TIMESERV.EXE: Time Synchronizing Service (Resource Kit Utility)

This service sets the system time accurately and keeps Windows NT Workstations and Servers synchronized with a specified primary or secondary timesource. TIMESERV always keeps the computer in sync, even when no one is logged on. This service can be run from either the Services option in Control Panel or the command prompt.

A *primary timesource* is one that provides the highest accuracy, such as a GPS-based board, NIST ACTS, or a radio clock. A *secondary timesource* is one that is set from a primary timesource, typically over a network. Typical clients set themselves from a secondary timesource by using the `NET TIME` command from the command line or its equivalent in TIMESERV. For convenience, you can set the LanmanServer timesource by typing **`timesource=yes`** in the TIMESERV.INI file; for more information on editing TIMESERV.INI, see the TIMESERV documentation in the Windows NT 4.0 Resource Kit.

The Time Synchronizing Service works with Windows NT 3.5 or later.

NetTime for Macintosh (Resource Kit Utility)

By default, no built-in mechanism enables Macintosh clients to synchronize their clocks with Windows NT Server. It is possible, however, to use NetTime to synchronize the local Macintosh clock to a given Windows NT server running the Services for Macintosh server on the network. NetTime for Macintosh requires ResEdit (Resource Editor) or another resource editor to change the zone and server name for the tool to which to synchronize. All Macintosh applications contain a resource fork that must be edited using this special tool.

NetTime for Macintosh is provided in NETTIME.HQX, a self-extracting archive file in BinHex 4.0 format. Most decompression utilities for the Macintosh include a BinHex translator to convert this utility. Make sure that this is translated under the Macintosh operating system.

Domain Name Service

When working with Windows NT, knowledge of DNS is helpful for several reasons: Internet connectivity, intranet name resolution, and the fact that Windows NT 5.0 DNS will be the primary naming platform for the Windows NT enterprise model. In the early days of the Internet, as the number of networks grew, so did the desire to establish a method of resolving a name to an IP address so that computers could communicate using these user-friendly names rather than cryptic IP addresses.

The first approach, which is still available, was a resolution file that was stored locally on the computer or server. This HOSTS file was simple in that it contained merely the IP address and the desired hostname. This file was later expanded to include both a simple local hostname and a multilevel Internet name. This approach soon became problematic for obvious reasons. As the number of machines grew, if there was to be a measure of consistency, every machine would need to have every other computer's hostname on the Internet stored locally. This would be a very large file—and an administrative nightmare.

There soon came a new idea: Having a centralized server or servers maintain a global host file that every computer on the Internet could connect to if they needed to resolve a user-friendly name. This quickly became an obsolete method, however, because it put a tremendous workload on those root servers involved.

Finally, what is now known as *DNS* or *NAMED* evolved from the idea of having each organization that participates on the Internet maintain a name server and link up to a global directory service of other DNS servers to resolve and exchange hostnames with one another.

The basic concept of DNS involves an organization registering a unique first-tier domain name (also called a *zone*) with the legislative body for Internet names (the InterNIC), and at the same time setting up at least two DNS servers to register with the InterNIC. One of these servers serves as a *Start of Authority (SoA)* in that it is the starting point for the local DNS hierarchy. The local hierarchy is responsible for answering queries internally and externally for those name records for that organization. They also opt to forward external requests coming from local computers to the root servers of the Internet. Those root servers then use the global InterNIC database to locate a DNS server for that organization.

If you plan on connecting directly to the Internet, it is necessary to obtain registered IP addresses from and register domain names with the InterNIC. You can also solicit the services of an ISP to maintain an organization's records. You can connect to the InterNIC at `ftp://ds.internic.net` to obtain information on registering a domain name. You can also do this through a third-party service, but will probably be paying an additional amount of money for using a "middleman." Most of them add a surcharge of up to $100 to the InterNIC charges.

Domain Name Uniqueness

The goal of InterNIC is to ensure domain name uniqueness.

Author's Note

The term domain *in this context refers to those names used to group Internet hosts in logical groups for user-friendly Internet name resolution. It is important to address this concern to ensure that you do not confuse these domains with the use of the term* domain *in describing units in Windows NT domain models, as mentioned in Chapter 1, "Developing an Enterprise Model."*

There are different types of DNS domain names. The one actually registered with the InterNIC (for example, `gc-consulting.com`, `microsoft.com`, `acm.org`) is referred to in DNS circles as a *zone*, as mentioned earlier. It is also referred to as a *second-level domain*. This is what must be unique with the Internet. Additional domain levels can be created after the zone has been registered and the SoA has been established through the Domain Name System.

Registering an Internet domain name requires that you provide the Internet domain name, your company information, an administrative contact for your company, and a password. Many Web sites, including the one at InterNIC (`http://www.internic.net`), can do a real-time search to see whether the selected domain name has been previously registered by another organization. If your domain name has not been used, proceed to register your information with InterNIC. The information is stored in the [InterNIC] database, as shown in Figure 3.5.

```
Gate City Consulting (GC-CONSULTING-DOM)
   301 S. Elm St, St 321
   Greensboro, NC 27401
   US

   Domain Name: GC-CONSULTING.COM

   Administrative Contact:
      Cardwell, Drew  (DC4199)  drewc@CCMAC.COM
      972-253-7109 (FAX) 972-273-2507
   Technical Contact, Zone Contact:
      Registration, NTX  (RN16-ORG)  ntxhostmaster@NTX.NET
      707-256-2853 (FAX) 707-256-1997
   Billing Contact:
      Thomas, Steven  (ST3432)  stevethomas@ACM.ORG
      336-373-9701 (FAX) 336-373-9702

   Record last updated on 12-Mar-98.
   Record created on 12-Mar-98.
   Database last updated on 14-Apr-98 03:43:25 EDT.

   Domain servers in listed order:

   NSX.NTX.NET                  209.1.144.216
   NSC.NTX.NET                  204.107.140.15
```

Figure 3.5. *The InterNIC domain record.*

Bear in mind that these records are considered public and can be accessed by anyone who looks up the zone record for an organization.

The DNS Hierarchy

The *DNS hierarchy* consists of a root followed by a series of top-level domains that have their databases distributed across the DNS root servers. The top-level domains consist of several worldwide generic domains followed by a domain for each country. The worldwide generic domains are as follows:

- *COM*. This domain was originally intended for commercial organizations such as corporations. It has been slightly used out of that spectrum and has become disproportionately larger in total size. This overused domain suffix has caused a rush to establish new domain suffixes that subdivide these entities. COM will only represent commercial entities in the future.

- *EDU*. This domain was developed strictly for educational purposes. This suffix currently contains universities, colleges, schools, educational service organizations, and educational consortia. An administrative decision was made recently by the U.S. government and the InterNIC to limit further registrations to only colleges and universities. This will enable others (community colleges, junior colleges) to only register in the U.S. domain (or their respective companies).
- *NET*. This domain was designed to store all the names of network service providers, telecommunication firms, and even ISPs. Some companies have registered in this location because of a conflict in the COM domain.
- *ORG*. This domain was designed as a miscellaneous top-level domain for organizations that didn't fit anywhere else. Originally it was proposed that nonprofit and certain public organizations reserve names under this domain.
- *INT*. This domain is for organizations established by international treaties.
- *ARPA*. These domains are maintained by DNS servers to designate reverse-lookup domains. They usually correlate with the zone databases maintained by a correlating DNS server.

United States-Only Generic Domains

United States-only generic domains are allowed only within the United States. There is a specific procedure for registering these domains as they are only allowed for specific government and military organizations. These organizations include the following:

- *GOV*. This domain was designed for any kind of government office or agency. It is restricted due to a recent decision that was made to register only agencies of the U.S. federal government. State and local agencies were originally allowed to register using this domain, but now are only allowed to be registered in the country domains.
- *MIL*. This domain is specifically allowed only for units of the U.S. military.

Country Code Domains

Country code domains are two character domains used to designate organizations within a specific country. They follow the ISO standard definitions that also are used by the CCITT X.500 standard.

A few examples include the following:

US	United States
DE	Germany
IE	Ireland
AU	Australia
CA	Canada
FI	Finland
FR	France
UK	The United Kingdom

These domains can provide registration of all kinds of entities in their respective countries on the basis of specific credentials. The US domain, for example, bases its information on geography.

Additional Branches Within the US Domain

The US domain now has a specific hierarchy for public organizations that includes a two-digit state code (for example, NC stands for North Carolina), followed by a locality such as a county, parish, or city. Most public organizations are then additionally defined by a series of categories. These include the following:

K12	Primary and secondary schools
CC	Community colleges
TEC	Technical schools
LIB	Libraries
MUS	Museums

For other types of public organizations, refer to RFC 1480, which has been designated for this purpose. Specific subunits of the US domain are designed to be the next level down from the US domain. These include the following:

FED	Agencies of the federal government
DNI	Distributed national institutes such as the National Park System

Installing the DNS Server in Windows NT

The DNS server can be installed by going to the Services tab in the Network Control Panel and selecting Add. After installing the DNS Server Service, reboot the computer. The DNS Manager appears as a new icon in the Administrative Tools group. The DNS Manager interfaces with the DNS Service, which is set to start automatically after its installation.

The DNS Manager looks to either the Registry or the standard DNS database files to determine its configuration. The Registry keys are found under the following:

HKEY_LOCAL_MACHINE\System\CurrentControlSet\Services\DNS

The database files are located under the following path:

%SystemRoot%\System32\DNS

Normally, earlier DNS systems ran on UNIX platforms and consisted of a simple daemon (service) followed by the configuration files. Windows NT provides a graphical interface to simplify the task of DNS management, as shown in Figure 3.6.

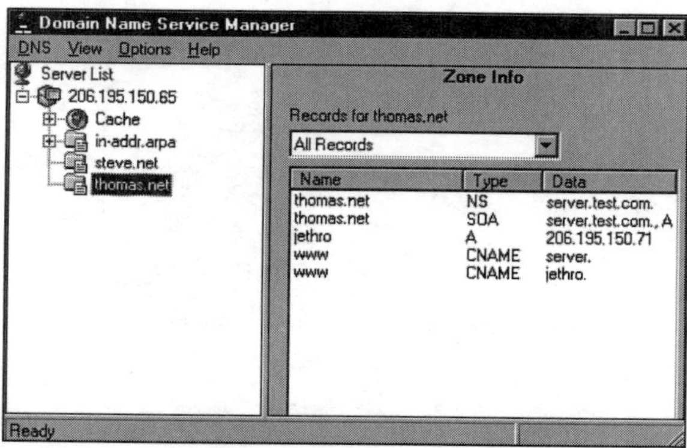

Figure 3.6. *The DNS Manager and its context-sensitive, menu-based utility.*

This provides a context-sensitive menu that enables you to adjust the properties of every entity involved. The following sections discuss these properties.

Servers

Right-clicking the Server icon and selecting Properties can set DNS Server properties. Figure 3.7 displays the multitabbed dialog box.

The following options can be configured under this dialog box:

- *Interfaces.* Only necessary to adjust on those machines that are *multihomed* (or that have multiple IP addresses). This is where you can tell a multihomed DNS which interfaces it will send and receive requests for. If the DNS server is not multihomed, there is only one interface.
- *Forwarders.* Where you can designate a forwarder to be the only DNS servers that will actually query information on the Internet.

- *Boot Method.* Not a configurable option; just denotes whether the DNS Service is configured to boot from the Registry, or by using the data files (standard DNS text files). This information is dependent on the following Registry key that may or may not exist. If it does not exist, the default will be to boot from the Registry. The Registry value is `EnableRegistryBoot` and it is found under the following Registry path:

```
HKEY_LOCAL_MACHINE\System\CurrentControlSet\Services\DNS\Parameters
```

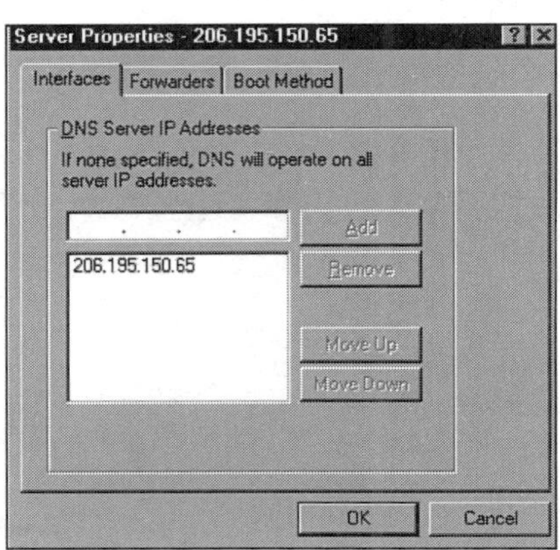

Figure 3.7. *The DNS Server Properties dialog box.*

DNS Zones and Zone Properties

DNS zones reflect second-tier and third-tier domains. You can think of a zone as a *partition*, or a portion of the global DNS database. The following options are available when configuring the properties of a zone. Most of them can be initially set when using the New Zone option. This invokes the Zone Wizard that simplifies the option of creating a zone.

The first tab under the Zone Properties dialog box enables you to select whether the server will be acting as a primary server for that zone or a secondary zone (see Figure 3.8).

The second tab is the SoA Record with which all zone files must start (see Figure 3.9). This record includes the name server that is the authority of this zone. The DNS Manager creates these records by default when you create a zone using the DNS Manager Zone Wizard. The secondary DNS servers in the zone cache the information in this zone. The Refresh and Retry Intervals govern the time span involved in updating these entries. The Expire Time is the last interval before the secondary server deletes the record.

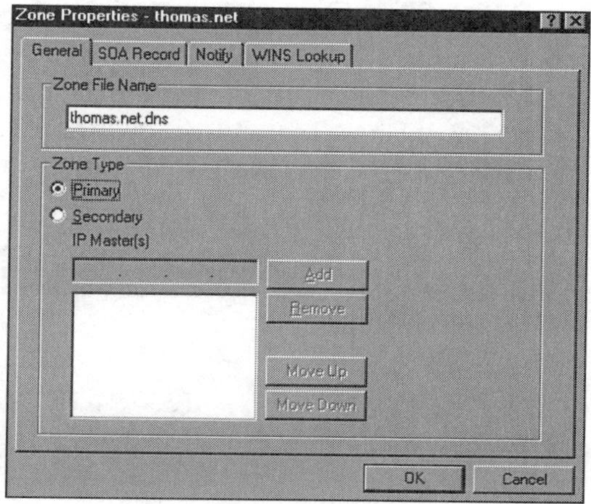

Figure 3.8. *The Primary/Secondary Zone Type options in the Zone Properties dialog box.*

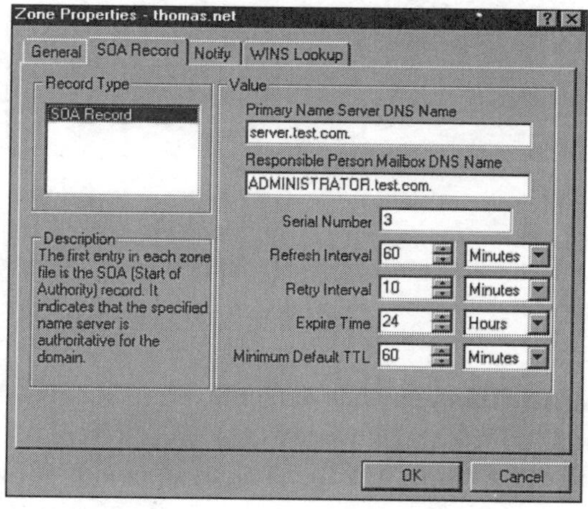

Figure 3.9. *The SOA Record tab.*

The Notify tab is where you list all the secondary DNS servers that need to be notified whenever there are changes to the DNS database. This tab also provides the option of selecting the box to only allow access from secondary servers included on the Notify List.

The WINS, shown in Figure 3.10, is where you can set the DNS server to offload requests to a WINS server if it is unable to resolve names. This is in the form of a recursive query. A *recursive query* is the act of forwarding the information to another DNS server. In this case, it is forwarding it to a WINS server. The zone file will include a proprietary record that is only supported by this DNS server package. It allows the completion of Microsoft's Dynamic Naming Solution.

The following option displays the option for WINS resolution. You can put in the option of using one or more WINS servers. For optimal performance, it is recommended to use the same server to reduce network traffic. You can also check the Settings Affect Local Server option to allow only this server to forward requests, as opposed to all the secondary DNS servers that may exist for that zone.

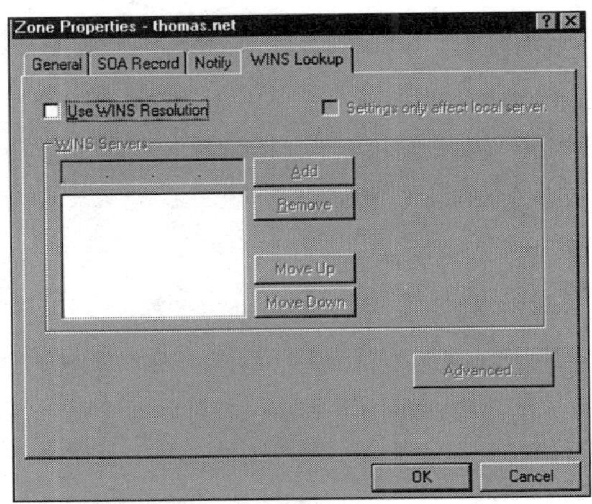

Figure 3.10. *The WINS Lookup tab in the Zone Properties dialog box.*

Other files are maintained as well. *Reverse lookup files* and *cache files* help cache out name queries and root server paths to help maintain optimal Internet queries.

DNS Zone Record Types

After initially setting up the zone, you can then begin to manually enter various records to be serviced by the DNS zone. The most common record is the *A record*, which is used for standard hostname mappings. Right-clicking the Zone object in the DNS Manager and selecting the New Host record can easily create this record.

Table 3.4 describes the various record types found in the zone database file for a DNS zone. The text file that contains these records never needs to be modified because of the Windows NT DNS Management utility.

Table 3.4. DNS resource record types.

Record Type	Description
A	An address record that maps a hostname to an IP address in a DNS zone. Its counterpart, the PTR resource record, is used to map an IP address to a hostname in a DNS reverse zone (those in the in-addr.arpa DNS domain).
AFSDB	Gives the location of either an Andrew File System (AFS) cell database server or a DCE (Distributed Computing Environment) cell's authenticated name server. The AFS system uses DNS to map a DNS domain name to the name of an AFS cell database server. The Open Software Foundation's DCE Naming Service uses DNS for a similar function.
CNAME	The canonical name resource record creates an *alias* (synonymous name) for the specified hostname. You can use CNAME records to hide the implementation details of a network from the clients that connect to it. `ftp.terraflora.com` is an alias (CNAME) for the real name of the computer that runs the FTP server, for example. This alias also allows the FTP server to be moved to a different computer; only the CNAME record needs to change.
HINFO	The host information resource record identifies a host's hardware type and operating system. The CPU type and operating system identifiers should come from the computer names and system names listed in RFC 1700.
ISDN	The Integrated Services Digital Network (ISDN) resource record is a variation of the A (address) resource record. Instead of mapping a hostname to an IP address, the ISDN record maps the name to an ISDN address. An *ISDN address* is a phone number that consists of a country code, an area code or country code, a local phone number, and, optionally, a subaddress. The ISDN resource record is designed to be used in conjunction with the RT (Route Through) resource record.
MB	The MailBox resource record is an experimental record that specifies a DNS host with the specified mailbox. Other related experimental records are the MG (Mail Group) resource record, the MR (Mailbox Rename) resource record, and the MINFO (Mailbox INFOrmation) resource record.
MG	The Mail Group resource record is an experimental record that specifies a mailbox that is a member of the mail group (mailing list) specified by the DNS domain name.
MINFO	The Mailbox INFOrmation resource record is an experimental record that specifies a mailbox that is responsible for the specified mailing list or mailbox.

continues

Table 3.4. Continued

Record Type	Description
MR	The Mailbox Rename resource record is an experimental record that specifies a mailbox that is the proper rename of the other specified mailbox.
MX	The Mail eXchange resource record specifies a mail exchange server for a DNS domain name. A *mail exchange server* is a host that will either process or forward mail for the DNS domain name. Processing the mail means either delivering it to the addressee or passing it to a different type of mail transport. Forwarding the mail means sending it to its final destination server, sending it using Simple Message Transfer Protocol (SMTP) to another mail exchange server that is closer to the final destination, or queuing it for a specified amount of time.
NS	The Name Server resource record identifies the DNS server(s) for the DNS domain. NS resource records appear in all DNS zones and reverse zones (those in the in-addr.arpa DNS domain).
PTR	The PoinTeR resource record maps an IP address to a hostname in a DNS reverse zone (those in the in-addr.arpa DNS domain). Its counterpart, the A (address) resource record, is used to map a hostname to an IP address in a DNS zone. The in-addr.arpa domain is discussed later in this chapter.
RP	The Responsible Person resource record indicates who is responsible for the specified DNS domain or host. You can specify multiple RP records for a given DNS domain or host. The record has two parts: an electronic mail address (in the same DNS format as the one in the SoA resource record), and a DNS domain name that points to additional information about the contact.
RT	The Route Through resource record specifies an intermediate host that routes packets to a destination host. The RT record is used in conjunction with the ISDN and X.25 resource records. It is syntactically and semantically similar to the MX record type and is used in much the same way.
SoA	The Start Of Authority resource record indicates that this DNS server is the authoritative source of information for the data within this DNS domain. It is the first record in each of the DNS database files. The SoA resource record is created automatically by DNS Manager when you create a new DNS zone.
TXT	The TeXT resource record associates general textual information with an item in the DNS database. A typical use is for identifying a host's location (for example, Location: Building 26S, Room 2499). The text string must be less than 256 characters, but multiple TXT resource records are allowed.

Record Type	Description
WINS	A record that contains the IP address of the WINS server configured on the DNS server for WINS name resolution. This record is automatically created when WINS lookup is enabled on the DNS server, and is not a record that can be manually created by using Add Record in DNS Manager.
WINS_R	This record instructs Microsoft DNS server to use a NetBIOS node adapter status (`nbtstat`) command to resolve a DNS client reverse lookup query. The reverse lookup query requests the name of a computer identified only by an IP address. This record is automatically created when WINS reverse lookup is enabled on the DNS server, and is not a record that can be manually created by using Add Record in DNS Manager.
WKS	The Well-Known Service resource record describes the services provided by a particular protocol on a particular interface. The protocol is usually UDP or TCP, but can be any of the entries listed in the PROTOCOLS file (\%systemroot%\system32\drivers\etc\protocol). The services are located below port number 256 from the SERVICES file (\%systemroot%\system32\drivers\etc\services).
X.25	The X.25 resource record is a variation of the A (address) resource record. Instead of mapping a hostname to an IP address, the X.25 record maps the name to an X.121 address. X.121 is the International Standards Organization (ISO) standard that specifies the format of addresses used in X.25 networks. The X.25 resource record is designed to be used in conjunction with the RT (Route Through) resource record.

The zone file is then automatically maintained and created by the manager without requiring manual editing. This reduces the chance for syntax error. Figure 3.11 shows an example zone file.

```
;
;  Database file thomas.net.dns for thomas.net zone.
;      Zone version:  41
;

@                        IN    SOA    server.test.com. ADMINISTRATOR.test.com.
(
                         4            ; serial number
                         3600         ; refresh
                         600          ; retry
                         86400        ; expire
                         3600       ) ; minimum TTL

;
;  Zone NS records
```

```
;
@                       IN    NS    server.test.com.

;
;  WINS lookup record
;

@                       0    IN    WINS    206.195.150.65

;
;  Zone records
;

elliemae                IN    A     206.195.150.72
granny                  IN    A     206.195.150.73
jed                     IN    A     206.195.150.74
jethro                  IN    A     206.195.150.71
www                     IN    CNAME    server.
                        IN    CNAME    jethro.
```

Figure 3.11. *An example zone file.*

The in-addr.arpa Domain (Reverse Lookups)

The in-addr.arpa domain is the zone used to create server queries. This is where reverse lookup records (PTR) are stored. The DNS Manager in Windows NT actually enables you to create this record automatically when a host record (A) is created. This only works if the in-addr.arpa domain actually exists.

The domain trees in this domain are the network portions of the address. Thus the reverse lookup is technically the IP address backward. If you had a host STEVE with an IP address of 206.195.150.112, for example, the PTR record would be 112.150.195.206 with a hostname of STEVE.

Figure 3.12 displays the PTR and in-addr.arpa options in the DNS Manager utility.

```
;
;  Database file in-addr.arpa.dns for in-addr.arpa zone.
;      Zone version:  31
;

@                       IN    SOA    server.test.com. ADMINISTRATOR.test.com.
(
                        3           ; serial number
                        3600        ; refresh
                        600         ; retry
                        86400       ; expire
                        3600      ) ; minimum TTL
```

```
;  Zone NS records
;

@                          IN    NS    server.test.com.

;
;  Zone records
;



;
;  Delegated sub-zone:  0.in-addr.arpa.
;
0                          IN    NS    server.test.com.
;  End delegation


;
;  Delegated sub-zone:  127.in-addr.arpa.
;
127                        IN    NS    server.test.com.
;  End delegation

71.150.195.206             IN    PTR    jethro.thomas.net.
72.150.195.206             IN    PTR    elliemae.thomas.net.
73.150.195.206             IN    PTR    granny.thomas.net.
74.150.195.206             IN    PTR    jed.thomas.net.

;
;  Delegated sub-zone:  255.in-addr.arpa.
;
255                        IN    NS    server.test.com.
;  End delegation
```

Figure 3.12. *Configuring reverse lookup records using the DNS Manager.*

The DNS Root Cache File

The name server needs to know which servers are the authoritative name servers for the roots, or the top-level domains, of the network. This is accomplished by priming the name server's cache with the addresses of these higher authorities. The location of this file is specified in the boot file, or the Registry, in the case of using the default components in Windows NT. Every now and then, you may need to obtain the updated cache file. The latest cache file also may be obtained from the InterNIC via FTP at `FTP.RS.INTERNIC.NET` under the directory /domain/named.root.

Migrating Data Files from Other DNS Servers

BIND (Berkeley Internet Name Domain) is a standard implementation of DNS, both server and client, found on UNIX platforms. Most of the development on the DNS protocols is based on this code. As a result, the BIND name server is the most widely used name server on the Internet.

BIND Boot File Commands

Table 3.5 describes the format of boot file commands. You can use any text editor to edit or create a boot file. Commands must start at the beginning of a line, and no spaces may precede the commands.

Table 3.5. Boot file command format.

Command	Description	Syntax
`Directory`	Specifies a directory where other files referred to in the boot file can be found.	`Directory` *`directoryname`*
`Cache`	Specifies a file used to help the DNS service contact DNS servers for the root domain. This command and the file it refers to must be present.	`Cache` *`filename`*
`Primary`	Specifies a domain for which this DNS server is authoritative, and a database file that contains the resource records for that domain in the zone file. Multiple primary command records can be entered in the boot file.	`Primary` *`domain filename`*
`Secondary`	Specifies a domain for which this DNS server is authoritative, and a list of master server Internet Protocol (IP) addresses from which to attempt downloading the zone information.	`Secondary` *`domain hostlist local filename`*
`Forwarder`	Identifies other DNS servers to which the local DNS server can send recursive queries when the local DNS server cannot resolve the queries itself.	`Forwarder` *`hostlist`*
`Slave`	Specifies that the local DNS server cannot resolve queries and must send the queries to DNS servers identified in the forwarder's host list. This command can only be used directly following the `Forwarder` command.	`Slave`

The following example shows a sample boot file that can be used to govern this information.

```
;BindSecondariesNoBindSecondaries
;CACHE FILE

cache       cache.dns

;PRIMARY DOMAINS
primary   gcci.com   gcci.com.dns

;REVERSELOOKUP

primary   150.195.206.in-addr.arpa     150.dns
;   SECONDARY DOMAINS
;secondary   gcci.com                   206.195.150.65   gcci.com.dns
;secondary   150.195.206.in-addr.arpa   206.195.150.65   150.dns
```

When booting the DNS server from the Registry, all of its information is obtained from the following Registry key:

HKEY_LOCAL_MACHINE\System\CurrentControlSet\Services\DNS

The specific information needed is found in the Parameters subkey as well as the Zones subkey.

Warning

If you switch the configuration of the DNS server from booting from the Registry to booting from the data files, the zone list information in the Registry will not be transferred and will immediately be purged. You might want to back up the Registry or configure the boot file prior to actually changing over.

Troubleshooting and Testing DNS

When experiencing problems testing or using DNS, the first thing you need to be aware of is that the HOST table is used before DNS is queried. After this has been eliminated, the best option to use next is NSLOOKUP. The utility NSLOOKUP is used to test resolution in both directions. You can even use the `debug` option in NSLOOKUP to get the DNS header information echoed to the screen as well as the answer. Normally the only option would be that of a protocol analyzer.

If testing DNS locally, and not using the Internet, you will want to use the `NSLOOKUP norecurse` option. This option does not recursively query other DNS servers to resolve a name. Usually, by default, the DNS server forwards the queries if they are unable to resolve the name.

The valid options for NSLOOKUP include the following:

- `NAME`. Attempts to resolve the DNS information, including the IP address using the default server.
- `NAME1 NAME2`. Similar to the preceding option, with the exception that `NAME2` is used as the DNS server.
- `set OPTION`. Sets a specific option for NSLOOKUP. They include the following:

`all`	Print options, current server, and host.
`[no]debug`	Print debugging information.
`[no]d2`	Print exhaustive debugging information.
`[no]defname`	Append domain name to each query.
`[no]recurse`	Ask for recursive answer to query.
`[no]search`	Use domain search list.
`[no]vc`	Always use a virtual circuit.
`domain=NAME`	Set default domain name to `NAME`.
`srchlist=N1 [/N2/.../N6]`	Set domain to N1 and search list to N1, N2, and so on.
`root=NAME`	Set root server to `NAME`.
`retry=X`	Set number of retries to `X`.
`timeout=X`	Set initial time-out interval to `X` seconds.
`querytype=X`	Set query type, for example, `A,ANY,CNAME,MX,NS,PTR,SOA`.

- `server NAME`. Sets the default server to `NAME`, using the current default server.
- `lserver NAME`. Sets the default server to `NAME`, using the initial server.
- `finger [USER]`. Fingers the optional `NAME` at the current default host.
- `root`. Sets the current default server to the root.
- `ls [opt] DOMAIN [> FILE]`. Lists addresses in `DOMAIN` (optional: output to `FILE`).

The available options for listing records and addresses include the following:

`-a`	List canonical names and aliases.
`-d`	List all records.
`-t TYPE`	List records of the given type (for example, `A,CNAME,MX,NS,PTR` and so on.)
`view FILE`	Sort an `ls` output file and view it with `pg`.
`exit`	Exit the program.

Dynamic Host Configuration Protocol

DHCP, the Dynamic Host Configuration Protocol, was developed in conjunction with the IETF, in which a Windows NT Server administrator specifies a range, or *scope*, of IP addresses on the server. Addresses are then automatically assigned, or *leased*, to individual nodes when those nodes connect to the network. Administrators no longer need to enter a unique IP address at every node machine. Additionally, DHCP prevents the assignment of the same IP address to more than one node.

Finally, DHCP helps conserve IP addresses because they are leased to network nodes. If a particular node no longer needs its IP address, the address can be leased to a different node. DHCP alleviates the burden on the administrator, freeing time for other, more productive tasks. The ultimate goal is reaching a level of automation that reduces the TCP/IP support burden.

IP Addressing with DHCP

Addresses are assigned dynamically to network nodes as needed. When services are idle, a certain amount of time is allotted before the address is retrieved and reassigned. This is referred to as a *lease expiration*.

The DHCP lease process is as follows (see Figure 3.13):

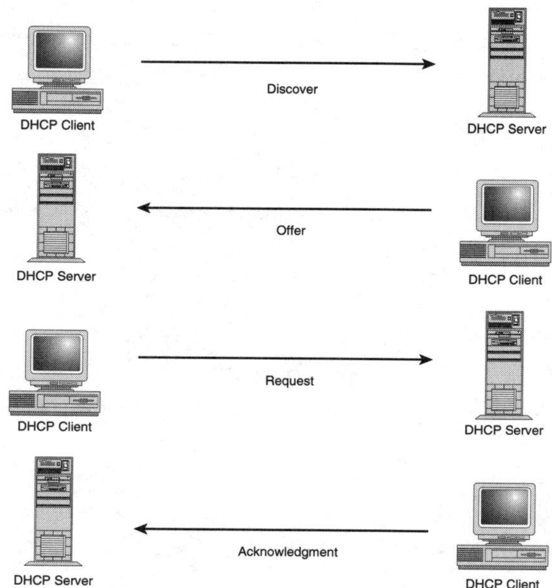

Figure 3.13. *The DHCP lease process consists of four packet exchanges: Discover, Offer, Request, and Acknowledgment.*

1. A DHCP client enters the network under an initializing state and broadcasts a Discover message on the local network. This message may be relayed to other networks to deliver it to DHCP servers on the Internet. Routers must be configured for BOOTP forwarding to support DHCP over internetworks.
2. Each DHCP server that receives the Discover message and can service the request responds with an offer message that contains an IP address and other associated configuration information.
3. The DHCP client enters a selecting state and examines the Offer messages that it receives from each DHCP server.
4. When the DHCP client selects one of the offers, it enters a requesting state, sending a Request message to the appropriate DHCP server.
5. The DHCP server grants the client with an Acknowledgment message that contains the IP configuration as well as a lease to use the configuration for a specific time.
6. The DHCP client receives the acknowledgment and enters a bound state in which the IP configuration is applied to the local TCP/IP protocols.
7. When the lease approaches expiration, the client attempts to renew its lease with the DHCP server.
8. If the lease cannot be renewed, the client re-enters the binding process and is assigned a lease to a new address. Nonrenewed addresses are returned to the scope.

Installation of the DHCP Server Service

The DHCP Server Service can be installed by navigating to the Network Control Panel and selecting the Services tab. Then, by selecting Add, you can add the service. After the DHCP Server Service is installed, the DHCP Manager utility appears in the Administrative Tools group (see Figure 3.14).

Troubleshooting Tip

If you install the DHCP Server Service after applying Service Pack 2 or later, you need to reapply the service pack or it will not function properly.

Tip

Clients can be configured to have reserved leases where the IP address is assigned to a specific MAC address.

Each subnet does not have to have a DHCP server. However, each subnet has to have a separate scope—only one subnet mask per scope. Scopes are created using the DHCP Manager utility using the Create Scope option, shown in Figure 3.15.

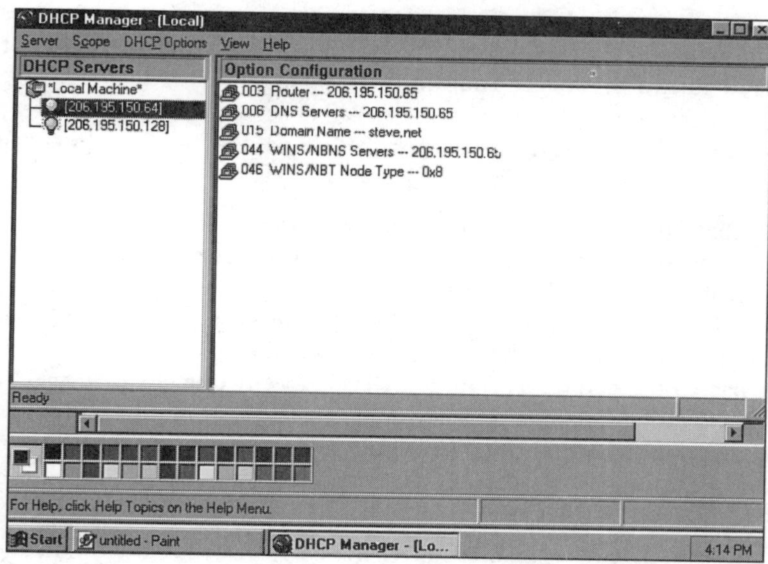

Figure 3.14. *The DHCP Manager utility.*

Create Scope - (Local)
IP Address Pool
Start Address: 206 .195 .150 .130
End Address: 206 .195 .150 .189
Subnet Mask: 255 .255 .255 .192
Exclusion Range:
Start Address:
End Address:
Add ->
<- Remove
Excluded Addresses:
Address 206.195.150.167
206.195.150.140 to 206.195.150.159
Lease Duration
Unlimited
Limited To: 3 Day(s) 00 Hour(s) 00 Minutes
Name:
Comment:
OK Cancel Help

Figure 3.15. *The Scope Properties dialog box in the DHCP Manager.*

Using the DHCP Manager, you can create and activate several DHCP scopes that can be managed for every subnet that you want to use this DHCP server. The IP Address Pool options enable you to specify a range along with an associated subnet mask. An exception-handling method ensures that the range and the associated mask are valid. After you have entered the scope information, you can then opt to exclude specific addresses or ranges within the address, as shown in Figure 3.13. These excluded addresses ensure that they will not be considered part of the scope. You can then use these for static-assigned addresses, such as DHCP server, routers, WINS servers, and DNS servers. It is also recommended, but not mandatory, that domain controllers do not use DHCP.

You can then specify the lease duration. The lease duration can be set to Unlimited, or to a specific interval. The interval is the maximum amount of time a client can use an IP address before the client must either release or renew the IP address. About halfway through the lease duration, the client will try to automatically renew the IP address. If the server is up and the address has not passed the database cleanup interval (specified in the Registry), it will renew. If the client is unable to renew at the halfway point, it will try again at seven-eighths of the way through the interval.

Client Reservations

Client reservations are when a client receives a preferred address that actually belongs to a scope and was not originally excluded. This is often confused with an excluded range. An *excluded range* is never part of the scope. The scope with reserved clients enables an administrator to have the best of both worlds. Computers can have fixed IP addresses, but can also be managed using a centralized utility.

Figure 3.16 shows the Add Reserved Clients dialog box, which enables you to add reservations.

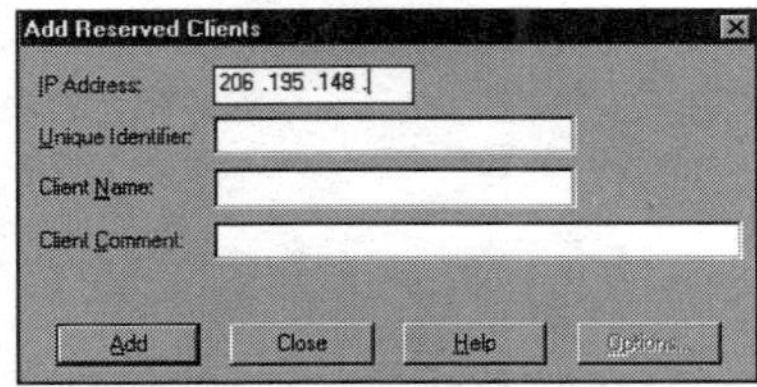

Figure 3.16. *The Add Reserved Clients dialog box in the DHCP Manager.*

The DHCP Administrator tool also enables the administrator to review the client lease information on a per-scope basis, which further enables the administrator to review the outstanding leases and associate them with the client names and their MAC layer addresses.

Options can be configured for the scope to provide additional configuration information for each scope member. The scope options contain an array of parameters that the DHCP Administrator can configure. Note that this same information can be set globally as well with the similar DHCP Options: Global dialog box (see Figure 3.17).

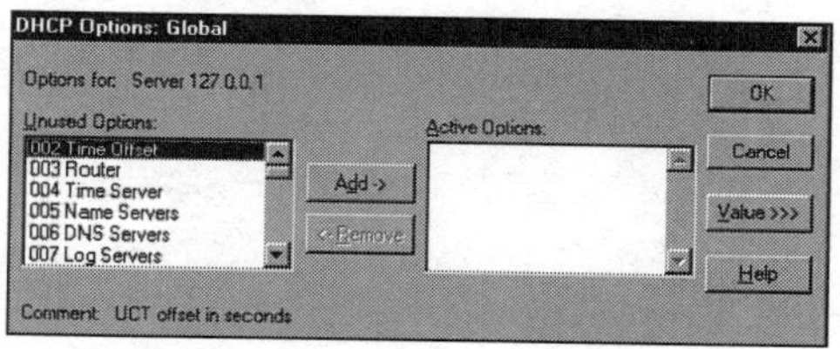

Figure 3.17. *The DHCP Options: Global dialog box.*

The DHCP Options include the following:

- *Global.* Those options that do not change from subnet to subnet and will pass down with all leases.
- *Local.* Those options that lie just within that scope (subnet).
- *Default.* If a value is not found globally or locally, it will search the default values.

Some options include the following:

- DNS Servers.
- NIS Servers.
- Domain Name.
- WINS/NBT Server IP Address.
- WINS/NBT Node Type. If this is a WINS client, it should be `0x2` (P-Node), `0x4` (M-node), or `0x8` (H-node). If you add the option for WINS first, you will see a warning message stating that this option will be required.
- Router (Default Gateway).

Viewing Active Leases

After addresses have been leased from the DHCP scope, you can then move to the Active Leases option in the DHCP Manager utility to monitor which clients have accessed which lease. You may need to do this when the scope has become full for a variety of reasons. You can also use this option to obtain MAC addresses of clients if you want to allow reserved leases (see Figure 3.18).

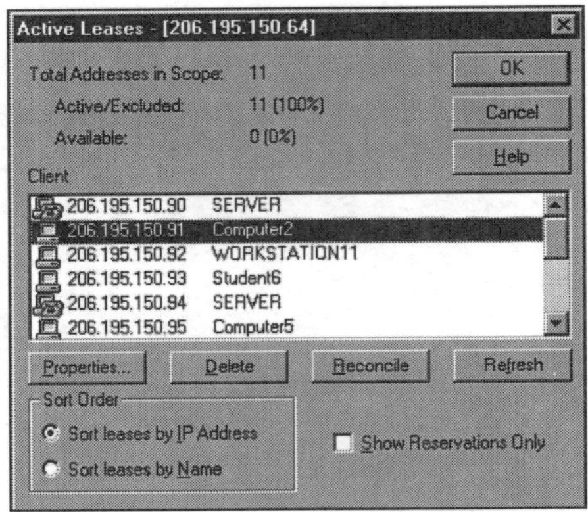

Figure 3.18. *The Active Leases options in the DHCP Manager.*

> *Author's Note*
>
> *From time to time, some of the leases have an icon that displays a telephone. This denotes that this address was leased from a Remote Access Server (RAS) service for the purpose of passing down to RAS clients.*

DHCP/BOOTP Relay

The DHCP Relay Agent enables the computer to receive and forward DHCP messages from and to IP interfaces across non-BOOTP routers.

The DHCP Relay Agent relays DHCP/BOOTP messages between a DHCP/BOOTP client and server when a router separates them (see Figure 3.19). Most of the DHCP/BOOTP network activity takes place as broadcasts that the routers will not pass, because routers do not ordinarily forward broadcasts.

In cases where a DHCP/BOOTP server is not available on the local network, but there is a DHCP/BOOTP server available at a remote network (across an IP router), the DHCP/BOOTP messages can be relayed to the server from the local network using the Relay Agent. Note that appropriate scopes need to be configured on the DHCP server to respond to the messages relayed by the Relay Agent.

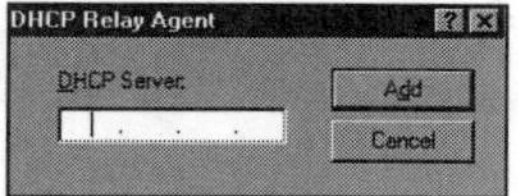

Figure 3.19. *The DHCP/BOOTP Relay Agent.*

DHCP Troubleshooting Issues

There are many problems that can arise when working with DHCP servers and clients. Many of these problems can be rectified by applying a patch or by working with additional utilities.

DHCP Security

Many people frown on using DHCP due to the possible security implications. There is no security implemented into DHCP by default. The primary function of bridges and switches is to forward frames. LAN switches and bridges work by examining frames that have been seen on the network and building a table that pairs the source hardware address with the port on which it was seen. As a result, the bridge or switch knows which devices are physically attached to each of its own ports.

In addition to using these data link devices to filter out collision packets, you can also use them for addressing the DHCP security issue. By placing restrictions on ports to where only computers with a specific MAC address can access it, unauthorized clients will not be able to obtain IP configuration.

Lease Renewal

DHCP clients first try to renew their lease halfway through the lease duration. To renew its lease, a DHCP client sends a directed `REQUEST` message to the DHCP Server from which it obtained the lease.

If permitted, the DHCP server will automatically renew the lease by responding with a `ACK` message. This `ACK` message contains the new lease as well as any configuration parameters so that the DHCP client can update its settings in case the administrator updated any settings on the DHCP server. If it fails to renew at this point, than it will wait for an additional rebinding interval. This rebinding interval occurs seven-eighths into the lease duration. At this point the DHCP client will attempt to contact *any* available DHCP server. Any DHCP server can respond with a `ACK` message renewing the lease or a `NACK` message (negative acknowledgment) that will force the DHCP client to re-initialize and obtain an IP address lease for a new IP address.

If the lease expires or a `NACK` message is received, the DHCP client must immediately discontinue using the IP address. However, the DHCP client can return to the initializing stage and attempt to obtain another IP address lease.

The NACK Packet

Once in while, you may notice that the event viewer may contain a few DHCP NACK messages. The NACK message is sent by DHCP servers to DHCP clients in order to inform the DHCP client that it has incorrect configuration information. This forces the DHCP client to release its IP address, return to the initializing state, and go through the process of acquiring an IP address lease again.

Using the DHCP Locator Utility

If you are concerned about unauthorized DHCP servers or are having trouble connecting to DHCP servers in general, you can use the Dhcploc utility to detect unauthorized DHCP servers on a subnet. This utility will display the DHCP servers that are active on the subnet. You can also use this utility to send an alert message when it detects unauthorized DHCP servers. This is a Windows NT Resource Kit utility and further documentation of this utility can be found there as well.

Service Pack 2 Enhancements to DHCP

If you have Service Pack 2 or later installed two additional troubleshooting options you can use with the DHCP Server service. In the DHCP Manager utility, when you navigate to the Server menu and select Properties, you will see a two-tabbed dialog box. Click on the General option and you will see these two options. The first one allows you to create a text-based DHCP log file of detailed DHCP events and details. The path to the log file is %systemroot%\System32\Dhcp\Dhcpsrv.log. When the activity log feature is enabled, DHCP server will keep this file open while the server is running. To delete the activity log file, you must first stop the DHCP Server service by typing the following at a command prompt:

```
NET STOP DHCPSERVER
```

There is also an option to enable conflict detection. This option will help to significantly reduce the possibility of accidental duplicate client addresses whether they are between dual DHCP clients or between a DHCP client and a static client. The way the conflict detection method works is that the DHCP server will PING the IP address it is about to lease to the DHCP client. If the DHCP server does not receive a response, then it will assume the address is valid for leasing. The General tab under the Properties dialog box allows you to set the number of conflict detection attempts.

NetBIOS Node Types

Before you can move to discussion of WINS, it is necessary to understand just what exactly WINS does. Unlike DNS, WINS provides an IP address-to-NetBIOS name mapping for every NetBIOS service that registers with the WINS server. It also is important to understand the order of how NetBIOS names are resolved on a network. There are various means of name-to-IP address mapping for name resolution, as shown in Table 3.6.

Table 3.6. Name-to-IP address mapping techniques.

Term	Definition
B-NODE	Broadcast nodes communicate using a mix of UDP datagrams (both broadcast and directed) and TCP connections. They interoperate with one another within a broadcast area, but cannot interoperate across routers in a routed network. B-nodes generate high-broadcast traffic. Each node on the LAN must examine every broadcast datagram.
P-NODE	Point-to-point nodes communicate using only directed UDP datagrams and TCP sessions. They relay on NetBIOS name servers, local or remote. If the name server is down, the p-node cannot communicate with any other system, even those on the same local network.
M-NODE	Mixed nodes are p-nodes that have been given certain b-node characteristics. M-nodes use broadcast first (to optimize performance, assuming that most resources reside on the local broadcast medium) for name registration and resolution. If this is unsuccessful, point-to-point communication with the name server is used. M-nodes generate high-broadcast traffic, but can cross routers and continue to operate normally if the name server is down.
H-NODE	Hybrid nodes (currently in RFC draft form) also are a combination of b-node and p-node functionality. H-nodes use point-to-point communication first. If the NetBIOS name server cannot be located, it switches to broadcast. H-nodes continue to poll for the name server and returns to point-to point communication when one becomes available.

Port Names and IDs

NetBIOS and NetBIOS over TCP/IP use hex IDs that append to their unique and group names to negotiate service access points and sessions. These are referred to as *port names* and *IDs*; you can also think of them as being analogous to TCP/IP sockets. The first 15 characters are a string value, and the 16th character is a hex digit. The hex digit denotes the actual service access point. Figure 3.20 displays these names and service IDs as they appear in a Dynamic WINS database. The following sections discuss each unique name and group ID definition.

Unique Names

```
\\computer_name[00h]
```

This is registered by the Workstation Service on the WINS client. Older Microsoft computers refer to this as the Redirector Service.

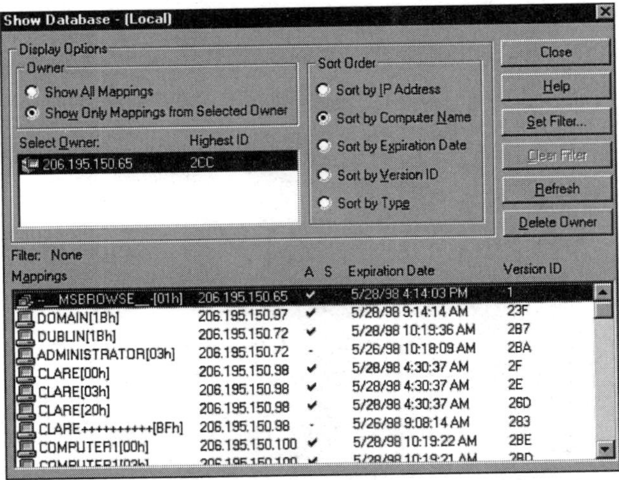

Figure 3.20. *NetBIOS names and IDs as they appear in a WINS database.*

`\\computer_name[03h]`

This is registered by the Messenger Service on the WINS client.

`\\computer_name[06h]`

This is registered by the Remote Access Server service (RAS), when started on a RAS server.

`\\computer_name[1Fh]`

This is registered by the NetDDE services, and only appears if the NetDDE services are started on the computer. By default under Windows NT 3.51 and 4.0, the NetDDE services are not started automatically.

`\\computer_name[20h]`

This is registered by the Server service on the WINS client.

`\\computer_name[21h]`

This is registered by the RAS Client service, when started on a RAS client.

`\\computer_name[BEh]`

This is registered by the Network Monitoring Agent service, and only appears if the service is started on the computer. If the computer name is not a full 15 characters, the name is padded with plus (+) symbols. The BONE (Bloodhound Network Entity) protocol is dependent on this.

`\\computer_name[BFh]`

This is registered by the Network Monitoring utility (included with Microsoft Systems Management Server). If the computer name is not a full 15 characters, the name is padded with plus (+) symbols.

`\\username[03h]`

Usernames for the currently logged on users are registered in the WINS database. The username is registered by the Server component so that the user can receive any `net send` commands sent to his or her username. If more than one user is logged on with the same username, only the first computer at which a user logged on with the username registers the name. For this reason, this name often conflicts.

Author's Note

When you configure administrative alerts using the Server Manager or the `NET NAME /ADD` *command, it causes additional names to be registered under this ID.*

`\\domain_name[1Bh]`

This is registered by the Windows NT Server Primary Domain Controller (PDC) that also is running as the Domain Master Browser and is used to allow remote browsing of domains. When a WINS server is queried for this name, a WINS server returns the IP address of the computer that registered this name.

`\\domain_name[1Dh]`

This is registered only by the Master Browser, of which there can be only one for each subnet (a rule that applies only to TCP/IP). This name is used by the backup browsers to communicate with the Master Browser to retrieve the list of available servers from the Master Browser.

Author's Note

WINS servers return the service request (`domain_name[1D]`*) with a positive response, even if it has not been registered in the database. This is why a client may still broadcast to resolve a domain controller when it is still using WINS. Additionally, if the client is a p-node client, this causes a failure in resolving this request.*

Group Names

`\\domain_name[00h]`

This is registered by the Workstation service so that it can receive browser broadcasts from LAN Manager-based computers. This is often not necessary in recent years.

`\\domain_name[1Ch]`

This is registered for use by the domain controllers within the domain and can contain up to 25 IP addresses. Therefore this affects planning for large-scale domain environments in which only 25 domain controllers are optional under this architecture. One IP address will be that of the PDC and the other 24 will be the IP addresses of Backup Domain Controllers (BDCs).

```
\\domain_name[1Eh]
```

This is registered for browsing purposes and is used by the browsers to elect a Master Browser. (This is how a statically mapped group name will register itself.) When a WINS server receives a name query for a name ending with `[1E]`, the WINS server always returns the network broadcast address for the requesting client's local network. When clients are configured not to act as browsers, they do not register under this service.

```
\\--__MSBROWSE__[01h]
```

This is registered by the Master Browser for each subnet. When a WINS server receives a name query for this name, the WINS server always returns the network broadcast address for the requesting client's local network.

The LMHOSTS File

Prior to WINS, the LMHOSTS file was the only option for resolving NetBIOS names. Now, it can still be used as either an alternative, or a supporting mechanism. The LMHOSTS file is a simple flat file that associates NetBIOS names with IP addresses. Select the Enable LMHOSTS Lookup option to activate the use of this file. This is found under the TCP/IP Properties dialog box after selecting Protocols from the Network Control Panel.

To load the LMHOSTS file from an existing file, click the Import LMHOSTS option (located in the same location) and provide the path to the file when prompted. LMHOSTS Lookup can be selected with DNS Windows Name Resolution. If both are selected, the system first checks the LMHOSTS file and then issues a DNS query if the NetBIOS name is not found in the file.

The LMHOSTS file looks like a UNIX /etc/hosts file and functions in a similar way. The difference is that the LMHOSTS file maps NetBIOS names to IP addresses, and the /etc/hosts file maps TCP/IP hostnames to IP addresses.

The following is a sample LMHOSTS file:

```
128.66.3.25     RHETT       #PRE    #DOM:TARA
128.66.3.26     SCARLETT    #PRE
128.66.3.27     PRISSY
128.66.3.28     ASHLEY
128.66.3.29     OLIVIA      #PRE    #DOM:TARA
#BEGIN_ALTERNATE
#INCLUDE \\RHETT\ATLANTA\LMHOSTS
#END_ALTERNATE
```

Each entry in an LMHOSTS file contains an IP address separated by white space from the NetBIOS name associated with that address. An entry must not exceed a single line, and comments begin with the pound sign (#).

The LMHOSTS file is stored in the WINDOWS directory on WfW, Windows 95, and Windows 3.1 systems and in the WINNT\SYSTEM32\DRIVERS\ETC directory under Windows NT, assuming that Windows NT is installed in `WINNT35`. Change the path accordingly if Windows NT is installed in another directory.

The same LMHOSTS file can be used on a WfW system or a Windows NT system, but the Windows NT version of the LMHOSTS file does have some features not supported by WfW. These special commands begin with pound signs (`#`) so that WfW systems treat them as comments, allowing the same file to be used on both systems. The Windows NT commands are discussed in the following sections.

`#PRE`

This command causes the entry to be preloaded into the cache and permanently retained there. Normally, NetBIOS names are only cached when used for name resolution, and that is only temporary. This option speeds up address resolution for frequently used hostnames.

`#DOM:domain`

This command identifies machines that are Windows NT domain controllers. Every domain controller in the LMHOSTS file should be identified by a `#DOM` command. If domains are not used, this command is not needed.

`#INCLUDE` *`file`*

This command specifies a remote file that should be incorporated in the local LMHOSTS file. This allows a centrally maintained LMHOSTS file to be loaded automatically. To provide redundant sources for LMHOSTS, enclose a group of `#INCLUDE` commands inside a pair of `#BEGIN_ALTERNATE` and `#END_ALTERNATE` statements. The system tries the various sources in order and stops as soon as it successfully downloads one copy of the LMHOSTS file.

`#MH`

This command associates a single, unique NetBIOS computer name to an IP address. You can create multiple entries for the same NetBIOS computer name for each NIC in the multihomed device, up to a maximum of 25 different IP addresses for the same name.

`#SG`

This command used to define a special group, such as printers or computers, that belong to groups on the intranet for easy reference, browsing, or broadcasting. Special groups are limited to a total of 25 members.

UDP Port 137 (NetBIOS Name Service Broadcasts)

Not all WANs will have problems browsing. Some routers can be configured to forward specific types of broadcasts and filter out others.

All NetBIOS over TCP/IP (NetBT) broadcasts are sent to the UDP port 137, which is defined as the *NetBT Name Service*. This usage is defined by RFC 1001 and 1002. Routers normally filter out these frames because they are sent to the hardware and subnet broadcast addresses. However, some routers allow all frames sent to this particular UDP port—which is used only by NetBT—to be forwarded. As a result, the browser looks as if it is on one big network segment. All computers, including Windows for Workgroups computers, see all domains and computers within the network segments.

Windows Internet Naming Service

Windows Internet Name Service (WINS) is a service that was developed by Microsoft specifically to provide NetBIOS name service for NetBIOS names over TCP/IP. The advantage of WINS is that it dynamically learns names and addresses from WINS client registration, and it also can be dynamically updated through DHCP clients. The only disadvantage of this is that it requires a Windows NT server, and it is a NetBIOS service. On strict TCP/IP networks, WINS is generally not used.

The benefit of WINS is that changes, additions, or deletions to the mapping information are automatically made to the WINS database. If a DHCP server leases an IP address to a new network node, for example, that address and the node's name are automatically entered into the WINS database. Network services that use machine names can now rely on WINS to resolve the names with their IP addresses. The administrator is not forced to manually update host mapping files, thereby reducing both administrative overhead and the opportunity for entry errors.

Figure 3.21 shows a view of the WINS architecture that includes WINS clients and WINS servers participating in a multisegment network.

WINS Proxy Agent

Windows NT Server, Workstation, Windows 95, and WFW computers can function as a WINS proxy agent receiving NetBIOS broadcasts and translating them to UDP- or TCP-directed messages to a WINS server. This allows older PCs that are not WINS-aware to participate in an NetBT network without having to have an LMHOSTS file. Windows NT, Windows 95, and WFW computers can all act as WINS proxy agents.

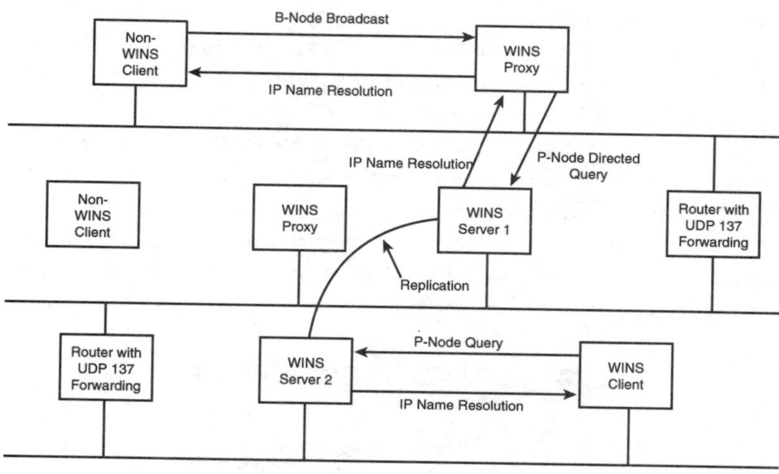

Figure 3.21. *The WINS architecture under Windows NT.*

A Windows NT computer is configured as a WINS proxy by going into the Registry, selecting the following key, and changing the value `EnableProxy` to `1`:

HKEY_LOCAL_MACHINE\System\CurrentControlSet\Services\NetBT\Parameters

Author's Note

It is important to note that the WINS proxy agent passes name resolution requests to the WINS server and it does not register NetBIOS names. Only one proxy agent should be configured on the subnet.

WINS Administration

The WINS Administration tool is designed to assist the network administrator in configuring the WINS-based servers and monitoring activity.

Author's Note

Note that the information presented is very detailed in nature. The following are key pieces of information:

- *The number of name queries received by the WINS-based server.*
- *The number of successful and less-than-successful responses.*

WINS Server Configuration

You can use the WINS Manager to set specific preferences on both servers. Figure 3.22 displays the Preferences dialog box, which can be accessed under the Options menu in the WINS Manager utility. The refresh interval of the statistics can be adjusted here in addition to start times and intervals of WINS database replication. The miscellaneous settings are important because you can actually set the manager to validate its cached information, or reconcile the information with the server. If the server cannot be found, a bit of a hang might be noticed while it times out this information. Everything else under this option deals with display style and format.

Figure 3.22. *The Preferences dialog box in the WINS Manager.*

For actual service configuration, select the Configuration option from the Server menu in the WINS Manager. By default, it displays only basic configuration options. All the options, including the advanced options, can be displayed by clicking the Advanced button. This is where you can adjust the life-cycle of WINS database entries. The life-cycle of WINS database entries are under the units separated by intervals.

If using WINS database replication, you can then use the advanced options to control the initial behavior of database replication. Beneath these options is advanced database-related information, including logging options, and whether unsolicited replication will be supported (see Figure 3.23).

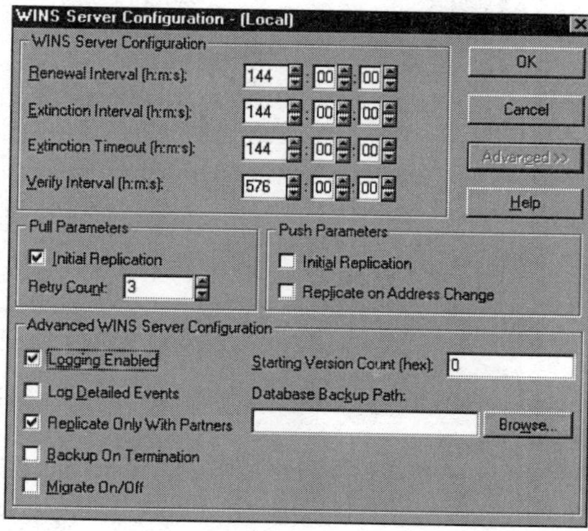

Figure 3.23. *The WINS Server Configuration dialog box.*

WINS Database Replication

To ensure that your clients can resolve all NetBIOS services, you can establish some redundancy by implementing multiple WINS servers and having them replicate their databases with one another. This gives the server an excellent means of fault tolerance and creates a highly reliable name service. You can also use WINS database replication to reduce NetBIOS name service traffic over routers. By putting WINS servers on different segments and replicating them with one another, all that will be passed over the router will be database replication traffic.

Each WINS server participating is referred to as a *replication partner*. Each partner can be configured as either a *PUSH partner* or a *PULL partner*, depending on the relationship. Although it is possible for a partner to be both at the same time, it is recommended that each partner be either/or. In many cases you can have multiple partnerships to handle network hierarchies. This is achieved in a daisy chain fashion of replication where a mechanism of transitivity is achieved by each partner passing its database up the hierarchy to the other WINS server. This would be similar to the way RIP works in routing.

PUSH and PULL replication partners can be adjusted by choosing Server, Replication in the WINS Manager utility (see Figure 3.24).

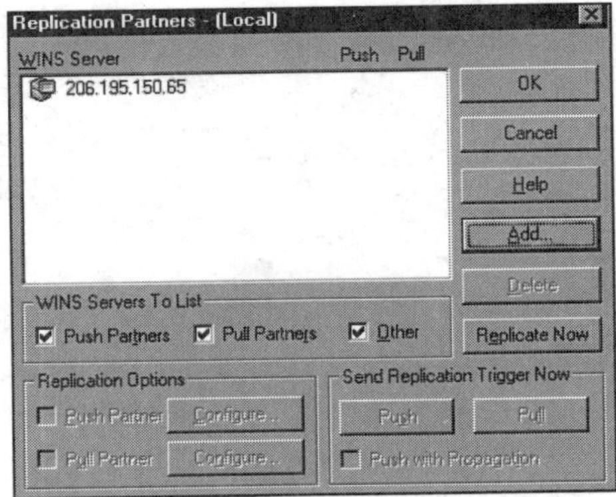

Figure 3.24. *The WINS Database Replication option.*

WINS Client Configuration

Windows NT clients using WINS configure the WINS options using the WINS option in the TCP/IP Properties dialog box. Figure 3.25 shows the WINS Address configuration tab, which allows a setting for both a primary and a secondary server. This is a means of fault tolerance in that the computer can register with the secondary server if the primary server is down.

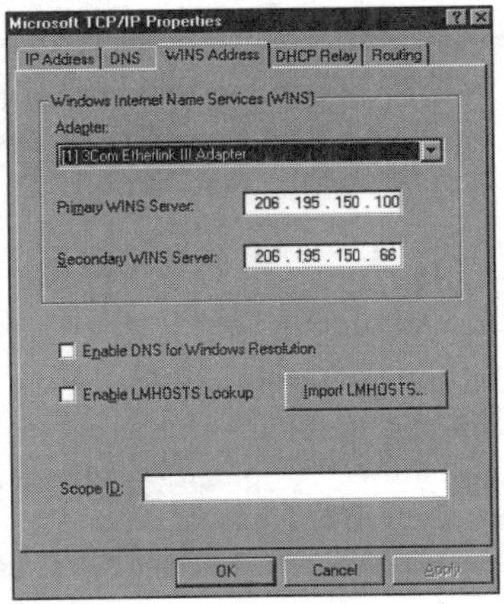

Figure 3.25. *The WINS Address tab in the TCP/IP Properties dialog box.*

The WINS Administrator tool enables the configuration of various parameters for the WINS-based server, including which WINS-based server to focus on, the static mappings for the server, the replication information, and the database in use.

The WINS Database

If a WINS client shuts down properly, it sends a name release request directly to the WINS server for each service. This is so that it can then be removed from the database to prevent others from believing it is still available on the network. When the release request occurs, if the database maps to a different IP address for that name, it sends a negative response to the client.

WINS Name Renewal

Halfway through the WINS lease duration (the value which is set after the client registers the name), the WINS client sends a name refresh request to the WINS server. This refreshes its registration and updates it with a new Time-To-Live (TTL) stamp. The default time to live is 144 hours, or six days.

WINS Database Entries

Each name and service mapping is listed individually in the WINS database. You can even think of these individual addresses as NBT socket addresses. Each entry in the WINS database is listed with a marking under A if it is an active lease. If that lease was entered in manually as a static mapping, it is also checked under the S option (for static). The possible values for the A column are as follows:

Check mark	Active entry.
Dash	Released state.
Cross	Extinct entry—soon to be deleted.

WINS Database Record Cycle

When the WINS client registers, it becomes active. After it becomes active, the lease is renewed halfway through the lease duration. If the lease is never renewed, it will be released after the renewal interval passes. The default value for this is 144 hours. After that point the lease is extinct until re-registered. It still remains in the database, however. After the extinction interval passes, the lease is then flagged as a tombstone entry (cross). This occurs after six more days. After the database entry is a tombstone, it has six more days to be registered before being purged from the database. Although extinct records are replicated, released records are not.

Static Mappings

A WINS server can create a WINS database by entering the service registrations sent to it directly from WINS clients. It can then maintain a dynamic database of NetBIOS name mappings. However, there will probably be times when you want to import static mappings or manually enter static mappings into the WINS database. Table 3.7 shows the types of static name mappings for NetBIOS.

Table 3.7. Types of static NetBIOS name mappings.

Type	Description
Unique	A unique name that maps to a single IP address. This contrasts with *Multihomed*.
Group	Also referred to as a *Normal* group. When adding an entry to Group by using WINS Manager, you must enter the computer name and IP address. The IP addresses of individual members of Group are not stored in the WINS database, however. Because the member addresses are not stored, there is no limit to the number of members that can be added to Group. Broadcast name packets are used to communicate with Group members. (Contrast with *Internet group*.)
Domain	A NetBIOS name-to-IP-address mapping that has 0x1C as the 16th byte. A Domain group stores up to a maximum of 25 addresses for members. For registrations after the 25th address, WINS overwrites a replica address or, if none is present, WINS overwrites the oldest registration.
Internet group	User-defined groups that enable you to group resources, such as printers, for easy reference and browsing. The default 16th byte of an Internet group name is set equal to 0x20. An Internet group can store up to a maximum of 25 addresses for members. When you add an Internet group, the following three unique records are added: InternetGroupName<0x20> InternetGroupName<0x3> InternetGroupName<0x0> This is similar to the Domain group. Internet group members can be added as the result of dynamic group registrations. A dynamic member, however, does not replace a static member added by using WINS Manager or importing the LMHOSTS file. (Contrast with *Group*.)
Multihomed	A unique name that can have more than one address and is used for multihomed computers. The maximum number of addresses that can be registered as multihomed is 25. For registrations after the 25th address, WINS overwrites a replica address or, if none is present, it overwrites the oldest registration. (Contrast with *Unique*.)

Troubleshooting WINS Servers

One of the best utilities, in my opinion, for helping you pinpoint any problems that may exist on the WINS server or within the WINS database is the Winschk utility. This is a command-line utility that checks various information on the WINS server. It can examine the following information:

- Name
- Version number
- Inconsistencies in WINS databases

It can also monitor replication activity, and verify replication configuration. Winschk has no switches but does have the following options:

Option	Action
0	Enable or disable interactive mode.
1	Test names on WINS servers.
2	Check for version number inconsistencies.
3	Monitor WINS servers and detect communication failures.
4	Verify replication configuration.
99	Exit Winschk.

Chapter 4

Remote Administrative Services

- **Remote Noninteractive Management Using the Server Management Utility**
  See this inherent mechanism for controlling server properties, services, and shares.
- **Use the r Commands to Implement Trusted Administration**
  Use this concept taken from UNIX and TCP/IP to transfer files and run remote processes on Windows NT computers running the Remote Shell service.
- **The Remote Console Service**
  Learn about the Resource Kit's Remote Console utility to run a remote interactive shell on another Windows NT computer to run command-line administrative tools.
- **Use a Telnet Service to Provide Remote Interactive Management**
  Learn about this possible solution, well known in the TCP/IP community, and compare it to the Remote Console utility.
- **Use Web-based Administration to Remotely Administer Windows NT**
  This new feature, designed for Internet Information Server, enables you to use a Web browser as an administrative interface for Windows NT Servers.

The Server Manager

The *Server Manager* is a separate program item in the Administrative Tools program group. You use the Server Manager to manage domains and workstations (see Figure 4.1).

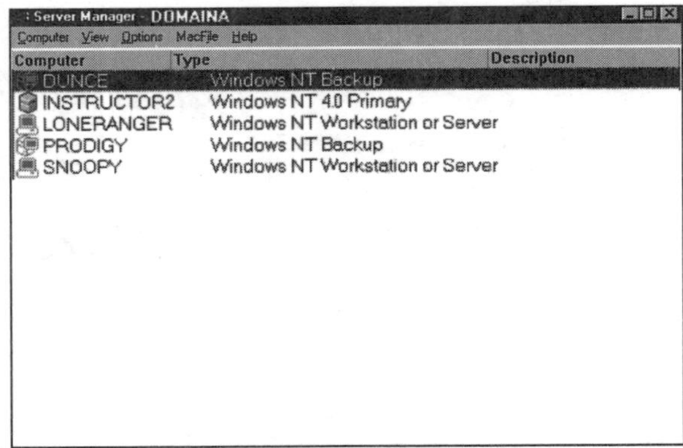

Figure 4.1. *The Server Manager utility enables you to remotely administer Windows NT Workstations and Servers.*

When a Workstation, Server, or Backup Domain Controller (BDC) is added to a domain, Windows NT generates an account for the machine name. The machine accounts serve various purposes, including linking BDCs with the Primary Domain Controller (PDC) and pairing up the trusting and trusted domains.

The permanent account types include the following:

- Windows NT 4.00 Primary
- Windows NT 4.00 Backup
- Windows NT 4.00 Server
- Windows NT 4.00 Workstation
- Windows NT 3.51 Primary
- Windows NT 3.51 Backup
- Windows NT 3.51 Server
- Windows NT 3.51 Workstation
- Windows NT 3.50 Primary
- Windows NT 3.50 Backup
- Windows NT 3.50 Server
- Windows NT 3.50 Workstation
- Windows NT 3.10
- Windows NT 3.10 Advanced Server

- Windows NT 3.10 Controller
- LAN Manager 2.x Controller
- LAN Manager 2.x Servers
- LM/X UNIX Server

The volatile account types include the following:

- Windows 95 (with authenticated user in the description)
- Windows for Workgroups (with authenticated user in the description)
- MS-DOS Peer Server (with authenticated user in the description)

Replication over WAN and RAS

Consideration should be given to the amount of traffic that account replication places on the wide area network (WAN) or a RAS dial-up line. In particular, avoid doing full synchronization across WAN links. Full synchronizations are required when first setting up a new PDC or bringing a new location online.

Full synchronizations are also initiated when more than 2,000 changes happen to user/groups within a short period of time (less than one hour). This is configurable by increasing the size of the Change log. If anticipating high change activity, you may wish to increase the value of this parameter.

The Computer menu is probably the most important menu in the Server Manager in that it provides the most options. Table 4.1 defines the Computer menu's commands.

Table 4.1. The Computer menu commands.

Command	Description
Properties	Brings up the Properties dialog box (see Figure 4.2). This dialog box is similar to the Server Control Panel in that it enables you to view the status of the remote machine's Server Service.
Users	Displays a list of connected users.
Shares	Lists shared directories.
Alerts	Defines which NetBIOS names the system alerts are sent to via the Messenger Service.
Replication	Defines Export and Import directory trees and servers.
Send Message	Sends a message to a workstation or server (see Figure 4.3). This dialog box enables you to send a message to

continues

Table 4.1. Continued

Command	Description
	all users connected to that computer. (This includes your machine as well.) Both systems must be running the Messenger Service.
Promote to Domain Controller	Makes a server in a domain the domain controller. The current domain controller is automatically demoted to a server.
Synchronize Entire account Domain	Manually synchronizes domain to downloading information from the domain controller to each. Synchronization occurs normally at regular intervals. Synchronize Entire Domain is only available when the domain controller is selected. It synchronizes the domain security database to all servers in the domain.
Synchronize with Domain	Available only when a controller server is selected. It replicates the Domain Security database to the selected server from the domain controller.
Add to Domain a Workstation	Used usually to add a Windows NT in a workgroup to domain.
Remove from Domain	Removes a server from a domain.

The commands on the View menu enable you to list different groups of systems in the main window of the Server Manager.

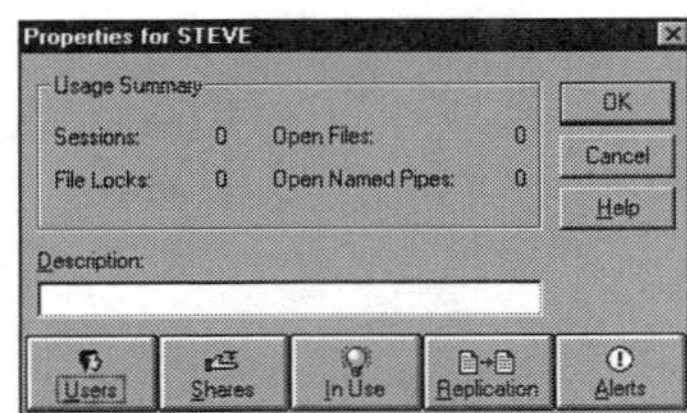

Figure 4.2. *The Properties dialog box.*

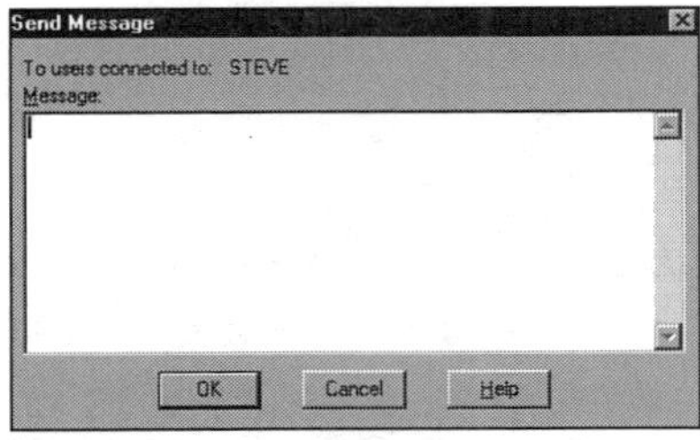

Figure 4.3. *The Send Message dialog box.*

You can choose to view individual workstations, servers, or only domain controllers. If you have any Windows NT Servers that have Services for Macintosh or the File and Print Services for NetWare running, you will also see links to these snap-in administrative modules.

Under the Options menu, notice the option to toggle back and forth between using and not using the low-speed connection option. A *low-speed connection* is used to eliminate information that may be unnecessary, and eliminates automatically refreshing the Server Manager's display. This is recommended when working with low-speed bandwidth.

Changing the Computer Name of a Workstation in a Domain

One of the major problems with using the Server Manager is that it does not enable you to change certain properties easily, such as the computer's name. This is not the easiest task in Windows NT. To change the computer name of a workstation in a domain, follow these steps:

1. On one of the domain controllers, run Server Manager to add a workstation with the new name.
2. Choose the Network icon in Control Panel, and then leave the current domain by joining a workgroup of any name.
3. Change the computer name. Make sure to click OK so that the changes will take effect immediately.
4. Reboot the computer.
5. Choose the Network icon in Control Panel, and then rejoin the domain.
6. Reboot the computer.
7. On the domain, run Server Manager and delete the old workstation name.

Run the `Synchronize Entire Domain` command in Server Manager for domains, in case the workstation is unable to log on to the domain after the name is changed.

The Remote Console Service

Remote Console is a client/server application in the Windows NT Resource Kit that you can use to run a remote command-line session. In this command-line session, you can start any other application remotely.

A Remote Console session resembles a Telnet session under UNIX, but differs significantly in the method of handling the terminal screen. It also is a multiprotocol solution in that it depends on the SMB protocol that can be bound on top of NetBEUI, NWLink, and TCP/IP. Telnet works only on top of TCP/IP. It is also more secure than Telnet in that it provides the option of added security.

The Remote Console Server service starts a CMD.EXE process for each client connection. (CMD is the command-line interpreter.) Remote Console then takes full control of the console in which CMD is running and notifies the client of any video memory change to that console. Because Remote Console does not redirect standard output, but directly takes control of video memory, you can use this tool to remotely run any command-line program that uses video memory, such as EDIT. Do not confuse this as being able to support GUI-based applications; it supports only command-line applications.

When you run Remote Console, the client sends all keyboard events to the Remote Console server so that these events are simulated in the CMD console on the server side.

The Remote Console client (RCLIENT.EXE) is compatible with any version of Windows NT Workstation or Windows NT Server, but runs only on the Windows NT platform.

The syntax for the Remote Console Client is as follows:

```
rclient [\\]servercomputername [/e[ncrypt]] [/logon[:[domainname\]username]
➥[password]] [/s[lowlink]]
```

The available options include the following:

- `/e[ncrypt]` Encrypts all data sent, so the contents of the console are only accessible to the Remote Console client. Encrypting data gives the user a way to keep the console contents secret. Depending on the language version of Windows NT, the encryption schemes vary. The `/encrypt` option is available only if both the client and the server are running Windows NT Server 4.0 or Windows NT Workstation 4.0. It does not work with NT 3.51.

- `/logon` Enables the server to give the CMD.EXE process, which runs on behalf of the client, a logon ID. With this logon ID, the CMD process uses the client's credentials (*`domainname`*, *`username`*, and *`password`*) to make network connections. Use this option if you are planning to use network connections after connecting to the server.

  If a username is not specified along with `/logon`, the current user is used. If the password has not been passed in the command line, the user is prompted to enter a password after Remote Console starts. After the user enters the password, the credentials are encrypted and sent to the server. Remote Console follows this process because Windows NT security does not support Security Delegation Mode, which allows propagating an access token from one server to another.

Author's Note

The `/logon` *option of the client now encrypts the password with a Data Encryption Standard (DES) algorithm. Password encryption is available only if both client and server are running Windows NT Server 4.0 or Windows NT Workstation 4.0.*

- `/slowlink` Low-speed connection. Use this option if the client and the server are linked with a low-speed connection (not a LAN)—for example, a RAS connection or a connection over a router. This option enables both the client and the server to tune their parameters so that the stream of data that goes across the wire relies on the link speed. If the `/slowlink` option is not used, the amount of data that goes across the wire is computed regardless of the link speed.

  If logged on to the local or remote workstation as administrator, you can also run RCONSTAT.EXE on the server, or remotely when connected to the server with the Remote Console client. RCONSTAT does not take any parameters and lists all the current connections.

Client Administrative Utilities

Client administrative utilities enable you to control a domain and domain controller from a remote machine that is not a domain controller. There are two sets of client-based administrative tools:

- \CLIENTS\SRVTOOLS\WIN95 Win32-based administrative tools. Originally designed for the Windows 95 platform (Win32 operating subsystem).
- CLIENTS\SRVTOOLS\WINNT Win32-based administrative tools. Originally designed for the WinNT operating subsystem.

The Windows NT Server tools for Windows NT Workstation clients are found on both Windows NT Server 4.0 and NT Server 3.51, and consist of the following:

- DHCP Manager
- WINS Manager
- User Manager for Domains

- System Policy Editor
- Remote Access Administrator
- Event Viewer
- Remoteboot Manager
- Server Manager

The Windows NT Server tools for Windows 3.x clients are found on the Windows NT 3.5x CD and consist of the following:

- User Manager for Domains
- Server Manager for Domains
- Event Viewer
- Print Manager for NT Server
- The File Manager Security Menu

The Windows NT Server tools for Windows 95 clients are found on the Windows NT Server 4.0 CD and Windows NT 3.51 Resource Kit, and consist of the following:

- Event Viewer
- User Manager for Domains
- Server Manager

Using Trusted Computing

When you speak of *trusted computing*, you are not talking about trust relationships like those discussed in Chapter 1, "Developing an Enterprise Model." *Trusted computing* refers to the act of trusted file management and application usage to certain host computers and usernames. The commands used to implement these are often referred to as `r` *commands*. By default, Windows NT supports only the client side of trusted computing, using the `RCP`, `RSH`, and `REXEC` commands.

RSH

`RSH` runs commands on remote hosts running the RSH service.

The syntax is as follows:

```
RSH host [-l username] [-n] command
```

- *host* Specifies the remote host on which to run the command.
- -l *username* Specifies the username to use on the remote host. If omitted, the logged on username is used.
- -n Redirects the input of RSH to NULL.
- *command* Specifies the command to run.

RCP

This connectivity command copies files between a Windows NT computer and a system running RSHD, the remote shell daemon. The RCP command can also be used for third-party transfer to copy files between two computers running rshd when the command is issued from a Windows NT computer. The rshd daemon is available on UNIX computers, but not on Windows NT; therefore, the Windows NT computer can only participate as the system from which the commands are issued. The remote computer must also provide the REP utility by running RSHD.

The syntax is as follows:

```
RCP [-a ¦ -b] [-h] [-r] [host][.user:]source [host][.user:] path\destination
```

- -a Specifies ASCII Transfer Mode. This mode converts the EOL characters to a carriage return for UNIX and a carriage return/line feed for personal computers. This is the default Transfer Mode.
- -b Specifies Binary Image Transfer Mode.
- -h Transfers hidden files.
- -r Copies the contents of all subdirectories; the destination must be a directory.
- *host* Specifies the local or remote host. If *host* is specified as an IP address, you must specify the user.
- *user* Specifies a username to use rather than the current username.
- *source* Specifies the files to copy.
- *path\destination* Specifies the path relative to the logon directory on the remote host. Use the escape characters (\ , “”, or ‘’) in remote paths to use wildcard characters on the remote host.

REXEC

REXEC runs a process on a remote computer.

The syntax is as follows:

```
REXEC host [-l username] [-n] command
```

- *host* Specifies the remote host on which to run the command.
- -l *username* Specifies the username on the remote host.
- -n Redirects the input of REXEC to NULL.
- *command* Specifies the command to run.

RSHSVC.EXE: TCP/IP Remote Shell Service

If you have the Windows NT Resource Kit, you can use the TCP/IP Remote Shell Service. TCP/IP Remote Shell Service, the server side of the TCP/IP utility RSH.EXE, provides a command-line shell or single command execution service for remote users. RSHSVC.EXE works like the UNIX Remote Shell Service. Any computer with an RSH client—which exists for nearly all major operating systems—can access this service.

Other Remote Administrative Utilities from the Resource Kit

The Resource Kit also contains many other command-line services and utilities that can further assist in remote administration.

RMTSHARE

RMTSHARE is a command-line utility that enables you to set up or delete shares remotely.

To run RMTSHARE, even to just view shares, you must have share-changing permissions on the remote computer.

REMOTE.EXE

The REMOTE utility is an external redirection element and enables you to run command-line programs on remote computers. This allows for collaboration using a single command as well as sharing so that others can attach to and view and share input and output.

When developing software, for example, you can compile code with the processor and resources of a remote computer while performing other tasks on the computer. You can also use REMOTE to distribute the processing requirements for a particular task across several computers.

To use `REMOTE`, you must first start the server end (by running `remote /s`) on the computer where you want to run the selected program. Then you connect to the server end from another computer (by running `remote /c`).

Troubleshooting Tip

`REMOTE` *does no security authorization, and permits anyone with a* `REMOTE` *client (*`remote /c`*) to connect to the* `REMOTE` *server (*`remote /s`*). This leaves the account under which the* `REMOTE` *server was run open to anyone who connects. By contrast,* `RCMD.EXE` *authenticates all users with standard Windows NT user-authentication procedures.*

Tip

`REMOTE` *cannot be used to control graphical Windows-based applications.*

Remote Killing

This service (RKILLSRV.EXE) with both GUI (WRKILL.EXE) and command-line (RKILL.EXE) clients enables a user to enumerate and kill processes on a remote computer. Only members of the Administrators group can kill a process remotely with this tool.

The service can be installed with INSTSRV.EXE or SRVINSTW.EXE.

Using a Telnet Daemon

Telnet Server Beta provides a solution for running command-line utilities, scripts, and batch files from clients on a network, independently of a client's operating system.

Telnet Server has two components: the service itself (TELNETD.EXE) and an underlying component, the Remote Session Manager (RSM.EXE).

The Telnet Server Service operates by connecting to the *Remote Session Manager (RSM)* component. RSM is responsible for initiating, terminating, and managing character-based remote Telnet sessions on a given system. RSM affects only the services provided in the Telnet Server Service; it does not affect the Microsoft Remote Access Service (RAS), or other layered products.

The second beta version of Telnet Server includes major enhancements such as an easier installation process, increased manageability, and improved performance.

The only sure way to determine whether an application can successfully be run in a Telnet session is to test it with Telnet Server. In most cases, graphics-based applications cannot be started successfully from within a remote session.

If such applications can start, they create a window on the desktop of the host computer, a situation that can be disconcerting to any local user on that computer.

Troubleshooting Tip

Applications that run properly in a remote text-based session but that display warnings or messages in graphical dialog boxes cannot display these warnings and messages when run in a Telnet session. Some applications compensate for this correctly.

In this version of Telnet Server Beta, the number of Telnet connections is no longer limited by the Telnet Server Service, although it might be constrained by memory, disk space, or other factors.

Web Administration of Windows NT Server

This ISAPI DLL enables limited remote administration of Windows NT Server via HTML browsers (including Internet Explorer 2.0 and later) from Windows, Macintosh, and UNIX platforms. The most recent version of Web Administration of Microsoft Windows NT Server is also available for download from the Microsoft Web site:

```
http://www.microsoft.com/
```

This tool does not replace existing administrative tools for Windows NT Server, but rather, assists administrators when they do not have access to existing tools—for example, when they are away from their normal administrative workspace. This tool is particularly useful for Windows NT administrators who are already experienced with the current administrative tools on Windows NT Server 3.51 and 4.0.

With Web Administration, “roaming” administrators can view performance and other server statistics and remotely manage the following:

- User and group accounts
- Services and devices
- Event logs
- Printers
- Shares and sessions

To use Web Administration, the administrator navigates through a series of HTML pages with a Web browser.

Using a Web Client to Manage NT Servers

The objective in this section is to successfully install the WebAdmin interface.

Part 1 is to be performed on the server. For Part 2, you need another computer that will be the client running the Web browser. Part 2 will be done at the client computer. The client can use any computer that runs Internet Explorer or Netscape Navigator, and the server should use Windows NT Server.

Part 1: The Server

1. Navigate to the C:\Classfiles directory and double-click Webadmin.exe.
2. Click Yes to accept the license agreement.
3. You are then prompted with the introductory screen. Click Continue to proceed.
4. After the files have finished copying, select Exit.

Part 2: The Client

1. To connect to the Web Administration home page, use a Web browser to navigate to the following URL:

   ```
   http://servername/ntadmin/ntadmin.htm
   ```

2. If you are not already authenticated to the server, you may be prompted for a username and password. This must be an administrative equivalent on the destination server.
3. After being authenticated, you can proceed to administer the server.

Installing and Using the Remote Console Service

The objective in this section is to successfully install the Remote Console Service as well as the Remote Console Client.

Tip

You need to have the Windows NT Resource Kit installed.

The following steps should be performed on both machines:

1. Right-click the Network Neighborhood and select Properties. The Properties dialog box appears. Click the Services tab. A list of installed services appears.
2. Click the Add button and select Have Disk. When prompted with the location of source files, type in the path field **`c:\ntreskit\rconsole`**. The dialog box shown in Figure 4.4 displays.

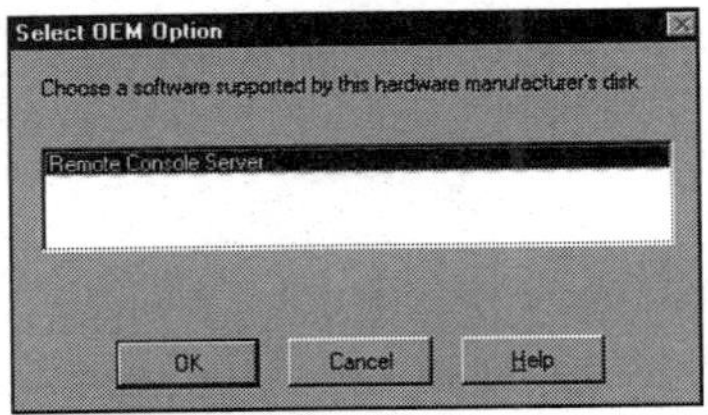

Figure 4.4. *The options needed to add the OEM service Remote Console Server.*

3. Click OK twice, and then restart the computer.
4. After the computer reboots, navigate to the Programs group and then select the command prompt.
5. Change to the C:\NTRESKIT\RCONSOLE directory.
6. You now are using the Remote Console Client utility. (If you have ever used an application like `xterm` or `rsh` using UNIX, you will notice that this is a similar command.) The following are the syntax options for `rClient`:

```
rClient [\\]computername [Options]
```

7. Type the following command:

```
rClient \\servername /logon:administrator administrator_password
```

8. What type of response occurred?
9. To verify the connection, type the following command within the console:

```
RCONSTAT
```

   What type of information displays?
10. What is the current working directory on the server?
11. What is your current user environment for `PATH` and `TEMP` on the server? (You can get this information by typing **`set`** within the remote console command prompt.)

12. Now, change the screen buffer size to 80×500 and the window size to 80×50. Type the following command:

    ```
    rconmode 80,500,80,50
    ```

13. Did the screen settings change?
14. Type the following command:

    ```
    winmsd
    ```

    Does the Windows NT Diagnostics program appear?
15. If so, which computer name appears in the WINMSD dialog box?
16. Navigate to the File menu and select Save Report.
17. Select the default settings. What is the default path? Is it located on your computer or the remote computer?

Installing and Using the Telnet Service

The objective in this section is to successfully install and use the Telnet Service.

Tip

You need to have the Windows NT Resource Kit installed.

1. Right-click the Network Neighborhood and select Properties. The Network Control Panel displays. Select the Services tab.
2. Click the Add button and select Have Disk. When prompted with the location of source files, type in the path field **`c:\ntreskit\telnet`**.
3. Select the Remote Session Manager.
4. Click the Add button and select Have Disk. When prompted with the location of source files, type in the path field **`c:\ntreskit\telnet`**. After the Select OEM Option dialog box (refer again to Figure 4.4) appears, select the Telnet Service Beta.
5. Click Close to continue. When prompted, reboot the computer.
6. After the computer has rebooted, using either Explorer or a command prompt, navigate to the C:\NTRESKIT directory.
7. Using Notepad, edit the RSMLOGIN.CMD and modify the contents. This is the file used as your welcome banner when users connect to your Telnet server. You can use this as your Telnet greeting.
8. Navigate to the Programs group and select Command Prompt.

9. Type the following command:

```
telnet HOSTNAME_OF_YOUR_NEIGHBOR
```

10. Log on to the host as administrator using the correct administrator account and password. A screen similar to that shown in Figure 4.5 appears.

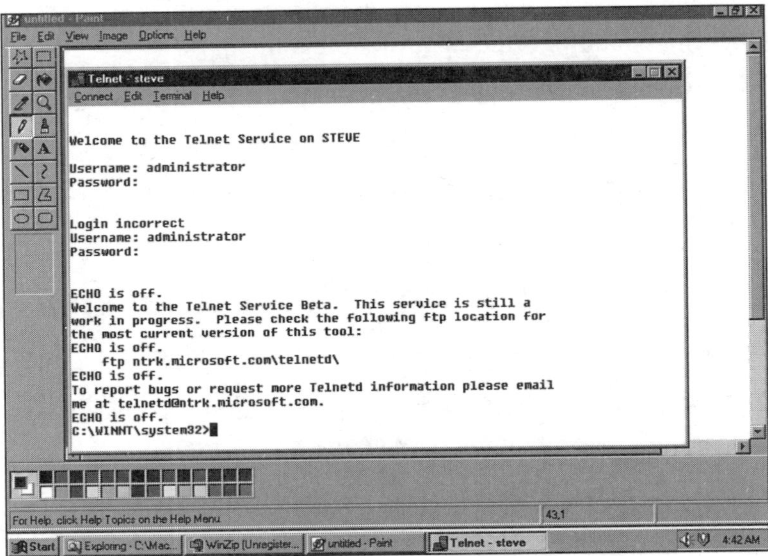

Figure 4.5. *Logging on to the Telnet Service.*

> ***Tip***
>
> *If the logon account does not seem to work, try it a few more times.*

11. What is the current working directory?

12. Type the following command:

```
dir
```

13. Now type an external command:

```
edit
```

This should invoke the MS-DOS editor on the remote machine.

14. Type the following command:

```
notepad
```

What happened to your computer? What happened to the remote computer?

Chapter 5

Network Management and Monitoring

- **Network Manager Tools**
  Utilities that give you the option of managing and monitoring Windows NT computers locally and/or remotely.
- **Network Monitor Utility**
  Learn about inherent utilities such as the Network Monitor utility and learn how the Network Monitor analyzes protocols and network traffic.
- **Performance Monitor**
  Learn how to use performance monitoring and metering utilities such as the Windows NT Performance Monitor.
- **Use SNMP to Manage Remote Computers**
  We will discuss in detail the SNMP manageable agent included with Windows NT.

The Tools of a Network Manager

From start to finish, many tools can assist a network manager. A network manager needs the following items to develop an internetwork design, manage the network, and troubleshoot:

- A plan (well laid out)
- Hardware (usually a private nonproduction workstation, a management console, a printer, and/or plotter)
- Software (used for documentation, network management data, and for establishing network blueprints)

- Spreadsheet or database program
- Graphics or drawing application
- Word processing application

The network administrator also needs tools and utilities that can enable him or her to monitor and manage network performance. This chapter focuses on performance management.

The Performance Monitor

The Performance Monitor is installed by default after the installation of Windows NT. To start the execution of the Performance Monitor, double-click its icon in the Administrative Tools program group.

The Performance Monitor has four view modes:

- Chart
- Log
- Alert
- Report

By default, Performance Monitor opens up in the Chart view.

Each of the views can be displayed in the Performance Monitor window using the icons in the toolbar or from the View menu.

Chart View

The Chart view, one of four main views, is brought up in an initialized state, as shown in Figure 5.1.

Several choices can be made when adding information to the Chart view. The first choice is the system to be monitored. It defaults to the local system.

You can then begin to add performance counters to the chart list for active monitoring, either by clicking the plus icon on the toolbar or by navigating to the Edit menu and selecting Add to Chart. Figure 5.2 displays the Add to Chart dialog box.

Any of the interconnected systems known to this system can be entered in the Computer text box. Objects for monitoring within the Chart view are chosen from the Object drop-down list box. The default object is Processor, which has the default counter of %Processor Time.

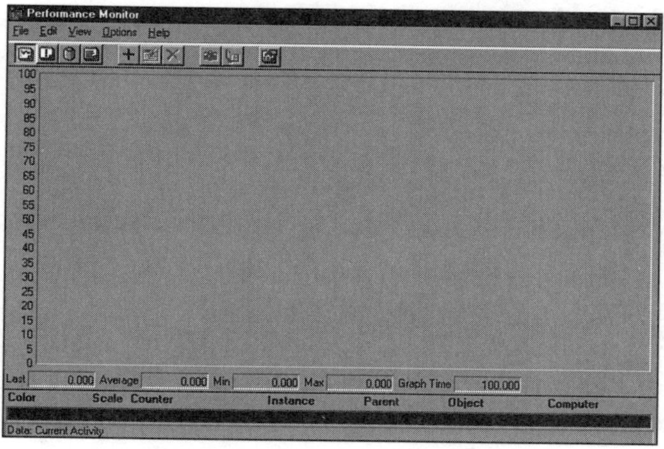

Figure 5.1. *The Chart view.*

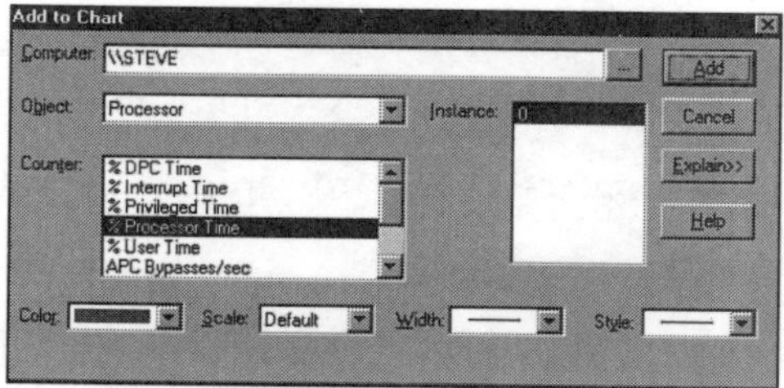

Figure 5.2. *The Add to Chart dialog box.*

The resulting chart can display separate lines for each counter for an object. Objects have varying numbers of counters that can be displayed. The following list shows the counters for the object Processor:

- Percentage DPC Time
- Percentage Interrupt Time
- Percentage Privileged Time
- Percentage Processor Time
- Percentage User Time
- APC Bypasses/sec
- DPC Bypasses/sec
- DPC Rate
- DPCs Queued/sec
- Interrupts/sec

As this list shows, the Processor object has many counters just for the processor and the instances of each process.

Tip

A large number of counters are available; the Explain button can be used to display an explanation of the selected counter, if necessary.

Commonly Used Counters

The objects commonly used for tracking can be chosen from the Chart view and include the following:

- *Cache*. File system cache.
- *Logical Disk*. Partitions and space usage.
- *Memory*. System memory.
- *Network Protocol Resources*.
- *Objects*. Certain parts of system software.
- *Physical Disk*. Counters relating to the physical disk systems.
- *Process*. Running programs.
- *Processor*. The CPU.
- *Redirector*. The file system redirector used to redirect file system requests to other systems.
- *Server*. Incoming network traffic due to share access.
- *System*. Common counters to all hardware and software.
- *Thread*. Running threads.

After selecting the object counter, click the Add button to add the counter line to the display. After all object counters are selected, click the Done button to display the chart, as illustrated in Figure 5.3.

> **Tip**
>
> *You can use the Ctrl+H keystroke to highlight your selected object counter so that you can more easily view its activity.*

The Edit Chart Line enables the color, scale, width, and style to be changed in the resulting display. The legend at the bottom of the window, above the status bar, shows what each color or style line represents, as illustrated in Figure 5.3.

The scale percent, a multiplier, allows an object counter display to fit within the boundaries of the current chart along with other object counters when they have widely varying values. The Instance specifies which of the object counters of the identical type is displayed.

Adjusting Chart Options

Click the Chart Options icon on the toolbar or choose Chart from the Options menu to change the characteristics of the chart. This brings up the Chart Options dialog box, as shown in Figure 5.4.

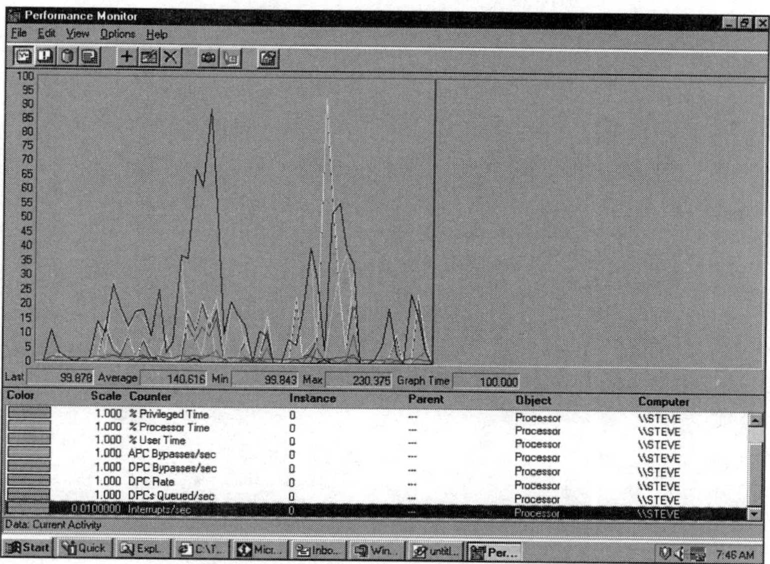

Figure 5.3. *Tracking real-time counters using the Performance Monitor.*

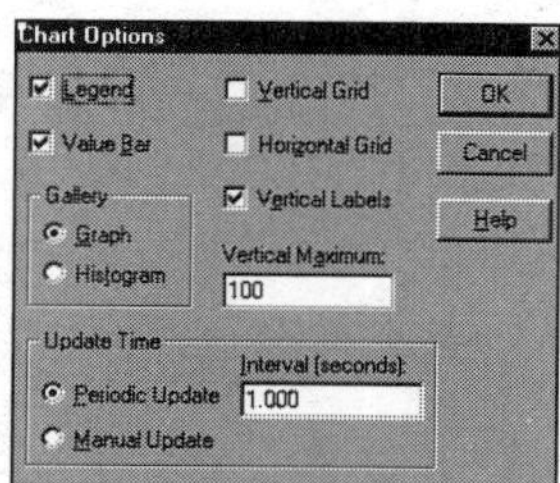

Figure 5.4. *The Chart Options dialog box.*

In the Chart Options dialog box, you can adjust the display properties and attributes of the Performance Monitor. Options in this dialog box enable you to make the following adjustments to the chart:

- The legend and counter values can be removed from the display.
- A vertical and horizontal grid can be added to the chart.
- The vertical maximum can be increased or decreased from a default of 100.
- The time or sample interval can be changed.
- The display or gallery can be changed from a default histogram to a bar graph.

The check box option Always on Top allows the Performance Monitor display to appear on top of any window you select, as illustrated in Figure 5.5.

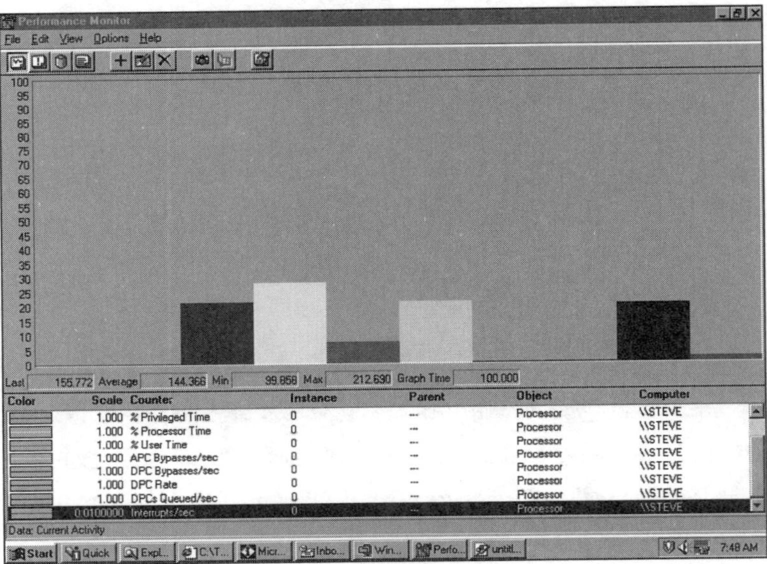

Figure 5.5. *Viewing histograms and other chart option changes in the Performance Monitor.*

Saving Settings

You can always save your settings to a .PMC file. This file can be used in conjunction with a Program Group icon to invoke a Performance Monitor session with the object counters automatically added to the chart.

Data Source

The data source explains the source of information the Performance Monitor is using. The default source for information is the current activity of this system. This source is shown on the status bar `Data: Current Activity` at the lower-left corner of the window (refer again to Figure 5.5). The alternative source for information is any log file in which previous activity has been recorded.

To change the source of data, choose Data From from the Options menu. This brings up the Data From dialog box, enabling you to change the source of the data. The default log file is perfmon.log. Figure 5.6 displays the Data From dialog box.

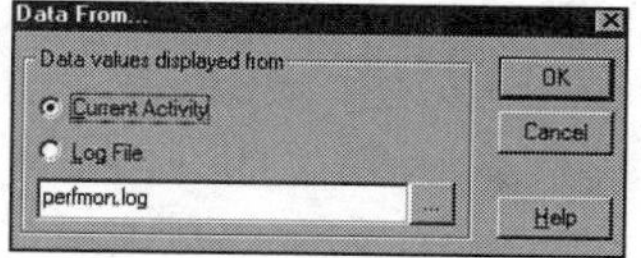

Figure 5.6. *The Data From dialog box.*

If the button to the right of the name of the log file is clicked, the Open Input Log File dialog box opens, allowing a log file to be selected from any path.

The Log View

The Log view enables you to select objects and their counters to be logged for subsequent display and analysis. Clicking its icon on the toolbar or choosing Log from the View menu can bring up the Log view. Like the other views, it is initialized by default; in other words, no object counters are defined for it. Figure 5.7 displays the Log view in the Performance Monitor.

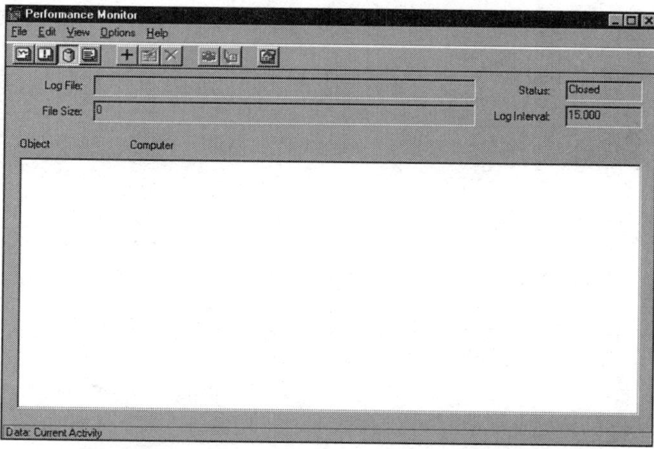

Figure 5.7. *The Log view.*

If Add to Log is selected from the Edit menu or clicked on the toolbar, the Add to Log dialog box displays, as shown in Figure 5.8. From this dialog box, you can select the object counters.

If you click the Done button (this button toggles with Cancel), the Performance Monitor window with the Log view is brought up, as illustrated in Figure 5.9.

The selected objects appear in the view with all counters collected for each object.

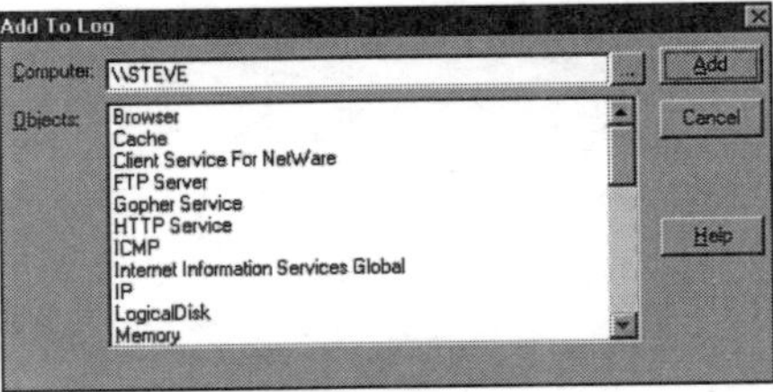

Figure 5.8. *The Add To Log dialog box.*

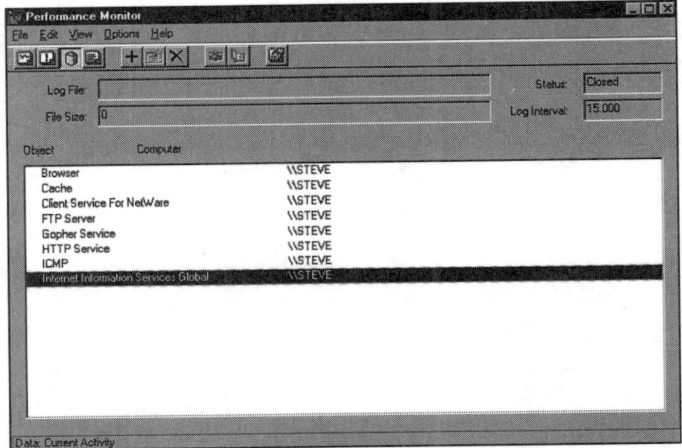

Figure 5.9. *Viewing the log status in the Performance Monitor.*

Log Options

Choosing Log from the Options menu or clicking the Options icon brings up the Log Options dialog box. Here, you can specify the name to be given to the log file and its location. The interval at which counters are written to the log file can also be specified. Figure 5.10 shows this.

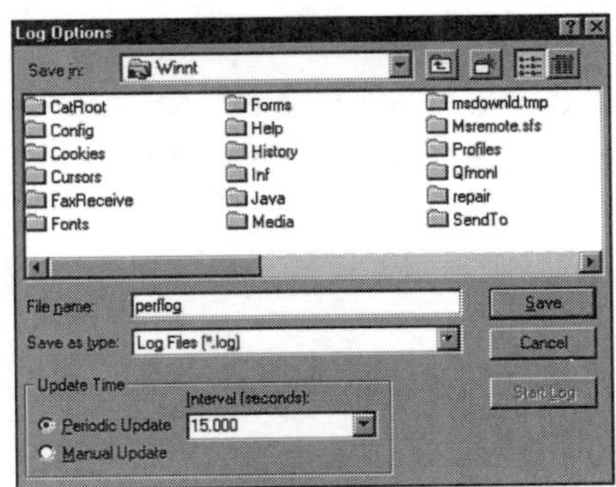

Figure 5.10. *The Log Options dialog box.*

The log can be paused with Pause or stopped with Stop.

Counters for the objects included in the log file are available for subsequent viewing. If the previously created log file is opened, for example, counters are only available for the Cache, Physical Disk, and Processor, as shown in Figure 5.11.

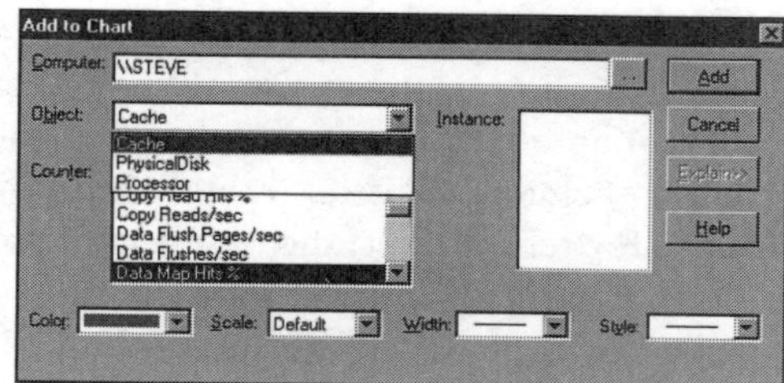

Figure 5.11. *Selecting the available counters from the input log file.*

After OK is clicked, the Performance Monitor window appears with the default Chart view. The status line at the bottom of the Performance Monitor window shows that the source of the data is from the log file. The graph time displays the duration for the log.

The Report View

The information collected by the Performance Monitor for object counters can be displayed in the form of a report rather than in a graphic representation.

The easiest way to begin a report is to click its icon on the toolbar. Alternatively, you can choose Report from the View menu. A new report is blank because no object counter information has been selected. Object counter information for a report is selected much like a chart.

Click the Add to Report icon to select object counters to be included within the report, as shown in Figure 5.12.

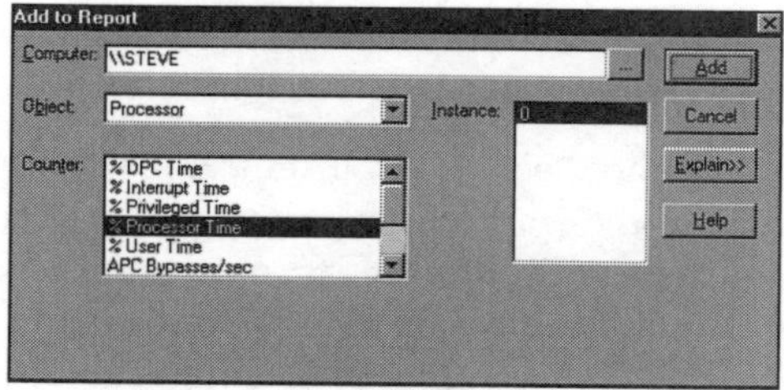

Figure 5.12. *The Add to Report dialog box.*

Because only object counter values are displayed in the report, only the object counter and instance can be selected. After the object counters have been chosen, click OK to display the report.

The objects organize the report with all counters for the same object group, together under a column header of the object.

The Alert View

An *alert* is a line of information returned to the Alert view of the Performance Monitor, when the value of an object counter is above or below a user-defined value. The entry in the log includes a date and timestamp, the actual object counter value, the criteria for returning it, the object value counter, and the system. Clicking its icon on the toolbar or selecting Alert from the View menu can bring up an Alert log. The Alert view, brought up in the Performance Monitor window, is initialized by default. Figure 5.13 displays the Alert view in the Performance Monitor.

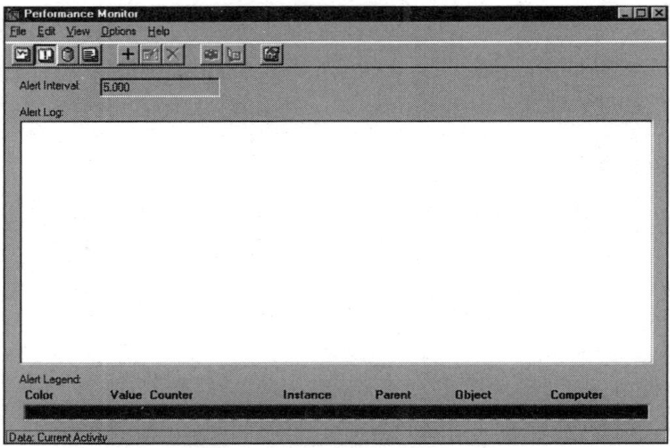

Figure 5.13. *The Alert view.*

Select Add to Alert from the Edit menu or click its icon on the toolbar to bring up the Add to Alert dialog box, as shown in Figure 5.14.

The computer, object counter, color, and instance, if appropriate, can be selected in a fashion similar to the way charts are selected. Alerts are different in that they result in the display of information only if the object counter value is greater than or less than a user-defined value. Optionally, a program can be specified to execute either the first time or each time an alert is recorded.

After you have finished adding object counters to the Alert log, click Done to display the Alert view as shown in Figure 5.15.

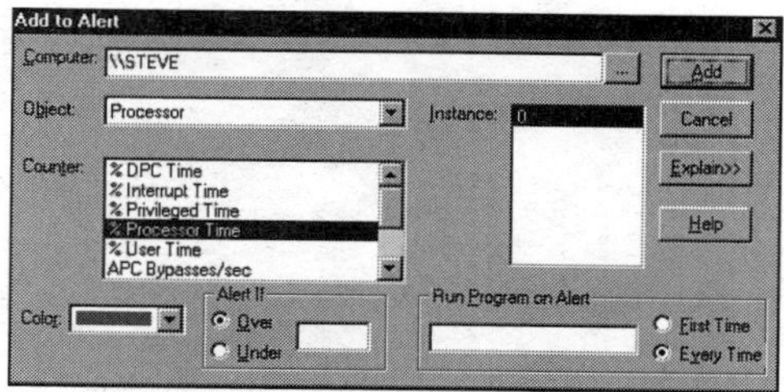

Figure 5.14. *The Add to Alert dialog box.*

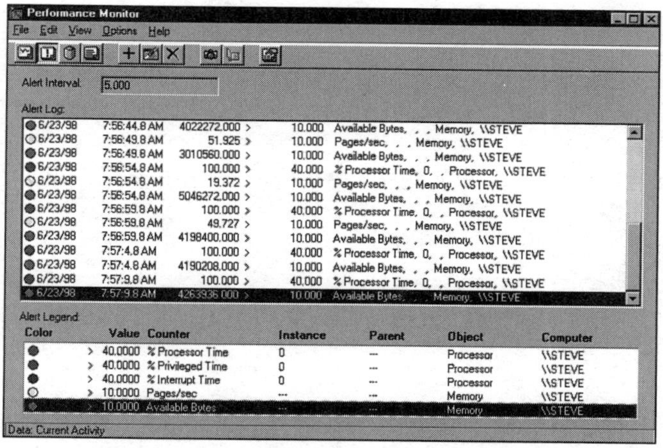

Figure 5.15. *The Alert view shown after adding object counters to the Alert log.*

In the example Alert log, the legend shows that alerts are logged under the following conditions:

- The processor uses more than 3% of its time executing Kernel Mode code.
- The number of available or free pages if memory drops below 1,000 pages.
- The average number of bytes written to the disk is less than 300.

The Alert options, brought up by choosing the Alert options icon, enable the automatic monitoring interval to be changed. Figure 5.16 shows the Alert Options dialog box.

Just like the Chart and Report option, the source of data for alerts can be changed using the Data From option: The source can either be the current activity of the system or any log file that contains previously recorded activities.

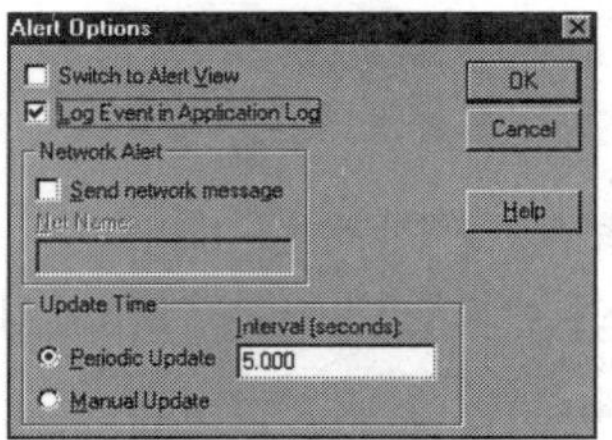

Figure 5.16. *The Alert Options dialog box.*

Isolating Bottlenecks

A *bottleneck* in the processor occurs when utilization sustains at 80% on a consistent basis. If the processor reaches 100% utilization, this usually indicates that the processor is inadequate. A second or faster processor would solve the problem. It is important to understand that acceptable processor usage can depend on computer activity.

Exporting Data

You can export data from charts and logs into other formats as well, as shown in Figure 5.17. This data can be read into charting programs such as Microsoft Excel or Lotus 1-2-3, as shown in Figure 5.18.

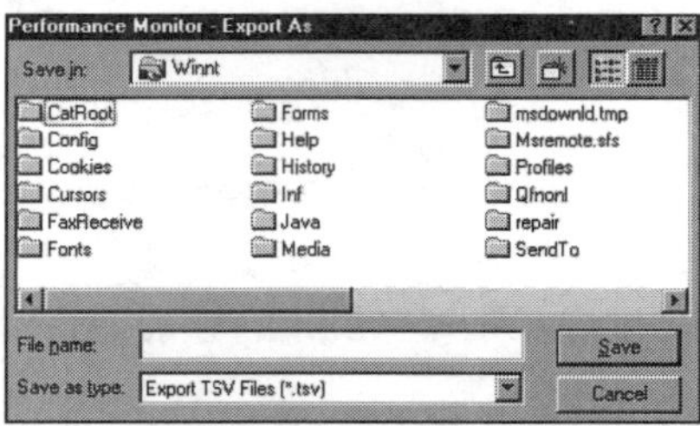

Figure 5.17. *Exporting data into a comma- or tab-delimited format.*

	A	B	C	D	E
1	Reported on \\STEVE				
2	Date: 6/23/98				
3	Time: 8:00:53 AM				
4	Data: Current Activity				
5	Interval: 1.000 seconds				
6					
7			% Interrupt Time	% Privileged Time	% Processor Time
8			0	0	0
9					
10			Processor	Processor	Processor
11	Date	Time	\\STEVE	\\STEVE	\\STEVE
12	6/23/98	7:59:29 AM			
13	6/23/98	7:59:30 AM	0	3.999	4.025
14	6/23/98	7:59:31 AM	0	1.001	0.947
15	6/23/98	7:59:32 AM	1	3.999	4.015
16	6/23/98	7:59:33 AM	1	14.001	17.997
17	6/23/98	7:59:34 AM	0	0	0
18	6/23/98	7:59:35 AM	0	2	1.996
19	6/23/98	7:59:36 AM	0	5	5.996
20	6/23/98	7:59:37 AM	0	10.998	12.014
21	6/23/98	7:59:38 AM	0	1	0.986
22	6/23/98	7:59:41 AM	7.938	30.349	37.433
23	6/23/98	7:59:41 AM	0	1.165	0.974
24	6/23/98	7:59:42 AM	0	0	0.006

Figure 5.18. *Viewing imported data using Microsoft Excel.*

PerfLog: Performance Data Log Service

This service is found in the Windows NT Resource Kit. This tool logs data from performance counters to tab- or comma-separated variable files. It enables you to choose which performance counters you want to log, and starts new log files automatically at selected intervals.

The text files to which PerfLog logs data can be used as input to spreadsheets, databases, and other applications, as well as to Performance Monitor. Unlike Performance Monitor logs, which store data in a compact, multidimensional C-language data format, PerfLog logs can be used as direct input without reformatting.

PerfLog uses the same objects and counters as Performance Monitor (included with the Windows NT operating system), but it enables you to select which counters you want to log for each instance of an object. You also can select the level of detail you need on an instance and let PerfLog select a set of counters for you. You can also view this data in the form of a report, which will give an average counter over the timespan of the log file. This is an excellent tool for collecting historical trends when you have to use the Performance Monitor in Interactive Mode.

Installing PerfLog

To install the Performance Data Logging service, follow these steps:

1. Navigate to the Administrative Tools group and select Performance Monitor.
2. From the Performance View menu, choose Log. From the Edit menu, choose Add to Log.
3. Add the objects you want to track to the log.
4. Navigate to the File menu and choose Save Settings As.
5. Save the settings file as a .PML file and save the file to the %SYSTEMROOT%\SYSTEM32 directory.
6. Navigate to the Options menu and choose Log.
7. In the Log File field, type the name of the log file you want in a .LOG format. Specify a log filename (*.LOG) and the logging interval, but do not start logging.
8. Save the settings file as a .PMW into your %SYSTEMROOT%\SYSTEM32 folder by using the Save Workspace command on the File menu.
9. Copy the file DATALOG.EXE from the Resource Kit directory into your %SYSTEMROOT%\SYSTEM32 folder.

To install the Data Logging service, type the following in a command prompt window in the %SYSTEMROOT%\SYSTEM32 directory:

```
monitor setup
```

This command registers the service with the Service Manager. You only need to run this command once. To use your settings file, type the following:

```
monitor filename.PMW
```

Type the following to start logging events and alerts immediately:

```
monitor start
```

To stop logging, type the following:

```
monitor stop
```

You can then view the log file in Performance Monitor. (You must stop the Monitor service before you can use the log file in Performance Monitor.)

You can also use this command to set the service to start automatically when Windows NT starts by typing the following:

```
monitor automatic
```

Viewing the Historical Data

To view historical data, follow these steps:

1. Navigate to the Administrative Tools group and select Performance Monitor.
2. From the Performance View menu, choose Chart. From the Options menu, choose Data From.
3. Change the option from Current Activity to the log file's complete path.
4. Your chart is now blank. You need to add the individual counters. You can do this by going to the Edit menu and choosing Add to Chart and selecting the counters you would like to view.

Author's Note

You can go back and forth, adjusting which counters are displayed, because the input is from a data file rather than current activity. You are not adding to the system load while doing this.

PERFMTR.EXE: Performance Meter

Performance Meter displays text-based information on the performance of a computer running Windows NT. You can think of this as a kind of command-line version of performance metering.

To use Performance Meter, follow these steps:

1. At the command prompt, type **`perfmtr`**.
2. Type a command (without pressing Enter) for any of the following:

`c`	CPU usage
`f`	File cache usage
`h`	Header
`i`	I/O usage
`p`	POOL usage
`r`	Cache Manager reads and writes
`s`	Server statistics
`v`	Virtual memory usage
`x`	x86 VDM (Virtual DOS Machine) usage

At any point while you are running this utility, you can change the option by typing the letter option. It keeps updating until you type the **`q`** key.

The Network Monitor

Windows NT 4.0 now includes a scaled version of the Network Monitor (see Figure 5.19). The Network Monitor tool enables a network manager to "sniff" the network for protocol analysis. This allows low-level network traffic analysis so that the various packet information can be filtered. This utility has limited parsing, restricted primarily to header information. The descriptions of the headers are excellent, however. I have always been a strong advocate of protocol analyzers because they make the best education tool for networking and data communications.

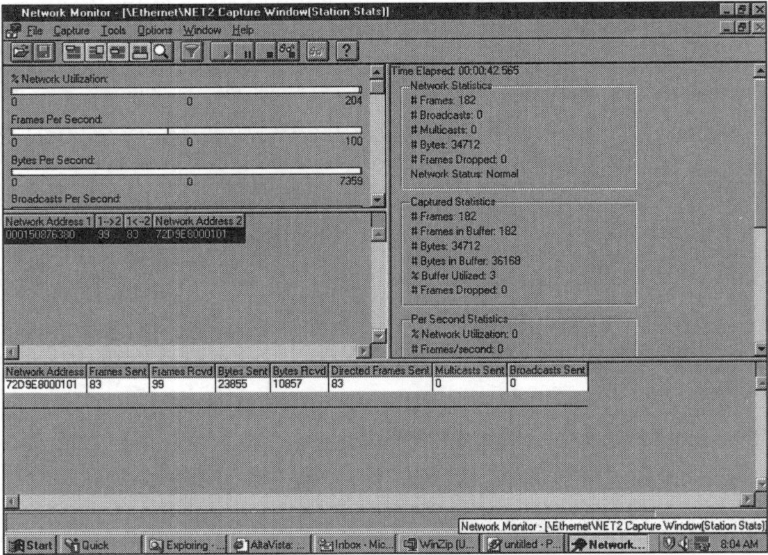

Figure 5.19. *A scaled version of the Network Monitor.*

A variety of options can be implemented with this utility. Available options include the following:

- Capturing data
- Filtering captures
- Registering network address information in databases
- Printing information
- Vendor adjustments

Captures can be saved for reference points in tracking historical performance.

Frame Types

Traffic captured by a network traffic analysis tool is displayed in segments called *frames*. A frame represents the addressing and protocol information, as well as the data transferred from one host to another on the network. The frame is merely a message. Any formatted message is a *protocol data unit (PDU)*. The frame is a PDU similar to a packet or a datagram. The PDU differs depending on the protocol. The term *frame* is used to describe data-link level PDUs, such as Ethernet and Token Ring.

There are three different types of frames:

- Broadcast
- Multicast
- Directed (unicast)

Broadcast

Broadcast frames are delivered to all hosts on the network. They may actually be destined for one specific host; because of protocol or addressing reasons, however, they are sent to all hosts.

Broadcasts are sent with the unique destination address of `FFFFFFFFFFFF`. No host can be configured with this address. All hosts on the network accept this frame, and process it up through its protocol stack until it determines whether to complete processing of the frame or discard it (as it is not meant for the local computer).

Multicast

Multicast frames are delivered to a portion of the hosts on the network. Similar to broadcast frames, they are not delivered to a specific destination media access control (MAC) address, but to a selected subset of the hosts on the network. Each host has to register the multicast address to become a member of that multicast subset. NetBIOS Extended User Interface (NetBEUI) and some TCP/IP applications make use of multicasts.

Directed Frames

Directed frames, or *unicasts*, are the most common type of frames. These frames have a destination address for a specific host on the network. All other hosts that receive this frame discard it because it does not contain the host's hardware address.

Each of the different protocols that ship with Windows NT 4.0 may differ in their implementation of broadcasts. TCP/IP and NWLink initiate broadcasts, for example, but NetBEUI sends multicasts rather than broadcasts.

Frame Encapsulation

The Network Monitor can capture information and store it in a buffer for analysis. The protocol analyzer then parses each frame. All the header information can be translated given that a corresponding DLL is available. The Network Monitor has header translation information for all the following protocols:

- AppleTalk
- TCP/IP
- Special Network Monitor
- Microsoft Services
- Novell Services
- IPX/SPX
- Remote Access
- Banyan VINES
- Routing

Even on a hybrid network, you can use this utility to analyze information. Figure 5.20 displays this information as it is shown in the Network Monitor.

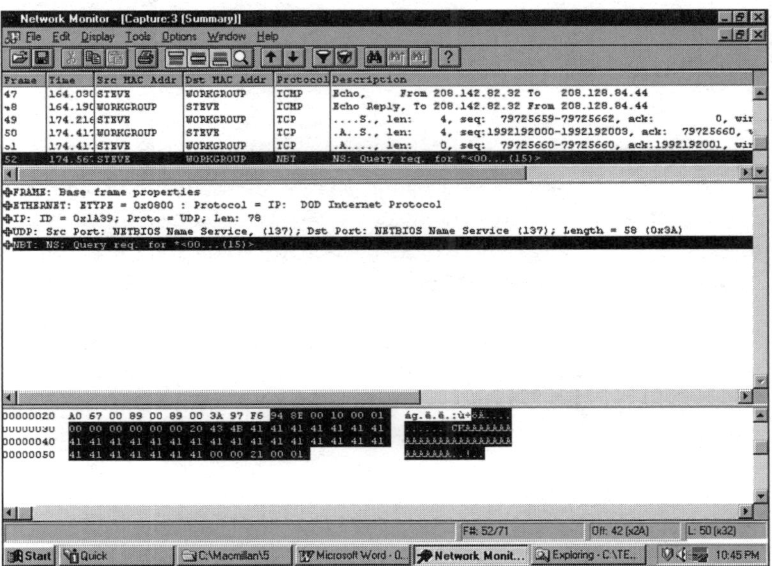

Figure 5.20. *The Capture window within the Network Monitor.*

The Capture window displays the following information in the upper pane:

- Frame number (for referencing within the capture)
- The time elapsed (offsets from the start of the capture)
- The source media access control address
- The target media access control address
- The highest layer protocol parsed
- The description of this protocol header
- Source other address (if used, a logical address—IP, IPX, and so on)
- Target other address (if used, a logical address—IP, IPX, and so on)
- Type other address (a Network Layer protocol, if found)

The following is an example of this using a NetBIOS over TCP/IP frame:

```
52 174.567 STEVE WORKGROUP NBT NS: Query req. for *<00...(15)> 208.142.82.32
➥208.131.160.103 IP
```

Double-clicking a frame invokes the multi-pane view dialog box. This is where two additional panes pop up below the frame list. The first new pane displays the parsed headers, which can be expanded to reveal every protocol field option. Each frame and all of its expanded fields can be copied to the Clipboard, if needed.

The following is a NetBIOS over TCP/IP frame in this format:

```
FRAME: Base frame properties
ETHERNET: ETYPE = 0x0800 : Protocol = IP:  DOD Internet Protocol
IP: ID = 0x1A39; Proto = UDP; Len: 78
UDP: Src Port: NETBIOS Name Service, (137); Dst Port: NETBIOS Name Service
➥(137); Length = 58 (0x3A)
NBT: NS: Query req. for *<00...(15)>
```

Finally, the bottom pane displays this information in raw hex or byte format. When a header is selected from the preceding pane, the corresponding bytes are selected in this pane as well. The following is that same information shown in byte format:

```
00000:  72 D9 E8 00 01 01 00 01 50 87 63 80 08 00 45 00
00010:  00 4E 1A 39 00 00 80 11 8C CC D0 8E 52 20 D0 83
00020:  A0 67 00 89 00 89 00 3A 97 F6 94 8E 00 10 00 01
00030:  00 00 00 00 00 00 20 43 4B 41 41 41 41 41 41 41
00040:  41 41 41 41 41 41 41 41 41 41 41 41 41 41 41 41
00050:  41 41 41 41 41 41 41 00 00 21 00 01
```

Capture and Display Filters

Filters can be invoked at any time when capturing data or working with a previous capture. When you implement a capture filter, you can tell the Network Monitor to include or exclude specific MAC addresses or logical addresses as well as protocols. You can use these same criteria to filter a display, which is for previously saved captures or an active capture that you have stopped. You can then save these criteria into a file with a .CF or .DF extension for use at a later time. The Network Monitor comes with two display and two capture filters. Each one has a default and a `NOBROAD` (which filters out broadcasts).

The addresses can come from the address database for the capture filter. In the case of the display filter, it would come from the current capture. For the protocols, which also are referred to as ETYPE and SAP (Service Access Point), you can filter based on all the available protocols:

AARP
ADSP
AFP
ARP_RARP
ASP
ATP
BONE
BPDU
BROWSER
CBCP
CCP
DDP
DHCP
DNS
ETHERNET
FDDI
FINGER
FRAME
FTP
ICMP
IGMP
IP
IPCP
IPX
IPXCP
LAP
LCP
LLC
MSRPC
NBFCP
NBIPX
NBP
NBT
NCP
NDR
NetBIOS
NETLOGON
NFS
NMPI
NSP
NWDP
OSPF
PAP
PPP
PPPCHAP
PPPPAP
RIP
RIPX
RPC
RPL
RTMP
SAP
SMB
SMT
SNAP
SPX
TCP
TMAC
TOKENRING
UDP
XNS
ZIP

The Address Database

The next time you design a capture filter that involves address pairs, you can use this database. If you assign the database the DEFAULT.ADR filename, it becomes your default address database. You can use the Address Database dialog box to add, delete, or edit addresses in an address database. You also can use this dialog box to save the current address database or load a different one.

Warning

I would not advise saving this information to the DEFAULT.ADR *if you plan to run this monitor on a machine moving from network to network, because the addresses may get confused.*

The Address List on this dialog box displays the following information about each computer:

- A friendly name
- The 12-digit hexadecimal network address
- The address type (for example, MAC or IP)
- The name of the vendor who created the network card
- A comment or additional information

With the address database, you can automatically pull up a capture display with the sources and target addresses resolved to a name automatically rather than a cryptic MAC address. This feature is a must for convenience on a regularly monitored LAN.

Additional Options

You can use the Network Monitor's advanced options to change between network devices, load a remote Network Monitor agent, and find routers, and query for other Network Monitor agents, utilities, and their current status. It is important to note that when you use these utilities, they will use special protocols, which also show up in a capture. These special protocols include the following:

- *BONE.* This is the Bloodhound Oriented Network Entity protocol. Each Network Monitor agent uses this protocol to perform station-to-station queries.
- *BOOKMARK.* This is used as a mark point method between Network Monitor agents. It also is used in the adjustment and retransmission of packets.

- *GENERIC.* This is an unused protocol designed for future versions of the Network Monitor utility.

Capture Triggers

Capture triggers allow the Network Monitor to not automatically capture unless a certain condition is met. You can use one of the following trigger types to determine the criteria:

Trigger	Description
Nothing	The default where no trigger is initiated.
Pattern Match	This initiates the trigger when the specified pattern occurs in a captured frame.
Buffer Space	This initiates the trigger when a specified amount of the capture buffer is filled. This is often used for a stop trigger.
Pattern Match Then Buffer Space	This initiates the trigger when the pattern occurs and is followed by a specified percentage of the capture buffer being filled. This is a popular one in that people use this to do a start trigger on the first one and a stop on the second one.
Buffer Space Then Pattern Match	This initiates the trigger when the specified percentage of the capture buffer fills and is followed by the occurrence of the pattern in a captured frame.

If the trigger condition has been met, you can tell the Network Monitor to perform a specific event.

Event	Description
No Action	This specifies that no action is taken when a trigger condition is met. This is the default. Even though you select No Action, the computer beeps when the trigger condition is met.
Stop Capture	This stops the capture process when the trigger condition is met.
Execute Command Line	This runs a program or batch file when a trigger condition is met. If you select this option, provide a command or the path to a program or batch file.

Different Network Monitor Versions

A Network Monitor version is included with Windows NT Server 4.0. This is the simple version and is not to be confused with the Microsoft Systems Management Server (SMS) Network Monitor extensions (full version).

Both versions can assist with network traffic analysis, although the full version of the product, included with SMS, offers more features and functions than does the version included with Windows NT Server 4.0.

Table 5.1 lists the product differences.

Table 5.1. Differences in the Network Monitor Simple and Full Versions.

Function	Network Monitor (Simple)	Network Monitor (Full)
Local capturing	To and from the local computer's Network Monitor agent	All devices on the entire subnet
Remote capturing	Not available	Yes
Determining top user of network bandwidth	Not available	Yes
Determining which protocol consumed the most bandwidth	Not available	Yes
Determining which devices are routers	Not available	Yes
Resolving a user-friendly name to a MAC address	Not available	Yes
Editing and retransmitting network traffic	Not available	Yes

Installing the SMS Network Monitor

To install the SMS Network Monitor, follow these steps:

1. Right-click the Network Neighborhood icon, and select Map Network Drive.
2. In the path field, type the path to the Network Monitor Extensions for SMS. This can be found on the SMS 1.x CD.
3. From an Explorer window or using a command prompt, open Setup.exe.
4. Accept the default network path and click Continue.
5. If you are prompted to create the directory, click OK.
6. When prompted for passwords, you can submit a password for control or not enter any. Proceed by clicking No Password.
7. When prompted for your username, type `administrator`.

8. Click OK again to confirm.
9. Click OK to continue. Then click OK again. The utility invokes the Network Control Panel application.
10. Click on the Services tab. Note that you will not see this option if the Network Monitor is already installed.
11. Click Add and select Network Monitor Agent, *not* Network Monitor Tools and Agent.
12. Click Close to exit out of the Network Control Panel.
13. When prompted to restart your computer, click Yes.

Network Monitor Command-Line Options

The Network Monitor has many command-line options that can be used for noninteractive use and/or for scheduling purposes.

The command-line version switches include the following:

- `/autostart` Start the Network Monitor in Capture Mode immediately.
- `/autostop` Stop capturing the moment the capture buffer is used.
- `/buffersize:`*`size`* Start the Network Monitor with a predetermined capture buffer size.
- `/remote:`*`name`* Connect to the remote computer's Network Monitor agent.
- `/net:`*`number`* Capture data from the network specified by the network number.
- `/quickfilter:`*`path`* Start capturing immediately using the filter specified by the path.
- `/displayfilter:`*`path`* Start the Network Monitor using the specified filter.

Monitoring Disk Usage

Disk performance is a big factor in overall network performance management. If the disk controller or the hard drive is encountering a bottleneck, file transfers can be significantly degraded. There are certain items to keep under consideration when monitoring disk usage on a computer, as described in the following sections.

Turning On the Windows NT Disk Performance Counters

To use utilities such as the Performance Monitor to keep track of physical disk usage, you must enable the Windows NT disk performance counters. By default, Windows NT does not enable physical disk performance counters. To enable disk performance counters, you need to use the `DISKPERF.EXE` command.

The syntax for `DISKPERF` is as follows:

```
Diskperf option
```

Available options include the following:

`-y`	Enable counters
`-n`	Disable counters
`-ye`	Enable counters for stripe sets, mirror sets, or stripe sets with parity

When you enable or disable counters, you must reboot Windows NT to actually complete the operation.

Test Your Server Hard Drive Performance

The hard drives and disk controllers are the most important part of a server's configuration and another critical part of performance management. Windows NT uses a lazy-write file system NTFS for its advanced file system option. If you decide to use NTFS, you will have additional overhead due to the file system's advanced structure, which includes extended attributes and transactional-tracking information. NTFS also does not automatically commit transactions to the disk like the FAT file system.

This is important to know because this forces your hard drives to be reliable and as fast as possible. One way to do this is to use additional utilities that can test and even enhance the performance of your disk drives.

DISKMAX

DISKMAX is found in the Windows NT Resource Kit. It is a response probe test to help you determine the maximum throughput of a disk drive. It can be excellent in testing the speed of your hardware. DISKMAX does sequential, unbuffered reads of 64KB records from a 20MB file. After you have performed the test using this utility, you can then use Performance Monitor to help you analyze the result.

To run DISKMAX, you first need to install the required files from the Resource Kit you want to test. The CD SETUP utility installs all files except for `Workfile.dat` as part of the Performance Tools group.

The following is the list of the files required from the Resource Kit:

```
Probe.exe         Diskmax.scp
Probeprc.exe      Diskmax.sct
Diskmax.scr       Workfile.dat
```

As noted previously, Workfile.dat is not installed by the SETUP utility, but you can copy it manually from the CD. Workfile.dat is a 20MB file filled with zeros that Response Probe uses to simulate a workload file. You can use Workfile.dat or you can create a zero-filled file of any size by using the CREATEFILE (Creatfil.exe) utility in the \Probe subdirectory. The CREATEFILE syntax follows:

```
creatfil <filename> [<filesize>].
```

`filesize` is optional; the default is 1,024KB.

If you haven't done so already, you need to enable the Performance Monitor disk counters using the DISKPERF utility discussed in the previous section.

Start a Performance Monitor log. If possible, write the log to a different physical drive. This helps ensure a realistic baseline. Log the Logical Disk object at a one-second update interval.

At the command prompt of the drive you want to test, change to the subdirectory where the .sc* files are stored (the default is Examples) and type the following:

```
<Path>Probe diskmax.scr 900
```

When the command prompt returns, stop the Performance Monitor log. Analyze the data from the test using the Response Probe output file, which is Diskmax.out, and your Performance Monitor log. Use the following Performance Monitor counters:

```
Logical disk: Avg. Disk Bytes/Read
Logical disk: Avg. Disk sec/Read
Logical disk: Disk Read Bytes/sec
Logical disk: Disk Reads/sec
```

Simple Network Management Protocol

You may want to look for a solution that enables you not only to monitor the important server and network resources, but also to modify them. A system or network management solution is viable for this.

For higher-scale heterogeneous networks, Windows NT supports SNMP (Simple Network Management Protocol). This is the Internet standard protocol for managing nodes on networks. The original implementation of SNMP allowed a predominant network-management protocol that is simple and inexpensive to implement. However, it could not communicate from manager to manager, did not support IPX, OSI, and AppleTalk, and above all did not address security. This protocol later evolved to support IPX, OSI, and AppleTalk networks as well as small levels of security. Figure 5.21 displays a typical SNMP environment.

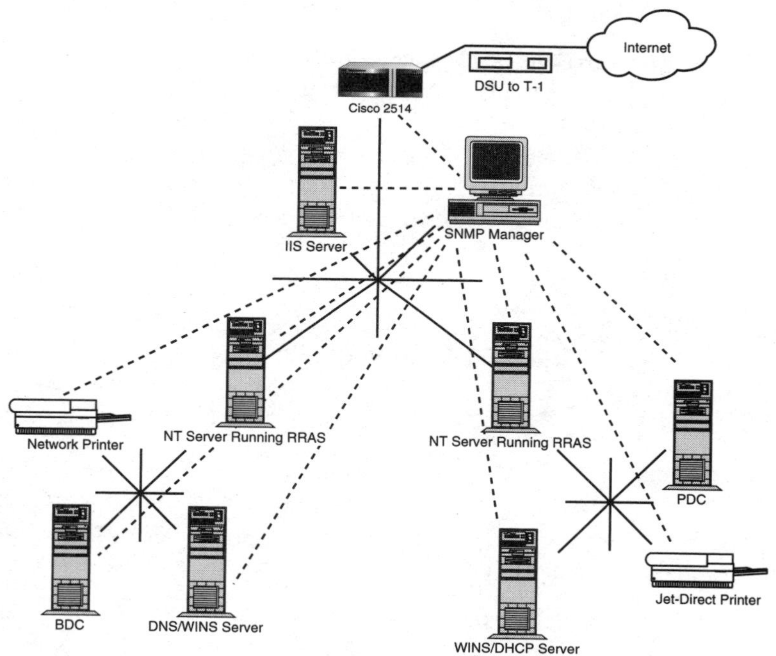

Figure 5.21. *Managing all major network entities with SNMP.*

SNMP 2, a new implementation, builds on features of SNMP, addresses more security and manager-to-manager communication, and provides for error return. It remains backward-compatible with the command set of SNMP version 1, but doubles the available command sets from four to eight.

SNMP uses databases known as *MIBs (Management Information Base)*. These are the set of parameters an SNMP management station can query or set in the SNMP agent of a network device. The Windows NT SNMP service includes the following:

- MIB II (based on RFC 1213)
- LAN Manager MIB II
- MIBs for DHCP and WINS servers

The SNMP service allows SNMP-based managers to perform standard SNMP commands, such as reading the counters in the standard MIBs included with the service. Windows NT SNMP has an extensible architecture, so it can be used to create custom functionality on a Windows NT Workstation or Server, such as starting and stopping specific services or shutting down the system. Later, we will discuss a utility that helps facilitate this.

The SNMP Model

The SNMP model is based on the manager-agent model. The SNMP Manager uses a network management application to submit the commands to the SNMP agents on the network entities. Lately, the applications have been developed primarily to provide a user-friendly interface for managers to seamlessly process these commands. Windows NT implements the SNMP agent as a service, but does not provide an SNMP Manager by default.

Object Identifiers

The network management platform is used by SNMP for object identification. It uses the available MODs as a dictionary of sorts. *MOD (manageable objects database)* refers to compiled MIBs. The MIB hierarchy is defined by using certain guidelines.

The main entities that comprise the MIB guidelines are the *OIDs (object identifiers)*, shown in Figure 5.22. They represent each manageable object with a unique sequence of numbers and names. SNMP uses the number as an abbreviated form of the name to make requests for data values and to identify the response that carries the values.

You can think of this as a directory service of manageable objects. Beneath the root of the hierarchy are three major areas:

- *ITU-T(0)*. This is the starting point for entities standardized by the International Telecommunication Union—Telecommunications.
- *ISO (1)*. This is where most of the major SNMP entities are found (Internet, and so on) under the International Standardization Organization.

- *Joint-ISO-ITU-T(2)*. This is an experimental area for joint entities.

Three basic types of MIBs are governed by their place in the MIB tree:

- Public—MIB 2 (Starts `1.3.6.1.2.1`)
- Experimental (`1.3.6.1.3.1`)
- Private Enterprise (`1.3.6.1.4.1`)

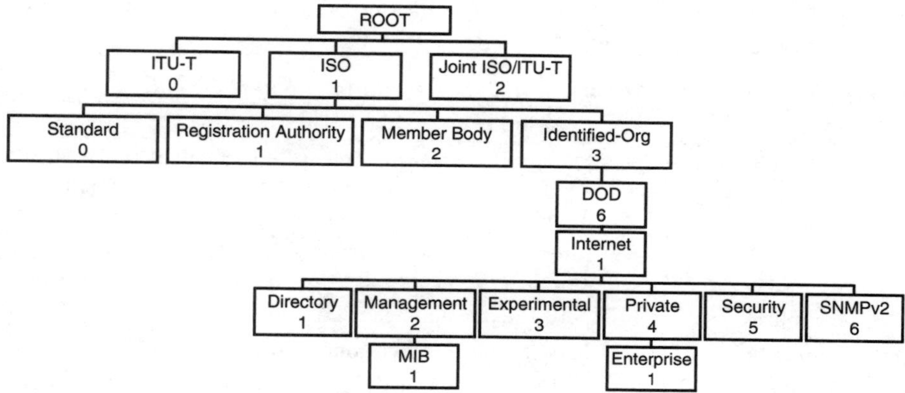

Figure 5.22. *The MID OID hierarchy.*

For the three MIBs we are focusing on, these OIDs are organized in a tree-like structure. The sequence of numbers identifies the various branches of the subtree that a given object comes from. The root of the tree is the *ISO (International Standards Organization) trunk*. Its value is 1. Each branch above the root (or below, depending on your perspective) further identifies the source of the given object.

All SNMP objects are members of the subtree identified by `iso.org.dod.internet` or `1.3.6.1`. Each additional component in this dotted notation further defines the exact location of an object. The numbers for each subtree are assigned by the IETF to ensure that all branches are unique.

The Enterprise numbers (beneath `1.3.6.1.4.1`) follow:

NCR 191	SGI 59
Banyan 1303	COM 43
NEC 119	Sun 42
LAN Manager 77	DEC 36
Network Associates 110	IBM 2

Oracle 111	UNIX 4
Microsoft 311	CISCO 9
Intel 343	HP 11
Apple 63	Novell 23

Installing SNMP

When you install SNMP on a Windows NT computer, you are only installing the SNMP agent. Table 5.2 describes the files installed on a Windows NT computer with the SNMP service installed.

Table 5.2. Files installed with SNMP when running Windows NT.

Filename	Description
Dhcpmib.dll	DHCP MIB extension-agent DLL, available only when the DHCP Server is installed on a computer running Windows NT Server.
Iis.dll	Internet Information Server DLL, available only if IIS is installed on a computer running Windows NT Server.
Inetmib1.dll	MIB-II extension-agent DLL.
Lmmib2.dll	LAN Manager extension-agent DLL.
Mgmtapi.dll	A Windows NT-based SNMP manager API that listens for manager requests. It sends the requests to and receives responses from SNMP agents.
Mib.bin	Installed with the SNMP service and used by the management API, Mgmtapi.dll, to map text-based object names to numeric OIDs.
Snmp.exe	SNMP agent service, a master (proxy) agent that accepts manager program requests and forwards the requests to the appropriate subagent-extension DLL for processing.
Snmptrap.exe	Receives SNMP traps from the SNMP agent and forwards them to the SNMP Manager API on the management console. Snmptrap.exe is a background process started only when the SNMP Manager API receives a manager request for traps.
Winsmib.dll	WINS MIB extension-agent DLL, available only when the WINS Server is installed on a computer running Windows NT Server.

Microsoft MIBs fall into the private enterprises category. Table 5.3 lists the base object names and their respective OID locations, along with the standard MIBs included with Windows NT.

Table 5.3. Standard MIBs Included with Windows NT.

MIB Name Base Object Name	Base Object Identifier (OID)	Description
Internet MIB-II mgmt.mib-2	iso.org.dod.internet. 1.3.6.1.2.1	Defines objects essential for either configuration or fault analysis. Internet MIB-II is defined in RFC 1213.
LAN Manager MIB-II private.enterprise. lanmanager	iso.org.dod.internet. 1.3.6.1.4.1.77	Defines objects that include such items as statistical, share, session, user,l and logon information.
Microsoft DHCP Server MIB private. enterprise.microsoft. software.dhcp	iso.org.dod.internet. 1.3.6.1.4.1.311.1.3	Contains statistics for the DHCP Server, and DHCP scope information.
Microsoft Internet Information Server MIB	iso.org.dod.internet. private.enterprise. microsoft.software. iis 1.3.6.1.4.1.311.1.7	The FTP, Gopher, and HTTP server MIBs are derived from the Internet Information Server base object.
Microsoft WINS Server MIB private. enterprise.microsoft. software.wins	iso.org.dod.internet. 1.3.6.1.4.1.311.1.2	Contains information about the WINS Server, including statistics, database information, and push and pull data.

With these MIBs running along with the SNMP service, a network administrator can do the following:

- View and change parameters in the LAN Manager and MIB-II MIBs by using SNMP Manager programs.
- Monitor and configure parameters for any WINS servers on the network by using SNMP Manager programs.
- Monitor DHCP servers by using SNMP Manager programs.
- Use Performance Monitor to monitor TCP/IP-related performance counters, which are ICMP, IP, Network Interface, TCP, UDP, DHCP, FTP, WINS, and IIS performance counters.
- Use the Windows NT Server Resource Kit utilities to perform simple SNMP Manager functions.

Table 5.4 describes SNMP-related utilities and files provided on the Resource Kit compact disc. If you ever plan to use SNMP to monitor and manage

Windows NT computers from another non-Windows NT operating system, your management application needs to have access to these precompiled MIB definition files.

You probably won't ever need these files if you are using a utility such as the Performance Monitor to monitor other Windows NT computers. If you are using an SNMP utility to track other Windows NT computers using strictly SNMP, however, you have to import these MIBs into the manager. You also need to download these files to a non-Windows NT computer to manage the nodes from a non-Windows NT computer.

Table 5.4. SNMP-related utilities and files.

Filename	Description
`Dhcp.mib`	DHCP server-managed objects. *
`Wins.mib`	Microsoft WINS server-managed objects. *
`Inetsrv.mib`	IIS-managed objects. *
`FTP.mib`	FTP server-managed objects. *
`Gopherd.mib`	Gopher server-managed objects. *
`Http.mib *`	HTTP server-managed objects.
`Lmmib2.mib`	LAN Manager MIB-II. *
`Mib_ii.mib`	MIB-II. *
`Smi.mib`	Structure of Management Information MIB, as specified in RFC 1155. This file contains the global definitions used to define the objects in the other MIBs.

Configuring SNMP

The SNMP service is installed when you check the related option in the Microsoft TCP/IP Installation Options dialog box. After the SNMP service software is installed on your computer, you must configure it with valid information for SNMP to operate (see Figure 5.23). The SNMP configuration information identifies communities and trap destinations (see Figure 5.24).

Tip

You must be logged on as a member of the Administrators group for the local computer to configure SNMP.

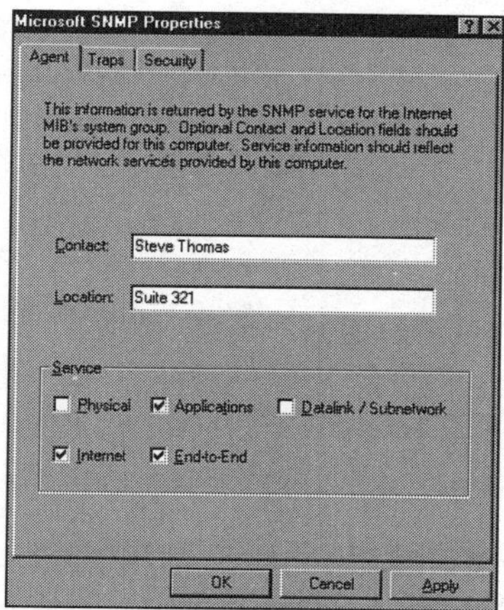

Figure 5.23. *Configuring SNMP network properties.*

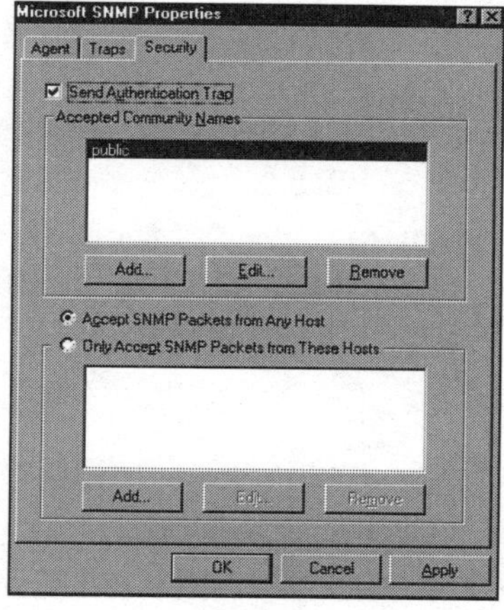

Figure 5.24. *Microsoft SNMP Properties dialog box.*

The SNMP configuration information identifies communities and trap destinations. A *community* is an ASCII name that represents a group of hosts to which a Windows NT computer running the SNMP service belongs. You can specify one or more communities to which the Windows NT computer using SNMP sends traps. The community name is placed in the SNMP packet when the trap is sent.

When the SNMP service receives a request for information that does not contain the correct community name and does not match an accepted hostname for the service, the SNMP service can send a trap to the trap destination(s), indicating that the request failed authentication. *Trap destinations* are the names or IP addresses of hosts to which you want the SNMP service to send traps with the selected community name.

You can also implement security at a higher degree by configuring the service to accept only certain community names. Then, you can configure the service to accept SNMP packets only from certain hosts within that community.

To configure the SNMP service, follow these steps:

1. Start the Network option in the Control Panel to display the Network Settings dialog box. On the Services tab, select SNMP Service, and choose the Configure button. The SNMP Service Configuration dialog box appears (refer again to Figure 5.23).

2. To identify each community to which you want this computer to send traps, type the name in the Community Names box. After typing each name, choose the Add button to move the name to the Send Traps With Community Names list on the left.

   Typically, all hosts belong to `public`, which is the standard name for the common community of all hosts. To delete an entry in the list, select it and choose the Remove button.

   Tip

   Community names are case-sensitive.

3. To specify hosts for each community you send traps to, after you have added the community and while it is still highlighted, type the hosts in the IP Host/Address or IPX Address box. Then, choose the Add button to move the hostname or IP address to the Trap Destination for the selected community list on the left.

   You can enter a hostname, its IP address, or its IPX address. To delete an entry in the list, select it and choose the Remove button.

4. To enable additional security for the SNMP service, choose the Security button. Continue with the configuration procedure.

5. To specify agent information (comments about the user, location, and services), choose the Agent button. Continue with the configuration procedure.

6. After you have completed all procedures, choose the OK button. When the Network Settings dialog box reappears, choose the OK button.

SNMPUTIL.EXE: SNMP Browser

SNMP Browser is a utility that enables you to get SNMP information from an SNMP host on your network. This is a pretty raw utility and uses the following syntax:

```
Snmputil command host community-name OID
```

Look at the following example:

```
snmputil getnext ip_address public .1.3.6.1.4.1.77.1.1.1
```

SNMP Command Set

SNMP uses a simple set of commands to set and retrieve values of objects in MIBs. There are three basic request types in SNMP: `Set`, `Get`, and `GetNext`. The basic SNMP protocol entity is referred to as a *PDU (protocol data unit).*

`Get` and `Set` operations are only allowed on object instances. Obviously, multiple objects may be retrieved or modified in a single PDU. SNMP specifies that, when modifying objects, if one `Set` fails in a PDU, none of the `Set` operation should be applied.

A `GetNext` request is slightly different from `Get` and `Set` operations. `GetNext` requests can specify any OID. The SNMP protocol specifies that when a `GetNext` request is issued to a particular agent, it will return the first value instrument by the receiving agent following the specified OID.

SNMP Traps

Traps are SNMP messages that originate from the agent to a preconfigured management station. They are used to notify management consoles of significant events.

The GENERICTRAP identifies what kind of trap this is. It can be one of any of the following:

- *SNMP_GENERICTRAP_COLDSTART*. This trap indicates cold start.
- *SNMP_GENERICTRAP_WARMSTART*. This trap indicates warm start.
- *SNMP_GENERICTRAP_LINKDOWN*. This trap indicates link down.
- *SNMP_GENERICTRAP_LINKUP*. This trap indicates link up.
- *SNMP_GENERICTRAP_AUTHFAILURE*. This trap indicates authentication failure.

- *SNMP_GENERICTRAP_EGPNEIGHLOSS*. This trap indicates EGP (Exterior Gateway Protocol) neighbor loss.
- *SNMP_GENERICTRAP_ENTERSPECIFIC*. This indicates an enterprise-specific trap.

Each SNMP command event is assigned a unique PDU number. In SNMP version 1, there are five PDUs (see Table 5.5).

Table 5.5. SNMP version 1 command PDUs.

PDU	Numbers
`Get`	0
`GetNext`	1
`GetResponse`	2
`SetRequest`	3
`TrapResponse`	4

For SNMP version 2, there were some changes with the command set. New PDUs were added but do not conflict with the previous events. Table 5.6 shows the changes in the PDUs that are available with SNMP version 2. The SNMP version 1 `Get`, `GetNext`, and `Set` requests will stay the same. The only change to the `GetResponse` is its name. With SNMP version 2, we will call it a *response*. The SNMP version 1 `TrapResponse` will become obsolete. The SNMP v2 Trap is its replacement.

Table 5.6. SNMP version 2 requests.

PDU	Numbers
`Get`	0
`GetNext`	1
`GetResponse`	2
`SetRequest`	3
`TrapResponse`	4
`GetBulk`	5
`Inform`	6
`SNMP v2 Trap`	7

Selected List of Object Identifiers

SNMP uses the data pointing structure of the Abstract Syntax Notation version 1 (ASN.1). This uses a tree structure to point at the item of data or object that we want. When we build OIDs out of this tree, we separate each branch with a period. These are often referred to as *dotted paths*. The next few pages list the most common branches beneath the MIB tree located at `1.3.6.1.2.1`.

Common MIB Paths

The first branches deal with the categories including the Systems Group, the Interfaces Group, the IP Group, the TCP Group, the UDP Group, the EGP Group, the Transmission Group, and the SNMP Group. They are in the following list:

```
system,1.3.6.1.2.1.1
interfaces,1.3.6.1.2.1.2
at,1.3.6.1.2.1.3
ip,1.3.6.1.2.1.4
icmp,1.3.6.1.2.1.5
tcp,1.3.6.1.2.1.6
udp,1.3.6.1.2.1.7
egp,1.3.6.1.2.1.8
cmot,1.3.6.1.2.1.9
transmission,1.3.6.1.2.1.10
snmp,1.3.6.1.2.1.11
```

MIB II Objects

These object are listed in order of their name, OID path, and a brief description (see Table 5.7).

Table 5.7. MIB II objects.

Name	OID Path	Description
sysDescr	1.3.6.1.2.1.1.1	A text description of the system supported by this agent.
sysObjectID	1.3.6.1.2.1.1.2	The vendor's OID of the agent in the system.
sysUpTime	1.3.6.1.2.1.1.3	The time in milliseconds since the agent was started.
sysContact	1.3.6.1.2.1.1.4	The contact for this agent and how to contact it.
sysName	1.3.6.1.2.1.1.5	An administrator-assigned name.
sysLocation	1.3.6.1.2.1.1.6	The physical location of this node.
sysServices	1.3.6.1.2.1.1.7	A value that indicates the set of services supported.
ifNumber	1.3.6.1.2.1.2.1	The number of network interfaces.
ifTable	1.3.6.1.2.1.2.2	A list of interface entries.
ifEntry	1.3.6.1.2.1.2.2.1	A row of the ifTable, containing objects for a logical interface.
ifIndex	1.3.6.1.2.1.2.2.1.1	A unique value for each interface.

continues

Table 5.7. Continued

Name	OID Path	Description
ifDescr	1.3.6.1.2.1.2.2.1.2	A text description of the interface.
ifType	1.3.6.1.2.1.2.2.1.3	The type of physical or link Interface protocol.
ifMtu	1.3.6.1.2.1.2.2.1.4	The maximum transmission unit (MTU).
ifSpeed	1.3.6.1.2.1.2.2.1.5	An estimate of the interface's current bandwidth.
ifPhysAddress	1.3.6.1.2.1.2.2.1.6	The interface's address at the Protocol Layer.
ifAdminStatus	1.3.6.1.2.1.2.2.1.7	The desired state of the interface.
ifOperStatus	1.3.6.1.2.1.2.2.1.8	The current operational state of the interface.
ifLastChange	1.3.6.1.2.1.2.2.1.9	The value of sysUptime at the time the interface became operational.
ifInOctets	1.3.6.1.2.1.2.2.1.10	The total numbers of octets received on the interface.
ifInUcastPkts	1.3.6.1.2.1.2.2.1.11	The number of subnet unicast packets delivered on the interface.
ifInNUcastPkts	1.3.6.1.2.1.2.2.1.12	The number of non-unicast packets delivered on the interface.
ifInDiscards	1.3.6.1.2.1.2.2.1.13	The number of non-error packets that were discarded.
ifInErrors	1.3.6.1.2.1.2.2.1.14	The number of inbound packets containing errors at a higher layer.
ifInUnknownProtos	1.3.6.1.2.1.2.2.1.15	Packets discarded due to an unsupported protocol.
ifOutOctets	1.3.6.1.2.1.2.2.1.16	The total of octets transmitted out of the interface.
ifOutUcastPkts	1.3.6.1.2.1.2.2.1.17	The total number of packets sent to a subnet unicast address.
ifOutNUcastPkts	1.3.6.1.2.1.2.2.1.18	The total number of packets sent to a non-unicast address.

Name	OID Path	Description
ifOutDiscards	1.3.6.1.2.1.2.2.1.19	The number of outbound packets that were discarded but did not have errors.
ifOutErrors	1.3.6.1.2.1.2.2.1.20	The number of outbound pack-ets that could not be sent because of errors.
ifOutQLen	1.3.6.1.2.1.2.2.1.21	The length of the output packet queue in packets.
ifSpecific	1.3.6.1.2.1.2.2.1.22	A reference to MIB definitions.
atTable	1.3.6.1.2.1.3.1	The network address-to-physical address table.
atEntry	1.3.6.1.2.1.3.1.1	Each entry contains one network address to physical address.
atIfIndex	1.3.6.1.2.1.3.1.1.1	The interface on which this entry's equivalence is effective.
atPhysAddress	1.3.6.1.2.1.3.1.1.2	The media-dependent physical address.
atNetAddress	1.3.6.1.2.1.3.1.1.3	The network address corresponding to the media-dependent physical address.
ipForwarding	1.3.6.1.2.1.4.1	The indicator that this system can forward datagrams received but not addressed to it.
ipDefaultTTL	1.3.6.1.2.1.4.2	The time-to-live field of the IP datagrams originated at this system.
ipInReceives	1.3.6.1.2.1.4.3	The total number of input datagrams received from interfaces.
ipInHdrErrors	1.3.6.1.2.1.4.4	The number of input datagrams discarded due to errors.
ipInAddrErrors	1.3.6.1.2.1.4.5	The number of datagrams discarded when the field was not destined for this system.
ipForwDatagrams	1.3.6.1.2.1.4.6	The number of datagrams received but not discarded because of an unknown protocol.
ipInUnknownProtos	1.3.6.1.2.1.4.7	The number of datagrams discarded because of an unknown or unsupported protocol.

continues

Table 5.7. Continued

Name	OID Path	Description
ipInDiscards	1.3.6.1.2.1.4.8	The number of IP datagrams received with no problems but still discarded by the system.
ipInDelivers	1.3.6.1.2.1.4.9	The total number of input datagrams successfully delivered to IP user-protocol.
ipOutRequests	1.3.6.1.2.1.4.10	The total number of IP datagrams that local protocols passed to IP.
ipOutDiscards	1.3.6.1.2.1.4.11	The number of outbound IP datagrams that were discarded but had no errors.
ipOutNoRoutes	1.3.6.1.2.1.4.12	The number of IP datagrams discarded because the system could not find a route.
ipReasmTimeout	1.3.6.1.2.1.4.13	The maximum number of seconds IP holds received fragments awaiting reassembly.
ipReasmReqds	1.3.6.1.2.1.4.14	The number of IP fragments needing reassembly.
ipReasmOKs	1.3.6.1.2.1.4.15	The number of IP datagrams successfully reassembled.
ipReasmFails	1.3.6.1.2.1.4.16	The number of failed reassembled IP datagrams.
ipFragOKs	1.3.6.1.2.1.4.17	The number of IP fragments that have been reassembled.
ipFragFails	1.3.6.1.2.1.4.18	The number of IP packets that have been discarded because they could not be fragmented.
ipFragCreates	1.3.6.1.2.1.4.19	The number of IP datagram fragments that IP has generated.
ipAddrTable	1.3.6.1.2.1.4.20	The table of IP addressing information.
ipAddrEntry	1.3.6.1.2.1.4.20.1	Information for one of the system's IP addresses.
ipAdEntAddr	1.3.6.1.2.1.4.20.1.1	The IP address to which this entry's addressing information pertains.
ipAdEntIfIndex	1.3.6.1.2.1.4.20.1.2	The index value that uniquely identifies the interface to which this entry is applicable.

Name	OID Path	Description
ipAdEntNetMask	1.3.6.1.2.1.4.20.1.3	The subnet mask associated with the IP address of this entry.
ipAdEntBcastAddr	1.3.6.1.2.1.4.20.1.4	The value of the least-significant bit in the IP broadcast address.
ipAdEntReasm	1.3.6.1.2.1.4.20.1.5	The size of the largest IP data-MaxSize gram that this system can reassemble from IP fragments.
ipRoutingTable	1.3.6.1.2.1.4.21	The IP routing table.
ipRouteEntry	1.3.6.1.2.1.4.21.1	An entry in the route table.
ipRouteDest	1.3.6.1.2.1.4.21.1.1	A route to a particular destination.
ipRouteIfIndex	1.3.6.1.2.1.4.21.1.2	The value that identifies the local interface through which the datagram should reach the next hop.
ipRouteMetric1	1.3.6.1.2.1.4.21.1.3	The primary routing metric for this route.
ipRouteMetric2	1.3.6.1.2.1.4.21.1.4	An alternative route metric for this interface.
ipRouteMetric3	1.3.6.1.2.1.4.21.1.5	An alternative route metric for this interface.
ipRouteMetric4	1.3.6.1.2.1.4.21.1.6	An alternative route metric for this interface.
ipRouteNextHop	1.3.6.1.2.1.4.21.1.7	The IP address of the next hop of this interface.
routeipRouteType	1.3.6.1.2.1.4.21.1.8	The type of route.
ipRouteProto	1.3.6.1.2.1.4.21.1.9	The way the system learned the route.
ipRouteAge	1.3.6.1.2.1.4.21.1.10	The number of seconds since IP last updated this route.
ipRouteMask	1.3.6.1.2.1.4.21.1.11	The mask to be logically ANDed with the destination.
ipNetToMediaTable	1.3.6.1.2.1.4.22	The IP address translation table for mapping IP to physical addresses.
ipNetToMediaEntry	1.3.6.1.2.1.4.22.1	Each entry contains one address to physical equivalence.
ipNetToMediaIfIndex	1.3.6.1.2.1.4.22.1.1	The interface on which this entry's equivalence is effective.

continues

Table 5.7. Continued

Name	OID Path	Description
IpNetToMedia	1.3.6.1.2.1.4.22.1.2	The media-dependent PhysAddress physical address.
IpNetToMedia	1.3.6.1.2.1.4.22.1.3	The IP address corresponding to NetAddress the media-dependent physical address.
ipNetToMediaType	1.3.6.1.2.1.4.22.1.4	The type of mapping.
icmpInMsgs	1.3.6.1.2.1.5.1	The number of routing entries that IP discarded even though they were valid.
icmpInErrors	1.3.6.1.2.1.5.2	The total number of ICMP messages that the system received.
icmpInDestUnreachs	1.3.6.1.2.1.5.3	The number of ICMP Destination Unreachable messages received.
icmpInTimeExcds	1.3.6.1.2.1.5.4	The number of ICMP Time Extended messages received.
icmpInParmProbs	1.3.6.1.2.1.5.5	The number of ICMP Parameter Problem messages received.
icmpInSrcQuenchs	1.3.6.1.2.1.5.6	The number of ICMP Source Quench messages received.
icmpInRedirects	1.3.6.1.2.1.5.7	The number of ICMP Redirect messages received.
icmpInEchos	1.3.6.1.2.1.5.8	The number of ICMP Echo requests received.
icmpInEchoReps	1.3.6.1.2.1.5.9	The number of ICMP Echo Reply messages received.
icmpInTimestamps	1.3.6.1.2.1.5.10	The number of ICMP Timestamp Reply messages.
icmpInTimestamp	1.3.6.1.2.1.5.11	The number of ICMP Reps Timestamp Reply messages received.
icmpInAddrMasks	1.3.6.1.2.1.5.12	The number of ICMP Address Mask request messages received.
icmpInAddrMask Reps	1.3.6.1.2.1.5.13	The number of ICMP Address Mask Reply messages received.
icmpOutMsgs	1.3.6.1.2.1.5.14	The total number of ICMP messages that the system attempted to send.

Name	OID Path	Description
icmpOutErrors	1.3.6.1.2.1.5.15	The number of ICMP messages that this system did not send due to ICMP problems.
icmpOutDest	1.3.6.1.2.1.5.16	The number of ICMP Unreachs Destination Unreachable messages sent.
icmpOutTimeExcds	1.3.6.1.2.1.5.17	The number of ICMP Time Exceeded messages sent.
icmpOutParmProbs	1.3.6.1.2.1.5.18	The number of ICMP Parameter Problem messages sent.
icmpOutSrcQuenchs	1.3.6.1.2.1.5.19	The number of ICMP Source Quench messages sent.
icmpOutRedirects	1.3.6.1.2.1.5.20	The number of ICMP Redirect messages sent.
icmpOutEchos	1.3.6.1.2.1.5.21	The number of ICMP Echo requests sent.
icmpOutEchoReps	1.3.6.1.2.1.5.22	The number of UCMP Echo replies sent.
icmpOutTimestamps	1.3.6.1.2.1.5.23	The number of ICMP Time Stamp messages sent.
icmpOutTimestamp	1.3.6.1.2.1.5.24	The number of ICMP Time Reps Stamp Reply messages sent.
icmpOutAddrMasks	1.3.6.1.2.1.5.25	The number of ICMP Address Mask Request messages sent.
icmpOutAddrMask	1.3.6.1.2.1.5.26	The number of ICMP Address RepsMask Reply messages sent.
tcpRtoAlgorithm	1.3.6.1.2.1.6.1	The algorithm used to determine the timeout value.
tcpRtoMin	1.3.6.1.2.1.6.2	The minimum, in milliseconds, for the retransmission timeout.
tcpRtoMax	1.3.6.1.2.1.6.3	The maximum, in milliseconds, for the retransmission timeout.
tcpMaxConn	1.3.6.1.2.1.6.4	The maximum number of TCP connections the system can support.
tcpActiveOpens	1.3.6.1.2.1.6.5	How many TCP connections transitioned to SYN-SET state from the CLOSED state.
tcpPassiveOpens	1.3.6.1.2.1.6.6	How many TCP connections transitioned to the SYN-RCVD state from the listen state.

continues

Table 5.7. Continued

Name	OID Path	Description
tcpAttemptFails	1.3.6.1.2.1.6.7	How many TCP connections have not completed the SYN handshake procedure.
tcpEstbResets	1.3.6.1.2.1.6.8	How many times TCP has gone to the CLOSED state from ESTABLISHED or CLOSE-WAIT state.
tcpCurrEstab	1.3.6.1.2.1.6.9	How many TCP connections are currently in the ESTABLISHED or CLOSE-WAIT state.
tcpInSegs	1.3.6.1.2.1.6.10	The total number of segments received, including those received in error.
tcpOutSegs	1.3.6.1.2.1.6.11	The total number of segments sent, excluding those containing only retransmitted octets.
tcpRetransSegs	1.3.6.1.2.1.6.12	The total number of segments retransmitted.
tcpConnTable	1.3.6.1.2.1.6.13	A table containing TCP connection-specific information.
tcpConnEntry	1.3.6.1.2.1.6.13.1	Information about a particular current TCP connection.
tcpConnState	1.3.6.1.2.1.6.13.1.1	The state of this TCP connection.
tcpConnLocal	1.3.6.1.2.1.6.13.1.2	The local IP address for this Address TCP connection.
tcpConnLocalPort	1.3.6.1.2.1.6.13.1.3	The local port number for this TCP connection.
tcpConnRemAddress	1.3.6.1.2.1.6.13.1.4	The remote IP address for this TCP connection.
tcpConnRemPort	1.3.6.1.2.1.6.13.1.5	The remote port number for this TCP connection.
tcpInErrs	1.3.6.1.2.1.6.14	The total number of segments received in error.
tcpOutRsts	1.3.6.1.2.1.6.15	The number of TCP segments sent containing the RST flags.
udpInDatagrams	1.3.6.1.2.1.7.1	The total number of incoming UDP datagrams.
udpNoPorts	1.3.6.1.2.1.7.2	The total number of UDP datagrams received where there were no ports on the receiving end.

Name	OID Path	Description
udpInErrors	1.3.6.1.2.1.7.3	The number of received UDP datagrams that are undeliverable, but not because of the UDP port.
udpOutDatagrams	1.3.6.1.2.1.7.4	The total number of UDP datagrams sent from this system.
udpTable	1.3.6.1.2.1.7.5	A table containing UDP listening information.
udpEntry	1.3.6.1.2.1.7.5.1	Information about a current UDP listener.
udpLocalAddress	1.3.6.1.2.1.7.5.1.1	The local IP address for this UDP listener.
udpLocalPort	1.3.6.1.2.1.7.5.1.2	The local port number for this UDP listener.
snmpInPkts	1.3.6.1.2.1.11.1	Total SNMP packets received.
snmpOutPkts	1.3.6.1.2.1.11.2	Total SNMP messages the agent sent to the transport service.
snmpInBadVersions	1.3.6.1.2.1.11.3	Total SNMP messages delivered with an unsupported SNMP version.
snmpInBad	1.3.6.1.2.1.11.4	Total SNMP messages sent with CommunityNames an unknown community name.
snmpInBad CommunityUses	1.3.6.1.2.1.11.5	Total SNMP messages with an operation not allowed by the community.
snmpInASNParse	1.3.6.1.2.1.11.6	Total ASN.1 errors found when Errs decoding SNMP packets.
snmpInBadTypes	1.3.6.1.2.1.11.7	Not used.
snmpInTooBigs	1.3.6.1.2.1.11.8	Total SNMP PDUs delivered with an error status of Too Big.
snmpInNoSuchNames	1.3.6.1.2.1.11.9	Total SNMP PDUs delivered with an error status of No Such Name.
snmpInBadValues	1.3.6.1.2.1.11.10	Total SNMP PDUs delivered with a status of Bad Value.
snmpInReadOnlys	1.3.6.1.2.1.11.11	Total SNMP PDUs delivered with an error status of Read-Only.
snmpInGenErrs	1.3.6.1.2.1.11.12	Total SNMP PDUs delivered with an error status field value of Generr (general error).

continues

Table 5.7. Continued

Name	OID Path	Description
snmpInTotalReqVars	1.3.6.1.2.1.11.13	Total MIB objects the agent retrieved successfully.
snmpInTotalSetVars	1.3.6.1.2.1.11.14	Total MIB objects the agent altered successfully.
snmpInGetRequests	1.3.6.1.2.1.11.15	Total SNMP Get-Request PDUs accepted and processed.
snmpInGetNexts	1.3.6.1.2.1.11.16	Total SNMP Get-Next PDUs accepted and processed.
snmpInSetRequests	1.3.6.1.2.1.11.17	Total SNMP Set-Requests PDUs accepted and processed.
snmpInGetResponses	1.3.6.1.2.1.11.18	Total SNMP Get-Response PDUs accepted and processed.
snmpInTraps	1.3.6.1.2.1.11.19	Total SNMP Trap PDUs accepted and processed.
snmpOutTooBigs	1.3.6.1.2.1.11.20	Total SNMP PDUs sent with an error status field of Too Big.
snmpOutNoSuchNames	1.3.6.1.2.1.11.21	Total SNMP sent with an error status of No Such Names.
snmpOutBadValues	1.3.6.1.2.1.11.22	Total SNMP sent with a status of Bad Value.
snmpOutReadOnlys	1.3.6.1.2.1.11.23	Total SNMP sent with an error status of Read-Only.
snmpOutGetErrs	1.3.6.1.2.1.11.24	Total SNMP sent with an error status field value of Generr (general error).
snmpOutGetRequests	1.3.6.1.2.1.11.25	Total SNMP Get requests sent.
snmpOutGetNexts	1.3.6.1.2.1.11.26	Total SNMP GetNext requests sent.
snmpOutSetRequests	1.3.6.1.2.1.11.27	Total SNMP Set requests sent.
snmpOutGetResponses	1.3.6.1.2.1.11.28	Total SNMP GetResponses sent.
snmpOutTraps	1.3.6.1.2.1.11.29	Total SNMP Trap PDUs sent.
snmpEnableAuthTraps	1.3.6.1.2.1.11.30	Indicates whether the agent can generate Authentication-Failure traps.

LAN Manager MIB

Although many of the following are obsolete, they still can be used for the purpose of some basic service management:

```
lanmanager,1.3.6.1.4.1.77
lanmgr-2,1.3.6.1.4.1.77.1
common,1.3.6.1.4.1.77.1.1
comVersionMaj,1.3.6.1.4.1.77.1.1.1
comVersionMin,1.3.6.1.4.1.77.1.1.2
comType,1.3.6.1.4.1.77.1.1.3
comStatStart,1.3.6.1.4.1.77.1.1.4
comStatNumNetIOs,1.3.6.1.4.1.77.1.1.5
comStatFiNetIOs,1.3.6.1.4.1.77.1.1.6
comStatFcNetIOs,1.3.6.1.4.1.77.1.1.7
server,1.3.6.1.4.1.77.1.2
svDescription,1.3.6.1.4.1.77.1.2.1
svSvcNumber,1.3.6.1.4.1.77.1.2.2
svSvcTable,1.3.6.1.4.1.77.1.2.3
svSvcEntry,1.3.6.1.4.1.77.1.2.3.1
svSvcName,1.3.6.1.4.1.77.1.2.3.1.1
svSvcInstalledState,1.3.6.1.4.1.77.1.2.3.1.2
svSvcOperatingState,1.3.6.1.4.1.77.1.2.3.1.3
svSvcCanBeUninstalled,1.3.6.1.4.1.77.1.2.3.1.4
svSvcCanBePaused,1.3.6.1.4.1.77.1.2.3.1.5
svStatOpens,1.3.6.1.4.1.77.1.2.4
svStatDevOpens,1.3.6.1.4.1.77.1.2.5
svStatQueuedJobs,1.3.6.1.4.1.77.1.2.6
svStatSOpens,1.3.6.1.4.1.77.1.2.7
svStatErrorOuts,1.3.6.1.4.1.77.1.2.8
svStatPwErrors,1.3.6.1.4.1.77.1.2.9
svStatPermErrors,1.3.6.1.4.1.77.1.2.10
svStatSysErrors,1.3.6.1.4.1.77.1.2.11
svStatSentBytes,1.3.6.1.4.1.77.1.2.12
svStatRcvdBytes,1.3.6.1.4.1.77.1.2.13
svStatAvResponse,1.3.6.1.4.1.77.1.2.14
svStatSecurityMode,1.3.6.1.4.1.77.1.2.15
svUsers,1.3.6.1.4.1.77.1.2.16
svStatReqBufsNeeded,1.3.6.1.4.1.77.1.2.17
svStatBigBufsNeeded,1.3.6.1.4.1.77.1.2.18
svSessionNumber,1.3.6.1.4.1.77.1.2.19
svSessionTable,1.3.6.1.4.1.77.1.2.20
svSessionEntry,1.3.6.1.4.1.77.1.2.20.1
svSesClientName,1.3.6.1.4.1.77.1.2.20.1.1
svSesUserName,1.3.6.1.4.1.77.1.2.20.1.2
svSesNumConns,1.3.6.1.4.1.77.1.2.20.1.3
svSesNumOpens,1.3.6.1.4.1.77.1.2.20.1.4
svSesTime,1.3.6.1.4.1.77.1.2.20.1.5
svSesIdleTime,1.3.6.1.4.1.77.1.2.20.1.6
svSesClientType,1.3.6.1.4.1.77.1.2.20.1.7
svSesState,1.3.6.1.4.1.77.1.2.20.1.8
svAutoDisconnects,1.3.6.1.4.1.77.1.2.21
svDisConTime,1.3.6.1.4.1.77.1.2.22
svAuditLogSize,1.3.6.1.4.1.77.1.2.23
```

```
svUserNumber,1.3.6.1.4.1.77.1.2.24
svUserTable,1.3.6.1.4.1.77.1.2.25
svUserEntry,1.3.6.1.4.1.77.1.2.25.1
svUserName,1.3.6.1.4.1.77.1.2.25.1.1
svShareNumber,1.3.6.1.4.1.77.1.2.26
svShareTable,1.3.6.1.4.1.77.1.2.27
svShareEntry,1.3.6.1.4.1.77.1.2.27.1
svShareName,1.3.6.1.4.1.77.1.2.27.1.1
svSharePath,1.3.6.1.4.1.77.1.2.27.1.2
svShareComment,1.3.6.1.4.1.77.1.2.27.1.3
svPrintQNumber,1.3.6.1.4.1.77.1.2.28
svPrintQTable,1.3.6.1.4.1.77.1.2.29
svPrintQEntry,1.3.6.1.4.1.77.1.2.29.1
svPrintQName,1.3.6.1.4.1.77.1.2.29.1.1
svPrintQNumJobs,1.3.6.1.4.1.77.1.2.29.1.2
workstation,1.3.6.1.4.1.77.1.3
domain,1.3.6.1.4.1.77.1.4
domPrimaryGroup,1.3.6.1.4.1.77.1.4.1
domLogonDomain,1.3.6.1.4.1.77.1.4.2
domOtherDomainNumber,1.3.6.1.4.1.77.1.4.3
domOtherDomainTable,1.3.6.1.4.1.77.1.4.4
domOtherDomainEntry,1.3.6.1.4.1.77.1.4.4.1
domOtherName,1.3.6.1.4.1.77.1.4.4.1.1
domServerNumber,1.3.6.1.4.1.77.1.4.5
domServerTable,1.3.6.1.4.1.77.1.4.6
domServerEntry,1.3.6.1.4.1.77.1.4.6.1
domServerName,1.3.6.1.4.1.77.1.4.6.1.1
domLogonNumber,1.3.6.1.4.1.77.1.4.7
domLogonTable,1.3.6.1.4.1.77.1.4.8
domLogonEntry,1.3.6.1.4.1.77.1.4.8.1
domLogonUser,1.3.6.1.4.1.77.1.4.8.1.1
domLogonMachine,1.3.6.1.4.1.77.1.4.8.1.2
```

Microsoft MIB Objects

The following MIBs are found under the Microsoft Enterprise object. There are more specific definitions found in the Microsoft Windows NT Resource Kit.

```
microsoft,1.3.6.1.4.1.311
software,1.3.6.1.4.1.311.1
systems,1.3.6.1.4.1.311.1.1
wins,1.3.6.1.4.1.311.1.2
par,1.3.6.1.4.1.311.1.2.1
parWinsStartTime,1.3.6.1.4.1.311.1.2.1.1
parLastPSvcTime,1.3.6.1.4.1.311.1.2.1.2
parLastAtSvcTime,1.3.6.1.4.1.311.1.2.1.3
pull,1.3.6.1.4.1.311.1.2.2
push,1.3.6.1.4.1.311.1.2.3
datafiles,1.3.6.1.4.1.311.1.2.4
```

```
cmd,1.3.6.1.4.1.311.1.2.5
dhcp,1.3.6.1.4.1.311.1.3
dhcpPar,1.3.6.1.4.1.311.1.3.1
parDhcpStartTime,1.3.6.1.4.1.311.1.3.1.1
dhcpScope,1.3.6.1.4.1.311.1.3.2
internetServer,1.3.6.1.4.1.311.1.7
ftpServer,1.3.6.1.4.1.311.1.7.2
ftpStatistics,1.3.6.1.4.1.311.1.7.2.1
totalBytesSentHighWord,1.3.6.1.4.1.311.1.7.2.1.1
totalBytesSentLowWord,1.3.6.1.4.1.311.1.7.2.1.2
totalBytesReceivedHighWord,1.3.6.1.4.1.311.1.7.2.1.3
totalBytesReceivedLowWord,1.3.6.1.4.1.311.1.7.2.1.4
totalFilesSent,1.3.6.1.4.1.311.1.7.2.1.5
totalFilesReceived,1.3.6.1.4.1.311.1.7.2.1.6
currentAnonymousUsers,1.3.6.1.4.1.311.1.7.2.1.7
currentNonAnonymousUsers,1.3.6.1.4.1.311.1.7.2.1.8
totalAnonymousUsers,1.3.6.1.4.1.311.1.7.2.1.9
totalNonAnonymousUsers,1.3.6.1.4.1.311.1.7.2.1.10
maxAnonymousUsers,1.3.6.1.4.1.311.1.7.2.1.11
maxNonAnonymousUsers,1.3.6.1.4.1.311.1.7.2.1.12
currentConnections,1.3.6.1.4.1.311.1.7.2.1.13
maxConnections,1.3.6.1.4.1.311.1.7.2.1.14
connectionAttempts,1.3.6.1.4.1.311.1.7.2.1.15
logonAttempts,1.3.6.1.4.1.311.1.7.2.1.16
httpServer,1.3.6.1.4.1.311.1.7.3
httpStatistics,1.3.6.1.4.1.311.1.7.3.1
totalBytesSentHighWord,1.3.6.1.4.1.311.1.7.3.1.1
totalBytesSentLowWord,1.3.6.1.4.1.311.1.7.3.1.2
totalBytesReceivedHighWord,1.3.6.1.4.1.311.1.7.3.1.3
totalBytesReceivedLowWord,1.3.6.1.4.1.311.1.7.3.1.4
totalFilesSent,1.3.6.1.4.1.311.1.7.3.1.5
currentAnonymousUsers,1.3.6.1.4.1.311.1.7.3.1.6
currentNonAnonymousUsers,1.3.6.1.4.1.311.1.7.3.1.7
totalAnonymousUsers,1.3.6.1.4.1.311.1.7.3.1.8
totalNonAnonymousUsers,1.3.6.1.4.1.311.1.7.3.1.9
maxAnonymousUsers,1.3.6.1.4.1.311.1.7.3.1.10
maxNonAnonymousUsers,1.3.6.1.4.1.311.1.7.3.1.11
currentConnections,1.3.6.1.4.1.311.1.7.3.1.12
maxConnections,1.3.6.1.4.1.311.1.7.3.1.13
connectionAttempts,1.3.6.1.4.1.311.1.7.3.1.14
logonAttempts,1.3.6.1.4.1.311.1.7.3.1.15
totalGets,1.3.6.1.4.1.311.1.7.3.1.16
totalPosts,1.3.6.1.4.1.311.1.7.3.1.17
totalHeads,1.3.6.1.4.1.311.1.7.3.1.18
totalOthers,1.3.6.1.4.1.311.1.7.3.1.19
totalCGIRequests,1.3.6.1.4.1.311.1.7.3.1.20
totalBGIRequests,1.3.6.1.4.1.311.1.7.3.1.21
totalNotFoundErrors,1.3.6.1.4.1.311.1.7.3.1.22
```

SNMP Monitor

The SNMP Monitor, found in the BackOffice and Windows NT Resource Kits, is a utility that can monitor any SNMP MIB variables across any number of SNMP nodes. It can then optionally log query results to a repository, which can be any ODBC data source (such as SQL Server), automatically creating any necessary tables. Logging can be enabled for all queries or limited to particular thresholds, and thresholds can be either edge- or level-triggered.

Rudimentary conditionals are also possible. SNMP Monitor can execute arbitrary command lines based on whether the node responded to the query, whether the node supported the requested variable, and whether the value was greater than, less than, or equal to a specified constant.

SNMP Monitor is a standalone executable that accepts a configuration file as input. By default, if no configuration file is specified, the SNMP Monitor does not successfully monitor anything. The configuration file is a text file that consists of one or more *monitored node definitions* separated by at least one blank line or C++-style comment line. A *definition* consists of the scope declaration followed by one or more conditional statements.

The syntax for the scope declaration is as follows:

```
<Node ID> <OID> <Poll interval> <Default log setting> [<ODBC data source> <ODBC
➥table name> <ODBC user ID> [<ODBC password>]]
```

Available options include the following:

- `<Node ID>` This could be a computer name without backslashes (for example, `STEVE`), a dotted IP address (for example, `128.11.100.4`), and a colon followed by the path to a text file containing a list of computer names or IP addresses. There must be one entry per line, and blank lines are ignored (for example, `:c:\snmpmon\config\nodes.snmp`).
- `<OID>` This is the dotted object identifier within the MIB namespace (for example, `1.3.6.1.2.1.1.3`).
- `<Poll interval>` This is the number of seconds between each poll of this monitored node.
- `<Default log setting>` This can be one of the following values:

  `0` Do not log any data unless specified by one of the conditionals.

  `1` Log all query results, ignoring the log settings in the conditionals.
- `<ODBC data source>` Refers to the name of the ODBC data source to which to direct logged data.

- `<ODBC table name>` Refers to the name of the table within the data source to which to direct logged data. If this table does not exist, it is created.
- `<ODBC user ID>` Refers to the user ID used to connect to the ODBC data source.
- `ODBC password>` Refers to the password used to connect to the ODBC data source. If this parameter is omitted, no password is used.

The scope declaration is followed immediately by any number of conditional statements. Each conditional has the following format:

```
<Condition> <Log trigger> [<Command-line trigger> <Command-line timeout>
➥<Command line>]
```

PERF2MIB.EXE: Performance Monitor MIB Builder Tool

Using PERF2MIB.EXE, Performance Monitor MIB Builder Tool, developers can create new ASN.1 syntax MIBs for their applications, services, or devices that use Performance Monitor counters. Administrators can then track performance of these components by using any system-management program that supports SNMP.

This tool also creates a .MIB file that can be used by an SNMP-based management console to perform SNMP requests for the performance data in question, and thus monitor performance remotely. This allows all performance data available through the HKEY_PERFORMANCE_DATA Registry key to be exposed through SNMP.

To use this utility, follow these steps:

1. From a command prompt, navigate to the Resource Kit directory.
2. Type the following command:

   ```
   perf2mib perfmib.mib perfmib.ini memory 1 mem processor 2 cpu "Network
   ➥Segment" 3 net PhysicalDisk 4 disk
   ```

   This helps translate the Performance Counter, proprietary to Windows NT, into a MIB (SNMP-compatible).
3. Type the following command to compile the MIB.

   ```
   mibcc -oc:\reskit\mib.bin -n -t -w2 c:\reskit\smi.mib
   ➥c:\reskit\LMMIB2.MIB c:\reskit\mib_II.mib perfmib.mib
   ```

4. Stop the SNMP agent by typing the following command:

   ```
   NET STOP SNMP
   ```

5. Rename the %systemroot%\system32\mib.bin to mib.old using the following command:

```
Ren %SystemRoot%\system32\mib.bin %SystemRoot%\system32\mib.old.
```

6. Transfer a few files from the Resource Kit directory to the System directory by typing the following:

```
XCOPY C:\RESKIT\perfmib.* %SystemRoot%\system32\
XCOPY C:\RESKIT\mib.bin %SystemRoot%\system32\
```

7. Register perfmib.reg using the following command:

```
REGINI PERFMIB.REG
```

8. Restart the SNMP agent by typing the following command:

```
NET START SNMP
```

Now you can use the Resource Kit utility SNMPUTIL.EXE to process SNMP requests.

Unicenter TNG Framework

This product, by CAI, allows full-scale enterprise management for IP and IPX environments. The Unicenter TNG base product offers an extremely rich set of management functions for network and systems management:

- Security
- Scheduling and workload
- Network management
- Storage
- Performance
- Output
- Resource accounting and chargeback
- Problem management
- Complete event management

All these functions are integrated on top of the framework and deliver, in one package, the core set of management functions needed for network and systems management.

The following is a selected list of features in Unicenter TNG:

- 2D and 3D user interface

- Object repository
- Autodiscovery of nodes
- Calendar management
- Virus detection
- Reporting
- Business-process views
- Event management

Command-Line Network Monitoring Utilities

There are two primary command-line utilities—NETSTAT and NBTSTAT—that are discussed in the following sections.

NETSTAT

NETSTAT displays TCP/IP protocol session information (see Figure 5.25).

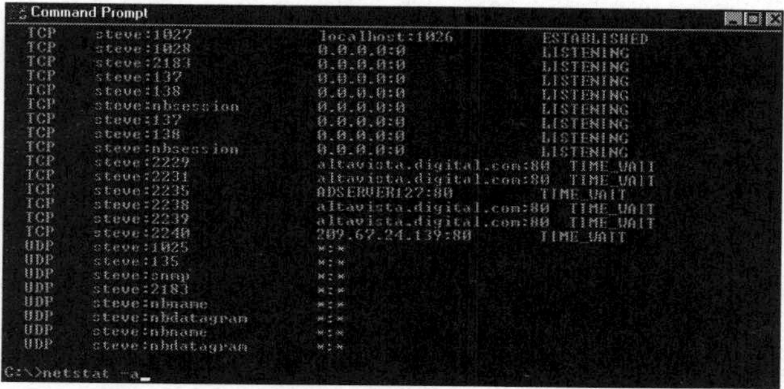

Figure 5.25. *NETSTAT.*

The syntax for NETSTAT is as follows:

```
NETSTAT [-a] [-e] [-n] [-s] [-p proto] [-r] [interval]
```

The following are switches:

`-a`	Displays all connections and listening ports. (Server-side connections are normally not shown.)
`-e`	Displays Ethernet statistics. This may be combined with the `-s` option.

`-n`	Displays addresses and port numbers in numeric form.
`-p proto`	Shows connections for the protocol specified by *proto*; *proto* may be `tcp` or `udp`. If used with the `-s` option to display per-protocol statistics, *proto* may be `tcp`, `udp`, or `ip`.
`-r`	Displays the contents of the routing table.
`-s`	Displays per-protocol statistics. By default, statistics are shown for TCP, UDP and IP; the `-p` option may be used to specify a subset of the default.
`Interval`	Redisplays selected statistics, pausing interval seconds between each display. Press Ctrl+C to stop redisplaying statistics. If omitted, NETSTAT prints the current configuration information one time.

NBTSTAT

NBTSTAT reports statistics and connections for NetBIOS over TCP/IP. The most common switch for NBTSTAT is `-r`, which reports complete name resolution statistics for Windows networking.

The syntax for NBTSTAT is as follows:

```
NBTSTAT [-a RemoteName] [-A IP address] [-c] [-n] [-r] [-R] [-s] [-S]
➥[interval] ]
```

The following are switches:

`-a`	(adapter status)	Lists the remote machine's name table given its name.
`-A`	(Adapter status)	Lists the remote machine's name table given its IP address.
`-c`	(cache)	Lists the remote name cache including the IP addresses.
`-n`	(names)	Lists local NetBIOS names.
`-r`	(resolved)	Lists names resolved by broadcast and via WINS.

`-R`	(Reload)	Purges and reloads the remote cache name table.
`-S`	(Sessions)	Lists sessions table with the destination IP addresses.
`-s`	(sessions)	Lists sessions table converting destination IP addresses to host names via the HOSTS file.

`RemoteName`	Remote host machine name.
`IP address`	Dotted decimal representation of the IP address.
`Interval`	Redisplays selected statistics, pausing interval seconds between each display. Press Ctrl+C to stop redisplaying statistics.

Service Pack 4 of Windows NT added an additional enhancement to the `nbtstat` utility. The Nbtstat.exe command now has the `-RR` command, which deletes and re-registers a user in WINS database without having to perform a system reboot.

Using the Resource Kit Management Tools

So far, we have mentioned built-in utilities that Windows NT provides for network management along with a few third-party utilities relating to disk and network management. The Resource Kit also has some graphical management utilities that enable you to further manage specific services in a much more detailed manner.

Domain Monitor

Domain Monitor is a Resource Kit utility that monitors the status of servers in a specified domain and its secure channel status to the domain controller, as well as to domain controllers in trusted domains. If any status shows errors, Domain Monitor displays various status icons, as well as the domain controller name and list of trusted domains. You can find the cause of errors by checking the error numbers reported in the Windows NT Messages database.

Domain Monitor connects to servers to retrieve status information using the current user's username and password. Therefore, if the current user account doesn't exist in a domain or in the database of a trusted domain, the status query may fail. Any user who is logged on can query the status information, but only administrators can use the Disconnect button to disconnect and restore connections.

The status of a domain is shown in one of following states:

- `Success` Indicates that all servers in the domain are running, and `PDCLinkStatus` and `TDClinkStatus` shows only successful connections (no errors).
- `Problem` Indicates a problem that may require attention. This icon appears when any server in the domain has an error under `PDCLinkStatus` or `TDClinkStatus` or when any server in the domain is down.
- `Warning` Indicates a severe problem that requires attention. This icon appears when the status for any server or domain controller shows an error or when the domain's domain controller is down.
- `Domain Down` Displayed when all servers in the domain are down.
- `Unknown` Displayed while Domain Monitor is checking connections.

The NET WATCH Utility

This Resource Kit utility shows which users are connected to shared directories. It also enables you to disconnect users and un-share directories. It can simultaneously monitor multiple computers. If a user or set of users reports being unable to access a server, you can check to see who can connect to it. To use NET WATCH, the Server Service must be started and you must be logged on as a member of the Administrators group for any computer you are trying to watch.

Look at the following syntax:

```
netwatch \\computername1 [\\computername2 ... \\computernameN]
```

computername1 to *N* are the names of the computers whose users you want to monitor.

To indicate the network connections you want to watch on the Options menu, click Show Open Files, Show Hidden Shares, or Show In Use Shares Only.

NET WATCH updates the list of connected users every 30 seconds or whenever you press F5. You can view more details on a resource by double-clicking it or by selecting it and pressing Alt+Enter. The Manage Shared Folders dialog box (Ctrl+S) lists and shows the paths of the shared folders of the computer.

REMOTE SHUTDOWN

REMOTE SHUTDOWN, a Resource Kit utility, is a batch file that runs either SHUTCMD.EXE when run with parameters, or SHUTGUI.EXE when run without them.

SHUTCMD.EXE and SHUTGUI.EXE are, respectively, a command-line utility and a GUI utility; both enable you to shut down or reboot a local or remote Windows NT Server or Windows NT Workstation.

Look at the following syntax:

```
shutcmd [/?] [\\computername] [/L] [/A] [/R] [/T:xx] [msg] [/Y] [/C]
```

/? (or shutdown without parameters)	Shows all command-line options.
computername	Specifies a remote computer to shut down. Note that if no name is given but the utility is started with any of the other options, the local computer name is used.
/L -	Specifies a local shutdown.
/A -	Aborts a system shutdown. This is only possible during the time-out period. If this switch is used, all others are ignored.
/R -	Specifies that the computer should reboot after shutdown.
/T:*xx* -	Sets the timer for system shutdown in *xx* seconds. The default is 20 seconds.
Msg -	Specifies an additional message, with a maximum of 127 characters allowed.
/Y -	Answers all following questions with yes.
/C -	Forces running applications to close.

Browser Monitor

The Browser Monitor Resource Kit utility monitors the status of browsers on selected domains. Browsers are shown on a per-domain and per-transport basis. In the main window, Browser Monitor displays various status icons and identifies the domain, transport, and Master Browser. Browser Monitor connects to servers to retrieve status information using the current user's username and password. Therefore, if the current user account doesn't exist in a domain, the status query may fail. Any user who is logged on can query the status information.

Chapter 6

Optimization and Capacity Planning

- **Guidelines for Capacity Planning**
  Find out how to properly plan resources for servers and Windows NT networks.
- **Hardware Planning**
  Look at ways to properly select practical and compatible hardware for Windows NT.
- **Network Traffic Planning and Optimization**
  Learn how to properly forecast network traffic and how to reduce and improve network traffic performance.
- **A Methodology of Avoiding Problems**
  Establish approaches to avoid having to spend an excessive amount of time troubleshooting and isolating problems.

Hardware Capacity Planning Guidelines

Planning is essential in any organization at many levels. When it comes to networks, especially Windows NT networks, ensuring that you have supported and tested adequate hardware will be the first step in the goal for establishing the most optimal performance. It is also a major step in avoiding unnecessary stress via troubleshooting.

Windows NT is scaled to fit right in with a regular LAN environment. The basic requirements for Windows NT are a 486DX/33 CPU with 16MB of RAM and 120MB of disk space.

Author's Note

When Microsoft published these requirements, people tended to interpret this more as a median requirement as opposed to what they really are—minimal—ground zero in terms of capacity planning.

Years ago, in 1992, Microsoft developed the requirements for Windows 3.1. The requirements were a 286 CPU with 2MB of RAM and 20MB of free disk space. Two years later, the average desktop running Windows 3.1 was a 486SX with at least 4MB of RAM and hard drives of at least 540MB.

Many got this baseline from combining the basic requirements and the applications they were running. This was the average workload for each operating system. A simple, yet necessary procedure designed primarily for client workstations. With a server and a network, you essentially are doing the same thing in determining the average workload, but there are many more variables.

With *server planning*, each basic hardware requirement must be examined thoroughly. There are also more specific hardware requirements. In addition to these specific hardware requirements, certain requirements that are deemed optional overall may be required for a specific situation to work.

Supported Processor Platforms for Windows NT

One of the first steps in properly planning a Windows NT server installation is determining an adequate CPU speed. Determining a proper CPU speed is essential no matter what the server's primary duties are. Windows NT can be installed on the following processor systems:

- Intel 486, Pentium, Pentium II, Pentium Pro, and Intel clones (such as Cyrix, AMD)
- MIPS (Silicon Graphics) R4000- and R4400-based systems
- Digital's Alpha AXP processor systems
- Systems based on the Motorola PowerPC

Author's Note

Although there are still products designed for MIPS and PowerPC, in 1997, Microsoft announced that it will no longer support MIPS and PowerPC platforms in future applications and versions of Windows NT.

Because the only supported CPUs for Windows NT as of 1998 are the Intel series and the Alpha series, many will suggest that the decision is based on whether you desire a RISC (Reduced Instruction Set Computer) CPU or a CISC (Complex Instruction Set Computer) CPU. CISC CPUs were made prevalent by the Intel x86 series CPUs. RISC-based CPUs include the IBM R6000, the DEC Alpha series, the NEC/SGI MIPS, and the Motorola PowerPC.

The Intel CISC CPUs went all the way to the 386SX/DX series. The 486 and the Pentium CPUs are actually more hybrid CISC/RISC CPUs. The 486 is the minimal Intel CPU for Windows NT. Clones of the 486 and Pentium are also supported, but the 486X series are not supported. Even if you have a 486 whose internal frequencies have been doubled or quadrupled (DX/2, DX/4), this will be a relatively slow CPU for Windows NT. Windows NT has been scaled to 32-bit processing and a 64-bit data structure. The best CPUs to accommodate this include the Intel Pentium, Pentium II, and the DEC Alpha.

Main Memory Requirements

Intel or compatible systems require a minimum of 16 megabytes for the server or a development system. MIPS R4000-, R4400- and Alpha AXP-based systems require 32 megabytes of memory. Again, like with the CPU, this is very minimal and should be treated as "ground zero" when planning applications, services, and workloads.

Disk Requirements

A Windows NT server system for an Intel x86 or compatible requires around 120MB, and 130MB for a RISC system. Of course, more disk space is desirable. It is recommended to allocate at least 250MB to the system file structure due to anticipated temporary space, space consumed by the addition of Windows NT OS components, and the space consumed by additional shared DLLs. Printers may also consume space (for spooling purposes).

Video Requirements

A VGA or higher resolution video driver is required, although a server really does not need more than 16 colors. The best choices are the 64-bit processor video boards, but check drivers for Windows NT compatibility *before* purchase.

Optional, but Recommended, Components

The following components may be useful in running Windows NT:

- Mouse or other pointing device
- SCSI CD-ROM drive (required for RISC-based systems)

- A supported network adapter card (required for network access)
- Tape backup device, including inexpensive QIC-80 drives (250MB) and SCSI (500MB) drives
- An uninterruptable power supply (UPS)

Hardware Detection

NTDETECT.COM, a program that runs during setup for x86-based computers, automatically detects the following items every time Windows NT boots:

- Bus/adapter
- Keyboard
- SCSI adapters
- Communication ports
- Video adapte
- Floating-point coprocessor
- Mouse
- Floppy drives
- Parallel ports
- Most IDE and PCI devices

This information will then be stored in the hardware portion of the Windows NT Registry.

Comments on Practical Planning

Planning is essential to a successful installation as well as successful systems administration. When a company markets software, especially an operating system, that company will publish the most minimal requirements to increase the market size. For a test machine, a Windows NT server with 16MB of RAM and 200MB of disk space will suffice.

If you are going to be running the entire MS BackOffice suite, however, it is woefully underpowered, especially in the memory and storage departments. Plan on partitioning almost 500MB for system files, and another 500MB or so for applications, which leaves only about a gigabyte for user storage.

In addition, if you're actually going to be running each BackOffice application on this system, plan on giving each application at least 16MB of RAM.

> NT Server + SQL Server + MS Mail and/or Exchange +
> SNA Server + File system cache =(minimum) 96MB of RAM

These are not necessarily Microsoft's recommendations *or* technical recommendations, but more so my practical recommendations based on realistic experiences.

In addition, it is recommended not to waste money on video for a server. It is nice if the card can do 1024×768, but it does not need to be fast, and the monitor should be usable but inexpensive. Also, is there any reason for having a sound card installed in it? More hardware installed just means more potential for conflicts. Instead, to make the system more cost effective, spend the extra money on a PCI-based Ethernet card (rather than ISA), and on a 4GB DAT backup drive.

Planning Information

Most organizations, especially large-scale ones, try to create server standards. These are curtailed to fit the needs of the organization. After these standards have been determined, they should be laid out on paper in the form of a policy. Appendix G, "Helpful Network Management Documents," contains some sample documents, including one for the server. A Windows NT server planning standard might look like this:

Operating System	Windows NT Server 4.0
Memory	32MB
Disk Space and	C: 100MB DOS Partition (FAT)
Partitioning	D: \WINNT35 System 1G E: User Directories 325MB F: Desktop Applications 400MB G: Server Applications 400MB
Fault Tolerance	Disk Duplexing
Backup Device	Exabyte 8500 (SCSI-II)
Backup Software	Arcada Backup, Exec Add-On
CPU	Pentium - 133MHz or higher
Licenses	Per Server (100)
Network Interface Card	NE 2000-compatible
Network Protocol	TCP/IP

Memory

When planning memory requirements practically, remember to properly add up memory starting with the basic 16MB requirement and adding additional memory based on the requirements. The following algorithm is recommended when computing initial memory requirements for Windows NT Server:

System Memory	Minimum Required	A
User Data	Average size of data files open per user.	B
	Number of users.	C
	Multiply *B* by *C*.	D
Applications	Average size of executables being run off the server.	E
	Number of applications being run off the Server.	F
	Multiply *E* by *F*.	G
Total Configuration	Memory required.	

Author's Note

A system operating on a standard ISA bus is not a logical choice for implementing a server. This architecture is scaled toward a memory ceiling of 16MB. It is best to deal with an EISA (Enhanced Industry Standard Architecture), MCA (Micro Channel Architecture), or a PCI (Peripheral Component Interconnect) bus. RISC-based servers in particular do not deal with the 16MB barrier.

Disk Space

When planning disk space, use a similar approach to how memory is determined. The minimum amount of disk space required is 250MB. The following algorithm is recommended when computing initial disk space requirements for Windows NT Server:

System Disk Space	Minimum required (including allocation for print spooling, pagefiles, and additional components).	A
Application Disk Space	Size of each application installation	B
	Number of applications being run off the Server.	C
	Multiply *B* by *C*.	D
User Data Disk Space	Budgeted disk space per user.	E
	Number of users.	F
	Multiply by 110% to get an additional margin for error.	G
	Multiply *E* by *F* by *G*.	H
Total Configuration	Disk space.	

Predicting Network Traffic

Many network administrators have had problems with network traffic in Windows NT. A lot of this has to do with the lack of understanding of what actually is going on behind the scenes. It is easy to lose sight of this when Microsoft hides all these entities behind a user-friendly, minimalist interface. A utility such as Microsoft's Network Monitor can assist in learning the amount of network traffic it will take for specific kinds of events.

The next few sections discuss common network components that exist on a Windows NT-based network. The assumption made in these sections is the use of TCP/IP as the primary transport protocol.

DHCP

If implementing DHCP, only two types of network events must be dealt with:

- DHCP client leasing
- Client renewal

Here are the frame counts and total bytes consumed during DHCP events:

Action	Traffic	Frequency
Acquire IP address	4 frames and 1,368 bytes.	Once per client.
Renew IP address lease	2 frames and 684 bytes.	Every startup and halfway through its lease life.

WINS

If implementing WINS for NetBIOS name resolution, you have to deal with two types of events as well. The WINS renewal occurs more frequently than the registration. In fact, it is often the woe of many network administrators in larger networking environments. Here are the frame counts and total bytes consumed during WINS events:

Action	Traffic	Frequency
Registration	2 frames and 214 bytes.	Once per service or application at startup.
Renewal	2 frames and 214 bytes.	Once per service or application halfway through its time to live.
Resolution	2 frames and 196 bytes.	Varying frequencies.

Logon Authentication

Logon validation is not as clear-cut as other network events. To authenticate is fairly clear-cut, but the extended properties are varying depending on whether you have policies, profiles, or logon scripts. Here are the frame counts and total bytes consumed during Logon Authentication events:

Action	Traffic	Frequency
Preparation	15 frames and 2,000 bytes.	Once per user logon.
Validation sequence	4 frames and 760 bytes.	Once per user logon.
Session breakdown	5 frames and 360 bytes.	Once per user logon.
Scripts, policies, profiles	Varying amount of traffic.	Once per user logon.

Browser Traffic

Probably one of the most cumbersome and annoying of the Microsoft networking services, the Browser Service generates different amounts of traffic. Often, what is generated will depend on the current browser roles. Here are the frame counts and total bytes consumed during Browser events:

Action	Traffic	Frequency
Host announcement	1 frame and 243 bytes.	Once per server computer every 12 minutes.
Local Master announcement	1 frame and 250 bytes.	After each announcement request or election.
Workgroup announcement	1 frame and 250 bytes.	Every 15 minutes.
Elections	Many frames and 235 bytes each.	After each computer capable of becoming the Master Browser initializes. This is multiplied by the total number of computers participating.
Finding a backup browser	2 frames and about 450 bytes.	Once per browsing at initial browse attempt.

File Session Traffic

Here are the frame counts and total bytes consumed during File Session events:

Action	Traffic	Frequency
Address resolution	2 frames and 120 bytes.	At each attempt to communicate with another TCP/IP host (when aged from ARP cache).
TCP session	3 frames and 180 bytes.	Once per first connection to each target TCP host.
NetBIOS session	2 frames and 186 bytes.	Once per first NetBIOS connection to a target computer.
SMB protocol negotiation	2 frames and about 350 bytes.	Once per first SMB connection to a target computer.
Connection sequence	2 frames and about 350 bytes.	Once per network resource access.
Session disconnection	5 frames and 360 bytes.	Once per final connection to TCP host has been disconnected.

As far as the actual file transfer process is concerned, this varies tremendously. You must consider the following variables:

- Directory listing transfers overhead
- SMB command processing overhead
- TCP sending and acknowledgment overhead
- IP fragmentation overhead

After you connect to a network share, for example, if the share has about 250 files in its directory, this may require 35,000 to 40,000 bytes of network traffic. To copy a 150,000-byte file, the additional overhead may cause the actual network traffic size to increase to 180,000 bytes. For TCP/IP, Microsoft helps to eliminate network overhead by implementing TCP sliding windows that allow a single acknowledgment for a series of packets.

Domain Database Synchronization

For domain database synchronization, you have a similar function just like file session traffic. You have a negotiation with an additional secure channel setup. The amount of database information that needs to be sent will depend on the Net Logon service settings as well as the total size of the changes. Here are the frame counts and total bytes consumed during domain database synchronization events:

Action	Traffic	Frequency
Find the PDC	4 frames and about 545 bytes.	Once per Backup Domain Controller bootup.
Establish session	11 frames and 1,200 bytes.	Every synchronization event.
Establish secure channel	8 frames and 1,550 bytes.	Every synchronization event.
Verify the databases	6 frames and 1,350 bytes.	Every synchronization event.
PDC update notice	1 frame and about 400 bytes.	Every synchronization event.
Establish a trust relationship	About 100 frames and 15,000 bytes of traffic.	Once per each trust relationship created.
Referencing trusted accounts	About 100 frames and 24,000 bytes of traffic for 11 trusted accounts.	Each attempt to import a referenced account into a trusting domain.
Pass-through authentication	20 frames and about 3,700 bytes of traffic.	Once for the first attempt to access a resource on a trusting computer, or log on to a trusted domain from a trusting computer.

Directory Replication

Although this has not been a popular service due to its many problems (directory replication did not work properly prior to Windows NT 4.0 Service Pack 2), it is still available for the purpose of automating the duplication of read-only files. Here are the frame counts and total bytes consumed during Directory Replication events:

Action	Traffic	Frequency
Announcement	1 frame and about 340 bytes.	Once per importing domain or server for every update of the export tree.
Establish session	9 frames and about 1,300 bytes.	Once from each import server for every update event.
Verify directory	22 frames and about 3,700 bytes.	Once from each import server for every update event.
Update directory	Various amounts of network traffic.	Once from each import server for every update event.

WINS Replication

If you have more than one WINS server in a large internetwork, you may configure your WINS servers to automatically replicate their databases with one another. Here are the frame counts and total bytes consumed during WINS (Windows Internet Naming Service) Replication events:

Action	Traffic	Frequency
Database verification	12 frames and about 900 bytes.	Once per update request to each replication partner.
Database update	About 14 frames and about 2,100 bytes (varies with number of updates).	Once per update request to each replication partner.

Mass Storage Device Issues

Often when planning for disk storage or any other type of secondary storage, all we hear about is disk space. Often, the method and speed of disk access is not heavily documented. Remember to consider the following three factors when choosing the server's data I/O architecture:

- 32-bit SCSI host adapters enhance system performance.
- Bus mastering host adapters also can reduce congestion.
- Always try to use any type of host adapter that allows for asynchronous input or output to take advantage of mirroring and striping across multiple physical disks.

There is also the problem of device support:

- SCSI drives are perceptibly faster than IDE drives running Windows NT.
- Basic IDE drives are limited to controlling two drives.
- SCSI controllers support seven drives, SCSI III up to 15.

16- or 32-bit SCSI controllers are more expensive than IDE controllers or 8-bit SCSI controllers, but they should be used on Windows NT systems. Eight-bit SCSI controllers are too slow and are not supported on Windows NT 4.0 anyway.

Many CD drives also can share a SCSI controller. Newer sound cards incorporate SCSI controllers for CDs. Make sure your SCSI controller has the added ROM support for more than a single drive.

Windows NT has built-in support for the following:

- 94 SCSI host adapters
- 72 CD-ROM drives
- 87 SCSI tape drives
- 24 SCSI removable media systems and scanners

Windows NT is also not compatible with certain BIOS LBA addressing. If using IDE drives greater than 540MB, make sure they follow the EIDE standard or are WD 1003-compatible. *Logical block addressing (LBA)* is a method of sector translation that allows the Enhanced IDE standard to go beyond the 540MB limit. This is a BIOS-level mechanism that is independent of the software or operating system installed on the system.

Computer Names

It is very important to use caution when selecting computer names. The chosen name will be the computer's NetBIOS name and can be the hostname if you are using LMHOSTS or WINS for NBT (NetBIOS over TCP/IP).

Troubleshooting Tip

Do not put spaces in the computer's name. It will cause problems trying to access from MS-DOS–based machines. Even in Windows NT, when you try to reference a server with spaces in its name from the command line, you must use quotation marks to distinguish it from a command-line argument.

Defragmentation Utilities for Windows NT

Regardless of the hearsay about Windows NT's NTFS, its I/O manager, and its improvement on previous file systems, you still have to deal with the problems of fragmentation on Server and Workstation hard drives. Older defragmentation utilities will not run on Windows NT, and special APIs are required for the NTFS file system. The next few paragraphs discuss a few third-party utilities that are available for Windows NT, because there is no inherent utility for Windows NT.

Diskeeper Lite

Diskeeper Lite is a file fragmentation analysis and defragmentation utility for Windows NT (see Figure 6.1). It is available from Executive Software. Contact information for Windows NT is available in Appendix E, "Multi-Vendor Command/Utility Reference and Translator." Figure 6.1 shows how a system can get fragmented by looking at the situation graphically through Diskeeper.

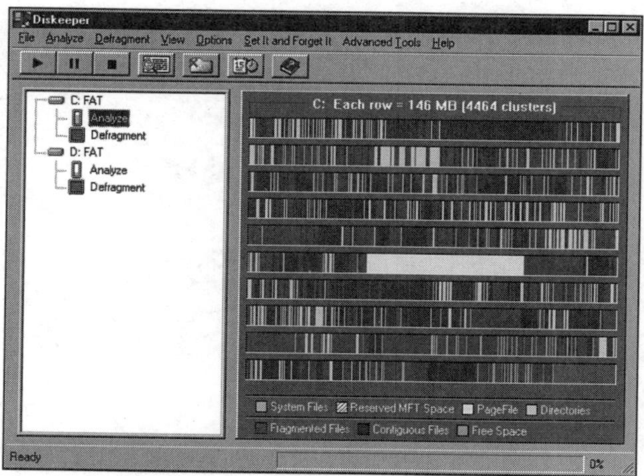

Figure 6.1. *Viewing a fragmented drive in Diskeeper 3.0.*

The Fragmentation Analysis portion on the right shows the state of file fragmentation on the disks. You also have the option to manually defragment the drive. Diskeeper works for all supported read-write file systems in Windows NT.

Author's Note

This utility is not intended to be run from a server to analyze remote disks over a network. To analyze local disks, install this utility on the local system to be analyzed.

Diskeeper

This utility is the full version of Diskeeper. It comes in two versions, one for Server and one for Workstation. It includes Executive Software's "set it and forget it" technology in which you can set a schedule for the service to defragment the drive at certain intervals or during periods of time in which the system is not being used.

Optimizing Domain Controllers

Often people think domain controllers take up a lot of server resources. That is not entirely true. Usually domain controllers are bogged down doing other things. The following recommendations should be followed when planning for and optimizing domain controllers:

- The recommended amount of RAM for a domain controller is roughly 2.5 times the size of the Security Account Manager (SAM).
- The maximum recommended size of the SAM is 40MB.
- The maximum number of objects in the SAM is 40,000.
- Each user takes 1KB of disk space.
- Each global group takes 512 bytes of disk space, plus 12 bytes per member.
- Each local group takes 512 bytes of disk space, plus 36 bytes per member.
- Each computer account takes 512 bytes of disk space.

The following guides can help you to figure out the capacity of servers. It can also give you information on the amount of network bandwidth that will be consumed.

The following steps show the formula used to calculate the number of users a server can support.

For password changes per month:

1. Divide the days before the password expires by 30.
2. Multiply the number of user accounts by the result received in step 1.

For additional changes per month:

1. Multiply the result of the preceding step 2 by .10.
2. Add the number of new user accounts, total group changes, and new computer accounts to the result from the preceding step 2, and the result of the previous step 1.
3. Multiply the result from step 3 by 1KB to get the total amount of data to be replicated each month.

If you need to calculate the number of groups a domain controller can support, you can use the following formula:

For calculating the space used by group accounts:

1. Multiply the total number of users by 12 for a global group. Or, for a local group, multiply the total number of users by 36.
2. To find out the total amount of space used, add the amount of group space to the result you received in step 1.

To calculate the SAM database size:

1. Multiply the total number of users by 1KB.
2. Multiply the number of computer accounts by 0.5 KB.
3. Add the space consumed by groups to the results received in steps 1 and 2 to get the total SAM database size.

Optimizing the Server Service

In terms of optimizing the Server Service, you actually have many built-in utilities to assist in doing this. The next section discusses these utilities.

Using the Command-Line Utility

The `NET CONFIG SERVER¦WORKSTATION /option` command enables you to view or modify the parameters relating to the Workstation or Server Service configuration.

Available configuration options for the Server Service include the following:

- `/autodisconnect:time` Sets the number of minutes a user's session with that computer can be inactive before it is disconnected. If you specify `-1`, the session will never disconnect. The upper limit is 65,535 (a little more than 45 hours).
- `/srvcomment:"text"` Adds a comment to a server for its display during a `net view` command.

- `/hidden: yes¦no` Enables you to hide or show a machine from the Browse List of server resources. The default is `no`.

Available configuration options for the Workstation Service include the following:

- `/charcount:`*`bytes`* Sets the amount of data that Windows NT collects before sending the data to a communications device. The default is 16, but the range goes from 0 to 65,535.
- `/chartime:`*`msec`* Sets the amount of time during which the machine collects data for transmittal before forwarding it to the communication device. The *`msec`* value is 0 to 655,350,000 ms. The default is 250 ms.
- `/charwait:`*`sec`* Sets the number of seconds that Windows NT waits for a communication device to become available. The range is 0 to 65,535 seconds. The default is 3,600.

Configuring the Server Service

The Service Control Manager allows only the startup control for a service. Many network services can be configured in the Network Control Panel application's Server dialog box (see Figure 6.2).

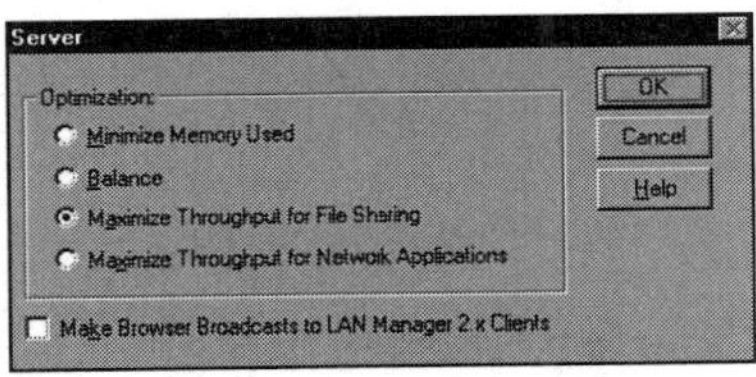

Figure 6.2. *The Server dialog box.*

The configurable options for the Server Service are as follows:

- *Minimize Memory Used* Minimizes its use and initially accepts a lower number of connections (up to 10).
- *Balanced* Initially allocates memory for up to 64 connections.
- *Maximize Throughput for File Sharing* Allocates memory for an unlimited number of connections (71,000 connections).
- *Maximize Throughput for Network Applications* Allocates memory for an unlimited amount of connections, but does not set aside as much memory for cache. This is appropriate for running client/server applications such as SQL Server, SNA Server, or any RPC server.
- *Make Browser Broadcasts to LAN Manager 2.1* Select this check box if there is a LAN Manager 2.x server on the network and you want that server to browse shared resources on this computer.

Table 6.1 shows the Server Service configuration parameter values.

Table 6.1. Server Service configuration parameter values.

Server Optimization	Parameter Values Per Level Server RAM (MB)							
Parameters	8	12	16	32	64	128	512	1024
Minimize Memory Used								
[MAX] Init work items	4	6	8	8	8	8	8	8
Max work items	32	48	64	64	64	64	64	64
Raw work items	8	12	16	16	16	16	16	16
Max Paged Memory (MB)	4	6	8	8	8	8	8	8
Max NonPaged Memory (MB)	2	3	4	4	4	4	4	4
Thread Count Add	2	2	2	2	2	2	2	2
Blocking Threads	2	2	2	2	2	2	2	2
Balance								
[MAX] Init work items	8	12	16	32	32	32	32	32
Max work items	64	96	128	256	256	256	256	256
Raw work items	16	24	32	64	64	64	64	64
Max Paged Memory (MB)	8	12	16	32	32	32	32	32
Max Nonpaged Memory (MB)	4	6	8	16	16	16	16	16
Thread Count Add	2	2	2	5	5	5	5	5
Blocking Threads	2	2	2	4	4	4	4	4
Maximize Throughput								
[MAX] Init work items	16	24	32	64	128	256	256	256
Max work items	128	192	256	512	1024	2048	4096	8192
Raw work items	32	48	64	128	256	512	512	512
Max Paged Memory (MB)	*	*	*	*	*	*	*	*
Max NonPaged Memory (MB)	*	*	*	*	*	*	*	*
Thread Count Add	2	4	5	8	8	8	8	8
Blocking Threads	2	3	4	8	8	8	8	8

***- unlimited**

Optimizing Browsing Traffic

This is probably the most troublesome of network traffic, so it should probably be addressed first. Because there are no built-in direct methods of optimizing this traffic, we have to dig deep into many of the factors that the Browser Service depends on. Several techniques enable us to reduce this traffic.

Disable Unnecessary Services

Disabling unnecessary network services can lessen WINS registration and renewal traffic. Each service that supports NetBIOS must register itself with WINS. If that service is never used, registration time and traffic are wasted, as well as the accompanying renewal traffic. If a computer is not providing NetDDE functions, for example, disable that service. The Server Service can also be disabled if the client is not providing any network resources.

Increase NetBIOS Name Cache

After a NetBIOS name has been resolved, it is placed in an internal NetBIOS name cache. The cache is checked before initiating a request to the WINS sServer whenever name resolution occurs.

By default, entries stay in the cache for 10 minutes (600,000 ms). Increasing this number to a large value will reduce WINS queries for frequently used servers.

To allow entries to remain in the local cache for a longer duration adjust the `HKEY_LOCAL_MACHINE\SYSTEM\CurrentControlSet\Services\NetBT\Parameters\CacheTimeout` to a higher value. This will require fewer resolution attempts for frequently used names.

Implement LMHOSTS

Another method of reducing WINS name resolution traffic is to use the LMHOSTS file. *LMHOSTS* provides resolution of NetBIOS names to IP addresses using a static ASCII text file. The disadvantage of the LMHOSTS file is that it is not dynamic like the WINS server. This means if a new server is brought online, it would need to be manually added to the LMHOSTS file.

Preloading an entry from the LMHOSTS file into the NetBIOS name cache will prevent any network traffic from occurring during resolution of that name, because it would be permanently entered into the NetBIOS name cache. This can be beneficial for a commonly accessed server or set of servers.

> **Tip**
>
> *You can add a* `#PRE` *statement in the LMHOSTS file to use an LMHOSTS file on a centralized server. This will produce network traffic at the startup, but will reduce name query attempts throughout the tenure of the server.*

Adjust Renewal Rate

Although it is possible to adjust the renewal rate (or TTL, time to live) of registered names using WINS Manager, it is not recommended. WINS renewal does not generate a large amount of traffic, so the default of six days is adequate. If there is justification to change the TTL, adjust the renewal interval in WINS Manager.

The Microsoft implementation of WINS configures the client computers to automatically renew their registered names halfway through the TTL duration. With default configuration, this will occur every 72 hours. Therefore, if a WINS client registered six names (for various network services) at startup, it will renew these same six names every 72 hours.

Most of the traffic generated by browsing is initiated automatically by the appropriate browsing computers. These are the Domain Master Browser, the Master Browsers, and the backup browsers. There are three general methods to reduce traffic:

- Reduce the network protocols used
- Reduce the number of browser entries
- Increase the amount of time between browser updates using optimization parameters in the Registry

Reduce Network Protocols

The browsing process operates separately on each installed and bound protocol. Therefore, if TCP/IP, NWLink IPX/SPX, and NetBEUI are all active on the network, each set of browser traffic, elections, host announcements, workgroup announcements, and so on, occur on each protocol independently. This triples the amount of network traffic related to browsing with the only product being a Browse List for three independent protocols. If possible, eliminate one or two of these protocols to greatly reduce the traffic generated for browsing.

Reduce Browser Entries

Disable the server component on computers that do not require sharing of resources. This will reduce the size of the Browse Lists, and therefore, the traffic passing between browser servers. Each type of client, whether Windows for Workgroups, Windows 95, or Windows NT, has a method for disabling the Server Service. Each entry in the Browse List is 27 bytes, plus space for the server comment, if any. Also consider reducing server comments.

Optimization Parameters in the Registry

Two parameters can be configured to control the amount of network traffic generated by the browser. Browsing parameters are found in the Registry in `HKEY_LOCAL_MACHINE\SYSTEM\CurrentControlSet\Services\Browser\Parameters`.

`MasterPeriodicity`

`MasterPeriodicity` specifies how frequently a Master Browser contacts the Domain Master Browser. The default is 720 seconds (12 minutes), with a minimum of 300 seconds (five minutes), and a maximum value of 0x418937 (4,294,967 seconds). This parameter is added as a `REG_DWORD` and can be changed dynamically without restarting the computer. This parameter should be added on the Master Browsers.

This parameter does affect WAN traffic, because each subnet within a domain has a Master Browser for the domain on that subnet.

`BackupPeriodicity`

`BackupPeriodicity` specifies how frequently a backup browser contacts the Master Browser. Adding this parameter as a reg_dword requires restarting the computer. The default value for `BackupPeriodicity` is 720 seconds. Configuring it to 1,800 (30 minutes) will reduce the frequency of Browse List updates. This parameter does not affect the WAN, because backup browsers always communicate with a local Master Browser, never with a remote one.

Optimizing File Session Traffic

The bulk of file session traffic happens after a session is established. However, session establishment traffic is repeated any time one computer needs to establish a session with another computer. There are at least two methods that can help limit the amount of traffic, described in the next few sections.

Remove Excess Protocols

The best way to optimize file session traffic is to remove any excess protocols, because connection requests are sent over all protocols simultaneously. Removing unnecessary protocols will reduce the number of frames on the network.

Provide Close Proximity Between Clients and Servers

Ensuring that commonly accessed servers are in close proximity to the users who most often access them can reduce the network traffic throughout the enterprise. If a single group of users on one subnet generate the most activity to a specific server, move that server to the users' subnet if possible. This will eliminate the traffic generated during file session activity from using valuable network bandwidth on other subnets.

Optimizing DNS Traffic

A simple address lookup takes only two directed frames. Optimization efforts should be focused on reducing recursion traffic that may result if a client's DNS server does not have the requested address. There are three methods for reducing recursion traffic:

- *Do not configure recursion.* Of course, this limits the functionality of DNS by not being able to provide all requested names, or it requires the addition of all host names to each DNS server, which is an administrative burden.
- *Ensure that the DNS server that will most likely resolve most of the names for a particular client is designated as its DNS server.* This reduces the chance of a recursive lookup and its associated traffic.
- *Increase the TTL of cached entries.* When one DNS server sends a name lookup request to another DNS server, the original DNS server, upon receiving the address, will cache that address for a period of time, which is the TTL of the record. By default, the TTL of a cached resolved name is 60 minutes. The default for a NetBIOS name resolved by a recursive lookup using WINS is 10 minutes. These TTLs are configurable using DNS Manager.

Optimizing Trust Relationship Traffic

Although trust relationships do not produce a high percentage of traffic, two areas can help reduce trust-related traffic. The next two sections discuss these areas.

Reduce the Number of Trusts

The obvious means of reducing trust relationship traffic is to reduce the number of trusts. This means giving up the benefits of the master resource domain model. It may be worth reviewing existing or planned resource domains, however, to ensure that each one is appropriate and necessary.

Verify that each one-way trust is appropriate. In an environment where two domains trust each other, for example, are both trusts really required? If not, break the nonessential trust.

There is very little maintenance traffic related to trust relationships. After the trust has been established, importing and verifying trusted accounts, and pass-through authentication generate most of the traffic.

Use Group Accounts

You can reduce the traffic associated with the verification of trusted accounts by applying either of the following methods:

- At the trusted domain, add the appropriate users to a global group.
- At the trusting domain, add the trusted global group to a local group or local resource.

By adding a set of users from a global group, as opposed to adding the users individually to a local group or resource, the traffic required to verify the security IDs (SIDs) and associate names with the SIDs can be reduced.

In a simple test, the lookup of a single SID for a global group used 552 bytes, whereas the same lookup for SIDs for two trusted user accounts used 636 bytes. Although this is not that much extra traffic, it was only for two users. Often, many users from a trusted domain are allowed access to a resource in a trusting domain. By using a global group, the traffic required to look up those accounts can be reduced; this could be substantial over a period of time.

Strategies for Reducing Domain Database Synchronization Traffic

The NetLogon service, unlike some other Windows NT Server services, cannot be disabled. Whether the domain design has a BDC at each remote location or BDCs located centrally, there is one way to reduce traffic: Change the default parameters for NetLogon synchronization and replication.

One of the primary jobs of NetLogon is to keep the user account database in sync on all the BDCs with the PDC. Most of the traffic generated by browsing is initiated automatically by the appropriate browsing computers, the Domain Master Browser, the Master Browsers, and the backup browsers.

The Registry path for the parameters for the NetLogon service is the following:

```
HKEY_LOCAL_MACHINE\System\CurrentControlSet\Services\Netlogon\Parameters
```

Author's Note

The NetLogon share name should also be in the path for logon scripts.

ChangeLogSize

This value has a data type of `REG_DWORD`. It can have a range from 64KB to 4MB, with a default of 64KB. This value defines the size (in bytes) of the Change log. The Change log exists both in memory and on disk at `%Systemroot%\Netlogon.chg`.

Because the setting of this value does not degrade system performance, it is advisable to leave it at the 0x4000000 (4MB) setting instead of returning it to the 64KB default setting. The 4MB setting ensures that the domain's database will not be completely replicated when large changes are made in the future.

The `ChangeLogSize` value should be the same on all BDCs to ensure that when a BDC is promoted to a PDC, it has the same `ChangeLogSize` value. The minimum (and typical) size of an entry is 32 bytes. Therefore, a 64KB Change log holds about 2,000 changes.

`MaximumMailslotMessages`

This value has a default data type of `REG_DWORD`. It can have a range from 1 to 0xFFFFFFFF messages, with the default value of 500. This value specifies the maximum number of mailslot messages that will be queued to the NetLogon service. Even though the NetLogon service is designed to process incoming mailslot messages immediately, it can get backed up when processing requests on a heavily loaded system. Each mailslot message consumes about 1,500 bytes of nonpaged pool until it is processed. By setting this entry to a low value, you can govern the maximum amount of nonpaged pool that can be consumed. If this value entry is set too low, NetLogon might miss important incoming mailslot messages.

`MaximumMailslotTimeout`

This value has a data type of `REG_DWORD`. It can have a range from 5 to 0xFFFFFFFF seconds. The default value is 10. This value specifies the maximum acceptable age (in seconds) of an incoming mailslot message. If NetLogon receives a mailslot message that arrived longer ago than this, it ignores the message. This allows NetLogon to process messages that are more recent. If this value entry is set too low, NetLogon will ignore important incoming mailslot messages.

Ideally, NetLogon processes each mailslot message in a fraction of a second. This value entry is significant only if the Windows NT server is overloaded.

`MailslotDuplicateTimeout`

This value has a data type of `REG_DWORD`, with a range from 0 to 5 seconds. It can have a default value of 2. This value specifies the interval (in seconds) during which a duplicate incoming mailslot message will be ignored. NetLogon compares each mailslot message received with the preceding mailslot message received. If the preceding message was received within this many seconds and the messages are identical, this message will be ignored.

Set this value entry to `0` to disable this feature. You should disable this feature if the network is configured so that this machine can see certain incoming mailslot messages but cannot respond to them.

For instance, a domain controller might be separated from a Windows NT Workstation–based machine by a bridge/router. The bridge/router might filter outgoing NBF broadcasts but allow incoming ones. Therefore, NetLogon might respond to an NBF mailslot message (only to be filtered out by the bridge/router) and not respond to a subsequent NBF mailslot message. You can solve this problem by disabling this feature (or preferably by reconfiguring the bridge/router). If you set this value entry too high, NetLogon will ignore retry attempts from a client.

`Pulse`

This value has a data type of `REG_DWORD` and can have a range from 60 to 172,800 seconds (48 hours). The default value is 300 (5 minutes). This value defines the typical pulse frequency (in seconds). All SAM/LSA changes made within this time are collected together. After this time, a pulse is sent to each BDC that needs the changes. No pulse is sent to a BDC that is up to date.

When this value is not specified in the Registry, NetLogon determines optimal values depending on the domain controller's load.

`PulseConcurrency`

This value has a data type of `REG_DWORD`. It can have a range from 1 to 500 pulses and have a default value of 20. This value defines the maximum number of simultaneous pulses the PDC sends to BDCs. NetLogon sends pulses to individual BDCs. The BDCs respond by asking for any database changes.

To control the maximum load, these responses place on the PDC, the PDC has only the number of pulses specified by `PulseConcurrency` "pending" at once. The PDC should be sufficiently powerful to support this many concurrent replication RPC calls. Increasing the value of `PulseConcurrency` increases the load on the PDC. Decreasing the value of `PulseConcurrency` increases the time it takes for a domain with a large number of BDCs to get a SAM/LSA change to all the BDCs.

`PulseMaximum`

This value has a default value of `REG_DWORD`. This can have a range from 60 to 172,800 seconds (48 hours). The default value is 7,200 (2 hours). This value defines the maximum pulse frequency (in seconds). Every BDC will be sent at least one pulse at this frequency regardless of whether its database is up to date.

`PulseTimeout1`

This value has a data type of `REG_DWORD`. It can have a range of 1 to 120 seconds, with a default value of 5. This value defines how long (in seconds) the PDC waits for a nonresponsive BDC. When a BDC is sent a pulse, it must respond within this time period. If it does not, the BDC is considered to be nonresponsive. A nonresponsive BDC is not counted against the limit specified by `PulseConcurrency`, allowing the PDC to send a pulse to another BDC in the domain.

If this number is too large, a domain with a large number of nonresponsive BDCs takes a long time to complete a partial replication. If this number is too small, a slow BDC might mistakenly be treated as nonresponsive. When the BDC finally does respond, it will partially replicate from the PDC, increasing the load on the PDC.

`PulseTimeout2`

This value has a data type of `REG_DWORD`. It can have a range from 60 to 3,600 seconds, with a default value of 300 (5 minutes). This value defines how long (in seconds) a PDC waits for a BDC to complete partial replication. Even though a BDC initially responds to a pulse (as described for `PulseTimeout1`), it must continue making replication progress or the BDC is considered nonresponsive.

Each time the BDC calls the PDC, the BDC is given the number of seconds specified by `PulseTimeout2` to be considered responsive. If this number is too large, a slow BDC (or one that has its replication rate artificially governed) will consume one of the `PulseConcurrency` slots. If this number is too small, the load on the PDC will increase because of the large number of BDCs doing a partial replication.

Author's Note

This value entry affects only the cases where a BDC cannot retrieve all the changes to the SAM/LSA database in a single RPC call. This happens only if a large number of changes are made to the database.

`Randomize`

This value has a data type of `REG_DWORD`. It can have a range from 0 to 120 seconds, with a default value of 1. This value specifies the BDC back-off period (in seconds). When the BDC receives a pulse, it backs off for a period from zero seconds to the number of seconds specified in `Randomize` before it calls the PDC. The pulse is sent to individual BDCs, so this value entry should be small.

The value of `Randomize` should be smaller than the value of `PulseTimeout1`. Consider that the time to replicate a SAM/LSA change to all the BDCs in a domain will be greater than:

```
[(Randomize/2) * NumberOfBdcsInDomain] / PulseConcurrency
```

When this value is not specified in the Registry, NetLogon determines optimal values depending on the domain controller's load.

`ReplicationGovernor`

This value has a data type of `REG_DWORD` and can have a range from 0 to 100%. By default, its value ranges all the way to 100%. This value defines both the size of the data transferred on each call to the PDC and the frequency of those calls. Setting `ReplicationGovernor` to 50%, for example, means a call will use a 64KB buffer rather than a 128KB buffer, and will have a replication call outstanding on the Internet only for a maximum of 50% of the time. If you set the `ReplicationGovernor` value too low, replication might never complete. A value of 0 causes NetLogon to never replicate, and the SAM/LSA database will get completely out of sync.

BDCs can be configured for the variances of WAN types. `ReplicationGovernor` allows the administrator to control the partial synchronization parameters. This value entry must be set individually on each BDC.

Author's Note

It is also possible to configure different replication rates at different times of the day by using a script file with the `AT` *command (for example,* `net stop netlogon`, `reg.ini scriptfile`, `net start netlogon`*). The script file contains the path to the* `RegistrationGovernor` *value and the new Registry entries.* `Regini.exe` *is included in the Windows NT Resource Kit.*

`Scripts`

This value has a data type of `REG_SZ`. The data for this value is actually a pathname. It specifies the fully qualified path to logon scripts. This value can be set by using Services in the Control Panel or by using the Server Manager.

`Update`

This value has a data type of `REG_SZ` and its range is either `Yes` or `No`. This value defaults to `No`. When this value is set to `Yes`, NetLogon fully synchronizes the database each time it starts.

Part II

Network Integration

Chapter 7

UNIX Integration

- **UNIX Basics**
  We will look at how UNIX differs from Windows NT.
- **Overview of UNIX and NT Inherent Integration**
  We will examine built-in utilities that enable UNIX and Windows NT to work together.
- **NFS Maestro—an NFS Server and Client Software for Windows NT**
  We will discuss how to connect back and forth between UNIX and Windows NT for file transfer purposes and directory mounting.
- **SAMBA - SMB Software for UNIX**
  We will discuss how to implement SAMBA to make UNIX file systems emulate Windows NT shares.
- **Trusted Computing Solutions**
  Learn about some utilities that allow for application transparency between Windows NT and UNIX.

UNIX Basics

The UNIX operating system originated as one of the most heavily used mainframe operating systems of the 1970s and 1980s. It has evolved into a cross-platform low- to mid-range solution for multi-user network environments. What makes UNIX strong is the fact that it revolves its rich processing and management around time slicing. It is also very portable, written in the C programming language. There are many different, but pretty much similar, versions of UNIX.

UNIX Flavors

These UNIX clones go by many different names; the most common are:

- Xenix
- SunOS
- Linux
- SCO
- Solaris
- System V
- Ultrix
- Ros
- IX/370
- Berkeley (BSD)

All of these flavors are usually grouped into two areas (or schools of thought): *Berkeley (BSD)* and *System V*. This evolution stemmed primarily from Bell Labs donating UNIX to universities in 1975. Most shells and commands have two implementations (see the following sections). But both of them share a common goal of a simple interface with a philosophy of doing things the best way, and not just the most expedient.

Linux

A college student developed *Linux* in 1991. It later grew into a cult operating system used and refined heavily by other students and programmers until it became one of the more popular flavors of UNIX. This was primarily because it was free, heavily documented on the Internet, and was developed for the Intel x86 platform. Linux uses Berkely's implementation.

UNIX Shells

The *UNIX shell* is the command interpreter program that accepts your input and carries out your commands. It is *not* the operating system itself, but rather the interface between the user and the operating system. The shell is a program that is executed when you are logged in, and when you end the shell program, you are logged out of the system. There is nothing special about the shell program—it is just a regular program, like any other on the UNIX system. In fact, once you are logged on, you can execute another shell just as you would execute a program. The ability to run multiple shell levels can be used to perform some interesting tricks that will be detailed later in this file.

There is also more than one kind of shell. All the shells perform the same basic function of interpreting the user's commands, but there are a few differences. Here is a list of the different shells, their unique characteristics, and how to tell which shell you are using:

- sh. The Bourne shell, the standard shell of UNIX System V, and the focus of this file. This shell gives user-level accounts a command prompt of `$`, and `#` for superuser accounts. On Berkeley BSD UNIX, this shell gives an ampersand (`&`) prompt.

- csh. The C shell, developed by the Berkely University Science department. This shell is pretty much the same as the Bourne shell, but features different shell programming control structures.
- ksh. The Korn shell, which combines features of both the Bourne shell and the C shell. It boasts the Bourne shell's easier shell programming, along with the C shell's aliasing and history.
- rsh. The restricted Bourne shell, used for accounts that the superuser wishes to restrict the commands available to. It will not allow you to execute commands outside of your search path, and will not let you change directories or the values of shell variables.
- bash. The Bourne Again shell. This is a very popular one used in Linux and enhances the original Bourne shell.

Daemons

Like services, *daemons* run independently of the currently logged on user or users. The first process `init` is responsible for starting all of the daemons and checks all of the file systems for consistency and stability. It is also responsible for determining run levels (single, multi-user) and it makes sure that the user logins (`gettys`) are ready and working. An instance of `getty` runs for each login.

UNIX System Administration

There are more than 1,000 official user and system administrative utilities and more than 100,000 unofficial. This of course means that there will be a substantial learning curve even greater than Windows NT. Some of the more common elements include:

- syslog. Responsible for logging error, warning, and other messages that are generated by the kernel and system processes.
- crontab. Scheduling batch processes and commands to run periodically using the `cron` command. Each user has their own separate crontab.
- mail. All messaging by default is managed through a mail transfer agent like sendmail or smail. On UNIX filesystems it is usually stored in /var/spool/mail.

The UNIX Filesystem

The UNIX filesystem is unusual in that it is one logical directory structure rather than a series of logical drives with separate drive letters. For each machine there is a root `/` that is stored on a local disk. It contains the operating system kernel and all of the necessary files for booting the system. Beneath the root on most flavors of UNIX, you will likely find these directory structures:

- /usr. Contains user commands, libraries, on-line manual pages, and other binary and unchanging files. This directory is usually heavily shared.
- /var. Contains files that change constantly such as print spool files, message spool files, log files, news, and the formatted man pages. All temporary directories and files are stored beneath this structure as well.
- /home. Contains the user's home directories. It is usually mounted as a physically separate file system for backup purposes.
- /bin. Contains system commands that will be needed during system bootup.
- /sbin. Contains commands like /bin that are system-based but not needed or used much.
- /etc. Contains system and network configuration files as well as startup scripts specific to the machine.
- /dev. The device directory which contains the special device files for all of the devices. They are named using special conventions. These files are first created during the installation but can be created later via a program or a script.

UNIX/NT Integration Issues

The main problem involves the fact that Windows NT and UNIX are two operating systems with their own clients and client services. There are many similarities between the two, and some differences that must be overcome. The biggest problem for integration is *seamless integration*: One or the other emulates the behavior of the other. Although Windows NT has seamless integration solutions for NetWare and Apple, they do not have all that many built-in solutions for UNIX integration other than the basic TCP/IP services.

Both operating systems provide the following:

- File and print services.
- Central administration of users and security.
- Advanced network services for users and administration.

With some specific software upgrades, they can provide their files and printers to clients from the other OS:

- Windows NT can provide file and print services to UNIX clients.
- UNIX can provide file and print services to Windows NT clients.

A Comparison of Windows NT and UNIX

Both UNIX and Windows NT are valued as *heterogeneous* in terms of capabilities because they both have the potential to support multiple network and transport protocols. Supporting multiple protocols is, however, more an issue in the UNIX world. In some cases, there is only TCP/IP inherently with certain flavors; in the case of Linux, however, there is arguably excessive potential.

SMB File Sharing is optional on UNIX but a major force by default in Windows NT. Macintosh File Sharing is also optional on the UNIX side. NFS File Sharing is common and, in some cases, a standard on most versions of UNIX; in Windows NT, on the other hand, it is left up to third-party applications. This is the same with X Application Support on Windows NT.

Both are very similar in security. They both require a mandatory user logon along with Discretionary Access Control. They both also offer extensive auditing and tracking capabilities.

Integration from Windows NT

File Manager or Explorer cannot browse UNIX file shares without the support of additional software. Mapping a connection to a share on UNIX can be performed the same way as for any Windows NT share using additional software, but does not occur by default. The only way to transfer files without additional software is through Internet Services.

Integration from UNIX

Remote file systems from Windows NT are mounted at local UNIX system file directory points for access via standard UNIX commands.

Network File System, or *NFS*, is the traditional UNIX network file sharing software. NFS shares can be accessed as if they were local to the UNIX file system. The NFS shares are "mounted" because a local directory NFS is not included with Windows NT by default, but can be included via third-party software.

Applications such as Telnet (see Figure 7.1) and FTP enable users from Windows NT computers to connect to UNIX hosts for certain services. These applications usually fall into these categories:

- TCP/IP-based utilities primarily used for network testing and services such as PING, TRACERT, and NSLOOKUP
- Remote command client services, such as RCP, RSH, and REXEC

```
Telnet - gc-consulting.com
Connect  Edit  Terminal  Help
-rw-r--r--   1 root  wheel       51 Jun  5 05:15 resolv.conf
-rw-r--r--   1 root  wheel      844 Jan 20  1997 rpc
drwxr-xr-x  11 root  wheel      512 Jan 29  1997 samba_samples
-rw-r--r--   1 root  wheel    14450 Jan 27  1997 security
-rw-rw-r--   1 root  wheel        0 Jan 20  1997 sendmail.cT
-rw-r-----   1 root  wheel    42808 Jun  4 10:47 sendmail.cf
-rw-rw-r--   1 root  wheel        0 Jan 20  1997 sendmail.cw
-rw-r--r--   1 root  wheel     4433 Jan 20  1997 services
-rw-r--r--   1 root  wheel      178 Jan 20  1997 shells
-rw-r--r--   1 root  wheel     3727 Jan 20  1997 shlib.map
-rw-r--r--   1 root  bin          0 Jan 20  1997 skeykeys
drwxr-xr-x   2 root  wheel      512 Jan 29  1997 sliphome
-rw-------   1 root  wheel   593920 Jun 24 00:11 spwd.db
-rw-r--r--   1 root  wheel     1557 Jan 20  1997 syslog.conf
lrwxr-xr-x   1 root  wheel       25 Jun 24 02:10 termcap -> ../usr/share/misc/
termcap
-rw-r--r--   1 root  wheel     1952 May 10 15:24 ttys
-r--r--r--   1 root  netdial  12238 Jan 27  1997 ttys.conf
-rw-r--r--   1 root  netdial   1512 May 10 15:24 ttys.conf.local
drwxr-xr-x   3 uucp  uucp       512 Jan 29  1997 uucp
-rw-r--r--   1 root  wheel    57344 Jun 24 17:05 vu.db
-rw-r--r--   1 root  wheel     1270 May 10 15:22 weekly
-rw-r--r--   1 root  wheel      493 Jan 20  1997 weekly.local
%
```

Figure 7.1. *Telnetting to UNIX from Windows NT.*

Mail Integration

Windows NT 4.0 provides an SMTP client that allows ease of messaging across Windows NT and UNIX platforms (see Figure 7.2). Most flavors of UNIX facilitate support for sendmail, which is an SMTP/POP3-compliant service for UNIX. Users can set up the Internet Mail option (see Figure 7.3), supply the UNIX hostname and user account/password combination, and can then download their mail to their local machines.

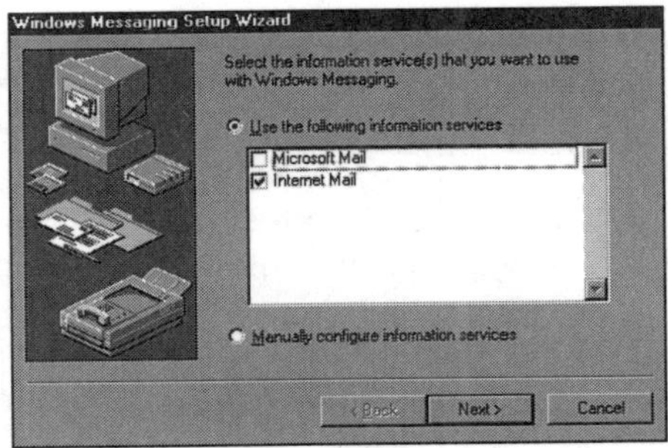

Figure 7.2. *The Windows Messaging Setup Wizard.*

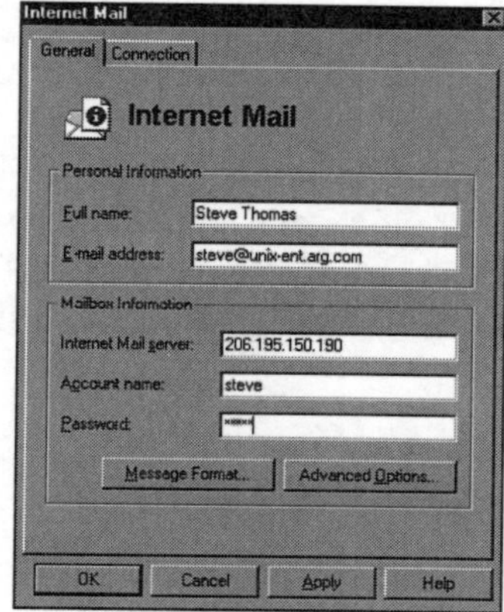

Figure 7.3. *The Internet Mail dialog box.*

Trusted Computing Solutions

In UNIX, the term *trusted computing* implies that certain users from certain computers have trusted access and run certain processes on a computer. This can provide an excellent facility for connectivity, application integration, and remote administration.

From Windows NT to UNIX

From Windows NT to UNIX, a few built-in utilities exist primarily as TCP/IP applications. We reviewed trusted computing earlier for remote administration purposes. We look at these same utilities as a means of integrating UNIX and Windows NT.

RSH

The RSH (Remote Shell) utility will run a command on any remote host running the RSH service.

The format for this utility is as follows:

```
RSH host [-l username] [-n] command
```

The available options include the following:

host	Specifies the remote host on which to run the command.
-l *username*	Specifies the username to use on the remote host. If omitted, the logged on username is used.
-n	Redirects the input of RSH to NULL.
command	Specifies the command to run.

RCP

This connectivity command copies files between a Window NT computer and another utility. The `rcp` command can also be used for third-party transfer to copy files between two computers running a Remote Shell service when the command is issued from a Windows NT computer. The remote shell daemon is available on UNIX computers, but not on Windows NT by default, so the Windows NT computer can only participate as the system from which the commands are issued.

The format for the rcp utility is as follows:

```
RCP [-a ¦ -b] [-h] [-r] [host][.user:]source [host][.user:] path\destination
```

Available options include the following:

`-a`	Specifies ASCII Transfer Mode. This mode converts the EOL characters to a carriage return for UNIX and a carriage return/line feed for personal computers. This is the default Transfer Mode.
`-b`	Specifies Binary Image Transfer Mode.
`-h`	Transfers hidden files.
`-r`	Copies the contents of all subdirectories; the copied destination must be a directory.
host	Specifies the local or remote host. If *host* is specified as an IP address, you must specify the user.
user:	Specifies a username to use rather than the current username.
source	Specifies the files to copy.
path\ destination	Specifies the path relative to the logon directory on the remote host. Use the escape characters (\ , ", or ') in remote paths to use wildcard characters on the remote host.

REXEC

Like RSH, REXEC runs a process on a remote computer. The only significant difference between this utility and RSH is the fact that the user causes the process to initialize wholly on that machine for the purpose of client/server interprocess communication. This is very useful in X Window environments.

Available options for REXEC include the following:

```
REXEC host [-l username] [-n] command
```

host	Specifies the remote host on which to run the command.
-l *username*	Specifies the username on the remote host.
-n	Redirects the input of REXEC to NULL.
command	Specifies the command to run.

From UNIX to Windows NT

Because Windows NT does not support a lot of server-side TCP/IP utilities, we are even shorter in the inherent support for UNIX to Windows NT integration. We can look to utilities, such as the Windows NT Resource Kit, to complete these solutions.

The Remote Shell Service for Windows NT

This service is offered in the Windows NT Resource Kit and allows such utilities as RCP, RSH, and REXEC to run from non-Windows NT or Windows NT computers *to* Windows NT computers. These three utilities in the preceding section can then be initiated on UNIX hosts to affect Windows NT computers. This would complete a trusted computing solution for UNIX and Windows NT.

It is important to note that these three utilities will differ possibly on certain flavors of UNIX.

The installation of the Remote Shell service is quite simple. After installing the Windows NT Resource Kit, copy Rshsetup.exe, Rshsvc.exe, and Rshsvc.dll to the %Systemroot%\System32 folder, and then run the following commands from the command prompt:

```
rshsetup %systemroot%\system32\rshsvc.exe %systemroot%\system32\rshsvc.dll
```

Then start the service by typing the following command:

```
net start rshsvc
```

You can also stop the service. At the command prompt, type:

```
net stop rshsvc
```

The RSH service in Windows NT is set up in the same capacity as it is in UNIX environments. To set up client access to the Remote Shell service, you must place a .rhosts file in the %Systemroot%\System32 folder\Drivers\Etc folder. The .rhosts file (see Figure 7.4) should contain one or more entries of the following type, each entry appearing on one line:

```
<hostname> <username1> <username2> <username3>
```

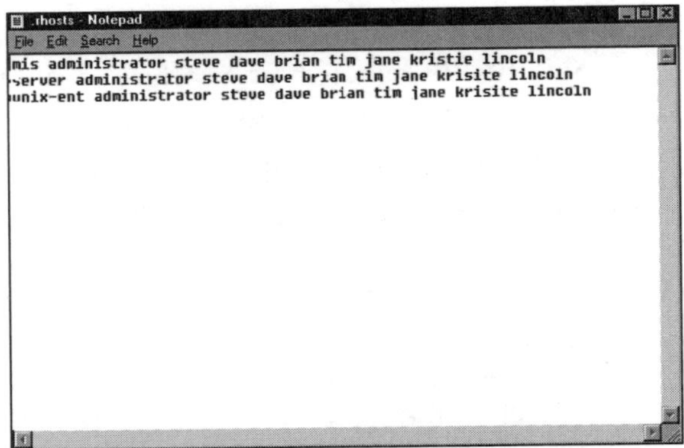

Figure 7.4. *Editing the .rhosts file in Notepad.*

The first field is the hostname of the computer that is allowed access. Every user who is allowed access then follows it on that host, separated by commas (refer to Figure 7.4).

Users can then use trusted computing commands on the UNIX side for Windows NT control and operation (such as the `rsh` command in Figure 7.5).

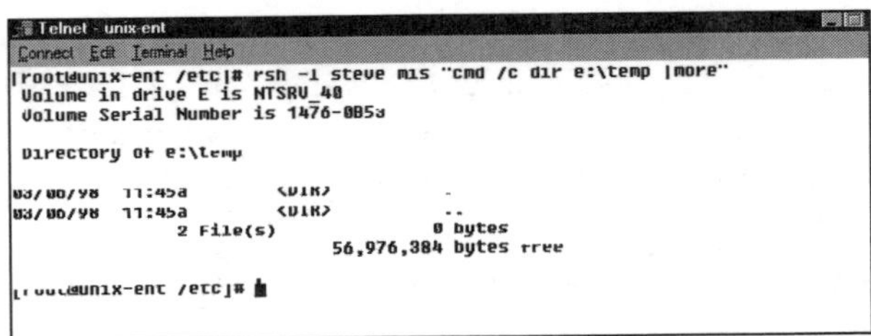

Figure 7.5. *The* `rsh` *command being run from a UNIX host.* `rsh` *is using the NT internal command* `dir`.

NFS Solutions

The most important add-on for UNIX and Windows NT integration will be NFS. The next few sections discuss NFS as well as NFS solutions for Windows NT.

NFS (Network File System)

NFS (developed by Sun Microsystems) provides directory points that can be exported (or shared out) to all or specified clients. It also provides local mount points for imported (mapped to) NFS file systems.

When designing NFS, Sun sought to provide universal network access to files on the network regardless of the operating system or machine platform. It also wanted to design a method where files on a remote file system could be accessed at a speed of at least 80% that of a local file system.

Seamless integration can be accomplished by allowing all participating nodes on the network to export some or all of their local file system using NFS. Defining these exports in UNIX is like sharing a file in UNIX. Using the TCP/IP host-to-host User Datagram Protocol (UDP) allowed for the speed goal, but does not give us the reliability that TCP does. The exported file systems are mounted by the client machines that assign what will appear to them as a "local drive" or a "directory name" to these remote junction points.

Hummingbird NFS Server

With Windows NT, you can install an NFS server package. This will allow UNIX hosts and Windows NT clients running NFS to connect to a Windows NT Server. Users can share local PC resources with other users on a LAN, including file services, CD-ROMs, and printers attached to the PC. Hummingbird offers two NFS products for the Windows NT environment: NFS Maestro for Windows NT-Client, and NFS Maestro Server for Windows NT.

Configuration Files

In traditional UNIX systems, configuration files are used to manage services (called *daemons*). The /etc/fstab is the most involved NFS setup file, but there are a few others, as described in the following sections.

The NFS configuration files in UNIX include the following:

/etc/fstab	This file contains entries that specify that certain local file systems are to mount from remote file systems.
/etc/hosts	This is the standard name-to-IP address mappings file.
/etc/exports	This file contains directory hierarchies that the server provides to other systems on the network, or the client received from the host.

The /etc/fstab file is not used in most Windows NT NFS packages. In UNIX, the /etc/fstab is the major NFS setup file. It contains the parameters to provide the `mount` command in terms of file systems and disk partitions. The `mount` command is invoked at the operating system startup using one of the /etc/rc.* files. Here are the parameters available with the /etc/fstab file:

share directory filesystem options freq pass

share	Source of the share to mount. It includes the following syntax: *hostname: share-directory*.
directory	The local drive on the local computer.
filesystem	The type of file system. Enter **nfs** here.
options	File system options, including hard or soft, bg or efg, rw or ro, and int. The normal set would be hard,bg,ro,intr.
freq	The number of days between dumps. Should be set to zero for NFS use.
pass	The partition check-pass number. Should be set to zero for NFS use.

NFS Maestro's Export Editor

Export Editor provides a graphical interface to the Exports configuration file (see Figure 7.6).

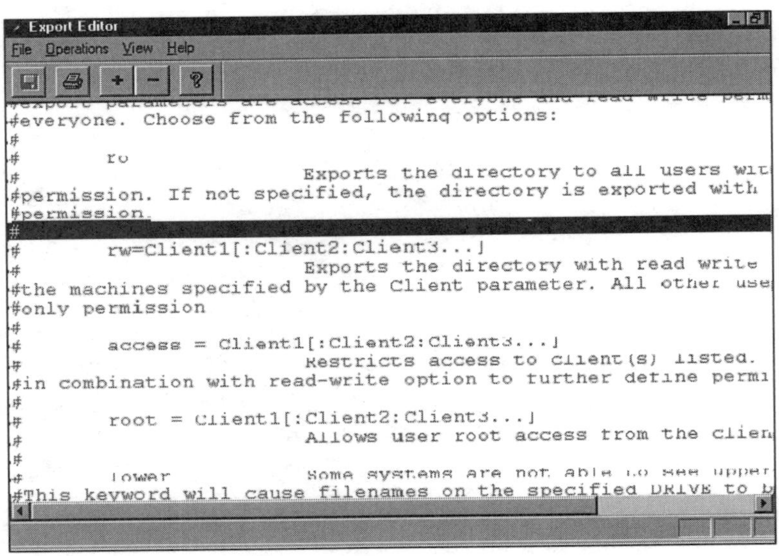

Figure 7.6. *The Export Editor.*

Export Filesystem Syntax

In the Exports file, blank lines and lines beginning with the # symbol are treated as comments and are ignored. Each non-comment line in the file specifies one remote mount point. The first field or item on a line is the mount point path, followed optionally by export options and specific hosts separated by white space.

Options include the following:

```
Resource [host1[:host2 ... :hostn]]

Resource [option[,option...]]
```

The `Resource` option refers to the queue name or pathname for the directory. UNIX-type entries are also valid. For example:

```
/usr/home=c:\usr\home
```

Hostname or IP address—client's machine name. By separating them with colons, you can enter more than one host. For example:

```
Gccidev1:gccidev2
```

`Option` specifies optional characteristics for the directory being exported. Separating the options with commas as shown earlier enables users to enter more than one option. The first option must be preceded with a dash. The default export parameters are access for everyone and read/write permission for everyone.

You can choose from the following options:

Option	**Result**
`ro`	Exports the directory to all users with read-only permission.
`rw=Client1:Client2`	Exports the directory with read/write permission to the machines `Client1` and `Client2`. All other users have read-only access.
`access=Client1`	Restricts access to the machine `Client1`. Access can also be used in combination with the `ro`/`rw` permission parameters to further define permissions.
`root=Client2:Client3`	Allows machines `Client2` and `Client3` root access.
`-lower`	Converts the exported file system to lowercase, because some systems cannot see uppercase file systems. Note that this parameter applies to the entire drive used in the file system specification, not just that file system. (That is, `/c/usr` applies to all the C: drive, not just `usr` on the C: drive.)

Windows NT permissions cannot be changed with permissions set in an exported file system. In other words, say LINC is a user with limited access on the Windows NT system HOST3, and the option `ROOT=HOST3` is used in exporting the file system. LINC will not have ROOT access on the exported file system because he does not have ROOT access on the Windows NT system in the first place.

Inetd Server Suite

Both Hummingbird NFS Maestro Client and Server provide support for Inetd32 (see Figure 7.7). This is a full-fledged INET daemon, which does an excellent job of filling the TCP/IP service gaps within Windows NT.

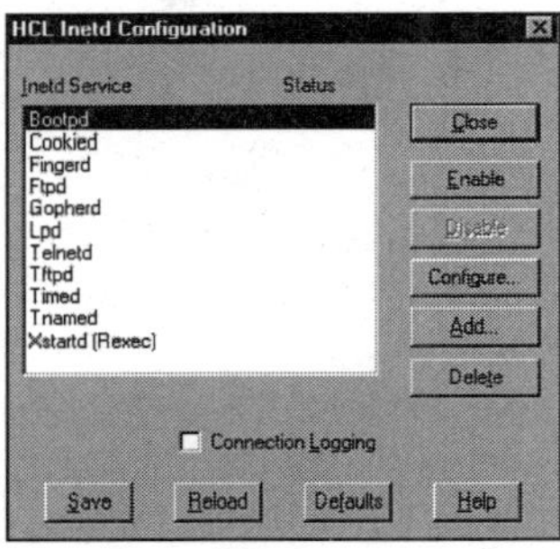

Figure 7.7. *The HCL Inetd Configuration dialog box.*

Desktop Integration

NFS Maestro also allows for Microsoft UNC support, so the user will have transparency when connecting to both Microsoft and UNIX resources. You can do this through virtually the same places where you access Microsoft resources because File Manager and Explorer browsing of NFS resources will be the exact same procedure as browsing for Microsoft resources.

Network Application Suite

Hummingbird Maestro products provide an extensive selection of high-performance TCP/IP client and server applications. For Windows NT and Windows 95 users, Hummingbird Maestro's native 32-bit TCP/IP applications are Internet Engineering Task Force (IETF)-compliant and integrate seamlessly, delivering the highest performance by using the multithreading and multitasking capabilities of 32-bit operating systems.

Hummingbird Maestro products include the following:

- TCP/IP applications such as Telnet and FTP
- Diagnostic tools
- Administrative utilities
- Advanced applications such as TN3270 and TN5250
- Integrated Internet/intranet applications, including Gather, the Columbus Web Browser, email, NetBook and Network News client

Hummingbird Maestro shared installation capability, Hummingbird Basic language WorkBench for script writing, Inetd daemon suite, Setup Configurator (Sconfig), and integrated Socks V4.2 security provide the most powerful and advanced administration functionality of any TCP/IP application suite today.

Telnet Profile Options

One strong feature that NFS Maestro provides for Windows NT is better Telnet clients and servers for Windows NT. The HOST Explorer utility provides a very powerful set of CRT emulators, host presentations, and terminal emulators, including Telnet, which offer many more options than the built-in Telnet.

Shares Maintenance

NFS Maestro Server provides a Share Editor to help translate Windows NT Server file systems and shares and translate them into NFS-compatible mount points. You can also establish bandwidth restrictions as well as UNIX-like access permissions.

RPC Info Utility

The RPC Info utility can be used to provide remote host Remote Procedure Call (RPC) information. You can use this to see whether NFS services are running on a remote machine.

The display information includes the following (see Figure 7.8):

- *Number*. The vendor's identification number for the program or service provided.
- *Ver*. The version of the protocol.
- *Port*. This displays the port number registered on the host.
- *Protocol*. Indicates whether the program supports the TCP or the UDP protocol.
- *Program*. Lists the name of the programs and services provided.

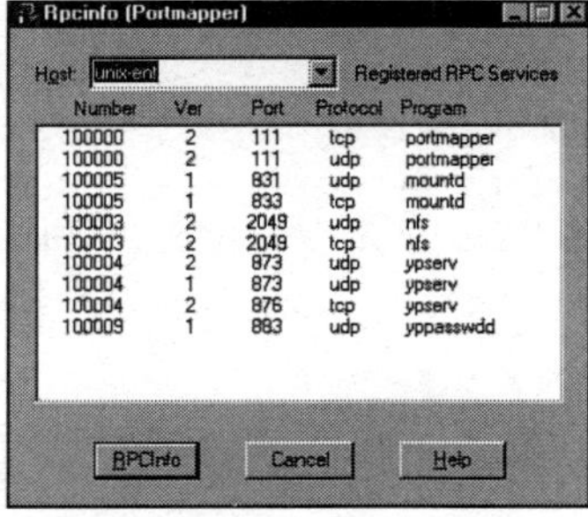

Figure 7.8. *The Rcpinfo dialog box.*

NIS Services Configuration

Like NFS, Sun also developed *NIS (Network Information System)*. NIS provides authentication for various facilities by employing a centralized database of information. NIS is based on RPC. It is made up of a server, a client library, and administrative tools. Originally NIS was called Yellow Pages, or YP, which it is often referred to. Yellow Pages is a registered trademark of British Telecom. Windows NT's Domain Model concept bears much influence from NIS.

The NIS Services dialog box is where you can specify NIS or YP, including the NIS Domain Name, Server Host Name, and IP Server Address (see Figure 7.9). In addition, passwords and other extended properties can be set as well. This allows the use of NIS as a *backbone* enterprise model for Windows NT.

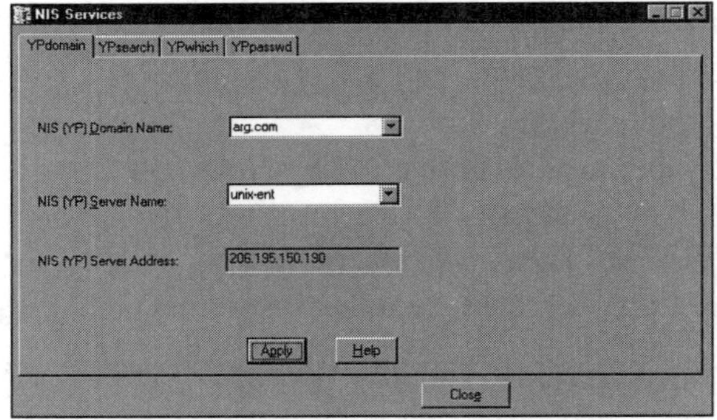

Figure 7.9. *The NIS Services dialog box in Hummingbird NFS Server.*

NIS maintains information in maps containing pairs. Maps are stored on a central host running the NIS server, from which clients can retrieve the information through various RPC calls.

PathWay NFS Server

This package is thought by most in Windows NT circles to be slightly easier to work with for setting up NFS servers on Windows NT. An evaluation is available from its manufacturer, Attachmate. It offers a quick installation and a multiple-tabbed centralized configuration dialog box in the Control Panel where NIS, Shares, and Performance can all be managed, as shown in Figure 7.10. This also avoids text-based configuration, which is still required with NFS Maestro.

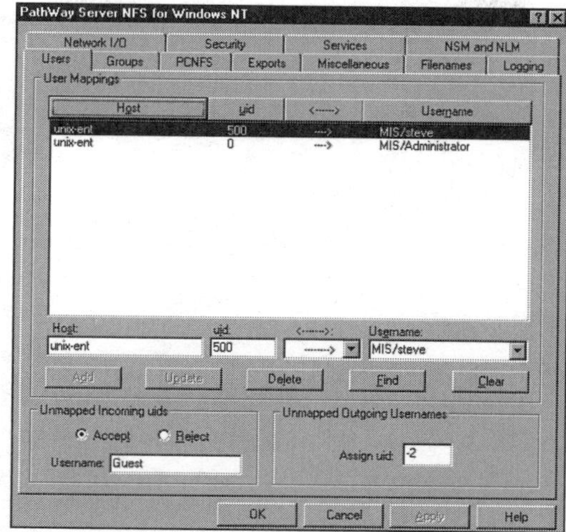

Figure 7.10. *PathWay Server NFS for Windows NT dialog box.*

Author's Note

I find that this NFS suite is somewhat easier to work with for UNIX-to-NT resource sharing. Whether you select Maestro, PathWay, or any other one, you will have to map out specific configuration information.

UNIX–NT Share Translation

Remember that UNIX does not have "drive" letters. Everything within the UNIX file system is built from a single root directory. This file system may exist on a single partition, or may actually span multiple volumes, even including other volumes on other network nodes.

Author's Note

When using NFS on NT, be sure to set up these shares on an NTFS file system in order to allow additional support for NTFS permissions. This can provide an extra level of security due to the fact the NFS permissions are not as discretionary as NTFS permissions on NT.

This is where NFS comes in. When creating the export, you must be aware that most flavors of UNIX will be using the export as a junction point within the UNIX machine's distributed file system. That is why you have to include a forward slash in front of the export share name, such as:

```
/ntstuff
```

The export would actually be linked to a drive and path on the Windows NT computer:

```
/ntstuff=e:\
```

Over on the UNIX side, you have to perform three basic steps to map a share over to the Windows NT NFS server:

1. Create the directory on the UNIX computer to be used as the local directory junction point. This would be equivalent to the drive letter in Windows NT. For example:

   ```
   Mkdir /NT
   ```

2. Then using the `mount` command, you can map or mount the directory using the following syntax found on most flavors of UNIX:

   ```
   mount -t nfs host:/exportpath /localpath
   ```

   In the case of our example, we would use this syntax:

   ```
   mount - nfs mis:/ntstuff /NT
   ```

3. On the UNIX side, change to the directory as if it were locally attached. (In a way, you may find this to be even more transparent than SMB sharing.) Figure 7.11 shows that this process occurs when you type `ls` on the UNIX host.

```
Telnet - unix-ent
Connect Edit Terminal Help
[root@unix-ent /NT]# ls -al
ls: pagefile.sys: Permission denieo
total 80
drwxrwxrwx  20 root     65534        364 Mar  9 01:41
drwxr-xr-x  17 root     root        1024 Mar  9 01:44 .
drwxrwxrwx   3 ruul     65534         46 Mar  9 01:14 ATM
-rwxrwxrwx   1 root     65534      51712 Nov 12 10:52 BLUESCRN.SCR
drwxrwxrwx   3 root     65534         45 Feb 17 23:52 ExecSoft
drwxrwxrwx   6 root     65534        104 Feb 28 19:02 InetPub
drwxrwxrwx  25 root     65534        552 Mar  7 16:15 Iomg_NT
drwxrwxrwx  23 root     65534        476 Mar  7 16:15 NM
drwxrwxrwx 356 root     65534       7940 Mar  7 16:15 NTRESKIT
drwxrwxrwx  15 ruul     65534        313 Mar  8 23:32 Pruyram Files
drwxrwxrwx  11 root     65534        490 Feb 20 11:31 RECYCLER
drwxrwxrwx   6 root     65534        105 Mar  5 09:55 Roamprofs
drwxrwxrwx  95 root     65534       2217 Mar  9 01:14 WINNT
drwxrwxrwx  98 root     65534       1965 Mar  7 16:14 bin
drwxrwxrwx   7 root     65534        129 Mar  7 16:15 ntdittn
drwxrwxrwx  50 root     65534       1064 Mar  7 16:15 ntzip
drwxrwxrwx   2 ruul     65534         27 Mar  9 01:12 Lemp
drwxrwxr-x  47 root     65534        814 Mar  4 14:11 users
drwxrwxrwx   3 root     65534         44 Feb 28 21:32 usr
[root@unix-ent /NT]#
[root@unix-ent /NT]#
[root@unix-ent /NT]#
```

Figure 7.11. *Working with the Windows NT file system from UNIX using NFS.*

GID and UID Mapping

Most NFS packages for Windows NT include support for NIS services. For example, both Hummingbird NFS and PathWay NFS include support for NIS.

When you decide to use NIS, you must first understand the differences between how Windows NT and UNIX handle their user accounts. While Windows NT uses security identifiers (SIDs) uniquely generated within an internal database, UNIX uses *user IDs (UIDs)* and *group IDs (GIDs)* to link access with usernames and group names. In both of the NFS solutions that we mentioned and on most every other one available, the Windows NT username, whether local- or domain-based, is mapped to a UNIX UID and GID.

Troubleshooting Tip

If you are not sure what the UID is for a particular UNIX user, you can find these mappings in the /etc/passwd *directory.*

SAMBA: An SMB Tool for UNIX

Windows NT and UNIX can be joined together through the support of the Server Message Block Protocol (SMB). SAMBA is a free SMB implementation that can be installed on UNIX platforms. SAMBA is available in archive format at `ftp://samba.anu.edu.au/pub/samba/samba-latest.tar.gz`.

You can do four things with SAMBA:

- Share a Linux drive with Windows machines
- Share a Windows drive with Linux machines
- Share a Linux printer with Windows machines
- Share a Windows printer with Linux machines

To install and configure SAMBA, download the archive from the preceding listed URL. You can also download this from the SAMBA Web site, shown in Figure 7.12. After extracting the archive, edit the makefile to decide which C compiler to use. Then, uncompress the flags that correspond to your operating system.

The code for SAMBA is cross-platform. it is supported by the following platforms:

- SunOS
- Solaris 2.2 and above
- Linux
- SVr4
- Ultrix
- Digital UNI
- SCO
- A/UX 3.0
- NeXT 3.2 and above
- Free BSD
- BSDI
- AIX

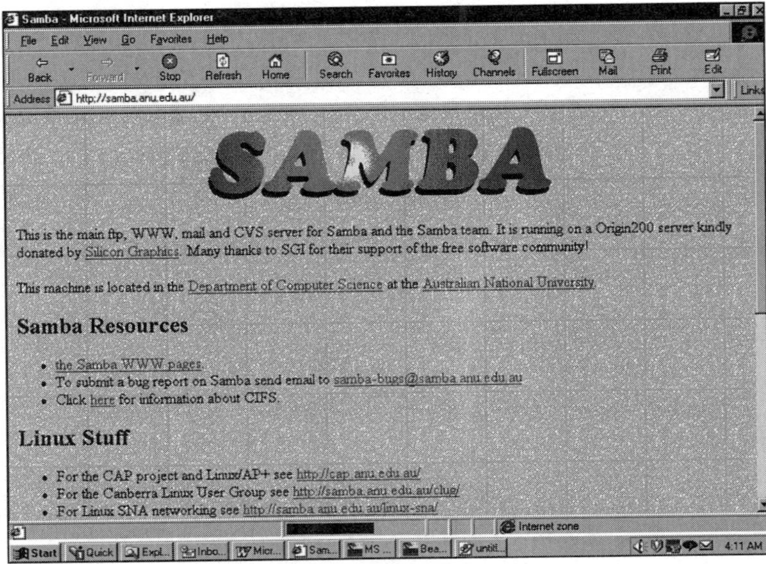

Figure 7.12. *The SAMBA Web site.*

When configuring the MAKEFILE, here are some of the options you might want to use:

```
BASEDIR=/usr/local/samba      LIBDIR=$(BASEDIR)/lib
BINDIR=/usr/local/bin         VARDIR=$(BASEDIR)/var
SBINDIR=/usr/local/bin
```

After you have configured these directories, you can then uncomment any setting that applies to your particular version of UNIX. You can then build and compile the source code using the following command:

```
make ¦ /usr/local/samba/buildlog.txt
```

You have the choice of using LAN Manager encryption to avoid using plaintext passwords. You could also use the libdes library. The SAMBA daemons are smbd and nmbd, and they are configured using the smb.conf file. This file has three main sections: global, home, and printers.

The global section contains workgroup information. Normally they browse the local network. To go across the internetwork, you must configure static mappings in either LMHOSTS or WINS.

> ***Warning***
>
> *You need to have entries for the* `IPC$`*; otherwise, you will see errors in the log files.*

Automatic Startup of SAMBA

The main control file is /etc/smb.conf. This file is a text file that enables the root user or administrator to set up SAMBA for his system. The Red Hat Linux 4.2 system has a well-written sample smb.conf file that can be used on any UNIX system with local modifications. If you are installing SAMBA on any other supported LINUX platform, a sample one will still be provided in the /etc directory.

To have smbd and nmbd start automatically upon reboot, add these lines to your equivalent rc script. You might want to keep a file called /etc/samba.rc to prevent the event from manually starting the dameons.

```
#!/bin/sh
# start samba servers
# start nmbd
if [ -f /usr/local/bin/nmbd ]
then
/usr/local/bin/nmbd -D
fi
# start smbd
if [ -f /usr/local/bin/smbd ]
then
/usr/local/bin/smbd -D
fi
```

Also note that file locations may differ depending on which version of UNIX is being used. Some examples include:

- *Solaris 2.x*. Save it to `/etc/rc3.d/SxxStartSamba`.
- *Red Hat Linux*. Save it to `/etc/rc.d/rc3.d/SxxStartSamba`.
- *SunOS or HP*. Add it to the end of `/etc/rc.local`.

Sample Samba SMB.CONF File

```
; The global setting for a RedHat default install
; smbd re-reads this file regularly, but if in doubt stop and restart it:
; /etc/rc.d/init.d/smb stop
; /etc/rc.d/init.d/smb start
;===================== Global Settings
=====================================
[global]
; workgroup = NT-Domain-Name or Workgroup-Name, eg: REDHAT4
   workgroup = UNIXGROUP
; comment is the equivalent of the NT Description field
   comment = UNIX Host Running Samba
; volume = used to emulate a CDRom label (can be set on a per share basis)
```

```
   volume = CD

; printing = BSD or SYSV or AIX, etc.
   printing = bsd
   printcap name = /etc/printcap
   load printers = yes

; Uncomment this if you want a guest account
   guest account = guest
   log file = /var/log/samba-log.%m
; Put a capping on the size of the log files (in Kb)
   max log size = 1000

; Options for handling file name case sensitivity and / or preservation
; Case Sensitivity breaks many WfW and Win95 apps
;   case sensitive = yes
    short preserve case = yes
    preserve case = yes

; Security and file integrity related options
   lock directory = /var/lock/samba
   locking = yes
   strict locking = yes
;   fake oplocks = yes
   share modes = yes
; Security modes: USER uses Unix username/passwd, SHARE uses WfW type passwords
;         SERVER uses a Windows NT Server to provide authentication services
   security = server
; Use password server option only with security = server
    password server = SERVER

; Configuration Options ***** Watch location in smb.conf for side-effects *****
; Where %m is any SMBName (machine name, or computer name) for which a custom
; configuration is desired
;   include = /etc/smb.conf.%m

; Performance Related Options
; Before setting socket options read the smb.conf man page!!
   socket options = TCP_NODELAY
; Socket Address is used to specify which socket Samba
; will listen on (good for aliased systems)
;   socket address = aaa.bbb.ccc.ddd
; Use keep alive only if really needed!!!!
;   keep alive = 60

; Domain Control Options
; OS Level gives Samba the power to rule the roost. Windows NT = 32
;    Any value < 32 means NT wins as Master Browser, > 32 Samba gets it
;   os level = 33
```

```
; specifies Samba to be the Domain Master Browser
;   domain master = yes
; Use with care only if you have an NT server on your network that has been
; configured at install time to be a primary domain controller.
    domain controller = SERVER
; Domain logon control can be a good thing! See [netlogon] share section below!
;   domain logons = yes
; run a specific logon batch file per workstation (machine)
;   logon script = %m.bat
; run a specific logon batch file per username
;   logon script = %u.bat
; Windows Internet Name Serving Support Section
; WINS Support - Tells the NMBD component of Samba to enable its WINS Server
;    the default is NO.
;   wins support = yes
; WINS Server - Tells the NMBD components of Samba to be a WINS Client
; Note: Samba can be either a WINS Server, or a WINS Client, but NOT both
; wins server = w.x.y.z
; WINS Proxy - Tells Samba to answer name resolution queries on behalf of a non
; WINS Client capable client, for this to work there must be at least one
; WINS Server on the network. The default is NO.
; wins proxy = yes

;============================ Share Declarations ==============================
[homes]
   comment = Home Directories
   browseable = no
   read only = no
   preserve case = yes
   short preserve case = yes
   create mode = 0750

; Un-comment the following and create the netlogon directory for Domain Logons
; [netlogon]
    comment = Samba Network Logon Service
    path = /home/netlogon
; Case sensitivity breaks logon script processing!!!
   case sensitive = no
   guest ok = yes
   locking = no
   read only = yes
   browseable = yes  ; say NO if you want to hide the NETLOGON share
   admin users = @wheel

; NOTE: There is NO need to specifically define each individual printer
[printers]
   comment = All Printers
```

```
   path = /var/spool/samba
   browseable = no
   printable = yes
   Set public = yes to allow user 'guest account' to print
   public = no
   writable = no
   create mode = 0700

 [tmp]
   comment = Temporary file space
    path = /tmp
    read only = no
    public = yes

; A publicly accessible directory, but read only, except for people in
; the staff group
[public]
   comment = Public Stuff
   path = /home/samba
   public = yes
   writable = yes
   printable = no
   write list = @users

; Other examples.
;
; A private printer, usable only by fred. Spool data will be placed in fred's
; home directory. Note that fred must have write access to the spool directory,
; wherever it is.
;[fredsprn]
;   comment = Fred's Printer
;   valid users = fred
;   path = /homes/fred
;   printer = freds_printer
;   public = no
;   writable = no
;   printable = yes
;
; A private directory, usable only by fred. Note that fred requires write
; access to the directory.
;[fredsdir]
;   comment = Fred's Service
;   path = /usr/somewhere/private
;   valid users = fred
;   public = no
;   writable = yes
;   printable = no
;
; a service which has a different directory for each machine that connects
```

```
; this allows you to tailor configurations to incoming machines. You could
; also use the %u option to tailor it by user name.
; The %m gets replaced with the machine name that is connecting.
;[pchome]
;  comment = PC Directories
;  path = /usr/pc/%m
;  public = no
;  writeable = yes
;
;
; A publicly accessible directory, read/write to all users. Note that all files
; created in the directory by users will be owned by the default user, so
; any user with access can delete any other user's files. Obviously this
; directory must be writable by the default user. Another user could of course
; be specified, in which case all files would be owned by that user instead.
;[public]
;   path = /usr/somewhere/else/public
;   public = yes
;   only guest = yes
;   writable = yes
;   printable = no
;
;
; The following two entries demonstrate how to share a directory so that two
; users can place files there that will be owned by the specific users. In this
; setup, the directory should be writable by both users and should have the
; sticky bit set on it to prevent abuse. Obviously this could be extended to
; as many users as required.
;[myshare]
;   comment = Mary's and Fred's stuff
;   path = /usr/somewhere/shared
;   valid users = mary fred
;   public = no
;   writable = yes
;   printable = no
;   create mask = 0765
```

Configuring the SMB Daemon

The file is divided up into several sections defined by nested headings. Unlike Windows NT, no Registry database is used and SAMBA is pretty much controlled exclusively by the settings in this configuration file. This file (smb.conf) is a traditional UNIX configuration file in that it leaves all options in by default commenting out the ones that are disengaged. The major sections are as follows:

[Globals Section]	Where workgroup settings, log file settings, global print settings, and guest account entries are stored.
[Performance Related Options]	Where settings governing how many resources are allocated to the daemons as well as optimization.
[Domain Control Options]	Where browser settings, domain settings, WINS, and logon script settings are stored.
[Share Declarations]	Where shares are declared in terms of description, security, and file systems.
[User Authentication]	Where user authentication can be set. You can set Share level, User level, or Server level security.

Browsing and Accessing SAMBA Resources

The preceding example allows the UNIX machine to be available in a workgroup called UNIX-ENT. It also creates the printer share as well as the three shares: public, root, and tmp (see Figure 7.13). Users running Windows NT can see this through the Network Neighborhood.

Browsing in SAMBA requires the nmbd daemon. This emulates the NetBIOS component. It is also responsible for facilitating named pipe support.

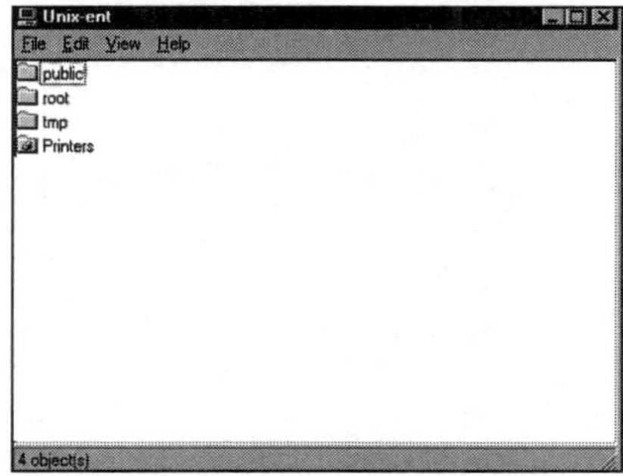

Figure 7.13. *Viewing SAMBA shares using the Network Neighborhood.*

You can also use the command prompt to access these resources. All the various SAMBA resources can be viewed and accessed using all the extensions of `NET.EXE` (see Figure 7.14), such as the following:

```
NET USE
NET VIEW
NET SEND
```

```
Command Prompt
Microsoft(R) Windows NT(TM)
(C) Copyright 1985-1996 Microsoft Corp.

C:\>net view \\unix-ent
Shared resources at \\unix-ent

Samba 1.9.16p11

Share name   Type         Used as  Comment

-------------------------------------------------------------------------------
HPLaserJ     Print                 HP LaserJet 5L
public       Disk                  Public Stuff
root         Disk                  Samba Network Logon
tmp          Disk                  Temporary File Space
The command completed successfully.

C:\>
```

Figure 7.14. *Using the* `NET VIEW` *command to view UNIX SAMBA shares.*

UNIX-to-NT Connectivity Using SAMBA

For UNIX file systems that need to map drives to Windows NT servers or workstations, you have a client tool that comes with SAMBA called *smbclient*. When you install SAMBA, the client application is automatically installed.

Some examples include the following:

```
Smbclient \\hawk\c -U NTSERVER
Smbclient -L hawk -I 206.195.150.190
./smbclient -L $MSservername
```

Tip

It is important to note that when accessing Universal Naming Conventions to access Microsoft resources, you must put in an extra back slash to connect to a Windows NT share and then enter a password, as follows:

```
\\\\$Msservername\\$sharename
```

The format for SMBCLIENT is as follows:

```
smbclient servicename [ password ] [ -A ] [ -E ] [ -L host ] [ -M host ] [ -I
IP number ] [ -N ] [ -P ] [ -U username ]  [ -d debuglevel ] [ -l log basename
] [ -n netbios name ] [ -W workgroup ] [ -O socket options ] [ -p port number ]
[  -c  command string ] [ -T tar options ] [ -D initial directory ]
```

Available options include the following:

servicename	The name of the service you want to use on the server.
password	The password required to access the specified service on the specified server. If supplied, the `-N` option (suppress password prompt) is assumed.
`-A`	If specified, causes the maximum debug level to be selected.
`-L`	Enables you to look at what services are available on a server. Type **`smbclient -L`** *host,* and a list should appear. The `-I` option may be useful if the NetBIOS names don't match your TCP/IP hostnames or if you are trying to reach a host on another network.
`-M`	Enables you to send messages, using the Messenger Service, to another computer. After a connection is established, you then type your message. If the receiving computer is running the Messenger Service, the user will receive the message and probably a beep. If the receiving computer is not running Messenger Service, the message will be lost, and no error message will occur.
`-E`	If specified, causes the client to write messages to the standard error stream (`stderr`) rather than to the standard output stream.
`-I` *IP number*	Specifies the IP address of the remote host if connecting to a multihomed computer.
`-P`	If specified, the service requested will be connected to as a printer service rather than as a normal filespace service. Operations such as `put` and `get` will not be applicable for such a connection.
`-D` *initial directory*	Enables you to change to the initial directory before starting. Probably would only be of any use with the tar (`-T`) option.
`-c` *command string*	A semicolon-separated list of commands to be executed instead of prompting from `stdin`.

After the client is running, the user is presented with a prompt: `smb: \>`. The backslash indicates the current working directory on the server, and will change if the current working directory is changed, as shown in Figure 7.15.

```
Telnet - (None)
Connect Edit Terminal Help

[admin@unix-ent admin]$ smbclient -M sidekick
Added interface ip=206.195.150.190 bcast=206.195.150.191 nmask=255.255.255.19
Connected. Type your message, ending it with a Control-D
Hello from UNIX Land
sent 22 bytes (status was 0-0)
[admin@unix-ent admin]$ smbclient \\\\sidekick\\moc carolina -U Administrator
Added interface ip=206.195.150.190 bcast=206.195.150.191 nmask=255.255.255.19
Server time is Wed Feb 11 15:06:13 1998
Timezone is UTC-5.0
Domain=[REDMOND] OS=[Windows NT 4.0] Server=[NT LAN Manager 4.0]
smb: \> dir
  .                                   DA        0  Wed Feb 11 22:34:13 1998
  ..                                  DA        0  Wed Feb 11 22:34:13 1998
  SIMULATIONS                         DA        0  Tue Feb 10 11:20:00 1998
  Videos                              DA        0  Tue Feb 10 11:23:21 1998

                37043 blocks of size 32768. 19748 blocks available
smb: \>
```

Figure 7.15. *Using the SMB client from UNIX to connect to a Windows NT Server.*

Chameleon UNIXLink 97

Chameleon UNIXLink 97 is another solution for PC-to-UNIX connectivity. One interesting new feature in this application is the first commercial connectivity solution that allows support for Broadway or Web-enabled X. This means that you can now use a Web browser to access UNIX applications.

Chameleon UNIXLink 97, like NFS Maestro, is also a complete solution, providing a suite applications for NFS; X Windows; host connectivity; Telnet terminal emulation for DEC, IBM and others; electronic mail; and File and Print Services.

X Windows Solutions

NFS is great for making file access between UNIX and Windows NT transparent. The *X Windows system* (also referred to as *X*) provides several other aspects of transparency. Most importantly, it provides a graphical Window interface similar to Apple Macintosh, MS Windows, and OS/2. In addition, it makes applications across these environments transparent. In a way, you can say that the network itself is transparent.

X allows for a windowing system that allows programs to display windows containing graphics or text on any node that supports the X Windows system without modifying, recompiling, or externally modifying the application. Each window that is displayed is equivalent to a terminal, so it is also imperative that a multi-user system be involved at least at one end of the client/server model.

X uses graphical controls such as pop-up menus, dialog boxes, input buttons, and mouse pointers to control aspects.

X Client and X Server

In the X Windows world, the terms *X client* and *X server* actually should be in reverse. They are opposite in meaning from other client/server models. In an X environment, the client usually resides on the host system, and the server resides on the local system.

Of course they can always both reside on the same system as well. The client is responsible for running the application. The server displays the output only. What makes the X server unique is that it can communicate with many different clients at the same time. Figure 7.16 shows the X Windows client/server architecture.

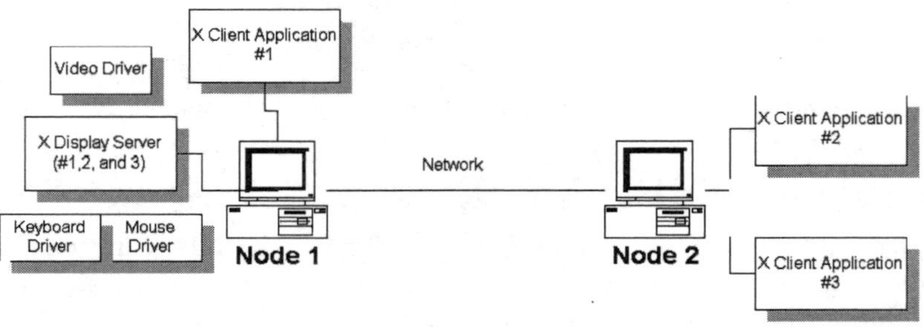

Figure 7.16. *The X Windows architecture: An X client processes the application and outputs it to a display server.*

Exceed

Exceed is Hummingbird Creative Lab's X Windows solution. It is most commonly implemented as an X display server for Windows NT, enabling those users to run utilities such as Motif and OpenLook using a UNIX computer that has the X client application source. Exceed includes a suite of X utilities as well as the INETD32 and the standard TCP/IP application suite.

Xstart

One of the most important application used in a Hummingbird X environment is Xstart. *Xstart* is an application for automating remote access and X client startup. You can use Xstart to also create custom startup script/configuration files referred to as Xstart (.XS) files.

Xstart is great for the Windows NT 4.0 environment. You can use it to install program items/shortcuts in a program group/folder to automatically establish a host connection, log on, and start an X client or a character-based application in a terminal emulator window, or run a script.

All the data required to start an X client using Xstart is stored in an Xstart file. When you run an Xstart file, Xstart will start the application based on the program type (X Windows or terminal emulator and the corresponding settings), using the start method that you indicated was supported by our host and transport software.

Because of Windows NT's association feature, you can start an X client by running its Xstart file.

Xsession

Also part of the Exceed suite, *Xsession* is an application that enables you to start the Exceed X server and multiple X clients/Windows programs whether they originate on one machine or several different machines. You can specify whether you want the X server to list the file in its Session Startup submenu or toolbar button, or if you want to automatically start the Exceed X server before running the clients/programs. If you want Xsession to start the server automatically, you can also specify the initial window and startup modes in the Server Options dialog box.

An Xsession file (.SES) contains a listing of all the individual files (.XS or .WS) that you want to start. When you run an Xsession file, Xsession will execute the individual files one at a time in the order you specified them in the Xsession window. You can specify whether you want to start the server when you run the Xsession file. If you do, you can also specify the window mode and startup mode to use.

Xconfig

Xconfig is the major configuration utility of the Exceed suite. Xconfig enables you to adjust the configuration parameters of the X display server. It enables you to set preferences for your host system if you are sponsoring X client applications (see Figure 7.17). You may want to think of this as the Exceed Control Panel.

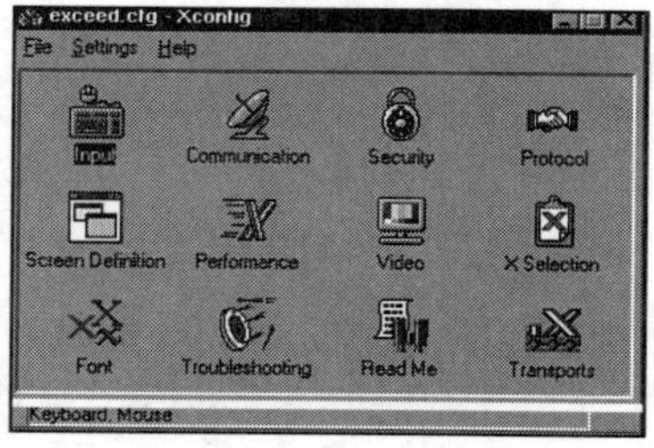

Figure 7.17. *The Xconfig Control Panel.*

The default Xconfig settings suit most systems. In most cases, the changes you make with Xconfig take effect immediately. If a setting cannot be changed immediately, the Exceed X server displays a message indicating the setting cannot be updated until the server is reset.

The Xconfig dialog box displays 12 icons (displayed in Figure 7.17) which, when double-clicked on, display the corresponding dialog box for that icon. Usually the default settings are sufficient for most systems. You can make changes, however, by altering the settings in a given dialog box and clicking the OK button. You can cancel any changes you make to an Xconfig dialog box by clicking the Cancel button.

Traditional X Windows on UNIX

X on UNIX technically is a work–in–progress. The most common releases in use are the varying degrees of version 11. They are referred to as X11r5, X11r6, and so on. The X consortium controls the progress of X development, but only in theory. The onset of Linux, GNU, and other free software movements along with the press not paying the X consortium any attention has led to a variety of different directions in X Windows. As a result, the common platform is still X11r5 and r6, even though they have been around for quite a few years now.

In UNIX, `xinit` and `xdm` have emerged as primary commands in starting an X display server. Of the two, `xinit` is the most common. It is usually found in the main X subdirectory, usually /usr/bin/X11.

The first method is `xinit`. The `xinit` command will start an X session on the local console by default. The only way to override this is to specify a default display for the X server. You can usually do this by typing the following command:

```
Setenv DISPLAY hostname:0
```

or

```
DISPLAY=tx600:0; export DISPLAY
```

You can usually initiate the X session using one of the following approaches:

- Via `xdm` and in .xsession file
- Via `xinit` and a .xserverrc file
- Via `xinit` and the .xinitrc file
- Via directly from the command line

The second method, `xdm` is a more recent development that uses the X Display Manager Control Protocol (XDMCP). The `xdm` application will act more like Windows NT in that it prompts for a logon to the GUI environment. It duplicates commands such as `init`, `getty`, and `login` because it starts the service, obtains a virtual terminal, and prompts for an initial logon.

Popular X Applications Under UNIX

The next few sections discuss popular applications found in most X11r5 environments. Consider these when incorporating UNIX X applications into a Windows NT environment.

Windows Managers

Several applications allow for X Windows to become more intuitive. A popular one is the Motif Window Manager or `mwm` as the command is known. In addition to Motif is `OpenWin`.

XTERM

The utility XTERM allows for a virtual terminal window that can contain its own security context, so it also establishes a user connection.

XCLOCK

The XCLOCK utility provides a graphical clock on the desktop similar to that of the Windows clock.

XPAINT

This is the X equivalent of the Microsoft PaintBrush application. It enables you to create bitmap images and edit them.

XCALC

The XCALC utility enables you to use a scientific calculator similar to that of the Windows calculator.

XBIFF

The XBIFF utility provides you with a pop-up menu informing you that a message has arrived from another machine.

XDPYINFO

The XDPYINFO utility displays information about the current X display.

XMAN

The XMAN utility enables you to use a graphical interface for viewing UNIX manual pages.

XWD

The XWD utility enables you to capture images in a window or on an entire screen, similar to the Alt+Print Screen option in Windows NT.

One reason people may not choose Exceed is its costs, although it is the most reliable and probably the most popular. If you are looking for an alternative with equivalent features, another option is KEA! X from Attachmate, descibed next.

KEA! X

KEA! X is an easy-to-use, full-featured PC X server that integrates the GUI-oriented X Windows environment (see Figure 7.18). KEA! provides a comprehensive implementation of the X11R6 Code Base. It also provides support for the newer X standards (font server support, XIE, XDMCP, true color support).

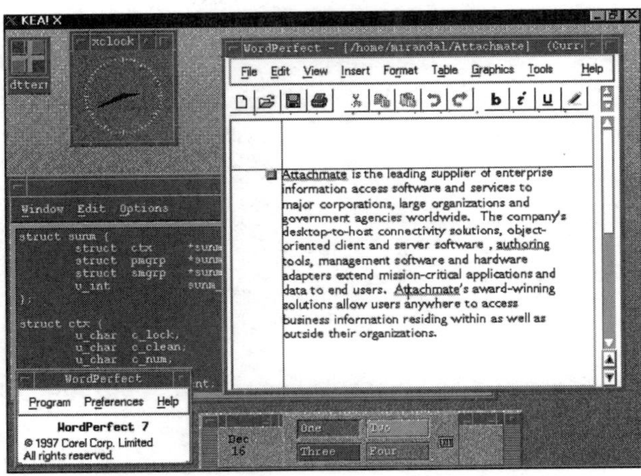

Figure 7.18. *Running X applications using UNIX as an X client and Windows NT as a KEA! X display server.*

UNIX Transparency on Windows NT

Throughout this entire section, we have been discussing options for UNIX connectivity. For the last part of this chapter, I want to introduce a few sets of utilities that help users and administrators migrating from UNIX to Windows NT.

Often people who are now in charge of Windows NT came from UNIX environments. These utilities make UNIX and Windows NT a bit more transparent in that they emulate UNIX commands and behaviors.

The POSIX Subsystem

Other tools that are available for Windows NT are the POSIX command utilities that come from the Resource Kit or from some third-party vendors such as MKS Tools. Inherent to Windows NT 4.0 is the POSIX subsystem that offers UNIX-like commands at the Windows NT command prompt. The source and documentation are also contained on the Windows NT 4.0 Resource Kit along with the compiled executables.

You can obtain free GNU utilities that use the Win32 subsystem as well as POSIX. You can obtain some of these free utilities at `ftp://ftp.cc.utexas.edu/microlib/nt/gnu/`.

Usually using the command followed by a `—help` will display the common usage for the command.

Common UNIX commands

UNIX commands tend to be very short and cryptic. The idea behind their development was efficiency rather than ease of use. Many of the basic commands were designed to be typed with alternating fingers on each side of the keyboard. Table 7.1 shows several useful UNIX commands.

Author's Note

When working with UNIX, all commands are considered case-sensitive.

Table 7.1. Useful UNIX commands.

Command	Description
`cat`	Displays a text file.
`cd`	Changes a directory.
`chmod`	Changes the file's access mode.
`chown`	(System V only.) Changes the file's ownership.
`p`	Copies the file.
`date`	Displays the current date.
`file`	Displays the type of file.
`find`	Finds the directory location of a file.
`grep`	Searches for a text string within a file.
`head`	Displays first lines of file.
`lp`	(System V.) Prints the file to a printer.
`lpr`	(BSD.) Prints the file to a printer.

continues

Table 7.1. Continued

Command	Description
`ls`	Lists directory contents.
`man`	Displays the manual (Help) pages for the command.
`mkdir`	Creates a directory.
`more`	Displays a file, one screen at a time.
`mv`	Moves an object.
`passwd`	Changes a logon password.
`pg`	Displays a file, one page at a time.
`ps`	Views the process list.
`pwd`	Prints the working directory.
`rm`	Removes an object.
`rmdir`	Removes a directory.
`sort`	Sorts an ASCII file.
`stty`	Changes terminal settings.
`tail`	Displays the last lines of the file.
`tty`	Displays the path name of the terminal.
`vi`	Invokes the Screen Editor.
`wc`	Displays the line, word, and character counts of file.
`who`	Displays the current active users.
`write`	Writes to user.

Resource Kit Utilities

The Resource Kit contains POSIX-compliant versions of the following commands:

```
ar      cat      cc     chmod    cp       find     ln       ls
make    mkdir    mv     rm       rmdir    sh       touch    wc
```

Chapter 8

Integration with NetWare Bindery-based Servers

- **NetWare Bindery Overview**
  We will discuss the basics of bindery-based NetWare servers and how they function in terms of administration and security.
- **Client Services for NetWare**
  This is Microsoft's solution for Windows NT Workstation-NetWare connectivity.
- **Gateway Services for NetWare**
  This is Microsoft's NT server-side solution for connecting to and allowing pass-through shares to NetWare servers.
- **File and Print Services for NetWare**
  This is Microsoft's add-on product that allows NetWare clients to connect to NT servers.
- **Directory Service Manager for NetWare**
  This is also a Microsoft add-on designed to synchronize bindery-based NetWare servers with NT domain controllers.

Bindery-based NetWare Overview

The most common versions of bindery-based NetWare servers in use today are versions 3.11 or 3.12. In fact, NetWare 3.12 is still so popular that Novell has recently made an enhancement pack available, referred to as *NetWare 3.2*.

The reason for the continued strength of NetWare 3.x is due to its bindery structure. While it is poor for enterprise networking models, it is strong for single-server networks. Small local area networks (LANs) that use a single file server and need to double as an application server find NetWare 3.x the best solution because it requires relatively minimal hardware requirements when compared to NT Server. While it does not have an interactive graphical logon, it does have a simple set of commands for basic operations. However, for any interactive management, a client workstation must be accessible.

The IPX/SPX Protocol

For years, the IPX/SPX protocol (mentioned in Chapter 2, "LAN/WAN Protocol Management") has been the primary backbone of NetWare connectivity. When installing IPX/SPX under Novell, it operated on top of an ODI-based (Open Data Link-based) network driver.

IPX stands for *Internet Packet Exchange*. This is a protocol derived from XNS and is now used by Novell, Microsoft, and certain flavors of UNIX. IPX is routable and operates primarily as a network transport. IPX provides a "best effort" delivery service and is equivalent to TCP/IP's IP.

SPX stands for the *Sequenced Packet Exchange*. It is primarily a NetWare communications protocol that ensures reliable data delivery. It uses IPX as its transport and is equivalent to TCP/IP's TCP.

Microsoft's NWLink IPX/SPX

The IPX/SPX network protocol is supported on NT by using the NWLink IPX/SPX Compatible Transport. This alone does not allow for complete capability. On top of this protocol, you need some tools to provide the integration. We will discuss those tools later in this chapter when we look at the Client and Gateway Services for NetWare.

NWLink Issues

NWLink is Microsoft's IPX/SPX implementation, modified to support NDIS technology. This is the major reason we refer to it as *NWLink* rather than *IPX/SPX*. NWLink is a full 32-bit implementation that provides support for two network APIs (Application Programming Interfaces):

- *Novell's Windows Sockets* provides the interface support for existing NetWare applications written to comply with IPX/SPX.
- NetBIOS links the NetBIOS interface with the NWLink transport protocol. This is actually the NWNBLink (NetBIOS-NetWare Link) that allows MS networks to use the NetBIOS interface for NetWare connectivity or to facilitate Microsoft networking using a routable protocol (instead of NetBEUI.)

NWLink IPX/SPX Network Numbers

The network number types have been a real large issue in dealing with NetWare and Windows NT integration. This is primarily because it is difficult to understand how network numbers relate to Windows NT and the Microsoft network, especially since this stack can be used regardless of whether or not you need NetWare connectivity. In fact, many organizations look to NWLink as their internetworking protocol of choice.

The NWLink IPX/SPX-compatible transport in Windows NT uses two distinctly different types of network numbers. This is where the confusion begins. Windows NT uses an IPX network number for routing purposes that is assigned to each configured frame type and adapter combination on your computer. In Novell NetWare networks, the network number is referred to as the *external network number*, and it must be unique for each network segment.

If you want to view your external network number and its associated frame type for each network device, go to a command prompt and type:

```
IPXROUTE config
```

to get this information. You can also view the external network number in the Network Control Panel as displayed in Figure 8.1.

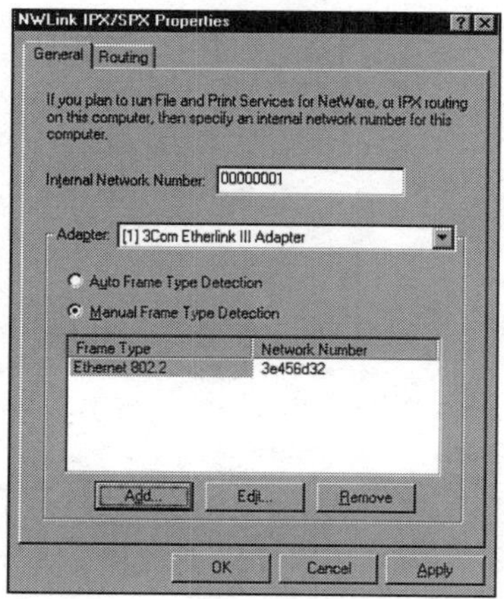

Figure 8.1. *Setting network numbers in the NWLink IPX/SPX Properties dialog box.*

Windows NT also uses an internal network number for internal routing purposes. The internal network number in Novell NetWare networks is known as a *virtual network number*. The internal network number uniquely identifies the computer on the internetwork. These two networks are totally different from each other.

The virtual network number must be unique for each network segment. Think of this as the subnet address. In fact, many administrators use a hexadecimal equivalent of a TCP/IP subnet address to ensure unique addressing and to maintain consistency on dual TCP/IP-IPX/SPX networks.

Troubleshooting Tip

If you do not set such a value for the IPX network number in the Registry, then it will default to a value of `0`, but the number itself will be assigned by Windows NT through auto-detection.

In most cases, it is acceptable to leave the network number at zero (`0`) unless you have FPNW (File and Print Services for NetWare) installed and have chosen multiple frame types or have NWLink bound to multiple adapters in your computer for routing purposes.

Frame Types

As mentioned earlier, NWLink automatically detects which frame type is being used on the network during initial startup and uses that frame type. This autoconfiguration first occurs when the NWLink protocol initializes.

The NWLink driver is temporarily set to 802.2 when the driver initializes under auto-detect configuration, but the protocol will still send out what is equivalent to a RIP for IPX (Routing Information Protocol) broadcast for network `0xFFFFFFFF` on all frame types supported by NT. This includes:

- Ethernet II
- Ethernet SNAP
- IEEE 802.2
- IEEE 802.3

If the server receives a response, it will re-bind using that frame type. If no frame type is detected, it will keep the default of 802.2. If multiple frame types are detected, then it will choose one frame type based on a pre-determined preference order. This order is as follows:

1. Ethernet 802.2
2. Ethernet 802.3
3. Ethernet II
4. SNAP

If you want to have multiple frame types supported, you will need to manually add these frame types.

Service Interoperability

Microsoft offers a full interoperability solution between NetWare file servers and Windows NT. This requires two major components:

- A compatible transport protocol
- Network API

Microsoft offers NWLink, which is an IPX/SPX-compatible transport protocol and NWNBLink, a Novell-compatible NetBIOS emulator that translates Novell's NCP (NetWare Core Protocol) packets into Microsoft's SMB (Service Message Block) packets. This allows file, print, and client-server application solutions to exist under both providers: the Microsoft Windows Network and the Novell NetWare Network (see Figure 8.2).

Table 8.1 shows this same approach implemented in earlier popular clients.

Table 8.1. Different types of early Novell clients and their drivers.

Client Type	Normal ODI Stack	Normal NDIS 2.0 Stack	WFW 3.11 Running Novell NetWare Software
Requestor/ Shell/ Redirector	VLM.EXE or NET.EXE	VREDIR.386	VLM.EXE VREDIR.386
Transport Stack	IPXODI.COM or IPX.COM	VNETBEUI.386	IPXODI.COM VNETBEUI.386
Link/Binding Manager	LSL.COM	PROTMAN.DOS	LSL.COM — ODIHLP.EXE
NIC Driver	NE2000.COM (or other network card driver)	NE2000.DOS (or other network card driver)	NE2000.COM (or other card driver)

Client Services for NetWare

Client Services for NetWare (CSNW) provides an NT Workstation with basic file and printer connectivity to NetWare. It supports both bindery and NetWare Directory Services. (The NetWare Directory Services support is very minimal, providing only access to File and Print Services.)

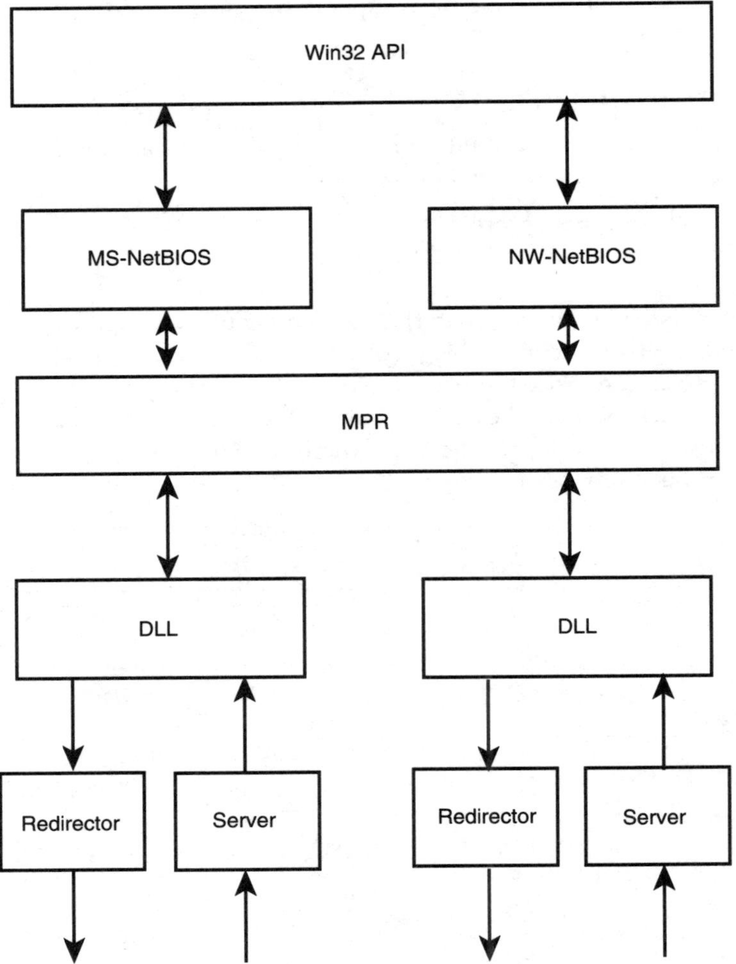

Figure 8.2. *Microsoft and Novell providers coexisting on Windows NT.*

CSNW is documented as being found only on Windows NT Workstation. The truth is that half of the Gateway Services for NetWare solution is the Client Services for NetWare. Therefore, both Server and Workstation have a client solution for NetWare.

Gateway Services for NetWare

Most newer Microsoft client software, including Windows for Workgroups 3.11, Windows NT Workstation, and Windows 95, support direct NCP connections to NetWare File and Print Services via the IPX/SPX transport protocol.

However, older Microsoft client software for MS-DOS and Windows only supports Microsoft's SMB File and Print Services protocol. As a result, Microsoft implemented the *Gateway Service for NetWare (GSNW)* and included it in Windows NT Server.

GSNW is a service that runs on a Windows NT server. It not only provides the client capabilities (similar to CSNW), but it can also act as a gateway to NetWare File and Print Services for any SMB client—for example, Windows for Workgroups (WFWG) or Windows NT. While you can simply use it for the client portion, if you run GSNW (and NWLink) on a Windows NT server, you can use NT as a gateway to NetWare 2.x, 3.x, and 4.x servers.

GSNW supports NetWare 4.x NDS servers in Windows NT 4.0. This provides you with the following capabilities:

- Browsing NetWare resources
- NDS authentication to multiple trees
- Processing logon scripts
- Access to print resources

Microsoft clients that would normally have to load dual redirectors to connect to both Windows NT and NetWare Servers can take advantage of this gateway service by accessing File and Print Services on NetWare without loading the second redirector. All that the client computers need is a common transport protocol. In the case here, it is IPX/SPX. The NT Server will act as a service-layer gateway, translating SMB and NetBIOS information into NetWare service information.

While it works well, it's likely that it would be a bottleneck if you were going to link large networks using this single gateway. The reason for this revolves around an interesting story. Microsoft uses a single client connection to the NetWare Server to facilitate the second half of the NetWare gateway. This account is configured using the Gateway Services for NetWare Control Panel. In fact, it is the only option that differs from the Client Services for NetWare's Control Panel. This account must match up with an identical user name and password on the NetWare Server. That account on the NetWare Server must also reside in a specially created group called NTGATEWAY. The Windows NT Server will then re-share that resource as if it were coming from the NT Server's local file system. The users will also assume that the gateway share will appear in the browse list just like any other share on the NT Server.

However, as Figure 8.3 demonstrates, multiple users can connect simultaneously to the NT Server's share and pass through the same SINGLE connection to the NetWare Server. Naturally, Novell was not happy about this. One major reason was that Microsoft provided a way for administrators and users to "cheat" the NetWare licensing structure which, up until now, was very strict and unforgiving.

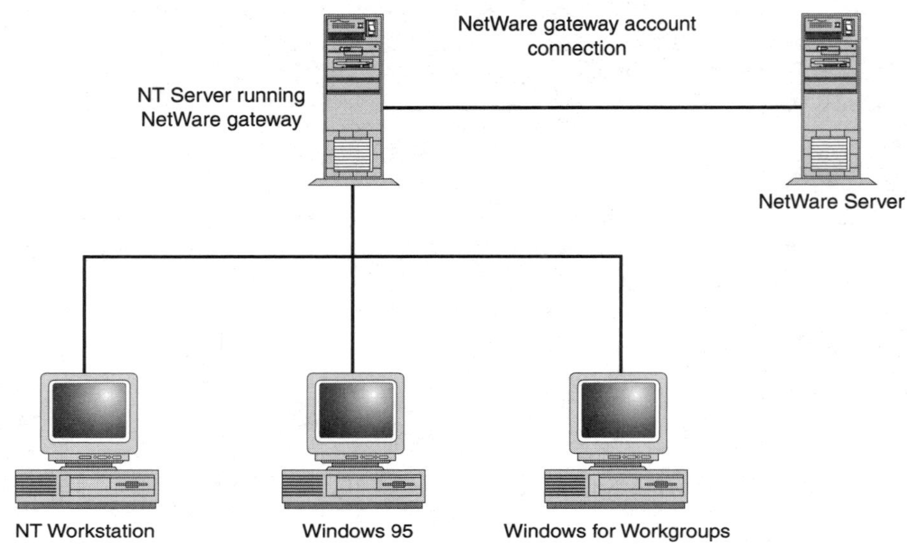

Figure 8.3. *The NetWare gateway account connection.*

Installing the Gateway Services for NetWare

Installation is pretty straightforward. One requirement for GSNW is the NWLink protocol stack, which will be automatically installed if it does not exist on the system when the GSNW package is being installed. Once you have that in order, start the Network Control Panel or right-click Network Neighborhood and select Properties. Click the Services tab and click Add. Then select Gateway (and Client) Services for NetWare and click OK.

Preparation on the NetWare Side

On the NetWare server, create the NTGATEWAY group and a user that is a member of that group on the NetWare server using SYSCON on 3.12 servers, or NWADMIN/NETADMIN on 4.0 or later. The user that you create will need to have matching credentials on the NT server as well.

Configuring the Gateway

Once you have installed the GSNW package and prepared the NetWare server, then you are ready to configure the gateway. You will notice that a GSNW Control Panel is created after rebooting your computer. Open that control panel and select the Gateway button; the Configure Gateway dialog box appears (see Figure 8.4). Enter the user account you created that is a member of the NTGATEWAY group.

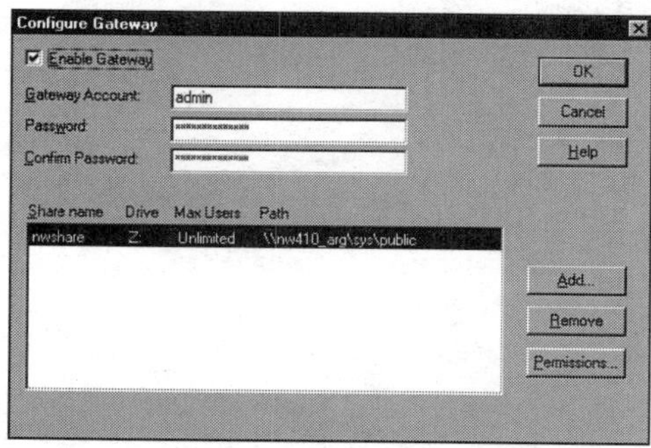

Figure 8.4. *Configuring the gateway.*

Attaching to NetWare 3.12 Servers

You can use the first dialog box in the GSNW Control Panel to initially attach to a NetWare server and select the server preference (see Figure 8.5). You can set a direct server preference, which would be appropriate for bindery-based NetWare servers or NetWare 4.x servers running under bindery emulation. You can also select a default NDS tree and NDS context for NDS authentication as well. For either option, you can allow the processing of a login script—this is a new feature in NT 4.0. You can also set default print options in this dialog box.

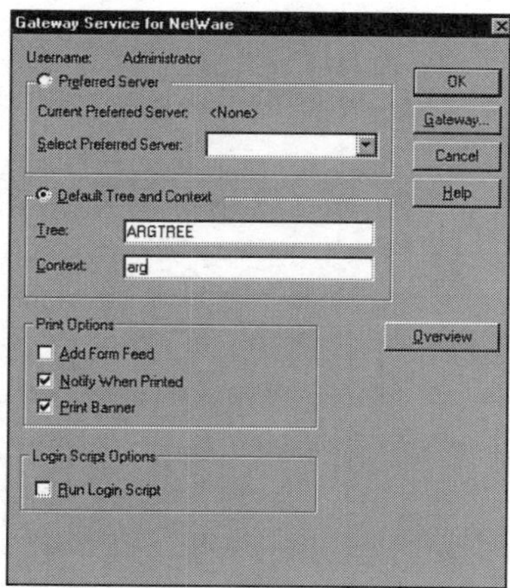

Figure 8.5. *The Gateway Service for NetWare dialog box.*

Fine-tuning Parameters

Many people find this solution to be low-end because of the lack of customizable options within the dialog box. Many NetWare administrators are used to using flat text files like the NET.CFG file for handling NetWare configuration options. There is no such equivalent in NT except for fine-tuning options in the Registry.

Accessing NetWare File Resources

There are several ways to access NetWare file resources once GSNW has been installed. There is the option for attachment, which only allows for authentication in the Control Panel. You can use these methods to access file resources:

- Use the Network Neighborhood (under NetWare or Compatible Network)—as shown in Figure 8.6. When you select a server that you have not been authenticated to, it prompts you with a NetWare Login dialog box.

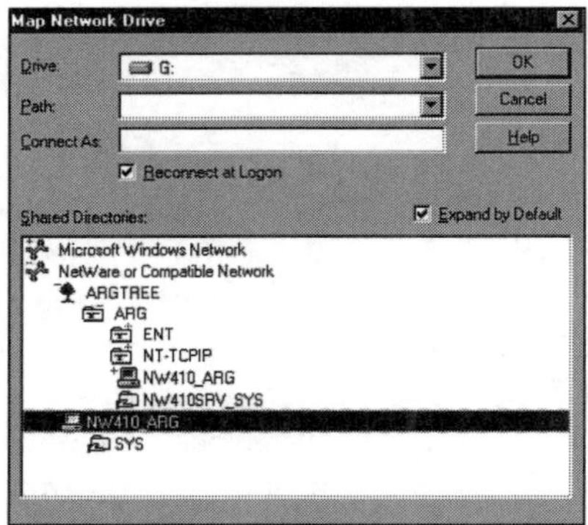

Figure 8.6. *The Map Network Drive dialog box.*

- Use the File Manager's Connect Network Drive (under NetWare or Compatible Network).
- From the command prompt, use the following command syntax:

```
NET USE [Drive:] \\NETWARESERVER\VOLUME\DIRECTORY
```

- From the command prompt, use the 16-bit DOS-based NetWare command MAP.EXE to connect to the NetWare drive. This will only work if the path to MAP.EXE exists in your local Windows NT path. The default location is the \\NETWARESERVER\SYS\PUBLIC in Microsoft UNC format. Note that when using the MAP.EXE utility, you will use the NetWare syntax and not the Microsoft UNC syntax for mapping the drive. The NetWare syntax is as follows:

```
MAP options [drive:] Server/Volume:Directory\Subdir,...
```

File and Print Services for NetWare

Today's NetWare clients, such as Windows-based computers running Novell's NetX or VLM client software, can also easily access Windows NT Server-based File and Print Services. This access is enabled by a new Windows NT Server utility called *File and Print Services for NetWare (FPNW)*. FPNW is a Windows NT Server utility that makes Windows NT Server look like a NetWare bindery-based file and print server. With FPNW, customers can deploy basic NetWare File and Print Services as well as powerful, advanced business applications on the same Windows NT Server-based machine—without changing their client software.

FPNW also gives the NetWare client greater capability. For example, when NetWare clients send an NCP file access request or print job to a Windows NT Server-based computer running FPNW, FPNW interprets the request and responds appropriately. If proper user access rights exist, an NCP-encoded response is sent to the file request. Similarly, print jobs are sent to the correct print queue. FPNW is an excellent option for NetWare sites wanting to deploy Windows NT Server without simultaneously modifying the client software and all of their NetWare client machines.

Deploying FPNW on Windows NT Server-based machines allows the administrator to take advantage of central administration of NetWare client user accounts while NetWare clients enjoy a single logon to all network file, print, and application service resources.

Some important aspects of the FPNW include the following:

- It provides for transparent networking making utilities available for NetWare clients such as `ATTACH`, `LOGIN`, `LOGOUT`, `SETPASS`, `MAP`, `SLIST`, `CAPTURE`, and `ENDCAP`.
- The security architectures are merged; however, the account parameters do not completely translate.
- It is dependent on the NTFS file system.
- An administrator can share directories and printers of a Windows NT server so they are accessible to NetWare clients.
- A Windows NT server computer can be used to manage NetWare printers. By doing so, you can also make the NetWare printers available to users of Microsoft client computers.

There is no support for the following:

- Workgroup managers
- Accounting
- User disk volume restrictions
- Setting Inherited Rights Masks (IRMs)
- NetWare loadable modules
- Transaction Tracking System (TTS)

Setting Up File and Print Services for NetWare

FPNW is installed from the Services tab by choosing Control Panel, Network. Even if you have File and Print Services for NetWare listed in your Network Service list box, do not select that. Instead, choose the Have Disk option and type the path where FPNW files are located. Figure 8.7 shows the installation options for FPNW. The default SYSVOL directory structure created by FPNW is similar to the SYS directory structure in NetWare and contains the subdirectories, described in Table 8.2.

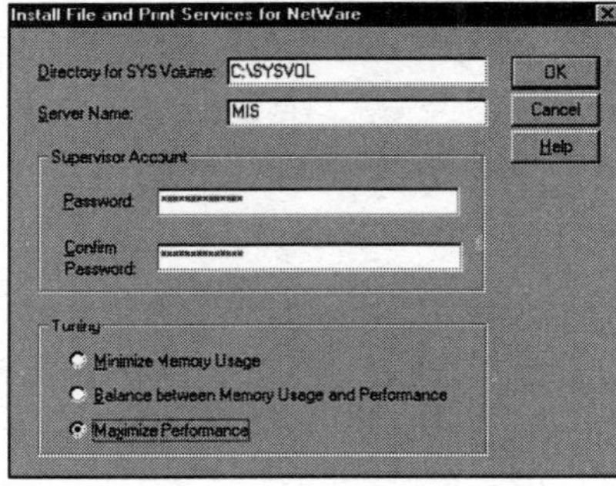

Figure 8.7. *The Install File and Print Services for NetWare dialog box.*

Table 8.2. FPNW subdirectories that emulate NetWare directories.

Subdirectory	Description
LOGIN	Contains the utilities that NetWare clients use to log in to Windows NT Server computers running FPNW. When NetWare clients first connect to the Windows NT Server computer, a mapping to the LOGIN directory is automatically created.
MAIL	Contains subdirectories for each user. The subdirectory is specified by the user bindery object identification. The user subdirectories contain the user login scripts.

Subdirectory	Description
PUBLIC	Contains the utilities that NetWare clients use for accessing and using resources on a server running FPNW. The utilities are `ATTACH`, `CAPTURE`, `ENDCAP`, `LOGIN`, `LOGOUT`, `MAP`, `SETPASS`, and `SLIST`.
SYSTEM	Contains the files for printing and print server support.

In the Directory for SYS Volume text box (see Figure 8.7), you should specify a directory located on an NTFS volume. Otherwise, you will not be able to take advantage of NTFS file- and directory-level security. Also, make sure you type the name of the server in caps in Server Name box. The default is the *server name*_FPNW.

Besides the Supervisor Account Password option, there are three tuning options available with FPNW. These are similar to the options used to tune the Server Service mentioned earlier in Chapter 5, "Network Management and Monitoring":

- Minimize Memory Usage
- Balance between Memory Usage and Performance
- Maximize Performance

The Minimize Memory Usage option will slow FPNW's performance. Select this option if the server is used for something other than File and Print Services (for example, if you run server applications).

The Balance Between Memory Usage and Performance option is suitable if your server is not only running applications, but is also a file and print server.

The third option, Maximize Performance, is best in situations where the server is primarily a network file and print server. In that case, FPNW will use more memory than the rest of the system resources.

The FPNW Service Account

If you are installing FPNW in a domain, a user account named FPNW Service account is created at installation. FPNW uses this account to log in and perform operations between domain controllers in a domain. During the installation, you are prompted to supply a password for the FPNW Service Account. You must supply the same password on all the domain's servers on which you are installing FPNW. The service account is automatically added to the Administrator's group.

Author's Note

The FPNW Service account is necessary to start FPNW on all servers in the domain. Do not delete this account. If you do, the service will fail to start.

When you install FPNW, it adds functionality to File Manager, Server Manager, User Manager for Domains, and an FPNW Control Panel. A NetWare Supervisor account is also created to which you can assign a NetWare password. The Supervisor account, which is created for administering NetWare servers, is automatically added to the Administrators group.

The Server Manager will have a new menu, FPNW, from where you can create, manage, and delete volumes that have been shared for NetWare clients. The same functionality is provided in both utilities. Server Manager has the additional menu called FPNW that allows you to view volumes, and FPNW server properties.

NetWare 2.x, 3.x and 4.x (running bindery emulation mode) customers can seamlessly integrate NT servers in their existing environment without changing their client software. This integration benefits NetWare shops in many ways:

- They can use FPNW during the transition from NetWare to NT, or integrate NT in their existing network by taking advantage of all the features that NT Server provides.
- NT offers an Intranet solution with Internet Information Server (IIS) and FrontPage in their existing environment at no extra charge.
- Furthermore, adding NT servers in a NetWare network gives customers the ability to benefit from NT solutions like Services for Macintosh, SQL Server, SNA Server and Remote Access Service (RAS).

Installing FPNW on an NT server gives you the ability to choose the Maintain NetWare Compatible Login check box, as shown in Figure 8.8.

This option can be pretty handy for the network administrators. You can set account information that applies to users who are logging on from a NetWare client. You can force a user to change the password at next logon from a NetWare client machine by checking the NetWare Compatible Password Expired box. Make sure they have at least one grace login so they can log on and change their password. You can also edit their personal login script, limit their grace logins, or limit concurrent connections to the server.

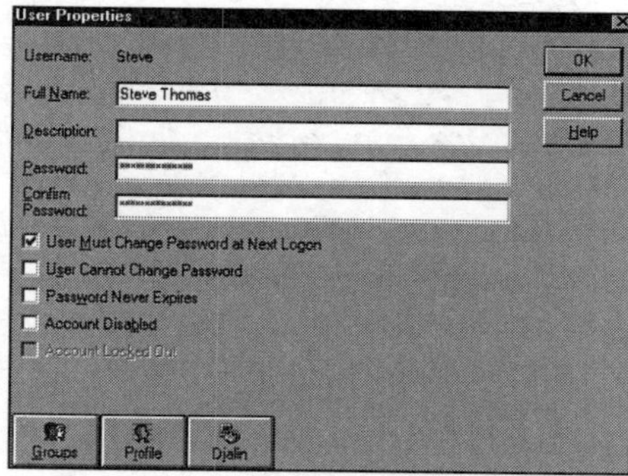

Figure 8.8. *Choosing to maintain the NetWare-compatible login.*

Warning

Do not use the Edit Login Script button to edit the system login script on a server, instead use another text editor (such as Notepad) to edit NET$LOG.DAT that resides in the SYSVOL\PUBLIC folder. You should handle this file in the same way that you handle NetWare in terms of how the system login script is maintained.

Securing access to volumes and management of user connections is provided by extensions added after the FPNW installation. These extensions are available in File Manager, User Manager, and Server Manager. An administrator can view resources that are being accessed by a NetWare user, send him a welcome message at logon, and maintain his account information.

NetWare clients also have the ability to use FPNW for printing. They can either print to a NetWare-compatible printer attached directly to the network that is serviced by an NT server, or print to a local printer attached to an NT server that will act as a print queue for them.

Issues with Novell's 32-Bit Client Redirector

The FPNW that shipped by default with Services for NetWare does not support access by the Novell Client32 packages for Windows 95 and Windows NT. Microsoft resolved this problem by making a fix available for free from either its Web site `http://www.novell.com`, or FTP site `ftp.novell.com`.

Troubleshooting Tip

On systems running FPNW, there are two checkboxes that are mutually exclusive: The Users Must Log On in Order to Change Password box (in the Account Policy) and the User Must Change Password at Next Logon box (in the User Properties). If you select the Users Must Log On in Order to Change Password box, then users who have the User Must Change Password at Next Logon box checked in their accounts cannot use `CHGPASS`*,* `SETPASS` *or* `LOGIN` *to change their passwords once they have logged on to the server. To work around this problem, only have one of them checked at a time.*

Troubleshooting Tip

On machines running FPNW, if you reboot and try to log on immediately, you may not be able to automatically restore connections between the FPNW server and NetWare server if you do not select a preferred server. This happens because the NT computer didn't have a chance to gather information about NetWare servers before it tried to restore connections.

Client Commands and Utilities Supported by FPNW

Since this service only emulates bindery-based servers for basic File and Print Services, the supported client command set is minimal. But this command set comprises about 90 to 95 percent of basic user duties. The NetWare commands that NetWare clients can use are described in the following sections.

Author's Note

The following commands are also identical to the NetWare commands, so users will see these utilities as totally transparent. When managing a NetWare server, those administrators not already familiar with NetWare can use these utilities to perform NetWare-specific management.

ATTACH

This utility provides access to a file server. It initially attaches to the SYS:LOGIN directory but it does not authenticate by itself. The LOGIN.EXE command actually completes the authentication transparently. This utility is obsolete in NetWare 4.x.

The syntax for `ATTACH` is as follows:

```
ATTACH ServerName/Username
```

CAPTURE

This command takes a local printer port and redirects its output to a NetWare print queue. This is only necessary for those older applications, which do not support network printing.

The syntax for CAPTURE is as follows:

```
CAPTURE options
```

Table 8.3 shows common options used with CAPTURE.

Table 8.3. Common options for CAPTURE.

Option	Description
AU	Automatically closes out a print job when exiting an application. This is automatically disabled by default.
NA	Does not automatically close out the job. This will require the use of the ENDCAP utility to close out the print job.
B	Sets up a banner page. A banner name can be any word or phrase up to 12 characters long that you will want to appear on the lower part of the banner page. The default is LST.
NB	Tells NetWare not to print a banner page.
C=*n*	Tells NetWare to print *n* copies.
CR=*file*	Instead of queuing the file to the printer, actually prints the raw output to the file.
FF	Sends a form-feed code to the printer at the end of each print job so that the next print job can start at the top of the next sheet of paper. It is not necessary to do this for applications that already submit form feeds. This will cause an extra blank page to be wasted.
NFF	Disables the Form Feed option.
L=*n*	Indicates which local LPT ports you want to capture. Valid choices are 1, 2, and 3.
NAM=*name*	The name can be any word or phrase up to 12 characters long that you would want printed at the top of the banner page. The default name is the username.
Q=*queuename*	The print queue name in which the print job was going to. If this failed to be specified by the client workstation, it will default to the queue to which spooler 0 has been assigned.
S=*name*	The name of the file server to which you are sending the print job and the server on which the print queue is located.
SHOW	Displays the current captured ports.

Tip

The CAPTURE *options that were introduced in NetWare 4 are not supported.*

CHGPASS

This utility allows the users to change their NetWare password. In the case of FPNW, it allows the NetWare user to change the NT password. The syntax for CHGPASS is as follows:

```
CHGPASS Servername
```

The user is then prompted for the old password and then the new password and confirmation.

ENDCAP

The ENDCAP utility ends the capture to the local port. By default, it ends capturing to LPT1 unless you specify otherwise. The syntax for ENDCAP is as follows:

```
ENDCAP options
```

Table 8.4 shows some common options used with ENDCAP.

Table 8.4. Common options for ENDCAP.

Option	Description
`Local n`	Indicates the LPT1 port from which you want to end capturing. *n* reflects the port captured.
`ALL`	Ends the capturing of all LPT ports.
`Cancel`	Ends the capturing of LPT1 and deletes any pending print jobs.
`Cancel Local n`	Ends the capturing of the specified LPT port and cancels all pending print jobs.
`Cancel ALL`	Ends the capturing of all LPT ports and deletes the data without printing it.

LOGIN

This command accesses your preferred server and will authenticate your connection as well as invoke your login script. The syntax for LOGIN is as follows:

```
LOGIN /option fileserver/username scriptoptions
```

Table 8.5 shows some common options used with LOGIN.

Table 8.5. Common options for LOGIN.

Option	Description
`/Script`	Processes the login script without authentication.
`/NoAttach`	Authenticates only.
`/ClearScreen`	Clears the screen before processing the login script.

Tip

New options in NetWare 4 are not supported.

LOGOUT

This is a simple command that logs you out of a server. The syntax for `LOGOUT` is as follows:

```
LOGOUT servername
```

MAP

This is the essential command that establishes network drive mappings. You can have up to 26 drive mappings. Of those, up to 16 can be search drives, which are used for your network path. This is reduced for DOS and Windows clients if the `LASTDRIVE` statement in the CONFIG.SYS is less than the letter Z. When this command is issued without any options, `MAP` displays the current drive mappings. You must be attached to at least one file server before you can map drives to it. The syntax for `MAP` is as follows:

```
MAP options drive:=network path
```

Table 8.6 shows some common options used with `MAP`.

Table 8.6. Common options for `MAP`.

Option	Description
`INS`	Allows you to change the order in which the mapped search drives are listed by inserting a new search drive between two existing search mappings.
`DEL`	Deletes a drive mapping.
`REM`	Removes (deletes) a drive mapping.
`Next`	Maps the next available drive letter to the specified path.
`ROOT`	Maps the path as a fake root on your computer so you cannot change to any parent directory from that drive. This is what occurs all the time in a Microsoft network when you use the `NET USE` command.

SETPASS

Like `CHGPASS`, this command simply changes the password. Its syntax is the same.

SLIST

This command displays the available file servers for the client workstation, which are dependent on the SAP (Service Advertising Protocol) information received by the client. The syntax for `SLIST` is as follows:

```
SLIST servername /C
```

The `servername` option is only available if you want to specify that you can connect to a specific server. Otherwise, it displays all advertised servers. The `/C` option allows `SLIST` to continuously scroll the screen rather than scroll the servers one page at a time.

The Directory Service Manager for NetWare

The Directory Service Manager for NetWare (DSNW) is named in a rather misleading manner. The words *Directory Service* imply a lot of things, including NDS support, which is not the case. DSNW is simply a synchronization agent that makes a bindery-based NetWare server act like a Backup Domain Controller. DSMN copies NetWare user/group accounts to NT Server and then propagates any changes back to the NetWare Server. This sharing of user/group information happens without you adding any software to the NetWare side at all.

DSNW provides a single network login as well as password synchronization. It also copies NetWare accounts to a domain (and any changes to those accounts gets propagated back). Additionally, it gives you the ability to merge multiple NetWare accounts into a single NT account.

Author's Note

It is seriously important to note that this utility, like the FPNW, only works with bindery-based NetWare servers, not any NDS servers, even those servers that are running under bindery emulation.

DSNW Options

DSNW gives you several options for setting up initial passwords, handling account deletions, and selecting which accounts should be propagated. In an NT environment, you only need a single account and password for each user. Unless you have already moved to NetWare 4.1 and NDS, you probably have numerous duplicate accounts on your NetWare 3.x servers for your users. DSMN gives you the opportunity to consolidate NetWare 2.x and 3.x binderies into Windows NT domain, thus providing you with a single point of administration to help ease your administrative burden.

Once these accounts are copied to a Windows NT domain, they are known as NetWare-compatible accounts and are bound by the account policy of the Windows NT server domain.

Trial Synchronization

Another nice feature of DSNW is *trial synchronization*. Running a trial synchronization before you perform the actual synchronization gives you the ability to read the logs, correct any possible errors, and then run the actual synchronization once you are satisfied with the results.

Synchronicity of Management

DSNW not only makes life easier for network administrators by providing them a single point of administration, it also offers several advantages to clients as well. Clients only need to remember one account name and password. They can access File and Print Services on NetWare and NT servers with a single logon. They can even change their password, both on NT and NetWare, by using the CHGPASS utility on NT. The change is automatically propagated to NetWare servers.

Using the Client-based Administrative Tools

DSNW also supports remote administration from a Windows NT or a Windows 95 machine. You can manage your users and group accounts on NT Server running DSMN either from a remote machine on your LAN, or use remote dial-up service. When you install Services for NetWare 4.0, the setup program installs 32-bit User Manager and Server Manager tools for remote management; however, Windows 95 is not as secure as Windows NT. As an extra security measure, users are prompted to re-enter their passwords when they attempt to run these tools. This prevents unauthorized users from simply walking up to a machine and administering the network.

Warning

Do not use previously released versions of remote administration tools when working with Services for NetWare. Use only the updated versions provided on Services for NetWare CD. Microsoft warns that using the older versions can corrupt the NetWare-compatible user accounts on your FPNW servers.

Network Performance Monitoring Objects

Once you have installed any of the services for NetWare, additional performance counter objects are made available. You can use the Performance Monitor, located in the Administrative Tools group, to monitor the following important objects that are related to NetWare Services:

- NWLink IPX
- NWLink SPX
- NWLink NetBIOS

NWLink also supports directing hosting with NetWare servers. Notice that browsing these NetWare resources is easier and quicker than browsing multiple domain Microsoft networks. This is because the support of direct hosting over IPX avoids the NetBIOS-based browsing mechanism.

A NetWare 3.x Primer

Many of us who work with NT sometimes find ourselves in situations in which we are working with other operating systems that we may not be familiar with. This book, of course, is not designed to serve as a beginner's guide to NetWare and is focused on Windows NT. But I would like to go beyond NT for a moment and give a basic overview of NetWare 3.x management.

Overall Account Database Management

Account restrictions are managed using the SYSCON utility. It requires access using the Supervisor account or an equivalent. When you open the SYSCON utility and select Supervisor Options, you see a series of options (as shown in Figure 8.9). These system-wide options only affect users created after the defaults have been set. The same options can also be set on individual users. These options allow you to do the following, among other things:

- Set the account expiration date.
- Limit the client workstation users can log in from.
- Set the user's home directory.
- Set the password restrictions for that account.
- Set the account credit limits.
- Set time restrictions.

Creating a User Using SYSCON

You can use MAKEUSER or USERDEF to automate mass user creation. SYSCON is recommended to use when you are creating a few users at a time. You can do this by accessing the User Information option. You will then see a list of existing users on the servers. Pressing the Insert key on the keyboard allows you to create the user and supply a home directory for the user.

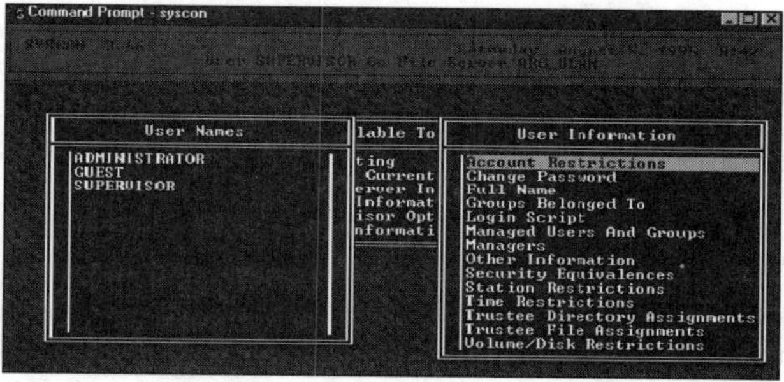

Figure 8.9. *The Main User option menu in the SYSCON utility.*

Creating Groups Using SYSCON

Groups generally serve the same function in NetWare 3.x that they do in Windows NT. They are designed to simplify the task of managing security for users. All newly created users are assigned to the group EVERYONE just as with Windows NT. Unlike Windows NT, NetWare's EVERYONE group is a manageable group in which you can control its membership. In the opening menu of SYSCON, select Group Information. It shows a list of current groups. You can press the Insert key to create the group. After creating the group, you can select the group, then the group options will appear. Selecting the Member List option will display the current users and groups that belong to that group. You can then select the Insert key and add a user.

Author's Note

At the least, you need to know the information contained in the preceding two sections to properly set up the Gateway Services for NetWare and the Directory Service Manager for NetWare.

Viewing File and Directory Information on NetWare Servers

You can view directory and file information on NetWare servers in many ways. There are the basic DOS-like or internal commands like `dir`. When viewing the complete context of files, including security attributes, owner information, creation and rights information, you need to use more NetWare-specific utilities.

`FILER` is a menu-based utility that enables you to view the current file or directory information or view information on other files and/or directories by selecting View/Set File (or Directory) Information.

You can also use external command line utilities like `NDIR` and `LISTDIR` to view this extended information.

NetWare Security

NetWare Security is handled at three levels:

- *Login.* You can lock out intruders and require them to log on to NetWare.
- *File/Directory.* You can assign attributes to directories and files that affect all users.
- *User/Group.* You can assign trustee rights to files and directories to groups and users. These trustee-based rights are similar to NTFS permissions on Windows NT.

Rights can be assigned to users and groups for directories and files. Specific trustee rights to a file within that directory can then override rights granted at the directory level. You can also restrict rights that flow down with the IRM.

NT Equivalents of NetWare Rights

Table 8.7 outlines the NetWare rights and their NT equivalents.

Table 8.7. NT rights and NT equivalents.

NetWare	Windows NT
Supervisor (S)	Full Control (All)
Read (R)	Read (RX)
Write (W)	Change (RWXD)
Erase	Change (RWXD)
Modify (M)	Change (RWXD)
Create	Add (WX)
File Scan (F)	List (RX)
Access Control (A)	Change Permissions (P)

The selected NetWare utilities and their options with Windows NT 4 are listed in Table 8.8.

Table 8.8. NetWare utilities and their Windows NT options.

Utility	Environment	NetWare 3	NetWare 4	MS Client Services for NetWare	Novell Client for NT
SYSCON	DOS	Yes	No	Yes	Yes
NETADMIN	DOS	No	Yes	No	Yes
PCONSOLE	DOS	Yes	Yes	Yes	Yes

Utility	Environment	NetWare 3	NetWare 4	MS Client Services for NetWare	Novell Client for NT
NWADMIN	Windows	No	Yes	No	Yes
NWADMIN-NT	Windows NT	No	Yes	No	Yes
RCONSOLE	DOS	Yes	Yes	Yes	Yes
PRINTCON	DOS	Yes	Yes	Yes	Yes
CAPTURE	DOS	Yes	Yes	Yes (with Shell Help)	Yes
VOLINFO	DOS	Yes	Yes	Slow	Slow
SESSION	DOS	Yes	No	Flaky	No

The NetWare 3.2 Enhancement Pack

The ongoing success of NetWare 3.x has led to the update package for NetWare. Named NetWare 3.2, it extends many NetWare capabilities. This meets a demand for those organizations that do not want to move to the large complexity of NetWare Directory Services but would like the network services updates and new NetWare Loadable Modules (NLMs). The NetWare Enhancement Pack brings many changes to NetWare 3.1x.

Updated NLSP

A newer version of the NLSP (NetWare Link State Protocol) is included, which updates for multi-server environments. This is Novell's proprietary link state solution for dynamic routing, which is preferred for those of us who may not like the traffic that the Routing Information Protocol (RIP) creates while sampling the network searching for optimal routes.

Patch Aggregation

As a major convenience, all of the patch update packages (Novell's euphemism for bug fix) that have been collecting and adding up have been fully integrated and packaged as a single solution.

The Year 2000 Issue

Novell is correcting all of Y2K problems with NetWare 3.1x by including updates and fixes into the enhancement pack. These updates have been verified as fully Year 2000-compliant by third-party evaluators.

Better Client and Administrative Utilities

For the clients, Novell comes with the enhancement patch Netscape Navigator versions 3.01 and 4.04. Do not expect Internet Explorer to be used anywhere near a NetWare product. For the administrators, it also bundles all of the recent client updates (including the Client32 solutions) for Windows 95 and Windows NT. A newer Windows-based SYSCON utility has also been provided to avoid using the DOS-based application under Windows 95, or in the case of the subject of this book, Windows NT.

Chapter 9

Integration with NetWare Directory Services

- **An Overview of NDS**
  Look at the recent versions of NetWare and IntranetWare and the overall concept and structures of NetWare Directory Services.
- **Novell's IntranetWare Client for Windows NT Workstation**
  This section examines how the IntranetWare Client can allow NT and NDS to coexist from a client-server perspective.
- **Configuration Issues**
  Learn what configuration issues exist with the IntranetWare client, including Redirector, IPX, and NetWare/IP issues.
- **The NetWare Administrator for Windows NT**
  Observe how a Novell administrator can manage an NDS tree using this utility from Windows NT Workstation.
- **The Novell Workstation Manager**
  Find out how to control Windows NT Workstation properties, user options, password synchronization, and other important aspects of NT workstations using this special NDS object.
- **The Novell Application Launcher**
  We will observe how to create these impressive NDS objects to push application parameters down to NDS user's desktops.

NetWare Directory Services

NetWare Directory Services (NDS) was released with NetWare version 4 in 1993. If you had been working with NetWare, this new release was a drastic change in the structure of NetWare. Instead of using a single-server, per-server database structure, Novell now used a multi-server single-database structure that could be distributed across multiple servers.

The first few releases of NetWare 4 had their share of problems. NetWare version 4.1 was the first stable release of NDS. It is still the major version of NDS in use as of 1998.

In late 1996, Novell decided to adjust the name for marketing purposes and to promote their additional Internet/intranet technologies by renaming NetWare to *IntranetWare*. Version 4.11 is referred to as *IntranetWare*. In 1998, Novell decided to change the name back to *NetWare* for version 5.0, scheduled to be released in late 1998 (code-named *Moab*.)

Structure of NDS

NDS allows enterprise network resources to be organized into objects called *leaf objects*. These leaf objects are then organized into a virtual directory using special types of objects called *containers*.

Author's Note

As mentioned in Chapter 1, "Developing an Enterprise Model," leaf objects are analogous to files while container objects are analogous to directories. This approach is based upon the CCITT X.500 standard in terms of object types, organizational structure, and naming guidelines.

NDS uses a standard guideline called a *schema* to determine the various leaf and container object types as well as all of their associated properties. NDS enables developers to extend that schema for additional purposes. Since 1997, the NDS schema has been extended to include various object types relating to Windows NT.

NDS Objects

The object-oriented view of the NDS tree is what lets you perform many routine functions for access and administrative control. Objects are named by a name value. Initials are actually used in place of their full type names when using them to name the *context*, or directory path, of an NDS object. Each object represents a type. These types usually fall into one of two categories; they are either containers or leafs. This holds true to the X.500 naming structure discussed earlier in Chapter 1. Table 9.1 describes the major name types and values used.

Table 9.1. NDS object type names.

Type	Value
C	Country
O	Organization (container)
OU	Organizational unit (container)
CN	Common name (leaf objects)

The NDS tree is defined as [ROOT] because it is the "root" of the directory. The NDS path to the object may be a complete path based from the root of the tree, or it may be the relative path from the current NDS context. The primary organized entity is always the leaf object just as the file is in the directory. Table 9.2 explains the most common types of leaf objects.

Table 9.2. Types of leaf objects.

Object	Description
User	Regular NDS user accounts
Server	NetWare Server or any server supporting the NetWare core protocol
Volume	A server volume
Bindery	A bindery-based object used for backward compatibility
Group	A group of users
Directory Map	A link to a specific file system directory
Alias	A symbolic link to another object
Print Server	A NetWare print server
Printer	A map to a printing device
Queue	A NetWare print queue
Profile	A login script shared among multiple users
AFP Server	An AppleTalk filing protocol supported by a NetWare server
Computer	A client computer

NDS objects can be referenced in two ways:

- A *distinguished name* refers to the direct path from the [ROOT] object. For example:

```
CN=SBTHOMAS.OU=JAMESTOWN.OU=TRAINING
```

- The *relative distinguished name* is named according to its parent container. For example, CN=SBTHOMAS would suffice if the current context was OU=JAMESTOWN.OU=TRAINING.

The syntax can fall into two areas: *typeful names* or *typeless names*. Typeful names is when the user or administrator is using the syntax

```
CN=SBTHOMAS.OU=JAMESTOWN.OU=TRAINING
```

to reference the object. The typeless names is when the user or administrator is simply using the syntax in the form of dotted paths:

```
SBTHOMAS.JAMESTOWN.TRAINING
```

The IntranetWare Client for Windows NT

The IntranetWare Client for Windows NT is provided for NT workstations and NT standalone servers designed to act primarily as NDS clients. Those organizations torn between the scalability, extensibility, and hierarchical structure of NDS and the security, application support, and robustness of NT Workstation as a business desktop solution can now literally have the best of both worlds.

This particular client package is an improvement upon the previous NetWare redirectors available for Windows NT. The Novell NetWare Clients Services package released with NT 3.51 was weak in that it required a separate ODI-based IPX/SPX stack and most of the NDS utilities needed to communicate via a DOS-based shell emulator.

Troubleshooting Tip

The IntranetWare Client simply works with Microsoft's built-in IPX/SPX compatible solution (NWLink). You cannot, however, have any Microsoft-based redirectors for NetWare like the Client Services for NetWare (CSNW) or the Gateway Services for NetWare (GSNW) installed. If you do have these products installed, Microsoft will prompt you to remove them. This makes a seamless operation for removing the Microsoft Redirector and installing the IntranetWare Client.

Installation

You can obtain the IntranetWare Client for free from Novell through direct order, Novell Support Connection (a CD subscription service of technical support and software from Novell), and their Web site (`http://www.novell.com`). There are two ways to install the client once you have obtained it:

- By using the Services tab from the Network Control Panel applet.
- By double-clicking the SETUPNW.EXE utility.

Either way, you will see the same startup screen shown in Figure 9.1.

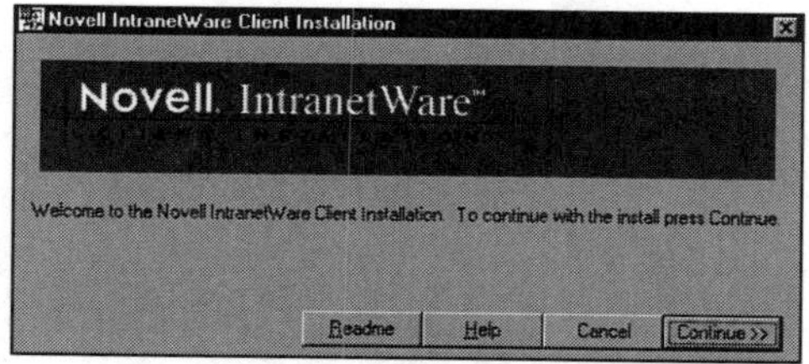

Figure 9.1. *The startup screen for the IntranetWare Client for NT installation.*

The installation is pretty simple in that it will not to prompt you for any specific configuration. You will have to do this after the files have finished copying and you have been prompted to reboot.

NetWare Graphical Interface Authentication

One of the first things you will notice that has changed is the login prompt. The IntranetWare prompt, shown in Figure 9.2, has replaced the Windows NT generic login screen. It still prompts you to press Ctrl+Alt+Delete.

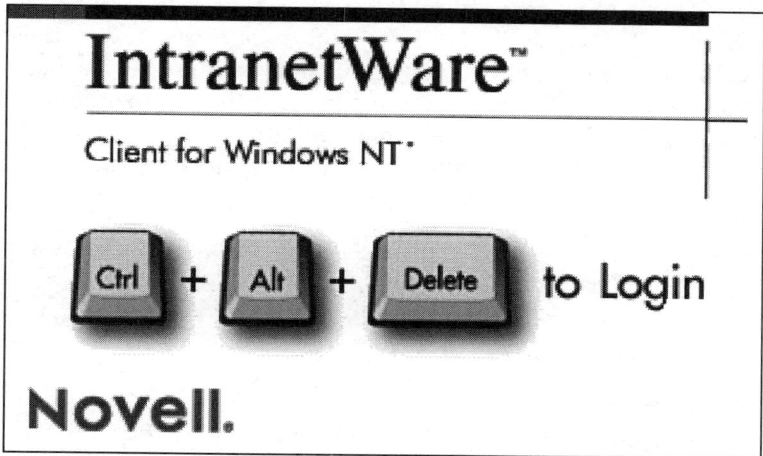

Figure 9.2. *The IntranetWare welcome screen.*

When you press Ctrl+Alt+Delete this time, you get a modified logon option. Windows NT added the NWGINA module to it. *NWGINA* stands for *NetWare Graphical Interface Authentication*. The most recent release as of this writing is version 4.11a. This dialog box is divided into six tabs:

- Login. The user submits his username, server or context, and password. If the user is logging on to Windows NT only, then this is where the NT username and password is specified. If the user is logging on to NDS with the Workstation Manager, or is performing a dual-logon with both NDS and Windows NT, he will put his NetWare username, NDS context, and password. If the Windows NT credentials are different (not using Workstation Manager) then the user is prompted for the NT username and password that follows immediately after a successful NetWare login. If the NetWare login fails, the user still has the option of doing an NT login only.
- IntranetWare. This is where NetWare and IntranetWare client login preferences can be set. If you are doing an NDS login, a preferred NDS tree and a preferred NDS server can be selected. You can also select the default context within the NDS tree. This should usually be the NDS path to the container object that contains your username. If you are using this for a NetWare bindery login, a preferred server is your only option.
- Windows NT. This is where you can put in your NT username (if different from your NetWare username) as well as the authentication authority for your NT username. If your NT workstation or server does not belong to a domain, then the only option you will have is for the local computer to authenticate you. If your NT computer does belong to a domain, you will be able to select that domain plus any other trusted domains in addition to your computer. You can also select to do a Windows NT login only, which will bypass NDS login altogether. This is great for NT users running NT Workstation on a laptop.
- Login Script. The user has the option of using alternative login scripts for his client. The bindery-based order of login script processing is as follows:

    The system login script

    The user's login script (if present)

    The default (if the user's login script is not available)

  In NDS, the scenario is a little bit different. The NDS order of login script processing is

    The user's container login script is run (if available).

    If a profile script is available, it will then run.

    Then (if available) a user login script is run.

    If the user login script is not available, then a default login script will run.

- Variables. This is where login script variables can be placed. You can define up to four variables to be used by the login scripts. You or your network supervisor can set up your login scripts to use these variables. For example, you might define one variable as `MAIL`. Your login script might use the `MAIL` variable to map drives to the mail server.
- Dial-Up. This page is only available with the Windows NT Dial-Up Networking component installed. Whether your are using this for NDS authentication, NT authentication, or both, this can very helpful for remote users.

Even if a user decides to log in to Windows NT only, she can still authenticate to a NetWare server or an NDS tree using the Network Neighborhood or by selecting the option to Map Network Drive from My Computer or the File Manager. When a user does this, she is prompted with the dialog box shown in Figure 9.3.

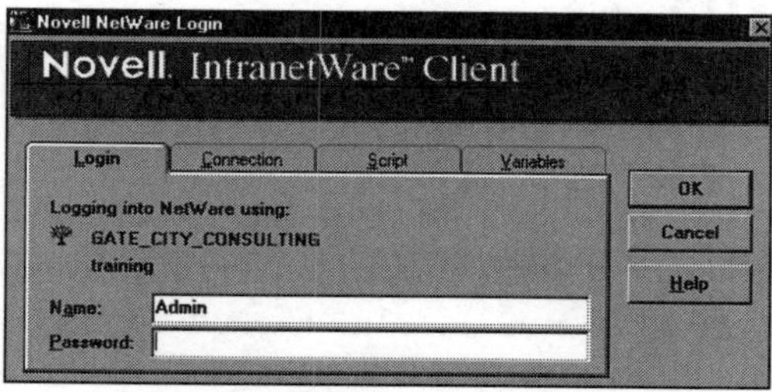

Figure 9.3. *Attaching authentication options using the IntranetWare Client.*

Including the Workstation Manager in Unattended Installations

As mentioned earlier in the book, Windows NT's setup management utilities allow the option for OEM components, including add-on products. This will be necessary in automating roll-outs of any Novell-based NetWare services. The Workstation Manager includes a pre-built template answer file which can be incorporated into unattended installations of Windows NT 3.51 and 4.0.

A special Novell Modified section is created containing information about the following areas:

- Protocol selections (TCP/IP, NWLink)
- Services (`NWFS = NovellNetWareClientParameters,` \OEM\NET\NTCLIENT\I386)
- License agreement

Author's Note

If the `AcceptLicenseAgreement` *is set to* `NO`*, all users will be prompted to accept the agreement individually when the client is installed.*

- The option to remove the MS NetWare Client
- Whether or not to use NWGINA
- Optional installation of NetWare IP
- Graphical login property page parameters (if selected)
- Novell NetWareIP property page parameters (if selected)

Viewing and Making NetWare Connections

With the IntranetWare Client, you have the option of browsing NetWare resources by server, or of browsing the NDS tree itself. Most likely, login connections will be established using login scripts when authenticating to NDS. To view your current connections, you can right-click the Network Neighborhood and select the IntranetWare Connection option. It then displays your NDS tree connections and server attachments. It also displays the username authenticated under NDS. Figure 9.4 shows this dialog box.

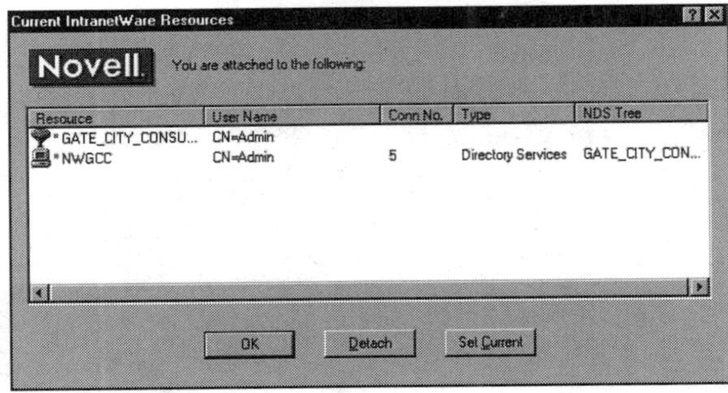

Figure 9.4. *The Current IntranetWare Resources dialog box.*

Drive Mappings

NDS drive mappings are under the same format as NT drive mappings in that they use the same Universal Naming Convention (UNC) format. This UNC format is slightly altered for NDS access. For example, to connect to the directory PUBLIC located on volume SYS in the server object:

```
CN=NWGCC.OU=JAMESTOWN.O=TRAINING
```

in the NDS tree GATE_CITY_CONSULTING using the UNC format, you would type the following:

```
\\GATE_CITY_CONSULTING\TRAINING\JAMESTOWN\NWGCC\SYS\PUBLIC
```

You could also connect strictly to the server using the following syntax if you are currently within the same NDS context as the server:

```
\\NWGCC\SYS\PUBLIC
```

Configuring the IntranetWare Client

The IntranetWare Client is configured as a network service. You can invoke this dialog box by navigating to the Control Panel and selecting Network, Services, Novell IntranetWare Client. This invokes the multi-tabbed dialog box.

Client Options

The first tab deals with basic client options (see Figure 9.5). This is where the first network drive setting can be used. Novell maps the first drive available to the first entry in the login script by default. This value is set to drive F: by default.

Troubleshooting Tip

The NetWare login script runs before any Windows NT logon scripts do. It also has precedence over any persistent connections you may have mapped under Windows NT. It is important to know this, because when trying to restore connections to Windows NT or other resources, you might encounter the error message `The device name is already in use.`

One bit of advice: Use drive letters not contained in login scripts, or use the following syntax when mapping drives from Windows NT logon scripts:

```
NET USE *

\\SERVER\RESOURCE /PERSISTENT:NO
```

You can also use the Client tab to set the preferred server and NDS tree, also shown in Figure 9.5.

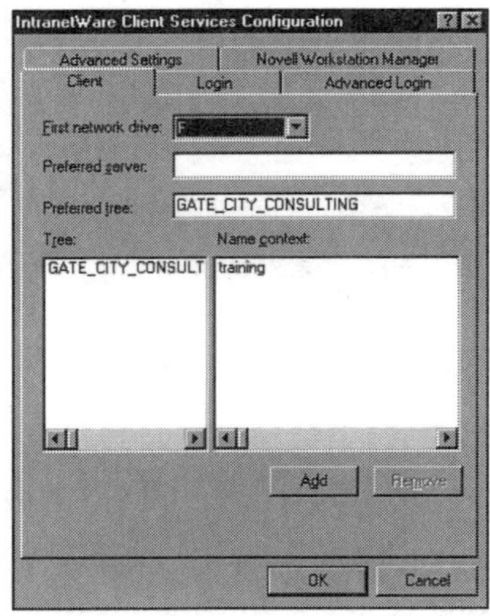

Figure 9.5. *The IntranetWare Client tab.*

Login Information

The second tab is the Login tab. The options within this tab determine which login tabs will be displayed on the screen when a user attempts to log on. You can also put in specific information about login scripts, profiles scripts, and even script variables. You can also turn on or off scripts completely using this tab, and even control how the results will be displayed. This is also the screen for enabling support for dialing up and accessing NetWare resources using Windows NT Dial-Up Networking, as shown in Figure 9.6.

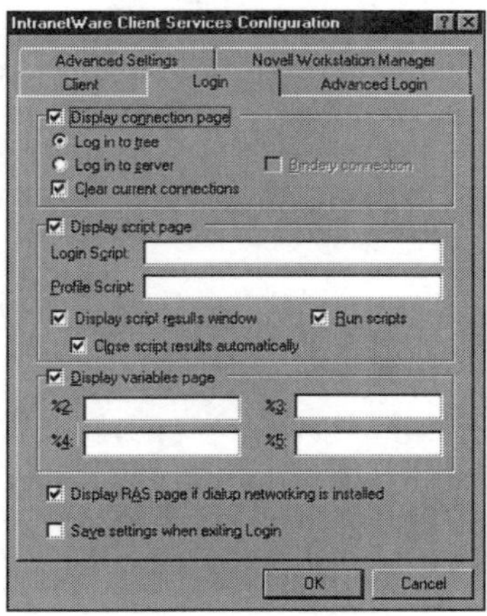

Figure 9.6. *The login options for the IntranetWare Client properties.*

Using Profiles and Policies

The Advanced Login tab in the IntranetWare Client Properties dialog box allows the IntranetWare Client to support Windows NT Profiles and Policies. The support extends as far as allowing policies to be accessed from NetWare servers and user profiles. You can also configure a custom welcome screen bitmap file to be used, such as a company's corporate logo.

As you can see in Figure 9.7, the policy is not accessed in the same manner as it is under Windows NT (using the domain controller's NETLOGON share and the filename NTCONFIG.POL). The policy can be stored on any accessible file system. The idea is that it can be stored on a NetWare file system to allow NetWare administrators to centrally manage policies. If they wish to do so, they either need access to Windows NT Server, or they need to use the System Policy Editor from Client-based Administrative Tools for Windows NT Server (which is also found on the Windows NT Server CD). The user profile can be stored in relation to the user's home or mail directory, or stored in a specific centralized file system directory.

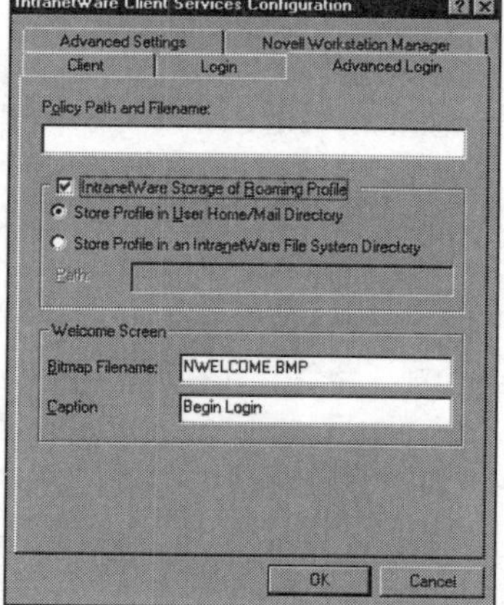

Figure 9.7. *The advanced login options for the IntranetWare Client.*

If you are implementing System Policies, you can control the IntranetWare Client configuration using a special System Policy template that you can snap into the Windows NT System Policy Editor. By default, when you pull up the System Policy Editor (POLEDIT.EXE), only two templates are loaded:

- One is COMMON.ADM, which is the template file containing common options for the Explorer shell in both Windows NT and Windows 95.
- The other is WINNT.ADM, which contains information specific to Windows NT.

An administrator has the option of also loading WINDOWS.ADM, which contains settings for Windows 95. This template is included so that the administrator has the option of creating system polices for Windows 95 as well as Windows NT.

IntranetWare Client also contains a special template that administrators can use to create system policies that not only control NT properties, but also can control IntranetWare Client properties. To install the policy template for the IntranetWare Client, select Policy Template under the Options menu in the System Policy Editor. You can then add the template by selecting Add and navigating to the path on the CD or disk that contains the NWNT.ADM template file. The NWNT.ADM file appears as a loaded template (see Figure 9.8).

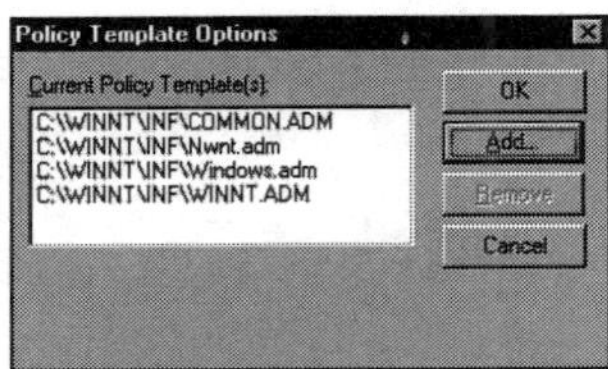

Figure 9.8. *The Policy Template Options dialog box.*

Once the Policy template is loaded, you can create a policy file for a computer that contains the same properties that are found in the Network Control Panel under the IntranetWare Client Properties. When a computer has been assigned a System Policy file, any changes that are made in the Policy file can be passed down to the client, and any modifications automatically take effect.

As shown in Figure 9.9, NetWare IP information can be adjusted as well via the System Policy Editor. I discuss NetWare IP issues later in this chapter. You can also enable support for the Novell Workstation Manager using a system policy.

If you are using profiles, the Intranetware Client saves the user's profile—whether it's a Windows NT 3.51 user profile or a Windows NT 4.0 user profile—to the destination specified. The Intranetware Client even enables the user to maintain separate roaming profiles for Windows NT 3.5 and 4.0.

Troubleshooting Tip

If you are enabling roaming profiles, you must first make sure the server has been adjusted to support the name space required by roaming profiles. By default, NetWare volumes are given long filename support. If you are working with NetWare version 4.1 or earlier, you need to load and add the OS2.NAM namespace module. If you are working with IntranetWare version 4.11 and later, you need to load and add the LONG.NAM namespace module.

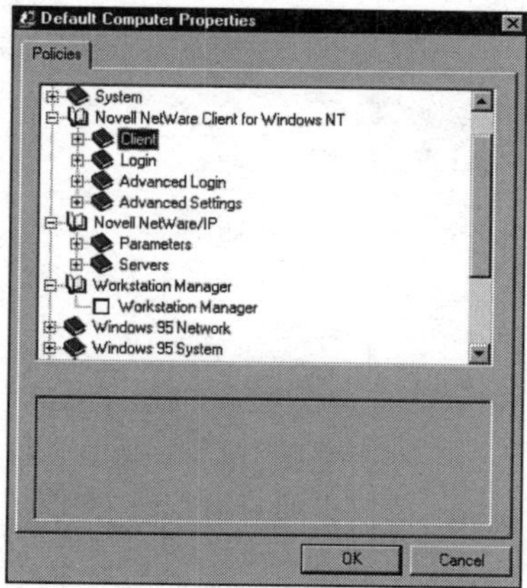

Figure 9.9. *Under the default computer, NetWare Client Properties can be set using the System Policy Editor.*

IntranetWare Client Advanced Options

Formerly, most DOS, OS/2, and Windows clients stored all of their basic and advanced settings in a file called NET.CFG. Because text-based configuration isn't used much in recent Windows-based operating systems, more of these options are being converted to graphical dialog boxes that serve as front ends to the configuration Registry.

Figure 9.10 shows the Advanced Settings tab.

Warning

These options should be adjusted only when absolutely necessary. In many cases, making certain adjustments improves performance significantly.

Several options need significant explanations. Following is a list of options with their definitions and available values:

- Receive Broadcast Messages. The available options are All, Server, and None. The default value is All. These options determine whether the client will receive all broadcast messages from NDS, from the server only, or none at all.
- DOS Name. This value sets compatibility for logon scripts. Normally, it is used to set the value of a workstation's particular version of DOS. With the IntranetWare Client, it defaults to WINNT.

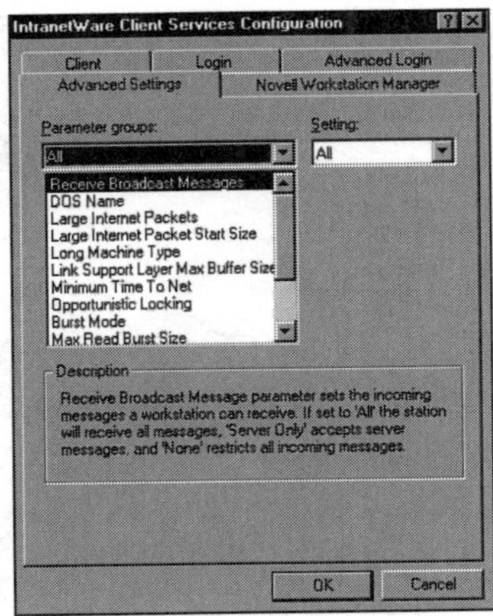

Figure 9.10. *The IntranetWare Client advanced options.*

- Large Internet Packets. This value is either turned On or Off. By default, it is set to On. This option increases performance for File and Print Services by telling the Workstation Client to use the maximum transmission size available. This varies between FDDI, Token Ring, Ethernet, and so on.
- Large Internet Packet Start Size. This value can range from 1 to 65,535 bytes. The default value is 65,535. This is the starting parameter for negotiating the Large Internet Packet size between a client and a server.
- Long Machine Type. This option is used by the `%MACHINE` variable used in NetWare login scripts. The default value is `IBM_PC`.
- Link Support Layer Max Buffer Size. This value can be from 638 to 24,682. The default value is 24,682 for the Link Support emulation facility.
- Minimum Time to Net. The range can be set from 0 to 65,535. The default value is 0. You may need to increase this value when working across slow WAN links or satellite links when the server is not using packet burst.
- Opportunistic Lockings. The value can have a range of On or Off. It defaults to Off. When you turn this value On, it can cache out information as a read-ahead method of improving network performance.
- Burst Mode. This value can have a range of On or Off. This value defaults to On. Packet Burst mode allows the maximum amount of information possible per fragment, which can reduce overhead and network traffic and improve overall network performance.

- Max Read Burst Size. This can have a valid range from 1 to 65,536. The default value is 36,000. This affects the read burst window. Both the read and write bursts are implemented as a sliding window. The window size changes according to the network utilization. Think of the window size being the amount of information that can be sent before an acknowledgment is required. The Max Read Burst Size is the maximum read size before an acknowledgment is mandatory.
- Max Write Burst Size. This can have a valid range from 1 to 65,536. The default value is 15,000. This is the maximum write size before an acknowledgment is mandatory.
- Signature Level. The default value is 1. Its levels are from 0 to 3, which designates the security level of the NetWare Core Protocol packet signature. The greater the level, the greater the security. This does, however, decrease performance on both the client and server ends.
- Short Machine Type. The default value for this is `IBM`. This is the machine name variable required when using older NetWare utilities.

Enabling the Workstation Manager

The last tab allows the workstation to trust NDS trees to adjust their client's setting using the NT Configuration NDS object (see Figure 9.11). This special type of object is added to the schema when the Novell Workstation Manager snap-in is installed. Often, when administrators are rolling out NT workstations using the IntranetWare Client, they simply configure this tab, then allow the Workstation Manager to take care of the rest of the configuration.

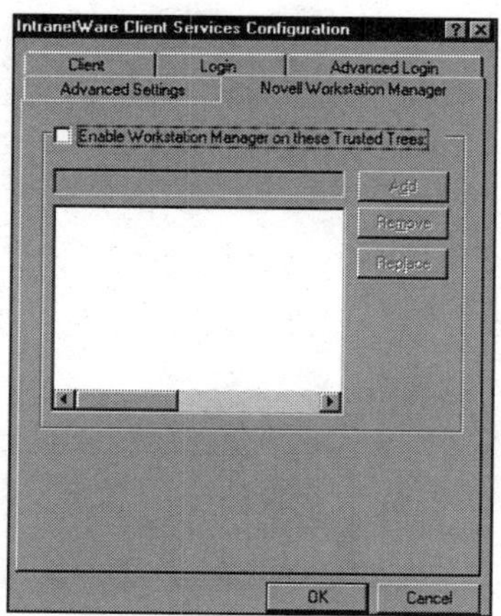

Figure 9.11. *The Novell Workstation Manager tab.*

NetWare/IP Configuration

One of the major benefits of the IntranetWare Client is that it facilitates the NetWare/IP stack that is a TCP/IP-based solution for NetWare. Connectionless oriented information, such as SAP (Service Advertisement Protocol) and RIP (Routing Information Protocol) is encapsulated using UDP (User Datagram Protocol). Connection-oriented information such, as NDS or NCP, is encapsulated using TCP (Transmission Control Protocol).

Auto-Configuration

Installing NetWare/IP requires you to install the IntranetWare Client first. Then the NetWare/IP component can be added under the Service option of the Network Control Panel.

The first thing you might want to have determined is whether or not you are using Custom Configuration or Auto-Configuration using Novell's DHCP (Dynamic Host Configuration Protocol). If you select Auto-Configuration when configuring NetWare/IP under the Control Panel (see Figure 9.12), you don't need to do any additional configuration.

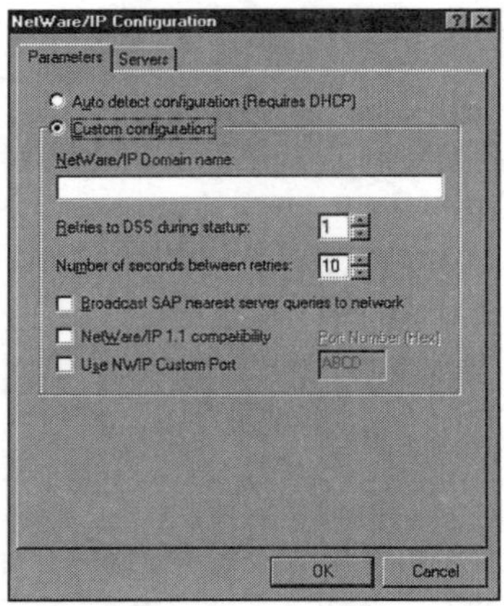

Figure 9.12. *The NetWare/IP Configuration dialog box.*

Custom Configuration

When performing custom configuration, the first thing you need to enter is a NetWare/IP domain name. NetWare/IP domains have the same syntax as any other DNS domain name (such as `gcci.com`). NetWare/IP domains have *DSS*

(Distributed SAP Service) servers. These servers allow NetWare clients and servers to send their SAP and RIP information back and forth in a point-to-point fashion similar to the way WINS handles NetBIOS name resolution. DSS consists of a primary DSS, multiple secondary DSS servers, and NetWare/IP servers. RIP and SAP entries are distributed in a hierarchical approach and stored in a Btrieve database where NetWare/IP servers exchange updates with secondary DSS servers who in turn exchange updates with the primary DSS. The default interval for the exchange is five minutes, although the administrator can configure it. Through this process, every server will have an identical view of the network.

When a NetWare/IP server starts up, it queries the DNS for the location of the DSS servers. It then sends SAP and RIP records to the nearest available DSS server, thus advertising its services to the NetWare/IP internetwork. While the NetWare/IP server is running, it continues to resend SAP and RIP information to the DSS server at defined intervals. If a SAP or RIP record has not been updated within a specific time frame, the DSS server deletes the record. This ensures that the data maintained by the DSS is accurate.

In addition to sending SAP and RIP information to the DSS server, the NetWare/IP server also downloads a copy of updated DSS database records to a local memory cache at a preconfigured interval. When a NetWare/IP client system starts, it can then directly query the server for available network services.

You can configure DSS information using the dialog box shown in Figure 9.12. The Retries to DSS During Startup and the Number of Seconds Between Retries options are usually left alone with defaults. The Broadcast SAP Nearest Server Queries to Network option is disabled by default and should not be needed unless there is not a DSS server on the same subnet.

The second tab is the NetWare/IP Servers tab. This is where you can set Nearest and Preferred DSS Servers. It is the recommended option to specify a preferred registration rather than the option to find the nearest one (via a broadcast).

Author's Note

There is one specific requirement for using NetWare/IP. The Microsoft NDIS driver must be loaded along with the TCP/IP stack. The NetWare/IP component will then be implemented as a tunneling driver. One big advantage of this feature is that you can then avoid using IPX/SPX and can strictly use TCP/IP.

Using the Administrative Utilities

The ADMSETUP.EXE utility that comes with the IntranetWare Client enables you to upload the NetWare Administrator and the Novell Workstation Manager for Windows NT.

Troubleshooting Tip

Bear in mind that ADMSETUP.EXE needs to be installed to the server only once.

Installing the NetWare Administrator

When installing the NetWare Administrator, you actually install two major utilities. You install the graphical-based NDS management utility NWADMINNT.EXE that allows you to manage all supported NDS objects. It also installs an NDS Manager for Windows NT, which enables you to control the database partitioning for the NDS database.

Installing the Novell Workstation Manager

If you elect to install the Novell Workstation Manager, you will then upload a series of snap-in DLLs to the SYS:PUBLIC\WINNT directory. This extends the schema of NDS to include support for the Novell Workstation Manager (labeled as NT Configuration). If you install the Novell Workstation Manager along with Windows NT, the option to install the Registry pointers will be made available (see Figure 9.13). If you select to update these values, you will then be able to use the NT Configuration object.

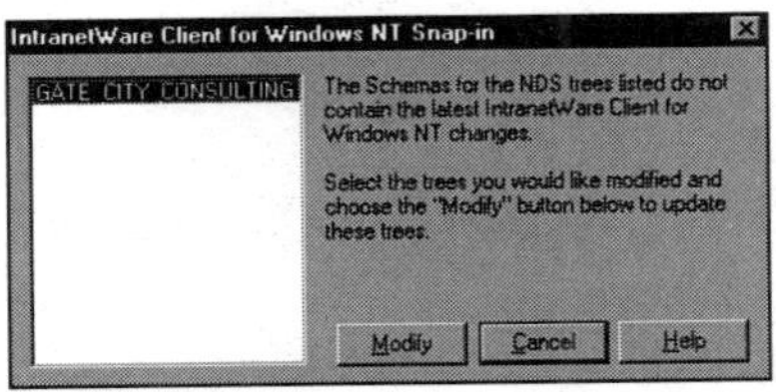

Figure 9.13. *The prompt to update the NDS Registry information.*

Since only one computer needs to run the Administrative setup per NetWare server, the question comes to mind, "How do the other computers use these utilities?" In order for them to use the NWADMNNT.EXE and NDSMGRNT.EXE utility, all they need to do is point to the two executables found under the default path: SYS:PUBLIC\WINNT.

Troubleshooting Tip

There is a problem with these clients running NWADMNNT.EXE using the Novell Workstation Manager to control NT computer objects. They will not have the proper Registry entries loaded that can point to the snap-in DLLs required for these schema extensions. As a result, these objects show up as being unknown objects, yet they still appear. These computers can use a Registry import file, called WORKMAN.REG, to load these new entries. The easiest way to load these entries into the Registry is to double-click the file—the information will automatically be imported. If the WORKMAN.REG file is unavailable, then you can create the file using Notepad or Edit and type in the following information:

```
1. REGEDIT4
2. [HKEY_CURRENT_USER\Software\NetWare\Parameters\NetWare
   Administrator\Snapin Object DLLs WINNT]
3. "APPSNPNT.DLL"=hex(7):41,50,50,53,4e,50,4e,54,2e,44,4c,4c,00
4. "AUDITNT.DLL"=hex(7):41,55,44,49,54,4e,54,2e,44,4c,4c,00
5. "REGEDTNT.DLL"=hex(7):52,45,47,45,44,54,4e,54,2e,44,4c,4c,00
6. "NWCSNAP"="NWSMGR32.DLL"
```

Using the NetWare Administrator

The NetWare Administrator allows an administrator to use a graphical administrative interface to control every object within the NDS database. The idea behind NDS was to create a single, flexible, and scalable management console. For the most part, it meets that duty if you have a client operating system that supports the utility.

Before the IntranetWare Client, only Windows 3.x and Windows 95 computers could run NWADMIN.EXE (shown in Figure 9.14), which was the original version of the NetWare Administrator. This utility would not run from an NT computer using the Microsoft CSNW because first, Windows NT did not support the DLLs used, and second, NDS administration is not supported.

All of the information is organized into an easily browsable tree in the NetWare Administrator. Container objects, such as Organizations and Organizational Units, serve as directories with specific icons designating their object types. Leaf objects emulate files in the directory tree.

Creating and Managing an NDS User

When creating an NDS user, only two properties are technically required:

- The username
- The user's last name

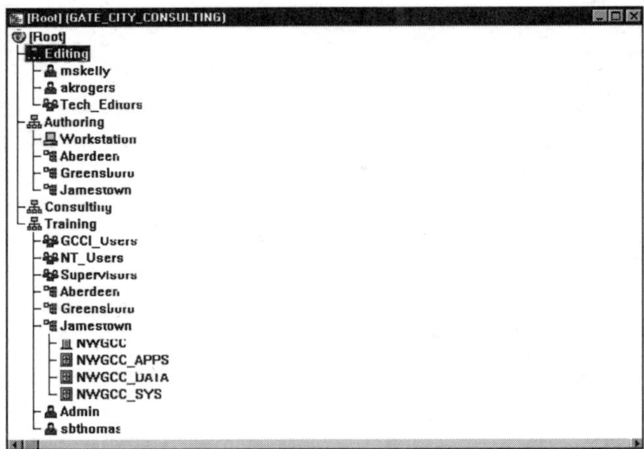

Figure 9.14. *The Novell NetWare Administrator can manage all of the objects in the NDS database.*

These two fields can be added by first selecting the context in which the user will belong. After that, select Create from the Object menu. A list of object types then appears. If you select a user object, then the properties available to users are available for the object, as shown in Figure 9.15.

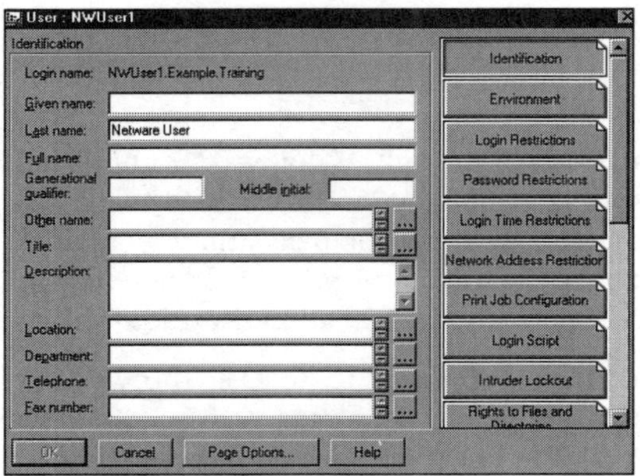

Figure 9.15. *The available user options when creating an NDS user.*

Passwords, home directories, rights, and other options are available to be associated with NDS users. When an object is selected or created, the schema tells the NetWare Administrator which options will be made available for adjustment. For example, when you select a NetWare server, the object properties are a bit different in that they relate more to the server, as shown in Figure 9.16.

You can use the object to view the server's error log, supported operators, and their users.

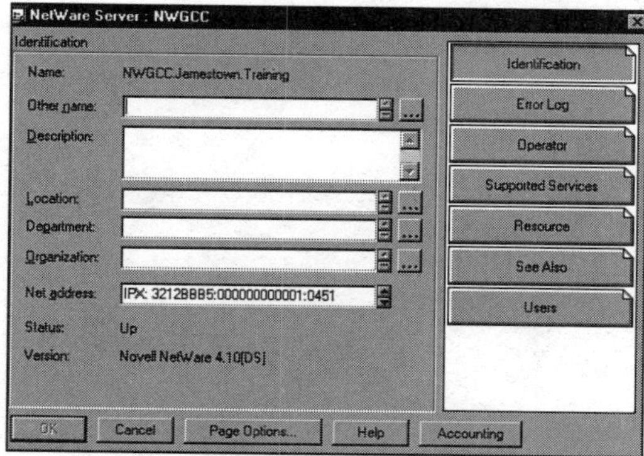

Figure 9.16. *Viewing a server object using the NetWare Administrator.*

A comprehensive discussion of NDS objects and their management within the NetWare Administrator goes far beyond the scope of this book.

Using the Novell Workstation Manager

If the Workstation Manager snap-ins have been loaded and registered, you can begin to create the NT Configuration object that you want to use to control one or more NT workstations running the IntranetWare Client.

Author's Note

Of course, bear in mind these affect only IntranetWare Client users who have the Workstation Manager enabled using either a policy or local configuration. If you are familiar with managing NDS objects, then most of the next few sections will be somewhat simple. Don't worry, though, if you are not familiar with creating an NDS object, because I step through every option.

The Identification Option

The first option is basic identification information for the object (see Figure 9.17). What an administrator puts here is simply information not pertinent to the configuration per se, but administrative information. Take advantage of this available field.

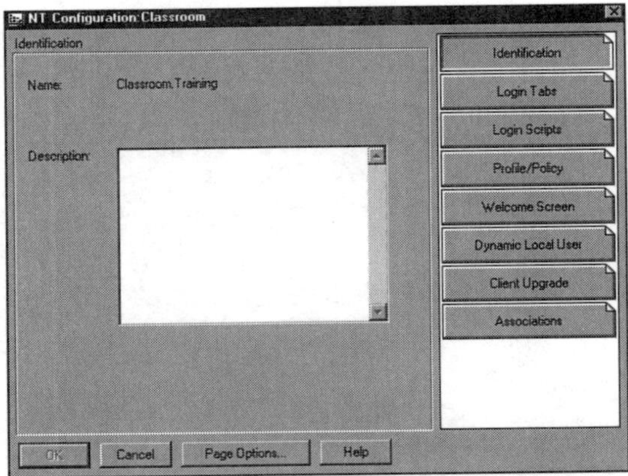

Figure 9.17. *The Identification tab of the NT Configuration object.*

The Login Tabs Option

The Login Tabs option is similar to the options available locally in that it allows you to determine which login tabs will be made available. In Figure 9.18, you see that this is a fairly simple and self-explanatory dialog box.

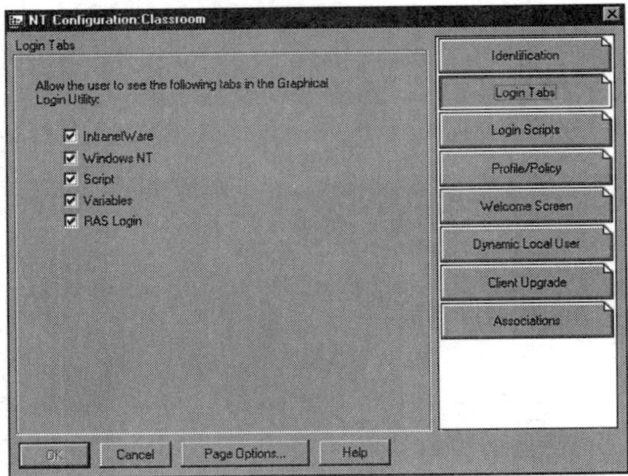

Figure 9.18. *The Login Tabs of the NT Configuration object.*

The Login Scripts Option

Figure 9.19 displays the Login Scripts options that can be set for the client. You can also put in specific information on login scripts, profiles scripts, and even script variables. You can also turn on or off scripts completely using this tab, as well as even control how the results will be displayed. You can define up to four variables to be used by the login scripts. You or your network supervisor can set up your login scripts to use these variables.

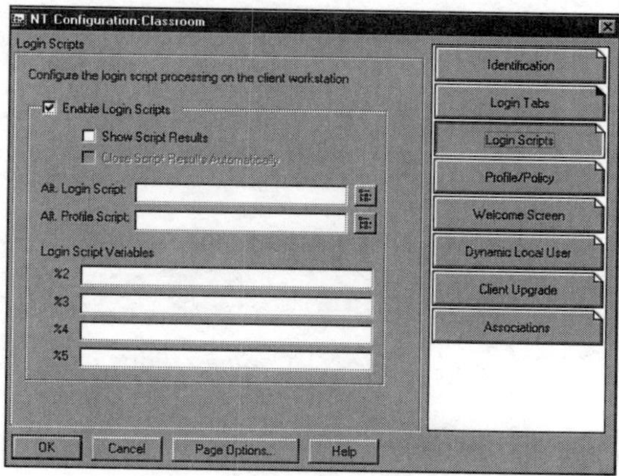

Figure 9.19. *The Login Scripts tab of the NT Configuration object.*

The Profile/Policy Option

The next option is Profile/Policy, which allows the Workstation Manager object to set the path for a Windows NT 3.51 or 4.0 profile. A path to a policy file is an option as well. For the most part, it makes the most sense to make the profile path relative to the user's home directory. Figure 9.20 displays the Profile/Policy option dialog box.

Troubleshooting Tip

If you are going to enable roaming profiles, you might want to first examine the current quota policy on the NetWare servers your users are accessing. Users may often place binary files and directories in shell folders, such as the desktop and the personal directory, which are then saved to the roaming profile location. If the total size of the profile is larger than the allotted disk quota space, then an error will occur when trying to log off. You will not be able to save your roaming profile.

As a way to avoid this problem, you might want to suggest to your users to create shortcuts only on the desktop and not to save large documents to any of the profile folders.

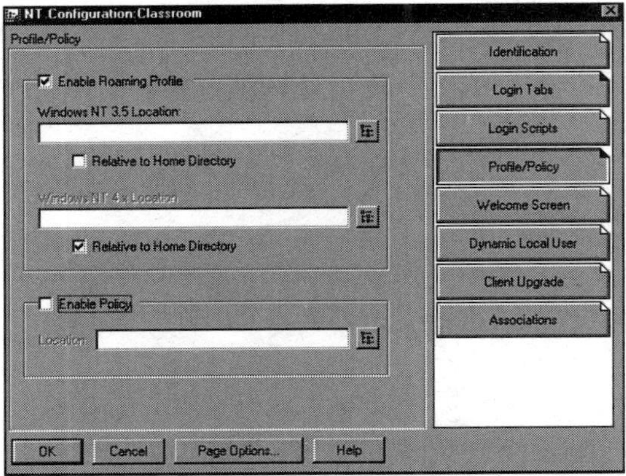

Figure 9.20. *The Profile/Policy tab of the NT Configuration object.*

Troubleshooting Tip

A problem arises if the network administrator also uses the COMMON.ADM template through POLEDIT.EXE (System Policy Editor) to specify the path to the policy file when configuring policies. This is because the template will add a different Registry key to the NT Registry. This key conflicts with the key that the Novell Workstation Manager needs to use. This conflict causes inconsistencies when the policies run.

The best way to avoid these inconsistencies is to use only the NT Configuration object to specify the path to the policy file when using the Novell Workstation Manager, and not to use the policy template.

The Welcome Screen Option

Figure 9.21 displays the Welcome Screen option. This is where you can assign a new title to the welcome screen that shows up on the Windows NT workstation. You can also use this option to control the bitmap image being used by the Workstation Manager object. This is a great way of allowing a corporate logo to appear in place of the default bitmap. By assigning all of your NDS users to this NT Configuration object, they would then have the same custom welcome screen.

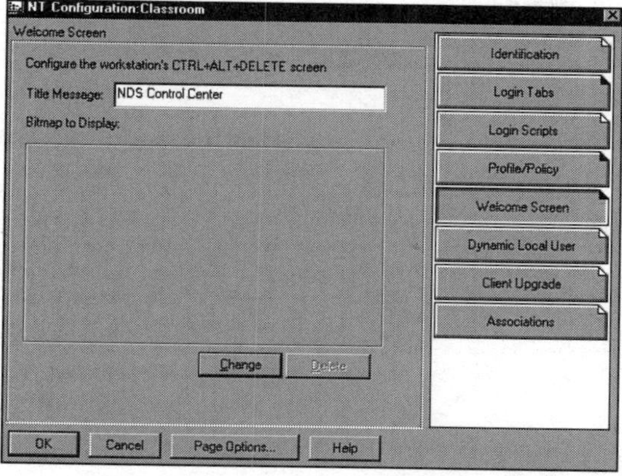

Figure 9.21. *The Welcome Screen tab of the NT Configuration object.*

The Dynamic Local User Account Option

This is probably the most important part of the Novell Workstation Manager. When you set this option, it can provide a single point of login for mixed NT and NetWare environments. This can also significantly reduce the individual user account management of NT workstations and, in some cases, even NT domains.

If you opt not to use the dynamic local user account creation option, what will occur first is the NDS authentication, unless it is turned off at the client. After the NDS authentication, users will authenticate to NT either locally or from a domain controller (if they are participating in a domain). They can use the same username or different usernames. They have to establish password synchronicity to enable the box to change their NT password to match their NetWare password. As you can see, not enabling the Dynamic Local User option leaves you with a totally manual, user-initiated process.

Enabling the Dynamic Local User creation allows the user to worry only about NetWare credentials. As seen in Figure 9.22, the user has three basic options:

- If the administrator wants, she can simply set the automatic account to be created using NetWare credentials, which means such properties as username, descriptions, passwords, and groups will be translated to the NT account. Each of these accounts is automatically created the first time the user logs on to a machine after it has been associated with that NT Configuration object.

- If the option to manage an existing NT account is selected, then an administrator can specialize a specific account that should already exist on the NT computer he is logging on to. The administrator, using this object, can adjust default group memberships.
- Using a volatile user account simply means that when a user logs on, an account is automatically created using the credentials set by the NT Configuration object, including the username, full name, description, and even the default group memberships (as shown in Figure 9.22). User Account Synchronicity, Password Synchronicity, and other security options are synchronized seamlessly using this option.

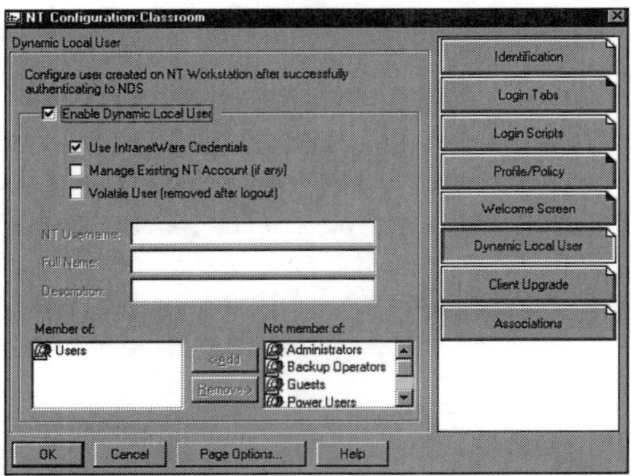

Figure 9.22. *The Dynamic Local User tab of the NT Configuration object.*

Advantages and Disadvantages of the Volatile User Account

The main advantages of the volatile user account are as follows:

- It prevents a large number of user accounts from building up in the local SAM.
- It forces users to authenticate using NDS before they can log on to the NT workstation. This is helpful when a large number of users are using the same workstation.
- The Volatile User option can also provide greater security. Users cannot log in if the workstation is not connected to the network.

Among the disadvantages of the volatile user account is that each time the user is created, it is assigned a unique SID (security ID). If NTFS is installed, users who save files to the local drive lose ownership and rights to those files. If using a FAT file system, then volatile users can access files on the local drive. Novell is aware of this issue and is working on a solution to it.

The Associations Option

The last tab available in the NT Configuration object is the Associations option. This option allows the direct NDS association to occur. In order for the Workstation Manager NT Configuration object to pass down correctly, a user using that workstation must be associated with that object.

Technically, any NDS object can be associated with another. Whether they can understand the association is another story. In the case of the NT Configuration object, users and groups can be associated. In larger environments, it makes much more sense to use the group options to associate users with NT Configuration objects. Figure 9.23 displays the Associations tab.

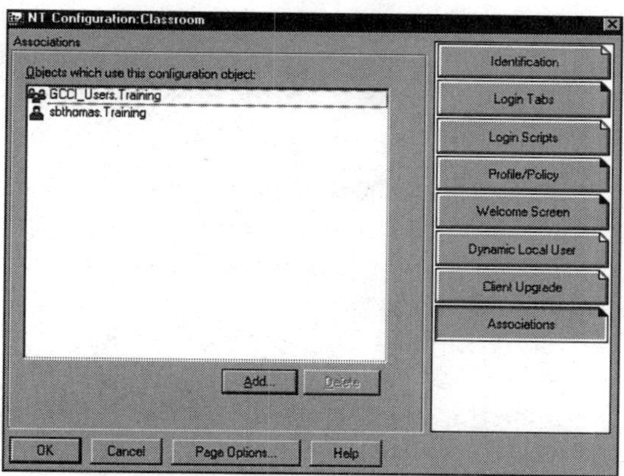

Figure 9.23. *The Associations tab of the NT Configuration object.*

Using the Automatic Client Upgrade

Another significant capability provided by the Workstation Manager is the capability to push an IntranetWare Client software upgrade to the workstation from a central location. This is possible with *Automatic Client Upgrade (ACU)*, which is performed through the login script process.

ACU works well for DOS, Windows, and other nonsecure operating systems, because all workstation users had unrestricted access to the local workstation. Windows NT, on the other hand, provides for workstation access control. Only users who have administrative privileges on the workstation can access and modify the operating system files. Thus, ACU can be used only when an administrator-level user is authenticating to the workstation. Workstation Manager can create this administrator user upon login and allow the client upgrade to take place.

Workstation Manager works with ACU to update the NT workstation without requiring a network supervisor to come to the workstation. To do this, the network supervisor uses NetWare Administrator to configure the NT Workstation object to perform a client upgrade when the next user logs in to the workstation.

The Novell Application Launcher

The *Novell Application Launcher (NAL)* reduces administration significantly, eliminates complexities associated with networked applications in mixed environments, provides for fault tolerance and load balancing among application servers, and provides true location independence—all from a single point of administration. This is accomplished by storing the information required to execute the application on the workstation within a directory object. Administrators can then assign applications by user, user group, or organization, and have appropriate applications dynamically appear on users' desktops.

Software assignment can be done once for a company group or department so those current and future members of this group will gain automatic access to a standard desktop configuration. The end user can have access to all applications assigned to them, on both IntranetWare and Windows NT servers, while the administrator can easily support this demand from the management console. The offering works with Windows 3.x, Windows 95, and Windows NT to automatically determine the desktop operating system platform upon which it is running.

NAL also lets the network administrator physically distribute software out to the desktop through automated installations, or allows users to pull applications to their desktop by providing them with setup programs.

Installing NAL

If you are going to install the Novell Application Manager first using POLEDIT.EXE (comes with the NT Resource Kit), you should implement the following steps:

1. Load the policy template sys:public\winnt\nalexp32.adm.
2. Save the policy in a network directory, for example sys:public\winnt\nwconfig.pol.
3. Create an NT Configuration object using the NetWare Administrator.
4. Associate the policy with the new one you have just created.
5. In the Dynamic Local User option of the NT Configuration object, make sure the user is a power user or administrator.

6. Install the application using the NetWare SNAPSHOT utility.
7. Log into the network as admin and as administrator to Windows NT. Log in using the NT Workstation Manager, and start NALEXPLD; the application is now able to be installed using NAL.

Other NetWare Administrative Utilities

There are several additional utilities that you can use to control NDS resources. In the interest of providing some additional information and knowledge, a select few (based on popularity) have been chosen for brief mention.

Remote Console

RCONSOLE.EXE is a DOS-based utility that allows the server's console to be projected to the client workstation. This is very helpful for administrators who need to manage servers from remote locations, especially different geographical sites.

In order for a server to be accessed using the Remote Console utility on a LAN, the server must have a module called REMOTE.NLM loaded, as well as a connection method (in the case of LANs it is usually the RSPX.NLM that is loaded). These steps can be automated by placing them in the NetWare server's AUTOEXEC.NCF startup utility. Figure 9.24 displays the Remote Console utility.

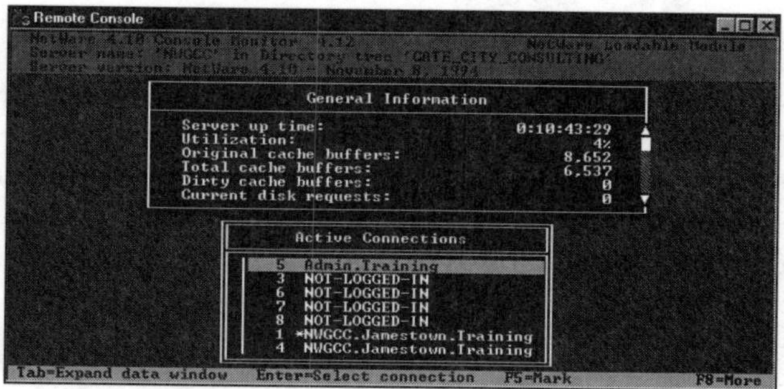

Figure 9.24. *The DOS-based Remote Console utility.*

Users can use additional menu-based NLMS that can help configure and manage the NetWare server once you have an RCONSOLE session established. Some of these useful NLMs include the INSTALL.NLM and the MONITOR.NLM.

AUDITCON

The AUDITCON utility allows the objects in the NDS tree to be audited, and enables the administrator to view these logs. AUDITCON can also be used to enable volume level auditing for those organizations that need lower levels of security.

The concept of extensive auditing using AUDITCON is new to NetWare 4. Like RCONSOLE, it is a DOS-based utility with no graphical NT-native equivalent. Figure 9.25 displays the AUDITCON utility.

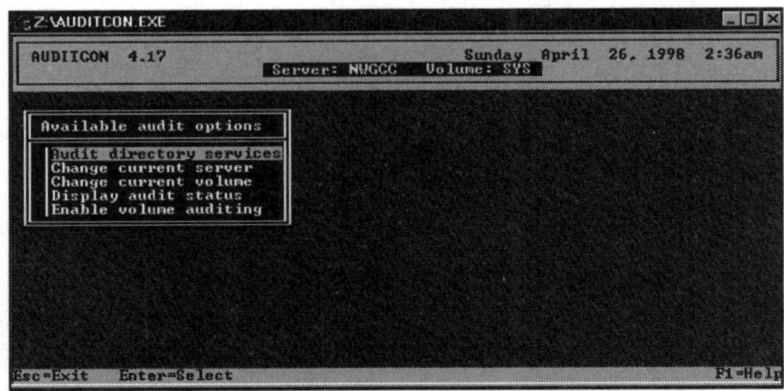

Figure 9.25. *The AUDITCON utility enables an administrator to enable NDS and volume auditing.*

FILER

FILER is another DOS-based utility that can enable a user or administrator to manage the file system rights and attributes of files and directories to which they have the proper access. The FILER utility can also be used to recover deleted files that have not yet been purged from the hidden DELETED.SAV directory found on every volume. As both a file management and security management utility, FILER is one of the more commonly used NetWare utilities. Figure 9.26 shows the FILER utility.

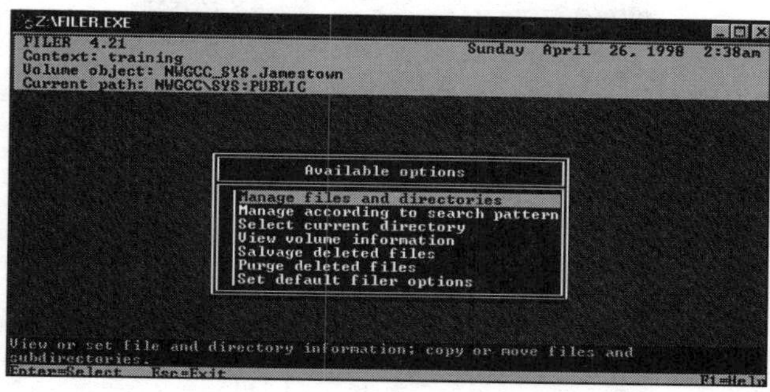

Figure 9.26. *The FILER utility.*

NETADMIN and PCONSOLE

These two utilities can serve as possible alternatives to the NetWare Administrator. They do not have the option of supporting many of the new snap-in modules, but can serve a purpose for basic NDS object management.

NETADMIN can control all of the default NDS schema using the same options as the NetWare Administrator, just using a less-intuitive interface. PCONSOLE is actually still preferably used instead of the NetWare Administrator in many circles due to its long history of being the main print management utility for NetWare. Bear in mind that like the preceding utilities, these are DOS-based utilities only so they perform somewhat slower on Windows NT. Figure 9.27 displays the NETADMIN utility.

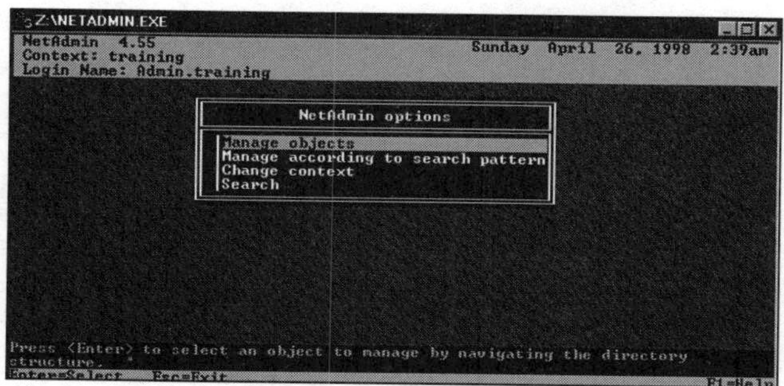

Figure 9.27. *The NETADMIN screen: A DOS-based NDS object management utility.*

Chapter 10

Apple Integration

- **Overview of Apple Networking**
  Learn how clients and servers interact on Macintosh networks using the AppleTalk transport as well as the Open Transport Mechanism. We will also discuss file formats and a few issues that need to be addressed in mixed environments.
- **Installing Services for Macintosh**
  Look at the features of Windows NT's Services for Macintosh and how to install this service. We will also discuss points to consider before installing this service.
- **AppleTalk Issues and Configuration**
  Review basic AppleTalk issues and configuration that were detailed previously in Chapter 2, "LAN/WAN Protocol Management."
- **Managing Mac Users**
  Discover how you can manage users originating from Macintosh clients using the same utilities that are used for volume management.
- **Macintosh Client Concerns**
  Look at specific troubleshooting concerns that can pop up specifically for Macintosh clients. We will look at which options do not transcend from Windows, Windows NT, and other PC clients to Mac clients.
- **Monitoring AppleTalk Performance**
  Examine how to track specific socket, node, and network connections between AppleTalk hosts.

Overview of Apple Networking

Networking in Apple environments originated with, and later evolved into, a more stable, complex version of the AppleTalk Network Stack. Like TCP/IP, AppleTalk is best described as a suite of protocols in that it comprises several components at all of the OSI layers. Phase 1 was the first implementation of AppleTalk. This was followed by Phase 2, which consisted of more complex internetworking capabilities and addressing.

The Application Layer is where we deal with the *AppleShare component*, which is accessed using the Chooser. This is where zone selection, file servers, and volumes can be accessed. The Chooser also prompts the user for authentication when accessible. Figure 10.1 displays the Chooser as it appears on Macintosh clients.

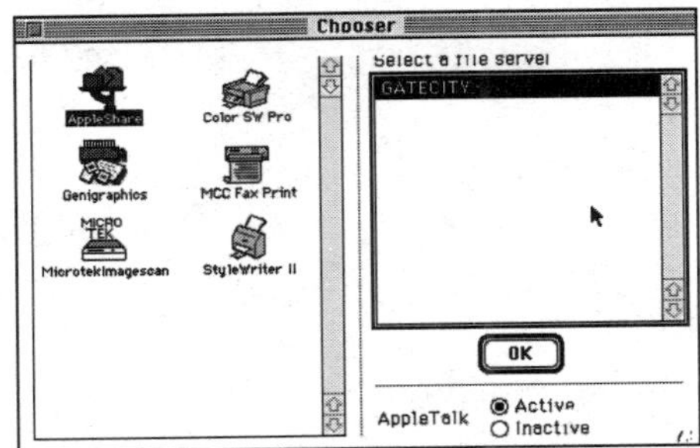

Figure 10.1. *The Macintosh Chooser that is accessible through the Apple menu.*

At the Presentation Layer are two specific components:

- The Apple Filing Protocol. This is the Macintosh network file system driver and the primary component of AppleShare.
- The PostScript Protocol. This is designed to translate PostScript code into raw vector-based data for printing.

There is only one protocol designed for establishing and controlling AppleTalk sessions at the Session Layer: *ASP—The Apple Session Protocol.* The ADSP or the Apple Data Stream Protocol, maintains full duplex data transmission (similar to TCP in TCP/IP). This is also the socket protocol, which also includes security. Printers use a specific protocol rather than ADSP, the PAP, or Printer Access Protocol. The ZIP, or Zone Information Protocol, is used by routers for exchanging information between each other about the regular zones and the networks with which they reconcile.

At the transport, or host, layer are more transaction-based mechanisms. Database applications use the *ATP*, or *AppleTalk Transaction Protocol*. The diagnostic protocol, or the error protocol, for the AppleTalk stack is the *AppleTalk Echo Protocol*. AppleTalk uses an interesting option for name resolution at the layer. Rather than use an application layer service, it uses the *Name Binding Protocol* to translate an AppleTalk character-based address to an AppleTalk node address or an IP address.

Also at the transport exists the primary distance-vector-based routing protocol for AppleTalk: the *Routing Table Maintenance Protocol*. This protocol updates routing tables via broadcasts in the same manner that RIP does for TCP/IP and IPX/SPX. More recent AppleTalk implementations use the *AppleTalk Update Routing Protocol*. Rather than sending constant broadcasts, this new routing protocol routes information only when there have been changes to the routing table.

At the network layer is the *Datagram Delivery Protocol*, which is the primary component of the AppleTalk stack. It is responsible for fragmenting, addressing, and routing through the network or internetwork. It works alongside the *AppleTalk Addressing Protocol*, which is used to map a media access control address with an AppleTalk address.

Finally, at the data link layer are the Access Protocol options, more commonly known as *EtherTalk*, *TokenTalk*, and *LocalTalk*. Ethernet and Token Ring logical rules and topologies are supported using their respective access methods.

LocalTalk

LocalTalk is not found in recent Mac environments. LocalTalk was the original solution, which consisted of *PhoneNet cabling*. This cabling was so titled due to the design of the cable using RJ-14 phone jacks. Serial connectivity used RS-422 cable rather than RS-232.

Unfortunately, the design of LocalTalk had many limitations. The bandwidth was limited to 230.4Kbps, it could not send and receive at the same time, and it was all proprietary media. However, it was very easy to use and was truly Plug-and-Play, which may explain why it is still used today for the sharing of printers.

AppleShare

As mentioned earlier, AppleShare is the network file system driver for Apple Servers. Prior to System 7, there were two types of AppleShare products:

- AppleShare File Server
- AppleShare Print Server

With System 7, AppleShare was integrated into the operating system. This gives the Macintosh a basic workgroup option to serve as both client and server simultaneously.

System 7's file sharing supports up to 30 users. However, AppleShare File and Print Servers are still available, allowing up to 120 users at one time.

AppleShare/IP

Recent implementations of AppleShare have evolved into *AppleShare/IP*. AppleShare/IP servers even allow for the support of Open Transport.

AppleShare/IP has recently been further enhanced to add support for Windows networking. This completes the full duplex connectivity solution that has been so desired for years from those hybrid environments. Windows NT Services for Macintosh allows Mac clients to connect to NT servers, and AppleShare/IP version 6 allows Microsoft Windows clients to connect to AppleShare servers.

One of the biggest innovations in AppleShare/IP is the new support for the SMB protocol. This allows AppleShare to provide File and Print Services for Windows NT and Windows 95 computers. However, the AppleShare file server must be configured to advertise itself properly using the Browser service mechanism. Unless there is a Windows 95, Windows NT, or other computer acting as either the Domain Master Browser or the Master Browser (for the IP segment), then the AppleShare/IP server will not work right—unless it is configured to be a Master Browser.

Windows machines are dependent upon Master Browsers to see anything in the Network Neighborhood. In TCP/IP, you must have at least one Master Browser per workgroup/domain and per IP subnet. AppleShare/IP does not support Domain Master Browser status; it only supports Master Browser status. As a result, there is no way for workgroup browse masters in different subnets to communicate their browse lists to each other, so you won't be able to see the ASIP server from other subnets if it is configured as a workgroup member.

If you have an NT server configured to be a primary domain controller, then make your ASIP server and your Windows 95 machine members of that domain. Domain members announce their presence to Master Browsers, who in turn announce their lists to Domain Master Browsers. Domains, as a result, enable browsing across subnets, whereas workgroups do not.

AppleShare IP 6.0 supports the NetBIOS Name Service, but only via TCP/IP. AppleShare IP would therefore advertise to a WINS server running on Windows NT. NetBIOS Name Service is very different from the AppleTalk Name Binding Protocol, the protocol Macs use to browse AppleTalk networks in the Chooser. When a Mac user opens the Chooser and selects AppleShare, the Mac sends out an NBP lookup request to the current zone asking for all AFP servers to identify themselves. This allows the user to get an immediately up-to-date list of all the available servers.

Merging Windows Browsing with AppleShare/IP

There are plenty of ways to make network browsing work in a larger complex internetwork, such as using LMHOSTS or WINS. No matter what network-browsing environment you use, the AppleShare IP setup remains the same. Your Windows clients do not have to be able to see your AppleShare/IP 6.0 server in the Network Neighborhood in order to connect to it.

To get AppleShare IP to appear in the Network Neighborhood, follow these steps:

1. Prepare the AppleShare IP server machine by making sure that the TCP/IP control panel is properly configured, the Web and File Server is running, the Windows File Sharing service is enabled, and the server's NetBIOS name and at least one share point name are valid for NetBIOS (less than or equal to 13—not 15—characters, generally avoiding punctuation and special characters).

2. Make sure all of your Windows client machines can do SMB via TCP/IP.

Troubleshooting Tip

AppleShare IP only supports SMB via TCP/IP. You must have the Microsoft SMB client and TCP/IP stack properly installed and configured on your Windows clients in order for them to connect to AppleShare IP's SMB service.

3. Make sure all of your client machines are on the same IP subnet without WINS or LMHOSTS. Your AppleShare IP server and your Windows clients must be on the same IP subnet.

4. Make sure your test machines are in the same NetBIOS workgroup. It is harder to do this step if you have to deal with more than one workgroup. In Windows 95 and NT, testing is performed in the Identification panel of the Network Control Panel. You can set AppleShare IP's NetBIOS workgroup in the Windows File Sharing panel of the Web and File Server Settings window of the Web and File Admin application.

5. Make sure exactly one of your test machines is acting as the Master Browser for your workgroup. AppleShare/IP cannot act as a Master Browser, so you need to have some other machine in the same IP subnet and NetBIOS workgroup acting as a Browse Master.

AppleShare/IP announces itself more often than other SMB servers, but due to limitations of the protocol, it can still take awhile for the AppleShare/IP server to show up. Selecting the Refresh command from the Network Neighborhood window's View menu doesn't help either. Rather than causing the SMB servers to reannounce themselves, it just asks the Master Browser for the most recent list, which may still be out of date.

System 7 AppleShare Options

System 7 AppleShare options function on top of all major AppleTalk Access Protocols, including LocalTalk, EtherTalk, TokenTalk, and Remote Only. These options are configured using the Networks Control Panel for AppleTalk configuration, as shown in Figure 10.2.

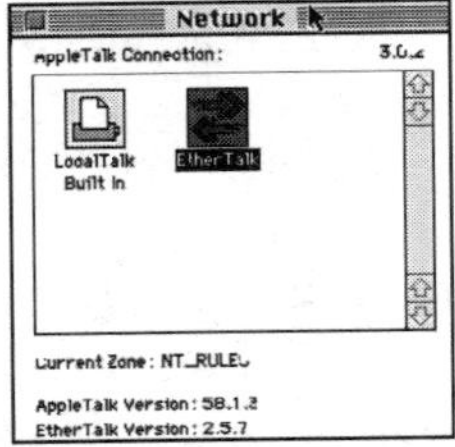

Figure 10.2. *The Network Control Panel, which resides under the Apple menu to adjust AppleTalk access support.*

For support of TCP/IP, you can adjust the access point using the MacTCP Control Panel, which is found in the same location as the Network Control Panel, under the Apple menu. Figure 10.3 displays the options for MacTCP.

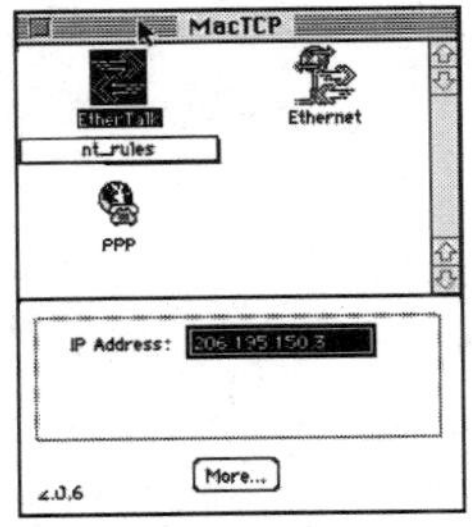

Figure 10.3. *The MacTCP Control Panel, which allows you to select the access point for TCP/IP.*

This is also where you can set specific configuration parameters, such as IP address, subnet mask, and advanced options (such as router and DNS configuration). For EtherTalk, you can also select the default zone, which will exist as your subnet as well.

The Sharing Setup Control Panel

The Sharing setup under System 7 is the mini-version of the AppleShare configuration options found on AppleShare server. This option enables the user to set the AppleShare identity, or its computer name. The computer name will be the one that resolves as the AFP server using the Name Binding Protocol. The owner, or administrator and his or her password can also be set up here to control administration levels.

You can also start and stop the AFP File Sharing setup, which can be used to enable Program Linking under this dialog box. This allows one Macintosh program to control another program on another Macintosh computer across the network. This is a fundamental concept of the Macintosh OpenDoc specification, which is similar to Microsoft's OLE and DCOM. Figure 10.4 depicts the Sharing Setup Control Panel, found under the Apple menu.

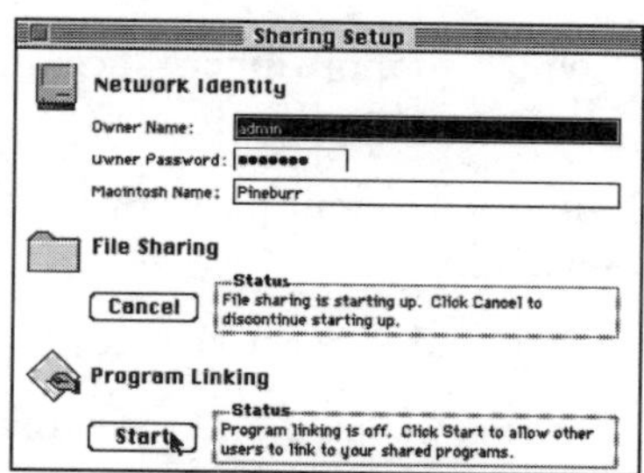

Figure 10.4. *The Sharing Setup Control Panel for System 7 AppleShare.*

The Users and Groups Control Panel

The Users and Groups Control Panel is where you can set up access levels for individual users and/or groups. You can create an icon for every user that you want to access your Macintosh. Just as with Windows NT, there is a guest user option as well. You can create a group, which contains a list of all of its users. They will inherit permissions that were assigned to the group.

Permissions for AppleShare volumes are placed when you select a directory and designate it for sharing using the Sharing option from the File menu. Figure 10.5 displays the Users and Groups window.

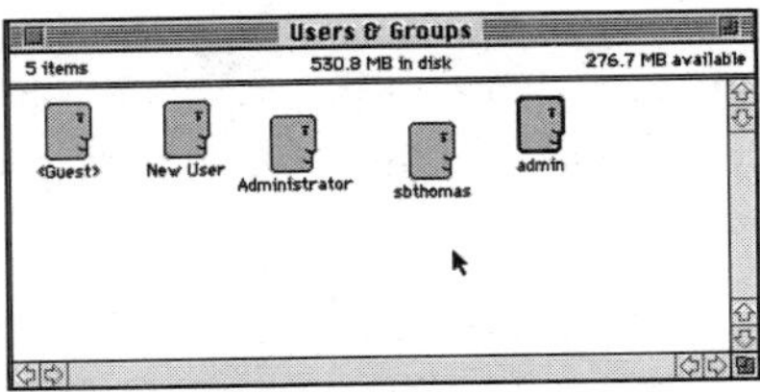

Figure 10.5. *The Users and Groups window for AppleShare.*

System 7 Enhancements to AppleShare

AppleTalk was enhanced in System 7 even for the workgroup version. Since System 7, AppleShare provides support for the following:

- Multitasking and modular components. Improves performance and allows for multiple transactions.
- Volume control. Provides the capability for controlling volumes with global permissions and passwords independent of user and group access.
- CD-ROM support. Provides the capability for mounting CD-ROMs as read-only volumes.
- Enhanced privileges, which support inheritance. Provides inherited permissions for both explicit and implicit access.
- Password control. Provides different password authentication modules for both volumes and users.
- Administrative overriding and super user use.
- Server message support. For sending and receiving messages from clients to servers and vice/versa.
- 250 users. Accepts up to 250 simultaneous users for access to the AFP server.

Open Transport

Newer Macintoshes running recent versions of the Mac OS (Systems 7.5.2 and later) have a built-in network stack called *Open Transport*. Think of Open Transport as a hybrid stack allowing support for both AppleTalk Phase 2 and TCP/IP. Open Transport adds support to Apple networking for the following:

- POSIX. The Portable API standard
- X/Open Transport Interface. Support for running X-compliant applications

- Streams. The UNIX streams protocol
- Data Link Provider Interface. An open bindings interface for multiple access points
- PPP. Support for the Point-to-Point Protocol
- SLIP. Support for the Serial Line Internet Protocol

With Open Transport, a new control panel called AppleTalk replaces the Network and MacTCP Control Panels. AppleShare 4.2, which is PowerPC native, supports 3,000 instances of 346 unique files and uses Open Transport 1.1 (requires System 7.5.3). Open Transport also provides support for Fast Ethernet.

Apple File Formats

When working with Apple computers, especially in a hybrid environment, you need to be aware of the different formats that may pop up for files being transferred back and forth from Apple computers to PC computers.

Forks

NT Server is able to truly emulate the NTFS file system because the file system also supports multiple data streams. Apple refers to these as *forks*. Mac files can have two forks:

- A data fork
- A resource fork

Most newer applications like MS Office have a file format that just uses a data fork to facilitate easier portability with PCs. *Data forks* contain data or programming code. *Resource forks* contain links to system firmware, font information, extended attributes, associations, sounds, and other specialty items.

Mac filenames can be up to 32 characters in length and can contain any character except a colon. The colon is used to separate a path portion (the way a backslash does this in NT, or a forward slash does in UNIX). All dates start at January 1, 1904. Files convert dates using a Julian system based on this starting point. Day 1 for a PC is usually January 1, 1980.

MacBinary

Certain file transfer protocols can corrupt Mac file formats because of the multiple fork issue. A binary transfer only transfers the data fork. A popular workaround is encoding this information using UUEncode or MIME. This converts both forks into a single text file, which then allows for seamless transfer on any platform, especially TCP/IP. If you have an application that supports MacBinary, it is best to use it for transfer since it will transfer both forks.

Installing Services for Macintosh

Windows NT is completely AppleShare-compliant. All AppleTalk protocols are supported; however, there is no complete support for Open Transport.

There are many other pluses to using Windows NT as a File and Print Server for AppleTalk networks. For starters, NT provides PostScript emulation for non-PostScript printers. Macintosh and other AppleTalk printers can be made accessible to the Microsoft Windows Network through a pass-through print share on the NT computer in order for PCs to access Macintosh printers. NT also allows for 255 simultaneous connections to its AFP server, with each access using only about 15K of RAM.

You can install Services for Macintosh under the Network Control Panel's Services option.

AppleTalk Configuration

In Chapter 2, we discussed the fine-tuning and addressing schematics of AppleTalk in detail. After you install Services for Macintosh, the AppleTalk Configuration dialog box pops up and enables you to configure seed routing, network range, and zone membership. The Services for Macintosh option under Services in the Network Control Panel is also where you go to adjust AppleTalk configuration.

During the installation, after you have entered the necessary AppleTalk configuration, you can reboot the computer. Usually, the minimum will be zone membership unless one has not been defined. In that case, you need to configure the NT server to act as a seed router or else no configuration node addresses will be obtained.

Using the File Manager for Volume Management

While the File Manager is considered a secondary option for file management in Windows NT 4.0 (behind Explorer), it is still the recommended option for MacFile, or Macintosh file management on Windows NT Server. MacFile, a new menu option, is available after you install Service for Macintosh.

Author's Note

There is an icon for the File Manager, but it is only found on NT Server, in the Administrative Tools group. You can also bring this up by typing `WINFILE` *at the command prompt, or by selecting the Run option from the Start menu.*

Creating the Volume

You can use the File Manager to create Mac-accessible volumes by selecting Create Volume from the MacFile menu. This brings up the dialog box shown in Figure 10.6.

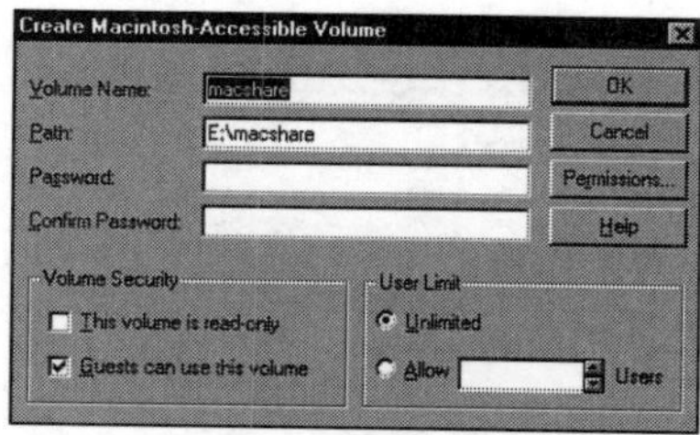

Figure 10.6. *The Create Macintosh-Accessible Volume dialog box.*

This is where you can select a directory path on an NTFS file system and allow it to appear as an AppleShare volume. The options that are available when creating a Mac-accessible volume include putting a global password on the volume to add an additional layer of password security. You can also set a global read-only flag that will affect the volume's access through the AppleShare. You can also determine whether or not you will allow AppleShare guests to access the volume. By default, the user limit option is set to unlimited, which actually means 255 users. You can reduce this number by selecting a specific number.

Author's Note

The default volume name is the same as the directory name; however, you can change it so that Macintosh users see a different name. The character limit is 27.

Setting Permissions

AppleShare privileges are fully supported on Windows NT Server. AppleShare permissions consist of three simple options:

- See Folders. If this option is not selected, then all folders within the share will not show and only the files directly at the root level of the share will be accessible.
- See Files. If this option is not selected, then files will not be shown beneath the directory and only folders will be seen. If both the See Folders and See Files options are deselected, then nothing will be seen on the share.

- Make Changes. If this option is selected along with the preceding two options, then the user will be able to duplicate, see, delete, and save changes to the files or folders beneath the shared directory.

Figure 10.7 lists the available options for AppleShare permissions within the Permissions dialog box.

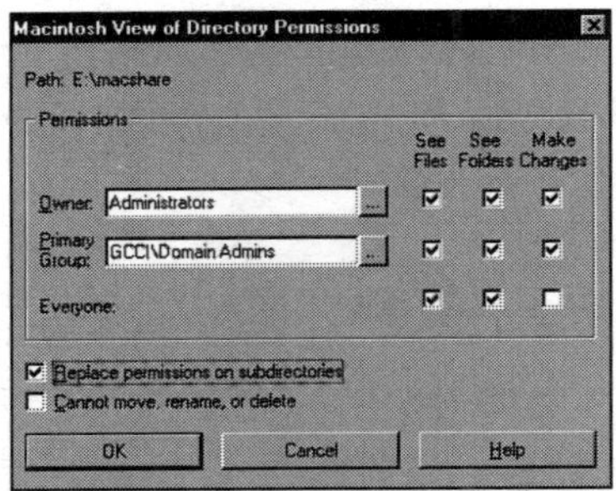

Figure 10.7. *The AppleShare Permissions dialog box.*

There are three groups to which you can assign AppleShare permissions on each Mac-accessible volume:

- The *Owner*, who by default will be the local group Administrator(s), should usually have complete control. You can specify a global or local group to serve as the owner.
- The *Primary Group* must be a global group from either the current domain or a trusted domain. This will correlate with the Primary Group option for users, as configured on Windows NT in the User Manager for Domains.
- The *Everyone Group*.

Troubleshooting Tip

When you select that a volume is read-only, the volume and all of its contents have read-only access. This option supersedes all directory permissions you set when using the Permissions option. In other words, if you give this volume read-only access, the permissions of directories with less restrictive access will not be honored. However, if you grant rights that are more lenient under permissions, read-only access will still take precedence.

After creating a volume initially, rebooting the machine and letting CHKDSK perform a check on this new structure is recommended. CHKDSK will also make additional stream pointers for both forks on this volume to support the Apple resource forks.

Modifying Volumes

You can also use the File Manager to modify the properties of those volumes you created. When you select this option from the MacFile menu, it displays the dialog box shown in Figure 10.8.

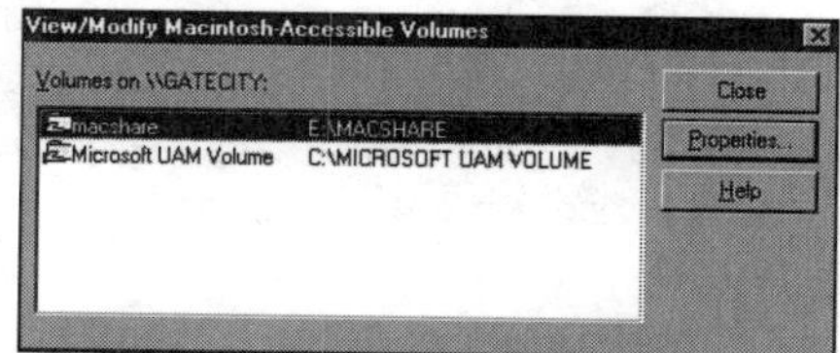

Figure 10.8. *Modifying the volumes using the File Manager.*

You will then see all of the volumes that you have created as well as the Microsoft UAM (User Authentication Module), which is created by default when you install Services for Macintosh. You can pull up the volume Properties button, which returns you to the same dialog box you used when you created the volume.

Microsoft User Authentication

AppleShare networks employ a UAM. This is a software module that prompts users for an account name and password before they log on to an AFP server. Apple's Chooser on System 6.x has a standard module built in, but this module only uses the clear-text password method of security.

Microsoft Authentication offers an additional level of security because it hashes out the password so that it cannot be picked up over the network, unlike the built-in module. If the system administrator for the computer running Windows NT Server has determined that encryption is an important security measure, you may be asked to use Microsoft Authentication when you log on to the server.

Installing the Microsoft UAM

The Microsoft User Authentication Module installation must be done from each Macintosh client that will be using the Microsoft UAM, so this may turn into a cumbersome task. You need to log on to the Microsoft UAM Volume on the computer running Windows NT Server, then look for the MS UAM file. This is the module you will need to drag the file to your AppleShare folder, which is found within your system folder.

Author's Note

Because the Apple System software up to version 7.1 does not fully support custom user authentication modules, Microsoft encourages you to install Microsoft User Authentication Module (MS UAM) only if you need increased security on your Windows NT Server computer.

Removing Volumes

You can remove volumes at any point by selecting the Remove Volume option from the File Manager's MacFile menu. Be very careful that you understand what this actually entails. As soon as you reboot, CHKDSK will clean up the volume and remove all stream pointers to resource forks. As a result, it may cause serious problems with those files that contained both elements. I have seen this occur numerous times. Recent packages, such as Microsoft Office products for the Macintosh, have gone out of their way to ensure that all of the critical components of each document are stored in the data fork for easier portability across Mac and PC platforms.

Warning

Do not copy files that were uploaded from Mac clients over to FAT partitions, away from the NTFS volumes where they are supposed to reside. This corrupts the files by stripping them of their resource fork. The FAT file system only supports the data fork portion of the Mac file. It sees the resource fork as a separate unknown file.

Adjusting Associations

Macintosh files divide their associations into two components:

- The *CREATOR component* refers to the application that created the software.
- The *TYPE* refers to the document type (which may have several possible creators, as do text files).

Figure 10.9 represents the Associate dialog box, found under the File Manager. This is where you can select an MS-DOS or NT-based extension type and associate it with a Macintosh CREATOR/TYPE association.

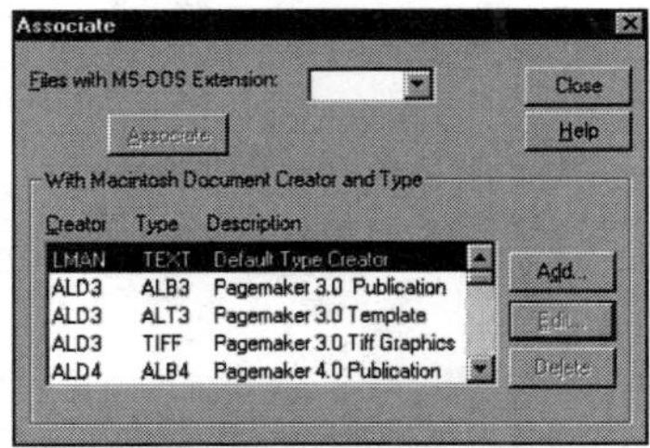

Figure 10.9. *Manipulating associations under the File Manager.*

These CREATOR/TYPE associations ensure that users see the correct icon on their computers for a file stored on the computer running Windows NT Server. Services for Macintosh does come with defined associations for the most common Mac application types, including Microsoft, Aldus, Adobe, and Claris products. You can, however, create new associations, or add, edit, or delete existing file creators and types.

Using the Server Manager to Manage Services for Macintosh

The Server Manager adds an additional snap-in module for Mac volumes when Services for Macintosh has been installed on an NT server. The first option that appears in this new menu is the MacFile Properties option. This dialog box represents more dynamic, user-based management of the NT AFP server. Figure 10.10 displays this properties dialog box.

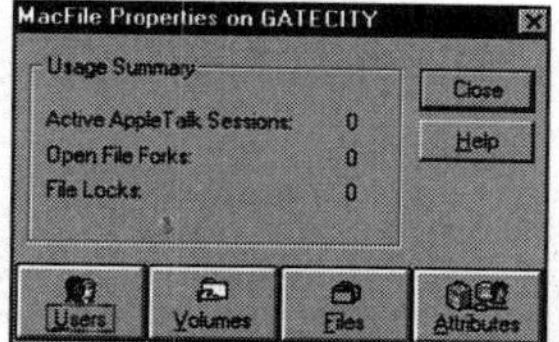

Figure 10.10. *Manipulating global MacFile Server properties using the Server Manager snap-in and the Control Panel.*

This option displays the current AppleTalk sessions as well as the available Apple File Forks and File Locks. This option also has links to manage Users, Volumes, Files, and Attributes. Think of this as being similar to the Server Manager's Properties option for NT Server computers, with the exception that this is for the AFP sessions and not for the sessions to NT's Server Service.

Author's Note

This same properties option can be found under the local NT server's Control Panel, under MacFile.

Managing Users

When you select the Users button, it invokes a list of all connected users, including the source location as well as the open files and the access time. The name found under Computer will be the AppleTalk node name that is configured in the Macintosh computer under Sharing Setup.

The Users option also breaks down the file access by each individual Mac share that may be accessing at that juncture. Figure 10.11 shows the Users dialog box.

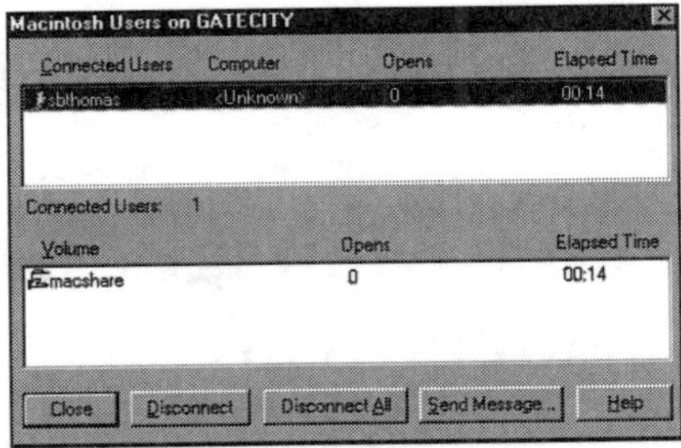

Figure 10.11. *Viewing connected users and their file access.*

You have the option of disconnecting an individual user or doing a blanket disconnect of all users connected to the AFP server. Notice that you also have the option of sending messages directly to the users themselves, or to all users, in case you need to inform them that the server will be going down. Figure 10.12 displays the Send Message dialog box.

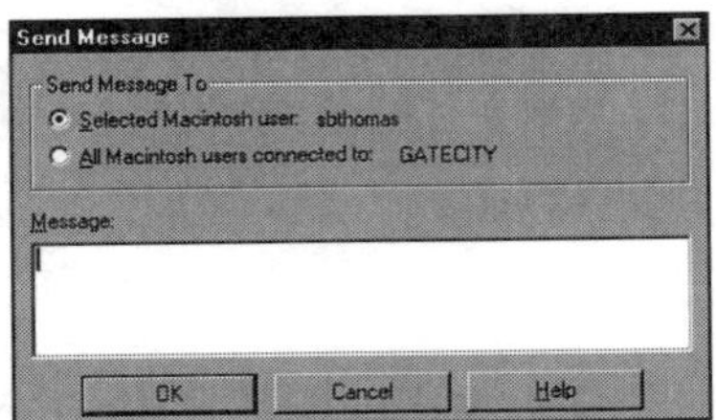

Figure 10.12. *Sending messages to Macintosh users.*

Troubleshooting Tip

You need to be aware of this option, especially since neither the regular `NET SEND` *command in Windows NT nor the option to send a message under the Server Manager Computer menu will send the message to the Mac users.*

Viewing Users by Volumes

The Volumes button allows you to manage users and their file access by individual volumes. When you select each share, it displays the number of uses as well as its link to the NT file system path. Each user is shown with his or her count of file uses and current use.

Figure 10.13 displays the option for viewing use by volumes.

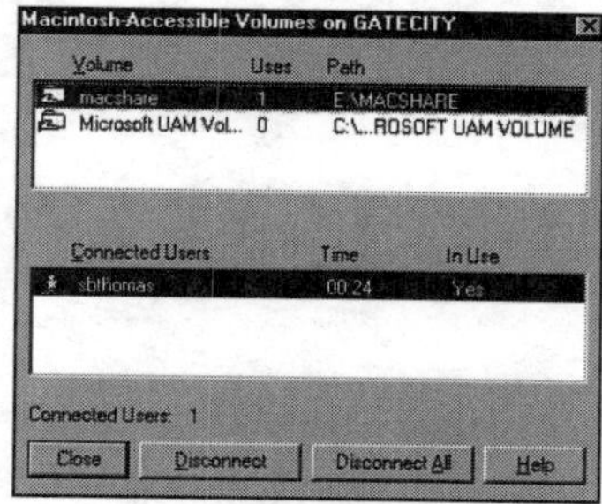

Figure 10.13. *Viewing user and file access by volumes.*

Viewing Files

The File option allows you to view each file that is currently opened for use by AppleTalk clients. It reveals the open file forks and whether the application has current locks on it via applications. Each file lists the user who has the file opened. The file is followed by the type of access, whether it is for Read Only or Read/Write. Then the type is followed by the locks count for the file. The locks count is followed by the NT file system path, which lists where the file is located. Figure 10.14 displays the Open Files dialog box.

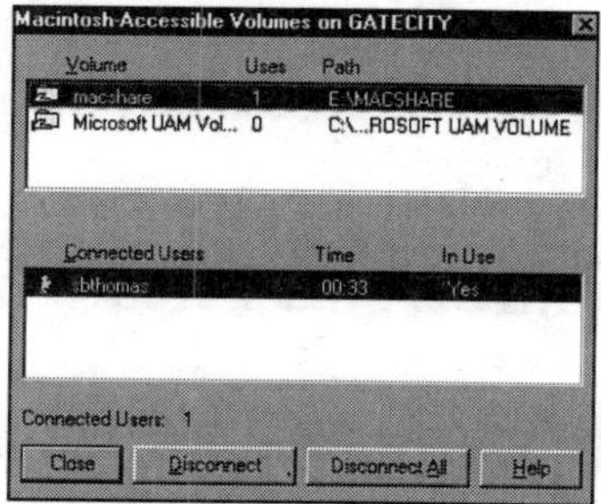

Figure 10.14. *Viewing opened file forks and locks using the MacFile Control Panel.*

You can use this option to close each fork individually or close all of them using a blanket fork close.

MacFile Attributes

The last option found in the Server Manager is the Attributes option. This is not for file attributes, but for general attributes relating to the AFP server. When you select this option, it displays the dialog box shown in Figure 10.15.

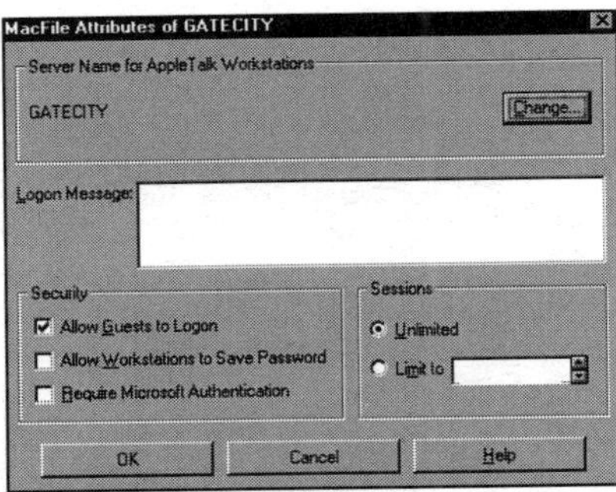

Figure 10.15. *Setting global AFP server settings options using the MacFile Attributes.*

This dialog box allows you to first change the name of the AFP server, which governs how the Mac clients see the server by name. This will be the name that the servers use to respond to Name Binding Protocol requests. You can also type in a customized logon message screen that will only be displayed to Mac clients.

The Security options found in this dialog box will not apply to a certain volume, but they will apply to the entire AFP server, including all of its volumes. The Security options enable you to disable Guest logon, allowing workstations to save the password and to force Microsoft User Authentication. You can also limit the total number of sessions to a specific number rather than the default, which is unlimited (actually 255 users).

Tip

You can also view volumes and send messages from the Server Manager's MacFile menu.

Viewing MAC Shares and Files Through Explorer

Explorer does not have any snap-ins to manage Mac files. Of course, you can use this utility to transfer files to and from the directory that is also the MacFile share. You may notice when working with these directories that a few important hidden elements will be added. If you have your View options set in Explorer to show hidden files, you will see these following options:

- Network Trash Folder. A desktop item that represents deleted items which have not yet been purged. This is similar to the Windows Recycling Bin.
- Desktop. A resource that maintains a database of properties to transcend to the Mac client's hierarchical file system manager. This is similar to the User Profile Folder on the Desktop.
- ICON. A resource element that uses the icon to display the Volume icon.

Figure 10.16 shows an example of a MacFile directory as seen through the Windows NT Explorer.

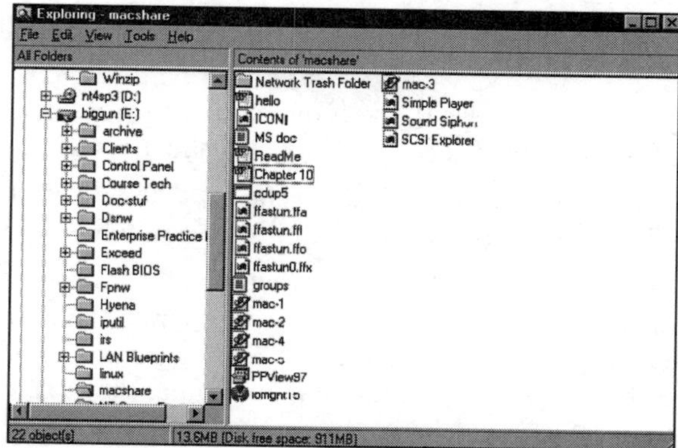

Figure 10.16. *Viewing resource fork files and special objects using the Explorer.*

Troubleshooting Tip

The Explorer will only show the file size of the data fork on those files found on Mac-accessible shares. This is why you may see some files that have a file size of zero—usually a file that has all of its information in a resource fork. Many Mac-oriented utilities consist only of resource forks.

The `MACFILE` Command

Windows NT 4.0 brought forth an excellent new command utility called the MACFILE utility. This utility goes far beyond its name by allowing you to completely control Windows NT Services for Macintosh from the command line.

This command is similar to the `NET` command in that it has a supporting set of subcommands in which each subcommand has its own set of command-line arguments.

`macfile volume`

This option allows you to add, change, or remove Macintosh-accessible volumes. The command syntax for `macfile volume` follows:

```
macfile volume {/add ¦ /set}[/server:\\computername] /name:volumename /path:
➥directory [/readonly:[true ¦ false]] [/guestsallowed:[true ¦ false]]
➥[/password:password] [/maxusers:number ¦ unlimited] macfile volume /remove
➥[/server:\\computername] /name:volumename
```

where:

`/add` Adds a volume based upon the specified settings. This fails if the volume already exists, so it should only be used for creating new volumes.

`/set` Changes a volume using the specified settings. The volume must exist for this command to work.

`/server:\\computername` Allows you to specify the NT server on which to add, change, or remove a volume. If the NT server isn't there, then it will assume the default computer is the argument.

`/name:volumename` Specifies the volume name to be added, changed, or removed. This parameter is required on this subcommand.

`/path:directory` Specifies the path to the root directory of the volume to be created. This option is only valid and required when adding a volume.

`/readonly: true or false` Specifies whether or not users can change files in the volume. You can use `true` or `false` to change the current setting of the volume. If this is not included when adding a volume, changes to files are allowed. If omitted when changing a volume, the read-only setting for the volume will remain unchanged.

`/guestsallowed:true or false` Specifies whether users logging on as guests can use the volume. When adding a volume, guests can use it by default. If omitted when changing a volume, this option for the volume remains unchanged.

`/password:password` Specifies a password required to access the volume. By default, no password is created. If omitted when changing a volume, the password remains unchanged.

`/maxusers:number ¦ unlimited` Specifies the maximum number of users that can simultaneously use files on the volume. When a volume is added, an unlimited number of users can use it by default. If omitted when changing a volume, this value remains unchanged.

`/remove` Removes the specified volume.

macfile directory

This option allows an administrator to modify the directories in Macintosh-accessible volumes. The syntax for `macfile directory` is as follows:

```
macfile directory [/server:\\computername] /path:directory [/owner:ownername]
➥[/group:groupname] [/permissions:permissions]
```

where:

`/server:\\computername` Specifies the server on which to change a directory. By default, the operation is performed on the local computer.

`/path:directory` Specifies the path to the directory to be changed on the Macintosh-accessible volume. The directory must exist; `macfile directory` does not create directories. This parameter is required.

`/owner:ownername` Changes the owner of the directory. By default, the owner remains unchanged.

`/group:groupname` Specifies or changes the Macintosh primary group associated with the directory. By default, the primary group remains unchanged.

`/permissions:permissions` Sets permissions on the directory for the owner, primary group, and world (everyone). This is similar to the `CHMOD` command in UNIX, where a numerical mask is used to set the permissions. The mask in this case is an 11-digit binary mask.

The number `1` grants permission while the number `0` revokes permission. The position of the digit determines which permission is set, as described in Table 10.1. By default, permissions remain unchanged. Table 10.1 displays the binary masks for the MacFile directory's `/permissions` option.

Table 10.1. Binary masks for the MacFile directory `/permissions`.

Position	Permission Option
First	`Owner: See Files`
Second	`Owner: See Folders`
Third	`Owner: Make Changes`
Fourth	`Group: See Files`
Fifth	`Group: See Folders`
Sixth	`Group: Make Changes`
Seventh	`Everyone: See Files`
Eighth	`Everyone: See Folders`
Ninth	`Everyone: Make Changes`
Tenth	The directory cannot be renamed, moved, or deleted.
Eleventh	The changes apply to the current directory and will propagate through subdirectories.

`macfile server`

This subcommand allows an administrator to change the Services for Macintosh server configuration. The syntax for `macfile server` is as follows:

```
macfile server [/server:\\computername] [/maxsessions:number ¦ unlimited]
➥[/loginmessage:message] [/guestsallowed:[true ¦ false]]
```

where:

`/server:\\computername` Specifies the server on which to change parameters. By default, the operation is performed on the local computer.

`/maxsessions:[number | unlimited]` Specifies the maximum number of users that can simultaneously use Services for Macintosh services. By default, the `maxsessions` setting for the server remains unchanged.

`/loginmessage:message` Changes the message Macintosh users see when logging on to the Services for Macintosh server. To remove an existing logon message, include the `/loginmessage` parameter but leave the message variable blank. By default, the `loginmessage` message for the server remains unchanged from the previous setting. The maximum number of characters for the logon message is `199`.

`/guestsallowed:[true | false]` Specifies whether users logging on as guests can use Services for Macintosh services. By default, the `guestsallowed` setting for the server remains unchanged.

macfile forkize

This is a subcommand designed for advanced users only and should be used with extreme caution. It joins the data fork and resource fork of a Macintosh file into one file. `macfile forkize` also can change the type or creator of the file. The syntax is as follows:

```
macfile forkize [/server:\\computername] [/creator:creatorname]
➥[/type:typename] [/datafork:filepath] [/resourcefork:filepath]
➥/targetfile:filepath
```

where:

`/server:\\computername` Specifies the server on which to join files. By default, the operation is performed on the local computer.

`/creator:creatorname` Specifies the creator of the file. The `creator` parameter is used by the Macintosh Finder to determine the application that created the file.

`/type:typename` Specifies the type of file. The file type is used by the Macintosh Finder to determine the file type within the application that created the file.

`/datafork:filepath` Specifies the location of the data fork that is to be joined. You can specify a remote path.

`/resourcefork:filepath` Specifies the location of the resource fork that is to be joined. You can specify a remote path.

`/targetfile:filepath` Specifies the location of the file created by joining a data fork and a resource fork or specifies the location of the file whose type or creator you are changing. The file must be on the specified server.

Working with the Macintosh Clients

Assuming that the network setup is correct on the Macintosh computer and the AFP server on the Windows NT Server is set up properly, the connectivity to an NT server is just like any other connection to an AppleShare server.

Connecting and Authenticating

When you select a zone under the Network Control Panel, by default all NT servers within the zone automatically appear in the Chooser when the AppleShare icon is selected. The user will have the option of connecting to the file server as either a guest or a registered user. You can also see in this option whether you are using a clear-text module or another module. Without the Microsoft Authentication module, it defaults to using Clear-Text. Figure 10.17 shows the Logon option on the Mac client computer.

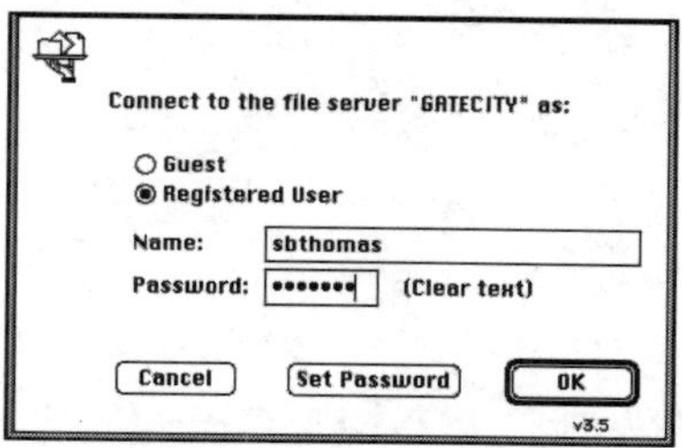

Figure 10.17. *The file server logon option on the Macintosh client.*

You will notice from looking at this dialog box that there is also an option for the user to set his or her password.

Once the user has successfully authenticated to the server, a list of available volumes appears for the user. If a volume is grayed out, the user either is not allowed access (possibly due to guest status) or has already connected to this volume. Figure 10.18 displays this option.

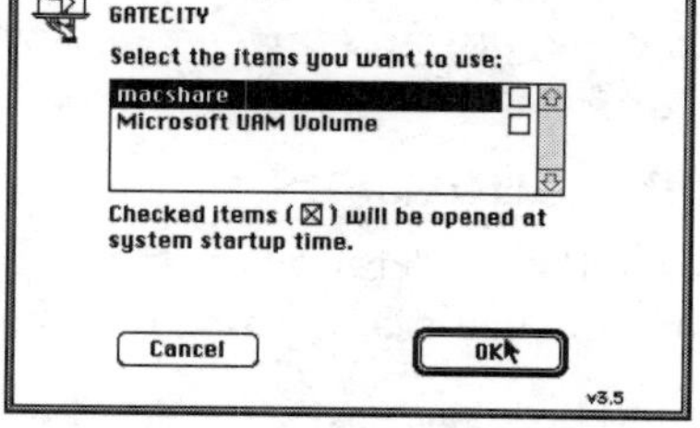

Figure 10.18. *Selecting a volume for access under AppleShare.*

This is where users can select a volume by highlighting a volume and clicking OK. After selecting a volume, the user returns to this dialog box and checks the box to ensure that he will reconnect to his volume when the Macintosh computer is rebooted. The user can even bring back the server in System 7.5 or later by going to the Recent Servers option under the Apple menu.

The volumes on the Windows NT server show up in a Mac window, just like any other volume or hard drive. If the associations have been set up properly, the user will see icons pop up, representing the application that created or can modify the object. The user will even see default icons for unassociated entities, such as PC Executables. Mac files that were uploaded to the volume will preserve all of their resources; therefore, all the icons and entities will remain. Figure 10.19 shows several files and their respective icons.

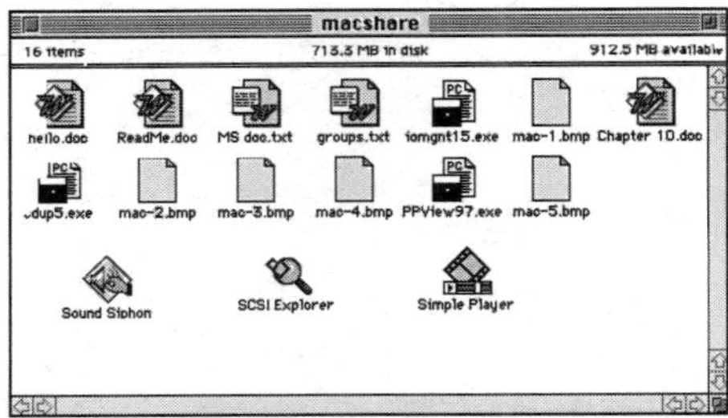

Figure 10.19. *Working with files on an NT server using a Mac client.*

While working with NT server Mac volumes, users can receive server messages initiated by an administrator or mandatory messages (such as errors or down-level server messages like the one shown in Figure 10.20).

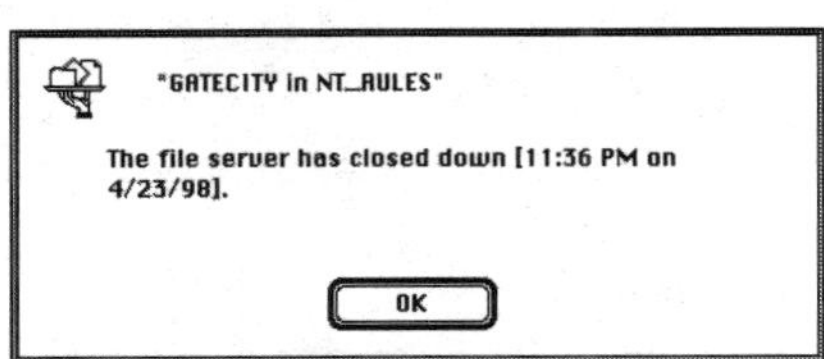

Figure 10.20. *Receiving down-level messages from the NT server.*

Macintosh Client Concerns

There are a few problems and considerations that pop up from time to time when dealing with Macintosh clients connecting to a Windows NT server.

First off, administrators need to be aware of some of the options that are available for Mac clients but that may not be available for other clients. For starters, Windows NT's Remote Access Service does not support Macintosh computers. This does not mean that Mac users cannot dial in using strictly PPP for TCP/IP applications, but it does mean the following:

- Services for Macintosh does not support connectivity over RAS mainly due to the lack of AppleTalk stack.
- Microsoft does not provide any support for any Mac attempt to connect over dial-up lines.

Mac clients do not execute login scripts, nor do they support user profiles. Mac clients cannot view or connect to domains at one time. They view and connect simply by servers. Mac clients cannot automatically synchronize time clocks with Windows NT servers. A manual NetTime option for the Macintosh is available through the Resource Kit. (NetTime was discussed earlier in Chapter 3, "Managing Enterprise Services," in the section "Time Services.")

NetTime can actually use any AppleShare server to synchronize client Macintosh clocks. However, in order to point it to a specific source, you need to use a resource editor, such as ResEdit, to modify the STR resources.

I recommend ResEdit because, as far as I know, it is the only one readily available for the Macintosh. In ResEdit, implement the following steps:

1. From the File menu, select Open.
2. Select Net Time, then click Open.
3. Look for the STR resource and double-click.
4. Located in the STR resource are four IDs, 128–131, with the names Zone, Server, Alt Zone, and Alt Server. Double-click Zone and type the zone where your server is located. If your network doesn't have a zone listing, type an asterisk (*).
5. Open the Server ID and type the name of your AppleShare server. Again, you don't need to put anything in the Data$ edit box.
6. Now close the window. NetTime will first use the server in Server in the zone in Zone. If it can't find the server, it will try to find the Alt Server in the Alt Zone.

If NetTime cannot find either server, it presents a dialog box telling you just that and recommending that you modify the STR resources accordingly, as shown in Figure 10.21.

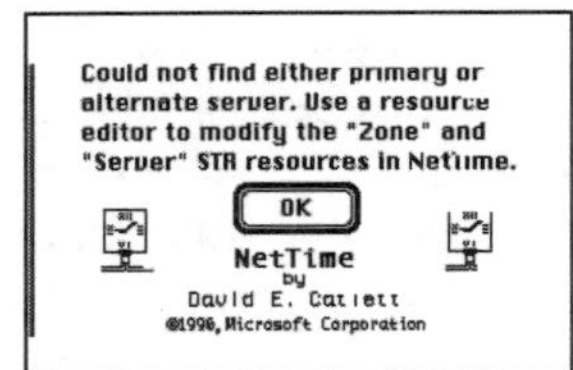

Figure 10.21. *The result of NetTime being unable to locate a time source.*

Author's Note

Microsoft recommends that you put NetTime in your Startup Items folder on your Mac. This folder is a subfolder in the System folder. This will ensure automatic synchronization every time your computer boots up.

Troubleshooting Tip

If the AppleShare client fails to connect to the NT server at startup, one of many reasons may be at fault. Some may even be beyond your control. In Chapter 11, "Enterprise Management," we look at the Knowledge Base, which is an excellent option for locating known problems and bugs.

There are some basic measures to take to try to eliminate obvious problems:

- *First, make sure the server is running and make sure the SFM services are started on the NT server.*
- *Also, make sure the volumes are set up and that the network is up.*

There are also some not-so-obvious measures to take:

- *Make sure the zone is set up and that there are available network numbers for dynamic assignment.*
- *Zap the PRAM on the Macintosh clients or run Disk First Aid or the Norton Disk Doctor. Disk First Aid is usually included with the Mac OS.*

Timbuktu Pro

There are many reasons why you may want to look to other options for Macintosh and Windows interconnectivity. Many of these reasons fall under two categories:

- The first is the lack of a built-in full-duplex solution built into Windows NT.
- The second is the Services for Macintosh on Windows NT being exclusively designed for and limited to AppleTalk.

Earlier in this chapter, we mentioned the recent enhancements to AppleShare/IP as an alternative option, especially for allowing your Windows NT clients to connect to AppleShare volumes as if they were Microsoft shares using the Server Message Block protocol. Using Timbuktu Pro is another alternative. Timbuktu Pro has been an excellent alternative because it has platform support for both Macintosh and Windows NT.

Figure 10.22 shows a connectivity sketch using Services for Macintosh, AppleShare/IP, and Timbuktu Pro to complete a multi-option full client-server connectivity solution between Windows NT and Macintosh computers.

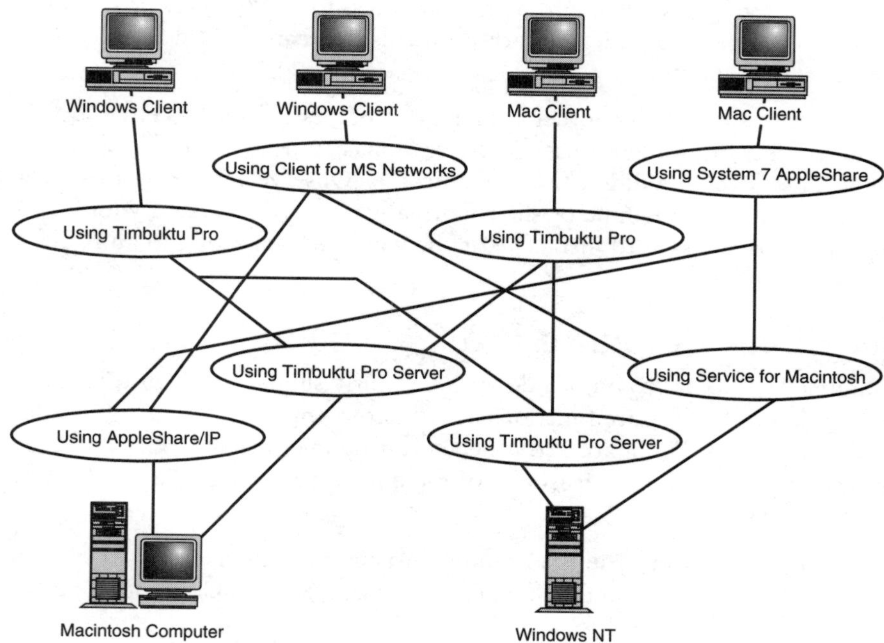

Figure 10.22. *A multiple solution schematic for NT and Macintosh connectivity.*

Timbuktu Pro for Windows NT and Macintosh allows you to connect your Windows NT and Macintosh to other Windows and Macintosh computers on your network. For example, you can share and exchange directories and files as well as send messages to one another or collaborate in a similar manner as you can with AppleShare and Windows NT.

Timbuktu Pro's capabilities fall into four categories of services:

- Sending FlashNotes and files. A point-to-point messaging system of sending messages, called FlashNotes, along with files similar to the way messages are exchanged using email or through Microsoft's NetMeeting.

- Exchange files between computers. You can exchange files in a method similar to the way the File Transfer Protocol works for TCP/IP networks.
- Control another user's computer. Remote administration and control is possible using Timbuktu Pro.
- Observe another user's desktop. Now if there were only a way to do this easily with Windows NT, life would be great.

With Timbuktu Pro, users are in charge of their computers. Users can send and receive FlashNotes and files from other computers that are running Timbuktu Pro. Access to the users' computers is completely in their control. They can assign the privileges available to users that access their Windows or Macintosh computer and designate the network protocols that can be used for access (AppleTalk or TCP/IP).

Interactive sessions with another computer can be established as either a registered user or as a guest user. These sessions can occur by using one of the following services: Send, Exchange, Control, or Observe Service. If a user connects as a registered user, he or she is normally required to log on with his or her name and a password just as he or she would if connecting to an NT or AFP server.

Installing Timbuktu Pro

Installing Timbuktu Pro on Windows NT is fairly simple (see Figure 10.23). The Timbuktu Pro Service functions as a desktop application that runs under the Systray menu. Timbuktu Pro is dependent upon either the TCP/IP or the AppleTalk protocol and at least one of these must be installed before Timbuktu Pro is installed.

During the installation, you are prompted to enter a Timbuktu Pro host name, which is used for access and communication using either TCP/IP or AppleTalk.

Remote Access

One thing lacking in Windows NT Services for Macintosh that Timbuktu Pro can provide is the capability for computers to send and exchange information with each other over dial-up PPP connections (see Figure 10.24). If you are operating as a remote node, you can dial in to a PPP server on a distant network. Once you're authenticated as a node on that network, you can use all Timbuktu Pro's functions with the workstations located on the distant network.

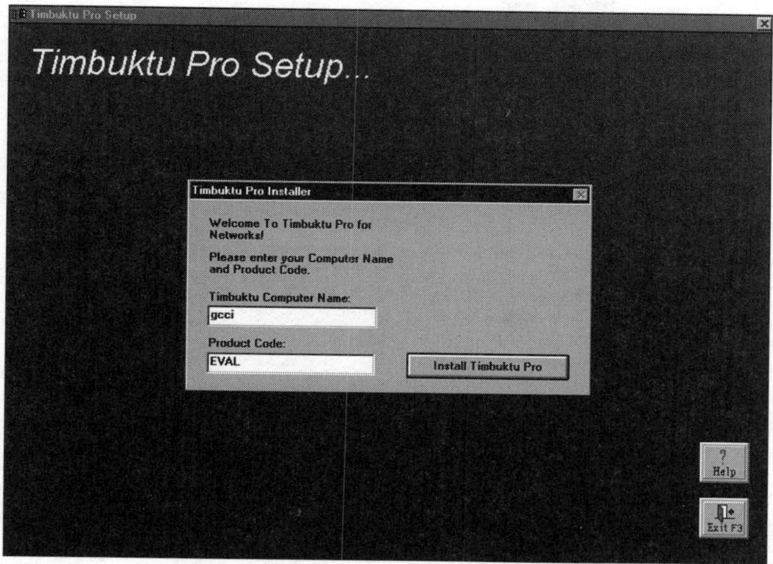

Figure 10.23. *Installing Timbuktu Pro.*

Figure 10.24. *In order for Timbuktu Pro to work over dial-up lines, Remote Access Services must be configured properly.*

Sending Notes and Files

The four options—Send, Exchange, Control, and Observe—appear as buttons on top of the Timbuktu Pro application. You will also see two test computers that Farallon has set up for use over the Internet, as shown in Figure 10.25.

To send a file to another computer, you can use the test computers or set up another connection. Select the remote addresses and click the Send button. If Timbuktu Pro asks you to log on with a name and password, enter them and click OK. The FlashNote window then automatically displays where you can send a message. If you want to include files with your message, click the Files button and make your selection in the Select Files to Send window.

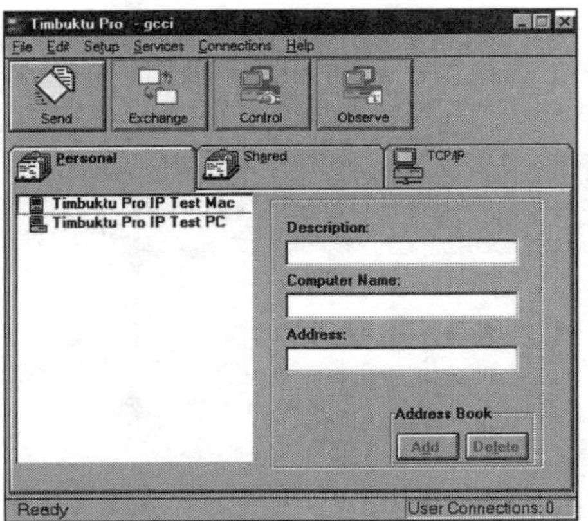

Figure 10.25. *The Timbuktu Pro main dialog box.*

If you wish, type a message in the FlashNote field. If you do not type a note, Timbuktu Pro sends a default note indicating the sender's computer name, date, and time. If you want to send the note and files to additional users, click the To button to display the Select Timbuktu Addresses dialog box. Select the next remote address from the appropriate connection tab. Click the Add button. Repeat it for each desired recipient.

If the Send Service denies your file transfer request, it could be for several reasons:

- The Send privilege is not granted to your user account on the remote computer.
- Timbuktu Pro is not running on the computer you are trying to contact. If you are using IP, the IP address of the remote computer may be incorrect.
- Another user is connected to that computer. Timbuktu Pro only allows one user at a time.

If you are sending files to a Macintosh, keep in mind that Timbuktu Pro handles messages slightly differently on the Macintosh.

Using the Exchange Service

When using the Exchange Service to copy files and directories to or from another computer, first select a remote address from a connection tab. Click the Exchange button. Depending on the privileges you have been granted on the remote computer, you may need to log on. Once you have successfully connected to the remote computer, the Exchange dialog box is displayed. The top panel in the dialog box lists the local drives, directories, and files on your PC. The bottom panel lists the same information on the remote computer. Choose the destination drive.

If you're copying files from your computer to the remote disk, go to the (Drive) field in the bottom half of the window, click the down arrow, and choose the desired drive from the drop-down list. If you're copying files from the remote disk to your computer, go to the (Drive) field in the top half of the window, click the down arrow, and choose the desired drive from the drop-down list. Display the destination directory. Folder icons represent directories.

If you're copying files from your computer to the remote disk, display the destination directory in the lower part of the window. If you're copying files from the remote disk to your computer, display the destination directory in the upper part of the window. If the desired directory is not at the root level of the disk, you'll need to work your way down to it by opening additional directories. If desired, create a new destination directory. Drag the files or directories or both from the source computer to the desired directory on the destination computer.

To select a group of consecutive filenames, click the first name in the list, hold down the Shift key, and click the last filename in the list.

To select nonconsecutive files, hold down the Ctrl key and click each filename. Timbuktu Pro begins to transfer the files immediately, with the status of the transfer appearing at the bottom of the Exchange dialog box. While the transfer is running, click outside the Exchange window or minimize it to return to other tasks on your PC. During an Exchange transfer, you'll notice a slight reduction in performance.

If you are exchanging files with a Macintosh and you are going back and forth to a FAT partition, the names of the files you receive from the Macintosh may be altered to conform to DOS filenaming requirements.

You can also transfer files to a remote computer while controlling or observing it. To use Exchange to remove files and directories from another computer, select the desired address and click the Exchange button. In the remote user's panel of the Exchange dialog box, open the necessary drive and directory and select the file or subdirectory you want to remove. Display the File menu by clicking the File Menu box in the upper-left corner of the Exchange window. Choose Delete. Timbuktu Pro will then display a message asking you to confirm your decision. To remove the file, click Yes.

Controlling Another Computer

To control another user's computer using Timbuktu Pro, first select the address of the computer you want to control. Click the Control button. Timbuktu Pro displays the other computer's desktop in a Control window. While the Control window is active, you can use your mouse and keyboard to operate the other computer. Clicking in a Control window makes it the active window. To return to your own PC, click outside the Control window. To stop controlling, choose Close from the Control menu of the Control window. Timbuktu Pro closes the window and ends the connection.

Troubleshooting Tip

If you fail, it could be because the Control privilege is not granted to your user account on the remote computer. It could be because Timbuktu Pro is not running on the computer you are trying to contact, or that two users cannot control the same computer simultaneously.

If you would like to enable or disable the Control privilege on your computer, you can do so in the Define Users dialog box. Figure 10.26 displays this option as it appears on Windows NT computers.

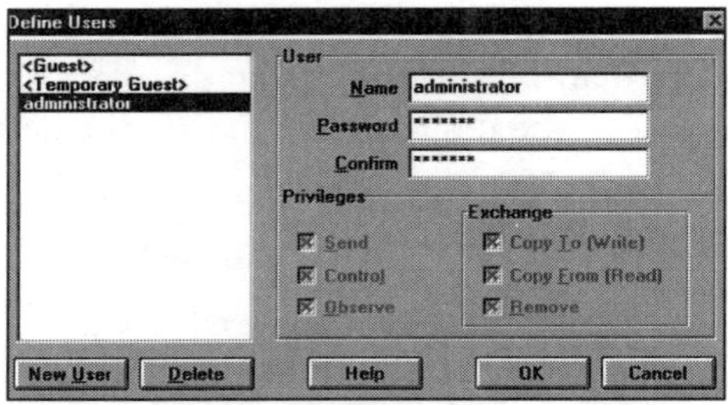

Figure 10.26. *The Define Users option under Timbuktu Pro for Windows NT.*

If you are controlling a Macintosh that has been equipped with more than one monitor, you can choose which monitor is to be displayed in your Control window. To switch between multiple Macintosh monitors, hold down the Shift, Ctrl, and Alt keys while pushing the left or right arrow key. Repeating these key strokes steps you through the loop of available monitors on the remote Macintosh.

To observe another user's computer, select the address of the computer you want to observe. Click the Observe button. Timbuktu Pro displays the other computer's desktop in an Observe window. To stop observing, choose Close from the Control menu of the Observe window and Timbuktu Pro closes the window and ends the connection.

If Timbuktu Pro turns down your request to observe, it is probably because the Observe privilege is not granted to your user account on the remote computer or that Timbuktu Pro is not running on the computer you are trying to contact. You can also use the Define Users option to enable or disable the Observe privilege on your computer.

Setting Preferences

You can use the Preferences option under Timbuktu Pro (both Macintosh and Windows NT) to control global options for the Timbuktu Pro server. Figure 10.27 shows the Preferences dialog box.

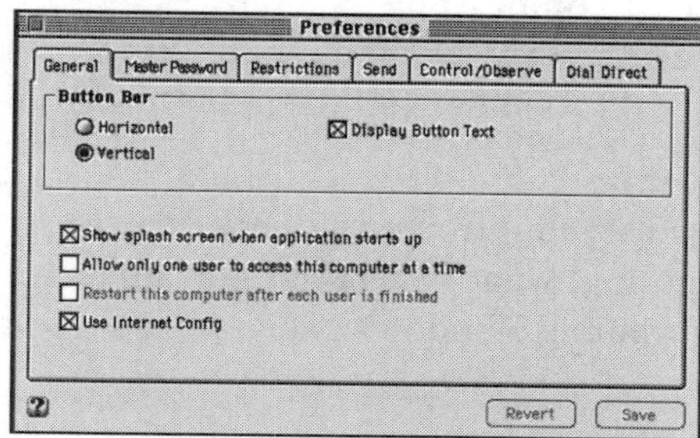

Figure 10.27. *The Timbuktu Macintosh Preferences dialog box.*

This is where you can opt to allow multiple user access, set a master password, and allow incoming access to specific users and even dial-up options.

Incoming Access

This option is very important because this is where you can set up the option to allow access by certain protocols. On Windows NT, this includes TCP/IP, AppleTalk, dial-up, and even using NetWare. On Macintosh computers, this can be using either TCP/IP, AppleTalk, and Dial-Direct. Figure 10.28 shows this option as its appears on the Macintosh.

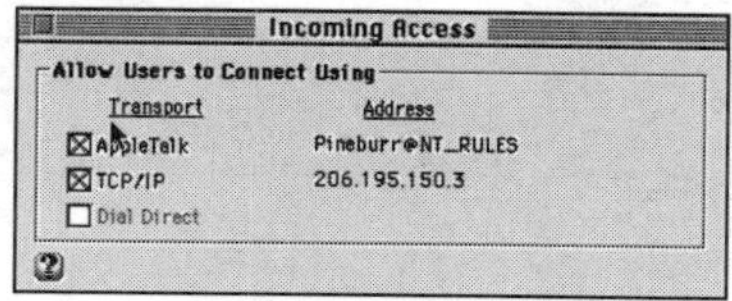

Figure 10.28. *The Incoming Access dialog box displays these options for protocol access.*

Monitoring AppleTalk Connections

Within Windows NT, there is only one built-in option for keeping track of AppleTalk activity. The Performance Monitor allows you to track performance counters relating to the Services for Macintosh, but it is unfortunately limited to tracking only those NT servers acting as AFP servers. Windows NT's SNMP Agent also is not an option in that it only allows SNMP support for the IP and IPX protocols and not the DDP (Datagram Delivery Protocol, AppleTalk's core protocol).

Using the AT Analyzer from the Resource Kit

This utility can allow you to track AppleTalk connectivity for all registered nodes on an AppleTalk network. It first performs an AppleTalk lookup for registered AppleTalk devices on an AppleTalk network on its initial start. The user can then perform a lookup of all AppleTalk devices by socket connections and listening ports. It can also use the Name Binding Protocol (NBP) and the Zone Information protocol (ZIP) to allow you to find information on specific networks and zones.

You can use this utility to find information about the AppleTalk network, such as what systems are routing, what system has a printer captured, or a list of printers or computers running Windows NT.

Warning

The computer that runs ANALYZER must have the AppleTalk stack installed through Services for Macintosh or it will fail.

Figure 10.29 displays the status on a zone lookup. Each entry is traced by individual socket. The first field refers to the network number, which is obtained from the seed router. The node number refers to the computer that is running AppleTalk. The socket refers to the service access point. Each socket has its own name in addition to the name of its computer running AppleTalk. The last column displays the zone.

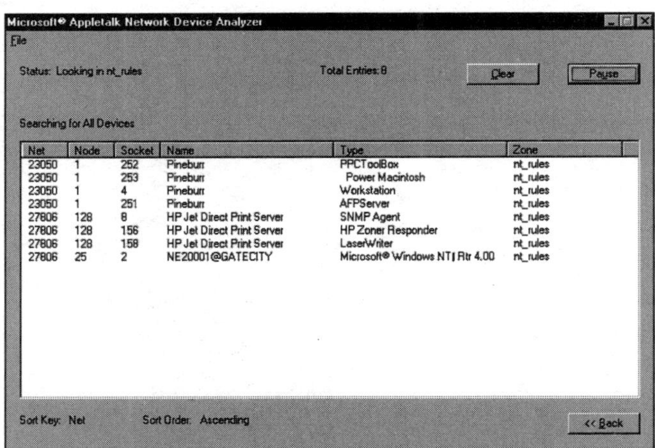

Figure 10.29. *The Search Results dialog box found under the ANALYZER utility.*

The initial screen for ANALYZER allows you to control the option for searching as well as the zone filter. By default, it uses the current zone of the one running the utility.

Part III

Advanced Topics

Chapter 11

Enterprise Management

- **24/7 Servers for Your Enterprise**
  Establish 24/7 servers for your enterprise.
- **Clusters**
  Learn about clusters and clustering technology.
- **System Maintenance**
  Learn tips and techniques for planning and conducting preventative maintenance on your systems.
- **Hardware Detection Problems**
  Find out how to troubleshoot hardware-detection problems.
- **The "Blue Screen of Death"**
  Learn about the "Blue Screen of Death" and what it means.
- **Disk Troubleshooting and Probing Utilities**
  Troubleshoot disk problems and utilities that will make it easier to resolve problems.
- **Helpdesk Assistance**
  Find out what role the Helpdesk has in the enterprise.
- **Those Problematic Laptop Users**
  Receive tips and techniques for supporting mobile users.

Establishing 24/7 Servers

Companies today require continuous access to data on the Enterprise network. This data is the essence of their business and must be available 24 hours a day, 7 days a week. With proper planning, it is easy to make servers available at any time.

Define the Need for Continuous Access

Proper enterprise planning and a scheduled preventative maintenance program are ways to ensure the availability of data. System engineers need to be aware of the technologies that are available to support fault-tolerance and high availability.

When planning enterprise systems, the planner must weigh several factors to determine the risks involved. Two big factors are cost and risk. Cost can be kept down if there is a higher assumption of risk on the part of the system planner. Risk can be controlled if the planner knows that a particular system can be down for 24 hours and that a replacement part can be obtained and installed in that time; then, the planner can assume the risk and the loss of that system for 24 hours. For example, what happens if the part is backordered? Or if the part is lost in shipment? The planner could also plan to keep spare parts on hand in case of a failure. Of course, if the system never fails, the stock of spare components might be considered a waste of money. These are all factors that the planner must take into consideration when developing a 24/7 enterprise network.

A study conducted by the University of Texas (Christensen, S. R., et. al, "Financial And Functional Impacts Of Computer Outages On Businesses," Center for Research on Information Systems, The University of Texas at Arlington) produced the following:

- On average, by the sixth day of an outage, companies experience a 25% loss in daily revenue; by the 25th day it is 40%.
- Financial and functional loss increases rapidly after the onset of an outage.
- 75% of organizations reach critical or total loss of functioning within two weeks of the loss of computer support.
- 43% of companies that experience a disaster but have no business recovery plan in place never reopen.
- Of companies that experience a disaster but have no tested business recovery plans in place, only one in ten are still in business two years later.

As the study indicates, companies that rely on computer systems risk serious financial losses if proper safeguards are not in place. Organizations that have properly planned their networks can significantly reduce the risk of financial loss in the event of a catastrophe. Companies that have a data recovery plan in effect can be back online with little or no interruption in service to the customer.

Fault Tolerance

Financial data systems used to be the only realm where you could find fault-tolerant (FT) systems. The cost and complexity were usually prohibitive to the average MIS department. The recent increase in the use of Windows NT in the enterprise and the decreased cost of Intel-based systems have resulted in an increased awareness for the need of FT systems. Many companies rely on revenue from systems that must be available 24 hours a day where even an hour's downtime could result in lost revenue.

There are many different levels and definitions for FT. The online Webopeadia (`www.pcwebopedia.com`) defines FT as:

> The ability of a system to respond gracefully to an unexpected hardware or software failure

The key aspect of FT is the ability of the system to continue operations after a critical component, hardware or software, has failed. Figure 11.1 shows an example of a fault-tolerant system.

Redundant Systems

PC companies today offer server platforms that have a wide variety of FT or redundant components. When deciding upon these types of components, the planner must know the technical capabilities of the MIS staff. Are they capable of replacing a failed power supply or hard disk?

Everything should have a backup. Again, assumption of risk is an issue. NASA's space shuttle uses four redundant computer systems, all running the same software, and a fifth computer running different software in case the software running on the first four has a fatal bug.

The use of *hot-swappable* components can reduce the downtime of systems by allowing the system engineers to replace critical components when they fail. System manufacturers offer many different hot-swappable components. Hot-swappable components allow you to replace failed components without shutting down the system or stopping processes. The most common of these are hard disks and power supplies. Hot swap PCI expansion cards are also available.

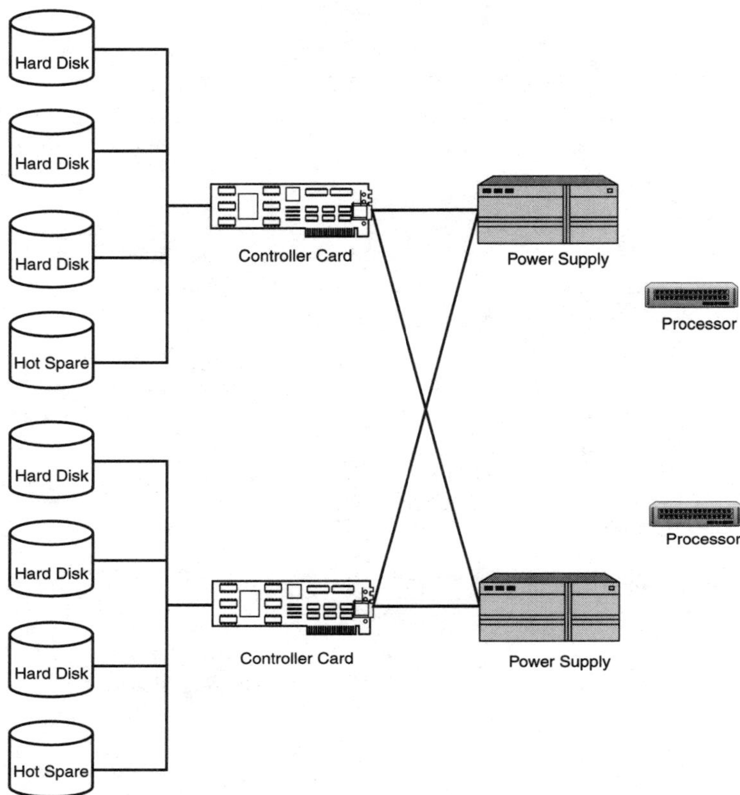

Figure 11.1. *An internal diagram of a fault-tolerant system.*

The planner must carefully examine every part of the enterprise and identify the areas where a failure would cause the greatest disruption in the system. Often, components like network hubs and switches are overlooked, but failure of these components can bring any enterprise to its knees. The planner must look for potential single points of failure and develop redundant systems to cover these points.

Uninterruptible Power Supply

It is common for a company to spend thousands of dollars to develop a sophisticated FT system and then connect it to a single Uninterruptible Power Supply (UPS). This is one of the most common single points of failure in the enterprise. Mission critical systems should have a secondary UPS that is not connected to the same power source as the primary UPS. In the event that the primary power throws a breaker, the secondary power system will be unaffected.

The UPS should be periodically tested. Many IS shops install a UPS and never test to see if it is working. Disconnect the power source and measure the time it takes to drain the batteries with a normal non-production server. This should be recorded and examined to determine if the UPS is losing storage capacity over time. Consult your UPS manual or manufacturer for proper maintenance procedures. Make sure to check for the following:

- Cracked, swelling, or leaking batteries
- Corroded or loose contacts
- Proper voltage

Tip

Keep a maintenance record on every component on every system in your shop. This record can be used to trace the lifespan of components and helps you to anticipate when they may fail.

Power Supply

Power supplies are a common failure point for servers. Many server manufacturers offer redundant, hot-swappable power supplies. Server/Class systems can be purchased with a single power supply to reduce the cost, but a spare power supply should also be purchased. This spare can be used as a backup for several single power supply servers.

When planning servers, remember to put mission critical data on servers with redundant power supplies. If the primary power supply fails, the alternate power supply will maintain power to the system, the system will remain viable, and there should be no loss of data. In a single power supply server, human intervention is required to switch to a spare power supply and the server will be down until the failed power supply is replaced. Any data that was being processed will most likely be lost. Again, you're dealing here with cost versus availability.

Processors

One of the most catastrophic failures is that of the processor. Replacing the processor can be time-consuming and may require an authorized technician. Processor failure on a single processor system will completely disable that server and will probably result in data loss. If a multiprocessor system loses a processor, chances are that no data will be lost. The server can be used until replacement parts and/or a technician is made available. The server can be shut down gracefully to avoid data loss at a time when the system load is low or at a scheduled maintenance period.

Disk Controllers

The disk controller is another important component in the computer system. It is responsible for making the data stored on the hard drives available to the system and users. Most high-end servers have the ability to use dual disk controllers.

It is important to understand the concepts of disk arrays and how they work in order to design a workable FT system. Using dual controllers allows one controller to completely fail, but keep in mind that many disk arrays require a minimum number of disks to be able to continue normal operation. If using dual controllers, make sure there are enough disks to recover in the case of a controller failure.

Controllers can contain cache, error correction, and other performance enhancements. Some of these controllers have batteries that can store the contents of the cache in the event that the system fails. Once the system comes back online, the data in the cache can be written back to the disks.

Hot Spare

Some controllers identify a disk as a *stand-by* or *hot spare*. If a disk within the array fails, the array can use the hot spare as a new disk. The array uses the parity data to rebuild the disk that failed. The failed disk can be removed and replaced with a new drive and the new drive then becomes the new hot spare.

RAID

RAID stands for Redundant Array of Inexpensive (or, more recently Independent) Drives. It is a technology that allows data to be intelligently and safely stored and accessed over multiple hard disks. Of the many different RAID configurations, the most common are 0 through 6, with RAID 5 being the most widely used. RAID uses error-correction data and parity disks to maintain data integrity in the event of a hard disk failure.

RAID can be either hardware or software in nature. Hardware solutions are much faster and have better performance; software solutions are usually less expensive.

The RAID levels consist of the following:

- RAID 0. This is not true RAID since no parity drive or error-correction is used. Data is spread over multiple disks. This is not a fault-tolerant configuration.
- RAID 1. This is disk mirroring or duplexing. Data is written to two drives simultaneously. If one drive fails, the data is safe on the other drive. This configuration has the highest performance overhead of all the RAID configurations.

- RAID 2. This configuration uses error correction on the controller and stripes the data at the bit level. This RAID level requires a large number of disks to do error correction. This configuration is rarely used.
- RAID 3. Data is striped in parallel at the byte level across multiple data disks. A separate disk is used to store the parity data. The parity disk can be used to rebuild data if a disk fails. However, the drives do not act independently and slow data access for multiple users.
- RAID 4. Similar to RAID 3 except data is striped in blocks rather than bytes. A separate parity disk is also used. The difference is that the disks can operate independently. Multiple reads are possible, but multiple writes are still prohibited because of the single parity disk.
- RAID 5. This is the most common RAID configuration. Data and parity information is written across all the drives in the array. Multiple reads and writes are possible because there is not a single parity disk. This increases I/O and is suitable for reading and writing large blocks of data at the same time.
- RAID 6. This is a combination of RAID 1 and RAID 5. Data and parity is spread across multiple disks but is also duplexed or mirrored to another set of disks.

High Availability

High availability solutions use multiple server platforms and/or storage enclosures to increase the availability of data. In the event that one or more servers fail or become unavailable, the other platforms can take over the responsibilities of the primary server. These types of solutions also provide a way to take down servers without disrupting service to users. This could be to conduct maintenance, upgrades, or to replace the server completely.

Clusters

Clusters were introduced in the mid-1980s by Digital Equipment Corporation (DEC) with its VMScluster product. *Clusters* are a group of servers that act as though they were one system on the network. Often, clusters share a storage device. A clustered system is less expensive than a fully fault-tolerant system. In a fault-tolerant system, expensive redundant components sit passively waiting for a failure. In a cluster, less expensive non-fault-tolerant servers can be used. If a server in a cluster fails, the other members of the cluster can take over for the failed server, and in some instances can even take over processes on-the-fly.

There are many different companies that offer clustering solutions. Some are tied into specific hardware manufacturers. Normally, a cluster consists of two servers and a shared storage device (see Figure 11.2). Companies like Tandem, Data General, Compaq, and DEC all provide excellent clustering solutions.

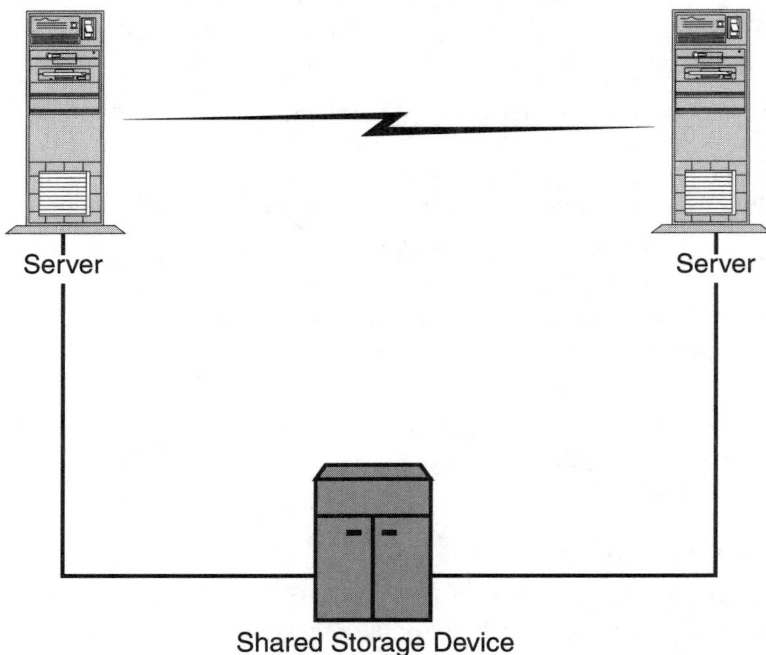

Figure 11.2. *A typical cluster.*

Server Replication (Mirror)

The best and most expensive fault-tolerant or cluster solutions cannot prevent data loss if your systems are destroyed from flood, fire, or other natural or man-made disasters. Current cluster solutions are limited to the distance that the shared storage device is from the servers. This is usually only several meters.

Although a complete backup is necessary and should be kept off-site, it does not allow for a rapid renewal of operations. Through a technology known as *server replication* or *mirroring*, an active server on the network can be replicated to another site in the same building or even another city or state (see Figure 11.3). This is a very fault-tolerant configuration that can greatly reduce downtime. This solution can also be beneficial in the event that network connectivity is lost to the primary data center.

This type of solution is almost always software-based. It can also cause a large amount of bandwidth utilization on the network. It would be best to configure a separate data channel for replication if this type of solution is utilized.

Author's Note

Don't confuse Server Replication with the Windows NT built-in Directory Replication. They are completely different. Windows NT built-in Directory Replication only replicates a specific part of the file system. Server Replication replicates the entire file structure. Changes that occur on the primary server are replicated to the secondary server as they occur.

There are several products on the market, such as OctopusHA+ from Octopus and Real Time Replicator for NT from Network Integrity, to name a few.

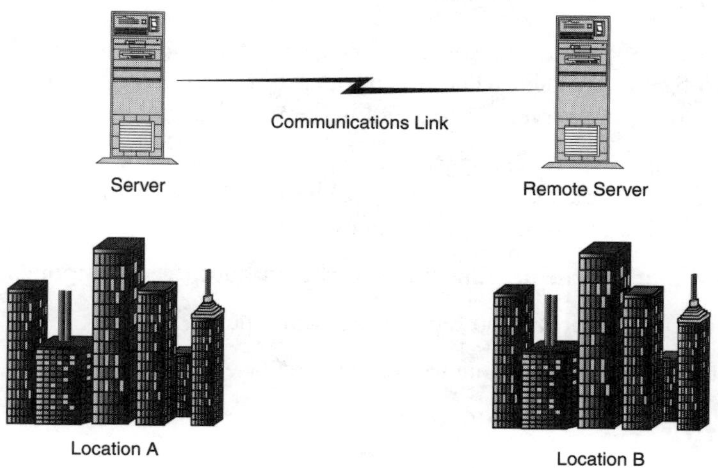

Figure 11.3. *A replicated server.*

Hot and Cold Spares

Many companies cannot afford any amount of downtime. One way to ensure that the network has the highest availability possible is to use hot and cold spare servers and workstations. This can be extended to include critical network components like routers and hubs.

A *hot spare* is a pre-configured computer workstation or server that is connected to the network and powered up. A replicated server or even a node member of a cluster could be considered a hot spare. Some data centers may have a system sitting off to the side to take over in the event of a failure.

A *cold spare* is a system that has been configured, but is either powered off or in off-site storage. Keeping the system powered off will prevent a catastrophic failure of the UPS from affecting the system. Storing cold spares off-site is a way to bring your operation back online in case the primary data center fails or is destroyed.

Troubleshooting Tip

Any time a system is planned, the planner must also plan disaster-recovery procedures and Continuation Of Operations (COOP). This plan should outline procedures to use in the event that the primary data center is destroyed or rendered inoperable. Take the mid-1990s, for example; corporate America suffered repeated floods, hurricanes, tornadoes, mudslides, and even terrorist bombings. It is estimated that as many as 15% of the businesses in the World Trade Center went out of business after the February 26, 1993 bombing.

Often, it is easier to take a system off-line to troubleshoot problems than to attempt to fix the problem when it is in operation. Maintaining a hot spare allows you to take a server off-line and maintain full coverage.

The concept of hot and cold spares can extend into any aspect of the data center, including UPS, disk drives (floppy and hard disks), network cards, etc. We come back to the assumption-of-risk questions:

- How long can the organization operate without these components?
- How long will it take to replace the components?
- Is it economically feasible to maintain replacements on-hand?

Testing

No matter what type of solution is implemented, it must be tested on a scheduled basis under operational loads. There is at least one grizzled veteran in every MIS department who will relate countless tales of failed backup tapes, dead UPSs, fail-over systems that crash, and fault-tolerant systems that aren't.

It is difficult to conduct scheduled testing on operational systems. It is inconvenient for users and unthinkable to production managers. These are the same irate users and managers who will be calling every 30 seconds to interrupt you while you are trying to find out why the backup tape is blank or why the UPS is dead (but the light is green!?).

Planning System Maintenance

Most organizations do not conduct any type of scheduled maintenance on their PCs. PCs today are very reliable and have few working parts that can fail. Since PCs become obsolete within two to three years, fans and disk drives often last beyond the usefulness of the PC. Organizations can reduce potential problems by conducting routine, scheduled maintenance on all of their systems.

Define the Need for Maintenance

Many system administrators will admit that they have never done any type of preventative maintenance on hardware under their care. Often, hardware will be upgraded or replaced with newer and better equipment before it ever fails. Hardware today can run for years without even being turned off.

So why perform preventative maintenance?

Preventative Maintenance

Preventative maintenance (PM) is the process of inspecting and testing critical hardware components on a regular basis in order to identify problems before they occur. This includes both hardware and software. PM gives the system administrators a chance to inspect wiring, update drivers, clean floppy and tape drives. UPS systems should be cleaned and tested, network contacts should be cleaned, and the list goes on.

One of the most common failures is in the system fans. Fans accumulate dust, and on some systems, the CPU fan tends to blow down onto the processor. This can cause a buildup of dust on the processor or motherboard components located near the processor. This dust buildup causes the components to heat up faster and possibly overheat. Fans can become clogged with dust and overheat themselves or just stop working. Newer computer systems, though, have internal heat sensors and can alert the administrator in the event of a problem.

Hard disks should be checked to make sure that their mounts are secure. If they are tray or removable, then the connector pins should be checked for corrosion. Internal hard disks often suffer from poor ventilation and can overheat quickly. Hard disks can also be optimized and checked for integrity. Check to make sure that expansion cards are securely seated and that they are secured with the proper screws. Heat expansion can cause cards and even chips to pop off or become loose. Tape and floppy drives should be cleaned of and inspected for debris and proper operation.

The area around the server should be inspected to ensure that there are no safety hazards like tangled power cords and cords that could trip someone. Make sure that there is adequate ventilation around the servers and workstations. People tend to stack paper on the top of computers and monitors; this is a very unsafe practice and could result in a real-world test of your recovery plan.

Don't forget to clean and check the mouse and keyboard. There's nothing like a crisis when the mouse and/or keyboard fails. This is also a good time to install patches and upgrades to the software. Preventative maintenance schedules should be rigidly enforced and supported by management.

System administrators should consult the computer manufacturer's manuals and Web sites for additional information on conducting maintenance on systems. Books like Que's *Upgrading and Repairing PCs* by Scott Mueller are also good sources of information on maintaining PCs.

Minimizing Server Downtime

PM practices can minimize the total downtime that servers experience. By taking the servers down periodically, the total available time for the server is greatly increased. The first time you find a potential catastrophic problem and correct it you will understand the reason for PM.

Hot/Cold Spares

Hot and cold spares, including both computer and components, are a great benefit in conducting PM. These components can be used to replace questionable components until a more thorough inspection can be performed.

Clusters

The very nature of clusters allows for node members to be taken down at will, enabling a less disruptive PM schedule. This is very evident when upgrading software. Often, software can be upgraded on each node member in a day without ever having to take down the network; the cluster is available the whole time.

Warning

You should test any new software in a lab environment if possible. Upgrades and patches do little good if they are incompatible with other software on the server, or completely take the server down. If you don't have a lab, make sure that you have a contingency plan in the event that the server fails during an upgrade or patch installation.

Hardware Detection Problems

It is possible that a particular combination of hardware in just the right places can cause unexpected behavior in computer systems. Today, most major server manufacturers offer a wide range of options and choices for server components.

The Microsoft Hardware Compatibility List

When a decision is made to add additional hardware to an existing system or during the planning stages of a new system, every aspect of the new component should be investigated. Contact the server manufacturer and the component manufacturer to ensure compatibility. Consult the Microsoft Hardware Compatibility List (HCL); this list is continually changing, so make sure that the most current one is used. Make sure that the most recent NT drivers are available. Once everything is in place, make sure that you test the configuration before moving it to a production environment.

Mission-critical servers should comply with the compatibility list to ensure that there is no question about whether the hardware is supported. Remember that hardware not listed on the HCL is not supported. If a problem should arise in the future, there will be limited resources to assist troubleshooting problems.

PCI Versus ISA

PCI or *Peripheral Component Interconnect* is a local bus standard developed by Intel. It replaces the older ISA or Industry Standard Architecture in most computer systems. As speeds increase, the ISA bus will be completely phased out.

PCI expansion cards are much easier to use than ISA and support plug and play. In 1993, Plug and Play ISA was introduced. Older ISA cards are not as easy to configure, usually relying on a complex mixture of jumper and software configuration settings to get them working properly. ISA is slower and has a smaller data path than PCI. The PCI bus controller allocates resources to PCI cards. This makes adding new cards quick and simple and reduces the potential for resource conflicts.

Troubleshooting Problems

If a problem arises where hardware is not detected, there are a limited number of options available. If the product is on the HCL, then you have many more options:

- Make sure you have the card or hardware correctly configured.
- Contact the manufacturer; most will supply technical support for a limited number of days.

- Read any Readme.txt files that are provided.
- Check the manufacturer's Web site for the latest drivers.
- Check on sites like `www.dejanews.com` to see if other people have experience with the product.
- Check the Microsoft Support Knowledge Base (`www.microsoft.com/support`) for any information related to the product.
- Use a compatible product from the HCL.

Interpreting the "Blue Screen of Death"

The infamous "*Blue Screen of Death*" *(BSoD)* (see Figure 11.4) has earned a reputation that is not deserved. When Windows NT encounters hardware errors, software errors, or inconsistent data, a kernel error, blue screen, or trap can occur. This is a normal function of Windows NT and can assist the system engineer in identifying hardware or software problems.

```
*** STOP: 0x0000000A (0x00000000,0x00000002,0x00000000,8038c240)
IRQL_NOT_LESS_OR_EQUAL*** Address 8038c240 has base at 8038c000 - Ntfs.SYS

CPUID:Genuine Intel 6.3.3 irql:1f SYSVER 0xf0000565

Dll Base DateStmp - Name                Dll Base DateStmp - Name
80100000 336546bf - ntoskrnl.exe        80010000 33247f88 - hal.dll
80000100 334d3a53 - atapi.sys           80007000 33248043 - SCSIPORT.SYS
802aa000 33013e6b - epst.mpd            802b5000 336016a2 - Disk.sys
802b9000 336015af - CLASS2.SYS          8038c000 3356d637 - Ntfs.sys
802bd000 33d844be - Siwvid.sys          803e4000 33d84553 - NTice.sys
f9318000 31ec6c8d - Floppy.SYS          f95c9000 31ec6c99 - Null.SYS
f9468000 31ed868b - KSecDD.SYS          f95ca000 335e60cf - Beep.SYS
f9358000 335bc82a - i8042prt.sys        f9474000 3324806f - mouclass.sys
f947c000 31ec6c94 - kbdclass.sys        f95cb000 3373c39d - ctrl2cap.SYS
f9370000 33248011 - VIDEOPORT.SYS       fe9d7000 3370e7b9 - ati.sys
f9490000 31ec6c6d - vga.sys             f93b0000 332480dd - Msfs.SYS
f90f0000 332480d0 - Npfs.SYS            fe957000 3356da41 - NDIS.SYS
a0000000 335157ac - win32k.sys          fe914000 334ea144 - ati.dll
fe0c9000 335bd30e - Fastfat.SYS         fe110000 31ec7c9b - Parport.SYS
fe108000 31ec6c9b - Parallel.SYS        f95b4000 31ec6c9d - ParVdm.SYS
f9050000 332480ab - Serial.SYS

Address  dword dump Build [1314]                                    - Name
801afc24 80149905 80149905 ff8e6b8c 80129c2c ff8e6b94 8025c000 - Ntfs.SYS
801afc2c 80129c2c 80129c2c ff8e6b94 00000000 ff8e6b94 80100000 - ntoskrnl.exe
801afc34 801240f2 80124f02 ff8e6df4 ff8e6f60 ff8e6c58 80100000 - ntoskrnl.exe
801afc54 80124f16 80124f16 ff8e6f60 ff8e6c3c 8015ac7e 80100000 - ntoskrnl.exe
801afc64 8015ac7e 8015ac7e ff8e6df4 ff8e6f60 ff8e6c58 80100000 - ntoskrnl.exe
801afc70 80129bda 80129bda 00000000 80088000 80106fc0 80100000 - ntoskrnl.exe

Restart and set the recovery options in the system control panel
or the /CRASHDEBUG system start option. If this message reappears,
contact your system administrator or technical support group.
```

Figure 11.4. *The infamous "Blue Screen of Death."*

Examination of Stop Messages

In order to quickly and correctly diagnose NT errors, the systems engineer or administrator needs to have an advanced knowledge of how the NT OS model works. One of the best references is *Inside Windows NT*, Second Edition, by David Solomon, available from Microsoft Press.

Most blue screens deal with specific hardware or software problems and are well documented in the Microsoft TechNet Subscription Service or from the Microsoft Support Knowledge Base (`www.microsoft.com/support`). Usually these errors are easy to identify and correct. Sometimes an error occurs that defies explanation.

In one case, a server was having continuous problems with a `STOP 0x00000077 KERNEL_STACK_INPAGE_ERROR`. This usually is an indication of a hard disk problem or a problem with the page file. It can indicate a possible impending hard disk failure. This error occurs when data is being paged into the page memory from the pagefile. SCSI termination, bad cables, and controller errors are but a few of the problems that can cause this error. In this case, the SCSI controller card was not fully seated in the expansion slot. The card was not attached with a screw, and when an external cable was connected to the external port, the card was unseated from the slot.

There are four parts to the STOP error message.

```
*** STOP: 0x0000000a (0x0000006c, 0x00000002, 0x00000001, 0x804029cc)
IRQL_NOT_LESS_OR_EQUAL
```

The first parameter identifies the address that was referenced improperly. The second parameter identifies the IRQL that was required to access the memory. The third parameter identifies the access (read or write). The fourth parameter identifies the instruction address that attempted to access the memory that was referenced in the first parameter.

Kernel Debugging

The Windows NT kernel debuggers are located on the NT CD in the \Support\Debug directory. The debuggers are platform-specific and are 32-bit executable files used on the host computer to debug a remote computer. The remote computer can be connected by either a null modem cable or through a modem connection and must have the same platform and NT version. Communications occur using a special debugging API and protocol.

Live Debugging

It may be necessary to run a debug session on an active server. Usually a support engineer does this since much of the output is unusable by the local system administrator. It may be possible to identify certain types of problems using this technique, but someone with development and programming experience is required. Debugging sessions can be conducted using a second NT computer connected using a serial port or through a modem. Live debugging can be used to allow a Microsoft support engineer to connect and debug the system over a phone line.

Memory Dump Files

Sometimes an error occurs that cannot be easily detected or defies every effort to identify. In cases like this, a dump of the system can be made. Windows NT can be configured to create a dump of all the data in the memory. This file is the same size as the system memory. A server with 128MB of memory would create a 128MB dump file. This is why the system pagefile must be larger than the system memory. By default, this file is created as %systemroot%\ memory.dmp.

To configure recovery options, implement the following steps:

1. Open the Control Panel.
2. Select the System applet (see Figure 11.5).
3. Select the Startup/Shutdown tab.
4. Select Recovery options as needed.

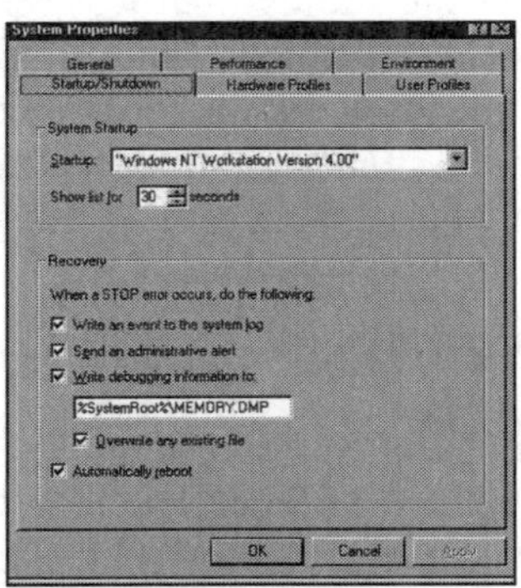

Figure 11.5. *The System Recovery Properties tab.*

Microsoft can analyze a dump file if it is sent to it. This can be a problem if you have a large dump file. High-density storage devices like Omega Zip disk or SyQuest Jet drives can be used to store the file so that it can be transported to Microsoft.

All the debug utilities require a symbol tree that contains the symbol files for the version of NT that you were running when the STOP error occurred. In order to correctly debug the system, you must construct a symbol tree on the system. The symbol files contain checked versions of the Windows NT systems files. These checked or debug versions of the files contain extra code that enables developers to find problems. These files are larger and execute slower than their counterparts. The symbol tree must include all the files that have been updated, such as service packs and hot fixes.

There are three utilities for preparing memory dump files prior to sending them to Microsoft technical support. These files are located on the NT CD under Support\Debug*platform* where *platform* is I386, Alpha, PowerPC or MIPS:

- `Dumpflop` `Dumpflop` is a command-line utility that can create floppies from the dump file that can be sent to Microsoft. `Dumpflop` can be used without setting up the symbol tree. There are many conditions that make `Dumpflop` the only option for creating something to send to technical support.

  This is the syntax to create a dump on floppy disks:

  ```
  Dumpflop options CrashDumpFile (%systemroot%\memory.dmp by default)
  ➥Drive:
  ```

  This is the syntax to pull a dump file from floppies:

  ```
  Dumpflop options Drive: CrashDumpFile
  ```

  In both cases the options are as follows:

  - `-?` Displays the command syntax.
  - `-p` Only Prints the crash dump header on an assemble operation.
  - `-v` Shows compression statistics.
  - `-q` Format floppies when necessary. When reading from floppies, overwrites existing dump file.

  If you execute `Dumpflop` without parameters, it will attempt to find the dump file in the %systemroot%\memory.dmp and write it to the A: floppy disk.

- `Dumpchk` This is a command line utility that can verify the integrity of the memory.dmp and make sure that it was correctly created. `Dumpchk` does not require access to the symbol tree.

  The syntax is:

  ```
  Dumpchk options CrashDumpFile
  ```

The options follow:

- `-?` Displays the command syntax.
- `-p` Prints the header only (with no validation).
- `-v` Specifies verbose mode.
- `-q` Performs a quick test.

`Dumpchk` reports any errors that are found during validation of the memory.dmp.

- `Dumpexam` This command line utility examines and extracts data from a memory dump file that is then written out to a text file. Often this text file can be sent to Microsoft Support instead of the full memory.dmp file. This utility requires a symbol tree.

  There are three files used by `Dumpexam`: dumpexam.exe, imagehlp.dll, and the third file depends on the platform: Kdextx86.dll, Kdexalp.dll, Kdextmip.dll, or Kdextppc.dll. These files must be in the same directory. `Dumpexam` creates a file called Memory.txt in the same directory as the Memory.dmp file. `Dumpexam` can also examine files from other NT systems as long as you replace the Kdext*.dll with appropriate hardware dll.

  The following is the proper syntax:

```
Dumpexam options CrashDumpFile
```

  The options follow:

  - `-?` Displays the command syntax.
  - `-p` Prints the header only.
  - `-v` Specifies verbose mode.
  - `-f` *`filename`* Specifies the output filename and path.
  - `-y` *`path`* Sets the symbol search path.

Tip

Detailed instructions for using these tools are located on the Windows NT Server Resource Kit.

Disk Troubleshooting and Probing Utilities

Hard disks are the single most common point of failure on a server. A properly configured fault-tolerant system will be able to recover from a disk failure.

Using hot spares and hot swappable disks, a faulty disk can be removed and a new disk can take its place. Proper backup procedures can be used to prevent data loss, but there is always a chance that a critical drive that contains important data will fail. In these instances, there are several tools available to help identify the problem and possibly repair and/or recover the data.

One critical tool for recovering from hard disk problems is the *Emergency Repair Disk (ERD)*. During the installation of Windows NT, there is a prompt to create an ERD. This should be skipped during the installation; wait until all the service packs and hotfixes have been applied and then create the ERD. Instead, running `RDISK` from the command line can create the ERD.

The following is the RDISK syntax:

- `RDISK /S` Skips the initial Create Repair Disk? dialog box and goes directly into saving the configuration.
- `RDISK /S` Also skips the initial Create Repair Disk? dialog box, saves the configuration, and the program quits.

The ERD is used to get the system back into a bootable state should something happen to the hard drive to corrupt system files or the boot sector. ERD can also be used to check the integrity of the system and find missing or corrupt system files.

A failed boot sector on the system drive can prevent the Windows NT Boot menu from displaying or it might display the following message on the boot loader screen:

```
Windows NT could not start because the following file is missing or corrupt
<%SYSTEMROOT%>\SYSTEM32\NTOSKRNL.EXE
```

Sometimes the ERD may not be able to automatically recover a corrupt boot sector. It may display a message stating:

```
Setup has determined that your file system is corrupt
```

If this occurs, corrupt boot sectors can be replaced using a utility called `DSKPROBE` available from the Windows NT Resource Kit.

Author's Note

The NT File System (NTFS) stores a copy of the boot sector on the disk. In NT 3.5x this copy is stored near the middle of the disk volume; in 4.0 it is stored at the end of the disk volume.

Helpdesk Assistance

It is important to have a knowledgeable staff manning the Helpdesk. Many problems can be quickly and efficiently resolved before involving a systems engineer.

Helpdesk personnel are the first point of contact for users and have the responsibility of making sure that problems are resolved.

Helpdesk personnel duties include the following:

- Providing support to incoming calls at the workstation and network levels, including logging the incoming calls in the problem-management system and escalating as necessary.
- Focusing on issues involving user attempts to log on to the Windows NT accounts domain, profile setup, and sending/receiving mail (including attachments).
- Calling users back when issues are resolved.
- Handling remote mail issues.
- Monitoring mail servers.
- Escalating problems.

Hours for the Helpdesk will depend greatly on the type of company and methods of operations. The Helpdesk should have access to all documents related to any product that is being used in the enterprise and be trained on those products. Also, Computer Based Training (CBT) materials should be available so that Helpdesk personnel can train during trouble calls.

It is vital that the Helpdesk personnel have access to the Internet. The Internet has a wealth of knowledge and chances are that someone else has encountered the same problem. Using newsgroups, mailing lists, and sites like DejaNews, Helpdesk personnel can access thousands of experts for free.

Microsoft TechNet

Microsoft TechNet (see Figure 11.6) is a subscription-based set of CDs that contains all the whitepapers, resource kits, Knowledge Base articles, service packs, client and server utilities, and so on, on all of Microsoft's products. It also contains monthly updates of drivers and supplemental files. This is a must-have for anyone working with Windows NT in an enterprise environment.

The Microsoft Developer's Network

The Microsoft Developer's Network (MSDN) is a subscription-based set of CDs related to development (see Figure 11.7). MSDN, just like TechNet, contains information on developing software, drivers, and so on. There are several levels of membership, the highest of which provides advanced copies of new products.

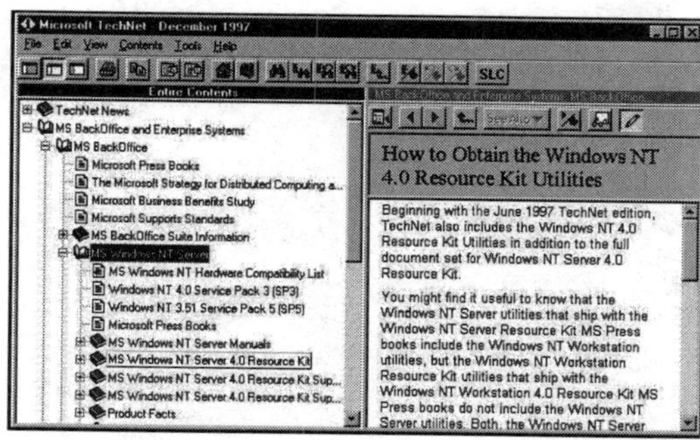

Figure 11.6. *The Microsoft TechNet interface.*

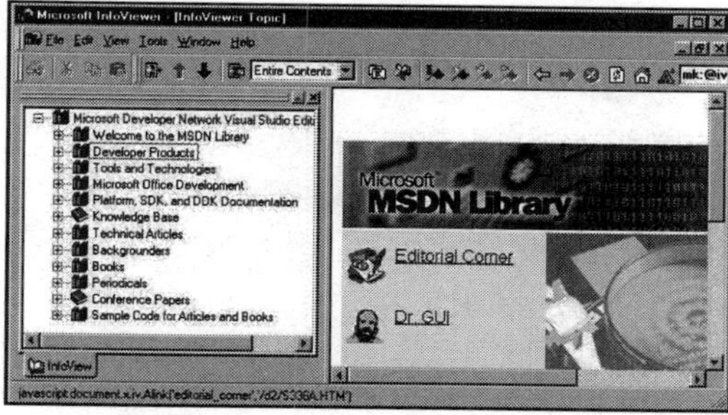

Figure 11.7. *The Microsoft Developer's Network interface.*

Microsoft Knowledge Base

The Microsoft Knowledge Base is a collection of whitepapers, technical tips, articles, and so forth. It is available from the TechNet CDs and on Microsoft's Web site, which can be accessed via Microsoft Direct Access at `http://support.microsoft.com/support`. The Web is the best place for the most up-to-date information (see Figure 11.8).

Using the Event Log Database

Both NT Server and NT Workstation have event logs. There are three event logs on Windows NT:

- System log. The system logs record system-specific events such as drivers that fail to load, successful loading of services, and so on.
- Security log. The security log is only accessible from the Administrator account. It contains events related to security, such as successful and unsuccessful logons, failed attempts to read files, and so on. Modifying the level of security auditing on the system can control what events are written to this log.

- Application log. Application-level events are written to this log. The application developer decides what events are written to the log.

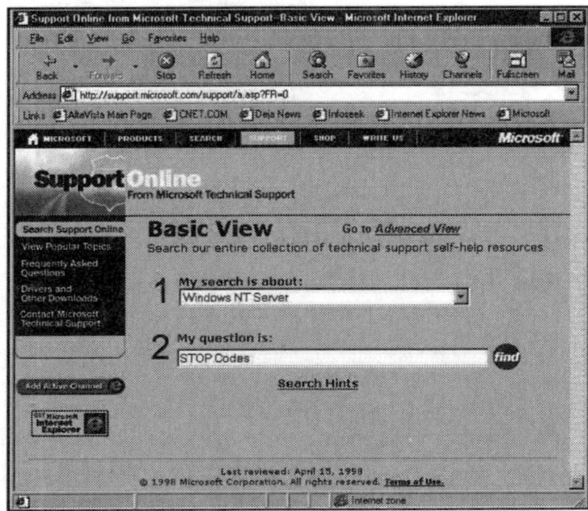

Figure 11.8. *The Microsoft Knowledge Base on the Web.*

In a large-scale environment it is impractical to try to monitor all the event logs on every system. There are third-party tools, such as SentryEm and LogCaster, that can monitor and filter events as they occur. This can be very useful because some events can be indicators of potential problems.

Event logs can be saved for future reference. The event logs can be saved in log file format, text file format, or comma-delimited text file format. Once saved, it is possible to create archives of past events and conduct pattern matching to see if a common problem occurs and on any type of recurring basis.

Using the Messages Database

The Messages database contains thousands of system-level messages with their probable causes and solutions and is searchable. The Messages database also includes the `STOP` error codes found on BSoDs.

The Messages database is included in the Windows NT Resource Kit (look for the ST NTMSGS.HLP file).

Using the Registry Database

The Windows NT Registry is a source of mystery for many NT administrators. Many are afraid to make any Registry-level changes for fear of rendering the entire system inoperable. It is important that systems engineers and administrators understand the Registry and how to correctly make changes to it.

The Registry is a database of system configurations. A good source for information is the *Concepts and Planning Guide*, located in the online books available on the NT CD \support\books.

Tip

Make sure that the Registry is backed-up before making any changes to the system.

Warning

Using the Registry Editor incorrectly can cause serious problems that may require you to reinstall your operating system. Use the Registry Editor at your own risk.

Those Problematic Laptop Users

Laptop users on the enterprise are a constant source of frustration for administrators and systems engineers. The mobile nature of laptops requires that several different configurations exist so that the users can work efficiently. There are three possible scenarios that exist for the laptop user:

- Connect to the LAN directly
- Connect to the LAN remotely
- Not connected to the network

Each scenario requires a different configuration for the laptop. NT has several options that allow the administrator to create different system profiles. When the user boots the laptop system, he will be presented with a choice of configuration options. The user chooses which configuration best suits his current connectivity requirement. The system continues to boot, enabling and disabling drivers to match the user's selection.

To create these hardware profiles, follow these steps:

1. Open the Control Panel.
2. Select the System applet.
3. Select the Hardware Profiles tab (see Figure 11.9).
4. Highlight the original configuration.
5. Select Properties.
6. Under the General tab, check the box This Is a Portable Computer. Under the Network tab, leave the box Network-Disabled Hardware Profile unchecked. This creates the Connected to the Network profile. Select OK.

7. Rename the original configuration to **`Connected to the Network`**.
8. Create a copy of the original configuration and rename it something like **`Not Connected`** or **`No Network`**. Select OK.
9. Highlight the new configuration.
10. Select the Properties button.
11. Select the Network tab and check the box Network-Disabled Hardware Profile. Select OK.

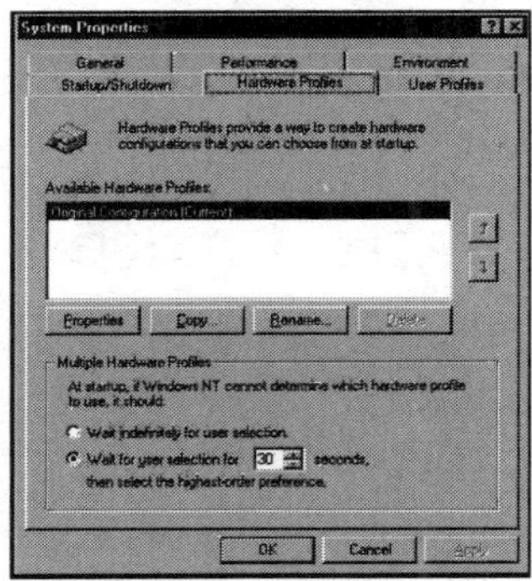

Figure 11.9. *The Hardware Profiles tab.*

The laptop now has two hardware profiles. If the user is not on the network, he will select Not Connected when prompted. Dial-in access may require some additional configuration, depending on the modem used.

Mail applications, like Microsoft Outlook, can be configured to work off-line. Mail that is created is queued until a network connection is made, then the mail is sent.

Chapter 12

Inventory Management

- **Windows NT Licenses**
  Learn the best ways to manage Windows NT licenses.
- **Software Metering**
  Survey various software-metering applications.
- **Quota Management**
  Learn how to use quota management utilities.
- **Advanced Systems Management Utilities**
  Survey ASM utilities.

Client Licenses Management

A *Microsoft Client Access License* is a legal document that provides the right for an individual computer to access a particular Microsoft server product. Client Access Licenses are required for compliance with the terms of Microsoft's server products licensing agreements. Client Access Licenses are available in single-client and 20-client configurations, and in volume quantities through Microsoft's select licensing program.

Licensing the Use of the Server Software

You may use one copy of the server software on one server, which may be connected at any point in time to an unlimited number of workstations or computers operating on one or more networks. You must, however, acquire a separate Client Access License to access or otherwise use the services of the server, whether you use the NCADMIN Client Software or third-party software to do so—unless it is otherwise noted in Section 2 of the License Agreement.

Each Client Access License must be dedicated to one unique computer or workstation. The license permits that computer or workstation to access or use the services of any server. This is known as using the Server Software in *Per Seat Mode*. If you choose Per Seat Mode, your choice is permanent. If you initially choose Per Server Mode, you have the right to change one time only to Per Seat Mode, as long as you acquire a Client Access License for each unique workstation or computer accessing or using the services of a server.

Licensing Limitations

The server software may be used by no more than four processors of the server at any one time (support for greater than four processors is available from authorized computer hardware vendors). You need a separate Client Access License for Windows NT Server in order to access or otherwise use the following Windows NT Server basic network services:

- File Services (sharing and managing files and/or disk storage).
- Printing Services (sharing and managing printers).
- Remote Access Service (accessing the server from a remote location through a communications link).

You do not need a separate Client Access License to use the Client software. The exception is for the Microsoft Windows 95 software; the CD on which Windows NT Server resides contains an upgrade copy of Windows 95 software. Note that in order to install or use this software, you must acquire a separate Windows 95 license.

Adding a New License

You can add new Client Access Licenses for products licensed in the Per Seat Mode. Keep in mind that unlike other major network operating systems such as Novell, you are adding these licenses to a pool of licenses, rather than to specific users. You are not replacing the license total, either; you are adding to it. As users access the product, they are assigned a license. When the pool of available licenses is depleted, license violations occur if new users access the product.

Author's Note

The Application log in Event Viewer on the master server reports license alerts.

The Master Server

The *master server* is a server in an organization that has been designated as the final centralized repository of all licensing data for that organization. It can be either the Primary Domain Controller (PDC) for that individual domain or a specified enterprise server. An enterprise server is the server to which multiple PDCs in a large organization replicate.

The PDC is the default master server for all servers in a domain and all Backup Domain Controllers (BDCs). Those servers replicate automatically to this PDC. Selecting and specifying a different enterprise server does not change that automatic functionality. You should only select the Enterprise Server option if your computer is one of the following:

- A standalone server in its own domain, but still part of a larger organization or enterprise
- The PDC for that domain, and you want to replicate to a higher server

Software Metering Options

One task that may become tedious with Windows NT is software management. Making sure users are keeping legal copies of software and not installing illegal software can drive administrators crazy.

Unfortunately, Windows NT does not have any built-in mechanism for software license metering or management. However, Windows NT *does* have a built-in License Manager, but it doesn't begin to address the concern of software metering. If you are looking for third-party software metering products, here are a few:

- *Express Meter* (manufactured by Express Systems)
- *CentaMeter* (manufactured by Tally Systems)
- *On Command Software Metering* (manufactured by On Technology)

Why is software licensed at all? As administrators, why should we purchase additional software metering packages? There are four basic reasons, as described in the following sections.

Fitness for Purpose

Many facilities and services are licensed when the provider of the service wants to control use for safety reasons: a driver's license, for example. A license therefore restricts use to certain conditions.

In software licensing, the software producer has manufactured the software for use under particular hardware/operating system(s). If the software purchaser uses the product outside of these parameters, the software producer will not be liable for the consequences. In any case, software is usually sold "as-is," with no guarantees attached in any event. Anyone who has worked with Windows NT more than a week or has had to install a service pack—much less five—can definitely understand this point.

Prevent Loss of Revenue

Take another example of licensing cable television hookups. One license covers all the TVs in one address (apart from the anomaly of battery-powered portables elsewhere). If a television viewer has two addresses, he needs two licenses—this is effectively a *site license.*

The same is true for software. A *software license* permits the use of the number of copies of the software that is specified in the license. For personal use, this usually means one copy. For use within the university, software is licensed under a variety of different terms and conditions; but a user should feel confident that the package he is using will be properly licensed if it is running from a file server.

Author's Note

The fact that software can be copied easily from disk to disk does not mean that license conditions do not matter. Much hard work has gone into production of the software, and further development needs to be funded from licensing receipts.

Protect Intellectual Property Rights

Software is copyrighted. The producer of the software grants certain rights to those using its software, which are set out in the license. It is the software (instructions/code) on the disk that is licensed, not the media (disk/CD-ROM) on which it is stored. Innovation usually occurs when a software producer can control how its software is used, without fear that a rival producer, or indeed its customers, can readily copy or imitate its work, which would devalue its efforts.

Keep Unwanted Software Installations

One reason people buy expensive software-metering packages does not fall into the actual issue of licenses. The main reason people buy these packages is to use the agents to prohibit *unwanted* installations of software—be it illegal or not. In this day and age of easy access to shareware and freeware on the Internet, there is more reason to be cautious of unwanted software. These software-metering agents often enhance the monitoring of process tracking.

Quota Management

Quotas will not be a concern with users who are allowed to manage their own desktop PCs. However, with client/server networks, the administrator needs to track disk space and manage users' quotas—jobs that Windows NT does *not* do!

QuotaAdvisor

Sunbelt's QuotaAdvisor is an excellent utility that provides up to five threshold levels of disk quotas. Each threshold can trigger an array of real-time action steps:

- Stop the current file write with an `Out of space` message.
- Issue a warning but let the job finish.
- Send a report to the user manager or administrator.
- Increase quotas by a preset amount.
- Provide simple tracking of disk usage.

Mass Configuration Deployment

Many organizations use *disk image cloning* to perform mass rollouts of Windows NT. This technique involves copying the disks of a fully installed and configured Windows NT computer onto the disk drives of other computers. These other computers effectively appear to have been through the same install process and are immediately available for use. The following sections introduce a few software solutions for this method.

DriveImage

DriveImage is a solution manufactured by PowerQuest and is designed for cloning workstations. It is recommended because it clones workstations very fast, is very flexible, and—as an added bonus—it is cheap. It uses a technology called SmartSector that provides imaging support for FAT32, FAT, NTFS, HPFS, EXT2FS, NetWare, and many UNIX file systems.

DriveImage is also integrated with PowerQuest's PartitionMagic, which allows for partition movements, resizing, and movement on-the-fly. It allows you to edit images as well as disk-to-disk copying on the same computer.

GHOST

GHOST (General Hardware Oriented System Transfer) is made by Innovative Software and is designed to minimize the installation times for operating systems such as Windows 95, Windows NT, and OS/2. This is particularly useful to organizations that have a large number of similarly configured workstations to install.

For example, GHOST reduces the time to install a typical 300MB Windows 95 system from an hour—with substantial operator input—to about five minutes with no operator input required. In addition, multiple workstations may be installed at the same time, further improving efficiency.

Hardware Solutions

The preceding solutions were for software-based image duplication. If you need large-scale mass production solutions with speed as a top priority, you may want to consider hardware solutions. They are more expensive, but will definitely solve your problem.

Image MASSter 2000

Intelligent Computer Solutions' Image MASSter 2000 is a hardware-based hard-disk duplicator and diagnostic utility. It can duplicate up to 16 Windows NT or 95 workstations in one minute on the high-end models. The more affordable models only allow duplication of four at a time.

While this method saves hours of work and hassle over other NT rollout approaches, it has one major problem: Every cloned system has an identical computer Security Identifier (SID). This fact compromises security in Windows NT Workgroup environments; and Microsoft has stated that Windows NT 5.0 Active Directory security will also be compromised in networks with multiple identical computer SIDs.

Demand from the NT community has lead PowerQuest, Ghost Software, and KeyLabs to develop programs that can change a computer's SID after a system has been cloned. However, PowerQuest's SID Changer and Ghost Software's GHOST Walker are sold only as part of each company's high-end product. Further, they both run from a DOS command prompt.

NTSID

NTSID is a program developed by the NT Internals group that changes a computer's SID. It is a free Win 32 program that comes with full source, meaning that it can easily be run on systems that have been previously cloned.

Establishing a Configuration Database

There are two approaches to keeping track of configuration on various machines. Built-in utilities within Windows NT, as well as utilities coming from inexpensive sources such as the Windows NT Resource Kit, can help you facilitate this. These are more cumbersome approaches that often require some tweaking and batch file scripting, but they work. There are also systems and desktop-management packages that can automate this information more easily, as described in the next few sections.

Windows NT Diagnostics

When managing inventory, hardware is probably the most crucial asset to track—especially internal components such as storage devices, hard drives, CPUs, BIOS, and video boards.

Windows NT Diagnostics, shown in Figure 12.1, allows an administrator to gather hardware and operating system parameters for troubleshooting, reporting, and configuration management. Windows NT Diagnostics can also read and display Registry data about the system resources used by drivers. Once you have opened the Windows NT Diagnostics dialog box, you can then click a tab to display data from the Registry.

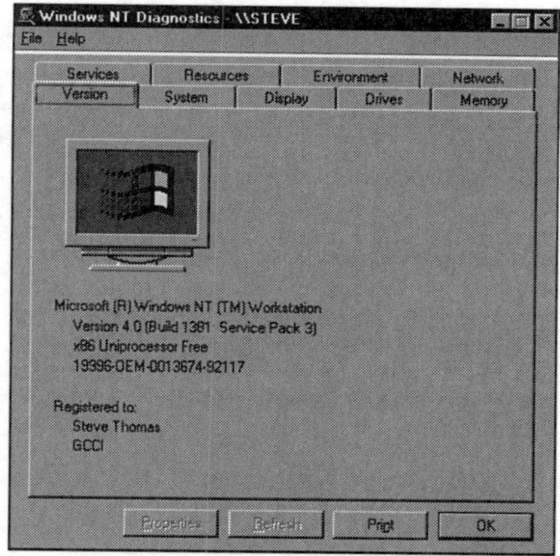

Figure 12.1. *The Windows NT Diagnostics dialog box.*

Troubleshooting Tip

It is important to understand that Registry entries cannot be edited by using Windows NT Diagnostics, so the Registry contents are protected while you browse for information. However, you can select and copy any value if you want to paste information by using the Registry Editor or a text editor.

Windows NT Diagnostics takes information from the following major Registry keys and displays it in a graphical, more user-friendly format (as shown in Figure 12.2):

HKEY_LOCAL_MACHINE\Hardware

HKEY_LOCAL_MACHINE\System\CurrentControlSet

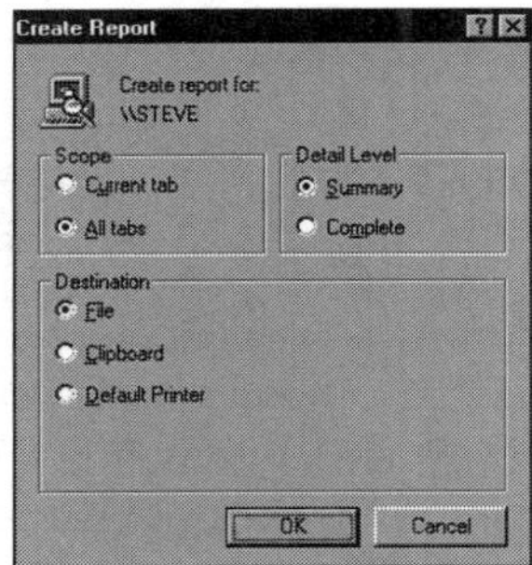

Figure 12.2. *Create a Windows NT Diagnostics report.*

It also takes dynamic system information such as memory loads, service, and device states and reports their statistics.

The areas reported in WinMSD include:

- Services and device status
- Resources, including IRQ, I/O Port, DMA, Memory, and Device information (see Figure 12.3)
- Environment: system and local user
- Network: General, Transports, Settings, and Statistics
- Memory with a Print button to grab statistics quickly
- Drives
- Display information
- System
- Version

> ***Tip***
>
> *Remember that most hardware component information is stored as binary data and can be displayed in the Registry Editor in hexadecimal or binary format.*

WinMSDP

WinMSDP is a command-line version of WINMSD.EXE. It requires the Windows NT Resource Kit and provides information about your system configuration and status.

The main advantage of WinMSDP is that it can run from the command line without a graphical interface. The regular version of WINMSD.EXE can print to a file, but this requires a user interaction.

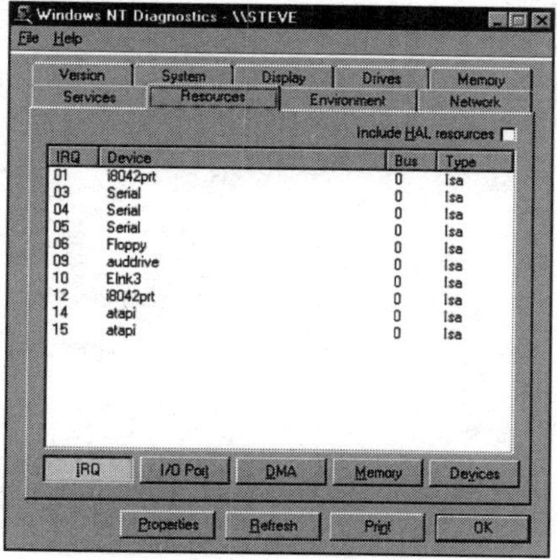

Figure 12.3. *The Resources tab.*

WinMSDP can be run from a remote command prompt like the one provided by RCMD.EXE or REMOTE.EXE. This allows users to run the utility over the network on remote systems, which is not possible with the standard version of WINMSD.EXE.

Viewing Drivers

The DRIVERS.EXE (from the Windows NT Resource Kit) application lists loaded drivers that display character-based information about the installed device drivers. There are no command-line arguments. When you type **DRIVERS** at the command prompt, you get this response:

```
ModuleName  Code  Data  Bss  Paged  Init  LinkDate  ModuleName  The
➥driver's filename
```

where:

- `Code.` The executable code in the image.
- `Data.` The non-.BSS data in the image.
- `Bss.` The .BSS section from the image. This is data that is initialized to `0`.
- `Paged.` The size of the data that is paged.
- `Init.` The size of the file on disk.
- `LinkDate.` The date that the driver was linked.

This application works very well within scripts. Be sure to redirect output to a text file. Normally you have to wait until you have an infamous "Blue Screen of Death" before you can see these modules.

Systems Management Server

Microsoft's Systems Management Server (SMS) works with your existing networked environment to provide a complete resource-management solution. SMS can work on many different networked environments such as Windows NT, LAN Manager 2.x, NetWare 3.1x and 4.x, Macintosh or a combination of environments. It's a very flexible system—you can implement SMS to fit your management, organizational, or functional requirements.

Inventory Management

SMS can collect and maintain hardware and software inventory for your entire enterprise. Inventory is collected at each site and forwarded to the site above it in the site hierarchy. The database at the topmost site (central site) contains inventory information for the entire system. By using the SMS Administrator from the central site, you can view the inventory for any computer at any site in your SMS system.

You can execute queries against the SMS inventory to gather information. You can view information about computers on your network (such as available disk space, processor type, operating system, installed software, and so on) to determine that the computers where you install software meet the software installation requirements.

Software Management

SMS enables you to distribute and install software on clients and servers. Using the SMS Administrator, you can perform any of the following tasks mentioned in the upcoming sections.

Software Distribution

When you distribute software to a site, the software is distributed to designated servers at the site, which are called *distribution servers*. From these distribution servers, users can manually access and install the software on their clients. You can also specify commands to automatically run applications or to automatically install software from the distribution servers to the clients.

Diagnostics

SMS provides several features for monitoring and reporting the status of your system and several troubleshooting utilities to diagnose and solve problems. The following sections discuss these features in detail.

Alerts

You can define alerts to detect specific conditions on your system and the actions that should take place when the alert occurs.

Events

SMS automatically monitors SMS system information, errors, and warnings and logs them into both the site database and the Windows NT event log. You can also define alerts to generate specific events.

Remote Troubleshooting Utilities

SMS provides the Help Desk and Diagnostics utilities, which allow you to directly control and monitor remote clients running MS-DOS, Windows version 3.1, and Windows for Workgroups. The Diagnostics utilities enable you to view the client's current configuration. The Help Desk utilities provide direct access to a client. SMS supports remote control across a RAS connection and across IPX- and IP-routed networks. You can also use these mechanisms to remotely take control of a user's desktop when he is encountering a lot of problems.

Network Monitor

SMS provides a powerful diagnostic component that enables you to monitor and identify problem areas on your network and appropriately tune the performance.

Microsoft SQL Server Database

The SMS system uses a Microsoft SQL server to store its system configuration and inventory data. By using DB-Library application programming interfaces (APIs), you can develop applications that access the SMS database and use the system or inventory information within your own applications.

SMS also provides the `SMSVIEW` utility that enables other applications to access and use information from the SMS database. The `SMSVIEW` utility creates Structured Query Language (SQL) views that enable other applications to easily access the computer inventory. It is important to note that SQL Server is required to run Microsoft's SMS package.

DMTF Compatibility

The SMS inventory system is based on the Management Information Format standard created by the Desktop Management Task Force (DMTF). You can add custom architectures and objects to the SMS database using a Management Information File (MIF).

SMS provides the *SMS Form Generator*, which enables you to create forms that users at clients can complete (using the MIF Entry program) and report back the information to the SMS system as MIFs. These MIFs are used to add the reported information to the SMS database.

SMS also provides a default form called *User Information* that can be automatically distributed to users at SMS clients.

Other Systems Management Software

There are also third-party packages available from many sources. Many of these are designed to focus on network management with additional systems management options added on to it. The key to many of these types of suites deals with heterogeneous management of multiple operating systems. We mentioned Computer Associate's Unicenter earlier in the book as a network management platform. It also serves as an excellent systems-management solution.

HP Openview Desktop Administrator

This is an excellent utility because it supports a large number of desktop clients including NetWare, NT, Banyan VINES, LAN Manager, OS/2, and Macintoshes. This program can be run from any Win32-compliant operating system. The package consolidates information across multiple applications and can trigger events such as license counts, data replication, or initiation of a distribution job.

Seagate Desktop Management Suite

This software gathers information about clients via the Internet and TCP/IP. It can meter software, check Year-2000 compliance, and install software. It does require Internet Explorer and a Windows NT Web server.

Chapter 13

Emerging Enterprise Concerns

- **Multi-user NT**
  We will take a look at the technology behind multi-user NT and see how it will shape the enterprise architecture of the future. Learn how UNIX users can access NT applications from the UNIX desktop.
- **NT/UNIX Integration and Migration Issues**
  This section provides a glance at integration and migration issues when moving from UNIX to NT.
- **Y2K (Year 2000) Concerns**
  What are the Y2K issues that will affect your enterprise? Learn how they will affect Microsoft products including Windows NT.
- **IPv6 Issues**
  We discuss the reasons why IPv6, the next generation of the Internet protocol, is being developed.
- **X.500 and LDAP**
  We will discuss the new directory services APIs forthcoming in Windows NT.
- **Virtual Private Networking**
  Learn more about the growing demand for Virtual Private Networking across the Internet.

Multi-user NT

Windows NT has been gaining a remarkable amount of market share in the last few years. Many companies have a large investment in other operating systems like UNIX. Some companies have limited resources and are unable to migrate their entire enterprise to a specific platform, but need to make sure all elements of the enterprise can access the same data and applications.

One way to accomplish this is with multi-user NT. Applications like NTerprise by Exodus Technologies and WinFrame by Citrix have open new markets in the NT world. These applications are designed to allow access to business critical applications from devices like the following:

- Other operating systems, like UNIX or Windows 3.11
- Platforms like NetPCs and older 386/486 computers
- Emerging technologies like Java and the Web

Citrix WinFrame

Citrix has introduced a new technology called *WinFrame*. WinFrame is a multi-user version of Windows NT Server produced under license from Microsoft. It supports thin-client architecture in that the processing of information occurs on the server and is displayed back to the client in frames. The client runs on a variety of platforms, from UNIX to Macintosh. Applications reside and are executed on the server and can be accessed across Dial-Up, LAN, WAN, and through the Internet. This occurs over a protocol developed by Citrix called *Independent Computing Architecture (ICA)*. Citrix WinFrame is based on the 3.51 version of Windows NT.

WinFrame provides a consistent look and feel for all users on the enterprise, regardless of the platform they are using. This makes it much easier for departments within the organization to communicate and collaborate.

There are a variety of companies that license and sell the WinFrame technology. These companies often add additional components to enhance the functionally of WinFrame and to meet specific needs. For example, in Figure 13.1 an NT 4.0 workstation is connecting to a Tektronix WinDD server. *WinDD* is a multi-user server platform that uses the WinFrame technology to provide support for Windows-based terminal clients.

Independent Computing Architecture (ICA)

ICA is the underlying protocol for WinFrame technology. It is lighter and less resource-intensive than the X Windows protocol and is designed to run over most of the standard industry network protocols like TCP/IP, NetBEUI, IPX, and PPP. It is designed for high performance over low bandwidth.

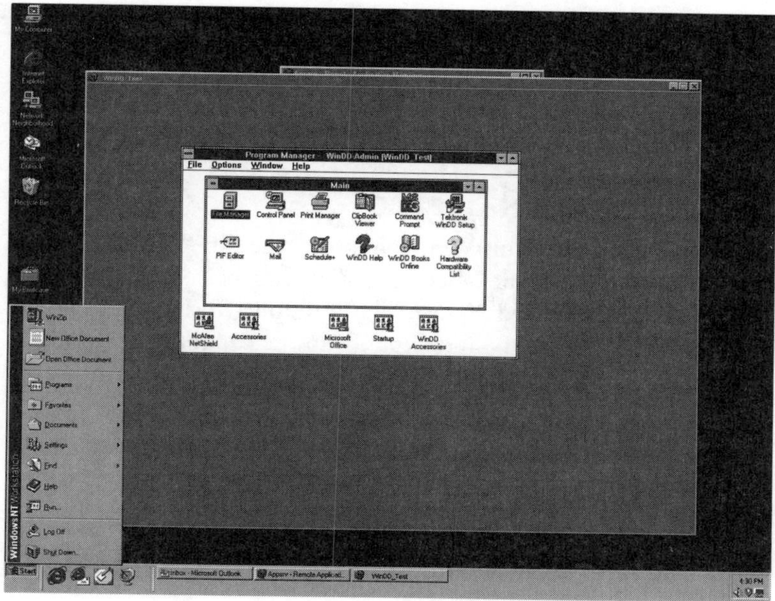

Figure 13.1. *A WinFrame client on an NT 4 workstation.*

Citrix MetaFrame

MetaFrame is client/server software that extends support for the Microsoft Windows Terminal Server to the following:

- MS-DOS operating systems
- 16-bit Windows
- 32-bit Windows
- Java-based devices
- Macintosh operating systems
- UNIX devices and operating systems
- ICA Windows-based terminals

Citrix is licensing the MetaFrame technology to other OEM vendors that will provide support for X Windows, NetPC, and other devices and protocols. MetaFrame is required to connect nonWindows-based clients to the Terminal Server.

Author's Note

For more information on this topic, read Windows NT Thin Client Solutions: Implementing Terminal Server and Citrix MetaFrame, *published by Macmillan Technical Publishing.*

Windows Terminal Server

Microsoft has licensed the MultiWin technology used in WinFrame from Citrix in May 1997 and produced the Microsoft *Windows NT Server, Terminal Server Edition*, formerly called *Hydra*. The Windows Terminal Server takes the technology developed by Citrix and expands on its capabilities. Terminal Server is based on the 4.0 version of Windows NT and is to be included with NT 5.0.

Terminal Server consists of three parts:

- The Terminal Server
- The Remote Desktop Protocol (T.share)
- The Terminal Server Client

Terminal Server is designed to operate only with Windows-based terminal devices, or PCs running Windows 95, Windows NT, or Windows 3.11. Support for other platforms is provided through Citrix MetaFrame and third-party vendors.

NT/UNIX Integration and Migration Issues

Windows NT is quickly becoming the operating system of choice for corporate America. NT's ease of use, cost, and the variety of available applications has enticed many companies to migrate from UNIX. Windows NT will not replace UNIX in many areas; there are some applications that NT is not yet mature enough to handle.

There are many aspects to migrating from UNIX to NT. Many companies elect to migrate only a part of the workforce and have a mixed environment of UNIX and NT. Some applications may need to be recompiled to run in the UNIX environment, while others may have to exchange data between both environments.

Integration

UNIX and NT can easily be integrated in a heterogeneous environment, but there are many issues that must be addressed and that require careful planning.

Some of the issues that the IS department will face include:

- Messaging
- Scheduling and calendaring
- File access
- Application support

This is by no means a complete list; each organization will have a variety of needs.

Messaging

Messaging is the most common application in use today. Most UNIX-based messaging systems are SMTP and POP3 compliant, which makes it easy to integrate most Windows NT mail clients. There are UNIX mail clients that work with NT-based messaging servers if the organization wishes to use an NT-based solution. The system planner must be aware of the behavior of applications that use the messaging system to make sure that they can operate with the messaging solution.

Scheduling and Calendaring

There are several products on the market that can provide cross-platform scheduling and calendaring. Scheduling and calendaring is usually difficult to implement due to its reliance on the messaging solution. Integration planners must take a careful look at how they are going to integrate messaging and scheduling.

File Access

File access can be accomplished in several ways. UNIX-side application like SAMBA can allow UNIX users access to the NT server and NT users access to UNIX servers. FTP can be used to move files between NT and UNIX machines. There are several third-party NT products that allow NT systems to access UNIX systems and allow UNIX systems to access NT systems.

Application Support

This is the most difficult aspect of integrating UNIX and NT. It is possible to create applications that can run on both UNIX and NT. Products like NuTCRACKER from DataFocus allow a programmer to port applications directly into NT code. Applications like OpenNT and Uwin enable you to run a UNIX shell in the NT environment.

Another way to support UNIX applications is to run an X Windows tool on the NT system. This gives users access to UNIX tools and applications through the X Windows interface. Again, these are third-party solutions.

Migration

A complete migration to UNIX is the easiest to accomplish. Since everyone is operating in the same environment, there will not be a need for cross-platform applications or communications. Applications on the UNIX side can be compiled and ported to run on the NT platforms.

User accounts can be migrated using the ADDUSER.EXE application from the Windows NT Resource Kit. A system administrator can take the passwd file from a UNIX system and create an ASCII text file. The file can then be used by the ADDUSER.EXE application to create user accounts on the NT server. User files can then be transferred over to the user's home directory on the NT system.

The most critical part of the migration is planning. Create a lab and test all aspects of the migration before you commit. Make sure that your solutions will work in the users' day-to-day environment. Don't forget to plan training for the users. Many users may have Microsoft Windows at home and will be comfortable using the desktop.

Author's Note

For more information, read Windows NT and UNIX Integration, *published by Macmillan Technical Publishing.*

Year 2000 Concerns

The Year 2000 question, sometimes called the *Y2K bug*, is a major concern of systems engineers and administrators. The basic problem is an inability of hardware and/or software to handle a four-digit year in the date field. Most of the recently released systems and software have been updated, but it is estimated that thousands of systems will be vulnerable to this bug. Many organizations are unprepared for this problem even though they have been aware of the issue for years. This is a problem on a global scale. Even if U.S. companies fix the issues before the year 2000, many other countries, such are Japan, are years behind in preparing for Y2K. This will have a great impact on the global economy.

Companies should conduct an audit of all software and hardware in the organization and either conduct their own Y2K testing or contact the manufacturer for instructions. Many manufacturers have produced patches and/or upgrades for their products that are vulnerable to the Y2K bug.

There are numerous things that can occur due to the Y2K bug. Applications may not accept orders after a certain date, users may not be granted access, and security safeguards may fail. Already some companies are experiencing this problem with programs that reject dates after the year 2000.

The most important thing is to make sure that a solid backup and recovery program is in place at your organization (see Chapter 11, "Enterprise Management"). A well-defined and maintained backup/recovery policy will help recover information in the event that a critical component within the enterprise fails due to the Y2K bug. Remember, this problem could cause interference with anything based on date calculations.

Of Microsoft's 60 core products, as of September 1998, only three do not meet Microsoft's definition of compliance. All three were released prior to 1995, and only one, Word 5 for DOS, requires an upgrade to a newer version. (Most Microsoft products function well into the 22nd century, and Windows NT handles dates more than 10,000 years into the future.)

Author's Note

For Windows NT and related Microsoft software, administrators can go to `http://www.microsoft.com/year2000`. *The site includes technical and business recommendations for organizations and results of compliance testing for Microsoft's core software and operating systems.*

Ways to Deal with the Y2K Problem

By now, if a readiness plan for Y2K compliance has not been set for your organization, you may be too late. Here are some steps you can take to ensure you are ready for Y2K compliance:

- First, ensure that you are using the most up-to-date, off-the-shelf software whenever possible. Y2K problems are rare in almost all software developed in the last two years.
- Use leading companies commercial products simply because they are more exposed to Y2K criticism and have as a result taken additional steps to ensure compliance.
- Sift through all of your vendors' definitions of *compliance*. There is no industry standard for Y2K compliance.
- Examine any custom-made software and solutions to ensure compliance. If possible, replace with commercial and complaint software when possible.
- Get the critical features of your main business systems running on newer systems and test that they work. Go back and add other features as you have time.

Author's Note

One thing you will not only need to do but will be obligated to do is notify your clientele and customer base. Many choose to do this through a formal letter. This could be letter to verify, or even a letter spelling out the products that have been tested compliant, non-compliant, as well as those pending testing.

IPv6 Issues

IPv6 is the next version of the Internet Protocol. It is also know as *IP Next Generation (IPng)*. The current version of IP is version 4. There are many reasons that a new version of IP is needed. One is the growth of the Internet. It is estimated that the number of computers on the Internet doubles every 12 months. With the numbers of other devices, such as WebTV and Java devices, the number of available IP addresses is rapidly dwindling. Another factor for developing a new version of IP is security, because all the previous versions of IP were not developed with security in mind.

IPv6 will be compatible with the older IPv4 and steps have been taken to ensure that the two versions are compatible. Microsoft currently has a prototype TCP/IP stack for NT 4 and NT 5 that supports IPv6.

The IP address field for IPv6 extends the address from 32 bits to 128 bits. This will drastically reduce the address problem. The address will also be specified in colon-hexadecimal notation rather than the dotted-decimal specifications as defined by IPv4.

The IP address architecture displays the address in the format as shown below:

Format Prefix	Address
n	128 - n

Like IPv4, many of the first prefixes will be reserved for organizational purposes including IPv6's support for IPX and NSAP allocation. To provide legacy support for IPv4 networks and IPv4 addresses, a special IPv6 unicast address will be supported with the first 96 bits being used to define the special unicast address. It will carry the IPv4 address in the low-order 32-bits (from the rightmost portion of the address). This can be used by routers and TCP/IP hosts to dynamically tunnel IPv6 packets over an IPv4 routing infrastructure.

More information is available at `www.6bone.net`. *6bone* is the IPv6 backbone that was established in 1995 for development of the IPv6 in the Internet. For official documentation, you can check the following RFCs:

- 1881: IPv6 Address Allocation
- 1883: IPv6 Specification
- 1884: IPv6 Addressing Architecture

X.500 and LDAP

One of the biggest of improvements that will come to Windows in future versions is the modification of the Directory Service Model. Windows NT 5.0 will include the *Active Directory Services*, which incorporates an X.500 directory model with the use of the Lightweight Directory Access Protocol (LDAP). X.500 was first mentioned in Chapter 1. Its namespace had become very common (being used in Banyan and Novell systems) because it is a hierarchical and explicitly defined.

X.500 is responsible for naming. With X.500, each entry is stored in a collection called an *X.500 Directory Information Tree (DIT)*. The object classes and attributes are stored along with it. The X.500 naming model defines the structure of the entries, but not the presentation format.

X.500 uses a bulky Directory Access Protocol (DAP) that is based at the OSI Application Layer. LDAP was created to allow access to X.500 with much less overhead. It does require TCP/IP exclusively.

Virtual Private Networking

With the growth of the Internet and the desire for companies to maintain secure remote connections without the long distance charges, Virtual Private Networking (VPN) is becoming very popular. A *VPN* is a secured network that is set up on the global Internet to where network traffic between a client and a server is tunneled under a complex encryption algorithm to prevent unauthorized analysis.

VPNs are solutions to many situations. You can create a VPN to let employees connect to your LAN without having to buy an expensive server-based modem solution. If you have a dedicated Internet connection and an ISP that supports PPTP (Point-to-Point Tunneling Protocol) filtering, you can take advantage of your existing infrastructure to create a VPN.

Part IV

Appendixes

Appendix A

Selected Network-Related Error Codes in Windows NT 4.0

Code	Name	Description
50L	ERROR_NOT_SUPPORTED	The network request is not supported.
51L	ERROR_REM_NOT_LIST	The remote computer is not available.
52L	ERROR_DUP_NAME	A duplicate name exists on the network.
53L	ERROR_BAD_NETPATH	The network path was not found.
54L	ERROR_NETWORK_BUSY	The network is busy.
55L	ERROR_DEV_NOT_EXIST	The specified network resource is no longer available.
56L	ERROR_TOO_MANY_CMDS	The network BIOS command limit has been reached.
57L	ERROR_ADAP_HDW_ERR	A network adapter hardware error occurred.
58L	ERROR_BAD_NET_RESP	The specified server cannot perform the requested operation.
59L	ERROR_UNEXP_NET_ERR	An unexpected network error occurred.
60L	ERROR_BAD_REM_ADAP	The remote adapter is not compatible.
61L	ERROR_PRINTQ_FULL	The printer queue is full.
62L	ERROR_NO_SPOOL_SPACE	Space to store the file waiting to be printed is not available on the server.
63L	ERROR_PRINT_CANCELLED	File waiting to be printed was deleted.
64L	ERROR_NETNAME_DELETED	The specified network name is no longer available.
65L	ERROR_NETWORK_ACCESS_DENIED	Network access is denied.
66L	ERROR_BAD_DEV_TYPE	The network resource type is incorrect.
67L	ERROR_BAD_NET_NAME	The network name cannot be found.

Code	Name	Description
68L	ERROR_TOO_MANY_NAMES	The name limit for the local computer network adapter card was exceeded.
69L	ERROR_TOO_MANY_SESS	The network BIOS session limit was exceeded.
70L	ERROR_SHARING_PAUSED	The remote server is paused or is in the process of being started.
71L	ERROR_REQ_NOT_ACCEP	The network request was not accepted.
72L	ERROR_REDIR_PAUSED	The specified printer or disk device has been paused.
80L	ERROR_FILE_EXISTS	The file exists.
82L	ERROR_CANNOT_MAKE	The directory or file cannot be created.
83L	ERROR_FAIL_I24	Fail on INT 24.
84L	ERROR_OUT_OF_STRUCTURES	Storage to process this request is not available.
85L	ERROR_ALREADY_ASSIGNED	The local device name is already in use.
86L	ERROR_INVALID_PASSWORD	The specified network password is incorrect.
87L	ERROR_INVALID_PARAMETER	The parameter is incorrect.
88L	ERROR_NET_WRITE_FAULT	A write fault occurred on the network.
89L	ERROR_NO_PROC_SLOTS	The system cannot start another process at this time.
109L	ERROR_BROKEN_PIPE	The pipe was ended.
110L	ERROR_OPEN_FAILED	The system cannot open the specified device or file.
111L	ERROR_BUFFER_OVERFLOW	The file name is too long.
119L	ERROR_BAD_DRIVER_LEVEL	The system does not support the requested command.
230L	ERROR_BAD_PIPE	The pipe state is invalid.
231L	ERROR_PIPE_BUSY	All pipe instances are busy.
232L	ERROR_NO_DATA	Pipe close in progress.
233L	ERROR_PIPE_NOT_CONNECTED	No process on other end of pipe.
234L	ERROR_MORE_DATA	More data is available.
240L	ERROR_VC_DISCONNECTED	The session was canceled.
254L	ERROR_INVALID_EA_NAME	The specified EA name is invalid.
255L	ERROR_EA_LIST_INCONSISTENT	The EAs are inconsistent.

Code	Name	Description
259L	ERROR_NO_MORE_ITEMS	No more data is available.
266L	ERROR_CANNOT_COPY	The Copy API cannot be used.
267L	ERROR_DIRECTORY	The directory name is invalid.
275L	ERROR_EAS_DIDNT_FIT	The EAs did not fit in the buffer.
276L	ERROR_EA_FILE_CORRUPT	The EA file on the mounted file system is damaged.
277L	ERROR_EA_TABLE_FULL	The EA table in the EA file on the mounted file system is full.
278L	ERROR_INVALID_EA_HANDLE	The specified EA handle is invalid.
282L	ERROR_EAS_NOT_SUPPORTED	The mounted file system does not support extended attributes.
317L	ERROR_MR_MID_NOT_FOUND	The system cannot find message for message number 0x%1 in message file for %2.
535L	ERROR_PIPE_CONNECTED	There is a process on other end of the pipe.
536L	ERROR_PIPE_LISTENING	Waiting for a process to open the other end of the pipe.
994L	ERROR_EA_ACCESS_DENIED	Access to the EA is denied.
1008L	ERROR_NO_TOKEN	An attempt was made to reference a token that does not exist.
1009L	ERROR_BADDB	The configuration Registry database is damaged.
1010L	ERROR_BADKEY	The configuration Registry key is invalid.
1011L	ERROR_CANTOPEN	The configuration Registry key cannot be opened.
1012L	ERROR_CANTREAD	The configuration Registry key cannot be read.
1013L	ERROR_CANTWRITE	The configuration Registry key cannot be written.
1014L	ERROR_REGISTRY_RECOVERED	One of the files containing the system's Registry data had to be recovered by use of a log or alternate copy. The recovery succeeded.
1015L	ERROR_REGISTRY_CORRUPT	The Registry is damaged. The structure of one of the files that contains Registry data is damaged, or the system's in-memory image of the file is damaged, or the file could not be recovered because its alternate copy or log was absent or damaged.

Code	Name	Description
1016L	ERROR_REGISTRY_IO_FAILED	The Registry initiated an I/O operation that had an unrecoverable failure. The Registry could not read in, write out, or flush, one of the files that contain the system's image of the Registry.
1017L	ERROR_NOT_REGISTRY_FILE	The system attempted to load or restore a file into the Registry, and the specified file is not in the format of a Registry file.
1018L	ERROR_KEY_DELETED	Illegal operation attempted on a Registry key that has been marked for deletion.
1019L	ERROR_NO_LOG_SPACE	System could not allocate required space in a Registry log.
1020L	ERROR_KEY_HAS_CHILDREN	An attempt was made to create a symbolic link in a Registry key that already has subkeys or values.
1021L	ERROR_CHILD_MUST_BE_VOLATILE	An attempt was made to create a stable subkey under a volatile parent key.
1022L	ERROR_NOTIFY_ENUM_DIR	A notify change request is being completed and the information is not being returned in the caller's buffer. The caller now needs to enumerate the files to find the changes.
1051L	ERROR_DEPENDENT_SERVICES_RUNNING	A stop control has been sent to a service upon which other services are dependent.
1052L	ERROR_INVALID_SERVICE_CONTROL	The requested control is not valid for this service.
1053L	ERROR_SERVICE_REQUEST_TIMEOUT	The service did not respond to the start or control request in a timely fashion.
1054L	ERROR_SERVICE_NO_THREAD	A thread could not be created for the service.
1055L	ERROR_SERVICE_DATABASE_LOCKED	The service database is locked.
1056L	ERROR_SERVICE_ALREADY_RUNNING	An instance of the service is already running.
1057L	ERROR_INVALID_SERVICE_ACCOUNT	The account name is invalid or does not exist.
1058L	ERROR_SERVICE_DISABLED	The specified service is disabled and cannot be started.
1059L	ERROR_CIRCULAR_DEPENDENCY	Circular service dependency was specified.

Code	Name	Description
1060L	ERROR_SERVICE_DOES_NOT_EXIST	The specified service does not exist as an installed service.
1061L	ERROR_SERVICE_CANNOT_ACCEPT_CTRL	The service cannot accept control messages at this time.
1062L	ERROR_SERVICE_NOT_ACTIVE	The service has not been started.
1063L	ERROR_FAILED_SERVICE_CONTROLLER_CONNECT	The service process could not connect to the service controller.
1064L	ERROR_EXCEPTION_IN_SERVICE	An exception occurred in the service when handling the control request.
1065L	ERROR_DATABASE_DOES_NOT_EXIST	The database specified does not exist.
1066L	ERROR_SERVICE_SPECIFIC_ERROR	The service has returned a service-specific error code.
1067L	ERROR_PROCESS_ABORTED	The process terminated unexpectedly.
1068L	ERROR_SERVICE_DEPENDENCY_FAIL	The dependency service or group failed to start.
1069L	ERROR_SERVICE_LOGON_FAILED	The service did not start due to a logon failure.
1070L	ERROR_SERVICE_START_HANG	After starting, the service hung in a start-pending state.
1071L	ERROR_INVALID_SERVICE_LOCK	The specified service database lock is invalid.
1072L	ERROR_SERVICE_MARKED_FOR_DELETE	The specified service has been marked for deletion.
1073L	ERROR_SERVICE_EXISTS	The specified service already exists.
1074L	ERROR_ALREADY_RUNNING_LKG	The system is currently running with the Last Known Good configuration.
1075L	ERROR_SERVICE_DEPENDENCY_DELETED	The dependency service does not exist or has been marked for deletion.
1076L	ERROR_BOOT_ALREADY_ACCEPTED	The current boot has already been accepted for use as the Last Known Good control set.
1077L	ERROR_SERVICE_NEVER_STARTED	No attempts to start the service have been made since the last boot.
1078L	ERROR_DUPLICATE_SERVICE_NAME	The name is already in use as either a service name or a service display name.
1079L	ERROR_DIFFERENT_SERVICE_ACCOUNT	The account specified for this service is different from the account specified for other services running in the same process.

Code	Name	Description
1115L	ERROR_SHUTDOWN_IN_PROGRESS	A system shutdown is in progress.
1116L	ERROR_NO_SHUTDOWN_IN_PROGRESS	An attempt to abort the shutdown of the system failed because no shutdown was in progress.
1118L	ERROR_SERIAL_NO_DEVICE	No serial device was successfully initialized. The serial driver will unload.
1130L	ERROR_NOT_ENOUGH_SERVER_MEMORY	Not enough server storage is available to process this command.
1131L	ERROR_POSSIBLE_DEADLOCK	A potential deadlock condition has been detected.
1142L	ERROR_TOO_MANY_LINKS	An attempt was made to create more links on a file than the file system supports.
1200L	ERROR_BAD_DEVICE	The specified device name is invalid.
1201L	ERROR_CONNECTION_UNAVAIL	The device is not currently connected but is a remembered connection.
1202L	ERROR_DEVICE_ALREADY_REMEMBERED	An attempt was made to remember a device that was previously remembered.
1203L	ERROR_NO_NET_OR_BAD_PATH	No network provider accepted the given network path.
1204L	ERROR_BAD_PROVIDER	The specified network provider name is invalid.
1205L	ERROR_CANNOT_OPEN_PROFILE	Unable to open the network connection profile.
1206L	ERROR_BAD_PROFILE	The network connection profile is damaged.
1207L	ERROR_NOT_CONTAINER	Cannot enumerate a non-container.
1208L	ERROR_EXTENDED_ERROR	An extended error has occurred.
1209L	ERROR_INVALID_GROUPNAME	The format of the specified group name is invalid.
1210L	ERROR_INVALID_COMPUTERNAME	The format of the specified computer name is invalid.
1211L	ERROR_INVALID_EVENTNAME	The format of the specified event name is invalid.
1212L	ERROR_INVALID_DOMAINNAME	The format of the specified domain name is invalid.
1213L	ERROR_INVALID_SERVICENAME	The format of the specified service name is invalid.
1214L	ERROR_INVALID_NETNAME	The format of the specified network name is invalid.

Code	Name	Description
1215L	ERROR_INVALID_ SHARENAME	The format of the specified share name is invalid.
1216L	ERROR_INVALID_ PASSWORDNAME	The format of the specified password is invalid.
1217L	ERROR_INVALID_ MESSAGENAME	The format of the specified message name is invalid.
1218L	ERROR_INVALID_ MESSAGEDEST	The format of the specified message destination is invalid.
1219L	ERROR_SESSION_ CREDENTIAL_CONFLICT	The credentials supplied conflict with an existing set of credentials.
1220L	ERROR_REMOTE_SESSION_ LIMIT_EXCEEDED	An attempt was made to establish a session to a LAN Manager server, but there are already too many sessions established to that server.
1221L	ERROR_DUP_DOMAINNAME	The workgroup or domain name is already in use by another computer on the network.
1222L	ERROR_NO_NETWORK	The network is not present or not started.
1223L	ERROR_CANCELLED	The operation was canceled by the user.
1224L	ERROR_USER_MAPPED_FILE	The requested operation cannot be performed on a file with a user mapped section open.
1225L	ERROR_CONNECTION_ REFUSED	The remote system refused the network connection.
1226L	ERROR_GRACEFUL_ DISCONNECT	The network connection was gracefully closed.
1227L	ERROR_ADDRESS_ALREADY_ ASSOCIATED	The network transport endpoint already has an address associated with it.
1228L	ERROR_ADDRESS_NOT_ ASSOCIATED	An address has not yet been associated with the network endpoint.
1229L	ERROR_CONNECTION_ INVALID	An operation was attempted on a nonexistent network connection.
1230L	ERROR_CONNECTION_ ACTIVE	An invalid operation was attempted on an active network connection.
1231L	ERROR_NETWORK_ UNREACHABLE	The remote network is not reachable by the transport.
1232L	ERROR_HOST_UNREACHABLE	The remote system is not reachable by the transport.
1233L	ERROR_PROTOCOL_ UNREACHABLE	The remote system does not support the transport protocol.

Code	Name	Description
1234L	ERROR_PORT_UNREACHABLE	No service is operating at the destination network endpoint on the remote system.
1235L	ERROR_REQUEST_ABORTED	The request was aborted.
1236L	ERROR_CONNECTION_ABORTED	The network connection was aborted by the local system.
1237L	ERROR_RETRY	The operation could not be completed. A retry should be performed.
1238L	ERROR_CONNECTION_COUNT_LIMIT	A connection to the server could not be made because the limit on the number of concurrent connections for this account has been reached.
1239L	ERROR_LOGIN_TIME_RESTRICTION	Attempting to login during an unauthorized time of day for this account.
1240L	ERROR_LOGIN_WKSTA_RESTRICTION	The account is not authorized to login from this station.
1241L	ERROR_INCORRECT_ADDRESS	The network address could not be used for the operation requested.
1242L	ERROR_ALREADY_REGISTERED	The service is already registered.
1243L	ERROR_SERVICE_NOT_FOUND	The specified service does not exist.
1244L	ERROR_NOT_AUTHENTICATED	The operation being requested was not performed because the user has not been authenticated.
1245L	ERROR_NOT_LOGGED_ON	The operation being requested was not performed because the user has not logged on to the network.
1246L	ERROR_CONTINUE	Return that wants caller to continue with work in progress.
1247L	ERROR_ALREADY_INITIALIZED	An attempt was made to perform an initialization operation when initialization has already been completed.
1248L	ERROR_NO_MORE_DEVICES	No more local devices.
1300L	ERROR_NOT_ALL_ASSIGNED	Not all privileges referenced are assigned to the caller. This allows, for example, all privileges to be disabled without having to know exactly which privileges are assigned.
1301L	ERROR_SOME_NOT_MAPPED	Some of the information to be mapped has not been translated.
1302L	ERROR_NO_QUOTAS_FOR_ACCOUNT	No system quota limits are specifically set for this account.

Code	Name	Description
1303L	ERROR_LOCAL_USER_SESSION_KEY	A user session key was requested for a local RPC connection. The session key returned is a constant value and not unique to this connection.
1304L	ERROR_NULL_LM_PASSWORD	The Windows NT password is too complex to be converted to a Windows-networking password. The Windows-networking password returned is a NULL string.
1305L	ERROR_UNKNOWN_REVISION	An encountered or specified revision number is not one known by the service. The service may not be aware of a more recent revision.
1306L	ERROR_REVISION_MISMATCH	Two revision levels are incompatible.
1307L	ERROR_INVALID_OWNER	A particular SID cannot be assigned as the owner of an object.
1308L	ERROR_INVALID_PRIMARY_GROUP	A particular SID cannot be assigned as the primary group of an object.
1309L	ERROR_NO_IMPERSONATION_TOKEN	An attempt was made to operate on an impersonation token by a thread that was not currently impersonating a client.
1310L	ERROR_CANT_DISABLE_MANDATORY	A mandatory group cannot be disabled.
1311L	ERROR_NO_LOGON_SERVERS	There are currently no logon servers available to service the logon request.
1312L	ERROR_NO_SUCH_LOGON_SESSION	A specified logon session does not exist. It may already have been terminated.
1313L	ERROR_NO_SUCH_PRIVILEGE	A specified privilege does not exist.
1314L	ERROR_PRIVILEGE_NOT_HELD	A required privilege is not held by the client.
1315L	ERROR_INVALID_ACCOUNT_NAME	The name provided is not a properly formed account name.
1316L	ERROR_USER_EXISTS	The specified user already exists.
1317L	ERROR_NO_SUCH_USER	The specified user does not exist.
1318L	ERROR_GROUP_EXISTS	The specified group already exists.
1319L	ERROR_NO_SUCH_GROUP	The specified group does not exist.
1320L	ERROR_MEMBER_IN_GROUP	The specified user account is already in the specified group account. Also used to indicate a group cannot be deleted because it contains a member.

Code	Name	Description
1321L	ERROR_MEMBER_NOT_IN_GROUP	The specified user account is not a member of the specified group account.
1322L	ERROR_LAST_ADMIN	The requested operation would disable or delete the last remaining administration account. This is not allowed to prevent creating a situation where the system could not be administered.
1323L	ERROR_WRONG_PASSWORD	When trying to update a password, this return status indicates the value provided as the current password is incorrect.
1324L	ERROR_ILL_FORMED_PASSWORD	When trying to update a password, this return status indicates the value provided for the new password contains values not allowed in passwords.
1325L	ERROR_PASSWORD_RESTRICTION	When trying to update a password, this status indicates that some password update rule was violated. For example, the password may not meet length criteria.
1326L	ERROR_LOGON_FAILURE	The attempted logon is invalid. This is due to either a bad user name or authentication information.
1327L	ERROR_ACCOUNT_RESTRICTION	A referenced user name and authentication information are valid, but some user account restriction has prevented successful authentication (such as time-of-day restrictions).
1328L	ERROR_INVALID_LOGON_HOURS	The user account has time restrictions and cannot be logged on to at this time.
1329L	ERROR_INVALID_WORKSTATION	The user account is restricted and cannot be used to log on from the source workstation.
1330L	ERROR_PASSWORD_EXPIRED	The user account's password has expired.
1331L	ERROR_ACCOUNT_DISABLED	The referenced account is currently disabled and cannot be logged on to.
1332L	ERROR_NONE_MAPPED	None of the information to be mapped has been translated.
1333L	ERROR_TOO_MANY_LUIDS_REQUESTED	The number of LUID (local user identifier) requested cannot be allocated with a single allocation.
1334L	ERROR_LUIDS_EXHAUSTED	There are no more LUIDs to allocate.

Code	Name	Description
1335L	ERROR_INVALID_SUB_AUTHORITY	The sub-authority value is invalid for the particular use.
1336L	ERROR_INVALID_ACL	The ACL (Access Control List) structure is not valid.
1337L	ERROR_INVALID_SID	The SID structure is invalid.
1338L	ERROR_INVALID_SECURITY_DESCR	The SECURITY_DESCRIPTOR structure is invalid.
1340L	ERROR_BAD_INHERITANCE_ACL	An attempt to build either an inherited ACL or ACE did not succeed. One of the more probable causes is the replacement of a `CreatorId` with an SID that didn't fit into the ACE or ACL.
1341L	ERROR_SERVER_DISABLED	The GUID allocation server is already disabled at the moment.
1342L	ERROR_SERVER_NOT_DISABLED	The GUID allocation server is already enabled at the moment.
1343L	ERROR_INVALID_ID_AUTHORITY	The value provided is an invalid value for an identifier authority.
1344L	ERROR_ALLOTTED_SPACE_EXCEEDED	When a block of memory is allotted for future updates, such as the memory allocated to hold discretionary access control and primary group information, successive updates may exceed the amount of memory originally allotted. Since quota may already have been charged to several processes that have handles of the object, it is not reasonable to alter the size of the allocated memory. Instead, a request that requires more memory than has been allotted must fail and the ERROR_ALLOTTED_SPACE_EXCEEDED error returned.
1345L	ERROR_INVALID_GROUP_ATTRIBUTES	The specified attributes are invalid, or incompatible with the attributes for the group as a whole.
1346L	ERROR_BAD_IMPERSONATION_LEVEL	A specified impersonation level is invalid. Also used to indicate a required impersonation level was not provided.
1347L	ERROR_CANT_OPEN_ANONYMOUS	An attempt was made to open an anony mous level token. Anonymous tokens cannot be opened.

Code	Name	Description
1348L	ERROR_BAD_VALIDATION_CLASS	The requested validation information class is invalid.
1349L	ERROR_BAD_TOKEN_TYPE	The type of token object is inappropriate for its attempted use.
1350L	ERROR_NO_SECURITY_ON_OBJECT	An attempt was made to operate on the security of an object that does not have security associated with it.
1351L	ERROR_CANT_ACCESS_DOMAIN_INFO	A domain controller could not be contacted or objects within the domain are protected and necessary information could not be retrieved.
1352L	ERROR_INVALID_SERVER_STATE	The SAM server was in the wrong state to perform the desired operation.
1353L	ERROR_INVALID_DOMAIN_STATE	The domain is in the wrong state to perform the desired operation.
1354L	ERROR_INVALID_DOMAIN_ROLE	The requested operation cannot be completed with the domain in its present role.
1355L	ERROR_NO_SUCH_DOMAIN	The specified domain does not exist.
1356L	ERROR_DOMAIN_EXISTS	The specified domain already exists.
1357L	ERROR_DOMAIN_LIMIT_EXCEEDED	An attempt to exceed the limit on the number of domains per server for this release.
1358L	ERROR_INTERNAL_DB_CORRUPTION	The requested operation cannot be completed due to a catastrophic media failure or on-disk data structure corruption.
1359L	ERROR_INTERNAL_ERROR	The SAM server has encountered an internal consistency error in its database. This catastrophic failure prevents further operation of SAM.
1360L	ERROR_GENERIC_NOT_MAPPED	Generic access types were contained in an access mask that should already be mapped to non-generic access types.
1361L	ERROR_BAD_DESCRIPTOR_FORMAT	A security descriptor is not in the required format (absolute or self-relative).
1362L	ERROR_NOT_LOGON_PROCESS	The requested action is restricted for use by logon processes only. The calling process has not registered as a logon process.
1363L	ERROR_LOGON_SESSION_EXISTS	An attempt was made to start a new session manager or LSA logon session with an ID already in use.

Code	Name	Description
1364L	ERROR_NO_SUCH_PACKAGE	A specified authentication package is unknown.
1365L	ERROR_BAD_LOGON_SESSION_STATE	The logon session is not in a state consistent with the requested operation.
1366L	ERROR_LOGON_SESSION_COLLISION	The logon session ID is already in use.
1367L	ERROR_INVALID_LOGON_TYPE	An invalid value that has been provided for `LogonType` has been requested.
1368L	ERROR_CANNOT_IMPERSONATE	An attempt which was made to impersonate via a named pipe was not yet read from.
1369L	ERROR_RXACT_INVALID_STATE	The transaction state of a Registry subtree is incompatible with the requested operation. For example, a request has been made to start a new transaction with one already in progress, or a request has been made to apply a transaction when one is not currently in progress. This status value is returned by the Runtime Library (RTL) Registry Transaction package (RXact).
1370L	ERROR_RXACT_COMMIT_FAILURE	An error occurred during a Registry transaction commit. The database has been left in an unknown state. The state of the Registry transaction is left as `COMMITTING`. This status value is returned by the Runtime Library (RTL) Registry Transaction package (RXact).
1371L	ERROR_SPECIAL_ACCOUNT	An operation was attempted on a built-in (special) SAM account that is incompatible with built-in accounts. For example, built-in accounts cannot be renamed or deleted.
1372L	ERROR_SPECIAL_GROUP	The requested operation cannot be performed on the specified group because it is a built-in special group.
1373L	ERROR_SPECIAL_USER	The requested operation cannot be performed on the specified user because it is a built-in special user.
1374L	ERROR_MEMBERS_PRIMARY_GROUP	A member cannot be removed from a group because the group is currently the member's primary group.

Code	Name	Description
1375L	ERROR_TOKEN_ALREADY_IN_USE	An attempt was made to establish a token for use as a primary token but the token is already in use. A token can only be the primary token of one process at a time.
1376L	ERROR_NO_SUCH_ALIAS	The specified alias does not exist.
1377L	ERROR_MEMBER_NOT_IN_ALIAS	The specified account name is not a member of the alias.
1378L	ERROR_MEMBER_IN_ALIAS	The specified account name is not a member of the alias.
1379L	ERROR_ALIAS_EXISTS	The specified alias already exists.
1380L	ERROR_LOGON_NOT_GRANTED	A requested type of logon, such as Interactive, Network, or Service, is not granted by the target system's local security policy. The system administrator can grant the required form of logon.
1381L	ERROR_TOO_MANY_SECRETS	The maximum number of secrets that can be stored in a single system was exceeded. The length and number of secrets are limited to satisfy the U.S. State Department export restrictions.
1382L	ERROR_SECRET_TOO_LONG	The length of a secret exceeds the maximum length allowed. The length and number of secrets are limited to satisfy the U.S. State Department export restrictions.
1383L	ERROR_INTERNAL_DB_ERROR	The Local Security Authority (LSA) database contains an internal inconsistency.
1384L	ERROR_TOO_MANY_CONTEXT_IDS	During a logon attempt, the user's security context accumulated too many SIDs. Remove the user from some groups or aliases to reduce the number of security IDS to incorporate into the security context.
1385L	ERROR_LOGON_TYPE_NOT_GRANTED	A user has requested a type of logon, such as interactive or network, that was not granted. An administrator has control over who may logon interactively and through the network.
1386L	ERROR_NT_CROSS_ENCRYPTION_REQUIRED	An attempt was made to change a user password in SAM without providing the necessary NT cross-encrypted password.
1387L	ERROR_NO_SUCH_MEMBER	A new member cannot be added to an alias because the member does not exist.

Code	Name	Description
1388L	ERROR_INVALID_MEMBER	A new member could not be added to an alias because the member has the wrong account type.
1389L	ERROR_TOO_MANY_SIDS	Too many SIDs specified.
1390L	ERROR_LM_CROSS_ENCRYPTION_REQUIRED	An attempt was made to change a user password in SAM without providing the required LM cross-encrypted password.
1391L	ERROR_NO_INHERITANCE	An ACL contains no inheritable components.
1392L	ERROR_FILE_CORRUPT	The file or directory is damaged and non-readable.
1393L	ERROR_DISK_CORRUPT	The disk structure is damaged and non-readable.
1394L	ERROR_NO_USER_SESSION_KEY	There is no user session key for the specified logon session.
1395L	ERROR_LICENSE_QUOTA_EXCEEDED	The service being accessed is licensed for a particular number of connections. No more connections can be made to the service at this time because there are already as many connections as the service can accept.
1700L	RPC_S_INVALID_STRING_BINDING	The string binding is invalid.
1701L	RPC_S_WRONG_KIND_OF_BINDING	The binding handle is the incorrect type.
1702L	RPC_S_INVALID_BINDING	The binding handle is invalid.
1703L	RPC_S_PROTSEQ_NOT_SUPPORTED	The RPC protocol sequence is not supported.
1704L	RPC_S_INVALID_RPC_PROTSEQ	The RPC protocol sequence is invalid.
1705L	RPC_S_INVALID_STRING_UUID	The string UUID (Unique User Identifier) is invalid.
1706L	RPC_S_INVALID_ENDPOINT_FORMAT	The endpoint format is invalid.
1707L	RPC_S_INVALID_NET_ADDR	The network address is invalid.
1708L	RPC_S_NO_ENDPOINT_FOUND	No endpoint was found.
1709L	RPC_S_INVALID_TIMEOUT	The timeout value is invalid.
1710L	RPC_S_OBJECT_NOT_FOUND	The object UUID was not found.
1711L	RPC_S_ALREADY_REGISTERED	The object UUID already registered.

Code	Name	Description
1712L	RPC_S_TYPE_ALREADY_REGISTERED	The type UUID is already registered.
1713L	RPC_S_ALREADY_LISTENING	The server is already listening.
1714L	RPC_S_NO_PROTSEQS_REGISTERED	No protocol sequences were registered.
1715L	RPC_S_NOT_LISTENING	The server is not listening.
1716L	RPC_S_UNKNOWN_MGR_TYPE	The manager type is unknown.
1717L	RPC_S_UNKNOWN_IF	The interface is unknown.
1718L	RPC_S_NO_BINDINGS	There are no bindings.
1719L	RPC_S_NO_PROTSEQS	There are no protocol sequences.
1720L	RPC_S_CANT_CREATE_ENDPOINT	The endpoint cannot be created.
1721L	RPC_S_OUT_OF_RESOURCES	Not enough resources are available to complete this operation.
1722L	RPC_S_SERVER_UNAVAILABLE	The server is unavailable.
1723L	RPC_S_SERVER_TOO_BUSY	The server is too busy to complete this operation.
1724L	RPC_S_INVALID_NETWORK_OPTIONS	The network options are invalid.
1725L	RPC_S_NO_CALL_ACTIVE	There is not a remote procedure call (RPC) active in this thread.
1726L	RPC_S_CALL_FAILED	The RPC failed.
1727L	RPC_S_CALL_FAILED_DNE	The RPC failed and did not execute.
1728L	RPC_S_PROTOCOL_ERROR	An RPC protocol error occurred.
1730L	RPC_S_UNSUPPORTED_TRANS_SYN	The transfer syntax is not supported by the server.
1731L	RPC_S_SERVER_OUT_OF_MEMORY	The server has insufficient memory to complete this operation.
1732L	RPC_S_UNSUPPORTED_TYPE	The type UUID is not supported.
1733L	RPC_S_INVALID_TAG	The tag is invalid.
1734L	RPC_S_INVALID_BOUND	The array bounds are invalid.
1735L	RPC_S_NO_ENTRY_NAME	The binding does not contain an entry name.
1736L	RPC_S_INVALID_NAME_SYNTAX	The name syntax is invalid.
1737L	RPC_S_UNSUPPORTED_NAME_SYNTAX	The name syntax is not supported.
1739L	RPC_S_UUID_NO_ADDRESS	No network address is available to use to construct a UUID.

Code	Name	Description
1740L	RPC_S_DUPLICATE_ENDPOINT	The endpoint is a duplicate.
1741L	RPC_S_UNKNOWN_AUTHN_TYPE	The authentication type is unknown.
1742L	RPC_S_MAX_CALLS_TOO_SMALL	The maximum number of calls is too small.
1743L	RPC_S_STRING_TOO_LONG	The string is too long.
1744L	RPC_S_PROTSEQ_NOT_FOUND	The RPC protocol sequence was not found.
1745L	RPC_S_PROCNUM_OUT_OF_RANGE	The procedure number is out of range.
1746L	RPC_S_BINDING_HAS_NO_AUTH	The binding does not contain any authentication information.
1747L	RPC_S_UNKNOWN_AUTHN_SERVICE	The authentication service is unknown.
1748L	RPC_S_UNKNOWN_AUTHN_LEVEL	The authentication level is unknown.
1749L	RPC_S_INVALID_AUTH_IDENTITY	The security context is invalid.
1750L	RPC_S_UNKNOWN_AUTHZ_SERVICE	The authorization service is unknown.
1755L	RPC_S_INCOMPLETE_NAME	The entry name is incomplete.
1756L	RPC_S_INVALID_VERS_OPTION	The version option is invalid.
1757L	RPC_S_NO_MORE_MEMBERS	There are no more members.
1758L	RPC_S_NOT_ALL_OBJS_UNEXPORTED	There is nothing to unexport.
1759L	RPC_S_INTERFACE_NOT_FOUND	The interface was not found.
1760L	RPC_S_ENTRY_ALREADY_EXISTS	The entry already exists.
1761L	RPC_S_ENTRY_NOT_FOUND	The entry is not found.
1762L	RPC_S_NAME_SERVICE_UNAVAILABLE	The name service is unavailable.
1764L	RPC_S_CANNOT_SUPPORT	The requested operation is not supported.
1765L	RPC_S_NO_CONTEXT_AVAILABLE	No security context is available to allow impersonation.
1766L	RPC_S_INTERNAL_ERROR	An internal error occurred in RPC.
1767L	RPC_S_ZERO_DIVIDE	The server attempted an integer divide by zero.

Code	Name	Description
1768L	RPC_S_ADDRESS_ERROR	An addressing error occurred in the server.
1769L	RPC_S_FP_DIV_ZERO	A floating point operation at the server caused a divide by zero.
1770L	RPC_S_FP_UNDERFLOW	A floating point underflow occurred at the server.
1771L	RPC_S_FP_OVERFLOW	A floating point overflow occurred at the server.
1772L	RPC_X_NO_MORE_ENTRIES	The list of servers available for `auto_handle` binding was exhausted.
1773L	RPC_X_SS_CHAR_TRANS_OPEN_FAIL	The file designated by DCERPCCHARTRANS cannot be opened.
1774L	RPC_X_SS_CHAR_TRANS_SHORT_FILE	The file containing the character translation table has fewer than 512 bytes.
1775L	RPC_X_SS_IN_NULL_CONTEXT	A null context handle is passed as an `[in]` parameter.
1776L	RPC_X_SS_CONTEXT_MISMATCH	The context handle does not match any known context handles.
1777L	RPC_X_SS_CONTEXT_DAMAGED	The context handle changed during a call.
1778L	RPC_X_SS_HANDLES_MISMATCH	The binding handles passed to a RPC do not match.
1779L	RPC_X_SS_CANNOT_GET_CALL_HANDLE	The stub is unable to get the call handle.
1780L	RPC_X_NULL_REF_POINTER	A null reference pointer was passed to the stub.
1781L	RPC_X_ENUM_VALUE_OUT_OF_RANGE	The enumeration value is out of range.
1782L	RPC_X_BYTE_COUNT_TOO_SMALL	The byte count is too small.
1783L	RPC_X_BAD_STUB_DATA	The stub received bad data.
1786L	ERROR_NO_TRUST_LSA_SECRET	The workstation does not have a trust secret.
1787L	ERROR_NO_TRUST_SAM_ACCOUNT	The domain controller does not have an account for this workstation.
1788L	ERROR_TRUSTED_DOMAIN_FAILURE	The trust relationship between the primary domain and the trusted domain failed.
1789L	ERROR_TRUSTED_RELATIONSHIP_FAILURE	The trust relationship between this workstation and the primary domain failed.

Code	Name	Description
1790L	ERROR_TRUST_FAILURE	The network logon failed.
1791L	RPC_S_CALL_IN_PROGRESS	An RPC is already in progress for this thread.
1792L	ERROR_NETLOGON_NOT_STARTED	An attempt was made to logon, but the network logon service was not started.
1793L	ERROR_ACCOUNT_EXPIRED	The user's account has expired.
1794L	ERROR_REDIRECTOR_HAS_OPEN_HANDLES	The redirector is in use and cannot be unloaded.
1795L	ERROR_PRINTER_DRIVER_ALREADY_INSTALLED	The specified printer driver is already installed.
1796L	ERROR_UNKNOWN_PORT	The specified port is unknown.
1797L	ERROR_UNKNOWN_PRINTER_DRIVER	The printer driver is unknown.
1798L	ERROR_UNKNOWN_PRINTPROCESSOR	The print processor is unknown.
1799L	ERROR_INVALID_SEPARATOR_FILE	The specified separator file is invalid.
1800L	ERROR_INVALID_PRIORITY	The specified priority is invalid.
1801L	ERROR_INVALID_PRINTER_NAME	The printer name is invalid.
1802L	ERROR_PRINTER_ALREADY_EXISTS	The printer already exists.
1803L	ERROR_INVALID_PRINTER_COMMAND	The printer command is invalid.
1804L	ERROR_INVALID_DATATYPE	The specified datatype is invalid.
1805L	ERROR_INVALID_ENVIRONMENT	The environment specified is invalid.
1806L	RPC_S_NO_MORE_BINDINGS	There are no more bindings.
1807L	ERROR_NOLOGON_INTERDOMAIN_TRUST_ACCOUNT	The account used is an interdomain trust account. Use your normal user account or remote user account to access this server.
1808L	ERROR_NOLOGON_WORKSTATION_TRUST_ACCOUNT	The account used is a workstation trust account. Use your normal user account or remote user account to access this server.
1809L	ERROR_NOLOGON_SERVER_TRUST_ACCOUNT	The account used is a server trust account. Use your normal user account or remote user account to access this server.
1810L	ERROR_DOMAIN_TRUST_INCONSISTENT	The name or SID of the domain specified is inconsistent with the trust information for that domain.

Code	Name	Description
1811L	ERROR_SERVER_HAS_OPEN_HANDLES	The server is in use and cannot be unloaded.
1812L	ERROR_RESOURCE_DATA_NOT_FOUND	The specified image file did not contain a resource section.
1813L	ERROR_RESOURCE_TYPE_NOT_FOUND	The specified resource type cannot be found in the image file.
1814L	ERROR_RESOURCE_NAME_NOT_FOUND	The specified resource name cannot be found in the image file.
1815L	ERROR_RESOURCE_LANG_NOT_FOUND	The specified resource language ID cannot be found in the image file.
1816L	ERROR_NOT_ENOUGH_QUOTA	Not enough quota is available to process this command.
1817L	RPC_S_NO_INTERFACES	The RPC server is unavailable to process this request.
1818L	RPC_S_CALL_CANCELLED	The server was altered while processing this call.
1819L	RPC_S_BINDING_INCOMPLETE	The binding handle does not contain all required information.
1820L	RPC_S_COMM_FAILURE	Communications failure.
1821L	RPC_S_UNSUPPORTED_AUTHN_LEVEL	The requested authentication level is not supported.
1822L	RPC_S_NO_PRINC_NAME	No principal name registered.
1823L	RPC_S_NOT_RPC_ERROR	The error specified is not a valid Windows RPC error code.
1824L	RPC_S_UUID_LOCAL_ONLY	A UUID that is valid only on this computer has been allocated.
1825L	RPC_S_SEC_PKG_ERROR	A security package specific error occurred.
1826L	RPC_S_NOT_CANCELLED	Thread is not canceled.
1827L	RPC_X_INVALID_ES_ACTION	Invalid operation on the encoding/decoding handle.
1828L	RPC_X_WRONG_ES_VERSION	Incompatible version of the serializing package.
1829L	RPC_X_WRONG_STUB_VERSION	Incompatible version of the RPC stub.
1830L	RPC_X_INVALID_PIPE_OBJECT	The IDL pipe object is invalid or corrupted. IDL stands for Interface Definition Library; it is a code library similar to C++ used to define interfaces when working with the Component Object Model (COM).

Code	Name	Description
1831L	RPC_X_INVALID_PIPE_OPERATION	The operation is invalid for a given IDL pipe object.
1832L	RPC_X_WRONG_PIPE_VERSION	The IDL pipe version is not supported.
1898L	RPC_S_GROUP_MEMBER_NOT_FOUND	The group member was not found.
1899L	EPT_S_CANT_CREATE	The endpoint mapper database could not be created.
1900L	RPC_S_INVALID_OBJECT	The object UUID is the `nil` UUID.
1904L	ERROR_ALREADY_WAITING	The specified printer handle is already being waited on.
1905L	ERROR_PRINTER_DELETED	The specified printer has been deleted.
1906L	ERROR_INVALID_PRINTER_STATE	The state of the printer is invalid.
1907L	ERROR_PASSWORD_MUST_CHANGE	The user must change his password before he logs on for the first time.
1908L	ERROR_DOMAIN_CONTROLLER_NOT_FOUND	Could not find the domain controller for this domain.
1909L	ERROR_ACCOUNT_LOCKED_OUT	The referenced account is currently locked out and may not be logged on to.
2138L	ERROR_NO_NETWORK	The network is not present or not started.
2202L	ERROR_BAD_USERNAME	The specified user name is invalid.
2250L	ERROR_NOT_CONNECTED	This network connection does not exist.
2401L	ERROR_OPEN_FILES	There are open files or requests pending on this connection.
2402L	ERROR_ACTIVE_CONNECTIONS	Active connections still exist.
2404L	ERROR_DEVICE_IN_USE	The device is in use by an active process and cannot be disconnected.
3000L	ERROR_UNKNOWN_PRINT_MONITOR	The specified print monitor is unknown.
3001L	ERROR_PRINTER_DRIVER_IN_USE	The specified printer driver is currently in use.
3002L	ERROR_SPOOL_FILE_NOT_FOUND	The spool file was not found.
3003L	ERROR_SPL_NO_STARTDOC	A `StartDocPrinter` call was not issued.
3004L	ERROR_SPL_NO_ADDJOB	An `AddJob` call was not issued.
3005L	ERROR_PRINT_PROCESSOR_ALREADY_INSTALLED	The specified print processor has already been installed.

Code	Name	Description
3006L	ERROR_PRINT_MONITOR_ ALREADY_INSTALLED	The specified print monitor has already been installed.
3007L	ERROR_INVALID_PRINT MONITOR	The specified print monitor does not have the required functions.
3008L	ERROR_PRINT_MONITOR_ IN_USE	The specified print monitor is currently in use.
3009L	ERROR_PRINTER_HAS_JOBS_ QUEUED	The requested operation is not allowed when there are jobs queued to the printer.
3010L	ERROR_SUCCESS_REBOOT_ REQUIRED	The requested operation is successful. Changes will not be effective until the system is rebooted.
3011L	ERROR_SUCCESS_RESTART_ REQUIRED	The requested operation is successful. Changes will not be effective until the service is restarted.
4000L	ERROR_WINS_INTERNAL	WINS encountered an error while processing the command.
4001L	ERROR_CAN_NOT_DEL_ LOCAL_WINS	The local WINS cannot be deleted.
4002L	ERROR_STATIC_INIT	The importation from the file failed.
4003L	ERROR_INC_BACKUP	The backup failed. Check to see if a full backup was done beforehand.
4004L	ERROR_FULL_BACKUP	The backup failed. Check the directory that you are backing the database to.
4005L	ERROR_REC_NON_EXISTENT	The name does not exist in the WINS database.
4006L	ERROR_RPL_NOT_ALLOWED	Replication with a non-configured partner is not allowed.
6118L	ERROR_NO_BROWSER_ SERVERS_FOUND	The list of servers for this workgroup is not currently available.

Appendix B

System STOP Messages

This appendix contains a list of system STOP messages that appear when a fault or other error occurs during the manipulation of a kernel mode object, a device driver failure, or a serious hardware error. These system STOP messages are also known in many circles as the *Blue Screen of Death*. Note that all numeric STOP codes are spelled out in the form of a 32-bit hexadecimal integer. The associated character serves as the title of the error code.

```
STOP: 0x00000001 (parameter, parameter, parameter, parameter)
APC_INDEX_MISMATCH
[Executive STOP]
```

This is a Windows NT Executive character-mode STOP message that indicates a mismatch of thread and asynchronous procedure call (APC) indexes. The most common reason to see this message is if a file system has a mismatched number in `KeEnterCriticalRegion` compared to `KeLeaveCriticalRegion`.

```
STOP: 0x00000002 (parameter, parameter, parameter, parameter)
DEVICE_QUEUE_NOT_BUSY
```

This is a Windows NT Executive character-mode STOP message that indicates that a device queue was expected to be busy, but was not.

```
STOP: 0x00000003 (parameter, parameter, parameter, parameter)
INVALID_AFFINITY_SET
```

This is a Windows NT Executive character-mode STOP message. It indicates a null of nonproper subset affinity.

```
STOP: 0x00000004 (parameter, parameter, parameter, parameter)
INVALID_DATA_ACCESS_TRAP
```

This is a Windows NT Executive character-mode STOP message. It indicates an invalid data access trap.

```
STOP: 0x00000005 (parameter, parameter, parameter, parameter)
INVALID_PROCESS_ATTACH_ATTEMPT
```

This is a Windows NT Executive character-mode STOP message. It indicates a problem with an owned mutex or a mutex with a process already attached.

```
STOP: 0x00000006 (parameter, parameter, parameter, parameter)
INVALID_PROCESS_DETACH_ATTEMPT
```

This is a Windows NT Executive character-mode STOP message. It indicates a problem with an owned mutex or an unclean APC state.

```
STOP: 0x00000007 (parameter, parameter, parameter, parameter)
INVALID_SOFTWARE_INTERRUPT
```

This is a Windows NT Executive character-mode STOP message. It indicates a level not within the software range.

```
STOP: 0x00000008 (parameter, parameter, parameter, parameter)
IRQL_NOT_DISPATCH_LEVEL
```

This is a Windows NT Executive character-mode STOP message. It indicates an attempt to remove a device not at the dispatch level.

```
STOP: 0x00000009 (parameter, parameter, parameter, parameter)
IRQL_NOT_GREATER_OR_EQUAL
```

This is a Windows NT Executive character-mode STOP message. It indicates that an internal request level (IRQL) was expected to be greater or equal, but was not.

```
STOP: 0x0000000A (parameter, parameter, parameter, parameter)
IRQL_NOT_LESS_OR_EQUAL
```

This is a Windows NT Executive character-mode STOP message. It indicates an attempt was made to touch pageable memory at a process IRQL that is too high. This is usually caused by drivers using improper addresses.

The fourth parameter in the message parameter list is the memory address at which the fault occurred. The second parameter shows the IRQL. If the IRQL was not equal to 2, then the interrupt most likely came from a driver.

Compare the memory address in the fourth parameter with the base addresses of the drivers in the driver table on the STOP screen to find the driver that is the problem. Note that the third parameter encodes read/write access (0 = read, 1= write).

```
STOP: 0x0000000B (parameter, parameter, parameter, parameter)
NO_EXCEPTION_HANDLING_SUPPORT
```

This is a Windows NT Executive character-mode STOP message. It indicates that exception handling was not supported.

```
STOP: 0x0000000C (parameter, parameter, parameter, parameter)
MAXIMUM_WAIT_OBJECTS_EXCEEDED
```

This is a Windows NT Executive character-mode STOP message. It indicates too many wait objects in a wait multiple structure.

```
STOP: 0x0000000D (parameter, parameter, parameter, parameter)
MUTEX_LEVEL_NUMBER_VIOLATION
```

This is a Windows NT Executive character-mode STOP message. It indicates an attempt to acquire a lower-level mutex.

```
STOP: 0x0000000E (parameter, parameter, parameter, parameter)
NO_USER_MODE_CONTEXT
```

This is a Windows NT Executive character-mode STOP message. It indicates an attempt to enter user mode with no context.

The STOP screen with trap 0x0000000E may be caused by an incorrect memory configuration.

To avoid this problem, check the following:

- Make sure the amount of memory installed on the computer is set correctly within the CMOS setup. If you have an EISA computer, make sure you run the EISA Configuration software to correctly configure the amount of memory.
- Some ISA bus computers experience problems running Windows NT Setup with more than 16M of physical memory. Reducing the amount of memory to no more than 16M may solve the problem.
- Make sure the memory chips have the same rated speed (for example, all chips 80 nanosecond) and manufacturer.

```
STOP: 0x0000000F (parameter, parameter, parameter, parameter)
SPIN_LOCK_ALREADY_OWNED
```

This is a Windows NT Executive character-mode STOP message. It indicates an attempt to acquire an owned spin lock.

```
STOP: 0x00000010 (parameter, parameter, parameter, parameter)
SPIN_LOCK_NOT_OWNED
```

This is a Windows NT Executive character-mode STOP message. It indicates an attempt to release an unowned spin lock.

```
STOP: 0x00000011 (parameter, parameter, parameter, parameter)
THREAD_NOT_MUTEX_OWNER
```

This is a Windows NT Executive character-mode STOP message. It indicates an attempt to release a thread by a mutex non-owner.

```
STOP: 0x00000012 (parameter, parameter, parameter, parameter)
TRAP_CAUSE_UNKNOWN
```

This is a Windows NT Executive character-mode STOP message. It indicates a trap from an unknown cause.

```
STOP: 0x00000013 (parameter, parameter, parameter, parameter)
EMPTY_THREAD_REAPER_LIST
```

This is a Windows NT Executive character-mode STOP message. It indicates the thread reaper list is corrupted (the reaper list became signaled, but no threads were present on the list).

```
STOP: 0x00000014 (parameter, parameter, parameter, parameter)
CREATE_DELETE_LOCK_NOT_LOCKED
```

This is a Windows NT Executive character-mode STOP message. It indicates that the thread reaper was handed a thread to reap, but the `CreateDeleteLock` for the process was not locked.

```
STOP: 0x00000015 (parameter, parameter, parameter, parameter)
LAST_CHANCE_CALLED_FROM_KMODE
```

This is a Windows NT Executive character-mode STOP message. This indicates that the last chance exception service was called from kernel mode.

```
STOP: 0x00000016 (parameter, parameter, parameter, parameter)
CID_HANDLE_CREATION
```

This is a Windows NT Executive character-mode STOP message, and indicates that a failure occurred creating a handle to represent a client ID.

```
STOP: 0x00000017 (parameter, parameter, parameter, parameter)
CID_HANDLE_DELETION
```

This is a Windows NT Executive character-mode STOP message. This indicates that a failure occurred deleting a handle to represent a client ID.

```
STOP: 0x00000018 (parameter, parameter, parameter, parameter)
REFERENCE_BY_POINTER
```

This is a Windows NT Executive character-mode STOP message. This indicates a failure occurred referencing an object by what should be a referenced pointer.

```
STOP: 0x00000019 (parameter, parameter, parameter, parameter) BAD_POOL_HEADER
```

This is a Windows NT Executive character-mode STOP message. This indicates a block of pool with a bad header was returned to the pool. There are many reasons why this would appear. Debugging the system would reveal the cause.

```
STOP: 0x0000001A (parameter, parameter, parameter, parameter) MEMORY_MANAGEMENT
```

This is a Windows NT Executive character-mode STOP message. It indicates a general memory management problem.

```
STOP: 0x0000001B (parameter, parameter, parameter, parameter) PFN_SHARE_COUNT
```

This is a Windows NT Executive character-mode STOP message. It indicates a memory management page frame number (PFN) database element has a corrupt share count.

```
STOP: 0x0000001C (parameter, parameter, parameter, parameter)
PFN_REFERENCE_COUNT
```

This is a Windows NT Executive character-mode STOP message. It indicates a memory management PFN database element has a corrupt reference count.

```
STOP: 0x0000001D (parameter, parameter, parameter, parameter)
NO_SPIN_LOCK_AVAILABLE
```

This is a Windows NT Executive character-mode STOP message. It indicates no spin locks are available to allocate.

```
STOP: 0x0000001E (parameter, parameter, parameter, parameter)
KMODE_EXCEPTION_NOT_HANDLED
```

This is a Windows NT Executive character-mode STOP message. It indicates a kernel mode exception was not handled. The second parameter in the parameter list is the memory address at which the unhandled exception occurred. Usually, the exception address pinpoints the driver/function that caused the problem. A common problem is `0x80000003`, which means a hard coded breakpoint or assertion was hit but the system started `\NODEBUG`.

Unfortunately, this can be a common error in C or assembler programming during the development stage. You can check the header in NTSTATUS.H.

Sometimes this error could even imply a problem in the file system. Run CHKDSK or another similar utility on the drive. Make sure your hardware is on the Hardware Compatibility List.

This is a very common bug check. Usually the exception address (the second parameter) pinpoints the driver/function that caused the problem. Always note this address as well as the link date of the driver/image that contains this address.

Restart and set the Recovery options in the System Control Panel or the `/CRASHDEBUG` system start option. If this message reappears, contact your system administrator or technical support group. Make sure that a debugger is attached to the computer and that the system is started with `/DEBUG`. Always note the address where the exception occurred as well as the link date of the driver/image that contains the address.

```
STOP: 0x0000001F (parameter, parameter, parameter, parameter)
SHARED_RESOURCE_CONV_ERROR
```

This is a Windows NT Executive character-mode STOP message. It indicates a shared resource conversion problem.

```
STOP: 0x00000020 (parameter, parameter, parameter, parameter)
KERNEL_APC_PENDING_DURING_EXIT
```

This is a Windows NT Executive character-mode STOP message. It indicates a kernel mode APC found pending during thread termination. The first parameter is the address of the APC found pending during exit. The second parameter is the thread's APC disable count. And the third parameter is the current IRQL. If the thread's disable count is non-zero, it is the source of the problem. The current IRQL should be 0. If not, a driver's cancellation routine returned at an elevated IRQL.

Restart and set the Recovery options in the System Control Panel or the /CRASHDEBUG system start option. If this message reappears, contact your system administrator or technical support group. Check the file systems and drivers installed on your computer.

```
STOP: 0x00000021 (parameter, parameter, parameter, parameter) QUOTA_UNDERFLOW
```

This is a Windows NT Executive character-mode STOP message. It indicates that quota was returned to a process, but that the process was not using the amount of quota being returned.

```
STOP: 0x00000022 (parameter, parameter, parameter, parameter) FILE_SYSTEM
```

This is a Windows NT Executive character-mode STOP message. This indicates a generic file system problem.

```
STOP: 0x00000023 (parameter, parameter, parameter, parameter) FAT_FILE_SYSTEM
```

This is a Windows NT Executive character-mode STOP message. It indicates a FAT file system problem.

```
STOP: 0x00000024 (parameter, parameter, parameter, parameter) NTFS_FILE_SYSTEM
```

This is a Windows NT Executive character-mode STOP message. It indicates an NTFS problem. All file system bug checks have encoded in their first ULONG the source file and the line within the source file that generated the bug check. The high 16 bits identifies the file, while the lower 16 bits identifies the source line in the file where the bug check occurred.

```
STOP: 0x00000025 (parameter, parameter, parameter, parameter) NPFS_FILE_SYSTEM
```

This is a Windows NT Executive character-mode STOP message. It indicates a named pipe file system problem.

```
STOP: 0x00000026 (parameter, parameter, parameter, parameter) CDFS_FILE_SYSTEM
```

This is a Windows NT Executive character-mode STOP message. This indicates a CD-ROM file system problem.

```
STOP: 0x00000027 (parameter, parameter, parameter, parameter) RDR_FILE_SYSTEM
```

This is a Windows NT Executive character-mode STOP message. It indicates a redirector file system problem.

```
STOP: 0x00000028 (parameter, parameter, parameter, parameter)
CORRUPT_ACCESS_TOKEN
```

This is a Windows NT Executive character-mode STOP message. It indicates that the security system encountered an invalid access token.

```
STOP: 0x00000029 (parameter, parameter, parameter, parameter) SECURITY_SYSTEM
```

This is a Windows NT Executive character-mode STOP message. It indicates a problem internal to the security system.

```
STOP: 0x0000002A (parameter, parameter, parameter, parameter) INCONSISTENT_IRP
```

This is a Windows NT Executive character-mode STOP message. It indicates that an IRP (I/O request packet) was encountered in an inconsistent state. For example, some fields of the IRP were inconsistent with the remaining state of the IRP.

```
STOP: 0x0000002B (parameter, parameter, parameter, parameter)
PANIC_STACK_SWITCH
```

This is a Windows NT Executive character-mode STOP message. It indicates a panic switch to the kernel stack because of stack overflow. This error may be caused by the kernel-mode driver using too much stack space or because a data corruption has occurred in the kernel.

```
STOP: 0x0000002C (parameter, parameter, parameter, parameter)
PORT_DRIVER_INTERNAL
```

This is a Windows NT Executive character-mode STOP message. It indicates an internal error in a port driver.

```
STOP: 0x0000002D (parameter, parameter, parameter, parameter)
SCSI_DISK_DRIVER_INTERNAL
```

This is a Windows NT Executive character-mode STOP message. It indicates an internal error in a SCSI hard disk driver.

```
STOP: 0x0000002E (parameter, parameter, parameter, parameter) DATA_BUS_ERROR
```

This is a Windows NT Executive character-mode STOP message. It indicates a data bus error that can be caused by a parity error in the system memory. This error could also be caused by a driver accessing an address that does not exist.

```
STOP: 0x0000002F (parameter, parameter, parameter, parameter)
INSTRUCTION_BUS_ERROR
```

This is a Windows NT Executive character-mode STOP message. It indicates an instruction bus error.

```
STOP: 0x00000030 (parameter, parameter, parameter, parameter)
SET_OF_INVALID_CONTEXT
```

This is a Windows NT Executive character-mode STOP message. It indicates an attempt to edit critical CPU instruction values when returning to kernel mode code.

```
STOP: 0x00000031 (parameter, parameter, parameter, parameter)
PHASE0_INITIALIZATION_FAILED
```

This is a Windows NT Executive character-mode STOP message. Initialization of the Windows NT Executive failed during phase 0 (this is during phase 4 of system startup). This can only happen during the relatively short period of time that the Windows NT Executive is being initialized. There may be a hardware problem.

```
STOP: 0x00000032 (parameter, parameter, parameter, parameter)
PHASE1_INITIALIZATION_FAILED
```

This is a Windows NT Executive character-mode STOP message. Initialization of the Windows NT Executive failed during phase 1 (this is during phase 4 of system startup). This can only happen during the relatively short period of time the Windows NT Executive is being initialized. There may be a problem with a device driver.

```
STOP: 0x00000033 (parameter, parameter, parameter, parameter)
UNEXPECTED_INITIALIZATION_CALL
```

This is a Windows NT Executive character-mode STOP message. Initialization of the Windows NT Executive failed during phase 1 (this is during phase 4 of system startup). This can only happen during the relatively short period of time the Windows NT Executive is being initialized. There may be a problem with a device driver.

```
STOP: 0x00000034 (parameter, parameter, parameter, parameter) CACHE_MANAGER
```

This is a Windows NT Executive character-mode STOP message. Initialization of the Windows NT Executive failed during phase 1 (this is during phase 4 of system startup). This can only happen during the relatively short period of time the Windows NT Executive is being initialized. There may be a problem with a device driver.

```
STOP: 0x00000035 (parameter, parameter, parameter, parameter)
NO_MORE_IRP_STACK_LOCATIONS
```

This is a Windows NT Executive character-mode STOP message. It indicates that the I/O system detected a call from one driver to another with no available IRP stack locations remaining in the packet for the invoked driver to use. Other memory problems may accompany this error.

```
STOP: 0x00000036 (parameter, parameter, parameter, parameter)
DEVICE_REFERENCE_COUNT_NOT_ZERO
```

This is a Windows NT Executive character-mode STOP message. It indicates an attempt was made to delete a device object whose reference count was non-zero. A *non-zero reference count* means that there are still outstanding references to the device. There may be a problem in calling the device driver.

```
STOP: 0x00000037 (parameter, parameter, parameter, parameter)
FLOPPY_INTERNAL_ERROR
```

This is a Windows NT Executive character-mode STOP message. It indicates a floppy disk driver internal error.

```
STOP: 0x00000038 (parameter, parameter, parameter, parameter)
SERIAL_DRIVER_INTERNAL
```

This is a Windows NT Executive character-mode STOP message. It indicates a serial device driver internal error.

```
STOP: 0x00000039 (parameter, parameter, parameter, parameter)
SYSTEM_EXIT_OWNED_MUTEX
```

This is a Windows NT Executive character-mode STOP message. It indicates that an attempt was made to exit a system service while owning one or more mutexes.

```
STOP: 0x0000003A (parameter, parameter, parameter, parameter)
SYSTEM_UNWIND_PREVIOUS_USER
```

This is a Windows NT Executive character-mode STOP message. It indicates that an attempt was made to unwind through the system service dispatcher into user mode.

```
STOP: 0x0000003B (parameter, parameter, parameter, parameter)
SYSTEM_SERVICE_EXCEPTION
```

This is a Windows NT Executive character-mode STOP message. It indicates that an exception was raised in a system service that was not handled by the system service.

```
STOP: 0x0000003C (parameter, parameter, parameter, parameter)
INTERRUPT_UNWIND_ATTEMPTED
```

This is a Windows NT Executive character-mode STOP message. It indicates an unwind operation was initiated in an interrupt service routine that attempted to unwind through the interrupt dispatcher.

```
STOP: 0x0000003D (parameter, parameter, parameter, parameter)
INTERRUPT_EXCEPTION_NOT_HANDLED
```

This is a Windows NT Executive character-mode STOP message. It indicates that an exception was raised in an interrupt service routine that was not handled by the interrupt service routine.

```
STOP: 0x0000003E (parameter, parameter, parameter, parameter)
MULTIPROCESSOR_CONFIGURATION_NOT_SUPPORTED
```

This is a Windows NT Executive character-mode STOP message. It indicates the multiprocessor configuration is not supported. For example, not all processors are at the same level or of the same type. There might also be mismatched coprocessor support.

Probably a subtle mismatch between the multiprocessor chips, such as a step level. If you can get the system up, the Windows NT Diagnostic application can check the step level of the chip. Other hardware mismatches can also occur.

```
STOP: 0x0000003F (parameter, parameter, parameter, parameter)
NO_MORE_SYSTEM_PTES
```

This is a Windows NT Executive character-mode STOP message. It indicates that no more system page table entries (PTEs) exist for mapping non-paged entities.

```
STOP: 0x00000040 (parameter, parameter, parameter, parameter)
TARGET_MDL_TOO_SMALL
```

This is a Windows NT Executive character-mode STOP message. It indicates a Multiple Definition Library (MDL) that was allocated to map a buffer is not large enough to contain the PFNs required to map the desired buffer. There might be a problem with the driver.

```
STOP: 0x00000041 (parameter, parameter, parameter, parameter)
MUST_SUCCEED_POOL_EMPTY
```

This is a Windows NT Executive character-mode STOP message. It indicates that there is no more must-succeed pool.

```
STOP: 0x00000042 (parameter, parameter, parameter, parameter)
ATDISK_DRIVER_INTERNAL
```

This is a Windows NT Executive character-mode STOP message. It indicates a hard disk device driver internal error.

```
STOP: 0x00000043 (parameter, parameter, parameter, parameter) NO_SUCH_PARTITION
```

This is a Windows NT Executive character-mode STOP message. It indicates a disk device driver called the I/O system to change a partition type on a specified partition, but the partition does not exist.

```
STOP: 0x00000044 (parameter, parameter, parameter, parameter)
MULTIPLE_IRP_COMPLETE_REQUESTS
```

This is a Windows NT Executive character-mode STOP message. It indicates an attempt was made to complete an IRP more than once, possibly by more than one driver.

```
STOP: 0x00000045 (parameter, parameter, parameter, parameter)
INSUFFICIENT_SYSTEM_MAP_REGS
```

This is a Windows NT Executive character-mode STOP message. It indicates an attempt was made to allocate more map registers than are allocated to an adapter.

```
STOP: 0x00000046 (parameter, parameter, parameter, parameter)
DEREF_UNKNOWN_LOGON_SESSION
```

This is a Windows NT Executive character-mode STOP message. It indicates a token was deleted that was not part of any known logon session.

```
STOP: 0x00000047 (parameter, parameter, parameter, parameter)
REF_UNKNOWN_LOGON_SESSION
```

This is a Windows NT Executive character-mode STOP message. It indicates a token was created that was not part of any known logon session.

```
STOP: 0x00000048 (parameter, parameter, parameter, parameter)
CANCEL_STATE_IN_COMPLETED_IRP
```

This is a Windows NT Executive character-mode STOP message. It indicates that an attempt was made to cancel an IRP, but the packet had already been completed so it was not in a cancelable state. There may be a problem with the driver. Or, although unlikely, more than one driver may be accessing the same packet.

```
STOP: 0x00000049 (parameter, parameter, parameter, parameter)
PAGE_FAULT_WITH_INTERRUPTS_OFF
```

This is a Windows NT Executive character-mode STOP message. It indicates a page fault occurred when interrupts were disabled. The instruction caused a page fault at an elevated IRQL, which is not permitted for performance reasons. Determine the system component that generated the message—it may be a user-written driver.

```
STOP: 0x0000004A (parameter, parameter, parameter, parameter)
IRQL_GT_ZERO_AT_SYSTEM_SERVICE
```

This is a Windows NT Executive character-mode STOP message. It indicates an attempt to exit from a system service with an IRQL greater than 0.

```
STOP: 0x0000004B (parameter, parameter, parameter, parameter)
STREAMS_INTERNAL_ERROR
```

This is a Windows NT Executive character-mode STOP message. This indicates an internal error in the Streams environment or in a Streams driver.

```
STOP: 0x0000004C (parameter, parameter, parameter, parameter)
FATAL_UNHANDLED_HARD_ERROR
```

This is a Windows NT Executive character-mode STOP message. This indicates a fatal hard error (STATUS error) occurred before the hard error handler was available. There are several reasons why this error might occur:

- A Registry hive file could not be loaded because it is either corrupt or missing.
- WinLogon or Windows unexpectedly did not start.
- A driver or system dynamic link library is corrupt.

Restart and set the Recovery options in the System Control Panel or the /CRASHDEBUG system start option. If this message reappears, contact your system administrator or technical support group. If you can, start an alternate operating system. If none is available, try reinstalling Windows NT after replacing the specified file with a new file.

```
STOP: 0x0000004D (parameter, parameter, parameter, parameter)
NO_PAGES_AVAILABLE
```

This is a Windows NT Executive character-mode STOP message. It indicates there are no physical pages available.

```
STOP: 0x0000004E (parameter, parameter, parameter, parameter) PFN_LIST_CORRUPT
```

This is a Windows NT Executive character-mode STOP message. It indicates the memory management PFN list is corrupt.

```
STOP: 0x0000004F (parameter, parameter, parameter, parameter)
NDIS_INTERNAL_ERROR
```

This is a Windows NT Executive character-mode STOP message. It indicates an internal error in the NDIS wrapper or an NDIS driver.

```
STOP: 0x00000050 (parameter, parameter, parameter, parameter)
PAGE_FAULT_IN_NONPAGED_AREA
```

This is a Windows NT Executive character-mode STOP message. It indicates a page fault in the address space reserved for non-paged data.

```
STOP: 0x00000051 (parameter, parameter, parameter, parameter) REGISTRY_ERROR
```

This is a Windows NT Executive character-mode STOP message. It indicates a Registry or configuration manager problem. An I/O error may have occurred while the Registry was trying to read one of its files. This could be caused by hardware or file system problems. Another reason this message may appear is because of a failure in a refresh operation that occurs when resource limits are encountered.

```
STOP: 0x00000052 (parameter, parameter, parameter, parameter)
MAILSLOT_FILE_SYSTEM
```

This is a Windows NT Executive character-mode STOP message. It indicates a mailslot file system problem.

```
STOP: 0x00000053 (parameter, parameter, parameter, parameter) NO_BOOT_DEVICE
```

This is a Windows NT Executive character-mode STOP message. It indicates no boot device driver was successfully initialized.

```
STOP: 0x00000054 (parameter, parameter, parameter, parameter)
LM_SERVER_INTERNAL_ERROR
```

This is a Windows NT Executive character-mode STOP message. It indicates an internal error in the Windows NT Server.

```
STOP: 0x00000055 (parameter, parameter, parameter, parameter)
DATA_COHERENCY_EXCEPTION
```

This is a Windows NT Executive character-mode STOP message. It indicates an inconsistency between pages in the primary and secondary data caches.

```
STOP: 0x00000056 (parameter, parameter, parameter, parameter)
INSTRUCTION_COHERENCY_EXCEPTION
```

This is a Windows NT Executive character-mode STOP message. It indicates an inconsistency between pages in the primary and secondary instruction caches.

```
STOP: 0x00000057 (parameter, parameter, parameter, parameter)
XNS_INTERNAL_ERROR
```

This is a Windows NT Executive character-mode STOP message. It indicates an XNS internal error. You may need to replace your network card.

```
STOP: 0x00000058 (parameter, parameter, parameter, parameter)
FTDISK_INTERNAL_ERROR
```

This is a Windows NT Executive character-mode STOP message. It indicates an inconsistency between pages in the primary and secondary data caches. It indicates a fault-tolerant disk driver internal error.

```
STOP: 0x00000059 (parameter, parameter, parameter, parameter)
PINBALL_FILE_SYSTEM
```

This is a Windows NT Executive character-mode STOP message. It indicates an inconsistency between pages in the primary and secondary data caches. It indicates an HPFS problem.

```
STOP: 0x0000005A (parameter, parameter, parameter, parameter)
CRITICAL_SERVICE_FAILED
```

This is a Windows NT Executive character-mode STOP message. It indicates that a critical service failed to initialize while booting the LastKnownGood control set.

```
STOP: 0x0000005B (parameter, parameter, parameter, parameter)
SET_ENV_VAR_FAILED
```

This is a Windows NT Executive character-mode STOP message. It indicates a critical service failed to initialize, but the LastKnownGood environment variable could not be set.

```
STOP: 0x0000005C (parameter, parameter, parameter, parameter)
HAL_INITIALIZATION_FAILED
```

This is a Windows NT Executive character-mode STOP message. Phase 0 initialization of the Hardware Abstraction Layer (HAL) failed. This can only happen during the relatively short period of time that the Windows NT Executive is being initialized, during phase 4 of Windows NT startup. This may be a hardware problem.

```
STOP: 0x0000005D (parameter, parameter, parameter, parameter)
HEAP_INITIALIZATION_FAILED
```

This is a Windows NT Executive character-mode STOP message. Phase 0 initialization of the heap failed. This can only happen during the relatively short period of time that the Windows NT Executive is being initialized, during phase 4 of Windows NT startup. This may be a hardware problem.

```
STOP: 0x0000005E (parameter, parameter, parameter, parameter)
OBJECT_INITIALIZATION_FAILED
```

This is a Windows NT Executive character-mode STOP message. Phase 0 initialization of the object manager failed. This can only happen during the relatively short period of time that the Windows NT Executive is being initialized, during phase 4 of Windows NT startup. This may be a hardware problem.

```
STOP: 0x0000005F (parameter, parameter, parameter, parameter)
SECURITY_INITIALIZATION_FAILED
```

This is a Windows NT Executive character-mode STOP message. Phase 0 security initialization failed. This can only happen during the relatively short period of time that the Windows NT Executive is being initialized, during phase 4 of Windows NT startup. This may be a hardware problem.

```
STOP: 0x00000060 (parameter, parameter, parameter, parameter)
PROCESS_INITIALIZATION_FAILED
```

This is a Windows NT Executive character-mode STOP message. Phase 0 process initialization failed. This can only happen during the relatively short period of time that the Windows NT Executive is being initialized, during phase 4 of Windows NT startup. This may be a hardware problem.

```
STOP: 0x00000061 (parameter, parameter, parameter, parameter)
HAL1_INITIALIZATION_FAILED
```

This is a Windows NT Executive character-mode STOP message. Phase 1 initialization of the HAL failed. This can only happen during the relatively short period of time that the Windows NT Executive is being initialized, during phase 4 of Windows NT startup. There may be a problem with a device driver.

```
STOP: 0x00000062 (parameter, parameter, parameter, parameter)
OBJECT1_INITIALIZATION_FAILED
```

This is a Windows NT Executive character-mode STOP message. Phase 1 initialization of the Object Manager failed. This can only happen during the relatively short period of time that the Windows NT Executive is being initialized, during phase 4 of Windows NT startup. There may be a problem with a device driver.

```
STOP: 0x00000063 (parameter, parameter, parameter, parameter)
SECURITY1_INITIALIZATION_FAILED
```

This is a Windows NT Executive character-mode STOP message. Phase 1 security initialization failed. This can only happen during the relatively short period of time that the Windows NT Executive is being initialized, during phase 4 of Windows NT startup. There may be a problem with a device driver.

```
STOP: 0x00000064 (parameter, parameter, parameter, parameter)
SYMBOLIC_INITIALIZATION_FAILED
```

This is a Windows NT Executive character-mode STOP message. Symbolic link initialization failed. This can only happen during the relatively short period of time that the Windows NT Executive is being initialized, during phase 4 of Windows NT startup. There may be a problem with a device driver.

```
STOP: 0x00000065 (parameter, parameter, parameter, parameter)
MEMORY1_INITIALIZATION_FAILED
```

This is a Windows NT Executive character-mode STOP message. Phase 1 memory initialization failed. This can only happen during the relatively short period of time that the Windows NT Executive is being initialized, during phase 4 of Windows NT startup. There may be a problem with a device driver.

```
STOP: 0x00000066 (parameter, parameter, parameter, parameter)
CACHE_INITIALIZATION_FAILED
```

This is a Windows NT Executive character-mode STOP message. Cache initialization failed. This can only happen during the relatively short period of time that the Windows NT Executive is being initialized, during phase 4 of Windows NT startup. There may be a problem with a device driver.

```
STOP: 0x00000067 (parameter, parameter, parameter, parameter)
CONFIG_INITIALIZATION_FAILED
```

This is a Windows NT Executive character-mode STOP message. Configuration initialization failed because the Registry couldn't allocate the pool needed to contain the Registry files. This can only happen during the relatively short period of time that the Windows NT Executive is being initialized, during phase 4 of Windows NT startup. There may be a problem with a device driver.

This initialization error also indicates that Windows NT is unable to communicate with the hard drive controller. Try the following:

- Slow down the direct memory access (DMA) transfer rate on the controller.
- Make sure both ends of the SCSI bus are terminated.
- Make sure there are no conflicts for IRQs or memory addresses.
- Make sure you are not using a faulty or unsupported driver.
- Make sure NTDETECT.COM is in the root of the boot drive partition.
- Make sure there are no missing Windows NT system files.

```
STOP: 0x00000068 (parameter, parameter, parameter, parameter)
FILE_INITIALIZATION_FAILED
```

This is a Windows NT Executive character-mode STOP message. File system initialization failed. This can only happen during the relatively short period of time that the Windows NT Executive is being initialized, during phase 4 of Windows NT startup. There may be a problem with a device driver.

```
STOP: 0x00000069 (parameter, parameter, parameter, parameter)
IO1_INITIALIZATION_FAILED
```

This is a Windows NT Executive character-mode STOP message. Phase 1 I/O initialization failed. This can only happen during the relatively short period of time that the Windows NT Executive is being initialized, during phase 4 of Windows NT startup. There may be a problem with a device driver.

Try the same suggestions for `STOP:0x00000067`.

```
STOP: 0x0000006A (parameter, parameter, parameter, parameter)
LPC_INITIALIZATION_FAILED
```

This is a Windows NT Executive character-mode STOP message. Local procedure call (LPC) initialization failed. This can only happen during the relatively short period of time that the Windows NT Executive is being initialized, during phase 4 of Windows NT startup. There may be a problem with a device driver.

```
STOP: 0x0000006B (parameter, parameter, parameter, parameter)
PROCESS1_INITIALIZATION_FAILED
```

This is a Windows NT Executive character-mode STOP message. Phase 1 process initialization failed. This can only happen during the relatively short period of time that the Windows NT Executive is being initialized, during phase 4 of Windows NT startup. There may be a problem with a device driver.

```
STOP: 0x0000006C (parameter, parameter, parameter, parameter)
REFMON_INITIALIZATION_FAILED
```

This is a Windows NT Executive character-mode STOP message. Reference monitor initialization failed. This can only happen during the relatively short period of time that Windows NT Executive is being initialized. There may be a problem with a device driver.

```
STOP: 0x0000006D (parameter, parameter, parameter, parameter)
SESSION1_INITIALIZATION_FAILED
```

This is a Windows NT Executive character-mode STOP message. Session Manager virtual memory allocation parameters failed during Session Manager initialization. This can only happen during the relatively short period of time that the Windows NT Executive is being initialized, during phase 4 of Windows NT startup. There may be a problem with a device driver.

```
STOP: 0x0000006E (parameter, parameter, parameter, parameter)
SESSION2_INITIALIZATION_FAILED
```

This is a Windows NT Executive character-mode STOP message. Session Manager virtual memory environment failed to initialize. This can only happen during the relatively short period of time that the Windows NT Executive is being initialized, during phase 4 of Windows NT startup. There may be a problem with a device driver.

```
STOP: 0x0000006F (parameter, parameter, parameter, parameter)
SESSION3_INITIALIZATION_FAILED
```

This is a Windows NT Executive character-mode STOP message. Session Manager process creation failed. This can only happen during the relatively short period of time that the Windows NT Executive is being initialized, during phase 4 of Windows NT startup. There may be a problem with a device driver.

```
STOP: 0x00000070 (parameter, parameter, parameter, parameter)
SESSION4_INITIALIZATION_FAILED
```

This is a Windows NT Executive character-mode STOP message. During Session Manager initialization, a resume thread operation failed. This can only happen during the relatively short period of time that the Windows NT Executive is being initialized, during phase 4 of Windows NT startup. There may be a problem with a device driver.

```
STOP: 0x00000071 (parameter, parameter, parameter, parameter)
SESSION5_INITIALIZATION_FAILED
```

This is a Windows NT Executive character-mode STOP message. During Phase 1 initialization of the Windows NT Executive, Session Manager terminated. This can only happen during the relatively short period of time that the Windows NT Executive is being initialized, during phase 4 of Windows NT startup. There may be a problem with a device driver.

```
STOP: 0x00000072 (parameter, parameter, parameter, parameter)
ASSIGN_DRIVE_LETTERS_FAILED
```

This is a Windows NT Executive character-mode STOP message. It indicates a drive letter assignment failed.

```
STOP: 0x00000073 (parameter, parameter, parameter, parameter)
CONFIG_LIST_FAILED
```

This is a Windows NT Executive character-mode STOP message. It indicates the system configuration link list failed. One of the core system hives is corrupt or unreadable, or some critical Registry keys and values are not present.

Restart and set the Recovery options in the System Control Panel or the /CRASHDEBUG system start option. If this message reappears, contact your system administrator or technical support group. Try starting the Last Known Good Configuration.

```
STOP: 0x00000074 (parameter, parameter, parameter, parameter)
BAD_SYSTEM_CONFIG_INFO
```

This is a Windows NT Executive character-mode STOP message. It indicates the system configuration information is corrupted.

```
STOP: 0x00000075 (parameter, parameter, parameter, parameter)
CANNOT_WRITE_CONFIGURATION
```

This is a Windows NT Executive character-mode STOP message. It indicates the system configuration information cannot be written. The system hive files cannot be expanded to accommodate additional data written to it between Registry initialization and phase 1 initialization. There may be no free space on the drive.

```
STOP: 0x00000076 (parameter, parameter, parameter, parameter)
PROCESS_HAS_LOCKED_PAGES
```

This is a Windows NT Executive character-mode STOP message. It indicates that a process terminated with pages locked for I/O.

```
STOP: 0x00000077 (parameter, parameter, parameter, parameter)
KERNEL_STACK_INPAGE_ERROR
```

This is a Windows NT Executive character-mode STOP message. It indicates an I/O error during a kernel stack paging operation. The requested page of kernel data could not be read. A bad block in the paging file or a disk controller error causes this. If the error was caused by a bad block, when your system is restarted, AUTOCHK.EXE will run and attempt to find the bad sector. If the error is a result of a paging error, upon system restart, AUTOCHK will attempt to map out the bad block. The second parameter identifies the cause of the error:

- 0xC000009A indicates a lack of non-paged pool resources.
- 0xC000009C and 0xC000016A both indicate a back block on the drive.
- 0xC0000185 indicates improper termination of a SCSI device, bad SCSI cabling, or two devices attempting to use the same IRQ.

```
STOP: 0x00000078 (parameter, parameter, parameter, parameter) PHASE0_EXCEPTION
```

This is a Windows NT Executive character-mode STOP message. It indicates an exception during phase 0 of the Windows NT executive. This basically means the operating system is unable to access the boot device. Often, this indicates a disk controller configuration problem, or error in accessing the hard disk. Other possible causes include the following:

- During initialization of the I/O system, the driver for the boot device failed to initialize the boot device (device not available, SCSI error).
- The file system could not recognize the data on the boot device.
- A virus has infected the boot sector.

```
STOP: 0x00000079 (parameter, parameter, parameter, parameter) MISMATCHED_HAL
```

This is a Windows NT Executive character-mode STOP message. It indicates a mismatched kernel and HAL image.


```
STOP: 0x00000079 (parameter, parameter, parameter, parameter) MISMATCHED_HAL
```

This is a Windows NT Executive character-mode STOP message. It indicates a mismatched kernel and HAL image.


```
STOP: 0x0000007A (parameter, parameter, parameter, parameter)
KERNEL_DATA_INPAGE_ERROR
```

This is a Windows NT Executive character-mode STOP message.

```
STOP: 0x0000007B (parameter, parameter, parameter, parameter)
INACCESSIBLE_BOOT_DEVICE
```

This is a Windows NT Executive character-mode STOP message. During I/O system initialization, the driver for the boot device may have failed to initialize the device the system is attempting to boot from. It is also possible that the file system failed to initialize because it did not recognize the data on the boot device.

If this error occurs during initial system setup, the system may have been installed on an unsupported disk or SCSI controller. Also, this error may occur because of the installation of a new SCSI adapter or disk controller or if the disk was repartitioned with the system partition.

During the initialization of the I/O system, the driver for the boot device may have failed to initialize the device that the system is attempting to boot from, or the file system that is supposed to read that device may have either failed its initialization or simply not recognized the data on the boot device as a file system structure. In the former case, the first argument is the address of a Unicode string data structure that is the ARC name of the device from which the boot was being attempted. In the latter case, the first argument is the address of the device object that could not be mounted.

If this is the initial setup of the system, this error may have occurred because the system was installed on an unsupported disk or SCSI controller. Note that only drivers that are in the Windows NT Driver Library (WNTDL), which requires the user to do a custom installation, support some controllers.

This error can also be caused by the installation of a new SCSI adapter or disk controller or by repartitioning the disk with the system partition. If this is the case, on x86 systems, the BOOT.INI file must be edited; on ARC systems, Setup must be run. For information on changing BOOT.INI, see the *Windows NT Advanced Server Administrator's Guide*.

```
STOP: 0x0000007D (parameter, parameter, parameter, parameter)
INSTALL_MORE_MEMORY
```

This is a Windows NT Executive character-mode `STOP` message. Windows NT requires at least 5M of memory to start.

```
STOP: 0x0000007F (parameter, parameter, parameter, parameter)
UNEXPECTED_KERNEL_MODE_TRAP
```

This is a Windows NT Executive character-mode `STOP` message. It indicates that a trap occurred in kernel mode. This means a trap occurred in privileged processor mode, and it is a trap the kernel is not allowed to have or catch. May indicate a computer RAM problem (mismatched SIMMs), a BIOS problem, or corrupted file system drivers. The first number in the bug check is the number of the trap. Consult an Intel x86 Family manual for the trap codes.

```
STOP: 0x00000080 (parameter, parameter, parameter, parameter)
NMI_HARDWARE_FAILURE
```

This is a Windows NT Executive character-mode `STOP` message.

```
STOP: 0x00000080 (parameter, parameter, parameter, parameter)
NMI_HARDWARE_FAILURE
```

A hardware error in which HAL reports what it can identify and directs the user to call the hardware vendor. This is a Windows NT Executive character-mode STOP message.

Restart and set the Recovery options in the System Control Panel or the /CRASHDEBUG system start option. If this message reappears, contact your system administrator or technical support group. You might also want to contact the supplier of your hardware.

```
STOP: 0x00000081 (parameter, parameter, parameter, parameter)
SPIN_LOCK_INIT_FAILURE
```

This is a Windows NT Executive character-mode STOP message.

Appendix C

Common Event Log IDs in the Windows NT Event Viewer

Event Source	Event ID	Explanation
BROWSER	8003	The subnet mask of the Windows NT client computer is incorrect or is different from the PDC. The client computer has attempted to promote itself to the master browser of the subnet and has failed because only one computer in a domain per subnet can act as a master browser.
BROWSER	8004	The computer is already at the highest level that it can reach. In the browser, computers are either client, potential, backup, or master, with client computers having the least power and master browsers having the most power.
BROWSER	8005	An inconsistency exists between the Browser service and the Server service.
BROWSER	8006	Another computer sent a packet that could not be recognized by your local computer.
BROWSER	8007	An error occurred in the Server service.
BROWSER	8008	Usually the browser cannot update its role if another computer in the domain has the same computer name.
BROWSER	8009	In a workgroup or domain, only one computer is allowed to be the master browser. Another computer in the workgroup or domain is functioning incorrectly as the master browser.
BROWSER	8010	The conversion of a name failed.
BROWSER	8011	You added a Windows NT domain name for the Browser Configuration Network Control Panel on the domain controller. The Browser Configuration Network Control Panel is used to add only LAN Manager domain names.
BROWSER	8012	If the user or system administrator sets log election in the computer's configuration information, each time an election occurs, the computer will register this information.
BROWSER	8013	This error occurred because the browser driver has forced a *number* because it was unable to find a master browser to retrieve a backup list on that network.
BROWSER	8014	This error occurred because the browser driver has forced an election on network *number* because it was unable to find a master browser for that network.

Recommended Action	Event Log Source	Type
Change the TCP/IP protocol configuration to the correct subnet mask.	System	Error
Verify that there is only one master browser and that browsing is functioning properly. Check browser registry entries on NT and Windows 95 computers and PROTOCOL.INI entries on Windows for Workgroups.	System	Warning
Stopping and restarting the Server Service will eliminate the error.	System	Error
No user action is needed.	System	Error
Check the Event log with Event Viewer for more details about the error.	System	Error
No action is needed.	System	Error
Change the TCP/IP protocol configuration to the correct subnet mask.	System	Error
No action is needed.	System	Error
To correct this problem, do the following on the domain controller: Open Network under Control Panel. Click the Services tab and double-click Computer Browser. Select the Windows NT domain name and choose Remove. Quit Control Panel. Shut down and restart.	System	Error
No user action is needed.	System	
No user action is needed.	System	
No user action is needed.	System	

Event Source	Event ID	Explanation
BROWSER	8015	This error occurred because the browser has forced an election on network %1 because a Windows NT server (or domain master) browser is started.
BROWSER	8016	The limit for the number of illegal datagrams that can be logged per minute has been exceeded.
BROWSER	8017	This error occurred because the browser has failed to start because the dependent service name had invalid service status code. There are seven status codes associated with this warning that indicated the status of the service: 1 Service Stopped 2 Start Pending 3 Stop Pending 4 Running 5 Continue Pending 6 Pause Pending 7 Paused
BROWSER	8019	The client has an incorrect or different subnet mask from the PDC. Because of this, the client has tried to promote itself to the master browser and failed.
BROWSER	8020	In any workgroup or domain, only one computer is allowed to be the master browser. Another computer in the workgroup or domain is functioning incorrectly as the master browser, but the computer is not recognized.
BROWSER	8021	The browser requested a list of servers from the master browser but did not receive the list.
BROWSER	8022	The browser requested a list of domains from the master browser but did not receive the list.
BROWSER	8023	This error occurred because the value for the parameter *parameter* <sent> to the browser service was illegal.
BROWSER	8024	The backup browser server %2 is out-of-date.
BROWSER	8025	The browser has retrieved a list of servers from remote computer %1 on transport %2. There were %3 entries read, and %4 total entries.
BROWSER	8026	The browser has retrieved a list of domains from remote computer %1 on transport %2. There were %3 entries read, and %4 total entries.
BROWSER	8027	The browser running on the domain controller has lost an election. The computer that won the election is %2, on the transport %3. The data contains the election version, election criteria, and remote computer time up, and the same information for the current computer.

Recommended Action	Event Log Source	Type
No user action is needed.	System	Warning
No user action is needed.	System	Warning
You may have attempted to start the browser while the Server or Workstation services were paused. Start or continue the Server or Workstation services.	System	Warning
Contact your network administrator. The network administrator can change the TCP/IP protocol configuration to the correct subnet mask.	System	Warning
Contact your network administrator to find the other computer.	System	Warning
Contact your network administrator.	System	Warning
Contact your network administrator.	System	Warning
Ask your network administrator to correct the parameter in your configuration information.	System	Warning
Consider upgrading this computer.	System	Warning

Event Source	Event ID	Explanation
BROWSER	8028	The browser running on this computer has won a browser election on network %2.
BROWSER	8029	The Registry contains invalid parameters.
BROWSER	8030	The browser driver has discarded too many mailslot messages.
BROWSER	8031	The browser driver has discarded too many GetBrowserServerList requests.
BROWSER	8032	The backup browser will stop being a backup when it tries and fails to retrieve the list more than 5 times. It will start again after one hour.
BROWSER	8033	The network must have a master browser.
BROWSER	8034	The browser has received a GetBrowserServerList request when it is not the master browser.
BROWSER	8035	A network administrator promoted or demoted a domain controller, so another master browser must be elected in order to keep the network functioning.
BROWSER	8036	The browser has failed to start because of an error in the DirectHostBinding parameter to the browser.
Dhcp	4001	The streams memory quota was exceeded or memory is unavailable for allocation.
Dhcp	4002	This may indicate a need to add more memory.
Eventlog	6000	The specified log file contains the maximum configured number of events.
Eventlog	6001	The log file may be read-only.
Eventlog	6002	The contents of the corrupt file will be deleted so that new data can be written to and read from the file.
Eventlog	6003	The Application log file is corrupted. The default log file will continue to be used as the log file until the Application log file is repaired and the system is restarted.
Eventlog	6004	The driver is functioning properly but is logging incorrectly formatted packets in the Event log.

Recommended Action	Event Log Source	Type
This computer is a member of a domain, so the domain controller should become the master browser. Check the Configuration parameters in the Registry. See the operating system documentation for information about valid configuration.	System	Warning
No user action is needed.	System	Warning
No user action is needed.	System	Warning
No action is needed unless you see this message on several different computers. In that case there may be problems with the master browser.	System	Warning
No user action is needed.	System	Warning
No user action is needed.	System	Warning
No user action is needed.	System	Warning
No user action is needed.	System	Warning
No action is needed unless you see this message frequently. Then add more memory.	System	Warning
No action is needed unless you see this message frequently. Then add more memory.	System	Error
Clear the log by using Event Viewer from the Administrative Tools group. Open Event Viewer, select Log, and then select Clear All Events.	System	Error
Ask your system administrator to examine the log files to determine why the specified file will not open. Events will be logged in the default log file.	System	Error
No user action is needed.	System	Error
Ask your system administrator to determine the cause of the corruption.	System	Warning
Examine the data in the Event log in Event Viewer for the Unicode version of the driver's name and replace the packets or contact the supplier of the driver.	System	Warning

Event Source	Event ID	Explanation
IPX/SPX	6005	The Event Log Service was started.
IPX/SPX	6006	The Event Log Service was stopped.
IPX/SPX	9501	Frame type is the way in which the network adapter formats the data to be put on the network. NetWare IPX clients and servers can be configured for different frame types, but for the computers to communicate, they must be configured for the same frame type.
IPX/SPX	9502	IPX servers use the Service Advertising Protocol (SAP) to automatically notify other IPX nodes of their presence and the services they provide.
IPX/SPX	9505	When you install NWLink, you must provide a value for Frame Type that specifies the frame format that the NWLink packets will use. There are default frame types you can choose from. However, if a computer that runs Windows NT, acting as an application server, it must have a frame type that matches the frame type for the computers running the client processes.
IPX/SPX	9507	The network adapter does not function correctly in Windows NT and Windows 95. If the part number ends in `-05N`, check the serial number. If the serial number is between 40B8D3 and 40CB2F hex, the network adapter must be replaced.
ndis	5000	The network driver failed to initialize due to an apparent conflict between the adapter card and some other hardware.
ndis	5001	The network driver could not allocate the necessary resources, usually memory, for operation.
ndis	5002	The network driver received an invalid response from the adapter.
ndis	5003	The network driver could not find the adapter.

Recommended Action	Event Log Source	Type
No user action is needed; however, it is a good practice to double-check that the correct frame type was detected.	System	Warning
No user action is needed.	System	Warning
Using any text editor, or by displaying the file at the MS-DOS command prompt, locate the Link Driver section under which the frame parameter is set. The NWLink `FRAME` parameter must be identical to the frame type specified in the NetWare client's Net.cfg.	System	Warning
Verify that the DLL for the interface driver is installed in the Windows NT System directory. Check the binding of the network adapter by clicking Network under Control Panel. If you cannot enable the binding of the network adapter, reinstall the device driver.	System	Warning
Contact your system administrator. Check the configuration of the adapter card by selecting Network in Control Panel. Make sure the adapter card is configured according to the manufacturer's specifications and that the configuration does not conflict with the hardware settings.	System	Warning
Remove some memory-intensive adapters or install more memory.	System	Warning
No action is needed. However, if you see this message frequently, ask your system administrator to make sure that the adapter card is configured properly and that its configuration does not conflict with the configuration of other hardware.	System	Warning
Contact your system administrator. Check the configuration of the adapter card by selecting Network in Control Panel. Make sure the adapter card is configured according to the manufacturer's specifications and that the adapter card's configuration does not conflict with the configurations of other hardware.	System	Warning

Event Source	Event ID	Explanation
ndis	5004	The network driver tried to connect to an interrupt that is in use by another device or adapter card.
ndis	5006	The network driver version number is incompatible with this operating system.
ndis	5007	The adapter card did not respond to a command.
ndis	5008	The network address for the adapter card is not configured properly.
ndis	5009	The parameters given to the driver are invalid.
ndis	5010	The adapter responded incorrectly to the driver.
ndis	5011	The driver parameters are invalid.
ndis	5012	The base address supplied in the Network option of Control Panel does not match the adapter card settings.
ndis	5013	Due to the space limitations of the adapter, your computer cannot use the full capabilities of the network.
ndis	5014	The adapter is not enabled.
ndis	5015	The adapter card and another device are configured to use the same I/O port.

Recommended Action	Event Log Source	Type
Use Network in Control Panel to change the jumpers of your adapter card or run the configuration utility that was supplied with the adapter. See your system administrator if you need assistance.	System	Warning
Contact the vendor to replace the network driver.	System	Warning
No action is needed. However, if this occurs frequently, ask your system administrator to check the adapter settings and/or replace the adapter card.	System	Warning
Ask your system administrator to reconfigure your card.	System	Error
Use Network in Control Panel to remove and then reinstall the driver. If you continue to see this error message, contact technical support.	System	Warning
Check the configuration of the adapter. If you see this message frequently, the adapter card may need to be replaced.	System	Error
Reinstall the driver using the Network option in Control Panel.	System	Error
Contact your system administrator. Your administrator should verify that the adapter card is configured properly and that the card's configuration does not conflict with the configurations of other hardware. Your administrator may want to replace your adapter.	System	Error
If possible, your system administrator may reconfigure the adapter card either to use more memory or to use memory more effectively. Otherwise, no action is needed.	System	Error
Contact your system administrator to run the adapter's configuration utility and then enable the adapter. Contact the vendor of the adapter if this does not correct the problem.	System	Error
Contact your system administrator. Check the configuration of the adapter card by selecting Network in Control Panel. Make sure the adapter card is configured according to the manufacturer's specifications and that the configuration does not conflict with the configurations of other hardware.	System	Warning

Event Source	Event ID	Explanation
ndis	5016	The adapter card and another device are configured to use the same I/O port or DMA channel.
ndis	5017	Both the adapter and another device are using the address specified. Each device should have a unique address.
ndis	5018	The network driver tried to connect to the specified interrupt, which is in use by another device or adapter.
ndis	5019	The adapter and another device are trying to use the specified DMA channel.
ndis	5021	`MaxReceives` specifies the maximum number of receive lists that the driver allocates for receive frames.
ndis	5022	`MaxTransmits` specifies the maximum number of transmit lists that the driver allocates for transmit frames. This number affects the number of packets that can be queued for transmission at any given time.
ndis	5023	`MaxFrameSize` specifies the largest frame size that can be handled by the driver. You specified a value that is out of range. The default value (`1514`) was used instead.
ndis	5024	`MaxInternalBufs` specifies the maximum number of transmit buffers. This number should be less than the `MaxTransmits` number.
ndis	5025	`MaxMulticast` specifies the maximum number of multicast addresses that can be set at one time by the driver.
ndis	5026	`ProductID` specifies the product ID of the adapter.

Recommended Action	Event Log Source	Type
Contact your system administrator. Check the configuration of the adapter card by selecting Network in Control Panel. Make sure the adapter card is configured according to the manufacturer's specifications and that the card's configuration does not conflict with the configurations of other hardware.	System	Warning
Contact your system administrator. Check the configuration of the adapter card by selecting Network in Control Panel. Make sure the adapter card is configured according to the manufacturer's specifications and that the card's configuration does not conflict with the configurations of other hardware.	System	Warning
Use the Network option in Control Panel to change the jumpers of your adapter card or to run the configuration utility that was supplied with the adapter. See your system administrator if you need assistance.	System	Warning
Contact your system administrator. Check the configuration of the adapter card by selecting Network in Control Panel. Make sure the adapter card is configured according to the manufacturer's specifications and that the configuration does not conflict with the configurations of other hardware.	System	Warning
	System	Warning
	System	Warning
	System	Warning
	System	Warning
	System	Warning
	System	Error

Event Source	Event ID	Explanation
ndis	5027	The lobe wire fault occurs when the cable is disconnected from the hub and the adapter continues to try to reinsert the token into the ring.
ndis	5028	The adapter had detected a loss of signal on the ring. The adapter will continue to try to reinsert back into the ring.
ndis	5029	The adapter has de-inserted from the ring because the ring was beaconing.
NetBIOS	4317	If this parameter contains a valid value, it will override the DHCP parameter of the same name. A blank value (empty string) will be ignored. Setting this parameter to the value "*" indicates a null scope and it will not be used.
NetBIOS	4318	This value also must not begin with a period. If this parameter contains a valid value, it will override the DHCP parameter of the same name. A blank value (empty string) will be ignored. Setting this parameter to the value "*" indicates a null scope and it will not be used.
NetBIOS	4319	A duplicate name has been detected on the TCP network. The IP address of the machine that sent the message is in the data.
NetBIOS	4320	A few network occurrences can cause this message. A computer on the network may have the same name, or you may be logging on to multiple computers with the same user name. If you are using WINS, you may have inactive or duplicate names in the WINS database.
NetBT	4306	You will not be able to use the Windows Internet Name Service (WINS) because the addresses of the WINS servers could not be added to your configuration.
NetBT	4309	The parameters in your configuration file are not correct.
NetBT	4313	The Registry may be corrupted.
NetBT	4314	The Registry may be corrupted.

Recommended Action	Event Log Source	Type
Check all cables and try another lobe media cable. Retry the operation. If unsuccessful, restart your computer and try again. Check all cables and try another lobe media cable. Retry the operation.	System	Error
If unsuccessful, restart your computer and try again.	System	Error
Check the network speed settings and cable connections and retry the operation. If the problem persists, contact your system administrator.	System	Error
Each label in the DHCP Scope cannot be longer than 63 bytes. Use the Control Panel, Network applet to change the scope.	System	Error
The NetBIOS name scope is too long. The scope cannot be longer than 255 bytes. Use the Control Panel, Network applet to change the scope.	System	Error
Use `nbtstat -n` at the command prompt to see which name is in the Conflict state.	System	Error
When you use the `nbtstat -n` command, if the IP address is all zeros, look for any Windows for Workgroups computers on the network with the same name. Windows for Workgroups computers sometimes return all zeros for their IP address with this error.	System	Error
	System	Warning
Verify the configuration parameters.	System	CoError
Ask your system administrator to reinstall the Registry from the ERD that was made when Windows NT was installed.	System	CoError
Ask your system administrator to reinstall the Registry from the ERD that was made when Windows NT was installed.	System	Error

Event Source	Event ID	Explanation
NetBT	4315	The Registry may be corrupted.
NetBT	4316	The Registry may be corrupted.
Rdr	3001	The redirector was unable to allocate memory.
Rdr	3002	Another device may exist with the device name you are trying to create.
Rdr	3003	Your computer may not have enough memory. Some operations might not work.
Rdr	3004	When the redirector creates system threads, the redirector sets the priority of these threads. The redirector was unable to set the priorities.
Rdr	3005	The redirector received a bad packet from a server.
Rdr	3006	The redirector received a bad packet from a server.
Rdr	3007	The specified server did not respond correctly.
Rdr	3009	Either the network went down or an application failure occurred. Data may have been lost.
Rdr	3011	Another error on the network may have caused this error. Data has been lost.
Rdr	3012	An unexpected network error has occurred on the virtual circuit to %2.
Rdr	3013	The server did not respond to a request from the redirector within the time specified by the `SESSTIMEOUT` entry in the configuration information. The default value for this entry is 45 seconds.
Rdr	3014	
Rdr	3015	
Rdr	3017	
Rdr	3018	The redirector does not support the security imposed by the server. The redirector will contact the server, but the connection will not be secure.
Rdr	3019	The workstation passed an invalid connection type to the redirector.

Recommended Action	Event Log Source	Type
Ask your system administrator to reinstall the Registry from the ERD that was made when Windows NT was installed.	System	Error
Ask your system administrator to reinstall the Registry from the ERD that was made when Windows NT was installed.	System	Error
Ask your system administrator to add more memory to your computer and then retry the command.	System	Error
Contact technical support to locate the other device on your computer.	System	Error
If you see this message often, contact technical support.	System	Success
Contact your technical support group.	System	Success
Your command could not be processed.Wait a few minutes, then retry the command. If you receive this message after retrying the command, contact your network administrator.	System	Error
Retry the command.	System	Error
Contact your network.	System	Error
Retry the command.	System	Warning
Retry the command. Check the Event log with Event Viewer for information about other network errors that are related to this error.	System	Error
Wait a few minutes, then retry the command.	System	Error
Retry the command. If this error occurs frequently, ask your network administrator to increase the value.	System	Error
No user action is needed.	System	Error
Contact your technical support group.	System	Error
Contact your technical support group.	System	Error
Contact your network administrator.	System	Error
Contact your technical support group.	System	

Event Source	Event ID	Explanation
Rdr	3021	The MAXCMDS parameter specifies the maximum number of work buffers that the redirector reserves for performance reasons. The default is 15. If your application performs more than 15 simultaneous operations, you might want to increase this value. Because increasing this value can be dangerous, it is recommended not to edit this value.
Rdr	3022	Your computer is running very low on memory. Other users may not be able to access any files that are shared.
Rdr	3023	The kernel on your computer does not match the version of your redirector.
Rdr	3024	A resource leak in the redirector may cause this error.
Rdr	3025	Data may have been lost.
Rdr	3026	An operation required more threads than the MAXTHREADS entry in your configuration information allows.
Rdr	3027	At startup, the redirector could not get the information it needed from the Registry because it is corrupted.
Rdr	3028	The time difference between the workstation and the server is larger than 24 hours, which indicates a configuration failure in one of the computers.
Rdr	3029	Your workstation could not be connected to this server.
Rdr	3031	
Sap Agent	8500	The application could not start because a key is missing from the Registry or is incorrect.
Sap Agent	8501	The application could not be started. You probably have an incompatible version of the WinSock interface.
Sap Agent	8502	The application could not start because a needed resource could not be obtained. The most likely reasons are that the Internetwork Packet Exchange (IPX) protocol could not be found or that the IPX WinSock information in the Registry is missing or in error.
Sap Agent	8503	The SAP agent encountered an error while setting a broadcast option on a socket.

Recommended Action	Event Log Source	Type
Ask your network administrator to increase the `MAXCMDS` value in the LanmanWorkstation section of the Registry to increase your network throughput.	System	Error
Contact your technical support group.	System	
Ask your network administrator to check your computer's configuration.	System	
No action is needed.	System	CoError
Retry the command or action.	System	Warning
Increase the number of `MAXTHREADS` in your configuration information.	System	Warning
Contact your network administrator.	System	Warning
Type **`TIME`** or **`DATE`** at the command prompt to determine whether the server or workstation has the incorrect time and then correct the time on that computer.	System	
Look up the error that caused this operation to fail, and take appropriate action. Then try again.	System	CoError
Use Windows NT Explorer or File Manager to delete this file.	System	Error
Use the Network option in Control Panel to remove and re-install the SAP agent.	System	Error
Make sure you are running the current version of both Windows NT and the SAP agent.	System	Error
Use the Network option in Control Panel to make sure the NWLink IPX/SPX Compatible Transport Driver is installed. If you still get this message, remove and re-install the NWLink IPX/SPX Compatible Transport Driver or have someone who is proficient in the configuration of NWLink do this.	System	
Restart your computer and try again. If you still get this message, call technical support.	System	

Event Source	Event ID	Explanation
Sap Agent	8504	The application could not be started because a resource is in use by another application or otherwise unavailable. Often the problem is insufficient free memory.
Sap Agent	8505	There was not enough memory to perform this operation. Resources that are accessed by using the SAP agent and services that depend on the SAP agent will not be available.
Sap Agent	8506	The application could not start because a needed option could not be set. Resources that are accessed by using the SAP agent and services that depend on the SAP agent will not be available.
Sap Agent	8508	If this message appears during initialization, the SAP agent cannot start and resources that are accessed by using the SAP agent and services that depend on the SAP agent will not be available. If this message appears while the SAP agent is running, the SAP agent is unable to communicate with the NWLink protocol.
Sap Agent	8510	The application could not start because a needed resource could not be created. Resources that are accessed by using the SAP agent and services that depend on the SAP agent will not be available.
Sap Agent	8511	The application could not start because a needed resource could not be created. Resources that are accessed by using the SAP agent and services that depend on the SAP agent will not be available.
Sap Agent	8512	The application could not start because a needed resource could not be created. Resources that are accessed by using the SAP agent and services that depend on the SAP agent will not be available.
Sap Agent	8513	The application could not start because a needed resource could not be created. Resources that are accessed by using the SAP agent and services that depend on the SAP agent will not be available.
Sap Agent	8514	The application could not start because a needed resource could not be created. Resources that are accessed by using the SAP agent and services that depend on the SAP agent will not be available.
Sap Agent	8515	There was not enough free memory for this application to run. Resources that are accessed by using the SAP agent and services that depend on the SAP agent will not be available.

Recommended Action	Event Log Source	Type
Close one or more applications and try again.	System	Warning
Close some applications and try again. If you get this message often you may be able to avoid it if you install more memory.	System	Error
Call technical support. Report both this message and the message that accompanies it.	System	Error
If this message appears during initialization, close some applications and try again. If you get this message often you may be able to avoid it if you install more memory. If this message appears while the SAP agent is running, no action is needed.	System	Error
Contact your technical support group. Report both this message and the message that accompanies it.	System	Error
Contact your technical support group. Report both this message and the message that accompanies it.	System	CoError
Contact your technical support group. Report both this message and the message that accompanies it.	System	Warning
Contact your technical support group. Report both this message and the message that accompanies it.	System	Warning
Contact your technical support group. Report both this message and the message that accompanies it.	System	Warning
Close some applications and try again. If you get this message often, have the system administrator install more memory to solve the problem.	System	Warning

Event Source	Event ID	Explanation
Sap Agent	8516	There was not enough free memory for this application to run. Resources that are accessed by using the SAP agent and services that agent and services that depend on the SAP Agent will not be available.
Sap Agent	8517	The application could not start because a needed resource could not be created. Resources that are accessed by using the SAP agent and services that depend on the SAP agent will not be available.
Sap Agent	8518	The application could not start because a needed resource could not be created. Resources that are accessed by using the SAP agent and services that depend on the SAP agent will not be available.
Sap Agent	8519	The application could not start because a needed resource could not be created. Resources that are accessed by using the SAP agent and services that depend on the SAP agent will not be available.
Sap Agent	8520	A client tried to communicate with this server, but the necessary memory could not be allocated on the server.
Sap Agent	8521	There was not enough free memory for this application to run. Resources that are accessed by using the SAP agent and services that depend on the SAP agent will not be available.
Sap Agent	8522	The application could not start because a key is missing from the Registry or is incorrect.
Sap Agent	8523	The application could not start because a needed resource could not be created. Resources that are accessed by using the SAP agent and services that depend on the SAP agent will not be available.
Sap Agent	8524	The application could not start because a needed resource could not be created. Resources that are accessed by using the SAP agent and services that depend on the SAP agent will not be available.
Sap Agent	8525	The specified name in the specified key of the Registry is not a valid name because it is too long. The application will work as usual except that this server name will be ignored during this session.
Sap Agent	8526	The application could not start because a needed resource could not be created. Resources that are accessed by using the SAP agent and services that depend on the SAP agent will not be available.

Recommended Action	Event Log Source	Type
Close some applications and try again. If you get this message often you may be able to avoid it if you install more memory.	System	Warning
Contact your technical support group. Report both this message and the message that accompanies it.	System	Error
Contact your technical support group. Report both this message and the message that accompanies it.	System	Error
Contact your technical support group. Report both this message and the message that accompanies it.	System	Error
Close some applications and direct the client to try again. If you get this message often you may be able to avoid it if you install more memory.	System	Error
Close some applications and try again. If you get this message often, have the system administrator install more memory to solve the problem.	System	
This key in the Registry should be changed to a value between 0 and 2, inclusive, by someone experienced with Regedit32.	System	
Contact your technical support group. Report both this message and the message that accompanies it.	System	Error
Contact your technical support group. Report both this message and the message that accompanies it.	System	Error
The server name should be changed in the Registry by someone experienced with Regedit32.	System	
Contact your technical support group. Report both this message and the message that accompanies it.	System	Error

Event Source	Event ID	Explanation
Sap Agent	8527	The application could not start because a needed resource could not be obtained. The most likely reasons are that the Internetwork Packet Exchange (IPX) protocol could not be found or that the IPX WinSock information in the Registry is missing or in error.
Sap Agent	8528	The application is unable to get status information about the wide area network (WAN). Resources that are accessed by using the SAP agent and services that depend on the SAP agent will not be available.
Sap Agent	8529	The application could not start because a needed resource could not be created. Resources that are accessed by using the SAP agent and services that depend on the SAP agent will not be available.
Sap Agent	8530	The application could not start because a needed resource could not be created. Resources that are accessed by using the SAP agent and services that depend on the SAP agent will not be available.
Sap Agent	8531	The application could not start because needed information could not be obtained. You may not have enough free memory. Resources that are accessed by using the SAP agent and services that depend on the SAP agent will not be available.
Sap Agent	8532	There was not enough free memory for this application to run. Resources that are accessed by using the SAP agent and services that depend on the SAP agent will not be available.
Sap Agent	8507	
Sap Agent	8533	The application could not start because a needed resource could not be created. Resources that are accessed by using the SAP agent and services that depend on the SAP agent will not be available.
Schedule	7901	When you used AT.EXE, the command did not start.
Security	512	This event record indicates that the system has been rebooted. This has several implications: All paired events (such as logon/logoff or open/close) from before the restart are terminated. Some number of audit event records might have been lost. This is a message that appears only if the audit policy designates the auditing of system startup and shutdown.

Recommended Action	Event Log Source	Type
Use the Network option in Control Panel to make sure the NWLink IPX/SPX Compatible Transport Driver is installed. If you still get this message, remove and re-install the NWLink IPX/SPX Compatible Transport Driver or have someone who is proficient in the configuration of NWLink do this.	System	Error
Contact your technical support group. Report both this message and the message that accompanies it.	System	Error
Contact your technical support group. Report both this message and the message that accompanies it.	System	Error
Contact your technical support group. Report both this message and the message that accompanies it.	System	Error
Close some applications and try again. If you still get this message, call technical support and report both this message and the message that accompanies it.	System	Error
Close some applications and try again. If you get this message often, have the system administrator install more memory to solve the problem.	System	Error
Restart your computer and try again. If you still get this message, call technical support.	System	Error
Contact your technical support group. Report both this message and the message that accompanies it.	System	Error
Look up the indicated error and take the appropriate action.	System	Error
	Security	Error

Event Source	Event ID	Explanation
Security	513	This event record indicates that the system is being shut down in an orderly fashion. This is not a guarantee that the system successfully shut down before power was turned off or the system stopped, because once the system has shut down it cannot write to the Event log.
Security	514	This event record indicates that the Local Security Authority has loaded an authentication package used for authenticating logon requests. Authentication packages are responsible for validating user identification and authentication information collected by the local security authority.
Security	515	This event record indicates that a logon process has registered with the local security authority. Logon requests will now be accepted from this source. Logon processes are trusted components responsible for collecting identification and authentication information.
Security	516	This event record indicates that audit event records have been discarded, due to overwriting of earlier records or to cessation of auditing, depending on the audit policy you have established; or by internal event queues exceeding their maximum length.
Security	529	This event record indicates an attempt to log on using an unknown user account or using a valid user account but with an invalid password. An unexpected increase in the number of these audits could represent an attempt by someone to find user accounts and passwords illegally.
Security	530	This event record indicates that an attempt to log on was made and rejected because the user tried to log on before or after the hours that the user is allowed to connect to the server.
Security	531	This event record indicates an attempt to log on using a disabled account.
Security	532	This event record indicates an attempt to log on to an account that has expired.
Security	533	This event record indicates an attempt to log on to an account that has been locked out.
Security	535	This event record indicates an attempt to log on using an account whose password has expired.
Security	536	This event record indicates that a logon attempt was made and rejected because the Net Logon service is not running.

Recommended Action	Event Log Source	Type
	Security	Error
	Security	Error
	Security	Warning
	Security	Error
	Security	
	Security	Error
	Security	Error
	Security	Error
	Security	CoError
	Security	
	Security	Error

Event Source	Event ID	Explanation
Security	537	This event record indicates that a logon attempt was made and rejected for some reason other than those covered by explicit audit records in this category.
Security	538	This event record indicates that a user has logged off.
Security	560	This event record indicates either that an object has been successfully opened or that an attempt to open an object was rejected.
Security	562	This event record indicates that a handle to an object has been closed. This event is only generated for handles that caused an audit to be generated when opened.
Security	576	This event record indicates that a privilege that is not auditable on an individual use basis has been assigned to a user's security context at logon. Some privileges are used so frequently that auditing their every use would flood the Audit log with excessive and repetitive entries.
Security	578	This event record indicates the use of privileges to operate on an object. For example, privilege is required to increase the base priority of a process and to change the primary token of a process.
Security	592	This event record indicates that a new process has been created.
Security	593	This event record indicates that a particular process has exited.
Security	594	A handle has been duplicated for the same or less access than previously granted. Handle duplication audit records always refer to kernel objects.
Security	595	One operation performed by Windows NT that causes an access check on an object when creating another object is connecting to an LPC port. This audit record is used to describe that operation.
Security	608	This event record indicates that a user right (privilege) has been assigned to or removed from a user account or group. Windows NT generates only successful forms of this audit event record. (Programs must first Create or Open the corresponding "privileged operation or service called.")
Security	609	This event record indicates that a user right (privilege or logon capability) has been taken away from the specified user account or group.
Security	610	This event record indicates that a new trusted domain has been added.

Recommended Action	Event Log Source	Type
	Security	Error
	Security	Error
	Security	Error
	Security	Error
	Security	
	Security	
	Security	Error
	Security	Error
No user action is needed.	Security	Error
	Security	Error
	Security	Error
	Security	Warning
	Security	Warning

Event Source	Event ID	Explanation
Security	611	This event record trusted domain has been removed.
Security	612	This event record indicates that audit policy has changed and contains the following information: subject's authentication ID, Audit category names, and current status (+ / -).
Security	624	This event record indicates that a user account has been created.
Security	625	This event record indicates that a user account type has been changed.
Security	626	This event record indicates that a user account has been enabled.
Security	627	This event record indicates that an attempt to change a password was made and rejected.
Security	628	This event record indicates that a user account's password has been set.
Security	629	This event record indicates that a user account has been disabled.
Security	630	This event record indicates that a user account has been deleted.
Security	631	This event record indicates that a Global Group account has been created.
Security	632	This event record indicates that a member has been added to a global group.
Security	633	This event record indicates that a member has been removed from a global group. This event occurs when a user account is deleted and removed from the built-in None group used internally by Windows NT.
Security	634	This event record indicates that a Global Group account has been deleted.
Security	635	This event record indicates that a local group account has been created.
Security	637	This event record indicates that a local group has been removed.
Security	638	This event record indicates that a local group has been deleted.
Security	639	This event record indicates that a change (other than group membership) has been made to a local group.
Security	640	This event record indicates that a change has been made to the Security Account Manager (SAM) database.

Recommended Action	Event Log Source	Type
	Security	Error
	Security	Error
	Security	Error
	Security	
	Security	Error
	Security	Error
	Security	Error
	Security	Error
	Security	Error
	Security	Error
	Security	Error
	Security	Error
	Security	Error
	Security	Error
	Security	Error
	Security	Error
	Security	Error
	Security	

Event Source	Event ID	Explanation
Security	641	This event record indicates that a change has been made to a global group.
Security	642	This event record indicates that a user account has been changed.
Security	643	This event record indicates that a change has been made to domain policy.
Security	517	This event record indicates that the audit log has been cleared. This event is always recorded, regardless of the audit policy. It is recorded even if auditing is turned off.
Security	518	This event record indicates that SAM has loaded a notification package.
Security	528	This event record indicates that a new logon has occurred.
Security	539	A logon attempt was made and rejected because the account has been locked out.
Security	636	This event record indicates that a new member has been added to a local group.
Security	1000	This event record indicates that the profile was loaded.
Security	1001	This event record indicates that the profile was unloaded.
Security	1002	This event record indicates that the user has been assigned a mandatory profile. The user can change environment settings during a logon session; however, these changes are not saved in the profile at the end of the session.
Security	1003	This event record indicates that the mandatory profile could not be located.
Security	1004	This event record indicates that the user cannot access the mandatory profile.
Security	1005	This event record indicates that the user does not have permission to read the keys in the indicated profile.
Security	1006	This event record indicates that the user was assigned the system default profile.
Security	1007	This event record indicates that the specified profile could not be loaded for the user.
Security	1008	This event record indicates that the specified profile could not be unloaded for the user.
Security	1009	This event record indicates that the user profile could not be copied back to the specified directory.

Recommended Action	Event Log Source	Type
	Security	Error
	Security	Error
	Security	Error
	Security	Error
	Security	Error
	Security	CoError
	Security	
	Security	Error
	Application	Error
	Application	CoError
	Application	CoError
	Application	CoError
	Application	
	Application	Warning
	Application	Error
	Application	
	Application	CoError
	Application	Success

Event Source	Event ID	Explanation
Security	1000	This event record indicates that a home directory could not be set for the user. A home directory can be assigned to each user for storage of personal files.
Security	1011	This event record indicates that the profile was not unloaded previously and that the user will see that profile from the last logon session.
Security	1012	This event record indicates that the user profile could not be loaded.
Security	1013	This event record indicates that a central profile for the user is not available.
Security	1014	The user default profile is the standard Windows NT profile. The user can modify this profile and save it as the user's personal profile. This event record indicates that the changes that the user made to the default profile were not copied to the local profile directory used for that user's local profile.
Security	1015	The system default profile appears when nobody is logged on. This event record indicates that the changes that the user made to the default profile were not saved to the local system. The user will have to use the system default profile at the next logon.
Security	1016	The user default profile is the standard Windows NT profile. The user can modify this profile, and save it as the user's personal profile. This event record indicates that the user's copy of the profile does not have the proper security and cannot be loaded.
Security	1017	The user default profile is the standard Windows NT profile. The user can modify this profile, and save it as the user's personal profile. This event record indicates that the user's copy of the profile cannot be loaded.
Security	1018	This event record indicates that an attempt was made to update a central profile for the user. The central profile could not be updated from that computer.
Security	1019	This event record indicates that an attempt was made to load a local cached profile for the user. The attempt was unsuccessful.
Security	1020	This event record indicates that a central profile was successfully copied over the user's cached profile.
Security	1021	This event record indicates that a user's cached profile was successfully copied over the central profile.

Recommended Action	Event Log Source	Type
	Application	
	Application	
Further explanation appears below the error message.	Application	
Further explanation appears below the error message.	Application	Error
	Application	Informa-tional
	Application	
	Application	Warning
	Application	
	Application	Error
	Application	Error
	Application	CoError
	Application	Error

Event Source	Event ID	Explanation
Security	1022	When you interactively log on (by using WinLogon) to an account not physically maintained on that Windows NT-based machine, the logon information is cached on the machine. Because of this, you can interactively log on to the same machine later even though the domain controller cannot be found on the network.
Security	1023	When you interactively log on (by using WinLogon) to an account not physically maintained on that Windows NT-based machine, the logon information is cached on the machine. Because of this, you can interactively log on to the same machine later even though the domain controller cannot be found on the network.
Service Control Manager	7000	The service could not be started.
Service Control Manager	7001	The specified service failed to start.
Service Control Manager	7002	None of the services in the specified group started. Because the service is dependent on other members of the group, the service did not start.
Service Control Manager	7003	The specified service could not be started because it is configured to depend on another service that does not exist.
Service Control Manager	7005	In order for the service controller to operate properly, the specified function call must be completed.
Service Control Manager	7006	The service controller could not set a Registry value for a function that it requires for operation.
Service Control Manager	7007	The current system configuration was unacceptable so the system restarted with the last saved configuration that worked. A service may have had an error that caused it to fail to start.
Service Control Manager	7008	The account name for the account in which the service is to run must contain a backslash. Unless the service is to run as a local system account, account names should contain a backslash, as in `<domain name>\\<user name>`.

Recommended Action	Event Log Source	Type
	Application	
	Application	Error
Contact your system administrator.	System	CoError
Contact your system administrator.	System	Success
Ask your system administrator to check the Event log with Event Viewer to locate any service-related errors that may have caused this error. Your system administrator should also check your computer's configuration.	System	Informa-tional
Ask your system administrator to check your computer's configuration.	System	Informa-tional
Contact your technical support group.	System	Informa-tional
Contact your technical support group.	System	Success
Check the Event log with Event Viewer to identify the configuration problems. The log has information about errors that preceded this one. You may need to contact the vendor of the component that failed.	System	Success
If this error occurs when setting up or configuring the system, create the account again by using a backslash to separate the domain name from the unique portion of the account name. Otherwise, contact the vendor of the service for which the account is being used to authenticate the service.	System	CoError

Event Source	Event ID	Explanation
Service Control Manager	7009	The service controller could not communicate with the service process within the specified time.
Service Control Manager	7010	The service controller could not communicate with the service within the specified time.
Service Control Manager	7011	A control message could not be sent to a service.
Service Control Manager	7012	The service controller cannot communicate with the service due to a problem with the system.
Service Control Manager	7013	An attempt to log on to a service account failed.
Service Control Manager	7014	The service controller made a second attempt to log on to a service by using an old password.
Service Control Manager	7015	A boot-start or system-start driver is dependent on another driver or service to start. These drivers should depend only on a group.
Service Control Manager	7016	The service controller cannot recognize the state code reported by the service specified.
Service Control Manager	7017	The specified service is dependent on a chain of other services. One of the other services is dependent on another service that appears earlier in the chain.
Service Control Manager	7018	An auto-start service is dependent on a chain of other services. One of the services in that chain is dependent on another service that appears earlier in the chain.
Service Control Manager	7019	The service specified depends on another service which is in a group that is configured to start later than the specified service.
Service Control Manager	7020	The service specified depends on a group that is configured to start later than the specified service.
Service Control Manager	7021	A critical service or driver failed to start; therefore the system will revert to the last saved configuration.

Recommended Action	Event Log Source	Type
Ask your system administrator to start the service again by using the Services option in Control Panel. If the service will not start, contact the service vendor.	System	CoError
Ask your system administrator to start the service again by using the Services option in Control Panel. If the service will not start, contact the service vendor.	System	CoError
Retry the operation. If the problem persists, ask your system administrator to stop and then restart the service. It may be necessary to contact the vendor of the service.	System	CoError
Contact your technical support group.	System	Success
Ask your system administrator to verify the current configured account information for the service. Use Event Viewer to examine the Event log an identify the service.	System	Success
Ask your system administrator to verify the current configured account information for the service. Use Event Viewer to examine the Event log an identify the service.	System	Informa-tional
Ask your system administrator to change the System dependency to refer to a group rather than another driver.	Success	
Report the code number to the service vendor's technical support group.	System	Success
Ask your system administrator to check the configuration of your system to review the chain of dependencies. Your administrator should remove the dependency that loops back.	System	Error
Ask your system administrator to check the configuration of your system to review the chain of dependencies. Your administrator should remove the dependency that loops back.	System	Error
Ask your system administrator to either change the dependency or change the order of the `GroupOrderList` in the Registry.	System	Warning
Ask your system administrator to either change the dependency or change the order of the `GroupOrderList` in the Registry.	System	Warning
Ask your system administrator to check the Event log with Event Viewer for details about the service or driver errors that preceded this one.	System	

Event Source	Event ID	Explanation
Service Control Manager	7022	The service specified is stuck in the start pending state. The service failed to indicate that it is making progress within the time period specified in its last status message.
Service Control Manager	7023	The service stopped due to an error.
Service Control Manager	7024	The service stopped due to an error.
Service Control Manager	7026	The drivers in the list failed to start.
Service Control Manager	7027	The system detected an incorrect configuration so the system reverted to the last correct configuration.
Service Control Manager	7028	The current permissions on the specified key in the control set do not allow full access to programs running in the Local System account (such as the Service Control Manager).
Service Control Manager	2510	The server was unable to a LAN Manager error code.
Service Control Manager	2511	The directory that was previously shared has been deleted.
Srv	2000	The server received `STATUS_INVALID_PARAMETER (c0000008)` when it called `NtQueryInformationFile (bc0)`. If a user application request is submitted illegally by a client operation, the server logs the failure. The server is failing a `SrvQueryBasic AndStandardInfo` subroutine (a basic system call).
Srv	2001	The page file has reached the maximum page file size and there are no more pages available, either in main memory or in the page file. This generally indicates a memory leak in another process.
Srv	2002	The server was started on a computer that does not have any memory free.
Srv	2003	The server was started on a computer that does not have any memory free.
Srv	2004	The server was started on a computer that does not have any memory free.

Recommended Action	Event Log Source	Type
Wait a few minutes to see if the service starts. If the service does not start, use the Services option in Control Panel to start the service manually. If the problem persists, contact the service vendor.	System	Success
Depending on the error, you should either restart the service using the Services option in Control Panel, contact your system administrator, or contact the service vendor.	System	Error
Contact your system administrator.	System	Error
Ask your system administrator to verify that the drivers in the list are not critical to your system's operation.	System	Error
Use Event Viewer to check the Event log for details about the incorrect configuration.	System	Informa-tional
Use the Registry Editor to find the key in the current control set and make sure the Local System account is given full access.	System	Error
Report this message to the vendor of the application.	System	Informa-tional
If you want to re-create the share, create the directory first.	System	Error
Contact your technical support group.	System	Error
Determine the process at fault by using the Performance Monitor to monitor each process's page file bytes or working set.	System	Error
Contact your technical support group.	System	Error
Contact your technical support group.	System	Error
Contact your technical support group.	System	Warning

Event Source	Event ID	Explanation
Srv	2005	There is a problem with the underlying transport.
Srv	2006	A client computer, using direct hosting over IPX, has written to a file on a Windows NT Server.
Srv	2007	The server was started on a computer that does not have any memory free.
Srv	2009	A client opened too many files or had too many active directory searches on the server.
Srv	2010	The server was started on a computer that does not have any memory free.
Srv	2011	The server pre-allocates I/O request packets to be the size specified by the `IRPSTACKSIZE` parameter in the configuration information. The value of this parameter must be as large as the size required by any transport or file system in the network.
Srv	2012	If you see many errors of this type in the Event log in Event Viewer, they indicate a network hardware or software problem.
Srv	2016	The page file has reached the maximum page file size and there are no more pages available, either in main memory or in the page file. This generally indicates a memory leak in another process.
Srv	2017	This non-critical message appears if the server is configured to use limited resources. If the server is configured to use an unlimited number of connections, some hidden parameters may need to be changed.
Srv	2018	This non-critical message appears if the server is configured to use limited resources. If the server is configured to use an unlimited number of connections, some hidden parameters may need to be changed.

Recommended Action	Event Log Source	Type
Contact the vendor of the transport.	System	Error
To work around this, do one or all of the following: Disable direct hosting over IPX on the client computer, disable direct hosting bindings on the Windows NT Server, or remove the IPX/SPX Compatible Transport Protocol (NWLink) and use another protocol on the server. This direct hosting mechanism uses unsupported file formats.	System	
Contact your technical support group.	System	Success
The client should either close some files or limit the number of simultaneous directory searches on the server.	System	Success
Contact your technical support group.	System	Informa-tional
Ask your system administrator to change the parameter in the server's configuration.	System	Informa-tional
Contact your network administrator.	System	Error
Determine the process at fault by using the Performance Monitor to monitor each process's page file bytes or working set.	System	Error
No action is needed unless the server has reached the maximum configured optimization setting. Then contact technical support. If the server is not configured to use the maximum number of connections, select Network in Control Panel. When the Installed Network Services dialog box appears, adjust the optimization for the Server service.	System	Error
No action is needed unless the server has reached the maximum configured optimization setting. Then contact technical support. If the server is not configured to use the maximum number of connections, select Network in Control Panel. When the Installed Network Services dialog box appears, adjust the optimization for the Server service.	System	Success

Event Source	Event ID	Explanation
Srv	2019	Nonpaged pool pages cannot be paged out to the paging file, but instead remain in main memory as long as they are allocated. An application is probably incorrectly making system calls and using up all allocated nonpaged pool. You may also see the following message: `Your system is running low on virtual memory….`
Srv	2020	The page file has reached the maximum page file size and there are no more pages available, either in main memory or in the page file. This generally indicates a memory leak in another process.
Srv	2501	The Registry is corrupted.
Srv	2502	The Registry is corrupted.
Srv	2503	There may be a problem with the underlying transport because it (they) did not load. If the server could bind to at least one transport, it would have started.
Srv	2504	There may be a problem with the underlying transport because it did not load.
Srv	2505	
Srv	2506	
Srv	2507	The Registry is corrupted.
Srv	2508	Either the SRV.SYS file is missing from your computer's driver directory or it is corrupted. The system refused to load the driver.
Srv	2509	
TCPIP	4188	

Recommended Action	Event Log Source	Type
To find the application, use the Performance Monitor to look at each application's nonpaged pool allocation. Or monitor the system with a utility such as PMON.EXE from the Windows NT Resource Kit.	System	Success
Determine the process at fault by using the Performance Monitor to monitor each process's page file bytes or working set.	System	Success
Ask your system administrator to reinstall the Registry from the ERD that was made when Windows NT was installed.	System	Success
Ask your system administrator to reinstall the Registry from the ERD that was made when Windows NT was installed.	System	Success
Check the Event log with Event Viewer for information about related errors. Contact your network administrator.	System	Success
Check the Event log with Event Viewer for information about related errors. Contact your network administrator.	System	Success
Ask your network administrator to change the server's name or to change the name of the other network computer.	System	Success
Ask your network administrator to remove the value from the Registry or to use the default for the Registry key.	System	Success
Ask your system administrator to reinstall the Registry from the ERD that was made when Windows NT was installed.	System	Error
Contact your system administrator.	System	CoError
Restart the server or, if the problem persists, contact your system administrator.	System	Informational
Get the correct subnet mask address from your network administrator. Double-click Network under Control Panel to specify this address in the TCP/IP configuration, then try again.	System	Informational

Event Source	Event ID	Explanation
TCPIP	4192	
TCPIP	4197	
Transport	9008	
Transport	9001	The resource pool is not available because the server is busy.
Transport	9002	Your server has reached the configured limit for NetBIOS.
Transport	9003	One of the Registry parameters, `MaxLinks` or `MaxConnections`, has been changed. The default for these parameters is unlimited.
Transport	9004	The specified device is not the correct version for the NDIS wrapper.
Transport	9005	The specified adapter did not load, is out of memory, or is not configured properly.
Transport	9006	A locally administered address that was assigned to a token ring adapter is a duplicate of an address already in use by another station on the ring.
Transport	9007	The NDIS driver has either a hardware or driver problem.
Transport	9008	There is either a hardware or driver problem with the NDIS driver.
Transport	9009	A hardware problem has occurred.
Transport	9010	Your computer created too many connections to the network.
Transport	9011	Your network is experiencing hardware problems or the software versions on the two computers may conflict.

Recommended Action	Event Log Source	Type
Get the correct gateway address from your network administrator. Double-click Network option under Control Panel to specify this address in the TCP/IP configuration, then try again.	System	Success
Use the Network option in Control Panel to remove some default gateways from the configuration for this adapter. Then try again.	System	Error
Use the `CD` command to reach the directory that contains the batch file, then type the filename.	Application	Error
Ask your system administrator to restart the server, or you can wait a few minutes and then try the operation again. If you see this message frequently, your system administrator may need to increase the server's memory.	System	Error
Ask your system administrator to increase the configured size of the protocol if it is not already configured to its maximum limit. The protocol's size can be changed by choosing Server in Network in Control Panel.	System	Error
Ask your system administrator to increase the `MaxLinks` or `MaxConnections` parameter in the Registry.	System	Informational
Ask your system administrator to reinstall the correct version of the device from the Setup disks.	System	Informational
Ask your system administrator to verify that the NDIS driver loaded correctly. Check the Event log with Event Viewer for related errors.	System	Success
Ask your system administrator to eliminate the address conflict.	System	Success
Check the Event log with Event Viewer for related errors.	System	Error
Check the Event log with Event Viewer for related errors.	System	Error
Check the Event log with Event Viewer for related errors that may indicate the hardware problem. If the related errors are serious, you should contact technical support.	System	Warning
Wait a few minutes, then retry the operation.	System	Informational
Contact your technical support group.	System	Informational

Event Source	Event ID	Explanation
Wins	4097	
Wins	4116	There are no active or tombstone records in the database. The records being requested by a remote WINS server may be released or nonexistent.

Recommended Action	Event Log Source	Type
No user action is required.	Application	Warning
Verify that the WINS server attempting to pull does not have a higher version ID than the WINS server being pulled from. If this is not the case, it means that no new records were available for replication.	Application	Error

Appendix D

Internetworking Protocol Reference

This appendix is a guide to the various internetworking protocols supported either directly or indirectly by Windows NT. These stacks (see Figure D.1.) come from the most common vendors of network operating systems. Also included are definitions of the various acronyms as well as pointers to additional Request for Comments (RFC) documents.

Application			Services for Macintosh (File Server)	Services for Macintosh (Print Server)
Presentation			Apple Filing Protocol (AFP)	PostScript
Session	Apple Data Stream Protocol (ADSP)	Zone Information Protocol (ZIP)	Apple Session Protocol (ASP)	Printer Access Protocol (PAP)
Transport	Routing Table Maintenance Protocol (RTMP)	Apple Echo Protocol (AEP)	Apple Transaction Protocol (ATP)	Name Binding Protocol (NBP)
Network	(DDP) Datagram Delivery Protocol			
Data Link	TokenTalk	EtherTalk	LocalTalk	

Figure D.1. *AppleTalk architecture.*

The AppleTalk stack is used in Windows NT to provide the Services for MacIntosh Network Service. The major component that provides Print Services is the Printer Access Protocol. The major component that provides File Services is the Apple Filing Protocol (AFP). Windows NT Services for MacIntosh supports AFP versions 2.0 and 2.1.

Figure D.2 represents the IPX/SPX-based protocol stack found in versions 3.x and 4.x of Novell NetWare. Windows NT is able to provide these higher layer services through both Microsoft and Novell-based solutions.

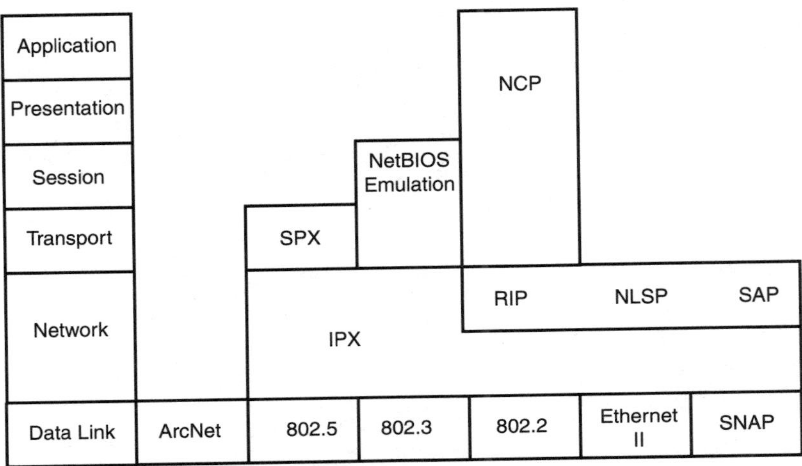

Figure D.2. *Novell Netware IPX/SPX architecture.*

The following is an explanation of the acronyms found in Figure D.2:

NCP	Netware Core Protocol
SPX	Sequenced Packet Exchange
IPX	Internet Packet Exchange
RIP	Routing Information Protocol
NLSP	Netware Link State Protocol
SAP	Service Advertising Protocol

Table D.1 describes the different frame types used in Netware and other operating systems. These help assist logical topology and other data link layer functions.

Table D.1. IPX/SPX frame types.

Frame Type	Common Protocol	Netware?	NT
Ethernet 802.2	IPX	Yes (Default NW 3.12, 4.x)	3.x, 4.x
Ethernet 802.3	IPX	Yes (Default NW 2.x, 3.11)	3.x, 4.x

Frame Type	Common Protocol	Netware?	NT
Ethernet II	TCP/IP, IPX, AppleTalk	Yes	3.x, 4.x
Ethernet Snap	AppleTalk	Yes	3.x, 4.x
Token Ring (802.5)	IPX	Yes	3.x, 4.x
Token Ring Snap	TCP/IP, IPX	Yes	3.x, 4.x

Figure D.3 represents the complete TCP/IP protocol stack, including all of the application services that are not found inherently within the Windows NT TCP/IP Protocol Stack.

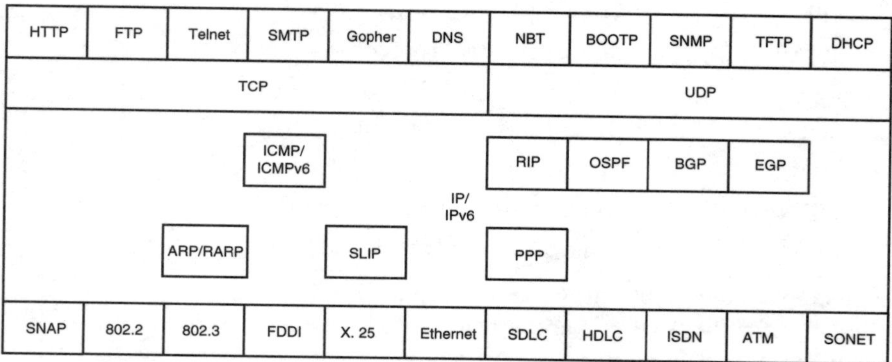

Figure D.3. *TCP/IP architecture.*

The following is an explanation of the acronyms found in Figure D.3:

HTTP	HyperText Transport Protocol
FTP	File Transfer Protocol
SMTP	Simple Mail Transport Protocol
DNS	Domain Name System
NBT	NetBIOS over TCP/IP
BOOTP	Boot Strap Protocol
SNMP	Simple Network Management Protocol
TFTP	Trivial File Transfer Protocol
DHCP	Dynamic Host Configuration Protocol
TCP	Transmission Protocol
UDP	User DataGram Protocol
ICMP	Internet Control Message Protocol

RIP	Routing Information Protocol
OSPF	Open Shortest Path First
BGP	Border Gateway Protocol
EGP	Exterior Gateway Protocol
IP	Internet Protocol
ARP	Address Resolution Protocol
RARP	Reverse Address Resolution Protocol
SLIP	Serial Line Internet Protocol
PPP	Point-to-Point Protocol
SNAP	Subnet Access Protocol
FDDI	Fiber Distributed Data Interface
SDLC	Synchronous Data Link Control
HDLC	High-Level Data Link Control
ISDN	Integrated Services Digital Network
ATM	Asynchronous Transfer Mode

There are well over 2,000 RFCs relating to internetworking. They were originally designed for the ARPAnet and other Internet networks. In recent years, RFCs have evolved into the source for most major network and internetworking standards. Table D.2 is a selected list relating to the topics discussed in this book.

Table D.2. Useful RFC documents.

RFC	Title
768	User DataGram Protocol
791	Internet Protocol
792	Internet Control Message Protocol
793	Transmission Control Protocol
821	Simple Network Management Protocol
826	Ethernet Address Resolution Protocol
854	Telnet Protocol
903	Reverse Address Resolution Protocol
959	File Transfer Protocol
1001	NetBIOS Over TCP/IP
1034	Domain Names-Concepts
1042	IP over IEEE 802 Networks
1055	Serial Line Internet Protocol
1058	Routing Information Protocol
1155	Structure of Management Information
1157	Simple Network Management Protocol

RFC	Title
1212	Concise MIB Definition
1213	Management Information Base – II
1245	OSPF Protocol Analysis
1270	SNMP Communication Services
1332	Internet Protocol Control Protocol
1377	OSI Network Layer Control Protocol
1378	AppleTalk Control Protocol
1390	Transmission of IP and ARP over FDDI
1418	SNMP over OSI
1419	SNMP over AppleTalk
1420	SNMP over IPX
1490	Multi Protocol Connectivity over Frame Relay
1547	Point-to-Point Protocol Requirements
1550	IPng White Paper Solicitation
1552	IPX Control Protocol
1570	Link Control Protocol Extensions
1583	OSPF ver. 2
1598	PPP in X.25
1602	The Internet Standards Process
1618	PPP over ISDN
1661	Point-to-Point Protocol
1661	Point-to-Point Protocol
1662	PPP in HDLC-like Framing
1663	PPP Reliable Transmission
1700	Assigned Numbers
1810	MD5 Performance
1881	IPv6 Address Allocation
1883	IPv6 Specifications
1901	SNMP V.2
1907	MIB for SNMPv2
1910	User-based Security Model
1968	Encryption Control Protocol
1973	PPP in Frame Relay
1990	PPP Multi-Link Protocol
1994	Challenge Handshake Authentication Protocol
2021	RMON2 MIB
2023	IPv6 over PPP

Table D.3 lists the IEEE family of network standards, in order.

Table D.3. The IEEE family of network standards.

802.1	Internetworking
802.2	Logical Link Control
802.3	Carrier-Sense Multiple Access with Collision Detection
802.4	Token BUS LAN
802.5	Token Ring LAN
802.6	Metropolitan Area Network
802.7	Broadband Technical Advisory Group
802.8	Fiber Optic Technical Advisory Group
802.9	Integrated Voice/Data Networks
802.10	Network Security
802.11	Wireless Networks
802.12	Demand Priority Access

Internet Resources

The next few pages assist network managers and engineers with implementing TCP/IP-based internetworks as well as connectivity to the worldwide Internet.

Internet Organizations

CommerceNet
URL: `http://www.commercenet.net/`
Email: `mailto:info@commerce.net`

Commercial Internet Exchange Association
URL: `http://www.cix.org/`
Email: `mailto:helpdesk@cix.org`

Internet Architecture Board
URL: `http://www.iab.org/`
Email: `iab-contact@isi.edu`

Internet Assigned Numbers of Authority
URL: `http://www.iana.org/`
Email: `mailto:iana@isi.org`

Internet Engineering Task Force
URL: `http://www.ietf.cnri.reston.va.us/`
Email: `mailto:ietf-web@ietf.cnri.reston.va.us`

Internet Society
URL: `http://www.isoc.org/`
Email: `mailto:isoc@isoc.org`

World Wide Web Consortium
URL: `http://www.w3.org/`
Email: `mailto:www-request@w3.org`

Internet Services

AT&T
Tel: 908-668-6587
Email: `mailto:admin@ds.internic.net`

Registration

Network Solutions, Inc.
Tel: 703-742-4777
Email: `mailto:admin@rs.internic.net`

Defense Data Network

Government Systems, Inc.
Tel: 703-802-4535
Email: `mailto:hostmaster@nic.ddn.mil`

RFC Repositories

RFCs are available via anonymous FTP from:

URL: `ftp://ds.internic.net/rfc`

URL: `ftp://nis.nsf.net/internet/documents/rfc`

URL: `ftp://ftp.jvnc.net/pub/RFC`

URL: `ftp://ftp.isi.edu/in-notes`

URL: `ftp://nic.ddn.mil/rfc`

Appendix E

Multi-Vendor Command/Utility Reference and Translator

The next few pages contain a series of tables arranged by common everyday categories. In each table, a function is mentioned followed by the command or utility that performs it within the major network operating systems. Refer to the command's documentation provided by the vendor for further detail into each utility.

It is also important to bear in mind these are all native commands within the respective operating systems. These tables do not include any third-party options that may be available.

Configuration

Function	NetWare 3.12	NetWare 4.x
Binding a Network Control protocol to a NIC	`BIND`	`BIND`
Setting startup parameters	Load install	Load install (*.NCF)
Adjust TCP/IP configuration	Load install	Load INETCFG
Adjust IPX/SPX configuration	Load install	Load IPXCON

Connectivity

Function	NetWare 3.12	NetWare 4.x
Authenticating to a Remote Server	`ATTACH`, `LOGIN`	`LOGIN`
Sends a user a message	`BROADCAST`, `send`	`BROADCAST`, `send`
Mount a remote network drive	`map`	`map`
Communicate in real-time to other clients	N/A	N/A

File Management

Function	NetWare 3.12	NetWare 4.x
Advanced directory information	`CHKDIR`	`NDIR`
Copy a file	`ncopy`	`ncopy`
Move a file	`move`	`move`
Create a directory	`md`	`md`
Rename a file	`ren`	`ren`
Rename a directory	`rdir`	`rdir`
Edit a text file	`load edit`	`load edit`
Create a batch file on standard input	`copy con`	`copy con`
Display a text file	`type`, `load edit`	`type`, `load edit`
View the file type	N/A	N/A
Compress files	N/A	`ADDSTOR`
Echo arguments to desired output	`echo`	`echo`
Search for file, strings, paths	N/A	N/A
Create a symbolic link	N/A	N/A
Delete a file	`del`	`del`
Delete a directory	`rmdir`	`rmdir`

BSD UNIX	System V UNIX	Windows NT
N/A	N/A	Network Control Panel
/etc/rc.	/etc/rc.	Services Control Panel, System Control Panel
ifconfig	ifconfig	Network Control Panel
N/A	N/A	Network Control Panel

BSD UNIX	System V UNIX	Windows NT
cu, rlogin	cu, rlogin	NET USE, Explorer, File Manager, Network Neighborhood
write	write	NET SEND
mount	mount	NET USE, File Manager, Explorer
talk	talk	WinChat

BSD UNIX	System V UNIX	Windows NT
ls	ls	Explorer, File Manager
cp	cp	copy, xcopy, File Manager, Explorer
mv	mv	move
mkdir	mkdir	MD, File Manager, Explorer
mv	mv	ren, File Manager, Explorer
mv	mv	ren, File Manager, Explorer
vi, pico, ex, emacs	vi, pico, ex, emacs	Notepad, edit
batch	batch	copy con
cat, more, less	cat, more, less	type
file	file	Quick View
compress/gzip	compress, gzip	File Manager, Explorer, compact
echo	echo	echo
find	find	find, Explorer
ln	ln	Create shortcut
rm	rm	del, File Manager, Explorer
rmdir	rmdir	rd, File Manager, Explorer

File System Management

Function	NetWare 3.12	NetWare 4.x
Mount/change a namespace/ filesystem	Add Name Space	Add Name Space
Break a mirror set	N/A	`Abort Remirror`
View free disk on filesystems	`dir, ndir`	`dir, ndir`
View volume information	`volinfo`	`volinfo`

System Management

Function	NetWare 3.12	NetWare 4.x
Shut down a server	`down`	`down`
Change the system time	`time`	`time`
Archive files	`sbackup`	`sbackup`
Schedule a process to run	N/A	N/A
View scheduled jobs	N/A	N/A
Back up files	`sbackup`	`SBACKUP`
Change the ystem date	`date`	`date`
Display environment variables	N/A	N/A
Adjust the priority of a process	N/A	N/A
System information	Load Monitor	Load Monitor
Display current username	`whoami`	`whoami`

Monitoring

Function	NetWare 3.12	NetWare 4.x
View a process	N/A	N/A
Keep track of performance	Load Monitor	Load Monitor
See who is logged on and/or connected	N/A	N/A

BSD UNIX	System V UNIX	Windows NT
mount	mount	CONVERT.EXE
N/A	N/A	Disk Administrator (SRV)
df	df	dir
df, du	df, du	Disk Administrator

BSD UNIX	System V UNIX	Windows NT
shutdown	shutdown	Explorer, Ctrl+Alt+Delete
date	date	time
ar	ar	backup
at, crontab	at, crontab	AT
atq	atq	AT
cpio, tar	cpio, tar	NTBACKUP
date	date	time
printenv	env	set
nice	nice	start
uname	uname	winver, WinMSD
whoami	whoami	Ctrl+Alt+Delete

BSD UNIX	System V UNIX	Windows NT
ps	ps	Task Manager
top	top	Performance Monitor, Task Manager
finger	finger	finger

Printing

Function	NetWare 3.12	NetWare 4.x
Redirect a printer port	Capture, SESSION	Capture, NetUser
Send a print job	nprint	nprint
View a print queue	pconsole	pconsole
Set up a print queue	pconsole	pconsole, NWADMIN

Security

Function	NetWare 3.12	NetWare 4.x
Managing security inheritance	ALLOW, FILER	FILER
View audit log	FCONSOLE	AUDITCON
Change user rights	SYSCON	NETADMIN, NWADMIN
Change file and directory security attributes	FILER	FILER

Troubleshooting

Function	NetWare 3.12	NetWare 4.x
Kill a process	N/A	N/A
Turn on or off messaging	CASTON/CASTOFF	CASTON/CASTOFF
Test TCP/IP configuration	N/A	load ping
Recover deleted files	salvage	edit

User and Group Administration

Function	NetWare 3.12	NetWare 4.x
Create a user	SYSCON	NETADMIN, NWADMIN
View a user's group membership	SYSCON	NETADMIN, NWADMIN
Create a group	SYSCON	NETADMIN, NWADMIN

BSD UNIX	System V UNIX	Windows NT
N/A	N/A	NET USE, Network Neighborhood, Print Manager, Explorer
lpq	lpstat	print, Explorer, File Manager
lpr	lp	Print Manager, NET PRINT
etc/printcap	etc/printcap	Print Manager, Printer Wizard

BSD UNIX	System V UNIX	Windows NT
umask	umask	Explorer, File Manager, CACLS
tail syslog	tail	Event Syslog Viewer
chmod	chmod	User Manager
chmod	chmod	CACLS, Explorer, File Manager

BSD UNIX	System V UNIX	Windows NT
kill	kill	Task Manager
mesg	mesg	net start (stop) Messenger
ping	ping	ping
N/A	N/A	N/A

BSD UNIX	System V UNIX	Windows NT
adduser	adduser	NET USER, User Manager
groups	groups	User Manager, NET GROUP, NET LOCALGROUP
/etc/passwd	/etc/passwd	User Manager, NET GROUP, NET LOCALGROUP

Appendix F

Resources Available for Windows NT

Product	Vendor	Type	Phone Number
PASSPORT	Zephyr	3270 emulator	1-800-966-3270
nu/TPU	A/Soft Development	32-bit text editor	1-603-666-6699
SoftImage 3D for NT	SoftImage	3D graphics design	1-800-576-3846
Solomon IV for Windows	Solomon Software	Accounting	1-800-4SOLOMON
InterCheck	ACT Sophos Data Security	Anti-Virus	1-513-755-1957
Carmel Anti-Virus	Carmel Software Engineering	Anti-Virus	972-48-416976
Inoculan for Windows NT	Computer Associates	Anti-Virus	1-800-CHEYINC
NetShield	McAfee	Anti-Virus	1-800-332-9965
VirusScan 2.5	McAfee	Anti-Virus	1-800-332-9966
Dr. Solomon's Anti-Virus Toolkit	S&S Software International	Anti-Virus	1-800-701-9648
SWEEP for Windows NT	Sophos	Anti-Virus	1-513-755-1957
Norton Anti-Virus Scanner 2.0	Symantec Corp.	Anti-Virus	1-800-441-7234
E-mail Virus Wall	Trend	Anti-Virus	1-800-272-3720
Borland C++ Development Suite	Borland International	Application Development	1-800-645-4559
Visual Basic 4.0	Microsoft	Application Development	1-206-882-8080
Watcom C/C++	Watcom International	Application Development	

Product	Vendor	Type	Phone Number
Dan Bricklin's Timelock	Lifeboat Publishing	Application Development	1-800-447-1955
Visual Slickedit for X Windows	Microedge, Inc.	Application Development	1-800-934-3348
Cenvi CMM Interpreter	Nombas, Inc.	Application Development	1-617-929-2500
CMM Macro Language ToolKit	Nombas, Inc.	Application Development	1-617-391-6595
Vision Storyboard	Vision Software Tools	Application Development	1-800-984-7638
Synon Obsydian	Synon	Application Development—BackOffice	1-800-94SYNON
File Archivists for NT	NTP Software	Archiving Software	1-800-226-2757
Visual Voice Pro	Stylus Product Group	Audio Application Development	1-617-621-9545
SQLStor 1.3	SQL Business Systems	Automated Database Backup	1-800-778-7410
Installation Expert	Great Lakes Business Solutions	Automated Installations	
Expose	Symantec Corporation	Automated Server Management	1-800-689-8727
Ultrabac	BEI Corporation	Backup Management	1-206-644-6000
ArcServe	Computer Associates	Backup Management	1-800-CHEYINC
Legato Networker	Legato Systems	Backup Management	1-800-747-7911
Webstor	McAfee	Backup Management	1-408-988-3832
Octopus	Octopus Technologies	Backup Management	1-800-919-1009
Backup Director	Palindrome	Backup Management	
Backup Exec	Seagate Technology	Backup Management	1-800-877-2340
Legato Networker 4.2 for Windows NT	Legato Systems	Backup/Storage Management	1-650-812-6000
Batch Services	Integraph	Batch Job Manager	1-800-689-8727
AQM/JSO	Argent Software	Batch Job Scheduler	1-860-489-5553
Wildcat 5	Mustang Software	BBS/Web Server	1-805-873-2400
mlab for Windows	Civilized Software	Business Software	1-800-672-6522
PowerPlay 5.0	Cognos	Business Software	1-800-223-2321
Daceasy Accounting and Payroll	DACEASY	Business Software	1-800-322-3279

Product	Vendor	Type	Phone Number
Datastore	Primavera Systems	Business Software	1-800-423-0245
SPS 3.5	Saratoga Systems	Business Software	1-408-371-9330
Tecumseh	Tippecanoe Systems	Business Software	1-510-416-8510
CyberShop 2.0	UHS	Business Software	1-613-722-1288
Microstation 95	Bently Systems	CAD	1-800-236-8539
Solid Works 95	Solid Works Corp.	CAD	1-508-371-2910
CAD/DRAW 4	Tommy Software	CAD	
Capacity Planner for Windows NT	Digital Equipment Corporation	Capacity Planning and Load Balancing	1-800-689-8727
Corel CD Creator	Corel Corp.	CD Recording	1-800-772-6735
Incat Easy-CD Pro	Incat	CD Recording	1-800-774-6228
Conference Room	WebMaster, Inc.	Chat Server	1-800-689-8727
Informer Enterprise Edition	Reportech	Client/Server	
Visual SQL	Blue Sky	Client/Server Development	1-888-831-6220
AcuCOBOL-GT	Acucobol	COBOL Development	1-619-689-7220
VB Compress Pro 4.0	Whippleware	Code Analyst/ Optimization	1-800-241-8727
WINport and RASport	LANSource Technologies	Communications Server	1-800-689-8727
NFS Maestro 5.1	Hummingbird	Complete TCP/IP Suite	1-800-689-8727
MultiActive Maximizer	MultiActive Technologies	Contact Management	1-800-804-6299
ACT! for Lotus Notes	Symantec	Contact Management	1-800-441-7234
Microsoft Outlook	Microsoft	Contact Management Software	1-800-426-9400
ACT!	Symantec	Contact Management Software	1-800-441-7234
Crystal Info	Seagate Technology	Crystal Report Interface	1-800-877-2340
Symbiator	Execusoft Systems	Data Replication	1-800-689-8727
FileMaker Pro Server 3.0	Claris	Database Management	1-800-544-8554
Zybase	Zylab	Database Management	1-800-544-6339
Paradox 8	Corel	Database Package	1-800-772-6735
Conference 1.1	Insitu	Data-Conferencing	
Design 4.0	Streetwise Software	Desktop Publishing	1-310-829-7827

Product	Vendor	Type	Phone Number
Approach 96	Lotus Development	Desktop/Client Database	1-617-577-8500
InstallShield 3.0	InstallShield Corporation	Development	1-847-240-9111
Lead Tools OCX32	LEAD Technologies	Development	1-800-637-4699
Synon	Synon	Development	1-800-94SYNON
Crescent ClassAction	Crescent	Development Aid	1-800-352-2742
LiveWire Pro	Netscape	Development for Web	1-800-421-8008
Optima++ Developer 1.0	Powersoft	Development Tool	1-800-395-3525
StreetTalk for Windows NT	Banyan	Directory Services	
Sentry 2020	MIS House	Disk Encryption	0-1622723400
Storage Accountant for NT	NTP Software	Disk Usage Managment	1-800-226-2756
MetaInfo DNS 2.0	Metainfo	DNS Server	1-206-521-2600
MailCheck	Baranof	Email Management System	1-800-689-8727
NTMail	Internet Shopper	Email Server	
Imail	Ipswitch	Email Server	1-617-676-5700
Krypton Internet Mail Server	Krypton Communications	Email Server	1-770-352-9704
Z-Mail	NCD Software	Email Server	1-800-600-6442
Post.Office	Software.com	Email Server	1-805-882-2470
CommPoint	Telephone Response	Enterprise Voice Mail	1-800-689-8727
Phoenix Disaster Recovery	On Technology	Fault-Tolerance and Clustering Software	1-800-381-5686
FAX Maker	GFI Fax and Voice	Fax - Exchange Integration	1-800-689-8727
Fax Development Toolkit	Black Ice Software	Fax C++ SDK	1-603-673-1019
Gold-Fax	Data Processing Design	Fax Client/Server Soultion	1-800-689-8727
FaxFacts	Copia International	Fax Server	1-800-689-8727
FAXport	LANSource	Fax Server	1-800-677-2727
Zeta Fax	TSP Communications	Fax Server	1-770-457-0630
FAXport 6.0	On Technology	Fax Software	1-800-381-5686
CommSuite 95	Delrina	Fax/Communications	

Product	Vendor	Type	Phone Number
Fax Sr.	Omtool	Fax/Communications	1-800-886-7845
MacOpener 1.0	Dataviz	File Conversion	
Iway-One	Bate Tech Software	Firewall Software	1-303-763-8333
Borderware Firewall	Borderware	Firewall Software	1-416-368-7157
Firewall-1	CheckPoint Software	Firewall Software	1-800-429-4391
Guardian	NetGuard	Firewall Software	1-214-738-6900
Firewall Plus	Network-1	Firewall Software	1-800-638-9751
On Guard Firewall	On Technology	Firewall Software	1-800-381-5686
Gauntlet	Trusted Information Systems	Firewall Software	1-888-347-3925
Process Model 2.0	PROMODEL, Corp.	Flow Charting Software	1-801-223-4600
Polar Link	Quadron	Frame Relay Routing Software	1-805-966-6424
FrameMaker 5.0	Adobe Systems	Full-Scale Publishing Software	1-800-421-8006
QuarkXPress	Quark	Graphic Design/Layout	1-800-676-4575
TriSpectives 4.0	3D/Eye	Graphics	1-800-946-9533
Photoshop 3.0.5	Adobe Systems	Graphics	1-800-833-6687
Photo/Graphic Edge Volume 1	Auto F/X Corporation	Graphics	1-800-839-2008
CorelDRAW 6	Corel	Graphics	1-613-728-8200
Painter	Fractal Design	Graphics	1-800-297-2665
Extreme 3D	Macromedia	Graphics	1-800-326-2128
Kai's Power Tools 3	Meta Tools	Graphics	1-805-566-6200
KPT Vector Effects	Meta Tools	Graphics	1-805-566-6200
MediaPaint 1.0	Strata	Graphics	1-800-678-7282
Visual Reality 2.0	Visual Software	Graphics	1-800-669-7318
Lotus Notes	Lotus	Groupware	1-800-343-5414
Lotus Organizer 97 GS	Lotus	Groupware	1-800-346-1305
PHD Professional HelpDesk	On Technology	Help Desk Software	1-800-381-5686
Action Request System 2.1	Remedy	Help Desk Software	1-415-903-5200
ForeHelp 2.95	ForeFront	Help File Creation	1-800-357-8507
Doc-To-Help	Wextech Systems	Help File Creation	1-800-939-8324

Product	Vendor	Type	Phone Number
Reflections for Windows	WRQ	Host Connectivity	1-800-872-2829
Web Factory Pro Image	Thunder and Lightning	HTML Editor	1-888-826-3520
LEADtools	LEAD Technologies	Image Development	1-800-637-1840
Fulcrum Knowledge Network	Fulcrum	Information Management	1-800-689-8727
Crystal's 101 Reports for BackOffice	Seagate Software	Information Management	1-800-689-8727
Internet Policy Manager	On Technology	Internet Access Control for Clients	1-800-381-5686
Internet Dashboard	Starfish Software	Interne Application Management	1-800-765-7839
CSM Proxy	Computer Software Manufaktur	Internet Gateway, Caching, Proxy, and Firewall Server	1-800-689-8727
CREW	Thuridion	Internet Groupware	1-408-439-9800
On Guard Internet Manager	On Technology	Internet Security Software	1-800-381-5686
WebScan	McAfee	Internet Virus Scan	1-206-882-8080
Jamba	Aimtech Corp.	Java Development	1-800-289-2884
JDesigner Pro 2.0	BulletProof Corp.	Java Development	1-800-421-8006
Java Workshop	Sun Microsystems	Java Development	1-800-786-7638
Visual J++	Microsoft	Java/ActiveX Development	1-800-426-9400
SoftICE for Windows NT	NuMega Technologies	Kernel-Mode Debugging Tools	1-800-468-6342
Analyst/Probe	Network Instruments	LAN Troubleshooter/ Sniffer	1-800-526-7920
Observer	Network Instruments	LAN Troubleshooter/ Sniffer	1-800-526-7919
WinEdit 95	Wilson Windoware	Large Text Editor	
KEAlink LAT	Attachmate	LAT Protocol	1-800-688-3270
SuperLAT	Meridian Technology	LAT Protocol	1-314-532-7708
Ventura 7	Corel	Layout Software	1-800-455-3169
NetTalk	WorldTalk Corporations	Mail Server, Email Connection Manager	1-800-689-8727
Domino	Lotus	Messenging/Mail/News	1-800-346-1305
Centameter 2.60	Tally Systems	Metering Software	1-800-262-3877

Product	Vendor	Type	Phone Number
Precise/CPE 3.0	Precise Software	Middleware	1-800-310-4777
Spartacom SAPS	SpartaCom	Modem pooling/ sharing	1-516-587-4279
WINport	LANSource	Modem Sharing	1-800-677-2727
SAPS	TSP Companies	Modem Sharing Software	1-800-689-8727
Elastic Reality	Avid Technology	Morphing/FX	1-800-875-4699
DSTune 2.1	Dubbledam Software	Multimedia	31-15-2135647
Flashware	Precept Software	Multimedia	1-408-446-7600
3D Studio Max	Autodesk	Multimedia 3D	1-800-964-6432
Innovous Multimedia	Innovous Corp.	Multimedia Authoring	1-800-433-1806
IconAuthor	AimTech	Multimedia Authoring Application	1-800-289-2884
Multimedia Toolbook	Asymetric	Multimedia Authoring Application	1-800-448-6543
Authorware	Macromedia	Multimedia Authoring Application	1-800-326-2128
Director	Macromedia	Multimedia Authoring Application	1-800-326-2128
System Commander	V Communications	Multiple Operating Systems	1-800-648-8266
Net Support	Markham	Multi-Protocol Remote Control	1-800-689-8727
Chameleon	NetManage	Multi-Services for TCP/IP	1-603-888-2800
Master Console	RCI	Multi-User Administration	
HP Openview Desktop Administrator	Hewlett-Packard	Multi-Vendor Network Management	1-415-857-4111
LANDesk Management Suite	Intel	Network and Desktop Management	1-800-628-8686
Who's Where	On Technology	Network Employee Time Clock and Notifier	1-800-381-5686
CANE	ImageNet	Network Engineering Solution	1-617-239-8197
Lotus Notes Server	Lotus Development	Network Groupware	1-800-343-5414
Final for NT Server	FastLane Technologies	Network Management	1-800-947-6752

Product	Vendor	Type	Phone Number
NTManage	Lanology	Network Management	1-713-975-8050
NFS Maestro	Hummingbird Communications	NFS File and Print Access	1-800-689-8727
DNEWS	NetWin Ltd.	NNTP Server	
DiskShare	Intergraph	NT/UNIX Client/ Server Solution	1-800-689-8727
OmniPage Pro	Caere Corp.	OCR Software	1-800-535-7226
Textbridge Pro 96	Xerox Corp.	OCR Software	1-800-248-6550
Wang Imaging Professional	Wang Technologies	OCR/Document Imaging	1-800-229-2973
FileMaker Pro	Claris	Office Suite	1-800-361-6075
Office 97	Microsoft	Office Suite	1-206-882-8080
Open File Manager	Computer Associates	Open-File Capturing	1-619-676-2277
Optiserver for NT	KOM	Optical Storage Solutions	1-800-668-1777
PartitionMagic	PowerQuest Corporation	Partitioning Software	
SmartAgent for NT	Landmark Systems	Performance Management	1-800-333-8666
Ghostscript Project	Aladdinx	Postscript Viewer	
Project	Microsoft	Project Management	1-206-882-8080
Open Sesame	Computer Manufaktur	Proxy Server/Gateway	1-801-547-0914
Internet Access Server	Microsoft	Proxy Server/Gateway	1-206-882-8080
IQ/Objects	IQ Software	Query and Reporting Tools	1-800-458-0386
Quota Server	Argent Software	Quota Management	1-860-489-5553
Quota Manager for NT	NTP Software	Quota Management	1-800-226-2755
Quota Advisor	Quinn	Quota Management	1-800-829-3453
Everstore RAID	Micropal	RAID cabinets	1-800-998-1638
Remote Access Manager	Virtual Motion	RAS Port Management	1-800-689-8727
Paradox 7	Borland	Relational Database	1-408-431-1000
Oracle 7 Workgroup Server	Oracle	Relational Database Management Server	1-800-633-0586
pcANYWHERE32 7.5 (w/ fix)	Symantec	Remote Access	1-800-441-7234

Product	Vendor	Type	Phone Number
SpartaCom	TSP Communications	Remote Access	1-770-457-0630
Allegra for NT	3COM	Remote Access	1-800-877-7533
Admin! NT	NetWin Software	Remote Control	1-800-689-8727
Remotely Possible	Avalan Technology	Remote Management	
SAPS	SpartaCom	Remote Management	
Domain Meter 7000	Technically Elite	RMON Tool	1-800-474-7888
Batch Job Server	Camelia Software	Scheduling	1-306-264-5307
Autosys	Platinum	Scheduling	1-708-620-5000
Kane Security Analyst	Intrusion Detection	Security Administration	1-212-348-8900
Enterprise Administrator	Mission Critical	Security Administration	1-800-814-9130
BINDVIEW EMS	Bindview Development	Security Manager	1-800-689-8727
Final !	fastlane Technologies	Security Manager	1-800-689-8727
Eagle NT	Raptor Systems	Security Manager Package	1-800-932-4536
DumpACL	Somar	Security Reporting Tool	1-415-776-7315
DumpACL	Somar	Security Reporting Tool	1-415-776-7316
DumpACL	Somar	Security Reporting Tool	1-415-776-7317
GemStone 4.1	GemStone Systems	SmallTalk Object Database	1-503-629-8383
SMS Toolset	CompuThoughts	SMS Add-On	44-2-879426
MailNet 3.1	Consensys Computers	SMTP Mail Gateway	1-800-388-1896
AltaVista Mail Server 97	Altavista Internet Software	SMTP/POP3 Mail Server	1-800-689-8727
NTMail	Internet Shopper	SMTP/POP3 Mail Server	1-800-689-8727
SendMail with POP3	Metainfo	SMTP/POP3 Mail Server	1-206-521-2600
Mail Server	Netscape	SMTP/POP3 Mail Server	1-800-421-8011
Netscape Mail Server 1.1	Netscape Communications	SMTP/POP3 Mail Server	1-415-937-2555
SLMailNT	Seattle Lab	SMTP/POP3 Mail Server	1-206-402-6003

Product	Vendor	Type	Phone Number
Open Administrator	Peregrine Systems	SNMP Management	1-800-638-5231
RouterManager/ Autobahn	StoneyBrook Software	SNMP Management	1-516-567-6060
Media Agent	Media Path	Software CD-ROM Management	1-800-357-0697
WinInstall	Tally Systems	Software Distribution	
ImageBlaster Pro	On Technology	Software Image Deployment	1-800-381-5686
Express Meter	Express Systems	Software Metering	
On Command Software Metering	On Technology	Software Metering	1-800-381-5686
CentaMeter	Tally Systems	Software Metering	
WinRunner 4.0	Mercury Interactive	Software Testing	1-408-523-9900
DBArtisan 2.5	Emarcadero	SQL Tools	1-415-834-3131
Dynamic C/S+	Great Plains Software	SQL Tools	1-701-281-0550
SPSS 7.0	SPSS, Inc.	Statistical Package	1-800-543-2185
OS/N for Windows NT	LaserData	Storage Management	1-508-649-4600
Vantage Point 2.0	Storage Dimensions	Storage Management	1-408-954-0710
RoboMon	Heroix	System Administration Tool	1-800-229-6500
ChamelonNFS/X	NetManage	TCP/IP Client/Server AppSuite	1-800-689-8727
Visual Internet ToolKit	Distinct Corporation	TCP/IP Development	1-408-366-8933
InterAccess TelnetD Server	Pragma Systems	Telnet Server	1-800-689-8727
Slnet	Seattle Lab	Telnet Server	1-800-689-8727
KEA! 340	Attachmate	Terminal Emulation	1-800-688-3270
KEA! 420	Attachmate	Terminal Emulation	1-800-688-3270
SmarTerm for Windows NT	Persoft	Terminal Emulation	1-800-368-5238
Rumba Office NT	Wall Data	Terminal Emulation	1-800-487-8622
Reflection 2	WRQ	Terminal Emulation	1-800-872-2829
Reflection 4	WRQ	Terminal Emulation	1-800-872-2829
Intelliterm	Distinct Software	Terminal Emulation	1-408-366-8933
CleanSweep95	QuarterDeck	Uninstaller	1-800-683-6696
OpenNT	Softway Systems	UNIX over WINNT	1-800-GET-UNIX

Product	Vendor	Type	Phone Number
Norton Utilities 2.0 for NT	Symantec	Utilities	1-800-441-7234
Enhanced CU-SeeMe	Whitepine Software	Video Conferencing	1-800-241-7463
Premiere	Adobe Systems	Video Editing	1-800-833-6687
Real Impact	Avid Technology	Video Editing	1-800-875-4699
Perception Video Recorder	Digital Processing Systems	Video Editing	1-606-371-5533
Speed Razor Mach III	in:sync	Video Editing	1-301-320-0220
VMT	Lightspeed Software	Vines to NT Migration	1-800-324-4291
Mobile VPN	On Technology	Virtual Private Networking	1-800-381-5686
Applet Designer	TV Objects	Visual basic to Java Code Translation	1-800-421-8007
BoundsChecker 4.0	NuMega Technologies	Visual C/C++ Debugger	1-800-4-NUMEGA
DV-Centro 1.2	Dataview	Visual Programming Language Builder	1-800-732-3300
RealAudio/RealVideo Server	Progressive Networks	Web Audio and Video Streaming	1-800-689-8727
Corel Web.Data	Corel	Web Authoring	1-800-772-6735
FutureTense Texture	Future Tense	Web Authoring	1-508-263-5480
InContext Spider 1.1	InContext	Web Authoring	1-800-263-0127
Microsoft FrontPage	Microsoft	Web Authoring	1-800-426-9400
HoTMetaL PRO 3.0	SoftQuad	Web Authoring	1-800-387-2777
WebAnchor 1.0	Iconovex	Web Browser	1-800-943-0292
CyberPilot	NetCarta Corp.	Web Browser	1-800-461-2449
Merchant Builder	The Internet Factory, Inc.	Web Commerce Package	1-800-689-8727
WebBoard	O'Reilly and Associates	Web Conferencing	1-707-829-0515
PointCast Server	PointCast	Web Conferencing NNTP Server	1-800-689-8727
Aspect dbWeb 2.0	Aspect	Web Database Management	1-808-539-3781
WebDBC	Normand	Web Database Management	1-206-448-1956
PolyForms	O'Reilly and Associates	Web Database Management	1-707-829-0515

Product	Vendor	Type	Phone Number
Visual InterDev ToolKit	Microsoft	Web Development	1-800-426-9000
Pageblazer	The Sapphire Group	Web Development	1-703-736-8090
Site Server	Microsoft	Web Information Server	1-800-936-5900
Web Mapper	NetCarta Corp.	Web Manager	1-800-461-2449
Netshow 1.0	Microsoft	Web Multimedia Assistant	1-800-426-9400
Web Publisher	askSam Systems	Web Publisher	1-800-800-1997
Common Ground	Hummingbird Communications	Web Publishing and Document Management	1-800-689-8727
Cold Fusion	Alltaire	Web Publishing Software	1-612-831-1808
Shockwave	Macromedia	Web Publishing Software	1-800-945-4061
Internet Studion (Blackbird)	Microsoft	Web Publishing Software	1-206-882-8080
Java	Sun Microsystems	Web Publishing Software	1-800-821-4643
SQL:Web	Sybase	Web Publishing Software	1-800-792-2731
WebTrends	e.g. Software	Web Reporting	1-800-689-8727
Catalog Server	Netscape	Web Search Engine	1-800-421-8010
Step Search	SAQQARA Systems	Web Search Engine	1-800-689-8727
Tecumseh Scout Pro	Tippecanoe Systems	Web Search Engine	1-800-689-8727
Alibaba 2.0	Computer Software Manufaktur	Web Server	1-801-547-0914
Interware	Consensys Computers	Web Server	1-905-940-2900
Internet Server 1.0	Cyber Presence International	Web Server	1-415-638-2582
MindWire NT	Durand Communications	Web Server	1-805-961-8700
InfoBase Server	Folio	Web Server	1-800-543-6546
Enterprise Server	Netscape	Web Server	1-800-421-8009
InterOffice Studio	Oracle	Web Server	1-800-633-0596
Website 1.1 Professional	O'Reilly and Associates	Web Server	1-707-829-0515

Product	Vendor	Type	Phone Number
Purveyor Encrypt WebServer	Process	Web Server	1-800-722-7770
Webserver32	QuarterDeck	Web Server	1-310-309-4261
SPRY WebServer	SPRY	Web Server	1-800-447-2971
Webstar/SSL Security Toolkit	Starnine	Web Server	
Commerce Builder Pro	The Internet Factory, Inc.	Web Server	1-916-939-1000
Internet Factory	The Internet Factory, Inc.	Web Server	1-510-426-7763
Corrider	Teubner and Associates	Web to SNA Software	1-405-624-2254
Surf Report NT	On Technology	Web Trend Analysis	1-800-381-5686
AltaVista Directory 97	Altavista Internet Software	Web-based Contact Management	1-800-689-8727
Chill! Reports	Chilli! Soft	Web-based Reporting Tool	1-800-689-8727
Ntrigue	Insignia Solutions	Win16/Win32 support over X-Terminals	1-508-682-7600
Wind/U -	Bristol Technologies	Windows API on UNIX	1-203-438-6969
Wireless Messaging Server	Integra	Wireless Messaging Server	1-206-637-5600
Track-It!	On Technology	Workstation Auditing	1-800-381-5686
eXceed for NT	Hummingbird	X-Window Solution	1-800-689-8727
EXTRA!	Attachmate	X-Windows	1-800-426-6283
Exceed	Hummingbird Communications	X-Windows	1-800-689-8727
Zip Tools	IOMega Corp.	ZIP Drive Interface	

Appendix G

Helpful Network Management Documents

This appendix provides document templates that will help an NT network administrator in a variety of duties.

Document 1: Installation Planning Sheet

This document helps an administrator install NT workstations and servers.

Table G.1. Planning sheet for NT installation.

Installation Item	Value
Backup Device	
Backup Software	
Computer Name	
CPU	
Disk Space and Partitioning	
Domain Name	
Fault Tolerance	
IPX Address	
IPX Frame Type	
Licenses and Mode	
Memory	
Network Interface Card	
Network Protocol at Install	
NIC I/O Base Address	
NIC IRQ Address	
NIC Transceiver Type	
Operating System	
Server Role	
TCP/IP Address	
TCP/IP Default Gateway	
TCP/IP Subnet Mask	
Host Name	
DNS Domain	
DNS Search Order	
Primary WINS Server Address	
Secondary WINS Server Address	

Document 2: Supported Hardware and Vendor List

This document lists the major hardware components and vendors used with Windows NT. While this list is dynamic, as it would be in any network operating system, it is still helpful to keep track of product lines and corresponding vendors. All major areas of hardware needs, from server hardware to multimedia use, are included.

Table G.2. Major hardware components and vendors.

Product	Vendor	Type	Phone Number
SyncLink WAN Adpater	Microgate	16 PVC Frame Relay	1-800-444-1982
R5000	MIPS Technologies	200Mhz 3D Graphics Microprocessor	1-415-960-1980
Intense 3-D	Intergraph	3D OpenGl Graphics Card	1-800-763-0242
Plextor 8plex	Plextor	8X CD-ROM Drive	1-800-886-3935
Nakamichi MJ-4.8S	Nakamichi	CD-ROM Changer	1-310-538-8150
Star Point CD-ROM	Axis	CD-ROM Server	1-800-444-2947
Hyper CD 30x	Procom Technology	CD-ROM Server	1-800-800-8600
Deskjet 820Cse	Hewlett-Packard	Color Inkjet Printer	1-800-752-0900
Raptor Reflex	DeskStation Technology	DEC Alpha 21164 Server	1-913-599-1900
RASER	RARE Systems	DEC Alpha Server	1-214-991-7273
Color Quick Cam	Connectix	Desktop PC Video Camera	1-800-950-5858
DS9000D	ADIC	DLT Storage System	1-800-336-1233
Twin Peaks	Aspen Systems	DUAL SMP 500mhz Alpha Server	1-800-992-9242
RAIDSTATION3	DPT Technology	Full-featured SCSI RAID Kit	1-800-860-4589
Imagine 128 Series 2	Number Nine Visual Technology	Graphics Accelerator	1-800-438-6463
Diamond 3D 2000	Diamond Multimedia	Graphics Accelerator	1-800-468-5846
Quantum Bigfoot 2.5 AT	Quantum Corp.	Hard Drives	1-800-624-5545
Web-300	Integraph	Hardware Web Server	1-800-763-0242
EdgeServer	U.S. Robotics	Information Access Server	1-800-877-7533
NCR S40 SMP Server	NCR	Intel Multi-Processing Server	1-800-543-2010

continues

Table G.2. Continued

Product	Vendor	Type	Phone Number
FX!32	Digital Semi-conductor	Intel Win32 Emulator	1-800-344-4825
ISDN Terminal Adapter IDC100I	Cardinal Technologies	ISDN Adapter	1-717-293-3000
Netopia ISDN Modem	Farallon	ISDN Modem	1-510-814-5000
SOHO Router	Accton Technologies	ISDN/Ethernet Router	1-408-452-8900
LaserJet 5, 5M, 5N	Hewlett-Packard	Laser Printers	1-800-752-0900
LaserJet 4000	Hewlett-Packard	Laser Printers	1-800-752-0900
Sharp QA-1800	Sharp Electronics	LCD Projection	1-201-529-8731
HotSwap Tower Drive	TAC System	Mass Storage Solution	1-800-659-4440
RAM	Kingston Technology	Memory Chips	1-888-435-5429
Sportster WinModem 28.8	U.S. Robotics	Modem	1-800-342-5877
Teleport 33.6 SpeakerPhone	Global Village	Modem/Faxmodem/ Speakerphone	1-800-329-9675
Appian Jeronimo J2	Appian Graphics	Multi-Monitor Spanning Graphics Card	1-800-727-7426
RADIO Cluster	Stratus	Multiple Server Clustering Solution	1-888-RADIO-PC
ChiliPorts	Consensys	Multi-Port Adapters	1-800-388-1896
RocketPort	ComTrol	Multi-Port Adapters	1-800-926-6876
8 port Digiboard PC-8e	Digi	Multi-Port Adapters	1-800-344-4273
Easy Connect	Stallion Technologies	Multi-Port Adapters	1-800-347-7979
Equinox SST-8I	Equinoz Systems	Multi-Port Adapters	1-800-275-3500
QuadRANT	Enterprise Communications	Multi-Port Adapters	1-619-674-6740
CyClom Y	Cyclades	Multi-Port Adapters	1-800-882-9252
SS Intelligent Multiport Controllers	Maxpeed	Multi-Port Adapters	1-800-877-7998
FaxPress	Castelle	Network Fax Server	1-408-496-0474
NTManage	Lanology	Network Management for NT	1-713-975-8050
NT Manager	Plasmon Data	Optical Jukebox Managers	1-408-956-9400
Evergreen 586/133	Evergreen Technologies	OverDrive Processor	1-800-733-0934

Product	Vendor	Type	Phone Number
EZFlyer 230	SyQuest	Parallel/SCSI External Drives	1-800-245-2278
ZIP Drive	IOMega	Parallel/SCSI External Drives	1-800-697-8833
2340-TX Adapter	Rockwell Network Systems	PCI-Fast Ethernet (100mbps) Adapters	1-800-262-8023
Etherlink III LAN+33.6	3Com	PCMCIA LAN/Modem Card	1-800-638-3266
IPDS Plug and Play Printing	QMS	Printer Protocol Converters	1-800-523-2696
Proxima Lightbook	Proxima Technology	Projector	1-800-447-7692
Sparta	NeTpower	Quad-Processor/RAID Server	1-800-801-0900
SuperFlex 3000	Storage Dimensions	RAID Storage Unit	1-408-954-0710
Olympus CD-R2 Internal	Olympus Image Systems	Recordable CD-ROM	1-800-347-4027
GyroPoint Pro	Gyration	Remote Pointer	1-800-316-5432
Sentry Shutdown	Server Technology	Remote Power Control	1-800-835-1515
Alpha 21164	Digital Equipment Corporation	RISC Processor - 266 - 500Mhz	1-800-437-7503
Microtek ScanMaker	Microtek Lab, Inc.	Scanner	1-800-654-4160
BusLogic Flashpoint LW	BusLogic	SCSI Controller	1-800-707-7274
SMART RAID IV	DPT Technology	SCSI RAID Controller	1-800-322-4378
SoundBlaster AWE32	Creative Labs	Sound Cards	1-408-428-6600
Audiotrix Pro	Media Trix	Sound Cards	1-819-829-8749
Synclink Internet Adapter	Microgate	T1-CSU/DSU Bus Mastering Adapter	1-800-444-1982
Spectra 4000 and 9000	UpTime Ltd.	Tape Backup Library	1-405-330-3033
Back-UPS Pro 4APC	American Power	Uninterruptible Power	
	Coversion	Supply	
Smart-Ups	American Power Coversion	Uninterruptible Power Supply	1-800-800-4APC
Play Snappy Video Snapshot	Play, Inc.	Video Capture Device	1-800-306-7529

Document 3: IRQ/IO Hardware Settings

This document may be overprinted but is a must for any management book that deals with PC-based local area networks.

Table G.3. Intel AT x86—hardware settings.

IRQ	Description
0	System Timer
1	CPU
2	EGA/VGA Graphics Adapter
3	COM2, COM4
4	COM1, COM3
5	LPT2, 8-bit Sound Cards
6	Floppy Controller
7	LPT1
8	Real-Time Clock
9	Redirected (2)
10	
11	
12	Mouse (PS/2)
13	Math Coprocessor
14	Hard Disk Controller
15	Controller

Table G.4. Base I/O port settings.

Range Start	Range End	Default
200	20F	Game Port
210	21F	
220	22F	
230	23F	Bus Mouse
240	24F	
250	25F	
260	26F	
270	27F	LPT3
280	28F	
290	29F	
2A0	2AF	
2B0	2BF	

Range Start	Range End	Default
2C0	2CF	
2D0	2DF	
2E0	2EF	
2F0	2FF	COM2
300	30F	Network Adapter Card
310	31F	Network Adapter Card
320	32F	Hard Disk Controller
330	33F	
340	34F	
350	35F	
360	36F	
370	37F	LPT2
380	38F	
390	39F	
3A0	3AF	
3B0	3BF	LPT1
3C0	3CF	EGA/VGA
3D0	3DF	CGA/MCGA
3E0	3EF	
3F0	3FF	Floppy Disk Controller, COM1

Document 4: EIA Twisted-Pair Cable Definitions

This document briefly discusses the five major EIA cable categories.

Table G.5. EIA cable categories.

Level	Description	Maximum Bandwidth
1 & 2	Used for voice and low speed data transmission	4Mbps
3	Used for Ethernet & high speed Token Ring LANs (such as IEEE 802.3 10Base-T or 802.5 4Mbps or 16Mbps)	16Mbps
4	Used for extended distance IEEE Ethernet and Token Ring LANs	20Mbps
5	Used for TPDDI (FDDI on TP instead of fiber) or ANSI X3T9.5 applications	100Mbps

Document 5: Management Cost and Delegation Sheet

Often a document like this is helpful if taped up on the wall next to an administrator's management console. It helps you to keep track of all major software and hardware costs as well as who is the delegated person to handle the management of that entity.

Table G.6. Managing cost and delegating personnel.

Product	Manufacturer	Requirements	Estimated Cost/yr	Contact Person	Telephone #
Admin Utility 1					
Admin Utility 2					
Admin Utility 3					
Cable Plant					
FAX Hardware					
FAX Software					
Intelligent Hubs/ MAUs					
NICs					
Operating System					
Print Servers					
Printers					
Routers					
Servers					
Tape Backup System					
Wiring Closets					

Document 6: Cost Estimation of Implementation and Integration

This document allows an administrator to avoid having integration costs run away from them. It also pinpoints where costs may run higher than normal in certain areas.

Table G.7. Cost integration management.

	Item
Section 1	
	Cable Plant
	Twisted Pair Implementation
	EIA Category *x* Twisted Pair Cable (x amount)
	RJ45 Connectors (x amount)
	Patch Panel, Interduct, Conduit, Panduit Installation (x amount)
	Installer Testing (Signal integrity/Continuity)
	Fiber Optic Implementation
	ST Connectors (x amounts)
	Fiber Optic Patch panel, Interduct, Conduit, Panduit Installation
	Installer Testing (Db loss, OTDR snapshots)
	General Cabling Requirements
	Cable Dressing and Labeling
	Documentation
	SUBTOTAL for Section 1
Section 2	
	Intelligent Hubs
	Installation, Configuration, Test, and Documentation
	Rack and Concentrator Installation
	Fiber Plant Connection and Cable Dressing
	Labeling (Cable, Panels, and Concentrators)
	Update of As-Built Documentation and Databases
	Install and Configure Network Management System
	Testing
	Document Ops, Troubleshooting, and Test Procedures
	SUBTOTAL for Section 2

	Estimated Duration (Hrs.)	Estimated Number of Staff	Estimated Total Staff Hours

continues

Table G.7. Continued

	Item
Section 3	
	Workstation and Network Interface Card
	RAM Memory Upgrade (1,000 users)
	Hard Disk Reconfiguration (NOS drivers) (1,000 users)
	Ethernet NIC Installation (1,000 users)
	Workstation Testing (1,000 users)
	Update of As-Built Documentation, Databases, Scheduling
	SUBTOTAL for Section 3
Section 4	
	Network Server Platform and NOS
	Server
	Tape Backup Hardware
	Documentation and Testing
	SUBTOTAL for Section 4
Section 5	
	NOS Administrative Utilities and Applications
	Server Configuration (Load processes, Partition Drives, Develop Scripts, and so on)
	Set Up Accounts, Directories, Privileges (1,000 Users)
	Move Data Files
	Install COTS Desktop Software
	Backup Software
	Menuing System
	Virus Protection
	Print Services
	Macintosh Connectivity
	Network Management Utilities
	Installation Team Testing
	Documentation
	SUBTOTAL for Section 5

Estimated Duration (Hrs.)	Estimated Number of Staff	Estimated Total Staff Hours

continues

Table G.7. Continued

Item
Section 6
Applications and Other Support Services
Electronic Mail
FAX Services
TCP/IP Services
NFS Services
Macintosh Connectivity with TCP/IP, NFS
SUBTOTAL for Section 6
Section 7
Engineering, Administration, and Planning
Project Management
Cable Plant Project Management
Configuration Management Plan
Quality Assurance/Test Plan and Test Procedures
Training Plan
LAN Master Transition Plan
User's Manual
System Operations and Configuration Manual
Training
SNMP and Network Management Software
TCP/IP
NOS Engineering
Network Management Utilities
Help Desk Staff
SUBTOTAL for Section 7
GRAND TOTAL

	Estimated Duration (Hrs.)	Estimated Number of Staff	Estimated Total Staff Hours

Document 7: Standard Request for Troubleshooting and/or Configuration Change Document

This is a sample document designed for a large-scale enterprise network that is occasionally dynamic with a variety of network operating systems. This expands upon the recommended approaches to documentation of troubleshooting using an example.

REQUEST FOR CONFIGURATION CHANGE

Send via fax to:
Network and Configuration Management
Fax #: 336-555-1234

From: ____________________
Phone: ____________________
DEPT: ____________________

PLEASE CHECK 1 BOX PER CATEGORY

INSTALL DATE/TIME ____/____/____ ____:____ (ET / GMT) Circle One

DURATION ____________________

REQUEST TYPE	RISK POTENTIAL/WORK TIME ZONE	REGION	CHANGE TYPE
EMERGENCY ☐ SCHEDULED ☐	NONE ☐ Not Attached to the Network (24x7)	**INTERNATIONAL** Latin America ☐ Europe ☐ Asia ☐	NSR/PROJECT ☐ #__________
VOICE ☐ (DATA) LAN ☐ WAN ☐ BACKBONE ☐ OTHER ☐ APPLICATION ☐ VENDOR DOCUMENTATION ☐	LOW ☐ Single User with Redundant Network Component(s) (7x1 7:00-06:00) MEDIUM ☐ Single User Without Redundant Network Component(s) Or Multiple Users With Redundant Network Component(s) (7x21:00-06:00) HIGH ☐ Multiple Users Without Redundant Network Component(s), Single/Multiple Users With Highly Sensitive Applications (Sunday 00:01-06:00) * IF CHANGE IS REQUIRED OUTSIDE OF THE SPECIFIED TIMES, OR IS AN EMERGENCY, OBTAIN USER SIGN OFF AND COMPLETE THE IMPACT STATEMENT SECTION.	**DOMESTIC** DP ☐ Accounting ☐ Retail ☐ Human Res. ☐ Corp. ☐ BA #1 ☐ BA #2 ☐ BA #3 ☐ OTHER ☐	TROUBLE ☐ #__________ SIR/ CHANGEMAN ☐ #__________ **MAINTENANCE** COB ☐ POWER ☐ SOFTWARE ☐ OTHER ☐

DESCRIPTION OF CHANGE OR PROJECT

NCC OPERATOR REQUIREMENTS

DESCRIPTION OF FALLBACK

*** IMPACT STATEMENT**

COMMENTS

EMERGENCY APPROVAL
(Division Head or above signature required)

Network Manager	**Implementor - Phone/Beeper -**	**NCC MGMT**	*** USER**
Configuration Manager		**Help Desk Manager Phone/Beeper -**	**INITIALS COMPLETED Y / N (circle one)**

Figure G.1. *Sample document for a large-scale enterprise network.*

Index

Symbols

A

B

C

D

E

G

H

I

K

L

M

N

O

P

Q-R

S

T

U

V

W

X

Y-Z